A HISTORY OF THE UNIVERSITY IN EUROPE

GENERAL EDITOR

WALTER RÜEGG

A HISTORY OF THE UNIVERSITY IN EUROPE

General editor and Chairman of the editorial board: Walter Rüegg (Switzerland)

This four-volume series, prepared under the guidance of an editorial board, has been directed by the Standing Conference of Rectors, Presidents, and Vice-Chancellors of the European Universities (CRE). The CRE, which is a non-governmental organization based in Geneva, has over 470 member universities in both eastern and western Europe. As coordinator of the whole publication, it delegated its assistant secretary general to ensure the administration of the project and to act as secretary to the editorial board.

The university is the only European institution to have preserved its fundamental patterns and basic social role and functions over the course of the last millennium. This *History* shows how and why the university grew to encompass the whole of knowledge and most of the world, how it developed an intellectual tradition common to all Europeans, and how it trained academic and professional elites whose ethos transcends national boundaries.

Volumes in the series

I   Universities in the Middle Ages
     Editor: Hilde de Ridder-Symoens

II   Universities in Early Modern Europe (1500–1800)
     Editor: Hilde de Ridder-Symoens
     Forthcoming (1992)

III Universities in the Nineteenth and Early Twentieth Centuries (1800–1945)
     In preparation

IV   Universities from 1945 to the Present
     In preparation

A HISTORY
OF THE
UNIVERSITY IN EUROPE

VOLUME I
UNIVERSITIES IN THE MIDDLE AGES

EDITOR

HILDE DE RIDDER-SYMOENS

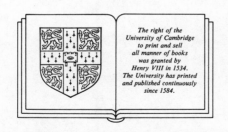

The right of the
University of Cambridge
to print and sell
all manner of books
was granted by
Henry VIII in 1534.
The University has printed
and published continuously
since 1584.

CAMBRIDGE UNIVERSITY PRESS

CAMBRIDGE
NEW YORK   PORT CHESTER
MELBOURNE   SYDNEY

Published by the Press Syndicate of the University of Cambridge
The Pitt Building, Trumpington Street, Cambridge CB2 1RP
40 West 20th Street, New York, NY 10011–4211, USA
10 Stamford Road, Oakleigh, Victoria 3166, Australia

© Cambridge University Press 1992

First published 1992

Printed in Great Britain at the University Press, Cambridge

British Library cataloguing in publication data

A History of the university in Europe.
Vol. 1, Universities in the Middle Ages.
1. Europe. Universities, history
I. Ridder-Symoens, Hilde de, 1943–
378.4

Library of Congress cataloguing in publication data

Universities in the Middle Ages / editor, Hilde de Ridder-Symoens.
p. c.m. – (History of the university in Europe: v. 1)
Includes bibliographical references.
ISBN 0 521 36105 2
1. Universities and colleges – Europe – History. 2. Learning and
scholarship – Europe – History – Medieval, 500–1500. 3. Education,
Medieval – Europe. I. Ridder-Symoens, Hilde de. II. Series.
LA177.U53   1991
378.4′09′02–dc20   90–33558 CIP

ISBN 0 521 36105 2 hardback

CONTENTS

Contents

Contents

Contents

Contents

MAPS

CONTRIBUTORS AND EDITORS

MONIKA ASZTALOS (Sweden) was born in Stockholm in 1953. She is associate professor of Latin in the Department of classical languages at the University of Stockholm. In 1987, she spent six months as visiting professor at the Pontifical Institute of Medieval Studies in Toronto.

ASA BRIGGS (United Kingdom) was born in Yorkshire in 1921. Provost of Worcester College, Oxford, Lord Briggs is a former vice-chancellor of the University of Sussex (1967–76), president of the British Social History Society and former chairman of the European Institute of Education and Social Policy in Paris.

ANTONIO GARCÍA Y GARCÍA (Spain) was born in Bretoña (province of Lugo) in 1928. Professor of the history of canon law at the Pontifical University of Salamanca, he is editor of the *Revista Española de Derecho Canónico* and of the *Synodicon Hispanum* series, as well as a member of the Institute of Medieval Canon Law at Berkeley.

ALEKSANDER GIEYSZTOR (Poland) was born in Moscow in 1916. President of the Polish Academy of Sciences and director of the Royal Castle in Warsaw, he is emeritus professor of history at the University of Warsaw.

NOTKER HAMMERSTEIN (Federal Republic of Germany) was born in Offenbach am Main in 1930. Professor of early modern history at the University of Frankfurt, he edited the *History of the University of Frankfurt* and is also a member of the editorial board of *History of Universities*.

GORDON LEFF (United Kingdom) was born in 1926 and educated at King's College, Cambridge. He is now professor of medieval history at the University of York.

PETER MORAW (Federal Republic of Germany) was born in Mährisch

Ostrau in 1935. He is professor of medieval history and of German national, economic, and social history at the University of Giessen.

PAOLO NARDI (Italy) was born in Siena in 1949. Professor of the history of Italian law at the University of Siena, he is also director of the review *Studi senesi*, published by the university.

JOHN NORTH (United Kingdom) was born in Cheltenham in 1934. Formerly at the University of Oxford, he is professor of the history of philosophy and the exact sciences at the University of Groningen in The Netherlands, and permanent secretary of the International Academy for the History of Science.

OLAF PEDERSEN (Denmark) was born in 1920. He is professor of the history of science at the University of Aarhus and a visiting fellow of St Edmund's House, Cambridge. He is vice president of the International Union for the History and Philosophy of Science and president of the Historical Commission of the International Astronomical Union.

HILDE DE RIDDER-SYMOENS (Belgium) was born in Sint-Jans-Molenbeek (Brussels) in 1943. Professor of medieval history at the Free University of Amsterdam, she is also a research associate for the Belgian National Fund for Scientific Research at the University of Ghent. Since 1985, she has been secretary general of the International Commission for the History of Universities.

JOHN ROBERTS (United Kingdom) was born in Bath in 1928. Warden of Merton College, Oxford, where he was previously fellow and tutor in modern history, he was also vice-chancellor of the University of Southampton for a number of years. From 1967 to 1976 he was joint editor of the *English Historical Review*. He is presently a governor of the British Broadcasting Corporation.

WALTER RÜEGG (Switzerland) was born in Zurich in 1918. Emeritus professor of sociology at the University of Berne, and former professor of sociology at the University of Frankfurt, he was rector of the latter from 1965 until 1970. He is the general editor of this *History of the University in Europe*.

RAINER CHRISTOPH SCHWINGES (Federal Republic of Germany) was born in 1943. He is now professor of medieval history at the University of Berne in Switzerland, after having taught at the University of Giessen.

EDWARD SHILS (United States of America) was born in Springfield, Massachusetts, in 1910. Founder and editor of *Minerva*, he is professor of social thought and sociology at the University of Chicago. He is also a fellow of Peterhouse, Cambridge, as well as of the London School of Economics.

NANCY SIRAISI (United States of America) was born in Yorkshire in 1932.

Professor of history at Hunter College of the City University of New York, she is also a member of the editorial board of *History of Universities*.

JACQUES VERGER (France) was born in Talence in the Gironde in 1943. He is *maître de conférences* in medieval history at the Ecole Normale Supérieure in Paris and vice-president of the International Commission for the History of Universities.

READER'S GUIDE

This series, although compiled by specialists, is destined for the general reader. The notes and bibliographies accompanying the different chapters have therefore been kept to a minimum. The notes are either bibliographical references to specific sources, generally the most important or recent works relating to the subject, or they have been introduced to justify quantitative data or explain any significant difference between two interpretations of a particular point. A select bibliography follows each chapter. These bibliographies are designed to stimulate further reading and are not exhaustive. The reader will find more complete bibliographical references in the works indicated. As a number of well-known works for the period are quoted in several chapters, abbreviations of the titles of these works have been used in the notes. A list of bibliographical abbreviations is included. Furthermore, the reader will find a more general bibliography and some maps at the end of chapter 2 (Patterns), as this chapter locates the presence and nature of universities during the Middle Ages. In order to avoid too many overlaps between the various chapters, the editors have made cross-references to other chapters in the text as well as in the notes, thereby informing the reader that more ample information on the subject can be found elsewhere in the volume (see also the geographical and subject index). The standard English version of proper names has been used throughout; when necessary, a form more commonly used in continental Europe is indicated by means of a cross-reference in the name index.

BIBLIOGRAPHICAL
ABBREVIATIONS USED IN
NOTES

Cobban, *Medieval Universities*
  A. B. Cobban, *The Medieval Universities: Their Development and Organization* (London, 1975).
CUP
  H. Denifle and E. Châtelain (eds.), *Chartularium Universitatis Parisiensis*, 4 vols. (Paris, 1889–97).
Denifle, *Entstehung*
  H. Denifle, *Die Entstehung der Universitäten des Mittelalters bis 1400* (Berlin, 1885; reprint, Graz, 1956).
Fournier (ed.), *Statuts*
  M. Fournier (ed.), *Les Statuts et privilèges des universités françaises depuis leur fondation jusqu'en 1789*, 4 vols. (Paris, 1890–2).
History of Oxford
  J. I. Catto (ed.), *The History of the University of Oxford*, vol. I, *The Early Oxford Schools* (general editor: T. H. Aston) (Oxford, 1984).
d'Irsay, *Histoire des universités*
  S. d'Irsay, *Histoire des universités françaises et étrangères des origines à nos jours*, 2 vols. (Paris, 1933–5).
Kaufmann, *Deutsche Universitäten*
  G. Kaufmann, *Geschichte der deutschen Universitäten*, 2 vols. (Stuttgart, 1888–96; reprint, Graz, 1958).
Kibre, *Nations*
  P. Kibre, *The Nations in the Mediaeval Universities*, Mediaeval Academy of America, 49 (Cambridge, Mass., 1948).
Kibre, *Privileges*
  P. Kibre, *Scholarly Privileges in the Middle Ages. The Rights, Privileges and Immunities of Scholars and Universities at Bologna – Padua – Paris – Oxford*, Mediaeval Academy of America, 72 (Cambridge, Mass., 1961).
Rashdall, *Universities*
  H. Rashdall, *The Universities of Europe in the Middle Ages*, 3 vols. ed. F. M. Powicke and A. B. Emden (Oxford, 1936; reprint, London, 1942–58; reprint, Oxford, 1988).

Renaissance and Renewal
R. B. Benson and G. Constable (eds.), *Renaissance and Renewal in the Twelfth Century* (Cambridge, Mass., 1982; reprint, Oxford, 1985).

Schulen und Studium
J. Fried (ed.), *Schulen und Studium im sozialen Wandel des hohen und späten Mittelalters* (Sigmaringen, 1986).

Schwinges, *Universitätsbesucher*
R. C. Schwinges, *Deutsche Universitätsbesucher im 14. und 15. Jahrhundert: Studien zur Sozialgeschichte des alten Reiches* (Stuttgart, 1986).

Università e società
Università e società nei secoli XII—XVI. Atti del nono convegno internazionale di studio tenuto a Pistoia nei giorni 20–25 settembre 1979 (Pistoia, 1982).

Universités en France
J. Verger (ed.), *Histoire des universités en France* (Toulouse, 1986).

Universities in the Late Middle Ages
J. IJsewijn and J. Paquet (eds.), *Universities in the Late Middle Ages*, Mediaevalia Lovaniensia, series 1, studia 6 (Louvain, 1978).

Universities in Politics
J. W. Baldwin and R. A. Goldthwaite (eds.), *Universities in Politics: Case Studies from the Late Middle Ages and Early Modern Period* (Baltimore/London, 1972).

FOREWORD

WALTER RÜEGG
(General Editor)

THE UNIVERSITY AS A EUROPEAN INSTITUTION

The university is a European institution; indeed, it is the European institution *par excellence*. There are various reasons for this assertion.

As a community of teachers and taught, accorded certain rights, such as administrative autonomy and the determination and realization of curricula (courses of study) and of the objectives of research as well as the award of publicly recognized degrees, it is a creation of medieval Europe, which was the Europe of papal Christianity. This is shown in the first volume of our history.

It is, moreover, the only European institution which has preserved its fundamental patterns and its basic social role and functions over the course of history; it has indeed been strengthened and extended in these respects – as the four volumes will show. Of the three acknowledged powers of medieval European society – *regnum*, *sacerdotium*, and *studium* – the first, political power, has undergone profound changes. The second has, in the Roman Catholic Church, preserved its structure and expanded over the whole planet but it has lost the monopoly which it once possessed of providing the conditions of salvation. The same may be said for the other institutional and cultural creations of the Middle Ages, i.e. the distinctively European forms of organization of a money economy, the plastic arts, architecture, and music.

No other European institution has spread over the entire world in the way in which the traditional form of the European university has done. The degrees awarded by European universities – the bachelor's degree, the licentiate, the master's degree, and the doctorate – have been adopted in the most diverse societies throughout the world. The four medieval faculties of *artes* – variously called philosophy, letters, arts, arts and sciences, and humanities – law, medicine, and theology have survived and have been supplemented by numerous disciplines, particularly the social sciences and technological studies, but they remain none the less at the heart of universities throughout the world. Even the name of the *universitas*, which in the Middle Ages was applied to corporate bodies of the most diverse sorts and was accordingly applied to the corporate organization of teachers and students, has in the course of centuries been given a more particular focus: the university, as a *universitas litterarum*, has since the eighteenth century been the intellectual institution which cultivates and transmits the entire corpus of methodically studied intellectual disciplines.

Moreover, the university is a European institution because it has, in its social role, performed certain functions for all European societies. It has developed and transmitted scientific and scholarly knowledge and the methods of cultivating that knowledge which has arisen from and formed part of the common European intellectual tradition. It has at the same time formed an academic elite, the ethos of which rests on common European values and which transcends all national boundaries.

The various efforts which were made after the Second World War to establish 'European' universities were largely unsuccessful because of the resistance of the existing universities, which regarded themselves as European. Indeed, they pointed out that the diversity of national traditions was a precious European heritage and that, by means of their different national components, they contributed to the European community of scholarship and scholars.

It may be asked whether this account does in fact characterize the present situation. Are not the universities of Europe equally, if not more deeply, marked by the differences among the European national states which began to take form in the late Middle Ages and during the Reformation and which, particularly since the nineteenth century, changed the universities of the European continent *de facto* – and often *de jure* as well – into parts of the governmental system? Do they perform genuinely European functions when, in any particular member state of the European community, only about 1 per cent of the student body is made up of those who come from any of the other member states of the community and when, in many European countries, professors from other countries cannot be appointed or can be appointed only in exceptional circumstances? Can the existing European universities be said to be performing their proper social role when the rising generation of European scientists and scholars prefers to continue its studies in universities of another country where the European traditions of scientific and scholarly research and of the academic ethic are pursued with more enthusiasm, seriousness, commitment, and effectiveness than they are in Europe?

Foreword

The growing significance for the commonwealth of scientific and scholarly knowledge and understanding and the unprecedented expansion of higher educational institutions which has flowed from the awareness of that significance have overtaxed the European universities. Despite the difference between the centrally, governmentally administered university systems of France, Italy, and Austria, the federal systems of the German Federal Republic and Switzerland, and the legally autonomous universities of Great Britain, their problems are essentially the same: the tasks which the universities are expected to perform are so multifarious, so subject to change, often so mutually contradictory, and also so immediately pressing that the universities are under unceasing pressure to deal with them and to bring them into harmony with their own traditional aims.

In response to this situation, representatives of the universities of fifteen European countries came together in Cambridge in 1955 for an exchange of experiences and ideas; in 1964 in Göttingen they formed the European Conference of Rectors.[1] Today more than 470 institutions of higher education from twenty-seven European countries belong to it. Its members meet every five years; every six months representatives of each country whose universities are members of the Conference meet to discuss the problems with which the universities are confronted owing to the deep social and cultural changes occurring in their respective societies.[2] In the course of these discussions a desire was often expressed for a more systematic understanding of the history of universities. The failure of the various attempts to reform the universities in the decades following the Second World War has shown that really effective solutions to the problems of the universities are unattainable without a better knowledge of their development and their long-standing traditions.

But the means of acquiring this better knowledge were lacking. It is true that there are innumerable works on the history of universities. The history of universities has over the past few decades become the object of many intensive investigations and of numerous conferences.[3] These have, however, been

---

[1] H.-A. Steger (ed.), *Das Europa der Universitäten, Entstehung der Ständigen Konferenz der Rektoren und Vize-Kanzler der europäischen Universitäten 1948–1962* (Bad Godesberg, 1964).

[2] *Europäische Rektorenkonferenz, III. Generalversammlung Göttingen 1964*, 2 vols. (Göttingen, 1964); J. Courvoisier (ed.), *Acts of the 4th General Assembly Geneva 1969* (Bologna, 1971); J. Roche (ed.), *Opening Address and Administrative Part of the 5th General Assembly held in Bologna September 1–6, 1974* (Bologna, 1977); CRE, *CRE VIth General Assembly* (Vienna, 1975); A. Barblan (ed.), *Actes de la VIIe Assemblée Générale tenue à Helsinki du 12 au 17 août 1979*, 2 vols. (Geneva, 1980); A. Barblan (ed.), *Actes de la VIIIe Assemblée Générale, tenue à Athènes du 9 au 14 septembre 1984* (Geneva, 1986); *CRE–Information*, quarterly, published by CRE from 1966, from 1988 onwards under the name *CRE–action*.

[3] S. Stelling-Michaud, 'L'histoire des universités au Moyen-âge et à la Renaissance au cours des vingt-cinq dernières années', in *XIe Congrès international des Sciences Historiques, Rapports*,

about various partial aspects of the larger subject: they have dealt with one or another epoch, with particular countries, universities, and disciplines, with the legal status of universities, with the statistics of admissions and graduation, with the lives of university teachers, etc. The last comprehensive history of universities is Stephen d'Irsay's *Histoire des universités françaises et étrangères des origines à nos jours*, which, for a long time, has been the standard work and was published in Paris in 1933–5; it needs revision in many of its details and it does not, in any case, go beyond 1860.[4]

For this reason, the Conference of European Rectors decided in 1982 to organize a collaborative investigation which would deal with the social setting, the social demands, the structures, and the major problems of the European universities as they have developed and changed in the course of their history. It was desired that the work should be performed in accordance with the highest standards of scholarly research, taking fully into account the results of the most recent research, and that it would be comparative, coherent, and comprehensive. The first step taken was the formation of a group of national correspondents who would be in a position to provide reliable information about the conditions of university life in their respective countries. With the assistance of this group, three programmes were initiated and carried out. The first was a set of expositions of the most important university problems seen historically in each country,[5] the second was the preparation and publication of a historical compendium of European universities,[6] and the third was the calling of an international conference, to be held in 1983, at which historians of universities from various European countries could discuss the changes in the social functions of universities; this conference was also expected to discuss the practical feasibility of a comprehensive, collaborative history of European universities.[7]

THE OBJECTIVE AND CONCEPTION OF THE PRESENT WORK

The present work as a comparative history of European universities has only one precursor. This is *Die Geschichte der Entstehung und Entwicklung der hohen Schulen unseres Erdtheils*, written by the British privy councillor and professor of 'worldly wisdom' at Göttingen, Christian Meiners, and

vol. I (Stockholm, 1960), 97–143; Italian translation with an up-to-date bibliography in G. Arnaldi (ed.), *Le origini dell'università* (Bologna, 1974), 153–217; J. Fletcher (ed.), *The History of European Universities, Work in Progress and Publications*, 1 (1974) – 5 (1981); from 1988 onwards the bibliography is published in *History of Universities* under the title 'Publications on University History since 1977: a Continuing Bibliography', ed. J. M. Fletcher and C. A. Upton; C. Schmitt and L. V. B. Brockliss (eds.), *History of Universities*, 1 (1981) onwards.

4 S. d'Irsay, *Histoire des universités françaises et étrangères des origines à nos jours*, 2 vols. (Paris, 1933–5).

5 'Interrogating the Past: in Search of the University', *CRE–Information*, 69 (1985).

6 L. Jílek (ed.), *Historical Compendium of European Universities* (Geneva, 1984).

7 'Town and Gown: the University in Search of its Origins', *CRE–Information*, 62 (1983).

published in four volumes between 1802 and 1805. Its goal was to set forth, as 'a pragmatic history of universities', 'the most important epochs of their establishment, their flowering and decay', as well as the 'most notable and distinctive features of universities in the cultivated states of Europe', and to do so 'in such a way that their misconduct, deficiencies, and faults would be recognized and corrected and their merits disclosed and emulated'.[8] The book is accordingly less chronological than thematic in its organization. The historical treatment of the origins focuses on 'nations' and faculties, the significance of colleges (*Kollegien*) and hostels (*Bursen*), the influence of external factors like the invention of paper, the printing of books, and the Renaissance and Reformation. Then there follows, in twelve books, the historical development of endowments, funds, privileges, academic courts, committees, offices, teachers, lecture rooms and classes, the conditions of study, and disciplinary measures. The work rests on a widely ranging but uncritical use of older monographs; thanks to the richness of its data, it was reprinted in 1973.

It was only after the critical assessment of the sources towards the end of the nineteenth century that it was possible to begin to write the history of the medieval universities in a genuinely scholarly way. The co-editor of the documentary sources for the history of the University of Paris, Denifle, presented in 1885 a historical account of the origins and the constitutional development of the various universities of Europe up to 1400.[9] Georg Kaufmann, a professor at the newly 'Prussianized' University of Strasburg, was charged by Althoff, the famous head of the Prussian higher education administration, to write a history of the German universities. In 1888, he showed in the first volume – which was a 'pre-history' of the German universities – the institutional development of the Italian 'city universities' (*Stadtuniversitäten*), that of the French and English 'chancellor universities' (*Kanzleruniversitäten*), and that of the 'state universities and Spanish universities' (*Staatsuniversitäten und spanische Universitäten*). In his concluding chapter, he attempted to depict the similarities in university development, especially with respect to academic degrees and founding charters. But he only managed to finish the first two volumes, both of which dealt with medieval universities.[10] Hastings Rashdall adopted a presentation by country and by university in his standard work in three volumes entitled, *The Universities of Europe in the Middle Ages*, first published in 1895 and revised in 1936 by Powicke and Emden, but he also added a detailed description of student life.[11] The only

---

[8] C. Meiners, *Geschichte der Entstehung und Entwicklung der hohen Schulen unseres Erdtheils*, vol. I (Göttingen, 1802; reprint, Aalen, 1973), 3ff.

[9] H. Denifle, *Die Entstehung der Universitäten des Mittelalters bis 1400* (Berlin, 1885; reprint, Graz, 1956).

[10] G. Kaufmann, *Geschichte der deutschen Universitäten*, vol. I, *Vorgeschichte* (Stuttgart, 1888; reprint, Graz, 1958).

[11] H. Rashdall, *The Universities of Europe in the Middle Ages*, 3 vols., ed. F. M. Powicke and A. B. Emden (Oxford, 1936; reprint, Oxford, 1988).

comprehensive work going beyond the Middle Ages is that of d'Irsay, which is an institutional and biographical history arranged according to centuries and intellectual currents, such as the Reformation, Romanticism, or positivism.

The editorial board appointed by the Conference of European Rectors in the autumn of 1983 had a more ambitious task. It was to set forth by sociological and comparative analysis the main intellectual and institutional features of the European academic world, with due attention to regional differences and historical changes.[12] In view of this, a pattern of analysis and presentation had to be devised which would permit the various periods of university history to be analysed in a way which enabled one epoch to be compared with another and which would do justice to the variegated aspects and changes in the functions of the university.

Accordingly, there are to be four volumes, all adhering systematically to an identical pattern. The first treats the rise and expansion of the universities in the Middle Ages, the second treats the regional, religious, and scientific and scholarly diversifications between 1500 and 1800; the third analyses the development of universities as scientific and scholarly institutions up to the Second World War; the fourth deals with the unprecedented expansion of scientific and scholarly research and teaching which has occurred since the end of the war. The boundaries between the periods are not interpreted as being more than a chronologically reasonable periodization of university history. Thus 1500 entails no decision regarding the disputed date of the end of the Middle Ages. It simply follows the periodization which has been applied in the standard works mentioned above on the history of universities. Undoubtedly, the universities of the sixteenth century, influenced by territorial–political and religious factors, are very different from those of the preceding period, which, despite their distinctive regional differences, were much influenced by the papal claim to universal legitimacy, which gave rise to a corresponding structural pattern. In a similar manner, 1800 marks, in a very general way, the beginning of two decisive though contradictory lines of development which are shared by the universities of the nineteenth century. The orientation of the centrally, governmentally organized educational system, perfected by Napoleon and aimed at immediate social utility, is one of these. The other pattern is that inspired by von Humboldt – research without practical ends and intended to serve the intellectual education of the human race. In the history of universities, the nineteenth century ends neither at 1900 nor at 1914. It is only after 1945 that the entire European higher educational scene and the individual universities present a quite different picture. In every scheme of periodization, the boundaries are always imprecise. That is also

---

[12] A. Barblan in 'Town and Gown' (note 7), 4ff. Concerning the concept of the project, see A. Barblan, A. de Puymège, and W. Rüegg, 'The History of the European University in Society: a Joint University Research Project', *History of European Ideas*, 8:2 (1987), 127–38.

the case here, and this will be made clear in the opening and concluding chapters of each volume as well as in all the others.

Each volume will consist of four major sections over which the fourteen or fifteen chapters will be distributed. Each will aim to provide the desired comparative analyses of the social functions of the European university as a whole. There will be no single portrayal of any particular university, but, through the use of the index, it will be possible to obtain from the various chapters a detailed idea of the significance of any particular university in the European situation as a whole.

The first part presents a thematic introduction and a comprehensive picture of the distribution and development of the universities in the period under consideration. Part II describes in three chapters the structures of the university, first, in relation to public authority, then in its internal organization, its financing, its buildings and equipment, its administrative and governing bodies and their ways of making decisions, and its academic staff – and, in the second, third, and fourth volumes, there will be a fourth chapter on the expansion of the European model of higher education to other continents. Part III deals in four chapters with one main task of the university, namely, the training of the students in scientific and scholarly knowledge, the social, economic, and intellectual preconditions of study at universities, the courses of study and the daily life of students generally, examinations, and careers. Part IV is devoted to the other main task of the university, namely, the validation, renewal, and expansion of human knowledge by the use of critical method. These four chapters are different in each volume corresponding to the prevailing kinds of science and scholarship in each epoch. In the first volume, attention is centred on the intellectual activities of the four faculties. In the second volume, the interplay between tradition and innovation within and outside the universities and the elaboration of the academic disciplines, the creation of systems in the humanistic subjects, and the significance of the universities in the 'scientific revolution' are highlighted. The third and fourth volumes deal with the modern specialized disciplines – from theology through philosophy, legal studies, and the natural and social sciences, to the medical and technological faculties, departments, and universities.

Such a work cannot be written by *one* person; this is self-evident. It was accordingly necessary to find, for each of fourteen or fifteen chapters, in the countries which shared the European tradition, an expert who could cover in a scholarly manner the subject-matter of that chapter. The larger the circle of collaborators, the greater the danger, in a work organized by themes, that the outcome would be a collection of unconnected essays, the sole unity of which would be constituted by their being bound together in a single volume. The editorial board, to avoid this, chose a rather complicated procedure. It began by working out, for each volume and for each chapter, an extensive set of substantive and methodical guidelines for the topics to be dealt with, and invited persons who expressed their readiness to collaborate on those terms to a first series of discussions. In these discussions, the prospective authors agreed on the division of labour, sometimes extending, sometimes contracting the subject-matter proposed for the chapters which they were being asked to write. In the course of these discussions, the consensus and mutual understanding necessary for such collaborative work were formed. At a second series of discussions the drafts of the various chapters were scrutinized and discussed in detail; national correspondents from the countries about which the editors and authors were insufficiently informed were invited to participate. The second drafts which followed these discussions were then worked over in detail by the editors in one or more meetings and, to the extent that this was possible by editorial procedures, the various chapters were coordinated with each other into a unified pattern.

Despite these efforts, the editors and the authors have not succeeded completely in eliminating either the – meaningful – inevitable stylistic and conceptual differences among individuals or the – less valuable – overlappings and disproportions in the treatments of particular topics. Overlaps could not be eliminated when a given phenomenon was important for several themes. The disproportionate attention paid to some regions or topics in relation to others is, in large part, a result of differences in the state of knowledge and the progress of research on those subjects. It has been a fundamental principle of our work that we have attempted to place the knowledge made available by the present state of research in the new perspective of a comparative synthesis. In this sense, each of the individual chapters represents a genuine achievement of research, even though they are not all equally the products of comprehensive investigations of archival sources.

THE SOCIAL ROLE OF THE EUROPEAN UNIVERSITY

By social function or role is implied the totality of the actions performed in response to the expectations of conduct which others direct toward the incumbent of the particular role. These expectations are based on values towards which conduct is oriented, and the values are translated into norms which guide the socially expected conduct. Expectations, values, and norms are delineated by the explicit and implicit interests of the various social actors and they are often mutually contradictory.

Conflicts are inherent in social roles, and not least in those of universities. Their fundamental values and the norms which are binding on their members are not homogeneous. The values of the universal validity of the criteria, methods, and results of scientific and scholarly research cannot always be adhered to in consequence of the limitations on and diversity of the cognitive powers of individual human beings. The equality of opportunity for admission to and continuance of studies at universities is in conflict with the inequality in the distribution of social and economic resources and of alternative uses for these resources. The precedence given to leisure and contemplation, which are necessary for scientific and scholarly research, represents an ideal of the *bios theoretikos*, which ever since the Greek philosophers has been contrasted and in conflict with the ideal of the *bios praktikos*, which gives precedence to social utility in the application of scientific knowledge and in the professional training provided by universities. The *amor sciendi*, which evaluates highly the search for truth by rigorous scientific and scholarly methods, is associated with indifference to the economic value of the results of research and teaching, and it stands in contradiction to the *ambitio dignitatis* and the *individia pecuniae*, the social and economic utilization of the fruits of academic study. Last but not least, the fundamental value of the academic freedom of the university as a corporate community stands in potential conflict, on two fronts: internally between the freedom of the individual and the collegial solidarity of the members of the university, and externally between the requirements of the university for autonomy and control by those who supply the necessary financial resources.

These and other conflicts are inherent in the social history of the university. To show the various forms which they have taken and the various solutions which have been attempted is the most important aim of our enterprise. Indeed, these conflicts, the tensions which arise from them, and the structures and mechanisms through which they are kept in a state of open equilibrium explain to a considerable extent the dynamics of the European universities. When one value becomes too preponderant and shifts the balance too markedly and too long to one alternative and away from the other, for example, to making the university into a governmental institution or into an ivory tower or into a vocational school or into a wholly self-contained scientific institution, the tensions lose their creative power and lead instead to somnolence or excessive superficial and fruitless agitation.

We certainly no longer share the view, which was put forward by Meiners and which was so characteristic of the Enlightenment, that the history of European universities can 'lead in part to the recognition and avoidance of their misconduct, deficiencies, and faults, and in part to the disclosure and emulation of their merits'.[13] Just as a machine can only be repaired and made operable once more when the significance of its parts and their interdependence is understood and tested, so the university, which is a very complex social institution, must from time to time be subjected to a fundamental analysis. This fundamental analysis of its structures and functions, which have developed in the course of history, is indispensable if the deeper aspects of its social role are to be understood and realistically improved.

[13] Meiners, *Geschichte* (note 8), 4.

ACKNOWLEDGEMENTS

The preparatory work for *A History of the University in Europe* has been generously supported by the Max and Else Beer-Brawand Fund of the University of Berne, the Donors' Association for the Promotion of Sciences and Humanities in Germany (*Stifterverband für die deutsche Wissenschaft*) in Essen, the European Cultural Foundation in Amsterdam, the Konrad Adenauer Foundation in Bonn, the Ramón Areces Foundation in Madrid, the Portuguese Secretary of State for Higher Education, the National Institute for Scientific Research, and the Calouste Gulbenkian Foundation in Lisbon, the António de Almeida Foundation in Oporto, the Volkswagen Foundation in Hanover, and the Fritz Thyssen Foundation in Cologne. We thank these patrons wholeheartedly. We are no less grateful to the universities at which our conferences and discussions have taken place, notably the Universities of Berne, Salamanca, Coimbra, Eichstätt, and Oxford. We should also like to express our thanks to Professors Grete Klingenstein of the University of Graz and W. Roy Niblett, emeritus professor at the University of London; as members of the editorial board in the early stages of the project, they helped to outline the framework of our *History*. Furthermore, we acknowledge the advice and support of Professor Nikolaus Lobkowicz, former president of the University of Munich and now president of the Catholic University of Eichstätt, who played a key role in defining and launching the whole undertaking. But, above all, we thank the secretary general, Andris Barblan, and the assistant secretary general, Alison de Puymège-Browning, of the Standing Conference of Rectors, Presidents, and Vice-Chancellors of the European Universities (CRE); it is they who, with tireless devotion and alertness, made possible the harmonious – indeed friendly – cooperation between so many European scholars.

PART I

THEMES AND PATTERNS

CHAPTER 1

THEMES

WALTER RÜEGG

No period in the history of universities has been more intensively studied than the Middle Ages.[1] Nevertheless, numerous gaps remain. Many archival documents, innumerable writings, and many of the lecture scripts of university teachers are still unpublished. Biographical accounts of teachers and students, their social and familial origins, their patterns of association in the course of their studies, and their subsequent careers are markedly lacking. Such prosopographical investigations, which have already been taken in hand for particular universities[2] or for certain regions of provenance,[3] are indispensable for a genuinely social history of universities.[4] Only when such

[1] J. M. F. Fletcher and J. Deahl, 'European Universities, 1300–1700, The Development of Research, 1969–1981 and a Summary Bibliography', in J. M. Kittelson and P. J. Transue (eds.), *Rebirth, Reform and Resilience. Universities in Transition 1300–1700* (Columbia, Ohio, 1984), 324–57; P. Denley, 'Recent Studies on Italian Universities in the Middle Ages and the Renaissance', *History of Universities*, 1 (1981), 198–205.

[2] A. B. Emden, *A Biographical Register of the University of Oxford to 1500*, 3 vols. (Oxford, 1957–9); D. E. R. Watt, *A Biographical Dictionary of Scottish Graduates to AD 1410* (Oxford, 1970); C. Renardy, *Le Monde des maîtres universitaires de Liège, 1140–1359. Recherches sur sa composition et ses activités* (Paris, 1979); C. Renardy, *Les Maîtres universitaires du diocèse de Liège. Répertoire biographique (1140–1350)* (Paris, 1981); J. Verger, 'Peut-on faire une prosopographie des professeurs des universités françaises du Moyen-Age?', *Mélanges de l'Ecole française de Rome, Moyen Age*, 100 (1988), 55–62; A. B. Emden, *A Biographical Register of the University of Oxford AD 1501 to 1540* (Oxford, 1974); H. de Ridder-Symoens, D. Illmer, and C. M. Ridderikhoff, *Le Premier livre des procurateurs de la nation germanique de l'ancienne Université d'Orléans. Seconde partie: Biographie des étudiants*, 3 vols. (Leiden, 1978–85).

[3] S. Stelling-Michaud, 'L'histoire des universités au Moyen Age et à la Renaissance au cours des 25 dernières années', in *XIe Congrès International des Sciences Historiques, Rapports*, vol. I (Stockholm, 1960), 121–30. For Switzerland: O. Vasella, 'Untersuchungen über die Bildungsverhältnisse im Bistum Chur mit besonderer Berücksichtigung des Klerus vom Ausgang des 13. Jahrhunderts bis um 1500', in 62. *Jahresbericht der Historisch-Antiquarischen Gesellschaft von Graubünden* (Chur, 1932); K. M. Zahnd, *Die Bildungsverhältnisse in den bernischen Ratsgeschlechtern im ausgehenden Mittelalter* (Berne, 1979). Further literature in W. Rüegg, *Humanistische Elitenbildung in der Eidgenossenschaft zur Zeit der Renaissance. Wolfenbütteler Abhandlungen zur Renaissanceforschung*, vol. 9 (Wiesbaden 1991), 95–133.

[4] Fletcher and Deahl, 'European Universities' (note 1), 327; L. Stone (ed.), *The University in*

studies have been done will it be 'possible to trace the channels of intellectual currents and influence, to reconstruct the composition and structure of intellectual groups and their connections with each other, and the lines of transmission and diffusion of certain intellectual traditions such as Aristotelianism in the thirteenth, Roman law in the fourteenth, humanism in the fifteenth, and the Reformation in the sixteenth centuries'.[5]

For these reasons, our project can reflect only the present state of research. The aim of this introductory chapter is to show, with reference to a few themes, which perspectives have been opened up through studies of medieval universities, which problems have arisen from those studies, and what knowledge can be drawn from them.

MYTHOLOGY AND HISTORIOGRAPHY OF THE BEGINNINGS

In 1988, the University of Bologna celebrated its nine-hundredth anniversary. However, neither our own investigation nor that of others into the history of medieval universities has produced any evidence for such a foundation of the University of Bologna in 1088. Rather, the upshot of these investigations is that no such event took place in 1088.[6] In fact, 1088 was chosen a century ago as the 'conventional date' by a committee under the chairmanship of the famous poet Giosuè Carducci; 1888 was to be the occasion for a grand jubilee to be celebrated in the presence of the royal family and rectors of universities from all over the world were to attend. The aim of the celebration was to imprint on the consciousness of the Italian people and of the whole world the knowledge that the recent and still not completely consolidated political unification of Italy could point for its legitimacy to the eight-centuries-long tradition of free research and teaching at the University of Bologna and its national and world-wide importance.[7] The celebration of the eighth centenary of the University of Bologna in 1888 was in fact one of the commemorative celebrations and related symbolic manifestations which were arranged in the course of the nineteenth century in order to remind the nations of their

---

Society, vol. I (Princeton, 1974), 4; P. Classen, *Studium und Gesellschaft im Mittelalter*, ed. J. Fried (Stuttgart, 1983), 18; J. Miethke, 'Die Kirche und die Universitäten im 13. Jahrhundert', in *Schulen und Studium*, 287; G. F. Lyttle, 'The Careers of Oxford Students in the Later Middle Ages', in Kittelson and Transue (eds.), *Rebirth* (note 1), 214; H. Coing (ed.), *Handbuch der Quellen und Literatur der neueren europäischen Privatrechtsgeschichte*, vol. I (Munich, 1973), 85 ff.; J. Verger, 'A propos de la naissance de l'université de Paris: contexte social, enjeu politique, portée intellectuelle', in *Schulen und Studium*, 88.

5 Stelling-Michaud, 'Histoire' (note 3), 121.

6 Rashdall, *Universities*, vol. I, 118; H. Grundmann, *Vom Ursprung der Universität im Mittelalter* (Darmstadt, 1957, 2nd edn 1960), 40. Even A. Sorbelli, *Storia della Università di Bologna*, vol. I, *Il Medioevo (Sec. XI–XV)* (Bologna, 1940), written on the occasion of the 850th birthday, does not mention the date.

7 U. Eco (ed.), *Bologna 1088–1988, Alma Mater Studiorum Saecularia Nona* (Milan, n.d. [1987]), [45]. W. Tega (ed.), *Lo Studio e la città. Bologna 1888–1988* (Bologna, 1987), 11–61.

past and its historical continuity and to fortify in them a sense of their national unity.[8]

Commemorative celebrations focus on a particular date. For that reason, a particular date had to be found and it had to be one which was as early as possible so that the politically important, symbolic function of the University of Bologna as the 'mother of European universities' could not be challenged on that occasion. Carducci and his medievalist colleagues based their claim on a document of the thirteenth century. According to this document, the 'famous Irnerius' (1055/60–1125) and an 'unknown' Pepo were the first to have delivered lectures on law in Bologna. Jubilees in most instances stimulate historical research.[9] Such research often corrects the date of foundation or shows the historical account of the alleged foundation to be a myth. Even more than the jubilee celebrations of other universities, the celebration of the eight-hundredth anniversary of the University of Bologna released a flood of publications on the history of universities. We know now that Pepo was by no means 'unknown'; he was referred to in 1190 as *'clarum Bononiensium lumen'*,[10] and presented himself at the court of Emperor Henry IV as an authority on Roman law.[11] In this regard, Carducci would not have chosen the 'conventional date' badly, if in fact Pepo was the founder, or at least a member, of a university. The booklet published on the occasion of the celebration of the nine-hundredth anniversary justified 1088 as the date of foundation of the university by the argument that, in that year, there appeared free arrangements for the teaching of law which were independent of the religious schools of Bologna and that such independence was the mark of a university.[12]

Is this argument defensible? No scholar doubts nowadays that, at various places in the eleventh and twelfth centuries, there existed significant schools and that successful teachers appeared as independent masters who gathered around themselves a circle of pupils. In Bologna, *legum doctores*, who were

[8] Cf. T. Nipperdey, 'Nationalidee und Nationaldenkmäler im 19. Jahrhundert', *Historische Zeitschrift*, 206 (1968), 528–85; E. Fehrenbach, 'Ueber die Bedeutung der politischen Symbole im Nationalstaat', *Historische Zeitschrift*, 213 (1971), 291–357.

[9] For the ambiguous relation between jubilees and the historiography of universities: N. Hammerstein, 'Jubiläumsschrift und Alltagsarbeit. Tendenzen bildungsgeschichtlicher Literatur', *Historische Zeitschrift*, 238 (1983), 601–33; J. Verger, 'Du bon et du mauvais usage des anniversaires', *Histoire*, 115 (Oct. 1988), 78–80. For Bologna: Denley, 'Recent Studies' (note 1), 193; Rashdall, *Universities*, vol. I, 88. For German Democratic Republic: W. Fläschendräger and M. Straube, *Die Entwicklung der Universitäten, Hochschulen und Akademien im Spiegel der hochschulgeschichtlichen Forschungen (1960–1969) – Literaturübersicht*, Informationen und Studien zur Hochschulentwicklung, 12 (Berlin, 1970).

[10] G. Cencetti, 'Studium fuit Bononie', in G. Arnaldi (ed.), *Le origini dell'università* (Bologna, 1974), 101–15.

[11] L. Schmugge, '"Codicis Iustiniani baiulus" – Eine neue Quelle zu Magister Pepo von Bologna', *Ius Commune*, 6 (1977), 1–9. H. G. Walther, 'Die Anfänge des Rechtsstudiums und die kommunale Welt Italiens', in *Schulen und Studium*, 138–44, does not recognize Pepo as a Bologna professor of law.

[12] Eco, *Bologna 1088–1988* (note 7), [14].

active as lawyers and judges, joined with their pupils to form free corporations.[13] There is also agreement among various investigators – as subsequent chapters show – that it was the associations of students (in Bologna) or of teachers and students (in Paris), which were granted special liberties and privileges in the thirteenth century, that first laid the basis for that form of higher education which in the Middle Ages was called *studium generale* and which later was designated as a university.

For this reason, Abelard, who taught in the first forty years of the twelfth century at Melun, Corbeil, and Paris, in part in a religious school and in part as probably the most famous independent teacher, has long since ceased to be regarded as the founder of the University of Paris.[14] Similarly, the medical school of Salerno has lost its reputation as the oldest European university;[15] it is, at best, regarded as a 'proto-university'.[16] This does not, of course, detract from its scientific significance as a school for physicians in the tenth century, as a medical centre in the twelfth century, and as a model of medical research and teaching in the thirteenth century.[17]

The origin of the first universities is a very complex process, as will be seen in the next chapter. Bologna or Paris may be called the oldest university depending on the weight which one attributes to one or another of the various elements which make up a university. If one regards the existence of a corporate body as the sole criterion, then Bologna is the oldest, but only by a slight margin. It was in Bologna that, towards the end of the twelfth century, the foreign students of law grouped themselves together as 'nations' and therewith developed a basic organizational form of the medieval European university. If one regards the association of teachers and students of various disciplines into a single corporate body as the decisive criterion, then the oldest university would be Paris, dating from 1208.[18]

The question of which university is the oldest is of practical importance only when it has to be decided which rectors should be granted precedence in academic ceremonies and processions. The date of foundation is more important because of the social and psychological significance of jubilees. Yet, as the next chapter will show,[19] it is very difficult and often arbitrary to assign

---

13 P. Weimar, 'Zur Doktorwürde der Bologneser Legisten', in C. Bergfeld (ed.), *Aspekte europäischer Rechtsgeschichte. Festgabe für Helmut Coing zum 70. Geburtstag* (Frankfurt, 1972), 422.

14 Rashdall, *Universities*, vol. I, 276–8. Cf. S. C. Ferruolo, *The Origins of the University. The Schools of Paris and their Critics* (Stanford, 1985), 24.

15 P. O. Kristeller, 'The School of Salerno, its Development and Contributions to the History of Learning', *Bulletin of the History of Medicine*, 17 (1945), 138–94; reprinted in P. O. Kristeller, *Studies in Renaissance Thought and Letters* (Rome, 1956), 495–551.

16 Cobban, *Medieval Universities*, 37.

17 P. O. Kristeller, 'The Curriculum of Italian Universities from the Middle Ages to the Renaissance', *Proceedings of the PMR Conference*, 9 (1984), 3.

18 *CUP*, vol. I, 67, no. 8; Verger, 'Naissance' (note 4), 86; Ferruolo, *Origins* (note 14), 5.

19 See pp. 45 ff.

an exact date to the foundation of a particular university. This is true not only for the oldest universities, which arose only gradually and which are officially acknowledged in various written documents as having 'grown through custom', *e consuetudine*, in a sequence of stages.[20] Even where the foundation of a university has occurred through an explicit decree or enactment, *e privilegio*, the question arises as to which particular event should be regarded as the date of foundation. Should it be the decision of a local authority to found a university or to recognize an existing school as a university, or should it be the recognition or endowment by papal, imperial, or royal authority, or should it be the executive decision by the local municipal authority, or the beginning of the teaching?

It is easier to answer the question as to whether the medieval university had forerunners or models. Very much like contemporary universities, the early universities dated their origins as early as possible. In Bologna, between 1226 and 1234, a founding document was forged, which asserted that the university was established in AD 423 by Emperor Theodosius.[21] The University of Paris thought that it had been founded by Charlemagne, and, through his action, it was able to see itself as a continuator of the tradition of Roman higher education.[22] Some claimed for Oxford an even earlier origin: when, following the destruction of their own city of Troy, the Trojans conquered Albion, it was said that they were accompanied by some philosophers who found a suitable place for themselves in Oxford. A more modest tradition contented itself with Alfred the Great (848–99) as the founder of Oxford.[23] All of these fictions, which were questioned or refuted by the humanists, may be traced back to the medieval practice of legitimating an institution by asserting the antiquity of its origin. The assertion of a line of descent which traced medieval universities back to antiquity does have some justification, inasmuch as essential features of their intellectual substance were of classical origin and then christianized by Saint Augustine and other church fathers. Medieval scholars regarded themselves as dwarfs who stood on the shoulders of their gigantic ancient ancestors and who for that reason could see further.[24] Nevertheless, the organizational form of the university cannot be traced to classical antiquity, nor was it influenced by Byzantium.[25]

[20] Cf. Miethke, 'Kirche' (note 4), 290; Denifle, *Entstehung*, 231.

[21] A. Borst, 'Geschichte an mittelalterlichen Universitäten', *Konstanzer Universitätsreden*, 17 (1969), 24–30.

[22] Stelling-Michaud, 'Histoire' (note 3), 99; Cobban, *Medieval Universities*, 14.

[23] J. Morris, *The Oxford Book of Oxford* (Oxford, 1978), 3ff.

[24] Cf. R. K. Merton, *On the Shoulders of Giants. A Shandean Postscript* (San Diego/New York/London, 1985; 1st edn, New York, 1965).

[25] Cobban, *Medieval Universities*, 20ff.; P. Speck, 'Die Kaiserliche Universität von Konstantinopel. Präzisierungen zur Frage des höheren Schulwesens in Byzanz im 9. und 10. Jahrhundert', *Byzantinisches Archiv*, 14 (Munich, 1973), 69–91; C. N. Constaninides, *Higher Education in Byzantium in the Thirteenth and Early Fourteenth Centuries (1203–ca 1310), Texts and Studies of the History of Greece*, 11 (Nicosia, 1982).

It seems more plausible to derive the organizational pattern of the medieval university from the Islamic schools of learning. (The importance of the latter for scholarly activity in philosophy, natural science, and medicine is evident in chapters 10 and 11.) British Islamic scholars give an affirmative answer to the question: 'Did the Arabs invent the university?' They maintain that Islamic institutions of learning were the source of the idea of organizing foreign students into nations and that they were also the source of the ideas of the universal validity of the qualification for teaching conferred by the *venia docendi*, of the academic robe, and of the title of the *baccalarius*.[26] Of course, the invocation of such affinities often confuses the *propter hoc* with the *post hoc*; it does not demonstrate whether and how the later forms emerged from the earlier ones. Furthermore, the discernment of such affinities requires an exact knowledge of both traditions. The term *baccalarius* could not be an Islamic importation of the twelfth century because it was already in use in the ninth century as the Latin designation of a preparatory or auxiliary status in a variety of social careers. The American Islamicist, Makdisi, who is to be taken more seriously, has discovered eighteen substantial affinities between the Islamic and the occidental patterns of the organization of learning and their transmission through institutional arrangements more or less like universities. He has concluded, however, that 'the university is a twelfth century product of the Christian West of the twelfth century, not only in its organization but also in the privileges and protection it received from Pope and King'. But the situation is different with regard to the colleges, which he does derive from Islamic models.[27]

The borrowings which the university made from other medieval institutions were more important. As the next chapter shows, the very idea of the *universitas* is drawn from the term for many kinds of cooperative associations. The term had, however, to be supplemented to refer to the special features of the university, namely *universitas magistrorum et scholarium* or *universitas studii*. The corporate features, privileges, statutes, seals, and oaths and the functions and titles of their officials all have a close affinity to contemporaneous legal and organizational forms.[28] Taken as a whole, the medieval university, as is apparent in the various chapters of this volume, is part of and an expression of its social environment.

---

[26] R. Y. Ebied and M. J. L. Young, 'New Light on the Origin of the Term "Baccalaureate"', *Islamic Quarterly*, 18:1–2 (1974), 1–7; R. Y. Ebied and M. J. L. Young, 'Did the Arabs invent the university?' *Times Higher Education Supplement*, 2 May 1975.

[27] G. Makdisi, *The Rise of Colleges, Institutions of Learning in Islam and the West* (Edinburgh, 1981), 287ff.

[28] Verger, 'Naissance' (note 4), 90; P. Michaud-Quantin, '*Universitas*'. *Expression du mouvement communautaire dans le Moyen-Age latin* (Paris, 1970).

THE UNIVERSITY: PRODUCT AND SHAPER OF SOCIETY

How is the origin of the university to be explained? Is it a resultant of the society in which it exists or is it a factor in the formation of society? Answers to this question are not dependent solely on the progress of research. The answers are affected by and are raised in the context of existing political conditions and of the current state of discussions about higher educational policy.[29]

Meiners' comparative history of universities, which has been mentioned in the 'Foreword', was written in 1802–5, immediately after the publication of the author's own large book on higher educational policy. In the latter, he emphasized the greater importance of scientific and theoretical education in comparison with education aimed at practical utility, and he recommended a number of reforms which were intended to counteract contemporary efforts to transform the universities into higher vocational training schools.[30] Accordingly, he viewed the earliest universities as 'a manifestation of the powerful progress of the spirit',[31] and he explained their origin in accordance with the ideas of the Enlightenment about the unceasing advance of the human striving for knowledge. Thus he explained the origin of the university by the substantial increase in the number of independent teachers in the twelfth century and the successful struggle of the scholars, who had achieved self-consciousness, for the recognition of their rights and privileges. He enquired, in a way which was astonishingly precise in view of the state of the sources available to him, into the emergence and development of academic communities in the Middle Ages. He had no doubt whatsoever that the universities were not epiphenomenal products of their social environment but had rather a formative role in shaping it. For this reason, he was really interested only in the benefits conferred and the damages inflicted on the university by its environing society.

This fundamental attitude was also to be seen in the works of Denifle, Kaufmann, and Rashdall, which were published between 1885 and 1895 and which proceeded in a more critical, scholarly way than did Meiners' own work. Even as late as 1923, 'the ancient and universal company of scholars' was at the centre of interest in the work of the American medievalist, Charles Homer Haskins;[32] d'Irsay, too, in his *Histoire des universités* published in

---

[29] Rashdall, *Universities*, vol. I, 12 n. 2, regards Kaufmann's controversy with Denifle as vitiated by an infusion of ideas suggested by the *Kulturkampf*.

[30] C. Meiner, *Über die Verfassung und Verwaltung der deutschen Universitäten*, 2 vols. (Göttingen, 1801–2; reprint, Aalen, 1970).

[31] C. Meiner, *Geschichte der Entstehung und Entwicklung der hohen Schulen unseres Erdtheils*, vol. I (Göttingen, 1802; reprint, Aalen, 1973), 7.

[32] C. H. Haskins, *The Rise of Universities* (New York, 1923), 126.

1933–5, regarded the history of universities as being primarily a part of intellectual history.[33]

According to Marxism,

> the thesis, so often and so variously reiterated by bourgeois and imperialistic historiography, that there is a pure idea of learning and of universities which has no relationship to classes and to class struggle ... has been shown by history to be an error and a falsification ... Schools and higher educational institutions are founded in order to train the persons who are needed to maintain the ruling class domination.[34]

Grundmann, in a lecture delivered at Jena and Leipzig in 1956, took a clear position against the somewhat more differentiated thesis that the university is determined by the 'needs of the ruling classes'. He said that the beginnings of the universities were favoured, it was true, by the social and economic developments which were concomitant with 'the efflorescence of commerce and transportation fostered by the crusades, the birth of a money economy or early capitalism with the growth of cities which had been affected by it, especially in Italy and France, and with the improvements in agriculture and in the position of the persons engaged in it'. But these developments in no way caused the universities.

> [Neither the] demand for persons with professional, vocational training or general education nor governmental, ecclesiastical, and social and economic demands and motives are the primary, constitutive, or really fundamental and determinative factors underlying the origin and nature of universities as wholly novel communities and as seats of teaching and study. Rather the contrary! Put in a nutshell, the stimulus to the emergence and growth of universities was scholarly and scientific interest, the desire to learn and to know, the *amor sciendi*.[35]

Grundmann's argument has been criticized as too idealistic or too ideological. Classen said in 1964 that the pure love of knowledge was better embodied in the cathedral school at Chartres than it was in the University of Paris; he asked how and why it happened that a university emerged here and not there. 'It seems that, in addition to the intellectual factors, there were other forces and motives which made possible the university as a new social form.' He cites Abelard's confession that he taught only from *pecunie et laudis cupiditas*, from greed and ambition, and a sentence of the broadly learned Peter of Blois, who later became a courtier (*c.* 1180): 'There are two

---

[33] d'Irsay, *Histoire des universités*, 1.

[34] G. Steiger and W. Fläschendräger (eds.), *Magister und Scholaren, Professoren und Studenten, Geschichte der Universitäten im Überblick* (Leipzig, 1981), 12; M. Steinmetz, 'Die Konzeption der deutschen Universitäten im Zeitalter von Humanismus und Renaissance', in *Les Universités européennes du XIVe au XVIIIe siècle, aspects et problèmes. Actes du Colloque international à l'occasion du VIe Centenaire de l'Université Jagellonne, Cracovie 6–8 Mai 1964* (Geneva, 1967), 115; W. Prahl, *Sozialgeschichte der Universität* (Munich, 1978), 13.

[35] Grundmann, *Ursprung* (note 6), 36, 39.

things which drive men hard to the study of jurisprudence; these are the pursuit of offices and the vain passion for fame [*ambitio dignitatis et inanis gloriae appetitus*].' For these reasons, Classen concluded that

> The schools of the twelfth century and the universities of the thirteenth century never set themselves the goal of providing the courts and municipalities with specialized experts. Nevertheless, the new social pattern which took form in the university was in part shaped by society, since it was the lively interest of wider social groups which made it possible for the higher schools to become enduring and independent institutions. From the very beginning, education was subject to the tension between the fundamental and primary impulse to seek the truth and the desire of many persons to acquire practical training. Conversely, without really wanting to do so, the schools formed the new academic stratum and changed the whole structure of society, enriching it and making it more complex.[36]

Most scholars nowadays share this view – not least as a result of the discussion of Grundmann's thesis.[37] Cobban and Esch lay more weight on the needs of an urbanized society and of an emergent ecclesiastical and governmental bureaucracy.[38] Le Goff and Southern lay more stress on the emancipation of the universities from social pressure.[39] But simple views are unacceptable; no serious historian disputes that the university neither descends on society from the heavens, nor simply emanates from it as a function of the social forces of production. The university and the society which environs it interact with each other, they influence one another. Without the intellectual stimulus of the rationally controlled search for knowledge, there would be no university. 'But the spirit alone cannot create its body.'[40] The new social institution, the university, could have arisen only in the particular economic, political, and social circumstances obtaining in certain cities of Europe in the early Middle Ages.

On the basis of the present state of knowledge, we cannot answer the question of what the decisive factors were or in which constellation they had to be combined so that beginners and mature scholars could be fused into a corporate body which would be guaranteed its rights and privileges by public authorities. Nevertheless, the histories of the foundation of the first universities do offer some suggestions.

The transformation of private schools of law into the university which first

[36] Classen, *Studium* (note 4), 25.
[37] Verger, 'Naissance' (note 4), 86; A. Seifert, 'Studium und soziales System', in *Schulen und Studium*, 604ff.; Arnaldi (ed.) *Origini* (note 10), 15ff.
[38] Cobban, *Medieval Universities*, 8; A. Esch, *Die Anfänge der Universität im Mittelalter. Rektoratrede Universität Bern 1985* (Berne, 1985), 8ff.
[39] J. Le Goff, *Les Intellectuels au Moyen Age*, Le Temps qui court, 3 (Paris, n.d. [1957]), 73; J. Le Goff, 'Les universités et les pouvoirs publics au moyen âge et à la Renaissance', in *Rapports du XIIe congrès international des sciences historiques*, vol. III, *Commissions* (Vienna, 1965), 189; R. Southern, 'From Schools to University', in *History of Oxford*, 35.
[40] Classen, *Studium* (note 4), 4.

occurred in Bologna might have arisen from the confluence of a number of external factors. These include the fact that Bologna was a nodal point of commercial routes and of the ways of pilgrimage from the north to Rome, as well as the interest of the emperor in the elaboration and application of Roman law as a means of legitimating his imperial claims. This interest moved Frederick I Barbarossa in 1155 to issue *Authentica Habita*,[41] and led to the strengthening of the municipality of Bologna after the decline of the Holy Roman Empire. All these external factors contributed to making Bologna into the seat of a university. No less important was the reputation of famous teachers throughout the entire twelfth century, which attracted students from various countries to Bologna. But the organization of a university occurred only when economically, socially, and politically powerful foreign students came together to protect their interests collectively against the town and their teachers.[42]

In Paris, which, with the consolidation of the Capetian monarchy, became a political, economic, and cultural capital, the competition among many schools under different religious authorities led, in the course of the twelfth century, to a concentration of famous teachers and to a corresponding influx of students. The kings, one of whom, Louis VII, had himself been a student, favoured these educational developments. The students were well provided with food but it was less easy for them to find suitable accommodation; in response to this situation, colleges for poor students were founded in 1180 and 1186.[43] As will be seen in the next chapter, the formation of the university was above all due to the efforts of the masters, supported by the king and the pope, to loosen local ecclesiastical supervision and, through the exercise of joint responsibility, to bring order into the anarchic arrangements for studies. Following fluctuating conflicts with the chancellor, the religious orders, and the citizens, between 1208 and 1231, this led also to the public recognition of the university.[44]

The royal court in London and the English episcopate employed more masters (*magistri*) in the twelfth century than the French monarchy and the church in France.[45] English scholars had studied in Europe; they had a special preference for Paris.[46] What led them, when towards the end of the century they wished to study in England, to decide on Oxford and not London? The

---

[41] See chapter 3, p. 78.   [42] Cobban, *Medieval Universities*, 49–55.

[43] Cobban, *Medieval Universities*, 79–82; Ferruolo, *Origins* (note 14), 22–6; 250–4; A. L. Gabriel, 'The Cathedral Schools of Notre Dame', in A. L. Gabriel, *Garlandia. Studies in the History of the Medieval University* (Frankfurt, 1969), 41ff.

[44] Cf. S. C. Ferruolo, 'The Paris Statutes of 1215 reconsidered', *History of Universities*, 5 (1985), 11; Verger, 'Naissance' (note 4), 75ff.

[45] J. W. Baldwin, 'The Penetration of University Personnel into French and English Administration at the Time of the Twelfth and Thirteenth Century', *Etudes Islamiques*, 44 (1976), 204–10.

[46] A. L. Gabriel, 'English Masters and Students in Paris during the Twelfth Century', in Gabriel, *Garlandia* (note 43), 1–57.

new *History of the University of Oxford* also asks this question. Oxford was a small provincial town, not to be compared with cathedral towns, and certainly not with London. But Oxford did acquire in the 1180s a certain strategic political significance as the seat of the royal administration and of the ecclesiastical courts. This encouraged some learned lawyers to move to Oxford and it encouraged some of them to offer instruction in the law. Within a decade, the Oxford school of law was the only one in England which was able to attract foreign students, even though they came from educationally backward areas like Friesland and Hungary. These developments also encouraged one of the best-known theologians of his time, Alexander Neckam, to take up teaching at Oxford. In 1209, the teachers refused to go on with their teaching in reaction against some excessive actions by the local authorities; they ceased their strike only in 1214, after the municipality, either as a result of the mediation of a papal legate or his command, had granted to the scholars liberties and privileges like those which were provided in Paris.[47]

In all three cities, the combination of political and economic advantages and the deference granted to the scholarly reputation of local teachers and their educational institutions attracted students and teachers in large numbers and of high quality. This assured both groups the protection of their interests against the local authorities. In Paris, it was also a means of constraining the otherwise unregulated competition among various teachers and schools, and of bringing about their amalgamation into 'universities'. In each city, the decisive factor was the interest of the teachers and students, first in a formal pattern of studies in which they could work on their own responsibility, then in the settlement of their disputes with the local authorities about freedoms and privileges, and finally in their support by the central authorities.

In Montpellier, where the school of medicine acquired the standing of a university at about the same time, the circumstances which attended the consolidation into a unitary corporate body are unclear. Nevertheless, this fourth of the oldest university cities shares with the others certain essential features; these were its economic importance, as the area of intersection of the Rhône valley, Spain, and Provence, a cultural efflorescence, and ultimately a flourishing seat of medicine and law schools which drew students from afar, as well as its special political position as a fief and outpost of the pope, who, in 1220, granted the university its statutes through the agency of a cardinal legate.

Where one or other feature or property was absent, such as the presence of famous teachers or royal or papal support, universities arose only later. This was the case with Pavia and Padua, which, as economically important entrepôts, had well-established schools of law.[48] The establishment only in 1346 of the first university in the Holy Roman Empire at Prague, which was at the

---

47 Southern, 'From Schools' (note 39), 4–36; R. W. Southern, *Robert Grosseteste. The Growth of an English Mind in Europe* (Oxford, 1986), 56.
48 Walther, 'Anfänge des Rechtsstudiums' (note 11), 121–35.

eastern periphery of the empire, although there were numerous politically and economically powerful German cities which had good schools of their own in the twelfth century but which were without universities, may be attributed to 'the insufficient support and uninterestedness of the dominant strata of German society'. These strata regarded noble birth as the criterion for appointment to higher positions in the church as more important than it was regarded in France, where 'scholarly distinction could enable even foreigners and non-nobles to become bishops'.[49]

These are only hypotheses. A conclusive explanation as to why there was no university in London and why universities were founded later in Rome (1303), Cologne (1388), and Mainz (1476) than in Bologna, Oxford, Montpellier, and Salamanca (1218–19) can only be given – if it can ever be given – after further source materials have been discovered and analysed, as we mentioned at the very beginning of this introduction.

EXPECTATIONS OF CHURCH, CROWN, AND MUNICIPALITY

What did the various social agents, the popes, the emperors, the territorial princes, the bishops, the municipal authorities, the aristocracy, the bourgeoisie, and, in the late Middle Ages, the peasantry on the one hand and the students and teachers on the other, expect of the universities? What defined their social role, which was a response to these diverse and often controversial expectations, and which cannot be conceived without taking these conflicts into account?

All of them hoped to gain from scholarly and scientific knowledge support in their struggle for existence; the political and ecclesiastical powers hoped to gain support and reinforcement of their dominion, the students and teachers sought knowledge and social advantage, the residents of university towns wanted improved well-being. But, for these purposes, there was really no need for universities.

As Frederick I Barbarossa said in 1155, in his fundamental law regarding academic liberties, it is by learning that the world is illuminated and the lives of subjects are shaped towards obedience to God and his servant, the emperor: *quorum scientia mundus illuminatur ad obediendum deo et nobis, eius ministris, vita subjectorum informatur.*[50] This rhetorical formulation delineated very precisely the dual expectations of the highest earthly power. The symbolism of light, so beloved in the Middle Ages, expresses the view that scholarship enriches knowledge and gives stability to the social order.

[49] J. Ehlers, 'Die hohen Schulen', in P. Weimar (ed.), *Die Renaissance der Wissenschaften im 12. Jahrhundert*, Züricher Hochschulforum Universität Zürich, E. T. H. Zürich, 2 (Zurich, 1981), 72.

[50] P. Krüger and T. Mommsen (eds.), *Corpus iuris civilis* vol. II (Berlin, 1877), 511; reprinted in Kaufmann, *Deutsche Universitäten*, vol. I, 165.

Pepo was surely not the founder of the University of Bologna but he was probably the first person to explain to an emperor – Henry IV – what new support for order the study of Roman law provides. At a criminal trial, conducted in the presence of the emperor, he protested against a ruling which decreed the usual punishment of the payment of *Wergeld* proportionately to the status of the person who had been killed by saying that the 'sacred laws of the emperor, i.e. Roman law, in accordance with the natural law of the equality of human beings, forbids the unequal treatment of a free person and one who is unfree'. However much Pepo impressed Henry IV with his argument, the emperors were more interested in the provisions of Roman law which strengthened their fiscal and political powers and they adopted them obviously with enthusiasm.[51]

Scholarship and scholars fulfilled such and similar expectations of earthly and ecclesiastical authorities before universities existed. Indeed, the founding of universities was regarded by some contemporaries as an impediment to the genuine cultivation and transmission of scholarly knowledge. The noteworthy theologian and poet, Philippus de Grevia, who became a *magister* at the University of Paris in 1206, and who was its chancellor from 1218 to 1236, complained about his colleagues that

> At one time, when each *magister* taught independently and when the name of the university was unknown, there were more lectures and disputations and more interest in scholarly things. Now, however, when you have joined yourselves together in a university, lectures and disputations have become less frequent; everything is done hastily, little is learnt, and the time needed for study is wasted in meetings and discussions. While the elders debate in their meetings and enact statutes, the young ones organize villainous plots and plan their nocturnal attacks.[52]

To be sure, Philippus was not an objective witness since he was the spokesman for the interests of the ecclesiastics, whose right of supervision over scholarly studies had been diminished by the university. Nevertheless, it was true that the independent teaching activities of individual masters during the twelfth century were not injurious to scholarship.

What, however, did the popes and monarchs expect when they conferred legal recognition on the universities which had already 'grown up' and later founded others by the grant of privilege? Obviously, corporate bodies made up of scholars who were granted liberties served their interests better than teachers who were controlled by the religious orders or their local bishops.

The popes were interested in the universities for three reasons. For one thing, they wished to strengthen the position of a rationally intelligible doctrine amidst the diverse and mutually contradictory beliefs of the various

---

[51] Schmugge, '"Codicis Iustiniani"' (note 11), 4–8.
[52] Verger, 'Naissance' (note 4), 76 n. 34.

religious orders and scholars; they were particularly concerned to carry on a battle against the expanding heresies. They were furthermore desirous of strengthening the central powers of the papacy against the claims and aspirations of the earthly powers and the regional feudal interests. They were also concerned with the recruitment of persons who could serve as the staff for their offices. The curia had acknowledged, as early as the twelfth century, the value of scholarly education for the solution of the dogmatic and legal problems of a consistent ecclesiastical policy. Scholars became cardinals. Two popes (Celestine II (1143–4) and Celestine III (1191–8)) were pupils of Abelard. Another pupil of Abelard, Alexander III (1159–81), whether he was the famous Colognese canonist Rolandus of Cremona or not, was called 'the first lawyer–pope, who initiated a new epoch in the history of the papacy'.[53] From the thirteenth century onward, the popes had in most instances attended university and they increasingly surrounded themselves with learned cardinals.[54] Thus, the popes looked upon the university as an institution which, under their direct jurisdiction and protection, could organize and control studies and could as a result deal with the three tasks in which the papacy was so interested. The increasing appointment of academically trained persons to ecclesiastical offices is dealt with in chapter 8 in a detailed manner.

How could the popes draw into their service not only individual university graduates but the universities as institutions? It was easiest – one would think – where they themselves had created the universities. This, however, occurred only very exceptionally; it happened for the first time in Toulouse in 1229, when they imposed on the count, once the war against the Albigensians was over, in order to build a bulwark against heresy, the founding and the financing of a university as a punishment. As is shown in the next chapter, the new foundation did not perform this task successfully. The popes acted directly only in Rome in 1245, when they founded their own curial university. In contrast with this, in the cases of other university foundations, they presented themselves by the issuance of a charter as their legal founders and their protectors; they were thereby able to bring them under their control. This included the institution of apostolic curators who were intended to protect the privileges which the popes had granted to the universities from being abridged or infringed on by local actions.[55] The popes also used the universities as a means of diffusion for decretals; they did this by sending their decrees to the universities for treatment and diffusion through lectures.[56]

The use of prebends, accorded to incumbents of ecclesiastical appointment

[53] P. Classen, 'Rom und Paris Kurie und Universität im 12. und 13. Jahrhundert', in Classen, *Studium* (note 4), 130.
[54] Miethke, 'Kirche' (note 4), 294–303; J. Verger, *Les Universités au moyen âge*, Collection SUP, l'Historien 14 (Paris, 1973), 70; R. Avi-Yonah, 'Career Trends of Parisian Masters of Theology', *History of Universities*, 6 (1986–7), 47–64.
[55] Miethke, 'Kirche' (note 4), 314.   [56] Classen, *Studium* (note 4), 292.

for the purposes of study at university, had deeper implications for the affairs of the church. The popes helped both the universities and the students who were priests and monks, and at the same time they placed them under obligation to themselves by exempting the recipients of prebends from the obligations of parochial residence ordinarily associated with a prebend. Papal support for study by the assignment of prebends was given a fixed institutional form in the fourteenth century by the periodical communication to the pope of the list of students and graduates, i.e. the *rotuli*.[57] 'The entire material existence of the academic institutions depended on the prebendal provision for their members by the church.'[58]

The award of the *licentia ubique docendi* by the *studia generalia* which were recognized by the pope – described in the next two chapters – had far-reaching historical significance. It is true that, from the very beginning, the qualification for teaching, which was, in principle, valid throughout the entire realm of papal Christendom, was, in fact, subject to restrictions and exceptions. The popes themselves limited the right for the benefit of those who had been awarded the qualification from Paris and Bologna. In addition to this limitation on the universal validity of teaching, the professorial colleges of the various universities sought to protect themselves from outside competition by the *numerus clausus*, which limited the appointment of ordinary professorships.[59] Furthermore, the authorities of particular universities refused to grant the right to teach anywhere in order to retain the services of their masters for their own universities.[60] The universal validity did not in fact apply so much to the appointment to teach as it did to the aptitude to teach. Even today, this is still the case and it reveals in a literal sense the fundamental significance of the *venia ubique legendi* for the university as an institution and indeed for the modern profession of learning as such. Through the papally legitimated universality of the validity of its final examinations, the university as an institution acquired the responsibility for the conduct of courses of study and final examinations according to a standard which obtained far beyond its own locality. This not only made the universities more autonomous but also had considerable impact on the history of learning and culture. The universal value of the quest for knowledge and of the transmission of knowledge, which has been recognized ever since antiquity, was thereby given an institutional setting in the university. It has remained so ever since then, even down to our own times; it is the common task, the responsibility – for good or ill – of the universal community of the

[57] A. Borst, 'Krise und Reform der Universitäten im frühen 14. Jahrhundert', *Konstanzer Blätter für Hochschulfragen*, 9 (1971), 55; Verger, *Universités* (note 54), 128ff.; D. E. R. Watt, 'University Clerks and Rolls of Petition for Benefices', *Speculum*, 34 (1959), 213ff.

[58] G. Ritter, *Die Heidelberger Universität*, vol. I, *Das Mittelalter* (Heidelberg, 1936), 44.

[59] See chapter 5, p. 145. Rashdall, *Universities*, vol. I, 14ff., comes to the conclusion: 'The Mastership was reduced to a universally recognized honour, but nothing more.'

[60] Borst, 'Krise und Reform' (note 57), 57.

holders of advanced university degrees, i.e. of the scientific and scholarly community, the community of learning.

Henceforth, conflicts between divergent doctrines, which ever since the twelfth century had often resulted in the condemnation of philosophical doctrines and teachers, or which two centuries later found expression in the rivalry between 'the ancients' and 'the moderns',[61] were fought out within the university, even though the external authorities had to put into practice the judicial consequences and often had also to settle the internal quarrels. Conflicts among scholars with each other and with persons and institutions outside the universities have contributed to the development of academic institutions. The fragile structures which emerged from these conflicts were fortified by the rules and practices for the regulation of conflict within universities and permitted the *studium* to take its place as the third power alongside the *sacerdotium* and the *regnum*.

The kings of France, England, and Spain, and later Portugal, Austria, Bohemia, Poland, and Hungary, as well as, following their example, dukes and princes, expected of their universities effective intellectual and individual help in establishing and consolidating the governmental and administrative institutions which they needed to overcome the centrifugal forces embodied in the landed and urban aristocracies. It is true that they often justified their founding of universities by reference to their concern for the young persons of their realms, whom they wished to save from the costly and burdensome alternative of studying abroad.[62] But they were, in fact, much more concerned to associate them with their own territorial policies, as happened in extreme form in the case of Frederick II's foundation of the University of Naples in 1224 and his attempt to dissolve the University of Bologna.[63] His prototype of a state university collapsed after five years and became a widespread institutional model only three centuries later.

What did the cities expect of the universities? The latter defended the collective interests of scholars and masters against the municipal authorities and citizenry through privileges, exemption from tolls and taxes, the fixing of maximal rents, and other constraints on municipal interests. Initially, the municipalities, for their part, did not need the universities to provide them with the knowledge which was necessary for the intellectual and legal support of their economic activities, ranging from the elementary arithmetic and bare literacy needed by merchants to the mastery of the language of documents by notaries and scribes, and to the higher education needed for

---

[61] See chapter 13, p. 438. In Heidelberg, after 1440 there were heavy discussions and also fighting, which were concluded by the intervention of the *Kurfürsten* and the institution of the rival studies of both *viae*; see P. O. Kristeller, 'Scholastik und Humanismus an der Universität Heidelberg', in G. Keil, B. Moeller, and W. Trusen (eds.), *Der Humanismus und die oberen Fakultäten*, Mitteilung XIV der Kommission für Humanismusforschung (Weinheim, 1987), 6.

[62] Borst, 'Krise und Reform' (note 57), 55.   [63] See chapter 3, p. 54.

the professions and offices of trans-local scope. All these needs could be satisfied without any contribution from the universities.

Where, however, famous masters and their schools had established themselves as useful for municipal policy and economy, the municipal authorities had an interest in more stable and continuing regulations than were possible through *ad hoc* arrangements. From the late thirteenth century on, the big commercial towns were well aware of the advantage of having universities which made provision for lawyers who could solve legal problems unknown to common law, as well as civil servants who could be a match for the princely authorities. They also had an interest in keeping the sons of citizens who had chosen an intellectual vocation at their own local university. Thus, they quickly recognized the advantage of the reliable partnership which was offered by the universities and they exerted themselves to gain control over the universities. In the city states, professors were more and more often paid salaries by the municipal government[64] and the university came under the control of local officialdom.[65]

Basle offers an interesting example of the expectation which in the late Middle Ages led to the founding of universities by municipalities. In 1431, the Council – which convened in Basle – established what was unique in the history of the medieval universities, namely a conciliar university, which was later dissolved, together with the Council, in 1449. After Aeneas Sylvius, who had been a scribe in the Council, became Pope Pius II in 1458, some of the Basle graduates of the conciliar university thought that it was a propitious moment to establish a municipal university. It was fairly easy, although not inexpensive, to obtain papal approval together with the reassignment of the prebends for professorial salaries. It was more difficult to persuade the sceptical citizenry of the value of a university of their own. They were persuaded in 1460 to proceed with the foundation of a university less by an appeal to their pride and the value of such an institution for Christian ideals than they were by economic and political arguments. They were more interested by the prospect of facilitating the entry of the sons of the citizens of Basle into the medical and legal professions and to higher ecclesiastical appointments and by the improvement in the competitive position of Basle *vis-à-vis* Freiburg im Breisgau in regional, political, and economic affairs – Freiburg im Breisgau had already decided to have a university but had not yet opened it. A not inconsiderable investment had already been made and they anticipated the economic benefits of an influx of wealthy students, which might help to offset the economic decline of Basle. The citizens of Basle were told that, if the

---

64 H. Koller, 'Stadt und Universität im Spätmittelalter', in E. Maschke and J. Sydow (eds.), *Stadt und Universität im Mittelalter und in der frühen Neuzeit*, Stadt in der Geschichte, 3 (Sigmaringen, 1977), 87; T. Bender (ed.), *The University and the City. From Medieval Origin to the Present* (New York/Oxford, 1988), 3–58.
65 See chapter 4, pp. 96–7.

university had one thousand students, they would spend an additional 20,000 guldens there every year.[66]

The calculation did not work straight away. The prebends which had been promised by the pope were not all vacated by their local incumbents. The foreign students who came to Basle were fewer than anticipated and there were, above all, fewer wealthy ones. This situation is illuminated by a contract of appointment from the first years of the university: it stipulates that the maximal salary would be paid on the condition that the professor in question would bring with him three very noble students of canon law and forty high-born students of civil law – and their attendents.[67] It was only a half-century later that the university, which drew into its immediate environment a very successful book-publishing industry, showed itself to be an economically viable investment for the city.

EXPECTATIONS OF SCHOLARS AND STUDENTS

What did scholars expect of the university? We have seen that it was not the *amor sciendi*, the desire for knowledge as such, but rather the uncertain status of students and teachers which was the occasion for the foundation of the first universities. The protection of the rights of the individual scholar, which imperial legislation assured to foreign scholars, became a dead-letter if the emperor was unable to enforce it. It was really the organized collective representation of the interests of the scholars before the local municipal and ecclesiastical officials, given force in extreme cases by the collective emigration to another town, which gave the individual the freedom and security from material exploitation and official arbitrariness which he needed for his scholarly studies. Membership in the university conferred, as has already been remarked and as is shown in greater detail in chapters 7 and 8, a number of legal and economic privileges. The *rotuli*, which have already been mentioned and which were compiled periodically by the university, brought substantial benefits to the members of the university. 'University education – then as now – offered the average student primarily an opportunity for a prospective prebendal income.'[68]

This exaggerated statement does apply to the large number of students who aspired to a position in the church or who already held one. But lay students were not altogether rare in universities of the Bologna type, and in the fifteenth century they became quite common in all universities, as shown in chapter 7. They, too, expected from their studies at university better quali-

[66] E. Bonjour, *Die Universität Basel von den Anfängen bis zur Gegenwart 1460–1960* (Basle, 1960), 21–38. Cf. Louvain: J. Paquet, 'Bourgeois et universitaires à la fin du Moyen-Age', *Le Moyen-Age*, 67 (1961), 312–40.

[67] J. Rosen, 'Die Universität Basel im Staatshaushalt 1460–1530', *Basler Zeitschrift für Geschichte und Altertumskunde*, 72 (1972), 177.

[68] Ritter, *Heidelberger Universität* (note 58), 44.

fications and – if they did not come from the traditional higher strata – improved opportunities for appointment to rewarding public offices. For this reason, they were very interested in an ordered course of studies such as a university could offer and they even insisted upon it – in Bologna, for example, where the student *universitates* in the beginning appointed the professors and supervised the punctuality and adequacy of their performance of their teaching obligations through the threat of fines, for the payment of which professors had to supply guarantees of payment through prior deposits of security money.

The social role of the medieval university consisted primarily of training for more rational forms of the exercise of authority in church, government, and society. This seems to contradict the fact that the courses of study, the examinations, and the degrees were not oriented to the provision of any training for occupations other than those of university teachers. The bachelor's degree as the culmination of the first stage of academic training certified nothing beyond the capacity and the right to serve as an apprentice in the art of teaching in a particular field under the supervision of a *magister*. The master's and doctor's degrees testified to the capacity and, as implied by the *licentia ubique docendi*, the formal right to deliver independent academic lectures, as well as, in many universities, the obligation to deliver such lectures in one's own faculty for a period of at least two years.[69] Thus, university teachers became a status group which transcended local and disciplinary boundaries and which possessed a distinctive corpus of knowledge and enjoyed a high degree of prestige; they came to conceive of themselves as a university élite with their own ethos appropriate to their status, and they were also accepted as such by society and its rulers. Symbolically, this internal university arrangement of academic qualification has persisted, as a reminder of its medieval origin, in the convocation at the University of Oxford, the highest governing organ of the university. It still comprises the teaching staff but it also includes the recipients of the degrees of masters of arts and doctors of theology, law, and medicine who are not active as members of the university as well as those recipients of other academic degrees who apply for it. Nowadays, the powers of this body are limited mainly to the election of the chancellor and of a professor of poetry.

Outside the universities, academic degrees were not entitlements to the practice of any particular profession. The study of theology was not a precondition for the priesthood but it could, where noble ancestry or charismatic qualities were absent, render it easier to enter higher ecclesiastical offices. As chapter 11 shows, physicians with university training were a minority in the Middle Ages but one which regarded itself as an élite; in the physicians' guild, however, they did not receive precedence over those without academic

[69] See chapter 5, p. 147.

degrees. In certain Italian university cities, it was necessary, in order to gain an appointment as a judge, to be educated in law, but not necessarily attested through the possession of an academic degree but rather through evidence of the possession of the most important law-books.[70] In general, the exercise of judicial office or of the profession of notary or teaching in a learned institution did not require an academic degree. Nevertheless, study at a university was so attractive to those who wished to engage in such activities as were practised in the public interest, and which could not be mastered by concrete experience or by tradition, that only relatively few students aimed to enter the academic profession as a lifelong career, which was in fact the professional objective postulated by university education.

At first, it was the knowledge and skill acquired in a faculty – in addition to social origin – that facilitated access to the performance of a corresponding practical activity. For the male offspring of the aristocracy and the *grande bourgeoisie* – as chapters 7 and 9 show – attendance at a university became in the fifteenth century a more or less extended episode in the predominantly knightly education received among peers. But a considerable percentage of the other students, who were increasingly coming from the middle classes, because of the high costs did not complete their studies to the point of taking a degree either. In the fifteenth century, the academic degree was recognized as evidence of scholarly qualification to such an extent that it became important in the competition for appointment to ecclesiastical and secular posts. In the filling of important pulpits and offices, the class of the degree was also taken into account. Thus, university education, at first without a degree and later with one, became a characteristic mark of professional élites engaged in the cure of souls, legal practice, governmental administration, medical care, and education.

Of course, it was not university education alone which determined the status of a practitioner of a learned profession; membership in a traditional ruling family or circle, as well as wealth and income and the prestige of the particular occupation were also relevant to the status of an individual, as is shown in chapter 8. Nevertheless, academic education by the end of the Middle Ages, thanks to the universities, became a mark of social distinction, and the doctorate approximated the noble title as a claim to deference.

With this, we return to the significance of the *amor sciendi* for the university. The social value of academic education for the professions, which is one of the chief interests of present-day research, could only be realized by the university because the learning and teaching of the rational pursuit of truth were the substance for which institutional regulations and collegially ordered courses of study provided the context. The heart of the university is the ill-famed ivory tower; its manifest function is to provide for the Aristotelian *bios*

[70] Walther, 'Anfänge des Rechtsstudiums' (note 11), 132.

theoretikos, intellectual training for its own sake. That its latent function is the preparation of professional experts for practical affairs, for the development of the *bios praktikos*, for which there is such a great demand, cannot belie the fact – indeed it confirms it – of the social value of the pure striving for knowledge. This practical function postulates the fundamental importance of the *amor sciendi*. Otherwise, the university, as a corporate body serving only material interests and freedoms, would have shared the fate of other medieval institutions; it would have long since disappeared. It was the collective responsibility for the organization and discipline of the striving for knowledge, of the *studium*, which gave some meaning to the liberties and privileges of scholars and masters, transcended their immediate material interests, and assured the persistence of the autonomy of the university in its most distinctive activity, which is that of scholarly and scientific teaching and research.

ORIGINS AND LIMITS OF FACULTY ORGANIZATION

When one seeks the earliest evidence of a collective responsibility exercised by the governing bodies of universities for the organization and supervision of the *studium*, one comes across a feature which down to the very present has been a criterion for the recognition of institutions of higher education as universities or their institutional equivalents. This is the award of academic degrees, and particularly the doctorate, on the basis of a decision by an academic committee (*collegium*) to which the responsibility for such a decision has been assigned.

In Paris in 1213, the chancellor issued the 'Magna Charta of the university'; in 1231, it was incorporated in the bull *Parens scientiarum* by Pope Gregory IX. It confirms the obligation of the chancellor to obtain the vote of the professors in matters connected with appointments for the teaching of theology and canon law; there had to be a collegial examination of candidates for appointment as university teachers.[71] It is true that the relationship of the individual teacher and his pupil remained basic to the medieval university. Subsequently, as in the past – as shown in chapter 6 – a person could become a student only in so far as he attached himself to a particular teacher. But, in contrast with earlier periods, it was no longer left to the individual teacher – anymore than to the ecclesiastical authorities – to assess the performance of his pupils. Henceforward, the teacher had to present his pupil to the colleagues in his discipline and the latter had to decide whether they should recommend to the chancellor the award of the *licentia docendi* and the acceptance of the pupil as a colleague. This could only be done once there was proof of the candidate's blameless mode of life and his progression through a proper course of studies.[72]

[71] See, for this and what follows, Verger, 'Naissance' (note 4), 8off.
[72] *CUP*, vol. I, 137, no. 79.

Collegial responsibility for decisions requires a minimum of common criteria for proper collegial behaviour as well as for the substance and procedure for reaching decisions. The examination for an ordered course of study was necessarily dependent – as it still is today – on a set of regulations which specified the required minimal period of study and the substance to be covered for each degree within each faculty. These regulations also specified rights and obligations of the teaching corps, the apparel to be worn at examinations, the appropriate ceremonies and burial and memorial services for deceased students and colleagues, the institutional obligations, the schedule of 'ordinary' and 'extraordinary' lectures, disciplinary powers, and the right of professors to strike against interventions by political authorities. Such collegially enacted and sworn rules of the University of Paris were recognized by Pope Innocent III in 1208–9 and then again in 1215 by the papal legate, Robert of Courson; they were confirmed and specified in 1231 in the bull *Parens scientiarum*.[73]

In Bologna, prior to 1219, the collegial collective doctoral examinations by the teachers of law formed the 'seed around which the community of doctors became crystallized'.[74] They also served in the co-optation into the circle of professors, but, unlike the first Parisian statutes, through a real examination by the professors in the presence of the ecclesiastical holders of the *licentia docendi*.[75] Nevertheless, in universities which followed the Bolognese pattern, the teachers did not form a corporate body with the power of fixing the statutes. Rather, it was the student corporations which, by their statutes, fixed the regulations governing courses of study and punished, by means of fines, as already noted, the unpunctuality or substantively deficient fulfilment of teaching obligations. Other obligations were fixed by municipal statutes. It was only at the beginning of the fourteenth century that colleges made up of a limited number of teaching and non-teaching doctors were formed; these colleges were later reserved for citizens of the municipality. The oldest known statutes of the Bolognese college of lawyers date from the year 1397.[76]

The problem of why the professorial colleges in the universities of the Bolognese type were able to establish themselves against the student corporations and the political authorities only relatively late, and then only in a limited measure, is still unsolved. Various causes have been adduced, which can all, in the last analysis, be reduced to the fact that in these universities the *scientiae lucrativae*, law and medicine, were most prominent and were to a large extent taught and practised by laymen. The latter were more dependent on fees and on fixed salaries than were the teachers of the *artes*, canon law,

[73] *CUP*, vol. I, 67ff., no. 8; 78ff., no. 20; 136–9, no. 79.
[74] Weimar, 'Doktorwürde' (note 13), 433.
[75] G. Cencetti, 'La Laurea nelle università medievali', *Studi e memorie per la storia dell'Università di Bologna*, 16 (1943), 259.
[76] Weimar, 'Doktorwürde' (note 13), 441

and theology, who drew their income from prebends and who were dominant in the universities based on the Parisian pattern. Furthermore, the link between teaching and practice was more direct among lawyers and physicians. 'Medieval legal education was not directed towards the training of law teachers but of professional legal practitioners.'[77] Accordingly, their colleges of doctors were open to the membership of practitioners and performed professional functions rather than those of collegial responsibility for the *studium*. It was the same in medicine, as is shown in chapter 11.

Nevertheless, a number of questions remain unanswered. In universities of the Parisian type as well, the teachers received lecture fees and fixed salaries, in other faculties as well as those of law and medicine. They, too, trained not only academic teachers but also future practitioners. In this case, as well as in the other, the academic degree confirmed nothing else than the capacity, and partly also the obligation, to teach the acquired knowledge and skills; the teachers of a faculty were collectively responsible for the assessment of the capacity to reach. Was it perhaps the lack of a far-reaching collective responsibility which accounts for the powerlessness of the professors in the Bolognese type of university and which led, in the fifteenth century, to the decline of the law school at Bologna, where nepotism became the rule in the doctors' colleges?[78] Was it, on the other hand, this lack of collegial responsibility for the *studium* which explains why new intellectual currents such as Averroism and humanism met with less resistance in Italian universities than was the case among universities of the Parisian type? In the latter, the faculties of arts became firmly attached to certain doctrines so that the composition of the teaching body was less influenced by social origin and professional interests than it was by doctrine and the particular form taken by the *amor sciendi*.

The faculties provided the institutional framework of the collegial responsibility for the *studium*. 'In the faculties, the teachers, who were assured of autonomy, and the students in a given discipline were amalgamated into a common body.'[79] The origins, significance, and development of the four typical faculties of the medieval university, the *artes*, medicine, law (both fields), and theology, are analysed in detail in chapter 4 and chapters 10 to 13. Why, however, were these intellectual disciplines taken into the universities and not others?

If 'social needs' had been taken into account, technological sciences like architecture, military technology, shipbuilding, machine manufacture, and mining, as well as the applied natural sciences like agriculture, veterinary medicine, and pharmacy, would have been taken up in the universities. For the cultivation of these disciplines, which were fundamental to society in the

77 Walther, 'Anfänge des Rechtsstudiums' (note 11), 161.
78 Cf. Cencetti, 'Laurea' (note 74), 273.
79 J. Verger, 'Fakultät, -en', in *Lexikon des Mittelalters*, vol. III (Munich/Zürich, 1987), cols. 215–17.

Middle Ages, the politically and economically powerful classes would have had to have been as interested in the scientific knowledge and developments and in the training of experts in these fields as they were in the subject-matters of the four faculties. Once more we see that it was not the demand for socially applicable knowledge which led to the foundation of the universities so much as the existence of certain disciplines which had shown themselves to be of value for dealing with certain social tasks.

What was the reason for the exclusion of the technological disciplines from the teaching programme of the faculties? At first sight, the explanation seems to lie in the medieval classification of the sciences, which made distinctions between the *artes liberales* and the *artes mechanicae*, between the 'liberal' and the 'mechanical' arts. But this is not necessarily derogatory. As early as the seventh century, mechanics was considered to be 'knowledge or theory in which, in a subtle manner, the *fabrica rerum omnia*, the creation of all things, comes together'.[80] In the twelfth century, Hugh of Saint Victor (1096–1141), attributed an even more subtle meaning to mechanics; in his *Didascalion*, he said that mechanics is the science by which man imitates nature in order to assist him in the satisfaction of his bodily needs. In his classification he attributed the same standing to the *artes mechanicae* as he did to the *artes liberales*. He distinguished seven sciences in 'mechanical' philosophy (which he placed alongside natural philosophy, moral philosophy, and the philosophy of language). Three of these sciences were concerned with things outside the body. The first was weaving, which dealt with all textiles (all materials used for clothing); the second dealt with all kinds of apparatus (such as pottery, stone-cutting, and masonry up to architecture, mining, woodwork, and metallurgy); and the third was nautics, which included all kinds of commerce. Four of these mechanical sciences serve bodily needs: the cultivation of the soil, hunting (including all forms of the preparation of food), medicine, and the theatrical arts. In 1250, Robert Kilwardby, a *magister* of the University of Paris and later archbishop of Canterbury, modified this scheme in his *De ortu scientiarum* by excluding 'pagan' theatrical art and assigning a special place of its own to architecture; at the same time, he replaced the excessively narrow categories with others which were more accurate in substance. For example, he substituted the art of textiles for weaving, commerce for navigation, farming for cultivation of the soil, and cooking for hunting. The *artes mechanicae* were regarded by Kilwardby as a part of philosophy, as they were by Hugh of Saint Victor, and as a part of the study of human things (as distinct from the study of divine things, which was theology).[81] On the basis of this

---

[80] B. Bischoff, 'Eine verschollene Einteilung der Wissenschaften' *Archives d'histoire doctrinale et littéraire du Moyen-Age* (1958), 16.

[81] R. Kilwardby, *De ortu scientiarum*, ed. A. G. Judy (London, 1976), Cap. 34–41, 122–37. Cf. J. A. Weisheipl, 'The Nature, Scope and Classification of the Sciences', *Studia Mediewistyczne*, 18 (1977), 85–101.

way of looking at the various kinds of knowledge, the university could have incorporated into itself from the very beginning not only the technological sciences but also the economic and empirical sciences as well as other practical specialities such as are not unusual in contemporary universities.

As it turned out, only one *ars mechanica*, namely medicine, became a university subject. As shown in chapter 11, medical schools were formed in the course of the preoccupation with Arabic medicine and with the aid of Arab and Jewish physicians. A Spanish philosopher and translator of Arabic commentaries on Aristotle, Dominicus Gundissalinus, in his *De divisione philosophiae*, written in about 1150, proposed that, instead of the distinction between *artes liberales* and *artes mechanicae*, every science should be divided into a theoretical and a practical part and that medicine, which has to do with human beings, who are the peak of nature, should be ranked as the highest of the natural sciences[82] and above the *artes liberales*. But this classification was not accepted. When it was desired to accord a high rank to medicine, it was placed among the *artes liberales*. Thus, in the preamble to the renewal of the statutes of the medical faculty of the University of Montpellier in 1239, medicine was compared with a star which illuminates the firmament of the sciences of the *artes liberales* with especial brightness.[83] As is mentioned in chapter 11, the study of the *artes* and the study of medicine were closely associated with each other and, in the Italian universities, they were placed in the same faculty. Many classifications of the sciences distinguished between practical medicine, including surgery, which would assign it to the *artes mechanicae*, and speculative medicine, which was to be regarded as being of the *artes liberales*.[84]

Thomas Aquinas, in his commentary on Boethius, *De Trinitate*, written between 1255 and 1259, rejected this distinction. Like alchemy, agriculture, and all sciences of this sort, medicine used the properties of natural things, like a handmaiden for practical purposes and it was thus subordinate to the natural sciences. All the mechanical sciences, to which medicine belonged, aimed not at knowledge but at a practical use and should therefore be considered as activities which belonged to the unfree part of the human being, i.e. to his body. They should therefore be regarded not as free arts but as servile arts, as *artes serviles*.[85] This theoretical distinction offered an argument welcome to those engaged in polemics against medicine. Petrarch, in his polemic, composed in 1355, 'against a physician', contrasted agriculture, as a useful *ars mechanica*, with harmful medicine.[86] Salutati, in his *De nobilitate legum et medicinae* of

---

[82] D. Gundissalinus, *De divisione philosophiae*, ed. L. Baur (Munich, 1903), 84–8.
[83] *Cartulaire de l'Université de Montpellier*, vol. I, (Montpellier, 1890), 185, no. 4.
[84] Library of Wolfenbüttel, Cod Guelf, 567, chart. XVs., fol. 113r.
[85] Thomas Aquinas, *Commentarii in Boethii De Trinitate*, Quaest. II, Art. 1, English translation by A. Maurer, *St Thomas Aquinas, The Division and Methods of the Sciences* (Toronto, 1953; 4th edn 1986), 19–22.
[86] F. Petrarca, *Invectiva contra medicum*, ed. P. G. Ricci (Rome, 1950), L. I. Cap. V; L. II, Cap. XVIII.

1399, based his argument regarding the superiority of jurisprudence on the attribution of medicine, for which he invoked Averroës (Ibn Rushd), to the category of the *artes mechanicae*.[87]

Why did medicine remain the only *ars mechanica* taught in the university? Even architecture, which was classified with medicine by Varro (116–27 BC) among the (nine) *artes liberales*, required a considerable amount of theoretical knowledge, particularly knowledge of mathematics, which was not inferior to the arithmetic and geometry taught in the *quadrivium* and which was superior to them in many respects.[88] In a comparison of the styles of scholastic philosophy and Gothic architecture, Panofsky traced their similarity to the common mental habit, the *habitus* of the philosophers and the architects. Panofsky said that the scholastic mode of thought affected the outlook of architects either through their own experience in schools and universities or through its absorption from the general cultural life of their times.[89] In fact, it is possible to demonstrate direct relations with the university only for a few master-builders. The latter, in their work in university towns on the construction of important churches and defence works, had charge of technologically, artistically, and organizationally demanding enterprises. These responsibilities afforded them a status in society which could call forth the envy of university teachers. From the thirteenth century on, there was an unprecedented increase in the amount of building. Master-builders became very prominent in the planning and supervision of large projects and enjoyed high social esteem as the heads of the building departments of municipalities and princely and royal courts. These projects gave rise to a great demand for architects who possessed not only practical but also theoretical knowledge.[90]

Neither the demands of society for architects nor the subject itself nor the classification of the sciences can explain the exclusion of architecture from the subjects taught in universities and the same is true for the other *artes mechanicae*.[91] There is no lack of ancient texts which would have permitted a theoretical justification of their inclusion in the syllabuses and a corresponding provision of teaching. Vitruvius offered the point of departure for a scientific treatment of the art of building. Such a treatment was indeed under-

---

[87] C. Salutati, *De nobilitate legum et medicinae, De verecundia*, ed. E. Garin (Florence, 1947), 24, 216.

[88] L. Mojon, *St Johannsen, Saint Jean de Cerlier, Beiträge zum Bauwesen des Mittelalters* (Berne, 1986), 23.

[89] E. Panofsky, *Gothic Architecture and Scholasticism*, Wimmer Lectures 1948 (Latrobe, Pa., 1951), 21–8.

[90] Mojon, *St Johannsen* (note 88), 20–7; M. Warnke, *Bau und Klosterbau, Soziologie der mittelalterlichen Architektur nach den Schriftquellen* (Frankfurt, 1976; reprint, 1984), 131–45.

[91] For a comprehensive overview of the *artes mechanicae* with an extensive bibliography, see E. Whitney, 'Paradise Restored, The Mechanical Arts from Antiquity through the Thirteenth Century', *Transactions of the American Philosophical Society*, 80, 1 (1990), 1–169.

taken by the private scholar and artist, Leon Battista Alberti, in his book *De re aedificatoria* of 1452. There were also the potentialities for a theoretical treatment of agriculture in Albertus Magnus's *De vegetabilibus et plantis libri* (VII), a botanical work of 1256, as well as in the widely known standard works on 'agriculture' by Walter of Henley (*Horsebonderie, c.* 1250) and Peter of Crescenci's *Ruralia commoda* (*c.* 1306), which was based on a discussion of Aristotle, Varro, and Columella. They all presupposed a university education but they did not become the subject-matter of such a programme of studies. This cannot be attributed to their objective, unlike medicine, of producing material artefacts. After all, the established university subjects of the *quadrivium* and physics – as is shown in chapter 10.2 – developed optical, astronomical, and musical instruments, which served practical purposes as well as research.

Perhaps we should not take the scholastic classification of the different kinds of knowledge so seriously. They also either made no room at all for the very important discipline of jurisprudence or made it into a subdivision of the *trivium* of grammar, dialectic, and rhetoric or alternatively of practical philosophy, neither of which was commensurate with its importance in the structure of the university. It is difficult to relate closely to each other the theoretical classifications of knowledge and the organization of intellectual activities in the university. This is true even for the *artes liberales*, which, from late antiquity through the Carolingian educational reforms and up to the twelfth century, were thought to be the *summum* of pagan science and philosophy and inferior only to theology. In the thirteenth century, the triumphant Aristotelian philosophy expelled them from their prominent position or assigned to them a subordinate position in the scholastic classification of kinds of knowledge.[92] The latter was utterly inconsistent with the name of the arts faculty and it became consistent with the programme of teaching of that faculty only when in 1253 – as is shown in chapter 10.1 – large numbers of the writings of Aristotle were admitted to the syllabus of the arts faculty of the University of Paris.

The persistence of the patterns of four faculties of the medieval university into the nineteenth century cannot be explained by the scholastic classification of types of knowledge or by the distinction between 'free' and 'mechanical' sciences or between 'speculative' and 'mechanical' philosophy. Rather, the adherence to the scheme of the four faculties is a result of the fundamental significance of the *amor sciendi*. Faculties emerged only where there were previously schools which transmitted knowledge as a public good and where attendance was basically open to everyone capable of performing at the required intellectual standard. Even the practically oriented field of

[92] R. McInerny, 'Beyond the Liberal Arts', in L. Wagner (ed.), *The Seven Liberal Arts in the Middle Ages* (Bloomington, Ind. 1983), 257ff; C. La Fleur, *Quatre introductions à la philosophie au XIIIe siècle* (Montreal/Paris, 1988).

medicine developed into a scientific discipline only when knowledge based on the study of theories of natural philosophy and medicine drawn from ancient and Arabic–Jewish texts, and from empirical observation, was introduced. The same thing happened in the schools of law. They, too, could become so attractive internationally only to the extent that universities were founded, when the reception of Roman law opened up their content, so that the derivation and exercise of jurisprudential principles and modes of thought became more important in teaching than the knowledge of formulae necessary for direct application in the practice of the law.

It was very different in building construction and in other *artes mechanicae*. In these, admission and training were dominated by guilds or corporate bodies formed on the basis of status; admission was often limited by connections of kinship. They were, moreover, oriented immediately towards the formation of practical occupational skills. In these fields, medieval societies did not provide generally accessible schools from which universities or university faculties could have grown. However much the hierarchical status system of medieval society affected the social composition of the student bodies and the profession of university teaching, in comparison with other spheres of life the universities did display a considerable degree of openness and even, indeed, of equality. This was not least a consequence of their manifest occupational objective, which was the acquisition and teaching of scientific and scholarly knowledge, while the acquisition of a professional or official qualification for an occupational activity within the framework of the hierarchical society was only a secondary objective or by-product.

As a matter of fact, a comparison between the socially no less relevant 'mechanical' sciences, which were transmitted through guild-like arrangements, and the subjects taught at university shows the significance for the development of academic disciplines of the opportunities allowed by the *scholè* for leisure as an emancipation from the immediate care of gaining one's daily bread which is characteristic of ordinary occupations. The preoccupation with the theoretical principles of the divine order of the universe and with the scholarly study of human things, freed from practical interests, was directly derived from the categories of Greek philosophy. This derivation notwithstanding, the search for the fundamental forms of the rational interpretation of reality is a characteristic feature of the scientific and scholarly methods of all the faculties. This search was also the basis of the peculiar idea of the medieval university that its fundamental structure was the outcome of a reform.

REFORMATIO IN MELIUS: THE ALPHA AND OMEGA OF THE UNIVERSITY

The first statutory regulations of the University of Paris, promulgated in 1215, arose in connection with the effort 'to reform and improve' the condition of the Parisian schools (*ut statui Parisiensium scholarum in melius reformando impenderemus operam efficacem*). As Classen showed in 1967, *reformatio* meant not only the re-establishment of dissolved universities and the re-enactment of old statutes but also the act which led to the founding or the statutory constitution or ordering of a university.[93] The officials who exercised supervisory powers over the universities in the Italian city states were often called the *reformatores studii*.[94] *Reformatio* had been used ever since the tenth century for the monastic reforms in its original meaning of the restoration of the proper or fundamental form. It meant the same for the universities; from the very beginning they had the task of realizing their proper form, their underlying idea, in the Platonic sense, or their entelechy, in the Aristotelian sense.

How could this, in fact, be done? On a very general level, it could be done by accepting models in which these proper forms had been embodied. This meant that, for the universities founded later, the patterns and regulations of either of the two most successful universities, Paris and Bologna, should be reproduced, at least in part, in detail. As is made clear in the chapters which follow, this explains the uniformity of the organization into faculties as well as of the courses of study, the degrees, the programmes of study, and the modes of teaching, which differ from each other only in minor respects. This astonishing unanimity as well as the remarkable phenomenon that one can classify the medieval universities as being of the Bolognese, of the Parisian, or of a mixed type is not attributable to any external unifying authority. Neither the emperor nor the pope was in a position, like a contemporary 'university planner', to lay down an ideal version of a Christian university and to carry it out in every detail! Rather, the first *reformationes* were the result of negotiations with various local individuals and institutions, churches, secular princes, municipal authorities, professors, and students of the various schools and nations. Later, they quite understandably turned to regulations which, having proved themselves in one place, might also have been equally applicable elsewhere. They had, however, to work them out with the other parties to the negotiations or at least to adapt them to local circumstances. The situation was different in the case of the first universities. These had no immediately available models. As a result they fabricated, as I mentioned at the beginning, historical forerunners in order to legitimate themselves, as a renewal, as the *reformatio*, of a form of university which they wanted to have already been realized in the past.

If we now enquire into what these regulations were in detail, in accordance with which the universities were to be reformed, we look in vain for ideas drawn from the theory of science, or of educational policy or of organization. As has already been indicated, the statutes not only fixed the rights and obli-

---

[93] Classen, *Studium* (note 4), 170ff.   [94] See chapter 4, p. 132.

gations of office-holders, the requirements for the award of academic degrees, the use and prohibition of certain textbooks, and the right of teachers to strike when their prerogatives were infringed on. They also set forth in very minute detail who was to be allowed to teach what and when and where, who might wear what academic robe and what form of academic hat and when and where, which teachers were to serve in the death vigil for colleagues, how many must participate in the burial services of scholars, etc. The aim of such regulations – as was already said by Robert of Courson in 1215 – was to assure the *tranquilitas scholarum*, the peace of the university.

However, in contrast with the reforms of universities introduced in recent decades with the same objective, the medieval prescriptions and prohibitions were directed at those kinds of actions which would prevent frictions among colleagues in the university and which would make possible the perfect performance of their tasks. In sermons and disputations they expressed, in the idiom of their time, ideas and values which were partly implicit and partly explicit and which are bound up with the ideal of the scientist and scholar. Alongside *amor sciendi* – intellectual integrity, broad learning, and conceptual clarity – they sought to sustain virtues like humility, love of one's neighbour, piety, fatherly solicitude towards students, loyalty and collegial solidarity towards the university, and deference towards the ecclesiastical and earthly incumbents of high university offices.[95] Here, too, it was a matter of *reformatio*, of the renewal of fundamental ethical forms in the context of a university community, which, as Christian and classical virtues and values, had first taken form in the basic works of the Western traditions.

If one attempts to formulate the essential outlines of an academic ethic in the process of formation, one may deduce in hypothetical form the following seven values which in the Middle Ages legitimated, in religious terms, the *amor sciendi* and the university which was its institutional form.[96] The seven evaluative propositions are:

(1) The belief in a world order, created by God, rational, accessible to human reason, to be explained by human reason and to be mastered by it; this belief underlies scientific and scholarly research as the attempt to understand this rational order of God's creation.

(2) The ancient understanding of man as an imperfect being and the Judaeo-Christian idea of a creature fallen into sin, and the proposition deriving from these ideas about the limitation of the human intellect, operated in the Middle Ages as driving forces impelling intellectual criticism and collegial

[95] A. C. Gabriel, 'The Ideal Master of the Medieval University', *The Catholic Historical Review*, 9 (1974), 1–40; G. Lebras, ' "Velut splendor firmamenti", le docteur dans le droit de l'église médiévale', in *Mélanges offerts à Etienne Gilson* (Toronto/Paris, 1959), 373–88; J. Leclercq, 'L'idéal du théologien au moyen-âge, textes inédits', *Revue des sciences religieuses*, 21 (1947), 121–48.

[96] W. Rüegg, 'The Academic Ethos', *Minerva*, 24:4 (1986), 393–412. Cf. Cobban, *Medieval Universities*, 13ff. See also chapter 5, p. 161 ff.

cooperation; they served as the foundation for the translation of general ethical values like modesty, reverence, and self-criticism into the image of the ideal scientist and scholar.

(3) Respect for the individual as a reflection of the macrocosm or as having been formed in the image of God laid the foundation for the gradually realized freedom of scientific and scholarly research and teaching.

(4) The absoluteness of the imperative of scientific truth already led in scholasticism to the basic norms of scientific and scholarly research and teaching such as the prohibition of the rejection of demonstrated knowledge, the subjection of one's own assertions to the generally valid rules of evidence, openness to all possible objections to one's own argument, and the public character of argument and discussion.

(5) The recognition of scientific and scholarly knowledge as a public good which is ultimately a gift of God had not, it is true, even before universities existed, prevented study and teaching for the sake of money. Nevertheless, there has been less interest within the universities in the economic use of scientific knowledge than there has been in the learned professions outside the university. This relatively smaller interest in the economic utilization of scientific knowledge has been an axiomatic value of the university.

(6) *Reformatio*, which regarded one's own scientific efforts as the renewal of previously established knowledge and its further development 'in the cause of improvement', laid a disproportionate weight in the medieval university on already established patterns of thought and older authors. Nevertheless, these were not accepted without criticism; they were critically scrutinized to test their veracity as the basis of one's own knowledge. They were a stimulus to new ways of seeing things and to new theories. This, as mentioned above, was expressed in the image of the later scientist, who, as a dwarf standing on the shoulders of a giant, sees further than the giant. Scientific and scholarly knowledge grows in a cumulative process, by building on earlier knowledge. In this sense, the progress of knowledge is a continuous process of *reformatio*.

(7) The equality and solidarity of scholars in confronting the tasks of science enable the universities to become the institutional centres of the scientific community. The acknowledgement of the scientific achievements of those who think and believe differently from ourselves and of those who are members of social strata different from our own and the readiness to correct one's own errors in the light of persuasive new knowledge, regardless of its source, permitted the rise of science. All these things contributed to the growth of scientific knowledge even before universities came into existence. The conception of the equality of human beings, which is part of natural law and which Pepo invoked from Roman law in the criminal trial mentioned on p. 15, first found an institutional arrangement for scientific and scholarly discussion in the setting provided by the university. However much modern

sociological historiography may emphasize the social inequalities within the university – set forth in chapters 6 to 8 – as far as scientific knowledge was concerned, differences in national and social origins played no role. Indeed, the more highly equality was evaluated, and the more it was joined to the common responsibility for the increase of knowledge, the better the university fulfilled its obligations. The less these values were respected, as was often the case in smaller universities of a local or regional nature, the greater was the decline in the level of scientific and scholarly activity. As a result, universities became sterile and some of them ceased to exist. This, too, is demonstrated by the history of the medieval universities.

CHAPTER 2

PATTERNS

JACQUES VERGER

No one today would dispute the fact that universities, in the sense in which the term is now generally understood, were a creation of the Middle Ages, appearing for the first time between the twelfth and thirteenth centuries. It is no doubt true that other civilizations, prior to, or wholly alien to, the medieval West, such as the Roman Empire, Byzantium, Islam, or China, were familiar with forms of higher education which a number of historians, for the sake of convenience, have sometimes described as universities. Yet a closer look makes it plain that the institutional reality was altogether different and, no matter what has been said on the subject, there is no real link such as would justify us in associating them with medieval universities in the West. Until there is definite proof to the contrary, these latter must be regarded as the sole source of the model which gradually spread through the whole of Europe and then to the whole world. We are therefore concerned with what is indisputably an original institution, which can only be defined in terms of a historical analysis of its emergence and its mode of operation in concrete circumstances.

THE UNIVERSITY AS *STUDIUM GENERALE*

This problem of definition naturally arose in the Middle Ages also. A term, *studium generale*, was therefore coined, together with a number of juridical criteria. A *studium generale* was an institution of higher education founded on, or, at any rate, confirmed in its status by, an authority of a universal nature, such as the pope or (less frequently) the emperor, whose members enjoyed a certain number of rights, likewise universal in their application, which transcended all local divisions (such as towns, dioceses, principalities, and states). These rights concerned, first of all, both collectively and individually, the personal status of teachers and students, who were placed under the immediate safeguard of the supreme authority, be it papal or imperial, which had founded the university in question; more especially, they received from the pope the right to enjoy the revenues from ecclesiastical benefices without actually having to take up residence in them. On the other hand, titles awarded in the universities were guaranteed by the founding authority and therefore regarded as being universally valid. This meant that the licences (*licentiae docendi*) granted by the universities were licences *ubique docendi*, entitling the holder to teach throughout Christendom and not merely in a particular diocese, as was the case with those offered by bishops or their representatives. As for the titles of doctor or master, the holding of them was regarded as a sign of the very highest intellectual competence and of equivalent value in all circumstances, no matter which university had granted them; and, as a consequence, they were supposed to allow access everywhere to the offices and honours reserved for the holders of this high rank.[1] Significantly enough, the pope had reserved for himself the right to grant doctorates in a sovereign manner, by special bull (the term *doctores bullati* was then in use), thus illustrating the delegated nature of the authority vested in the universities.

The truth is that, even though the term *studium* had acquired, from the twelfth century on, in addition to its classical and somewhat abstract meaning of 'study', the further, more institutional one of 'school', the notion of a *studium generale* only gradually emerged after the first universities had in fact already been founded. There are a few rare instances of this term in the early decades of the thirteenth century but the expression only became a common one towards the middle of the same century, that is to say, at a time when the civil and ecclesiastical authorities began to set about creating new universities from scratch, deriving a universally applicable legal form from already existing models (Paris and Bologna, in particular). From this time on, all the founding charters of new universities mentioned that these latter were in fact *studia generalia*. Indeed, among the very oldest universities, a number of them (Montpellier in 1289, Bologna in 1291, and Paris in 1292) nevertheless received at that date confirmation from the pope of their official status as *studium generale*, even though they had for long had all the features of such an institution, and had in fact played a large part in defining it in the first place. Admittedly, the University of Oxford never received such a confirmation and can hardly be said to have suffered from the want of it.[2]

Not only was the notion of *studium generale*, as it was elaborated in medieval law, a relative latecomer, but it has the additional drawback of being, for the historian's purposes, too vague. Admittedly, it allows one more or less to circumscribe the world of the university during the Middle Ages and to dis-

---

[1] G. Ermini, 'Il concetto di "Studium generale" ', *Archivio giuridico*, series V, 7 (1942), 3–24.
[2] On the use of the expression *studium generale* see Cobban, *Medieval Universities*, especially 21–36.

tinguish between universities in the strict sense and all the other types of schools existing in the same period (cathedral or municipal schools, the *studia* of the mendicant orders, private law schools, etc.). Some of these establishments, whose teachers were sometimes university graduates themselves, may have reached, at one time or another in their history, a level, as regards the actual content of their curricula, comparable to that of some universities. But the fact that they were exclusively answerable to local authorities, whether civil or religious, that their pupils did not benefit from the special privileges accorded to those at universities and therefore could not have their studies ratified by official degrees, in short, the fact that these institutions lacked the very qualities to which the adjective 'general' referred, had always meant that they were confined to a junior position, could not spread their influence outwards, and enjoyed very little social prestige.

There were in fact a few exceptions to this rule. In the thirteenth century, especially, pupils at schools that were indisputably not universities might on occasion be granted one or other privilege that was normally restricted to members of the *studia generalia* (for example, exemption from residence for holders of benefices). In a number of cases, the most famous of which is that of the schools of medicine in Salerno, one should speak of quasi-universities.[3] But these hybrids were rare and had virtually disappeared by the fourteenth century. From then on, contemporary witnesses seem to be quite clear as to which were (or were not) the genuine universities; lists of universities were compiled and chroniclers' descriptions of countries always mention them.

THE UNIVERSITY COMMUNITY: INDEPENDENCE AND INFLUENCE

But what, in more concrete terms, were these universities? If we look more closely at the vocabulary in use at the time, we find that the commonest term in texts, especially in the thirteenth century, would seem to be *universitas* and not *studium generale*. An abstract word in classical Latin (meaning 'the totality' or 'the whole'), *universitas* had become, for medieval jurists, the general term used to designate all kinds of community or corporation (a guild, a trade, a brotherhood, and so on). The term very often had this sense in medieval Latin, from the twelfth century on, a period which had in fact been marked by a proliferation of institutions of this sort.[4] One had therefore to specify the object to which one was referring so that, if teaching was the topic, one would talk of 'the university of students' or 'the university of masters and students' (*universitas scholarium* or *universitas magistrorum et scholarium*) of such and such a place. These expressions may be found throughout the first university cartularies and there is even some probability

---

[3] See p. 52.
[4] P. Michaud-Quantin, *Universitas. Expressions du mouvement communautaire dans le Moyen-Age latin* (Paris, 1970).

that fairly early, at any rate in everyday language, the word 'university' was sometimes used on its own, without any further qualification, with the same meaning as today.

The interest of formulae such as *universitas magistrorum et scholarium* lies in the fact that it places the emphasis upon the human reality of the medieval universities, which was all the more fundamental given that for a long time these universities scarcely knew any other reality, remaining content with the strict minimum, as we shall see, in buildings and finances. The medieval universities were therefore, first of all, organized communities of individuals responsible, in certain towns, for higher education, or for the *studium: universitas studii* X, as it was sometimes put. This notion of a community would seem to be fundamental to the definition of the medieval university, whatever limitations and mishaps were involved in practice.[5] It implied a degree of independence and internal cohesion. A university was a group which one freely joined, assuming that one was granted admittance. It was a moral entity, able to issue deeds sealed with its seal, to sue in a civil action in its own name, to endow itself with statutes, and to enforce obedience of such statutes on the part of its members. However, we should not entertain too juridical a view of the university community as a moral entity; for it already enjoyed such a status as early as the thirteenth century, before the first written statutes that have survived were drafted (which only date from 1215–31 in Paris, from 1220 in Montpellier, and from the 1250s in Oxford, Cambridge, and Bologna), and before the university's official seal appeared (1246 in Paris, 1276 in Oxford).

Independence of this sort did not of course rule out the interference or control, more or less strict depending upon circumstances, of the external lay or religious authorities. Still less did it rule out internal subdivisions and hierarchies within the universities themselves. Almost invariably, only a part of the members of the *universitas*, of the university community, would enjoy all of the rights and prerogatives that this independence established. The others, who were generally regarded as the mere *suppositi* of the university, were subject to its authority, but were unable to take part in the exercise of responsibilities (participation in assemblies and councils, the holding of university offices). In universities based on the Oxford or Paris model, only the masters were in this sense full-fledged members of the university. Since, however, many students in theology, law, or medicine were already masters of arts, these universities were in fact much less hierarchical than their usual appellation of 'masters' universities' would lead one to suppose. Indeed, it was actually these masters of arts, since they were the most numerous, the youngest, and the most turbulent, who tended to exercise a good part of the control over the whole of the university. The only people who were really

[5] J. Verger, 'Université et communauté au Moyen Age', *CRE–Information*, 62 (1983), 21–44.

excluded were plain students of arts, who were often merely children or adolescents, together with all those (servants of masters or pupils, beadles, scribes, booksellers, etc.) who, gravitating around the university, were under its authority and could benefit from its protection, without, however, having access to its councils.

In the so-called students' universities (Bologna, Padua), on the other hand, the university consisted only of the students, the teachers simply being hired through annual contracts that were agreed with the university itself or with the commune, which did not stop them from fairly rapidly creating their own organization, the 'college of doctors', whose particular responsibility was for examinations and the conferring of degrees. To be more precise, one should also note that, at Bologna or Padua, there were not one but several students' universities, enrolment at which was determined either by one's geographical origin or by the subject taught. Thus, students of law belonged to the 'cis-montane' universities or to the 'ultramontane' universities, depending upon whether they were Italian or not; students of the arts or of medicine belonged to another, wholly independent university. The masters were likewise organized in distinct doctoral colleges depending upon their particular exper-tise. These universities did, however, cooperate very closely with each other. In Padua, the two universities for students of law actually fused in 1473.

In southern France, the Iberian peninsula, and eastern Europe, the univer-sities belonged to a mixed type, in which the students were in control, to a degree, of certain university offices (councillor, rector), but in which the colleges of doctors were integrated into the university. The latter was gen-erally a single university but at Montpellier, in spite of a vain attempt at unification in 1289, a distinction was still made between the university of medicine (the oldest one, proud of its traditions and of its international pres-tige) and that of law, which was completely separate, not to speak of a modest 'university of arts', which would, however, appear not to have kept its independence for long. At Prague, between 1372 and 1415, the faculty of law separated off from the others (organized according to the Paris model) in order to form a 'university of law' with a student rector.

One should note, however, that, no matter what the definition and the outline, the university communities were generally subdivided into a certain number of elements, often as old as the university itself, or sometimes even older. In many universities, especially those with a fairly large recruitment, the students were divided up in terms of their geographical origin, into 'nations'. Thus, there were some twenty nations at Bologna, ten at Orléans, four at Paris, and four also at the main universities of the Holy Roman Empire and of eastern Europe (Prague, Vienna, Leipzig, Louvain, etc.) and at Salamanca. The geographical denomination of these nations obviously varied from one university to another and their role was of varying importance, sometimes being a simple system of organization of electoral colleges, and sometimes being highly structured and fairly independent institutions within the university.[6]

Almost all universities were also subdivided into distinct faculties for the masters and students of a particular discipline. The classical faculties were those of the 'arts' (i.e. the liberal arts), theology, law (although the faculty of canon law was often distinguished from that of civil law), and medicine. Yet there were others. At Toulouse, for example, there was a faculty of grammar as well as a faculty of arts.

In cities such as Bologna, Padua, or Montpellier, where there were whole universities devoted to a single discipline, the very notion of faculty had no real justification. But, in the majority of cases, faculties were essential and somewhat autonomous units within the university, with their own statutes, their own council, and often their own dean. Their immediate interests, which were bound up with a specific recruitment of students and with their own particular purposes, were not all the same, and relations were therefore often tense.

There is little point at this stage in the argument in lingering any longer over this question of the structures and internal subdivisions of the medieval universities. There was an almost limitless variation as regards matters of detail; they developed over the centuries and they should not at any rate be allowed to obscure the fundamental notion: that of an independent university community. But it must be realized that this community, even if perceived by contemporaries as a whole, almost invariably had an organization of the federal kind, in which the reciprocal play of the various constituent elements could just as well be an essential factor in its dynamism as an ever-present threat of dislocation. This may be treated as sufficiently general to serve as a defining feature of the medieval universities.

Another matter to be considered is that of the influence of the universities, which may more particularly be measured through considering the geo-graphical area from which students were recruited. Admittedly, as we shall see below, it was very rare in the Middle Ages for universities to attract students consistently from the whole of Christendom. Only the Universities of Paris and Bologna, and just possibly that of Padua during the fifteenth century, could fairly make this claim and, even in those cities, there was always a core of students recruited from the surrounding regions. Everywhere else – including universities with a reputation for intellectual achievement that was not in dispute (Orléans, Oxford, Salamanca, Prague, Louvain, etc.) – the area of recruitment was mainly 'national' (in so far as this word had a meaning in the Middle Ages), or, indeed, regional, or even local. From the fourteenth century on, university and state took various measures designed rather to discourage than to favour student mobility.

6 Kibre, *Nations*.

Nevertheless, it has always been allowed that the universities had, at least in ideal terms, a universalist vocation. Although of course situated in a particular town or country, they could wield an influence over an area whose extent was not determined by the limits of any pre-existing ecclesiastical or political circumscription (diocese, province, principality, or kingdom) but simply by their intrinsic capacity to attract. This was, in turn, determined by the fame of their traditions and by the quality of their teaching. The journey to and the sojourn in a given place of study were regarded as two indissociable parts of university life, during which the student enjoyed to the same degree the same privileges. Medieval students were, by definition, foreigners. Moreover, at Bologna, those students who were strictly speaking natives did not belong to the university since, as citizens of Bologna, they continued to be members of the city community and enjoyed the rights and freedoms of the commune.[7]

SCHOLASTIC PEDAGOGY

Finally, medieval universities might be defined in terms of the kind and level of education available. It is not sufficient to speak only of 'higher education'. We must not elaborate here on questions to be discussed in the chapters of this history devoted to the various faculties, but it is important to bear in mind that, for the most part, medieval universities were structured in terms of pedagogic conceptions and classifications of knowledge which the twelfth-century schools had bequeathed to them and which were often of a much more ancient provenance, dating from the Carolingian reformers (Alcuin), from the church fathers (Saint Augustine, Saint Jerome), and from theorists of antiquity (Quintilian, Varro, Boethius, Cassiodorus, etc.), who had themselves drawn their inspiration from Aristotle and Cicero.[8]

This inheritance was a threefold one, involving a classification, a hierarchy, and a method.

The classification culminated in a fixed list of disciplines, which were themselves defined, for the most part, by the 'authorities', that is to say, the basic texts and the most 'authoritative' commentaries which served as their basis and elements of which, more or less complete by the twelfth century, would be used almost unchanged for university teaching in the following centuries. These disciplines were those which gave their names to the various faculties, namely, theology, law, medicine, and the liberal arts. In practice, a number of additional disciplines could be taught in the margins, as it were, and these were under the control of the traditional faculties (the 'notarial art'

---

[7] Cobban, *Medieval Universities*, 69–70.
[8] R. R. Bolgar, *The Classical Heritage and its Beneficiaries from the Carolingian Age to the End of the Renaissance* (Cambridge, 1958); A. Piltz, *The World of Medieval Learning* (Oxford, 1981).

alongside law, and surgery alongside medicine, at Bologna, for example); within particular faculties, one or another secondary branch, especially in the scientific 'arts' of the *quadrivium* (astronomy at Bologna and Padua, music at Salamanca), might also be developed to such an extent as to give rise to independent teaching or even the conferring of degrees. Such innovations were, however, rare and did little to alleviate the rigid character of the framework of disciplines and faculties which the universities had inherited and perpetuated. The main consequence of this way of proceeding was to debar whole branches of knowledge, which were not recognized by the traditional classifications, from university teaching. This was true of history, poetry, customary law, and the 'mechanical arts' (by which we would understand the applied sciences and technology).

The cultural and pedagogic tradition of antiquity and of the early Middle Ages bequeathed to the universities, along with this rigid classification of the disciplines, the idea that there was a hierarchy among the disciplines themselves. This hierarchy was governed by positive criteria such as the more or less directly religious character of each discipline, its social usefulness, and its intellectual dignity; conversely, a discipline would be downgraded, or even excluded outright, if it in any way seemed 'profane', 'lucrative' (i.e. yielding profits to an individual), or 'mechanical' (i.e. concerned with matter). Any hierarchy constituted in this manner and expressing itself more concretely in university life, in terms of the according of precedence, powers, and prestige, was obviously bound to place the faculty of theology at the summit, with the faculties of law and medicine coming just below it and the faculty of arts being ranked last. One should not conclude from this, as we shall see, that this latter was, as has sometimes been suggested, merely a 'preparatory faculty' for the other so-called 'superior' faculties, or that arts students and teachers were necessarily excluded from every form of 'university power'. But the fact remains that no recognized medieval university was ever restricted to arts schools. Although the latter were, in various forms, fairly plentiful in the medieval West (above all, from the fourteenth century on), they were only granted university status when they were associated with, at the very least, a faculty of theology, law, or medicine.

It was, however, rare in the Middle Ages to find a university with all of the various faculties. Prior to the 1360s, when the new faculties of theology proliferated, such universities were only to be found at Paris (although civil law had not been taught there since 1219), Oxford, and Cambridge. The other universities tended to have only two or three faculties or, indeed, just one (law in the case of the University of Orléans, for example). Those universities which had been founded from the 1380s onwards, were usually granted, on paper at least, the right to have 'all the authorized faculties' but, in practice, certain of these faculties, especially those of theology and medicine, had very low numbers or even a very intermittent existence.

But the crucial point to grasp here is that, for the men of the Middle Ages, there could only be a university or *studium generale* where a discipline was taught that was 'higher', that is, perfect and completed, as much in terms of the 'authenticity' of the knowledge that it contained as in terms of its social purpose. In spite of the tireless attempts of medieval philosophers and scientists to affirm the independence and the lofty nature of their discipline, the arts never ceased to labour under the suspicion of being irredeemably marked by their profane origins in antiquity. As a consequence, they were never accorded anything other than a propaedeutic value, since incomplete disciplines in a Christian culture could claim no legitimate role other than that of helping one to gain access to the truly higher and self-sufficient forms of knowledge.

In theory, as I have already said, all universities with the same faculties were supposed to guarantee the same level of teaching and to confer degrees that were equally valid throughout Christendom. In practice, as we shall see below, there were considerable disparities and the most important universities, especially Paris as regards theology and Bologna as regards law – which claimed, in their own favoured domain, a founding role, a genuine superiority, and a kind of mastery over the whole of Christendom – refused to admit that the degrees obtained in the other *studia generalia* were of equal value to their own.

Finally, the methods of teaching adopted tended to be much the same in all the medieval universities. Admittedly, there were significant differences, in matters of detail, from one faculty, university, or period to another. However, considered overall, there was a kind of common spirit which could fairly be described, if one so wished, as scholastic. This was still, for the most part, an inheritance derived from the main centres of scholarship of the twelfth century, namely, the schools of logic and theology in Paris, the law schools in Bologna, and the schools of medicine in Salerno.

What were the main features of this tradition? Apart from the general and exclusive use of Latin as the language of scholarly debate, one should note the primacy of two basic types of exercise, in all faculties, namely, the 'lecture' and the 'dispute'. The former consisted of a reading, with commentary, of the texts contained in the official syllabuses, thereby giving the student mastery of the 'authorities' who served as the basis of each discipline; the latter, an oral debate conducted according to the rules of Aristotelian syllogistics, depending upon constant references to the 'authorities' and serving to establish, defend, or refute a particular thesis or 'case', allowed one to resolve and to develop into a body of consistent doctrine problems of every kind (philosophical, juridical, theological, etc.) which arose out of the study and comparison of texts.

The prevalence of this type of pedagogy, which was all the more pervasive for being defined as compulsory by the university statutes, had a whole range of different consequences. Firstly, it gave a crucial, propaedeutic role to grammar and dialectic, disciplines which were indispensable for anyone wishing to arrive at a good understanding of texts and at logically impeccable reasoning which was itself regarded as the primordial means of access to the truth. Secondly, it established the respective importance, within this form of teaching, of writing, which was a necessary support of the authorities and of the 'authorized' gloss, and of the spoken word, the normal medium for lectures and still more for disputes. Thirdly, and as a consequence of the above, it gave considerable importance to the personal relation between master and pupil. Fourthly, it also required constant recourse to memorizing and therefore to repetition, which generally demanded very long durations of study. These durations, which increased throughout the thirteenth century and only began to shorten to any extent in the fifteenth, varied from university to university and from faculty to faculty, ranging from four or five years in the arts faculties (and even seven or eight at Oxford) to twelve or thirteen at certain law faculties (Toulouse) and as many as fifteen or sixteen at the faculty of theology in Paris.

So committed were the medieval universities to this form of pedagogy that they took it to excesses which many deemed paralysing. Indeed, they were virtually cut off from every other form of intellectual procedure, whether traditional (mystical exegesis, beloved of monastic culture) or innovatory (experimentation and measurement, philological and historical analysis); these latter, championed by the humanists, only began, with great difficulty, to make inroads into university teaching around the late fifteenth and early sixteenth century. Up until then, only the liveliest forms of doctrinal opposition had managed to achieve some sort of expression within this stiflingly uniform framework.

The universities did not have a monopoly over 'scholastic' pedagogy. It also prevailed, albeit in an often simplified form, in the thirteenth and fourteenth century, in many urban schools and mendicant *studia*. Yet it was the universities that were responsible for perfecting scholasticism. More particularly, they were the only institutions – and this was one of the great innovations of the medieval university system – to link teaching and examinations closely together. Even if in fact, for various different reasons, many medieval students defaulted, as we shall see, before actually taking their exams, the examination was conceived as the normal culmination of a course of study, which entitled one to an official degree. The examinations were mainly oral and were subject to the most meticulous specifications (although this concern with minutiae obviously did not rule out deception and cheating); they served to confirm that a student had mastered the knowledge and techniques which had been inculcated in him, and that he was capable of reproducing the exercises where he had up until then been a merely passive listener. The *baccalariatus*, where it existed, generally involved carrying out a simplified 'reading', whereas the granting of the *licentia* depended upon the winning of a dispute, and a doctorate was nothing other than the solemn inauguration of an 'ordinary' teaching post.

The above is obviously no more than a general, fairly abstract framework, whose concrete application, local peculiarities, and long-term transformations will be illustrated in subsequent chapters.

To summarize the argument so far: a medieval university was not only a papal foundation guaranteeing its members a range of different privileges; it was also an independent community, with an often complex internal structure, committed to a specific type of teaching, and recruiting its members from the whole of the geographical area over which it wielded influence (an influence which could, ideally speaking, be extended across the whole of Christendom).

THE DIVERSITY OF MEDIEVAL UNIVERSITIES

Our first task was obviously to attempt a definition of the medieval university. Yet, were we to stop short at this point, the reader would be left with a far too uniform and static idea of the phenomenon, for the sixty or so universities of the medieval West were in fact extremely various as regards their numbers, their intellectual orientation, their social role, and the university institutions themselves.

This diversity was the product of both history and geography. Indeed, the particular qualities of each medieval university can largely be accounted for in terms of the date of its establishment, the conditions under which it was founded, and the social and political situation of the town and region in which, whether by chance or design, it was installed. It is therefore appropriate now to retrace in broad outline the chronology of the university foundations which occurred in medieval Europe, together with a brief account of their respective localities.[9] Yet this seemingly simple task runs up against a number of practical difficulties.

Since the first universities arose gradually out of pre-existing schools, the fixing of an exact date of birth is always awkward. If, for example, one were to accept the solemn papal confirmations or the first written statutes which have survived (1215 and 1231 for Paris, 1220 for Montpellier, 1252 for Bologna), one would invariably end up with dates that are clearly too late. If, in spite of all the complications involved, one can generally agree, as we shall see below, that a decisive change in the nature of the institutions involved occurred within a 'fork' of ten to fifteen years (as was the case at Bologna, Paris, Montpellier, and Oxford, all four of which would seem to have become genuine universities between 1200 and 1215, or possibly a little earlier in the

---

[9] Save where contrary information is available, I have followed Rashdall, *Universities*; L. Jílek (ed.), *Historical Compendium of European Universities* (Geneva, 1984).

case of Bologna), there are a number of other cases in which such a change would seem to have dragged on interminably, as was the case at Orléans (where the word *universitas* was first used in 1236, with the papal bull being dated 1306) or at Angers (where we know of schools of law as early as 1230, but where the first use of the expression *studium generale* dates from 1337, and where the papal confirmation only occurred in 1364).[10] In the latter instances, the choice of a date of birth can only be arbitrary.

For the more recent universities, there is usually a clearly dated papal letter of foundation (sometimes preceded or followed by a princely charter). But the real launching of such institutions often occurred a few years later and, most crucially, there were false starts. Thus, the University of Toulouse, although officially created in 1229, enjoyed a somewhat precarious existence up until the 1260s. The University of Vienna, founded in 1365, only really became active in 1383, with the arrival of teachers who had been hounded out of Paris by the Great Schism. The University of Cracow, which was established in 1364, rapidly disappeared from sight, being revived only in 1400, upon the initiative of King Ladislaus Jagello, with new papal bulls. In cases such as these, it obviously makes no sense to hold to one date only.

There were also many projects for the foundation of universities which were stillborn, even if things sometimes proceeded as far as the granting of a papal bull. Rashdall's classic manual on the subject cites some fifteen 'paper universities' of this kind, and his list is almost certainly incomplete.[11] Such failures are invariably of interest to the historian. A number of them, being no more than projects arising out of a prince's whim or a chance concatenation of circumstances, are easily explained. Others are more difficult to understand. Why, for instance, did the universities projected for Lucca, Lyon, or Geneva never see the light of day? Each of these cases requires a monograph by itself. But, for our present purposes, these failed attempts must be set to one side.

Studia generalia which indisputably existed but which were ephemeral, intermittent, or in decline pose a much more serious problem for the historian. This category would include, for example, various *studia* of northern Italy (Vicenza in 1204–10, Arezzo in 1215–55 and then again around 1338, Vercelli from 1228 to the end of the thirteenth century) which arose as a consequence of the migration of teachers and students from the two main universities, Bologna and Padua, and which, for the most part, fell into decline and disappeared fairly quickly, after a few years of activity, when the majority of their members returned to their universities of origin, once the conflict which had led to their departure had been settled. A number of other universities, mostly fourteenth-century foundations, failed to develop sufficiently, either because of the general 'troubles' of the period, or because a

[10] *Universités en France*, 41–2.   [11] Rashdall, *Universities*, vol. II, 325–31.

favourable social or political milieu was lacking. A few continued neverthe-less to lead a humdrum, even vegetative, existence right up until modern times, as for example the Universities of Cahors and of Orange in France, the University of Huesca in Aragon, and that of Ferrara in Italy. Others were obliged to shut their doors fairly rapidly, as, for example, the University of Palencia in Castile, the University of Grenoble in Dauphiné, and the Univer-sities of Treviso, Florence, and Piacenza in Italy. Such matters are all the more difficult to assess, as one can well imagine, given the fact that the decline and disappearance of these institutions generally left no other trace than that of increasing gaps and silences in the documentation. But one should not therefore disregard these universities, whose character as *studia generalia* is usually well established.

While, in spite of everything, it is relatively easy to draw up a list of the universities founded during the Middle Ages, the real difficulty is to establish which, at any given date, were the truly active *studia generalia*. The maps assembled at the end of this chapter are intended to give some idea of this, but they have the drawback of making no distinction between big and little universities, between complete universities and universities with one or two faculties, and between universities which wielded some influence over a large area and universities which were merely local. It would seem difficult, not least because of the present state of research, to imagine any system of repre-sentation that would be sufficiently fine to bring out the interplay of these various parameters (which themselves vary over time). But one should at least bear this problem in mind when one seeks to understand the place and the role of universities in medieval society and civilization.

THE BIRTH OF THE UNIVERSITIES

Broadly speaking, one can distinguish three different phases in the develop-ment of the medieval universities.

The first phase, obviously, is that of the birth of the universities. The crucial event here was the emergence of the Universities of Paris and Bologna, which, although very different from each other, would continue to be the most famous ones up until the end of the Middle Ages. One should not, of course, exaggerate the differences between these two universities or, above all, overemphasize the extent to which they served as models for all sub-sequent foundations. Nevertheless, the crucial role that they played in the first elaboration of the university as an institution justifies our pausing a moment to consider the conditions surrounding their birth.

Let us begin with Bologna, which clearly deserves, because it was a handful of years ahead of any other, the somewhat vain title of oldest European uni-versity. We cannot, however, assign an exact date to this birth. It seems more important to stress that the University of Bologna inherited a long tradition of law teaching.[12] Private law schools had existed in Bologna since the second half of the eleventh century. Although their origin is obscure, the context in which they arose is quite clear, namely the particularly precocious renewal of urban life in northern Italy and the revival of written law in places that were, from 1075 onwards, the main theatre for the great political confrontation between the papacy and the empire. The first professors at Bologna of whom we know were Pepo, who taught around 1070–1100, and, more especially, Irnerius, whose presence there is attested for the years between 1112 and 1125 and to whom we owe the restructuring of the whole of the *Corpus iuris civilis* (that is to say, the whole of Roman law as codified in the sixth century by the Emperor Justinian) and the beginnings of the 'Gloss' (that is to say, the commentary upon the text of the *Corpus* in accordance with the rules of dialectic). Towards the year 1140, the monk Gratian, who was also at Bologna, performed a similar service in relation to canon law.

The progress of the Bolognese schools was such that, in 1155, the Emperor Frederick I Barbarossa placed their students under his direct protection and declared them subject only to the jurisdiction of their masters or of the bishop of Bologna (and not to that of the local civil authorities).[13] There is no indication, however, that, up until around 1180, the Bolognese law schools were anything other than private schools opened and run by each master after his own fashion, gathering together the students who had entered into an agreement with him and paid him fees (*collectae*) in return for his teaching. The crucial change would seem to have taken place around the years 1180–90.[14] The number of students, often from very distant countries (Germany, France, England), was growing even faster. Rival schools were developing in neighbouring towns (Modena). At Bologna itself, the commune, whose independence was growing even greater, sought to win more control over the masters and students, while at the same time preventing them from fleeing to rival towns. The masters, who were themselves mainly Bolognese in origin, agreed from 1189 to swear an oath to the commune not to seek to transfer the *studium* elsewhere. The students, on the other hand, began to group themselves in 'nations', according to their places of origin (we hear of the Lombard nation as early as 1191), and these were soon federated into 'universities' with elected rectors at their head. These associations were meant to guarantee the mutual aid and protection of the students against the exactions of the local people and local authorities. After a few false starts, the classical

---

[12] With regard to the beginnings of the university of Bologna, see, in addition to Rashdall, *Universities*, and Cobban, *Medieval Universities*, M. Bellomo, *Saggio sull'università nell'età del diritto comune* (Catania, 1979).

[13] On the Bologna schools of the twelfth century see G. Cencetti, ' "Studium fuit Bononie" ', *Studi Medievali*, series III, 7 (1966), 781–833 (republished in G. Arnaldi (ed.), *Le origini dell'Università* (Bologna, 1974), 101–51).

[14] J. K. Hyde, 'Commune, University, and Society in Early Medieval Bologna', in *Universities in Politics*, 17–46.

system of the two cismontane and ultramontane universities would seem, around 1230–40, to have assumed its definitive shape. The rectors, unlike the doctors, refused to swear an oath to stay in the one place, whereas the commune, with the agreement of the teachers, sought by means of various statutes (1211, 1216–17) to check the further development of student universities which were already well and truly constituted and, in addition, enjoyed the support of the pope. The latter, by presenting himself as the defender of the 'liberty of the students', managed to extend his authority over institutions that had up until then been mainly secular. Thus, in 1219, he decided that from then on it would be the archdeacon of Bologna who would confer a *licentia*, after a rigorous examination; up until then, the awarding of titles would seem to have been left to the masters' discretion.

The struggle was a protracted one, but the energy of the students, the growing threat to the very existence of the *studium* of Bologna posed by the emergence of those of Arezzo (1215), Padua (1222), and Naples (1224), and, finally, the development of Bologna's communal government, in which the 'popular' party, more favourably disposed towards the schools, had gained the upper hand, allowed a compromise to be reached. The town recognized the independence of the universities, which were therefore under the jurisdiction of their rectors, whilst at the same time giving the students, as far as lodgings, provisions, and access to credit and justice were concerned, the same guarantees as were enjoyed by the citizens of Bologna. These concessions, which had already been implied in the communal statutes of 1245, were solemnly ratified only in 1274–90. To understand the nature of this development, one should bear in mind that the law students in Bologna were generally adults, often recruited from fairly high up in the social scale, and sometimes the holders of offices or benefices, which naturally conferred independence and maturity upon them.

In the meantime, these same student universities had also succeeded in assuming virtually total control of the organization of studies. Thus, it was they who hired the teachers, by means of a yearly contract which fixed their fees and committed them to a strict schedule for the reading of the specified books of the *Corpus iuris civilis* or of the *Corpus iuris canonici*. This system is known to us through the university statutes of 1252, which are the oldest surviving ones and whose drafting may be taken to symbolize the moment at which the university became definitively stabilized as an institution.[15]

So it was that the university which was to serve as a model for the whole of southern Europe was born. Since the model was for a 'students' university', the doctors, although they did not lose their undeniable social prestige, and

---

[15] D. Maffei, 'Un trattato di Bonaccorso degli Elisei e i più antichi statuti dello Studio di Bologna nel manoscritto 22 della Robbins Collection', *Bulletin of Medieval Canon Law*, new series, 5 (1975), 73–101.

although they did in the end establish colleges of their own,[16] found themselves marginalized in institutional terms. In addition, the fact that it was a model for a university which was, above all, juridical played a large part in consolidating the role of jurists in every aspect of life in the societies and states of western Europe.

In the course of the thirteenth century, other forms of instruction were also established, in the wake of the juridical universities, at Bologna. 'Arts' schools undoubtedly existed there from before 1220. The training of students attending such schools, many of whom were subsequently to become jurists, involved the teaching, above all, of grammar and of rhetoric (in the educational form of the *ars dictaminis*, that is, the epistolary art), together with a fair amount of logic, but with almost no natural philosophy. The schools of medicine made their appearance around 1260. Gradually, a university of arts and of medicine was established, with institutions directly inspired by those of the juridical universities; it was only in 1316, however, that its full independence, under an elected rector, was recognized by the universities of law and by the commune.

The University of Paris, which came into being at almost the same time as that of Bologna, had very different qualities.[17] It owed its origin to the schools which appeared in Paris from the end of the eleventh century. However, one should distinguish between the traditional ecclesiastical schools, the principal one being that of the chapter of the cathedral of Notre-Dame, and the private schools opened by independent masters (although obliged, at any rate after 1150, to request a 'licence to teach' from the chancellor of Notre-Dame). The school of Notre-Dame was, above all, a school of theology and it was run, in the second half of the twelfth century, by a series of famous masters, such as Peter Lombard, Peter Comestor, and Peter the Chanter, who composed the manuals upon which the teaching of theology, until the end of the Middle Ages, depended. The content of the courses taught in the private schools was more varied for, although their speciality was dialectic, grammar, law, and medicine were also taught there.

In the closing decades of the twelfth century, such schools undoubtedly proliferated. More and more students, often from distant parts (England, Germany, Italy), flocked to them. This rapid, almost uncontrolled growth gave rise to many problems, both material (lodgings, provisioning, and public

---

[16] There is considerable controversy regarding the date at which the Bolognese 'doctors' colleges' first appeared. Some scholars believe that embryonic forms already existed as early as the end of the twelfth century, but P. Weimar, 'Zur Doktorwürde der Bologneser Legisten', *Aspekte europäischer Rechtsgeschichte. Festgabe für Helmut Coing zum 70. Geburtstag* (Frankfurt, 1982), 421–43, reckons that their final organizational form was not achieved until 1291.

[17] J. Verger, 'Des écoles à l'université: la mutation institutionnelle', in R.-H. Bautier (ed.), *La France de Philippe Auguste. Le temps des mutations* (Paris, 1982), 817–46; J. Verger, 'A propos de la naissance de l'université de Paris: contexte social, enjeu politique, portée intellectuelle', in *Schulen und Studium*, 69–96.

order) and institutional and intellectual. The new masters chafed at the power over them, limited though it was, that the bishop and the chancellor claimed to wield; the latter were themselves troubled, as were many of the masters, by the proliferation of the schools and by the resulting 'confusion' in instruction, the major dangers in their eyes being obviously the advance of the 'lucrative disciplines' (law) and the success of Aristotle's philosophical texts, the translations of which were then becoming current in Paris.[18]

Given these conditions, the birth of the University of Paris can be interpreted as a kind of compromise between the parties involved. It allowed the masters, and the masters of arts in particular, certainly as early as 1208–10, to form themselves into an autonomous guild, to endow themselves with statutes, to co-opt their new colleagues, and to elude the direct control and exactions of the chancellor of Notre-Dame – in short, to form a university in the sense defined above. On the other hand, the ecclesiastical authorities, together with the already established masters, the masters in theology in particular, benefited from the institution of obligatory syllabuses, detailed curricula, rigorous examinations, and valuable guarantees against the proliferation of new schools and the anarchic 'confusion' of disciplines; it imposed, through the bias of the university institutions themselves and, more especially, through the distinctions between the various faculties, a respect for the classifications and hierarchies upon which Christian knowledge had traditionally been based.

This compromise was not achieved without struggles, which lasted up until 1231. Indeed, they would have continued longer, had the king of France and the pope not intervened and acted as arbiters, very much in the schools' favour. The king allowed the students the personal privileges of clerics as early as 1200, and the pope solemnly granted the university its first official statutes, in 1215 and in 1231. Yet this support was counterbalanced by other factors. The popes, in particular, set out to supervise the organization of teaching and to have the new institution serve their own ends, namely the defence and exposition of orthodox doctrine against the threat of heresies, and the training of effective theologians and preachers. Having prohibited the teaching of civil law in Paris in 1219, on the grounds that it was too profane, they lost no time in compelling the university to incorporate the theology schools of the new mendicant orders (1220) and, in spite of the very violent dispute between mendicant friars and secular masters (1250–6) which finally erupted in relation to this issue, they remained unyielding.[19] It was during this same dispute, and in the years that followed, that the University of Paris finally settled upon the institutions that it was to keep until the end of the

[18] S. C. Ferruolo, *The Origins of the University. The Schools of Paris and their Critics. 1100–1215* (Stanford, 1985).

[19] M.-M. Dufeil, *Guillaume de Saint-Amour et la polémique universitaire parisienne. 1250–1259* (Paris, 1972).

Middle Ages, with the constitution of the 'four' nations (from 1220 on), the creation of the office of rector, who was elected from the company of the masters of arts (around 1240), and the emergence of the 'higher' faculties, with their own statutes and dean (around 1260).

Throughout this long history of conflict, the university essentially consisted of the masters. The University of Paris was in fact a 'university of masters', a federation of schools in which, while maintaining their personal authority over their own pupils within their particular school, the masters, by means of their councils and their elected officers, collectively administered the whole of the *studium* and abided by a common agreement as regards all matters concerning teaching and examinations. As explained above, the majority of these masters, who therefore dominated the nations and elected the rector, were the young masters of arts, often themselves students or about to be students of theology, law, or medicine. This fact had an indisputably 'democratic' impact upon the operation of the University of Paris as an institution, even if it was bound to lead to repeated clashes with the masters of the 'superior' faculties.

If so much space has been devoted to the two oldest European universities, it is not only because, up until the end of the Middle Ages, they continued to be the most famous, with the largest teaching staff and the widest geographical influence, but also because they generally served as models for the majority of the more recent foundations. A more rapid listing seems appropriate for the latter, however.

Some of them are, in fact, almost as old as Bologna or Paris. As we have already seen, the schools of medicine at Salerno did not really undergo much development in the course of the thirteenth century; the statutes granted them in 1231 by the Emperor Frederick II established a degree system but denied them all independence. On the other hand, the schools of medicine at Montpellier, whose existence is attested at least as early as the 1130s but whose origin remains obscure, became a genuine 'university of medicine' in the course of the thirteenth century. The statutes this university received in 1220 from a papal legate placed it under the authority of the church but also confirmed the doctors' authority over the *studium*.

In these same years, the University of Oxford was born. The siting of the first English university in this small market-town, which was not even the seat of a bishop, is somewhat surprising, and chance must have played a part in it. One should bear in mind, however, that Oxford had long had several ecclesiastical establishments, which may have provided a point of departure. At any rate, even if it is certain both that a series of contributions from the University of Paris played a part in developing it further and that its institutions took their inspiration from the Parisian ones, it was indisputably an autochthonous and original university. There were schools in operation in Oxford from at least as early as the middle of the twelfth century; an embryonic university organization was in existence from 1200, even before the first papal statutes (1214), which were complemented by royal charters, had established its first institutions (the chancellor, the proctors of the nations, and the 'congregations' of the masters), while at the same time guaranteeing its independence from both the bishop of Lincoln and the local population and civil authorities.[20]

The two principal ways in which, up until the end of the Middle Ages, a university came to be founded, the 'swarm' or the establishment of such an institution by prior decision of the civil or ecclesiastical authorities, were already familiar in the first decades of the thirteenth century.

A swarm involved a group of masters and students leaving their university of origin, generally after a dispute with the local authorities, establishing themselves in a new town, and recreating a university there. Migrations of this sort were generally provisional, with settlement of the dispute resulting in a return to the original university. Yet, where conditions were favourable, a new university might be founded.

This is precisely what happened in Cambridge, with masters and students fleeing Oxford between 1209 and 1214 (following the arrest and execution of a few students, upon the orders of the mayor and the king). In France, the ancient schools of Orléans and Angers undoubtedly benefited from the flight of masters and students from Paris in 1229–31 (they were seeking reparation for the death of a number of students at the hands of the royal serjeants), even if, as we have seen, it was only much later that they won official recognition of their university status.

Yet it was northern Italy that was the heartland of university migrations, very probably because of its economically developed condition, its division into rival city states, and, as noted above, its system of student universities, which were especially suited to geographical mobility. In addition, the various disputes which, in the first half of the thirteenth century, marred relations between the University of Bologna on the one hand, and the commune and the emperor on the other, gave rise to a series of secessions. However, only one of these gave birth to an important university, that of Padua (1222). Yet this university, whose institutions and intellectual orientation clearly reflected its descent from the University of Bologna, did not really make any noteworthy advances until after 1260.[21] There may have been a university at Reggio Emilia from around 1188, and there were undoubtedly universities at Vicenza between 1204 and 1209, at Arezzo in 1215 and up until around 1255, at Vercelli (the result of a migration from Padua between 1228 and 1244), and at Siena from 1246 to 1252, but all of these institutions shone brightly for a brief period, only to disappear after a few years, leaving behind

---

[20] *History of Oxford*, vol. I, 1–95.
[21] G. Arnaldi, 'Le origini dello studio di Padova dalla migrazione universitaria del 1222 alla fine del periodo ezzeliniano', *La Cultura*, 15 (1977), 388–431.

them a local memory which would serve to justify, in the fourteenth century, a number of generally vain attempts to revive them.

It was also in the thirteenth century that the civil or ecclesiastical authorities first, of their own accord, took the decision to create or, as the saying went, to 'plant' universities. Even where there were founding acts of this nature, earlier schools often existed and, indeed, provided the basis for the new university. Yet such acts generally implied recourse, with varying degrees of completeness, to an established institutional model. In addition, one can interpret them as signs that clearly conceived social and political aims were invested in the new foundations from the very beginning, even if they were not always fully realized subsequently.

The University of Naples, which was founded in 1224 by the Emperor Frederick II to compete with that of Bologna and to train the jurists whom he required, was one of the first of this type. Although closely supervised by royal officers, it was granted the minimum of corporate organization that would enable one to speak of a university. Furthermore, very probably because of southern Italy's troubled development in the thirteenth century, it did not manage to develop much further, in spite of a series of 'general reforms', effected as much by Frederick II and his immediate successors as under the Angevin dynasty.[22]

The first foundation of this type in France was that of the University of Toulouse, which was established through the Treaty of Paris, after the crusade against the Cathars and the count of Toulouse (1229). This foundation, which was obviously fairly unpopular locally, took a long time to gain ground, and only did so, during the 1260s, at the price of a fairly profound alteration in its nature. Instead of the religious, proselytizing university that had first been planned, there developed a predominantly juridical university, which was more in harmony with the southerners' expectations.[23]

Our list of 'created' universities ought also to include the one that Pope Innocent IV chose to establish in the curia itself (*studium curiae*, 1245).

Yet it was undoubtedly in the Iberian peninsula that, from the thirteenth century, the political authorities interfered most directly in the development of the universities, a fact which can very probably be explained by the tendency of the Spanish sovereigns to take the whole of the organization of their kingdoms into their own hands, as they were constituted through the gradual advance of the *Reconquista*. As early as 1208, Alfonso VIII, king of Castile, introduced salaries for the teachers at the cathedral school of Palencia. It is hard to decide if these privileges, confirmed in 1220 by a papal bull, served to create a genuine university. Be this as it may, the *studium* of Palencia, which remained in operation for a number of years, above all for the liberal arts and

---

[22] G. Arnaldi, 'Fondazione e rifondazioni dello studio di Napoli in età sveva', in *Università e società*, 81–105.

[23] *Les Universités de Languedoc au XIIIe siècle*, Cahiers de Fanjeaux, 5 (Toulouse, 1970).

theology, would seem to have disappeared around 1250. In the meantime, royal favour had shifted to Salamanca. Indeed, a chronicler records that, in the winter of 1218–19, Alfonso IX of León had founded a university at Salamanca. Royal privileges of 1254, ratified by a papal bull of 1255 and reiterated in the famous juridical compilation known as the *Siete partidas* (around 1260), culminated in the definitive recognition of a genuine *studium generale* at Salamanca, which was under the strict control of the local ecclesiastical dignitaries but clearly endowed with all the traditional privileges. Its organization, which we only know of through a series of very late statutes (1411, 1422), was undoubtedly of a mixed type, borrowing more elements from Bologna than from Paris. Another *studium generale* of the same type was founded at Valladolid before the end of the century, endowed by the king of Castile and enjoying his full protection, although the papacy did not fully recognize its status as a university until 1346.

The University of Lisbon was of much the same kind, and was founded and endowed by Denis, king of Portugal, and by a number of the kingdom's ecclesiastical dignitaries (the Cistercian abbot of Alcobaça, in particular) around 1288, a foundation which was confirmed by the pope in 1290.

So it was that, by the end of the thirteenth century, the universities, although still few in number, had become institutions of central importance in European cultural life, places dedicated to the production and diffusion of ideas, indeed, even sites of genuine 'intellectual power',[24] as well as for the training of ecclesiastical or civil élites. Eighteen *studia generalia* emerged prior to 1300,[25] of which fifteen (or sixteen, if one includes Salerno) were very probably quite active at this date. A number of them had certainly already attracted several thousand students, of very varied origin; these would continue to be the main European universities up until the end of the Middle Ages (Bologna, Paris, Montpellier, Oxford, Padua, Salamanca, Cambridge). Other universities had a strong influence locally.

UNIVERSITIES AT THE END OF THE MIDDLE AGES

Given that new universities were still being founded, possibly in even greater numbers, in the course of the fourteenth and fifteenth centuries, there is cause to question the traditional diagnosis which has it that the universities 'declined' at the end of the Middle Ages.

The first phase may be said to end in 1378, when the Great Schism began. This phase, as well as involving the definitive recognition of the university status of centres founded prior to 1300, such as Orléans, Angers, and Valla-

---

[24] H. Grundmann, ' "Sacerdotium – Regnum – Studium": zur Wertung der Wissenschaft im 13. Jh.', *Archiv für Kulturgeschichte*, 34 (1952), 5–21.

[25] The number would be twenty-three if one were to include the disputed cases of Salerno, Reggio, Piacenza (papal bull of 1248, but very probably without effect), Palencia, and Seville.

dolid, saw the creation of nineteen new universities, namely Lérida (1300), Avignon (1303), Rome (1303), Perugia (1308), Treviso (1318), Cahors (1332), Grenoble (1339), Pisa (1343), Prague (1347), Florence (1349), Perpignan (1350), Huesca (1354), Arezzo (1355), Siena (1357), Pavia (1361), Cracow (1364), Orange (1365), Vienna (1365), and Pécs (1367).[26] A total number of twenty-eight (or thirty-one if one includes Salerno, Verona and Lucca), would seem to have been genuinely in operation in 1378.

Without going into details regarding these later foundation, their general characteristics should none the less be reviewed. First of all, the initiative of the authorities, whether ecclesiastical or, as was more and more the case, civil, was from now on the crucial factor – even if the presence of earlier schools and, more broadly, the existence of a favourable social and cultural milieu were common and, indeed, virtually necessary elements in the successful development of a new foundation. In Avignon, Perugia, and Prague, for example, such new foundations began by confirming the elevation to university status of important pre-existing schools. On the other hand, in places such as Treviso, Grenoble, and Huesca, where virtually nothing existed, the universities seem to have been fairly arbitrarily implanted and quite often languished or even disappeared at the end of a few years. Adopting an overall view, prior to 1378, only universities with relatively low numbers and slight influence – Prague excepted – arose in the course of the fourteenth century.

The majority of these universities (fifteen out of nineteen) were located in southern Europe, and the dominant faculty was generally that of law, the others being non-existent or, at best, having low numbers and a mediocre level of achievement. Consequently, these universities generally adopted statutes modelled on those of Bologna, but they usually adapted them to the local social and political situation and tried to avoid the complete separation of student universities and doctors' colleges that characterized the system at Bologna itself.

If one excepts Paris and Oxford, southern Europe had been the favoured terrain for universities, because of its higher levels of urbanization, because of its traditions of written law, and, possibly, because of the earlier progress made by lay elements in society there. However, a movement for the creation of new universities outside this area arose in the middle of the fourteenth century, the turning-point being the founding of the University of Prague in 1347. Up until then, the Holy Roman Empire and central Europe had remained a little outside this movement, very probably because of the preponderance of the nobles. As the latter were able, when they so desired, to send their sons to study in Paris or in Bologna, they had little desire to see the

---

[26] Or twenty-one if one were to regard the *studia* of Verona (it was granted a papal bull by Pope Benedict XII in 1339) and Lucca (imperial bull in 1369) as enjoying university status. One should also bear in mind that Arezzo and Siena had already fostered *studia generalia*, for a period of some years, in the thirteenth century.

emergence of autochthonous universities, which would be easier to enter, thereby providing the children of the bourgeoisie and the peasantry with opportunities for social climbing and by the same token reinforcing the political weight of the church and of the towns. Yet economic development and the awakening of national sentiments made the movement for the creation of new universities ever more powerful. In 1347, it prevailed, with the help of the pope and, above all, that of the new emperor, Charles IV – a prince of French culture and a man very much in favour of the university as an institution.[27] After some years, the University of Prague met with considerable success, attracting hundreds of German, Czech, and Polish students.[28] This success spawned a number of imitations, whose early stages were, however, far more laborious: in Austria the University of Vienna, which was created in 1365 but languished up until 1383; in Poland the University of Cracow, which was founded in 1364 but was very soon in trouble and had to be re-established in 1397–1400; and in Hungary the University of Pécs, founded in 1367, but which only lasted ten years.

As in so many other areas of European history, the Great Schism, which began in 1378, represents a genuine rupture in the history of the universities, which was all the more dramatic for unfolding against a background of crisis (plagues, wars, and economic depression). The unit of medieval Christendom was irremediably shattered, and universalist pretensions, such as were cultivated at the University of Paris, were no longer in fashion. Here one is witness to the birth of the modern state and to the awakening of national sentiments.

Given this context, it is not hard to understand why universities should have proliferated. Indeed, seven were founded or reopened between 1378 and 1400, eighteen between 1400 and 1450 (indeed, twenty, if one is prepared to count Parma and Gerona), and twenty-two between 1451 and 1500. The twenty-eight (or thirty-one) universities operative in 1378 became thirty-one (or thirty-four) in 1400 and sixty-three (or sixty-six) in 1500. New foundations sprang up throughout Europe, with seven in the Iberian peninsula (or eight with Gerona), eight in France, fifteen in Germany (to which one can add the University of Louvain, founded in 1425 by the duke of Brabant), nine in the kingdoms situated on the western and eastern fringes of old Europe (Scotland, Scandinavia, Poland, and Hungary), and, finally, eight in Italy. There it was admittedly not so much a question of genuinely new foundations, save at Ferrara (1391), Turin (1404), and Catania (1444), as of the reopening of

---

[27] In addition to Prague, the Emperor Charles IV granted diplomas either founding or ratifying the foundation of *studia generalia* in Cividale in Friuli (1353, but it remained a dead-letter), Arezzo (1355), Perugia (1355), Siena (1357), Pavia, (1361), Florence (1364), Orange (1365), and Lucca (1369).

[28] P. Moraw, 'Die Universität Prag im Mittelalter. Grundzüge ihrer Geschichte im europäischen Zusammenhang', in *Die Universität zu Prag*, Schriften der sudetendeutschen Akademie der Wissenschaften und Künste, 7 (Munich, 1986), 9–134.

universities in towns which had already given shelter to *studia generalia* in the thirteenth or fourteenth century. England alone was untouched, with no new foundation emerging to challenge the age-old monopoly of Oxford and Cambridge.

Far more than had been the case in the past, these new universities were mainly founded upon the initiative of princes or of towns, which would grant them, along with their first privileges, their initial material and financial endowments. Being simultaneously the founders and protectors of these institutions, they derived both prestige and a crucial nursery of clerics, preachers, and jurists from them. However, a confirmatory papal bull was generally required and, needless to say, many of these new foundations in fact depended upon pre-existing schools.

This does not mean that, by the end of the fifteenth century, the European university network was virtually complete. After all, new universities were still being founded in the sixteenth century. However, a number of people began to grow anxious, in the course of the fifteenth century, about the proliferation of new foundations. The ancient universities tried, with varying degrees of success, to preserve their local monopoly. Thus, the University of Paris, believing that the towns of Caen and Bourges were too close, sought to check the creation of new universities there. In the kingdom of Aragon, the University of Lérida never ceased reminding the world at large of the monopoly granted it in 1300 by its founder, King Diego II, in order to impede plans for the founding of universities in other cities, in Barcelona in particular.[29] Likewise, in Italy, Pavia managed to establish its right to remain the one and only university within the duchy of Milan, and thus to restrict the claims of existing or projected schools in Piacenza, Parma, and Milan itself.

On the other hand, it should be appreciated that very few of the universities founded after 1378 foundered altogether, since many managed to survive at a fairly mediocre level, both as regards numbers and as regards the influence of their teaching. The most dynamic foundations of the fifteenth century were undoubtedly in the northern half of the kingdom of France (Poitiers, Bourges, Caen), in Louvain, in Cracow, and in Germany. These universities were large institutions, often with several hundred students of varied origin, and their numbers rose steadily in the course of the century.[30] Further, these universities were favourably regarded by the local people and by the local civil and ecclesiastical authorities, and were therefore the recipients of generous donations, benefiting the university itself, the colleges, and the university teachers. The Hanseatic Universities of Rostock and Greifswald are outstanding instances of this type of university. Finally, they

---

[29] C. Carrère, 'Refus d'une création universitaire et niveaux de culture à Barcelone: hypothèses d'explication', *Le Moyen Age*, 85 (1979), 245–73.

[30] The increasing size of the student body in German universities of the fifteenth century has been established by R. C. Schwinges, in his *Universitätsbesucher*.

were intellectually ambitious universities, capable of retaining the services of masters of some renown. These institutions thereby succeeded in promoting new currents of thought and original teaching (the new astronomy at Cracow, humanism at Vienna, 'nominalism' at Tübingen), in short, in reviving, for their own benefit, the creative vocation which had seemed up until then to be the prerogative of the oldest centres of learning, such as Paris or Oxford.

These new universities in the northern half of Europe generally took the main features of their organization from the Parisian model. They therefore tended to have the four 'classical' faculties (arts, theology, law, and medicine), the most important being the arts faculty, which had the largest numbers and the theology faculty, in which secular masters and mendicants shared out the teaching between them. These were 'masters' universities', although at Prague, for example, or at Vienna or St Andrews, the students were sometimes able, at least in the early years, to play a part in certain elections and decision-making processes. At Prague, Vienna, Louvain, St Andrews and Glasgow, there were, as in Paris, four 'nations', but the masters of arts never achieved the kind of dominance they enjoyed at Paris or at Oxford. Each faculty had its own dean, and authority over the whole university was wielded by a council of masters, from all the faculties, which generally elected the rector.

The universities which had been founded in the fifteenth century were usually equipped, at any rate officially, with 'all the authorized faculties', either right from the start or else after a few years (at Rostock, the theology faculty was only inaugurated in 1431, a full twelve years after the founding of the university). Conversely, the majority of those born before the middle of the fourteenth century were incomplete, and could only boast one, two, or three faculties. To be more specific, the popes, concerned to exercise strict control over the teaching of theology and the proliferation of the prestigious degree of master of theology, had only sanctioned its teaching at a university level in Paris, Oxford, and Cambridge and at the *studium* of the curia.[31] This policy was abandoned from the 1360s, undoubtedly upon the initiative of Pope Urban V.[32]

The call for a degree of decentralization of theological instruction was now being heard on all sides, for the teaching in Paris, torn apart by the quarrels between 'nominalists', Scotists, Thomists, and so on, could no longer provide such guarantees of orthodoxy as would justify the virtual monopoly which it

---

[31] Which obviously did not stop numerous theology *studia*, often of a very high level, from functioning within the mendicant orders' own educational networks; *Le scuole degli ordini mendicanti (secoli XIII–XIV)* (Todi, 1978); F.-B. Lickteig, *The German Carmelites at the Medieval Universities* (Rome, 1981).

[32] E. Delaruelle, 'La politique universitaire des papes d'Avignon – spécialement d'Urbain V – et la fondation du Collège Espagnol de Bologne', in *El Cardenal Albornoz y el Colegio de España*, vol. II (Bologna, 1972), 8–39.

enjoyed. Furthermore, there was now a more rigorous definition of the notion of the *studium generale*, and there were increasing local and national pressures for the establishment of autochthonous theology faculties. The end of the Middle Ages therefore saw the constitution of numerous such faculties by papal bull, namely Toulouse and Bologna in 1360, Padua in 1363, Pavia in 1389, Salamanca in 1396, Lisbon in 1400, Avignon in 1413, Montpellier in 1421, Lérida in 1430, Valladolid in 1436, and Perpignan in 1447, amongst others. Around the end of the fourteenth century, Vienna and Cracow received the right to have theology faculties, although they had been explicitly refused that right twenty or thirty years earlier, at the time of their original foundation (at Prague, admittedly, the theology faculty had existed from the start). In general, however, this proliferation of theology faculties mainly affected the southern universities and, in practice, it often led to already existing mendicant *studia* being granted university status (which gave then the right to confer degrees), through their integration into the local university.

UNIVERSITY COLLEGES

No typology of medieval universities, even if a cursory one, would be complete without a mention of university colleges.

The first university colleges appeared in Paris, at the end of the twelfth century. These were nothing more than modest pious foundations, serving to provide shelter for a handful of students, often in the midst of other 'poor clerics'. The first genuine colleges were established in Paris, and then in England, in the second half of the thirteenth century, at a time when the rate of expansion of the universities was beginning to pose serious practical problems. In Paris, mention should be made of the colleges of the Sorbonne (1257) and of Harcourt (1280); in Oxford, there were Merton (1263–4), Balliol (1261–6), and University College (around 1280), and, at Cambridge, Peterhouse (1284). Their mode of organization took its inspiration in the main from that of the mendicant monasteries, which had been established as early as the 1220s within these universities, for the use of students belonging to these orders. Endowed with land, properties, and rents, these colleges considered it their mission to take in a given number of students for a specified period of time. The first colleges included establishments reserved for the use of the monks of a particular abbey or order and which were more or less assimilated to priories, such as the colleges of Saint-Bernard (Cistercian – 1248), of Cluny (around 1260), and of Saint-Denis (around 1263), all at Paris, and the colleges of Gloucester (1283) and of Durham (1289), at Oxford. However, the majority of colleges were meant for secular students (with the family or compatriots of the founder often enjoying priority). In the years before 1300, a total of nineteen colleges were founded at Paris, six at Oxford, and one at Cambridge.

Although there were more colleges at Paris than elsewhere, they were often small establishments, meant for young students of arts; they had very little independence and were strictly supervised by the external authorities, whether ecclesiastical or university. The English colleges were more independent and more democratic, their fellows being predominantly bachelors of arts and theology students.

As an institution, the university college was most successful in the fourteenth century: between 1300 and 1400, thirty-seven were founded in Paris, five in Oxford, and seven at Cambridge. The Parisian colleges continued in general to be more modest than the English ones, yet the most important for a long time was the College of Navarre, founded at Paris in 1304, for seventy students; it was to be rivalled only by New College, Oxford, founded in 1379, also for seventy students. Colleges spread in the fourteenth century in the southern universities, where they had been unknown up until then, but they were never to be as important there as at Paris or Oxford. Fifteen colleges were founded in the south of France (eight of which were at Toulouse), eleven in Italy (the only important one being the Spanish College founded in Bologna in 1367), and two in Spain. The new universities of the Holy Roman Empire and of central Europe adopted this institution (eight foundations, in all) but a fairly particular type of college (often called *collegium maius*) was involved here, in which masters enjoyed precedence. Such colleges were then supposed to supervise the running of the faculties, whose teaching body they, for the most part, assembled.

Colleges were still being founded in the fifteenth century, at a slower rhythm in the oldest universities (thirty-six in France, twelve of which were in Paris; nine in England; eight in Italy), but enjoying considerable support elsewhere (twenty-seven in the Empire; three in central Europe; three in Scotland; six in the Iberian peninsula, destined to have a glorious future). It was rare indeed for a medieval university to have no college, as was the case with Orléans.

Whoever their founders were, whether princes, important officers, ecclesiastical dignitaries, or former regents, the colleges of the fourteenth and fifteenth centuries were regarded less as simple lodging-houses for 'poor scholars' and more as privileged institutions serving to guarantee their members, at the price of a degree of discipline, the best conditions for work and study, in other words, to constitute a student élite.[33] Wealthier students, especially students of law, were therefore admitted. The ever larger donations benefiting the colleges, or, at any rate, those which had not been ruined by the wars, enabled them to extend their libraries and, crucially, to constitute

---

[33] A. L. Gabriel, 'The College System in the Fourteenth-Century Universities', in F.L. Utley (ed.), *The Forward Movement of the Fourteenth Century* (Columbus, 1961), 79–124; A. L. Gabriel, 'Motivations of the Founders of Mediaeval Colleges', *Beiträge zum Berufsbewusstsein des mittelalterlichen Menschen*, Miscellanea Mediaevalia, 3 (Berlin, 1964), 61–72.

themselves as genuine teaching institutions, with a proper body of regents and with new and more progressive pedagogic methods. Such colleges were therefore increasingly in a position to compete with the faculties, whose role tended to be reduced to the conferment of degrees.

Only the main colleges became '*collèges de plein exercice*' (colleges providing a full course) but, from the end of the fourteenth century, some gave the impression of being genuine centres of intellectual life, indeed, far more dynamic than the rest of the university. The role played by the College of Navarre and by Magdalen College in the first spread of humanism at Paris and at Oxford is well known.[34] This process was very probably less pronounced in the countries of the Holy Roman Empire, where the poor students continued to constitute an important part of the enrolment of the colleges. At any rate, the colleges still only received a minority of students (between 10 per cent and 20 per cent at Paris, Oxford, and Cambridge and even less at other places) but, in France, England, and Germany, they were henceforth the place where the pedagogic model which was to exert the greatest influence upon the evolution of practices of secondary and higher education in modern Europe was elaborated.

LIST OF EUROPEAN UNIVERSITIES IN THE MIDDLE AGES

Those *studia* whose status as universities is open to dispute have been placed in brackets.

(Salerno) (twelfth century) – statutes granted by the Emperor Frederick II in 1231
Bologna (end of the twelfth century)
(Reggio) (1188) (schools continued to be active up until the end of the thirteenth century)
Vicenza (1204) (disappeared after 1209)
(Palencia) (1208) (disappeared around 1250)
Paris (beginning of the thirteenth century)
Oxford (beginning of the thirteenth century)
Montpellier (beginning of the thirteenth century)
Cambridge (1209–25)
Arezzo (1215) (disappeared around 1260 – a new foundation in 1355, disappeared around 1373)
Salamanca (before 1218–19)
Padua (1222)
Naples (1224)

---

[34] G. Ouy, 'Le collège de Navarre, berceau de l'humanisme français', in *Enseignement et vie intellectuelle (IXe–XVIe siècle). Actes du 95e Congrès national des sociétés savantes*, vol. I (Paris, 1975), 275–99.

Vercelli (1228) (disappeared in the fourteenth century)

Toulouse (1229)

Orléans (around 1235) (officially recognized as a *studium generale* in 1306)

Studium of the Roman curia (1245)

Siena (1246) (disappeared around 1252 – new foundation in 1357)

(Piacenza) (1248) (there is some doubt as to how effective its opening in 1248 really was; it was active once more from 1398 to 1402, when the University of Pavia transferred to Piacenza)

Angers (around 1250) (officially recognized as *studium generale* in 1337)

(Seville) (1254–60) (founded by the king and the pope, this *studium* may not have been a genuine university – disappeared around 1270)

Valladolid (end of the thirteenth century) (officially recognized as *studium generale* by the pope in 1346)

Lisbon (1290) (transferred to Coimbra from 1308 to 1338 and from 1354 to 1377)

Lérida (1300)

Avignon (1303)

Rome (1303) (disappeared at the end of the fourteenth century – re-established in 1431)

Perugia (1308)

Coimbra (see Lisbon)

Treviso (1318) (very probably disappeared in the fourteenth century or, at the latest, in 1407)

Cahors (1332)

Grenoble (1339) (disappeared in the middle of the fourteenth century)

(Verona) (1339) (this *studium*, whose status as university is doubtful, disappeared in the fifteenth century)

Pisa (1343) (disappeared around 1360 – re-established at the beginning of the fifteenth century)

Prague (1347)

Florence (1349) (transferred to Pisa, and thereby closed, in 1472)

Perpignan (1350)

Huesca (1354) (disappeared in the first half of the fifteenth century – re-established in 1464)

Pavia (1361) (transferred to Piacenza in 1398, and thereby suppressed – re-established in 1412)

Cracow (1364) (disappeared prior to 1370 – re-established in 1397)

Orange (1365)

Vienna (1365)

Pécs (1367) (disappeared at some point after 1376)

(Lucca) (1369)

Erfurt (1379)
Heidelberg (1385)
Cologne (1388)
Buda (1389) (disappeared around 1400 – re-established in 1410, disappeared around 1460)
Ferrara (1391) (disappeared in 1394 – re-established in 1430)
Würzburg (1402) (disappeared after 1413)
Turin (1404)
Leipzig (1409)
Aix-en-Provence (1409)
St Andrews (1411)
(Parma) (1412) (this *studium* claimed to be *generale* between 1412 and 1420)
Rostock (1419)
Dole (1422)
Louvain (1425)
Poitiers (1431)
Caen (1432)
Bordeaux (1441)
Catania (1444)
(Gerona) (1446) (royal charter in 1446, but only became a real university in the sixteenth century)
Barcelona (1450)
Glasgow (1451)
Valence (France) (1452)
Trier (1454)
Greifswald (1456)
Freiburg im Breisgau (1457)
Basle (1459)
Ingolstadt (1459)
Nantes (1460)
Bourges (1464)
Pozsony (1465) (disappeared at the end of the fifteenth century)
Venice (1470) (college of physicians authorized to grant doctoral degrees)
(Genoa) (1471) (only opened in 1513)
Saragossa (1474)
Copenhagen (1475)
Mainz (1476)
Tübingen (1476)
Uppsala (1477)
Palma, Majorca (1483)
Sigüenza (1489)
Aberdeen (1495)

Frankfurt-on-Oder (1498) (only opened in 1506)
Alcalá (1499)
Valencia (1500)

SELECT BIBLIOGRAPHY

Bibliographies

Bibliographie internationale de l'histoire des universités, vol. I, *Espagne – Louvain – Copenhague – Prague*, by R. Gilbert, J. Paquet, S. Ellehój, F. Kavka, and J. Havránek, Geneva, 1973; vol. II, *Portugal – Leiden – Pécs – Franeker – Basel*, by A. Moreira de Sà, R. Ekkart, M. Fényes, A. de Kalbermatten, and L. Haeberli, Geneva, 1976.

Coing, H. (ed.) *Handbuch der Quellen und Literatur der neueren europaïschen Privatrechtsgeschichte*, vol. I, Munich, 1973, 39–128.

Craigie, J. *A Bibliography of Scottish Education before 1872*, London, 1970.

Ermann, W. and Horn, E. *Bibliographie der deutschen Universitäten*, 3 vols., Leipzig/Berlin, 1904–5; reprint, 1965.

Fletcher, J. M. (ed.) *The History of European Universities. Work in Progress and Publications*, 5 vols., Birmingham, 1977–81.

Fletcher, J. M. and Deahl, J. 'European Universities 1300–1700: the Development of Research 1969–81, and a Summary Bibliography', in J. M. Kittelson and P. J. Transue (eds.), *Rebirth, Reform and Resilience: Universities in Transition 1300–1700*, Columbus, Ohio, 1984, 324–57.

Fletcher, J. M. and Upton, C. A. 'Publications on University History since 1977: a Continuing Bibliography', *History of Universities*, 7 (1988), 371–468. This is a current bibliography which is published every year.

Gabriel, A. L. *Summary Bibliography of the History of the Universities of Great Britain and Ireland up to 1800, Covering Publications between 1900 and 1968*, Notre Dame, Ind., 1974.

García y García, A. 'Bibliografía de historia de las universidades españolas', *Repertorio de historia de la ciencias eclesiásticas en España*, 7 (1979), 599–627.

Guenée, S. *Bibliographie de l'histoire des universités françaises des origines à la Révolution*, 2 vols., Paris, 1978–81.

Hammerstein, N. 'Jubiläumsschrift und Alltagsarbeit. Tendenzen bildungsgeschichtlicher Literatur', *Historische Zeitschrift*, 236 (1983), 601–33.

Hammerstein, N. 'Neue Wege der Universitätsgeschichtsschreibung', *Zeitschrift für Historische Forschung*, 5 (1978), 449–63.

Hammerstein, N. 'Nochmals Universitätsgeschichtsschreibung', *Zeitschrift für Historische Forschung*, 7 (1980), 231–36.

Petry, L. 'Deutsche Forschungen nach dem zweiten Weltkrieg zur Geschichte der Universitäten', *Vierteljahresschrift für Sozial- und Wirtschaftsgeschichte*, 46 (1959), 145–203.

de Ridder-Symoens, H. 'Universiteitsgeschiedenis als bron voor sociale geschiedenis', *Tijdschrift voor Sociale Geschiedenis*, 10 (1978), 87–115.

de Ridder-Symoens, H. and Paquet, J. 'Bibliografisch Overzicht Universiteitsgeschiedenis der Nederlanden', *Batavia Academica*, 2 (1984), 18–21. This is a current bibliography which is published every year.

Scheurkogel, J. 'Nieuwe universiteitsgeschiedenis in de late middeleeuwen', *Tijdschrift voor Geschiedenis*, 94 (1981), 194–204.

Stark, E. *Bibliographie zur Universitätsgeschichte. Verzeichnis der im Gebiet der Bundesrepublik Deutschland 1945–1971 veröffentlichen Literatur*, ed. E. Hassinger, Munich, 1974.

Steiger, G. and Straube, M. 'Forschungen und Publikationen seit 1945 zur Geschichte der deutschen Universitäten und Hochschulen auf dem Territorium der DDR', *Zeitschrift für Geschichtswissenschaft*, 7 (special issue), (1960), 563–99.

Stelling-Michaud, S. 'L'histoire des universités au Moyen Age et à la Renaissance au cours des vingt-cinq dernières années', in *Rapports du XIe Congrès international des Sciences historiques*, vol. I, Stockholm, 1960, 97–143; revised Italian translation: 'La storia delle università nel medioevo e nel Rinascimento: stato degli studi e prospettive di ricerca', in G. Arnaldi (ed.) *Le origini dell'Università*, Bologna, 1974, 153–217.

Straube, M. and Fläschendräger, W. 'Forschungen zur Geschichte der Universitäten, Hochschulen und Akademien der DDR (1960–1970)', *Zeitschrift für Geschichtswissenschaft*, 18 (special issue) (1970), 187–209.

Verger, J. 'Tendances actuelles de la recherche sur l'histoire de l'éducation en France au moyen âge (XIIe–XVe siècles)', *Histoire de l'Education*, 6 (1980), 9–34.

Vico Monteoliva, M. 'Bibliografía sobre historia de las universidades españolas', *Historia de la Educación*, 3 (1984), 281–90.

Zanella, G. 'Bibliografia per la storia dell'università di Bologna dalle origini al 1945, aggiornata al 1983', *Studi e memorie per la storia dell'Università di Bologna*, new series, 5, (1985).

General works

Cobban, A. B. *The Medieval Universities: Their Development and Organization*, London, 1975.

Denifle, H. *Die Entstehung der Universitäten des Mittelalters bis 1400*, Berlin, 1885; reprint, Graz, 1956.

Fried, J. (ed.) *Schulen und Studium im sozialen Wandel des hohen und späten Mittelalters*, Sigmaringen, 1986.

d'Irsay, S. *Histoire des universités françaises et étrangères des origines à nos jours*, 2 vols., Paris, 1933–5.

IJsewijn, J. and Paquet, J. (eds.) *Universities in the Late Middle Ages*, Mediaevalia Lovaniensia, series 1, studia 6, Louvain, 1978. This volume is also published as Paquet, J. and IJsewijn, J. (eds.) *Les Universités à la fin du moyen âge*, Publications de l'Institut d'Etudes Médiévales, 2nd series, 2, Louvain, 1978.

Jílek, L. (ed.) *Historical Compendium of European Universities – Répertoire historique des universités européennes*, Geneva, 1984.

Kaufmann, G. *Geschichte der deutschen Universitäten*, 2 vols., Stuttgart, 1888–96; reprint, Graz, 1958. Volume I deals with European universities.

Kibre, P. *Scholarly Privileges in the Middle Ages. The Rights, Privileges and Immunities of Scholars and Universities at Bologna – Padua – Paris – Oxford*, Cambridge, Mass., 1961.

Le Goff, J. *Les Intellectuels au Moyen Age*, 2nd edn, Paris, 1985.

Pedersen, O. *Studium generale. De europæiske universiteters tilblivelse*, Copenhagen, 1974.

Rashdall, H. *The Universities of Europe in the Middle Ages*, 3 vols., ed. F. M. Powicke and A. B. Emden, Oxford, 1936; reprint, Oxford, 1988.

Università e società nei secoli XII–XVI. Atti del nono convegno internazionale di studio tenuto a Pistoia nei giorni 20–25 settembre 1979, Pistoia, 1982.

Les Universités européennes du XIVe au XVIIIe siècles: Aspects et problèmes. Actes du colloque international à l'occasion du VIe centenaire de l'université Jagellone de Cracovie, Geneva, 1967.

Verger, J. *Les Universités au Moyen Age*, Paris, 1973.

Verger, J. 'Universités et écoles médiévales de la fin du XIe à la fin du XVe siècle', in G. Mialaret and J. Vial (eds.), *Histoire mondiale de l'éducation*, vol. I, Paris, 1981, 281–309.

Wieruszowski, H. *The Medieval University: Masters, Students, Learning*, Princeton, N.J., 1966.

Individual countries

Ajo González de Rapariegos y Sáinz de Zúñiga, C. M. *Historia de las universidades hispánicas. Orígenes y desarrollo desde su aparición a nuestros días*, 11 vols., Madrid, 1957–77.

Barcala Muñoz, A. 'Las universidades españolas durante la Edad media', *Anuario de Estudios medievales*, 15 (1985), 83–126.

Bellomo, M. *Saggio sull'università nell'età del diritto comune*, Catania, 1979.

Boehm, L. and Müller, R. A. (eds.) *Universitäten und Hochschulen in Deutschland, Oesterreich und der Schweiz. Eine Universitätsgeschichte in Einzeldarstellungen*, Düsseldorf, 1983.

Cadini, F. and others (eds.) *La crisi del sistema comunale*, Storia della società italiana, 7, Milan, 1982.

Cobban, A. B. *The Medieval English Universities: Oxford and Cambridge to c. 1500*, Cambridge, 1988.

Coissac, J. B. *Les Universités d'Ecosse depuis la fondation de l'université d'Aberdeen jusqu'au triomphe de la Réforme (1410–1560)*, Paris, 1914.

Engelbrecht, H. *Geschichte des österreichischen Bildungswesens*, vol. I, Vienna, 1982.

Guenée, S. *Les Universités françaises des origines à la Révolution. Notices historiques sur les universités, studia et académies protestantes*, Paris, 1982.

Kaufmann, G. *Geschichte der deutschen Universitäten*, 2 vols., Stuttgart, 1888–96; reprint, Graz, 1958. Volume II deals with German universities.

Paulsen, F. *Die deutschen Universitäten und das Universitätsstudium*, Berlin, 1902.

Paulsen, F. *Geschichte des gelehrten Unterrichts auf den deutschen Schulen und Universitäten vom Ausgang des Mittelalters bis zur Gegenwart*, vol. I, 3rd edn, Leipzig/Berlin, 1919.

Rosłanowski, T. 'Universitäten und Hochschulen in Polen', in E. Maschke and J. Sydow (eds.), *Stadt und Universität im Mittelalter und in der frühen Neuzeit*, Sigmaringen, 1977, 166–9.

Verger, J. (ed.) *Histoire des universités en France*, Toulouse, 1986.

1   Medieval university towns. The political divisions are those of *c.* 1490. Dates in brackets are uncertain. See the list at the end of chapter 2 for further details. Adapted, with permission, from H. Rashdall, *The Universities of Europe in the Middle Ages*, ed. M. M. Powicke and A. B. Emden, Oxford, 1936; reprint, Oxford, 1988

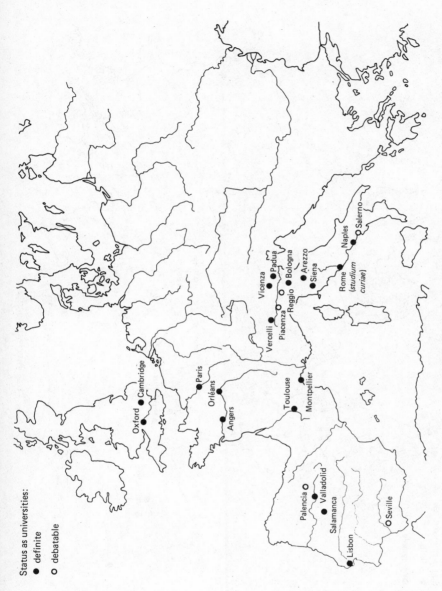

Status as universities:

● definite

○ debatable

Oxford ● ● Cambridge

Paris ●

Orléans ●

Angers ●

Toulouse ●

Montpellier ●

Vercelli ●

Piacenza ○

Vicenza ●

Padua ●

Reggio ●

Bologna ●

Arezzo ●

Siena ●

Rome
(*studium
curiae*) ●

Naples ●

Salerno ○

Palencia ○

Valladolid ●

Salamanca ●

Lisbon ●

Seville ○

2 Foundations prior to 1300.

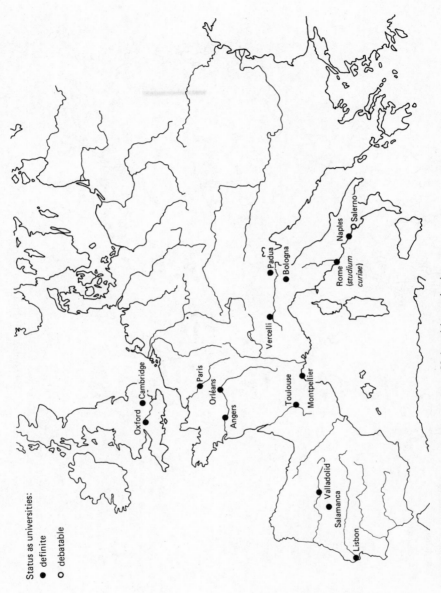

Status as universities:

● definite

○ debatable

3　Universities active in 1300.

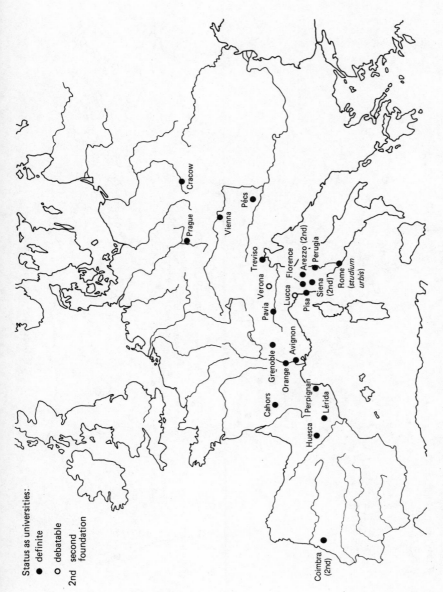

Status as universities:

● definite

○ debatable

2nd second
  foundation

Cracow

Prague

Vienna

Pécs

Treviso

Verona

Pavia

Lucca

Florence

Arezzo (2nd)

Perugia

Pisa

Siena
(2nd)

Rome
(studium
urbis)

Avignon

Grenoble

Orange

Cahors

Perpignan

Lérida

Huesca

Coimbra
(2nd)

4 Foundations 1300–78.

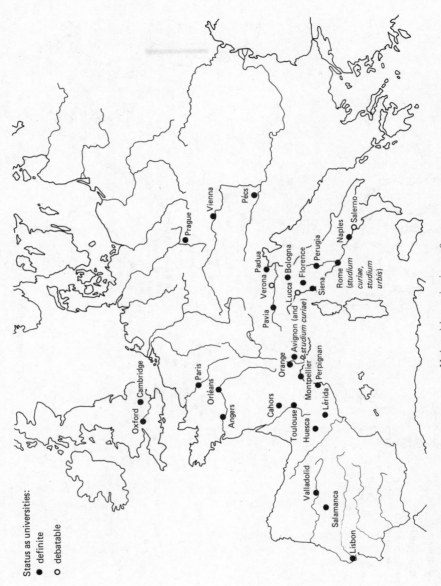

Status as universities:
● definite
○ debatable

Oxford ● Cambridge

Paris ●

Orléans ●

Angers ●

Cahors ●

Toulouse ●

Huesca ●

Lérida ●

Perpignan ●

Montpellier ●

Orange ●

Avignon (and ○ studium curiae)

Pavia ●

Verona ○ Lucca ○

Padua ●

Bologna ●

Florence ●

Perugia ●

Siena ●

Rome
(studium
curiae, studium
urbis) ●

Naples ●

Salerno ○

Prague ●

Vienna ●

Pécs ●

Valladolid ●

Salamanca ●

Lisbon ●

5 Universities active in 1378.

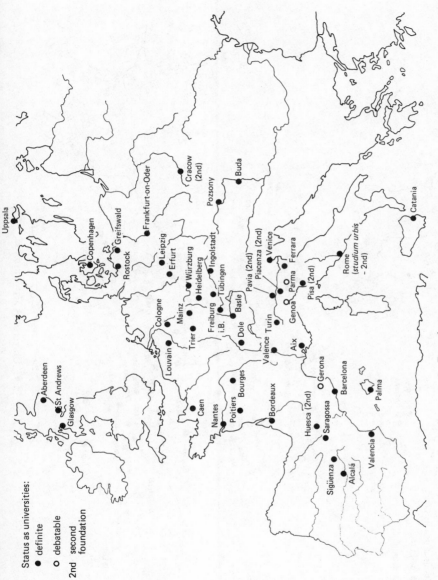

Status as universities:

● definite
○ debatable
2nd second
  foundation

Uppsala

Copenhagen
Greifswald
Rostock
Frankfurt-on-Oder
Leipzig
Erfurt
Cologne
Mainz
Trier
Louvain

Aberdeen
St Andrews
Glasgow

Caen
Nantes
Poitiers
Bourges
Bordeaux

Cracow
(2nd)
Pozsony
Buda

Würzburg
Ingolstadt
Heidelberg
Tübingen
Freiburg
i.B.
Basle
Dole
Valence Turin
Aix
Valence

Pavia (2nd)
Piacenza (2nd)
Venice
Ferrara
Parma
Genoa
Pisa (2nd)
Rome
(studium urbis
– 2nd)

Catania

Gerona
Barcelona
Palma
Valencia
Alcalá
Sigüenza
Saragossa
Huesca (2nd)

6 Foundations 1378–1500.

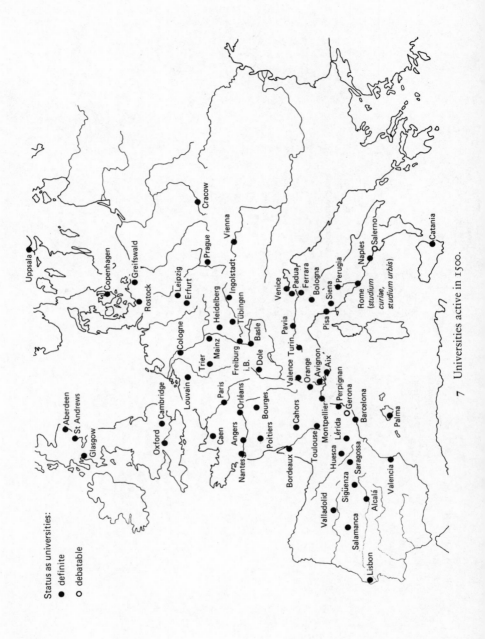

Status as universities:

● definite

○ debatable

7   Universities active in 1500.

Uppsala

Copenhagen
Greifswald
Rostock

Cracow

Vienna

Prague
Leipzig
Erfurt
Ingolstadt
Heidelberg
Tübingen

Cologne
Mainz
Trier
Freiburg i.B.
Basle
Dole

Venice
Padua
Ferrara
Bologna
Perugia
Siena
Pisa

Rome
(studium
curiae,
studium urbis)
Naples
Salerno

Catania

Aberdeen
St Andrews
Glasgow

Oxford
Cambridge

Louvain

Paris
Orléans

Angers
Caen
Nantes

Poitiers
Bourges

Pavia
Turin
Valence
Orange
Avignon
Aix

Perpignan
Gerona
Barcelona
Palma

Bordeaux
Cahors
Toulouse
Montpellier
Huesca
Lérida
Saragossa

Valladolid
Sigüenza
Salamanca
Alcalá
Valencia

Lisbon

PART II

STRUCTURES

CHAPTER 3

RELATIONS WITH AUTHORITY

by PAOLO NARDI

by PAOLO NARDI

PAPACY, EMPIRE, AND SCHOOLS IN THE TWELFTH CENTURY

Recent historical studies clearly show that the theory that the imperial authorities intervened directly in higher education from the early twelfth century onwards must be rejected. There is nothing, for example, to show that the University of Bologna was founded at the instance of Countess Matilda of Canossa after her appointment as Vicar of the Holy Roman Empire in May 1111.[1] In the first few decades of the twelfth century not even the church found it necessary to institutionalize the new schools arising in Europe, in spite of the close ties that, from the Gregorian reform onwards, firmly linked ecclesiastical circles with the study of theology and law. The way the schools were organized did not make for closer official relations, for they flourished at a time when the institutional location of education was less important than the personality of a teacher able to attract a group of pupils willing to follow him anywhere.[2] Also, it was widely believed that hankering after riches led directly to the propagation of false doctrine; accordingly, the Councils of Clermont (1130) and Reims (1131) and the second Lateran Council of 1139 solemnly forbade monks and regular canons to study medicine and civil law after taking holy orders and pronouncing religious vows.[3] On the other hand the papal curia did not neglect contacts with the principal schools – the Bologna school of law (Cardinal Aimericus, Chancellor of the Holy Roman Church from 1123 to 1141, was in close touch with the famous

---

[1] E. Cortese, 'Legisti, canonisti e feudisti: la formazione di un ceto medievale', in *Università e società*, 208–9.

[2] R. W. Southern, 'The Schools of Paris and the School of Chartres', in *Renaissance and Renewal*, 114ff., 123ff. In the same volume, see especially the essays by J. Leclercq, 'The Renewal of Theology', 68–87, and S. Kuttner, 'The Revival of Jurisprudence', 299–322.

[3] D. Diepgen, *Studien zur Geschichte der Beziehungen zwischen Theologie und Medizin im Mittelalter*, vol. I, *Die Theologie und der ärztliche Stand* (Berlin/Grünwald, 1922), 16ff.

glossator Bulgarus)[4] and the school of theology in Paris (in 1144 Cardinal Robert Pullen,[5] an English theologian who had taught in Paris, was appointed Chancellor of the Holy Roman Church).

The first important manifestation of imperial interest in the demands and activities of teachers and scholars was undoubtedly the *Authentica Habita*, a constitution issued by the Emperor Frederick I Barbarossa in 1155 when he first came to Italy to receive the crown.[6] In May 1155, near Bologna, he met the masters and students of the school of law. According to the anonymous author of the *Carmen de gestis Frederici I*, they begged him to forbid the exercise of the right of reprisal against foreign scholars (seizure of person or property to satisfy debts incurred by their compatriots) and to grant all of them freedom of movement 'so that all men minded to study be free to come and go and dwell in security' (*ut nemo studium exercere volentes/impediat stantes nec euntes nec redeuntes*).[7] Frederick I Barbarossa immediately issued the celebrated constitution, in which he affirmed the pre-eminent value of scientific knowledge, and recognized as praiseworthy and deserving of protection all persons who in pursuit of it were obliged to live far from their own country. He granted professors of civil law and students the privilege of freedom of movement and safe residence in all seats of learning. Secondly, expressing compassion for persons who spent all their substance and braved all sorts of dangers in order to survive in a foreign country, he decreed that no one should dare to harm or wrong scholars or, above all, to recover from them debts contracted by their countrymen, on penalty of having to reimburse four times the amount (the *quadruplum*). This sanction was enforceable against all transgressors, and magistrates neglecting to enforce the law were disgraced and barred in perpetuity from their office. Thirdly, Frederick I ordered that any scholar summoned to appear in court could choose whether to be tried by his own masters or by the bishops' courts. A plaintiff applying to another judge was punished by losing his case even if it was good in law. The effect of this order was to extend the benefit of clergy (*privilegium fori*) already enjoyed by clerics to lay students, and to confirm an old imperial rule (which since it came from Justinian's *Omnem* constitution was well known to the masters of Bologna) empowering the bishop and professors of Berito to judge students of that city. Frederick I caused the *Habita* to be inserted in Justinian's *Codex*; this clearly showed his wish to revive Roman law and incorporate it in the legal system of the Holy Roman Empire (the *Sacrum Imperium*). His plan exactly suited the masters in Bologna, who as the inter-

[4] H. Kantorowicz, *Studies in the Glossators of the Roman Law* (Cambridge, 1938), 68, 71.

[5] P. Classen, *Studium und Gesellschaft im Mittelalter*, ed. J. Fried, Schriften der MGH, 29 (Stuttgart, 1983), 9–10.

[6] W. Stelzer, 'Zum Scholarenprivileg Friedrich Barbarossas ("Authentica Habita")', *Deutsches Archiv für Erforschung des Mittelalters*, 34 (1978), 123–65.

[7] I. Schmale-Ott (ed.), *Carmen de gestis Frederici I. imperatoris in Lombardia*, MGH Scriptores (Hanover, 1965), 17–18, 496–7.

preters and teachers of Justinian's laws, had every interest in getting them generally recognized and applied.[8]

Frederick I was not, however, in a position to put the *Habita* into effect; the political aims that appeared feasible when he first visited Italy proved to be beyond his reach. The war of 1159–62 with the communes of the Lombard League, culminating in the sieges of Crema and Milan, affected his relations with the scholars studying in Bologna, if we are to treat as genuine a letter said to have been sent to him at the time by four masters in Bologna, begging him to revoke the order expelling from Bologna students from Milan, Brescia, and Crema.[9] On that occasion Frederick I ignored the *Habita* constitution, and addressed himself only to the political situation of the moment. Later on, when the city joined the Lombard League, the emperor showed no further interest in Bologna's professors and scholars.[10]

In September 1159 Cardinal Rolando Bandinelli became pope. He was an expert theologian and consummate politician. As Chancellor of the Holy Roman Church from 1153 onwards he had favoured closer contact between the papal curia and the principal schools, fully realizing because of his education and political acumen the growing importance of teaching theology and law. Immediately after his bitterly contested election (which led to a schism) Pope Alexander III sent letter after letter to prominent persons and institutions, explaining the facts and presenting himself as legitimate pope. Among the recipients were the teachers of civil law, and all other masters, in Bologna. This was probably the first official solemn recognition of their importance by the ecclesiastical authorities.[11] When Alexander, as a fugitive from the enmity of the Emperor Frederick I, stayed in France from April 1162 to September 1165, he gained a profound knowledge of conditions in the numerous and flourishing episcopal schools of the kingdom of the Franks (*regnum Francorum*). On his return to Italy the pope decided to order the abolition of the evil custom (*prava consuetudo*) of masters in the diocesan schools of exacting a money payment for the award of the licence to teach (*licentia docendi*). He accordingly issued a decretal, addressed principally to the French bishops, ordering that persons considered capable of teaching in schools (*regere scholas*) should be able to do so without making payment and without let or hindrance, as it was not lawful for knowledge to be bought or sold. He later

---

8 G. Cencetti, 'Il foro degli scolari negli Studi medievali italiani', *Atti e memorie della R. Deputazione di storia patria per l'Emilia e la Romagna*, 5 (1940), 165; J. K. Hyde, 'Commune, University and Society in Early Medieval Bologna', in *Universities in Politics*, 32ff.; R. L. Benson, 'Political Renovatio: Two Models from Roman Antiquity', in *Renaissance and Renewal*, 359–86.

9 J. Fried, *Die Entstehung des Juristenstandes im 12. Jahrhundert*, Forschungen zur neueren Privatrechtsgeschichte, 21 (Cologne/Vienna, 1974), 54–5.

10 G. De Vergottini, 'Lo Studio di Bologna, l'Impero, il Papato, in *Scritti di storia del diritto italiano*, vol. II, Seminario giuridico della Università di Bologna, 74 (Milan, 1977), 744ff.

11 K. W. Nörr, 'Institutional Foundations of the New Jurisprudence', in *Renaissance and Renewal*, 325. For Rolando Bandinelli see Classen, *Studium* (note 5), 130ff.

confirmed this principle and fixed the procedure for recognition of the candidate's ability to teach, laying down that the candidate must be recognized as able to teach only after examination by the 'greater and wiser part' (*maior et sanior pars*) of the chapter of canons of the cathedral (1173).[12] He ordered that, if the dignitary authorized to confer the *licentia docendi* infringed the order not to require payment, the bishop should appoint someone else in his place. Finally, at the third Lateran Council of 1179 the pope confirmed that both the *licentia docendi* and teaching should be free of charge, and provided that masters should be paid by benefices. Thus to repress simony and corruption Alexander reformed the educational practices of the church, encouraged an influx of poor students admitted not for their fortune but for their merit, and saw to it that teachers were adequately paid; moreover, he laid the foundations of the *studia* of western Europe and especially of the Paris *studium*.[13]

During the pontificate of Alexander III (1159–81) the teaching of law was vigorously encouraged, to the particular advantage of the school in Bologna, which consolidated its position as the most important centre in Europe for the study of Roman and canon law, although other schools appeared, mainly outside Italy.[14] It has been roundly denied that the Bologna school was an ecclesiastical foundation;[15] but the bishop of Bologna was unquestionably the only authority to be given jurisdiction over scholars by the emperor himself. Later the conflict between the emperor and the commune of Bologna strengthened Bologna's links with the papacy. The Holy See had its own lively interest in promoting the teaching of law, as may be inferred from the great output of canon law rules at the time, and from the appointment to high office of many prelates trained in law. The first mention of an order by a papal legate regarding the scholars and teachers of Bologna dates from 1176–7: the bishop of Porto-Ostia Guglielmus forbade them on penalty of excommunication to compete for lodging in the *hospitia* (halls of residence) by promising to pay landlords a higher rent, either in consideration of the advantages of the lodging or for the vainglory of seeming richer than their colleagues, and protected the tenants of the *hospitia* by forbidding masters and scholars to apply to the landlord for an already occupied lodging before the expiry of the current lease or without the tenants' consent. Some years later, and certainly before August 1182, the Legate Pietro, bishop of Tusculum, confirmed the prohibition, threatening transgressors with anathema –

---

12 Classen, *Studium* (note 5), 245 n. 14a (note added by J. Fried); A. E. Bernstein, 'Magisterium and License: Corporate Autonomy against Papal Authority in the Medieval University of Paris', *Viator, Medieval and Renaissance Studies*, 9 (1978), 292ff., appears to be unaware of the document mentioned by Fried.

13 P. Delhaye, 'L'organisation scolaire au XIIe siècle', *Traditio*, 5 (1947), 258ff.; G. Post, K. Giocarinis, and R. Kay, 'The Medieval Heritage of a Humanistic Ideal: "scientia donum Dei est, unde vendi non potest" ', *Traditio*, 11 (1955), 195–234.

14 S. Kuttner, 'Revival' (note 2), 319. See also chapter 12, 'The faculties of law'.

15 G. Cencetti, 'Studium fuit Bononie. Note sulla storia dell'università di Bologna nel primo mezzo secolo della sua esistenza', *Studi medievali*, 3: 7 (1966), 781–833, especially 815.

banishment from the Christian community. Lastly, between July 1184 and November 1185, Pope Lucius III repeated the prohibition and furthermore charged the bishop of Bologna to read out the decretal *Ex rescripto* constitution every year to the assembled masters and scholars (*in communi audientia magistrorum et scholariorum*).[16] The pope thereby specifically reaffirmed the bishop's jurisdiction on a very sensitive issue, since it concerned the relationship of the citizens of Bologna with all members of the Bologna *studium*.

At about this time the commune of Bologna became actively interested in the schools (*scholae*) in its territory, which brought the city prestige and its inhabitants riches. It began to devise ways of preventing the masters from emigrating to other cities with their pupils in their train. The case of the jurist Pillius, who in 1182 or thereabouts entered into secret negotiations with the people of Modena to transfer his school there, led the commune to require all masters to swear on oath not to transfer their residence out of Bologna for at least two years. Other teachers were subsequently required to swear similar oaths and in this way the *Habita* constitution, granting teachers the *beneficium* of freedom of movement to carry out their teaching, was repeatedly violated. These serious acts of interference with the academic life of Bologna probably encouraged the students to form a *universitas*, that is, a corporation similar to the contemporary trade guilds, or associations of members of certain professions within a city, formed to defend members' interests by appointing their own representatives and by special jurisdictions reserved to themselves.

THE CONTRIBUTION OF THE CHURCH IN THE TWELFTH AND THIRTEENTH CENTURIES

At the end of the twelfth century and in the first twenty years of the thirteenth century the hegemony in European politics assumed by the papacy and the ecclesiastical hierarchy undoubtedly led to an increase in the number of 'ecclesiastical clerks'[17] attending the principal *studia*. At that time, even in a kingdom with as many schools as France, there were not many masters even in cathedral chapters; but between the second and third decades of the thirteenth century Boncompagno da Signa had no hesitation in affirming that teachers and scholars (*ordo scholasticus*) were the mirror of the church (*speculum Ecclesiae*) because many of the highest ecclesiastical dignitaries were drawn from academic circles (*ab ipso [ordine] quidem trahuntur omnia principalia et secundaria Ecclesiae membra*), to such an extent that the world

[16] P. Landau, 'Papst Lucius III und das Mietrecht in Bologna', in S. Kuttner (ed.), *Proceedings of the Fourth International Congress of Medieval Canon Law. Toronto, 21–25 August 1972* (Vatican City, 1972), 511–22.

[17] For the distinction between ecclesiastical and scholar (or lay) clerks, see J. W. Baldwin, *Masters, Princes and Merchants. The Social Views of Peter the Chanter and his Circle* (Princeton, 1970), vol. I, 73; vol. II, 51 n. 57.

of study appeared to be identical with the church itself (*cum ex ipsis* [sc. *viris scholasticis*] *et in ipsis consistere videatur* [*Ecclesia*]).[18]

The Holy See's interest in promoting and organizing higher education therefore revived, and greatly increased under Pope Innocent III (1198–1216), a theologian, jurist, and politician of great acumen and indisputable authority. His laws aimed at amplifying the rules laid down by Pope Alexander III for the episcopal schools, and, especially in Paris and Bologna, establishing the status of teachers and students. Such was the purpose of the decretal *Tuae fraternitatis*, issued in 1207, authorizing clerics going to study at an important centre of learning to go on drawing the income from their benefices in absence from them. Such was also the purpose of the rules promulgated at the fourth Lateran Council of 1215, repeating the order to cathedral churches to open schools, run by masters of recognized ability paid by benefices, for priests and poor laymen, and requiring schools of theology, also with paid teachers, to be set up in metropolitan dioceses.[19] Nor was Innocent III indifferent to the demands of the *universitates* then coming into being; his decretal *Quia in causis* confirmed to the scholars of Paris assembled in a *universitas* their right under the *ius commune* (the two universal codes of Roman law and canon law) to appoint their own representatives in a legal action; and by his decretal *Ex literis* he acted as interpreter and supreme guarantor of the rules which the *societas* of teachers of theology, canon law, and arts in Paris had sworn to obey; he laid down the principle that any person excluded from the *universitas* for disobedience (*propter contumaciam*) could be readmitted if he made adequate amends. All these rules figured in two decretal collections: *Compilatio III*, promulgated by Innocent III in 1210 and sent to all masters and students dwelling in Bologna for faithful observance in and out of school, and *Compilatio IV*, drawn up in 1215–16 by a prominent jurist of Bologna in close touch with the curia.[20]

The efforts of Innocent III to regulate higher education would have fallen short of their goal had they not been completed by the special regulations issued by his cardinal legates and by the jurisprudence of the prelates appointed to adjudicate controversies. Thus in Paris the Cardinal Legate Guala Bicchieri's shrewd legal mind laid down the methods to be followed by the masters and ecclesiastical authorities in the exercise of their jurisdiction over the scholars. Teachers were first to admonish the students in general

---

18 De Vergottini, 'Studio di Bologna', (note 10), 790 n. 120.

19 G. Post, 'Masters' Salaries and Student-fees in the Mediaeval Universities', *Speculum*, 7 (1932), 181ff.

20 K. Pennington, 'The Making of a Decretal Collection: the Genesis of Compilatio Tertia', in S. Kuttner and K. Pennington (eds.), *Proceedings of the Fifth International Congress of Medieval Canon Law. Salamanca, 21–25 September 1976* (Vatican City, 1980), 67–92; S. Kuttner, 'Johannes Teutonicus, das vierte Laterankonzil und die Compilatio quarta', in S. Kuttner, *Medieval Councils, Decretals and Collections of Canon Law. Selected Essays* (London, 1980), essay no. X, 608–34.

(*generaliter*) and threaten transgressors with excommunication. Then, after granting the students time to submit their defence, they were to repeat their admonishments and threats in school, naming the rebels and all persons evading trial. Finally, if the guilty persons failed to mend their ways, the chancellor of the cathedral chapter was to pronounce on them a sentence of excommunication from which only the bishop or abbot of Saint Victor could absolve them (1208). Later the *universitas* of masters and scholars entered into a long dispute with the chancellor of the chapter over the award of the *licentia docendi* and the exercise of jurisdiction. Innocent III appointed the bishop of Troyes to settle the dispute, and the bishop of Paris to act as depositee of, and to approve, the agreement reached by the parties. This stipulated that candidates for the *licentia docendi* should not be required to pay for it or to swear fidelity, and that if the chancellor refused to grant it the bishop should award the *licentia* to all candidates recognized by a majority of the teachers in the disciplines concerned as suitable to hold it. The masters in Paris were thus officially recognized as possessing the same prerogatives as those held by cathedral chapters at least since the time of Alexander III.[21] Lastly, in 1215 the Cardinal Legate Robert of Courson (Robert of Kedleston), a former master in Paris, drew up a comprehensive set of rules for the Paris *studium*. These laid down teaching programmes and procedure, regulated academic custom at official gatherings and clothing and occasions for mourning, confirmed the rules for examinations for the *licentia docendi* fixed two years before by agreement between the *universitas* and the chancellor, and repeated that masters should exercise jurisdiction over scholars. Without explicitly referring to the decretal of Lucius III on tenancies in the *hospitia*, he drew attention to its contents; and he indicated the matters which the *universitas* was competent to decide by requiring masters and scholars to swear an oath to observe certain rights and duties – preparation of the defence of scholars who had been seriously wronged, where justice had not been done; the fixing of rents for rooms in the *hospitia*; and settling times and procedures for lessons and disputations. This was the fullest and most detailed definition of *studium* organization ever formulated by the ecclesiastical authorities.[22]

Ecclesiastical authority also tried to influence the Oxford *studium*. However, although Oxford scholars were formally subject to the supervision and jurisdiction of the bishop of Lincoln, to whose diocese Oxford belonged, Lincoln was far away and his practical influence small. The excommunication of King John by Innocent III in March 1208 caused the first diaspora of the 'clerks' of Oxford, who feared reprisals by the king. In the following year a murder committed by a scholar led the authorities to arrest some of his

[21] G. Post, 'Parisian masters as a corporation, 1200–1246', in G. Post, *Studies in Medieval Legal Thought. Public Law and the State, 1100–1322* (Princeton, 1964), 34ff., 44–6.

[22] S. C. Ferruolo, 'The Paris statutes of 1215 reconsidered', *History of Universities*, 5 (1985), 1–14.

colleagues. Two or perhaps three students were condemned to death with royal approval. The result was an exodus of masters, followed by their pupils, in protest against the violation of the benefit of clergy (*privilegium fori*). Only five years later, in 1214, the rules made by the Cardinal Legate Nicolaus de Romanis restored the *studium* to life; he ordered that scholars arrested by the secular authorities should be handed over to the bishop of Lincoln, or to the archdeacon or the chancellor of the chapter; and he made these authorities responsible for administering the compulsory payment extracted from the citizens of Oxford in aid of poor students. The legate also confirmed the system then current of fixing rents in the *hospitia*, to ensure compliance with the regulations made by Lucius III to prohibit competition, basing their amount on the valuations agreed by scholars and citizens jointly prior to 1209; a committee of four masters and four citizens was appointed to settle cases in which the necessary valuations had not been made.[23]

The troubles in Oxford in the early thirteenth century are a clear example of the difficulties and bitter disputes between a university and secular authorities – especially locally – at a time of crucial importance to the formation and growth of the *studia*. Similar events elsewhere were settled by closer control of the ecclesiastical authorities. In Paris, for instance, following the murder of several students by a band of serjeants guided by the *prévôt*, Philip II Augustus was obliged in 1200 to grant the scholars a privilege assuring them that he would prosecute with special rigour any persons doing them harm, and undertaking to allow scholars accused of criminal offences to be tried by the ecclesiastical authorities.[24] Meanwhile in Bologna the *universitas* of scholars was gathering strength and becoming more firmly established, to the alarm of the commune, which feared the growth in its midst of a cosmopolitan body and a jurisdiction parallel to that of its own *podestà*. In 1211 the city was governed by the *podestà* Guglielmo da Pusterla, who supported the Emperor Otto IV recently excommunicated by Innocent III. One of the laws enacted by Guglielmo as *podestà* prohibited the formation of groups whose members swore to lend each other mutual aid and support, other than associations of men of war and artists taking such oaths *ad honorem et utilitatem* of the commune. The intention was obviously to prevent the formation of scholars' *universitates*. But in the same year the pope came down firmly on the side of the students, exhorted the people of Bologna to leave the party supporting the emperor, and threatened to excommunicate the city and transfer the *studium* elsewhere. By this means he succeeded in bringing about a new balance of power in Bologna favouring the party supporting the papa-

23 R. W. Southern, 'From Schools to University', in *History of Oxford*, 26, 29–32; C. H. Lawrence, 'The University in State and Church', in *History of Oxford*, 97–100, 133, 136, 140.
24 J. Verger, 'Des écoles à l'université: la mutation institutionnelle', in R.-H. Bautier (ed.), *La France de Philippe Auguste. Le temps des mutations. Actes du Colloque international organisé par le CNRS (Paris, 29 septembre – 4 octobre 1980)* (Paris, 1982), 821ff.

cy.[25] Subsequently, in 1215 or thereabouts, the teachers renounced jurisdiction over lay scholars in criminal cases, and it passed almost entirely to the commune (cases involving clerics remaining under the jurisdiction of the bishop). Although recognizing the existence of the *universitas*, the commune forbade scholars to associate themselves *in sectam vel conspirationem* to leave Bologna, and demanded that the rectors, as representatives of the association, should swear never to promote the transfer of the *studium*. The scholars reacted strongly, and found that the most effective defence of their *libertas* was the protection of the church: in the spring of 1217 the new pope Honorius III exhorted the *podestà* to revoke his order, or not to apply the regulations restricting scholars' freedom of movement, and advised the scholars to resist the demands of the city authorities without using violence, and to leave Bologna rather than give way. Later, in 1220, addressing the people of Bologna, he condemned the laws restricting academic *libertas*, calling them harmful to the interests of the city; he ordered their repeal and declared the *podestà* to be released from the oath he had taken on them. The year before, the Holy See had reaffirmed that it was for the ecclesiastical authorities to award the *licentia docendi*, and had ruled that, in Bologna, only the archdeacon could confer it – after diligent examination so as to prevent unqualified persons from occupying the professorial chair, as, it was complained, they often did, to the detriment of the entire teaching profession.[26]

Honorius III showed similar solicitude for the Paris *studium*. On learning that the bishop of Paris had excommunicated the *universitas* on the grounds that it had framed its own statutes without the explicit consent of the local ecclesiastical authorities, the pope took the scholars under his protection as his dearly beloved sons (*tamquam filios speciales*) and ordered the excommunication to be cancelled; but meanwhile he took over direct control of the *universitas*, and until the dispute was settled issued instructions on the use of the seal, the exercise of jurisdiction by the masters, the appointment of officials to punish misconduct, and participation in funeral rites. He also settled the function and role of the Paris *studium* in his decretal *Super speculam* of 22 November 1219, forbidding civil law to be taught in Paris and neighbouring cities and localities, on the grounds that in France laymen did not use the laws of the Roman emperors, and that in few ecclesiastical suits was resort to Roman law essential. The decretal also attempted to control the teaching of theology by extending the provisions of the Council of Tours of 1163 forbidding regular and secular clergy to study civil law and medicine,

---

[25] G. Rossi, ' "Universitas scholarium" e Comune (sec. XII–XIV)', *Studi e memorie per la storia dell'Università di Bologna*, new series, I (1956), 197–227; A. Hessel, *Storia della città di Bologna dal 1116 al 1280*, ed. G. Fasoli (Bologna, 1975), 92.

[26] M. Bellomo, *Saggio sull'università nell'età del diritto comune* (Catania, 1979), 87–9; P. Weimar, 'Zur Doktorwürde der Bologneser Legisten', in C. Bergfeld (ed.), *Aspekte europäischer Rechtsgeschichte. Festgabe für Helmut Coing zum 70. Geburtstag* (Frankfurt-on-Main, 1982), 427–9.

and by granting to teachers of theology, for so long as they continued to teach, and to students, for a period of five years, the privilege of drawing the income of their benefices even when absent from them, notwithstanding any provisions to the contrary, whether written or customary.[27]

At the same time the Holy See also intervened in minor *studia* such as that of Montpellier. In 1220 the Cardinal Legate Conrad of Urach, in agreement with certain bishops of the region and the teachers and scholars of the medical *universitas*, issued comprehensive regulations 'in the general interest', ordering that no person should teach in public unless approved by the bishop of Maguelone and the college of teachers, or style himself a scholar unless subject to a master. In the matter of jurisdiction the legate ordered that civil cases should in the first instance be heard before a master chosen by the bishop and a college of three teachers. The bishop himself was to act as judge of appeal in civil cases and as sole judge in criminal cases. Other regulations were issued on relations between masters and scholars, the duration of lessons and disputations, funeral honours, and the obligation to receive the tonsure incumbent on any person who had received an ecclesiastical benefice or taken holy orders. Lastly, each master was required, when entering upon his career as a teacher, to swear to observe the legate's statutes. These were to be read out publicly at every *inceptio* – the master's official inception of his duties as a licensed teacher – *in audientia communi*, before the assembled masters and scholars.[28]

It may be concluded that in the papacies of Innocent III and Honorius III the church, realizing that new organizations such as the *universitates* were growing up in the most important centres of study in Europe, issued increasingly detailed regulations on higher education with the intention of effecting reform and improvement (*reformatio in melius*) in the most authoritative schools – a reform that would not merely regulate relations with the nascent corporations of teachers and scholars, but would cover every detail of the organization of the *studia*. One reason, incidentally, for the violent disputes between the universities and the lay authorities was that, judging by the small numbers of royal officials with academic qualifications, particularly in the French court, the lay authorities were not interested in encouraging the formation of an educated ruling class.

THE POLICY OF EMPEROR FREDERICK II AND THE POPES

On the day of his coronation, 22 November 1220, the Emperor Frederick II

---

[27] *CUP*, vol. I, 88–90, nos. 30–1; 102–4, no. 45; 90–3, no. 32; Post, 'Parisian masters' (note 21), 37, 39, 47–9. For the problems concerning the *Super speculam*, see S. Kuttner, 'Papst Honorius III und das Studium des Zivilrechts', in S. Kuttner, *Gratian and the Schools of Law 1140–1234* (London, 1983), essay no. X, 79–101 (for *retractationes*: 43–7).

[28] *Cartulaire de l'Université de Montpellier*, vol. I, *1181–1400* (Montpellier, 1890), 180–3, no. 2; Fournier (ed.), *Statuts*, vol. II, 4–6, no. 882.

promulgated the constitution entitled *De statutis et consuetudinibus contra libertatem Ecclesiae editis* safeguarding the immunities and privileges of the clergy, and ordered the jurists of Bologna to insert it in the great *Corpus* of Roman law.[29] He thereby showed that imperial policy was still interested in the law schools, following a tradition going back to the *Habita* constitution but soon interrupted by war and the dynastic crisis preceding his ascension of the throne. Nevertheless, the Emperor Frederick II had no intention of competing with the pope as protector of the Bologna *studium*, but he had other and more ambitious plans, as the years of his vigorous rules in Italy were to show. His first important act of scholastic policy was to found the Naples *studium* to train the ruling class of the kingdom of Sicily, a territory no less dear to Frederick II than the Holy Roman Empire. In 1224 a letter to all dignitaries in the kingdom, stating the reasons for his decision and the way in which it was to be carried out,[30] echoed parts of the *Habita* constitution and followed some of its directives. But it was for quite other reasons; for, whilst both documents showed the intention of preserving scholars and teachers from the discomforts of the status of foreigners (*peregrini*), the *Habita* constitution offered protection to all possible seats of learning and forbade reprisals of any kind, whereas the 'circular' of 1224 restricted protection to persons frequenting the Naples *studium*. It forbade any person to leave the kingdom to teach or study, and threatened to punish the parents of any subjects of the king of Sicily who did not return to their home country by Michaelmas (29 September). The privileges it granted to scholars were naturally similar to those enjoyed by their colleagues in the principal *studia* of the time; as in the *Habita* constitution, the safety of their person and property was guaranteed and they were made subject to the jurisdiction of their teachers, but only in civil cases (this was analogous to the papal legate's provisions for the Montpellier *studium*). To prevent competition for tenancies of the *hospicia*, rents there were to be fixed by a joint committee of scholars and citizens and might in no case exceed a stated amount. This last provision was not very different from that made by the papal legate a decade before for the Oxford *studium*. The main differences between Frederick II's *studium* and the most important seats of learning in Europe was that in Naples the ecclesiastical authorities had no authority to recruit teachers, award the *licentia docendi*, or exercise jurisdictional powers.

Thereafter, between 1226 and 1240, the emperor pursued his scholastic policy of depriving Bologna of its primacy and sought to make Naples the most prestigious centre for the teaching of law in the kingdom of Sicily and in

---

[29] Weimar, 'Zur Doktorwürde' (note 26), 431; S. Kuttner, 'A New Eyewitness Account of the Fourth Lateran Council', in Kuttner, *Medieval Councils* (note 20), essay no. IX, 167–71.

[30] F. Torraca, 'Le origini. L'età sveva', in *Storia della Università di Napoli* (Naples, 1924), 3–15; G. Arnaldi, 'Fondazione e rifondazioni dello studio di Napoli in età sveva', in *Università e società*, 81–105.

the whole empire. On several occasions, in 1226, 1234, and 1239, Frederick II sent pressing invitations to teachers and scholars in Bologna and to his other subjects, Italian or ultramontane, to attend the Naples *studium*. He forbade them to go to Bologna to teach or study, and formed in Naples a teaching staff of great eminence, whose jurists were especially remarkable. His intention was no longer merely to train the ruling class of his kingdom of Sicily; he aspired to nothing less than creating a great intellectual élite to sustain the imperial throne with the instruments of law and the prestige of culture. In this belief, and paraphrasing Justinian's summons to the aspiring law students (*cupida legum iuventus*) of his time when he promulgated his Institutes, Frederick II affirmed that the imperial throne should be mighty by force of law as well as by force of arms.[31] With that lofty aim in view, in 1238 he sent a jurist devoted to him, a former professor in Naples, to teach civil law in the Vercelli *studium* founded shortly before by a migration of students from Padua. At that time the emperor's policy of centralization to benefit Naples caused a crisis in other centres of learning such as Modena, Arezzo, and Padua, which had come into being spontaneously, at the end of the twelfth century and in the first decades of the thirteenth, through migrations of teachers and scholars from Bologna, and had then flourished for some years.[32]

The emperor's tactics, vigorous and tenacious though they were, did not deter the popes from their policy of assiduous guardianship and tight control of the *studia* traditionally linked with the ecclesiastical authorities. At the same time they granted concessions and privileges to schools of more recent formation, and promoted the foundation of new centres of learning. Above all, they continued to show the highest consideration for the Bologna *studium*; in 1226, at the very time when the emperor was sending out the first of his invitations to desert Bologna, Pope Honorius III appointed the jurist Tancred, archdeacon of the diocese of Bologna, to draft the *Quinta compilatio* of decretals, and instructed him to see that it was adopted in all law courts and schools (*tam in iudiciis quam in scholis*).[33] In 1234 Pope Gregory IX repeated this significant gesture by publishing his great collection of decretals, the *Liber extra*, addressing it to the academics of Bologna (and Paris) in the very words of Innocent III promulgating the *Tertia compilatio*. Especially under the heading *De magistris*, the new *Compilatio* included all the principal regulations for higher education from the time of Pope Alexander III, and so

---

[31] E. M. Meijers, 'L'Università di Napoli nel secolo XIII', in E. M. Meijers, *Etudes d'histoire du droit*, vol. III (Leiden, 1959), 149–60; P. Nardi, 'Comune, Impero e Papato alle origini dell'insegnamento universitario in Siena', *Bullettino senese di storia patria*, 90 (1983), 55ff.

[32] E. Cortese, 'Scienza di giudici e scienza di professori tra XII e XIII secolo', in *Legge giudici giuristi* (Milan, 1982), 117, 122.

[33] L. E. Boyle, 'The Compilatio Quinta and the registers of Honorius III', *Bulletin of Medieval Canon Law*, 8 (1978), 9–19.

sanctioned the discipline elaborated by the Church of Rome over nearly three-quarters of a century.[34]

Meanwhile in 1231 Gregory IX successfully concluded his mediation in the controversy between the university community of Paris and King Louis IX of France. His bull *Parens scientiarum* recalled teachers and scholars to Paris, confirmed and clearly recapitulated the regulations made by Cardinal Robert of Courson, and introduced further measures to protect scholars and teachers, authorizing them to suspend lessons whenever their privileges were seriously infringed. At the same time the pope exhorted the king to renew the privileges granted to scholars by his predecessor Philip II Augustus, and in particular asked him to agree that rents in the *hospitia* should be fixed by a joint committee of two masters and two citizens.[35]

The most significant order made by Gregory IX in scholastic affairs is contained in his bull of 1233 to the Toulouse *universitas* of masters and scholars,[36] and to the bishop and Count Raymond. This granted the students of Toulouse equal privileges with their colleagues in Paris, and made the signal concession that anyone examined and awarded the *licentia docendi* in Toulouse could freely *regere ubique*, that is, teach anywhere without undergoing further examination. This important concession aroused so much apprehension that hardly a year later the pope had to send the bishop of Paris assurances that the privilege granted to the Toulouse *studium* would not prejudice the privilege of the Paris *studium* relating to the award of the *licentia*. A few years before, Gregory IX had exempted several masters of arts and medicine who had taught in Angers and Orléans from further examination before they were allowed to teach in Paris. By the will of the pope, therefore, a rift was opening in the system of recruiting teachers, a system founded on the privileged position rightly enjoyed by the oldest and most authoritative *studia* as teacher-training centres for the whole of western Europe. Henceforth the Holy See's scholastic policy was strongly to encourage the formation of new schools, especially outside Italy and in territories not *de facto* subject to imperial jurisdiction and therefore not directly controlled by the Emperor Frederick II. Thus in 1233 Pope Gregory IX conferred important privileges on the Cambridge *studium*, founded in 1209 by a migration from Oxford; he recognized the existence of the scholars' *universitas*, and granted its members the right of trial only within the diocese of Ely, to which Cambridge belonged (*ius non trahi extra*).[37] A few years later the same pope sent a brief to the bishop of Orléans authorizing the teaching of Roman law in

---

[34] A. Friedberg (ed.), *Corpus iuris canonici*, vol. II (Leipzig, 1879), 1–4, coll. 768–71 (X.5.5); coll. 14–15 (X.1.2.11); coll. 215–16 (X.1.38.7); coll. 520–1 (X.3.18.1); coll. 463 (X.3.4.12).

[35] *CUP*, vol. I, 136–9, no. 79; 140, no. 82.

[36] C. E. Smith, *The University of Toulouse in the Middle Ages. Its Origins and Growth to 1500 AD* (Milwaukee, Wis., 1958), 57ff.

[37] M. B. Hackett, *The Original Statutes of Cambridge University. The Text and its History* (Cambridge, 1970), 51, 53ff.

Orléans, Honorius III having forbidden it in Paris. In doing so Gregory bowed to the wishes of many doctors of law and scholars, on condition that the scholars were not members of the clergy with cure of souls, who were again forbidden to study civil law.[38]

The higher education policy of Gregory IX was continued by Innocent IV (Sinibaldo Fieschi of Genoa), who ascended the papal throne in the summer of 1243, when Frederick II was consolidating his hegemony over the ecclesiastical hierarchy, especially in Italy. In the autumn of 1244, fearing complete subjection to the will of the emperor, the new pope fled to France, where he turned his attention mainly to the transalpine *studia* and schools. In the university community in Paris he found little to add to the firmly based system of privileges and guarantees set up by his predecessors; it remained for him only to confirm previous provisions and agreements, and to grant the *ius non trahi extra* in 1245. At the same time Innocent IV extended to the Toulouse *studium* the rules made for Paris in the bull *Parens scientiarum* of Gregory IX, and granted secular students of theology at the Dominican *studium* in Dijon rights equal to those of their colleagues in Paris, and especially the privilege allowed by Honorius III of continuing to draw the income of their benefices even in their absence. But the most significant results of Sinibaldo Fieschi's university policy during his stay in Lyon were the foundation of the papal *studium* (*studium curiae*) in 1244–5 and the Piacenza *studium* in 1248, and his concessions to the teachers and scholars of Narbonne in 1247. In every case the pope provided that teachers and students should enjoy the same privileges, indulgences, freedoms, and immunities as their colleagues in the *studia generalia*. Turning in particular to the bishop, clergy, and people of Piacenza he quoted as an example of a *studium generale* the one in Paris.[39] These were important innovations in official language; never before had the public authorities used the term '*studium generale*' or indicated the Paris *studium* as a prototype. When the Emperor Frederick II proclaimed in 1226 that he had founded the Naples *studium* 'in the general interest' (*ad generale commodum*) of all persons wishing to study and be trained in the disciplines of scholars, the expression was probably not used in a technical sense to mean a *studium generale*. In the late 1230s and early 1240s, however, the term *studium generale* was used with an exact meaning in the works of authoritative masters of canon law such as Goffredo of Trani and Bernard of Botone. For them it was an institution in a city of royal foundation (as opposed to *villae* and *castella*) which could be frequented by students 'from almost any part of the world' (*quasi de omnibus partibus mundi*), who if they were

[38] E. M. Meijers, 'L'Université d'Orléans au XIIIe siècle', in Meijers, *Etudes* (note 31), 28.

[39] E. Falconi and R. Peveri (eds.), *Il Registrum Magnum del Comune di Piacenza*, vol. I (Milan, 1984), 303–4, no. 146; R. Creytens, 'Le "Studium Romanae Curiae" et le Maître du Sacré Palais', *Archivum fratrum praedicatorum*, 12 (1942), 23ff.; M. Bellomo, 'Intorno a Roffredo Beneventano: professore a Roma?', in M. Bellomo (ed.), *Scuole diritto e società nel Mezzogiorno medievale d'Italia*, vol. I (Catania, 1985), 172.

theologians could continue to draw their prebends during their absence. Understandably, as a trained jurist Pope Innocent IV was disposed to accept officially a term formerly generic but fast acquiring a precise technical meaning.[40] His concessions of 1244–8 did not put the new *studia* on a completely equal footing with the *studium generale* of Paris, particularly as they made no mention of the award of the *licentia docendi* and so conveyed that the function of the *studia* was merely to teach.

On the death of the Emperor Frederick II in 1250 his plans for higher education collapsed. Innocent IV returned to Italy and followed the traditional papal policy of support to university communities. He was perfectly familiar with their theoretical as well as practical problems, having dealt fully in his legal works with the nature and character of a *universitas*. In 1253 he approved the statutes of the community of scholars (*universitas scholarium*) in Bologna. These, as far as is known, regulated *inter alia* the time allowed scholars to pay the masters' fees, feast-days, the obligation to hold disputations at the beginning of the academic year, and (perhaps later) the *puncta* – the time in which teachers were required to 'read' (expound) the books of law – and penalties for non-compliance.[41] The texts as we know them are probably not complete, so that it is impossible to say to what extent the Bologna *universitas* had become independent of the commune and the church; but for a long time past the rectors' powers must have included jurisdiction in civil lawsuits and minor criminal cases. In 1252 Innocent IV had granted special privileges to the *universitas* of masters and scholars in Siena, whom he declared to be completely immune from taxes and forced labour (*servitia, tallia, collecta,* and *angariae*) levied on their person or property by the city of Siena. Finally he confirmed the *universitas* of scholars and masters in Oxford in the full enjoyment of the immunities, freedoms, customs, and statutes already being observed by them.

The same policy of ubiquitous intervention in the universities' internal affairs was followed by Pope Alexander IV, especially towards the Paris *studium*, of whose superiority to the *studia generalia* of more recent foundation he was very well aware. In a striking phrase he compared its role in the church to 'the tree of life in God's paradise' (*lignum vitae in Paradiso Dei*), and accordingly issued orders in April 1255 abolishing, modifying, or making innovations in some of the statutes of the University of Paris, including those on the suspension of courses as a sign of protest, the procedure for co-opting new teachers, and the powers of the chancellor. The ecclesiastical authorities' extreme zeal and interest in the discipline and activities of the Paris *studium*

---

[40] On the *studium generale* concept, see E. Cortese, 'Sulla scienza giuridica a Napoli tra Quattro e Cinquecento', in Bellomo (ed.), *Scuole diritto* (note 39), 44–6; Nardi, 'Comune, Impero e Papato' (note 31), 62–5.

[41] D. Maffei, 'Un trattato di Bonaccorso degli Elisei e i più antichi statuti dello Studio di Bologna nel manoscritto 22 della Robbins Collection', *Bulletin of Medieval Canon Law*, 5 (1975), 85–101.

led them after a few years to condemn severely philosophical doctrines judged heterodox, such as those professed by Siger of Brabant, Boethius of Dacia, and other exponents of Latin Averroism. These were definitively condemned in 1277 by Stephen Tempier, bishop of Paris.[42]

RELATIONS BETWEEN SECULAR AUTHORITIES AND UNIVERSITIES IN THE THIRTEENTH CENTURY

The privileges granted by the thirteenth-century popes would never have been put into effect but for the constant collaboration of the secular authorities, whether royal or local. A striking example is Piacenza, where in spite of the foundation of the *studium generale* by Innocent IV the ruling class of citizens failed to provide conditions in which a *studium* could be formed or grow up.[43] In contrast, the kings of England strongly supported the *studium* at Oxford and Cambridge. From 1231 onwards Henry III issued orders confirming and consolidating the privileged position already enjoyed by masters and scholars as a result of ecclesiastical concessions. The privilege granted to the Oxford *universitas* by the papal legate in 1214, of directly controlling rents of scholars' lodgings through committees appointed for the purpose, could never have been put into practice without the cooperation of the secular authorities. It was they too who enforced the rule (also applied in Paris and Montpellier) that students must be entered on a teacher's list; the sheriff was ordered to imprison students who did not register as scholars within a fortnight of their arrival. These and other royal orders became part of the statutes of the *universitas* of Cambridge issued around 1250. In 1244 King Henry III granted the chancellor of the *universitas* at Oxford wide powers of jurisdiction, making him competent to try cases of debt, the fixing of rents for lodgings, the hire of horses, breaches of contract, and purchase of victuals where one of the parties to the lawsuit was a member of the *universitas*. In 1248 the king granted the *universitas* further privileges, conferring upon it authority to superintend trade in victuals within the city.

No less decisive was the action taken by the kings of Castile and León in Spain; Alfonso VIII of Castile (1158–1214) founded a *studium* in Palencia, engaging Italian and French teachers of theology, canon law, and arts, and Alfonso IX of León (1188–1229) founded the *studium* of Salamanca. The latter foundation was confirmed and reorganized by Alfonso X the Wise (1252–84), who regulated the stipends of professors and the jurisdiction of the

---

42 *CUP*, vol. I, 279–85, no. 247; 543ff., no. 473; M. Grabmann, *Mittelalterliches Geistesleben. Abhandlungen zur Geschichte der Scholastik und Mystik*, vol. III (Munich, 1956), 159–96; J. Châtillon, 'L'exercice du pouvoir doctrinal dans la chrétienté du XIII siècle: le cas d'Etienne Tempier', in J. Châtillon, *D'Isidore de Séville à Saint Thomas d'Aquin. Etudes d'histoire et de théologie* (London, 1985), essay no. XV, 13–45.

43 E. Nasalli Rocca, 'Lo "studium generale" di Piacenza nel sec. XIII. Contributo alla storia delle Università', *Bollettino storico piacentino*, 51 (1956), 129–41.

bishop and *alcalde* of the city.[44] The secular authorities, however, had first to enlist the cooperation of the local ecclesiastical authorities (the bishop of Palencia, and the bishop and chapter of Salamanca) and then to apply to the Holy See to obtain for both foundations the dignity and privileges of *studia generalia*, albeit with certain restrictions. Thus in 1255 Pope Alexander IV solemnly confirmed the foundation of Salamanca and granted it the prerogatives of a *studium generale*, including recognition of the *licentia ubique docendi*, except in Paris and Bologna.[45] And in 1263 Pope Urban IV granted the masters and students of Palencia the usual immunities, freedoms, and indulgences enjoyed by their colleagues in Paris and other *studia generalia*, in the same terms as for Piacenza but (as for that city) without mentioning the *licentia ubique docendi*.

In the thirteenth century kings and princes became more anxious to have the services of university-trained administrators. Already at the end of the twelfth century officials known as *magistri* were working in the English royal chancery, but only in the reign of Louis IX did university-trained officials become numerous and influential in the French bureaucracy and court. From the latter half of the thirteenth century onwards, and especially after Philip the Fair became king in 1285, many jurists entered the *Parlement* and the royal curia, most of them from the Orléans *studium* or trained in Roman Law at that school, and some of them vigorously upheld the French monarchy's ambitions to take the place of the Holy Roman Empire and assume its prerogatives and rights of dominion. When an Angevin ascended the throne of the kingdom of Sicily after the Hohenstaufen dynasty became extinct, the relations of the Orléans Law school with the house of Anjou were just as close. Thus in 1266 Charles I re-established the Naples *studium*, attracting to it teachers from Orléans, and employing some of them in high offices of state rather than in teaching.[46]

Although the transformation of law into 'a culture of officials' was 'typical of monarchies', even then and even in the *studia* in the Italian communes it was becoming common for *doctores* to produce works intended mainly for the legal profession and the town magistrates, and among the latter appeared the first important authors of legal works of great technical value.[47] The time had long gone by when the professors of Bologna had deplored the ignorance of judges; city governments were now increasingly interested in subsidizing

---

[44] A. Pérez Martín, 'Importancia de las universidades en la recepción del derecho romano en la Península ibérica', *Studi sassaresi*, 8 (1980–1), 285–8.

[45] V. Beltrán de Heredia, *Bulario de la Universidad de Salamanca (1219–1549)*, vol. I (Salamanca, 1966), 322–3, no. 15; see also 320ff., nos. 11–14 and 16.

[46] Meijers, 'Université d'Orléans' (note 38), 5–24; Meijers, 'Università di Napoli' (note 31), 149–66; D. Maffei, 'Il giudice testimone e una "quaestio" di Jacques de Revigny' (Ms. Bon. Coll. Hisp. 82)', *Tijdschrift voor Rechtsgeschiedenis*, 35 (1967), 71–3; J. R. Strayer, *Les Gens de justice du Languedoc sous Philippe le Bel* (Toulouse, 1970).

[47] Cortese, 'Legisti, canonisti e feudisti' (note 1), 272; Cortese, 'Scienza di giudici' (note 32), 117–29.

and regulating their own schools. Thus in Padua, after 1260, the commune decreed that new professorial chairs should be set up at the university and undertook to pay the stipends of foreign teachers, drawing up rules for students' mutual benefit societies, the production of manuscripts, and the availability and rent of lodgings, and so set in motion a fruitful process of 'refoundation' which was to have important results, especially at the turn of the thirteenth century. Similarly, the communes of Perugia, Siena, and Modena in the latter half of the thirteenth century took it upon themselves to engage masters and recall scholars, offering them excellent living conditions in accordance with the provisions of ordinary law relating to their safety and privileges.[48] The commune of Bologna, in particular, steadily extended its influence and control over the *studium*, granting the students the right to compensation for damage suffered in riots or fires and concessions regarding rents, food purchase, and the validity of contracts and wills made in a form other than that required by the laws of the city. It also granted them a status similar to that of the citizens of Bologna as regards liability to 'reprisals' in conformity with all the provisions of the *Habita* constitution of more than a century before. As a corollary, however, the jurisdiction of the town magistrates was extended and that of the rectors restricted, and the commune gradually took over the recruitment of teachers and the burden of paying masters' salaries, previously paid by the scholars' contributions (*collectae*), so that the scholars lost an ancient and important prerogative. In this way municipalization of the Bologna *studium* was greatly stimulated. It could no longer be checked at the end of the thirteenth or the beginning of the fourteenth century, when the commune intervened more rigorously in the life of the *universitas*, interfering in the election of rectors and making secular scholars completely subject to municipal jurisdiction in criminal cases. The latter provision, whilst admittedly confirming a long-standing practice, finally deprived the scholars of an ancient privilege dating back to the *Habita* constitution, but left clerics under the bishop's jurisdiction.

Despite the universally recognized primacy of the *studia* of Paris, Bologna, Montpellier, Oxford, and Cambridge, they lacked any official declaration of the right to confer the *licentia ubique docendi*. Only a universal power (*potestas generalis*) could grant this right, as it had done in Toulouse and Salamanca, which had received this important privilege from Pope Gregory IX and Pope Alexander IV, respectively. The special status of the Paris and Bologna *studia* was implicitly recognized by the refusal of Pope Alexander IV to permit teaching there by *licentiati* from the *studium generale* of Sala-

---

48 G. Arnaldi, 'Il primo secolo dello Studio di Padova', in *Storia della cultura veneta*, vol. II, *Il Trecento* (Vicenza, 1976), 14–17; M. Bellomo, 'Studenti e "Populus" nelle città universitarie italiane dal sec. XII al XV', in *Università e società*, 69ff.; G. Ermini, *Storia della Università di Perugia*, vol. I (Florence, 1971), 15ff.; C.G. Mor and P. Di Pietro, *Storia dell'Università di Modena*, vol. I (Florence, 1975), 12–19; Nardi, 'Comune, Impero e Papato' (note 31), 87ff.

manca. Pope Nicholas IV granted official recognition of the *licentia ubique docendi* to Montpellier in 1289, to Bologna in 1291, and to Paris in 1292. Oxford failed to obtain it, in spite of the efforts of King Edward I and King Edward II between 1303 and 1317, but in 1318 Pope John XXII issued a papal bull appointing Cambridge a *studium generale*, which henceforth also implied the grant of the *licentia*. At the end of the thirteenth century and in the first two decades of the fourteenth, the papacy was in fact pursuing its higher education policy with renewed vigour, as is shown by the decisions of Nicholas IV and his successors Boniface VIII and Clement V. Thus in 1290 Nicholas IV granted *studium generale* status to the school founded in Lisbon by King Denis the Just of Portugal in 1288–9 and in 1291 to the school founded at Gray by Count Otto IV of Burgundy in 1287. Boniface VIII instituted the *studium generale* of Rome in 1303 and that of Pamiers in 1295. He raised Avignon to university status in 1303, as did Clement V the already famous schools of Orleans (in 1306) and those of Perugia (in 1308).[49] Clement V issued orders for the foundation of chairs of Hebrew, Arabic, and Chaldean in the *studia* of Paris, Bologna, Oxford, and Salamanca, not all of which complied, and forbade newly graduated doctors to spend more than three thousand silver *turonenses* to celebrate the award of their degree. These orders completed the regulations made by the church on higher education, and were incorporated into the collection of *Clementinae* decretals issued by his successor John XXII on 1 November 1317 and sent to many *universitates*.[50]

Among the documents of that period the decree for the foundation of the *studium generale* in Rome is of special interest. It was promulgated by Pope Boniface VIII (Benedict Caetani) at Anagni on 6 June 1303, towards the end of his conflict with King Philip the Fair of France and the clergy supporting him, and a few months before the pope's humiliation and death. As well as making the customary provisions for the institution of the *studium generale* and the grant to masters and scholars of all the privileges, freedoms, and immunities conferred upon their colleagues in other *studia generalia*, the decree regulated in detail the status to be enjoyed by professors and students, so recapitulating in essentials the entire discipline for *studia generalia* gradually built up and consolidated over more than a century on the model of Paris and Bologna. This is a highly significant event, taking into account that

[49] M. Meyhöfer, 'Die kaiserlichen Stiftungsprivilegien für Universitäten', *Archiv für Urkundenforschung*, 4 (1912), 396ff.; G. L. Haskins, 'The University of Oxford and the "Ius ubique docendi" ', *English Historical Review*, 56 (1941), 281–92; A. García y García, 'Aspectos de la Universidad Portuguesa Medieval', in *Universities in the Late Middle Ages*, 134ff., 139.

[50] *Clementinae* 5.1.1 and 5.1.2, in A. Friedberg (ed.), *Corpus iuris canonici*, vol. II (Leipzig, 1879), coll. 1179–80. On the application of *Clementinae* 5.1.1 see D. Maffei, 'Alberico di Metz e il suo apparato sulle Clementine', *Bulletin of Medieval Canon Law*, 1 (1971), 44 n. 4; F. Soetermeer, 'The Origin of Ms. D'Ablaing 14 and the *Transmissio* of the Clementines to the Universities', *Tijdschrift voor Rechtsgeschiedenis*, 54 (1986), 108–12.

the pontificate of Boniface VIII and with it the political apogee of the papacy were drawing to an end, and that the Avignon 'captivity' of the Church of Rome was about to begin.

THE GROWING SUPPORT OF SECULAR AUTHORITIES IN THE FOURTEENTH CENTURY

In the first half of the fourteenth century the secular authorities became much more active in higher education. In many parts of Europe princes and communities of citizens joined the ecclesiastical authorities in promoting and organizing new and old centres of learning. At the beginning of the century the Angevins showed particular solicitude for the Naples *studium*, giving it special protection,[51] and for the *studium* of Avignon in Provence, which Charles II sedulously protected, granting the masters and scholars many privileges and trying to ease their poverty by giving them leave to appoint a banker to lend them money.[52] He attempted, however, to encroach upon the independence of the *universitas* of doctors and students there by ordering that an official from his curia should be appointed to the committee fixing rents for accommodation in the *hospitia*, to act as referee in case of disputes between the *universitas* and the town. Meanwhile, as part of his conflict with Boniface VIII, King Philip the Fair of France repeatedly interfered in the internal affairs of the Paris *studium*, in pursuance of the plans for his hegemony elaborated by his court and the Orléans school of law. King Diego II of Aragon gave Lérida a *studium* adequately protected and furnished with professorial chairs paid for by the town, and obtained for it from Boniface VIII privileges equal to those of Toulouse. Some years later, in 1318, Frederick of Habsburg, king of the Germans and pretender to the imperial throne, granted the town of Treviso permission to found a school for the teaching of law and any other discipline *solemniter et generaliter*, that is, to standards as high as in a *studium generale*.

In the northern part of central Italy communes boasting a respectable cultural tradition, and which for many decades, although not continuously, had financed professorial chairs and schools of higher education, spent great sums of money in an effort to deprive Bologna of the supremacy it had enjoyed since the twelfth century. In the first decades of the fourteenth century Padua, Perugia, Siena, and Florence, taking advantage of the crisis opposing the town of Bologna and the scholars of its *studium*, spared no pains to attract teachers and students, promising them ideal living conditions and continuance of their existing privileges. Some communes made extraordinary efforts of organization to put their *studium* on a sound financial basis and consolidate their

---

[51] F. Sabatini, *Napoli Angioina: cultura e società* (Naples, 1975), 18ff., 223ff.
[52] G. M. Monti, 'Da Carlo I a Roberto d'Angió. Ricerche e documenti', *Archivio storico per le province napoletane*, 57 (1932), 127ff., 130ff.

administration, appointing 'wise men' or 'officers' to look after the requirements of the *studium* and approach illustrious teachers, to whom they offered
lavish rewards and good lodgings to attract their services. Relations between
the university and the local authorities accordingly became closer and the
authorities exercised stricter control over their *studia*; but any attempt to
improve organization would have failed had not the competent authorities
granted the title and privileges of a *studium generale*, without which no
academic institution could now survive. Municipal governments, especially
those of Perugia, Siena, and Florence, therefore had to make protracted
efforts to get the popes to bestow the prestigious title and its corollary, authority to grant the degree of doctor; only Perugia managed to obtain this in
time to take full advantage of the crisis of 1321 in the Bologna *studium*,
especially in the teaching of law.[53]

One after the other, princes outside Italy promoted the foundation of new
studia – the Dauphin Humbert II at Grenoble in 1339 and, more importantly,
Charles IV of Luxemburg at Prague in 1347.[54] The secular authorities were
eager to found a university because they wanted a steady supply of better
trained and more cultivated officials, and even more because they aspired to
possess and control a centre of education that would rival the most ancient
and famous seats of learning, and spare their subjects the discomforts of
having to study abroad.

For some years after his coronation as emperor in 1355, Charles IV of
Luxemburg successfully opposed the papal monopoly of the award of the title
of *studium generale* and the privilege of *ubique docendi*. Breaking with the
policy of his predecessors, who from the time of Frederick II onwards had
taken no interest in higher education, he hastened to grant a *studium generale*
to the Italian cities of Arezzo, Perugia, and Siena, and later to Pavia, Florence,
Lucca, and Orange. It is, however, significant that the charters of Charles IV
confirmed the regulations established long ago, predominantly by the church,
and repeated the organization of the *studia generalia* as modelled mainly by
the church. This was particularly so in respect of the privileges of *universitates* – exemption from taxes, dues, or 'reprisals' (seizure of person or property), and the award of academic degrees. These had to be awarded by the
bishop or his representative from the council of doctors and masters of the
studium (*de consilio doctorum et magistrorum studii*).[55] In this way the *studia
generalia*, founded by the public authorities and substantially uniform in
organization and purpose although located far apart and living under dissimilar

[53] Especially for Siena: G. Prunai, 'Lo Studio senese dalla "migratio" bolognese alla fondazione
della "Domus Sapientiae" (1321–1408)', *Bullettino senese di storia patria*, 57 (1950), 3–54. For
Florence: E. Spagnesi, 'I documenti costitutivi dalla provvisione del 1321 allo statuto del 1388',
in *Storia dell'Ateneo fiorentino. Contributi di studio*, vol. I (Florence, 1986), 109–45.
[54] A. Vetulani, 'Les origines et le sort des universités de l'Europe centrale et orientale fondées au
cours du XIVe siècle', in *Universities in the Late Middle Ages*, 150ff.
[55] Meyhöfer, 'Kaiserlichen Stiftungsprivilegien' (note 49), 320–30.

political systems, began their functional relationship with the papacy and the empire, which in the medieval view were authorities complementing each other.

Ecclesiastical interest in higher education did not slacken in the fourteenth century, in spite of the growing involvement of secular rulers and the end of papal hegemony in European politics. During the Avignon 'captivity' (1309–76), the universities of the south of France and Provence benefited most from papal grants and from the influx of intellectuals having connections with the papal court. The Avignon *studium* in particular had as masters famous jurists who were also employed on official duties for the papal curia.[56] In 1339 the Montpellier *studium* received from the Cardinal Legate, Bertrand de Deaux, new regulations which ensured that the bishop should control the award of academic degrees and have powers of jurisdiction, and confided responsibility for day-to-day administration to the students, and for teaching to the masters. The statutes of the Toulouse *studium* were reformed, Pope John XXII, born in Cahors, founded a *studium* there in 1332, and in 1339 Benedict XII raised the Grenoble *studium* to the rank of *studium generale*. Especially in the first part of the fourteenth century, however, the popes continued to exercise tight control in Paris, still the most important centre for the teaching of theology, and proved willing to entertain applications from other sources. Thus Clement VI (1342–52) conferred the title of *studium generale* on Valladolid in 1346 at the request of King Alfonso XI of Castile, on Prague in 1347 at the request of King Charles IV (the future emperor), and on the *studia* of Pisa (1343), Padua (1346), and Florence (1349). Later, perhaps because of the energetic policy of the Emperor Charles IV, papal policy towards the universities became more selective. Pope Urban V (1362–70) in particular did not stop short at granting privileges and titles, but tried to regulate the establishment of faculties of theology, found more university colleges, and reaffirm ecclesiastical prerogatives, especially for the award of academic degrees. The most significant features of his policy were his confirmation of the *studium generale* and *licentia ubique docendi* to three European rulers: Casimir III of Poland for the *studium generale* of Cracow in 1364, Duke Rudolf IV of Austria for the *studium generale* of Vienna in 1365, and King Louis I of Hungary for the *studium generale* of Pécs in 1367; but the pope did not grant these three *studia* a faculty of theology, being of the opinion that, in those parts, conditions were not favourable to the formation of theological schools. He did, however, found the theological faculty in Padua, and agreed to improvements in the operation of the theological faculties in Bologna, Toulouse, and Florence, mainly to decentralize theological

---

56 J. Verger, 'Les rapports entre universités italiennes et universités françaises méridionales (XII–XV siècles)', in *Università e società*, 157ff., 174ff.; J. Verger, 'L'Université d'Avignon au temps de Clément VII', in *Genèse et débuts du Grand Schisme d'Occident* (Paris, 1980), 185–200.

studies but probably also to promote criticism of the Ockhamist doctrines professed by the doctors and scholars of Paris, and to revive the Thomist doctrines that he himself professed. Urban V strongly asserted that the award of academic degrees was an ecclesiastical prerogative; he even declared that Casimir's order to the royal chancellor of Cracow to exercise that function was invalid, and that only the bishop was entitled to perform it. In Urban's time and that of his immediate predecessors and successors, many more colleges for poor students were founded in Italy and elsewhere, either by the popes or by prelates of high rank.[57]

Although in the fourteenth century many universities were founded and others were granted the privileges of a *studium generale*, only those universities assiduously supported by their founders or administrators proved viable for long. In central and eastern Europe, in spite of the solemn foundation of *studia* in Vienna, Cracow, Pécs, and Prague, a flourishing university grew up only in Prague, principally because of the support of the Emperor Charles IV, who endowed each faculty with a building and provided for the subsistence of the masters in various ways, even founding the Collegium Carolinum for twelve of them in 1366.

Meanwhile, in Italy universities flourished and took firm root in the great cities where governments, either directly or through their nominees, issued strict and detailed regulations for the organization of the *studium*, closely supervised its operation, and did not cut their spending on education to supply more pressing demands such as those for weapons of war. Prosperity and crisis alternated in the Universities of Perugia, Padua, Siena, and Florence, as the city authorities alternatively showed them care and neglect, and the Naples *studium* became an emblem of decay when in the reign of Queen Joan I (1343–81) it ceased to receive any support worthy of mention. In fact, in the kingdom of Naples, from the time of Robert the Wise (1309–43) onwards, the dearest ambition of many teachers in the university was to leave it and take up high office in the government and the church, as indeed many teachers of civil and canon law did.

Many local authorities in the south of France were similarly indifferent to the needs of universities. In Montpellier, for example, the city consuls did not trouble to apply the regulations for the control of rents in the *hospitia* issued by Cardinal Bertrand de Deaux, who in 1344 threatened to revoke the privileges of the *studium* and even to transfer it elsewhere.

Troubles infinitely more serious broke out between town and gown in Oxford, culminating on St Scholastica's Day (10 February 1355) in nothing

---

[57] A. L. Gabriel, 'The College System in the Fourteenth-Century Universities', in F. L. Utley (ed.), *The Forward Movement of the Fourteenth Century* (Colombus, 1961), 79–124 (especially 84ff.); A. L. Gabriel, 'Motivation of the Founders of Mediaeval Colleges', in A. L. Gabriel, *Garlandia. Studies in the History of the Mediaeval University* (Frankfurt-on-Main, 1969), 211–23.

less than a massacre of students by the citizens with the connivance of the bailiffs. The king took over the protection of the *studium* and appointed a panel of judges, which arrested the mayor and aldermen of Oxford and deprived the sheriff of office. Only when its existing privileges were confirmed, and further privileges granted by the royal charter of 27 June 1355, did the *studium* resume its activities: Oxford was sentenced to pay heavy reparations, and was humiliated by subjection of its civic representatives to the university.

THE CONSEQUENCES OF THE GREAT SCHISM

The crisis following the Great Schism profoundly affected the *studia generalia* most closely linked to the papacy and church. From 1380 onwards there were two popes, Urban VI in Rome and Clement VII in Avignon. University communities were at once faced with a dilemma: recent practice required them to send the pope the *rotuli* (rolls) of petitions for benefices for the 'clerks';[58] which pope should they declare for? At first they attempted to find a legalistic way round the difficulty by trying to establish which of the two elections was in accordance with canon law, and famous teachers including Baldus de Ubaldis and Giovanni da Legano gave their own authoritative opinion. Their views commanded respectful attention in Italian and foreign universities, but not unanimous agreement, particularly in the latter. Everywhere, on the contrary, there were conflicting loyalties, uncertainty, and fierce quarrels such as those between the Urbanist universities of Bologna or Prague and the French and Provençal universities, which were of course Clementist. The Paris *studium* offered the most intense turmoil and the most bitter internal divisions between its nations and the faculties until the supporters of Clement VII won the day with the decisive backing of the French kings.[59] It was in the Paris *studium*, more than in any other European intellectual centre, that the debate on how to end the Schism was most advanced, and that the foundations were laid on the conciliarist theories so profoundly influential in the ensuing decades. But, meanwhile, the firmly Clementist attitude of the French crown caused irremediable divisions among the teachers of the Paris *studium*, preventing freedom of discussion and driving opponents into exile (1383). Nor did Urbanist ardour abate; in 1384 Pope Urban VI launched an active university policy, granting Vienna a faculty of theology and in 1385 founding the Heidelberg *studium*, whose masters at once refused to recognize academic degrees awarded in Paris by the Clementist chancellor. Between 1386 and 1389 Urban VI, pursuing the same policy, granted the privileges of *studium generale* to Cologne, Lucca, Kulm, and Erfurt in an attempt to extend

---

[58] D. E. R. Watt, 'University Clerks and Rolls of Petitions for Benefices', *Speculum*, 34 (1959), 213–29.
[59] R. N. Swanson, *Universities, Academics and the Great Schism* (Cambridge, 1979), 22–44, 58.

his influence, but was disappointed in his expectations. The net result was that more university institutions were founded in central and eastern Europe, and that *studia* such as those of Prague and Vienna flourished, benefiting by the exodus from Paris of the masters of the German nation. The universities in the south of France, however, suffered defections, even by Clementist masters, and entered upon a decline that spared only Avignon, obviously because of the curia there, which still strongly attracted masters and students whose ambitions lay in an ecclesiastical career.

The Schism continued under the successors of Urban and Clement, keeping alive the debate in and between the universities on how to escape from a situation of growing confusion and danger to the church. The Paris *studium* was, as before, one of the most active parties; it pressed for an agreement, preferably that both popes should abdicate (1395), but both European academic circles and the most active architects of the Schism had grave doubts as to the wisdom of this course. In May 1398 the French universities were admitted to the Council of the French Church assembled to consider the question of obedience to the pope in Avignon (the Spaniard Pedro de Luna), but only the University of Paris exercised much influence, particularly towards the end of the Council, when it managed to push through the decision to withdraw obedience (*subtractio oboedientiae*) from Benedict XIII so as to end the feud between Avignon and Rome. That decision proved ineffective and doomed to failure when the University of Paris had again to swear obedience to Benedict XIII, under pressure from the French crown and from the minor *studia* of Angers, Montpellier, Orléans, and Toulouse (1403).

In the first years of the fifteenth century conciliarist views came to be regarded as those most likely to end the Schism, and so gained ground in the principal *studia* of Europe; but the authority of the university doctors was on the wane, and they now supplied only a gloss of theory to each move by the ecclesiastical and temporal powers. The universities had in fact never regarded themselves as institutions responsible for reuniting the church, but only as counsellors of the religious and temporal authorities, leaving them the onus of policy and action. Consequently, the universities were not allowed to take part in decision-making, either during the attempts to end the Schism or in the General Councils that took place in Europe from 1409 until the mid-fifteenth century, although many academics took part in the discussions, stating their views and exercising great personal influence.

The bitter quarrels that had marked the Schism and continued to divide the church in the conciliar period encouraged popes and anti-popes alike to interest themselves in the universities. At the end of the fourteenth century and in the first decades of the fifteenth, both Rome and Avignon were prodigal in granting privileges to religious and secular authorities wishing to set up *studia* in the territories under their jurisdiction. Evidently the rival popes realized that they needed the intellectual support of part of the academic world. They therefore encouraged the foundation of universities in areas on whose fidelity they could count.[60]

Meanwhile the bitter controversies between the religious authorities, in which sovereigns too were involved, weakened what had been the function of the *studia generalia* from their very beginnings: that of supranational centres propagating an international culture. Instead, the universities were more closely associated with sovereigns and secular authorities and became, in effect, schools for the intellectual élite and ruling classes of the states in which they were situated. A striking example of this is the Prague *studium generale*. Still as an offshoot of the original idea of the university as a universally-minded pan-European institution, the Prague *studium* was founded in 1348 on the model of both Paris and Bologna. Its foundation was due to royal interest and a royal decision. Situated well away from a traditional older Europe racked by the notorious crises caused by the Schism, Prague University, elaborating on an existing *studium generale* of the religious orders, owed its existence and the favourable political terms that guaranteed its privileges and success to the patronage of a great sovereign, Charles IV. Before long – in 1372 – it was divided into a university of law and faculties of arts, medicine, and theology. It could draw on a wide supraregional recruitment area for its students and teachers, and consequently soon enjoyed an importance comparable to that of the older universities.

The intention of Charles IV was not to give what might be called a 'modern national Bohemian' education, however modern he might have appeared at the time, but to glorify the abstract principles of dynastic prestige and the universal preservation of sovereignty. At Charles's death his university was still not strong enough to ride out the political and religious troubles which cast a shadow over King Wenceslas's reign, and consequently declined. The narrow pro-Czech policy applied by the university at the time of the struggle between the archbishop and the supporters of Wyclif, especially later on, when John Huss became active, and between the king and the princes of the Holy Roman Empire, plunged the university into meaningless mediocrity at the beginning of the fifteenth century. The non-Czech professors and students left Prague in a body, to the great benefit of Vienna,

---

60 H. Millet, 'Les Pères du Concile de Pise (1409): édition d'une nouvelle liste', *Mélanges de l'Ecole française de Rome. Moyen Age. Temps modernes*, 93 (1981), 713–90; M. C. Miller, 'Participation at the Council of Pavia–Siena, 1423–1424', *Archivum historiae pontificiae*, 22 (1984), 389–406; P. Uiblein, 'Zu den Beziehungen der Wiener Universität zu anderen Universitäten im Mittelalter', in *Universities in the Late Middle Ages*, 188; A. Black, 'The Universities and the Council of Basle: collegium and concilium', in *Universities in the Late Middle Ages*, 513.

Heidelberg, and most of all Leipzig, which most nearly became the successor of Prague University.[61]

Prague University of course set the princes and authorities of the empire and of eastern central Europe an example worth imitating of a really successful national *studium generale*, a *studium* in the guise of an old universal European institution, but with a new look. It was this that inspired many of them in the fifteenth century to set up similar institutions of their own. But neither the Schism nor the new conciliar outlook could alter the fact that these *studia* needed papal privileges. It was consequently easier than ever to get these, but they no longer meant universal recognition; their importance was merely formal. Even so, adopting and adapting the statutes of older European universities did suggest an apparently universal equilibration and a uniformity not confined by frontiers.

In reality the authorities founded the new universities for their own political and religious ends; the foundation of universities at Leipzig (1409) and Rostock (1419) was quickly followed by that of seven others in the territory of the Holy Roman Empire, mainly at the expense of the secular authorities. But although these universities seemed to follow the traditional model and ideals, they had a distinctly regional slant. They were no longer founded for genuinely European reasons; it was rather the steady development of the Holy Roman Empire in the late Middle Ages as a group of independent territories that led princes and cities to found these universities, which enjoyed papal privileges granted by the popes to ensure papal supremacy. The universities were founded for a variety of reasons – a sovereign's ambition, the growing usefulness of scholars in public business, a prince's desire for prestige, and even piety or to bring economic relief to depressed areas, as in Louvain, Mainz, and Trier. All those universities, although superficially resembling their older universally-minded sisters, slowly changed in character. Their connections with the burghers and court circles were much stronger. Certainly, in spite of their outward conformity with the intentions of their founders, the universities enjoyed great freedom in their internal affairs, no less than their older sisters. They were not yet subject to the religious stranglehold of the state, as they were in the Reformation period. Spiritual and temporal interests could co-exist peaceably to a great extent and could even work together for a common purpose without disagreement.[62]

No less significant was the turn taken in the first half of the fifteenth century in the relationship between the Paris *studium* and the secular authorities, especially towards the end of the Hundred Years War. The university's

[61] P. Moraw, 'Die Universität Prag im Mittelalter. Grundzüge ihrer Geschichte im europäischen Zusammenhang', in *Die Universität zu Prag*, Schriften der sudetendeutschen Akademie der Wissenschaften und Künste, 7 (Munich, 1986), 9ff.
[62] E. Schubert, 'Motive and Probleme deutscher Universitätsgründungen des 15. Jahrhunderts', in P. Baumgart and N. Hammerstein (eds.), *Beiträge zu Problemen deutscher Universitätsgründungen der frühen Neuzeit*, Wolfenbütteler Forschungen, 4 (Nendeln, 1978), 13ff.

prospensity to intervene in political and religious affairs (so evident at the time of the Schism) continued during the spread of English domination in France and the foundation there of the dual monarchy. At the crucial points of this long crisis the University of Paris never failed to play a part of the first importance. Its apparently inconsistent behaviour towards the rival parties was in line with the openly pacifist views of its academics, who had no hesitation in proclaiming fidelity to the king of France, even if that king were an Englishman; but they did so to obtain the favour and protection of the crown, as they looked upon the *studium qua studium* as an institution governed by privileges granted by the popes as universal rulers. The representatives of the royal power, however, declared that the king of France was emperor in his kingdom and was not subject to any other authority there; but it was for the king only, and not for the pope or any other person, to create bodies such as the university and endow them with privileges; and that the University of Paris could therefore enjoy its privileges only by submitting to royal control and jurisdiction. The controversy – never a bitter one – ended in 1446 when Charles VII ordered all cases, including civil cases, relating to the University of Paris to be dealt with by the *Parlement*.[63] In 1452 the Cardinal Legate Guillaume d'Estouteville promulgated a general reform of the statutes of the University of Paris, mainly at the instigation of high officials of the crown, including the president of the *Parlement*, in obedience to the orders of the king himself.

Henceforth France tended to restrict drastically the immunities and privileges which the academics of the twelfth to fourteenth centuries had enjoyed before the complete consolidation of the French monarchy. Toulouse University, for example, recognized the *Parlement* of Toulouse as a referee in university controversies, and in the second half of the fifteenth century relied more and more on it to settle administrative difficulties in the university.[64]

At the end of the Middle Ages nearly all the principal states of Europe had universities of their own, founded on the authority of pope or emperor, but the supreme authorities of the *Respublica christianorum* did no more than grant certain initial privileges. Therefore the institutions they founded were completely dependent on their local authorities, especially the secular ones, for their administration and operation. Let us take as an example the Louvain *studium*, founded by Martin V in 1425 at the request of John IV, duke of Brabant, the inhabitants of the city, and the chapter of St Peter: the ecclesiastical authority reserved the right to award the *licentia ubique docendi*, and the provost of the chapter of St Peter was appointed chancellor with the power to award academic degrees, but the *studium* began to function only because of the financial support of the duke and citizens, who sincerely

---

63 J. Verger, 'The University of Paris at the end of the Hundred Years' War', in *Universities in Politics*, 47–78.
64 Smith, *University of Toulouse* (note 36), 183ff.

wanted to have efficient university schools.[65] Rulers were convinced of the
social importance of universities, not least as training centres for their own
civil servants. At the petition of Louis II, king of Sicily and count of Provence,
Alexander V created by bull in 1409 a *studium generale* in Aix-en-Provence
with the privileges of Paris and Toulouse. To be sure of the viability of the
new institution, Louis II compelled his Provençal students to study at Aix
only.[66]

In fourteenth- and fifteenth-century Italy, as the free communes and citizen
Signorie were replaced by larger territorial states, the organization and distribution of the *studia* were correspondingly affected. Most of them had come
into being spontaneously in the thirteenth and fourteenth centuries, and had
been consolidated by the zeal of the local government. Like rulers elsewhere,
the fifteenth-century Italian princes and republican oligarchies were ambitious to possess *studia* renowned for the quality of their teaching and able to
train a ruling class and a professional élite. Thus both the Visconti and the
Sforza dynasties of the dukes of Milan, tried to make the Pavia *studium
generale* the principal university in the dukedom, to the especial detriment of
Parma. They restricted as much as they could the rector's jurisdiction and the
powers of the *universitas* to make its own regulations, and tried to transfer
them to the ducal government; and, by taking over the financial administration of the *studium*, they assumed control over the selection and payment of
teachers and regulation of its teaching.[67]

The Aragonese sovereigns of Naples adopted similar methods when they
refounded the old Hohenstaufen *studium generale*, which had suffered a
serious decline towards the end of Angevin rule. They renewed 'public participation in the organization of the school and in the formation of a body of
teachers paid from the public purse'. The Aragonese princes had previously
founded a *studium* in Sicily: in 1434 Alfonso V the Magnanimous approved
the opening of a university in Catania, probably at the suggestion of dignitaries of the royal council having connections with that city, and perhaps to
compensate Catania for the transfer of the royal court to Palermo. The new
studium generale was granted privileges by Pope Eugenius IV, and from the
very beginning was controlled and administered by the central authority and
the citizen commune, in conflict with the bishop-chancellor (who was
empowered to award doctorates) over the collection of income for the benefit

---

[65] E. J. M. van Eijl, 'The Foundation of the University of Louvain', in *Universities in the Late
Middle Ages*, 29–41.

[66] For the Aix *studium*: D. Maffei, *Giuristi medievali e falsificazioni editoriali del primo Cinquecento* (Frankfurt-on-Main, 1979), 7–9, 13–15, 40–2, 68.

[67] M. C. Zorzoli, 'Interventi dei duchi e del Senato di Milano per l'Università di Pavia (secoli
XV–XVI)', in *Università e società*, 553–73; M. G. Di Renzo Villata, 'Scienza giuridica e legisla-
zione nell'età sforzesca', in *Gli Sforza a Milano e in Lombardia e i loro rapporti con gli Stati
italiani ed europei (1450–1535)* (Milan, 1982), 65–145. For the Parma *studium*: C. Piana,
'L'Università di Parma nel Quattrocento', in *Parma e l'Umanesimo italiano* (Padua, 1986), 108.

of the university. The college of teachers and the *universitas scholarium* never had any influence to speak of.[68] The popes lavished special care on the Rome *studium*, behaving towards it like secular princes, and the citizens of Florence did much to help their *studium*, spending large sums to pay its teachers.[69] The Venetian republic tightened its grip on the Padua *studium*, and the counts (later dukes) of Savoy and the Turin commune established and organized a prestigious centre of learning.[70] Even minor Italian states like the marquisate of Este and the republic of Siena worked zealously to provide themselves with schools and teachers of a high standard, competing with richer cities able to offer greater inducements.[71]

As has recently been pointed out,[72] all the *studia* that flourished in Italy in the late Middle Ages vied with each other in recruiting masters at high salaries and offering students better living conditions. This explains why governments had to enact protectionist laws, why they carefully administered the finances of the *studium*, and why it was general practice to restrict the powers of rectors of *universitates* to civil law cases, and sometimes as well to minor criminal cases. All in all, Italian centres of learning gradually became provincialized, although some of the best teachers remained continually on the move from one *studium* to another[73] and there was an influx of students of various nationalities. Academics in Italy thus became more and more closely associated with the ruling oligarchy, composed of the richest families, who filled the principal public offices and the most sensitive diplomatic posts, and who acted as subtle mediators between the universities and the shifting kaleidoscope of politics and society.

---

68 A. Romano, *'Legum doctores' e cultura giuridica nella Sicilia aragonese. Tendenze, opere, ruoli* (Milan, 1984), 183–92. For Naples: Cortese, 'Sulla scienza giuridica' (note 40), 43 n. 24.

69 D. S. Chambers, 'Studium Urbis and Gabella Studii: the University of Rome in the Fifteenth Century', in C. H. Clough (ed.), *Cultural Aspects of the Italian Renaissance. Essays in Honor of Paul Oskar Kristeller* (New York, 1976), 68–110; K. Park, 'The Readers at the Florentine Studio According to the Communal Fiscal Records (1357–1380, 1413–1446)', *Rinascimento*, 20 (1980), 249–310.

70 For the Padua *studium* and Venice: F. Dupuigrenet Desroussilles, 'L'Università di Padova dal 1405 al Concilio di Trento', in *Storia della cultura veneta*, vol. III: 2 (Vicenza, 1980), 616ff. For Turin: E. Bellone, *Il primo secolo di vita della Università di Torino (sec. XV–XVI). Ricerche ed ipotesi sulla cultura nel Piemonte quattrocentesco* (Turin, 1986).

71 Piana, 'Università di Parma' (note 67), 104. For Siena: L. Zdekauer, *Lo Studio di Siena nel Rinascimento* (Milan, 1894).

72 P. Denley, 'Recent Studies on Italian Universities of the Middle Ages and Renaissance', *History of Universities*, I (1981), 200–1.

73 P. Nardi, 'Umanesimo e cultura giuridica nella Siena del Quattrocento', *Bullettino senese di storia patria*, 88 (1981), 244–53.

SELECT BIBLIOGRAPHY

Baldwin, J. W. and Goldthwaite, R. A. (eds.) *Universities in Politics. Case Studies from the Late Middle Ages and Early Modern Period*, Baltimore/London, 1972.

Benson, R. L. and Constable, G. (eds) *Renaissance and Renewal in the Twelfth Century*, Cambridge, Mass., 1982; reprint, Oxford, 1985.

Classen, P. *Studium und Gesellschaft im Mittelalter*, ed. J. Fried, Schriften der M.G.H., 29, Stuttgart, 1983.

Kuttner, S. 'Papst Honorius III und das Studium des Zivilrechts', *Gratian and the Schools of Law 1140–1234*, London, 1983, 79–101.

Lawrence, C. H. 'The University in State and Church', in J. I. Catto (ed.), *The History of the University of Oxford*, vol. I, Oxford, 1984, 97–150.

Meyhöfer, M. 'Die kaiserlichen Stiftungsprivilegien für Universitäten', *Archiv für Urkundenforschung*, 4 (1912), 294–314, 395–413.

Post, G. 'Parisian Masters as a Corporation, 1200–1246', *Speculum*, 9 (1934), 421–45 (reprinted in G. Post, *Studies in Medieval Legal Thought. Public Law and the State, 1100–1322*, Princeton, 1964, 27–60).

Rossi, G. '"Universitas scholarium" e Comune (sec. XII–XIV)', *Studi e memorie per la storia dell' Università di Bologna*, new series, I (1956), 197–227.

Swanson, R. N. *Universities, Academics and the Great Schism*, Cambridge, 1979.

Università e società nei secoli XII–XVI. Atti del nono convegno internazionale di studio tenuto a Pistoia nei giorni 20–25 settembre 1979, Pistoia, 1982.

CHAPTER 4

MANAGEMENT AND RESOURCES

ALEKSANDER GIEYSZTOR

GENERAL UNIVERSITY STRUCTURE

The history of the European university is the history of many universities, of which some eighty existed in the Middle Ages. They varied greatly in antiquity, permanence, and the quality of their teaching and research. Nevertheless, it is possible to detect some regularities, notably in the shaping influence of two archetypes, those of Bologna and Paris (see chapter 2), and in the use of the two main Latin terms which designated the medieval university: *studium generale* (or more simply *studium*) and *universitas scholarium* (or *universitas magistrorum et scholarium*). These reflect two features of its organization. A *studium generale* arose spontaneously or was founded by papal or imperial charter, and had the right to grant its alumni permission to teach at any university (*licentia ubique docendi*). The term *universitas* was of much wider scope. In law, it meant any type of corporation or community.[1]

Like every corporate body in the Middle Ages the universities were, to some extent, distinguished by their privileges or, as they were then called, their 'liberties and immunities'. The first and most important of these privileges was autonomy, that is, the university's recognized right to act as a corporate body in dealing with the outside world, to supervise the recruitment of its members, whether teachers or students, and to make its own regulations and enforce them by exercising some degree of internal jurisdiction. Other privileges, though, were enjoyed by individuals as members of the corporate body. Teachers and students alike enjoyed a personal status. This appeared in the twelfth century and took firm shape in the thirteenth. It owed much to canon law, supplemented by the *Authentica Habita* (1155), the scholar's statute. This was both the cause and outcome of a growing ecclesiastical authority over universities, including the Mediterranean universities of

---

[1] O. Weijers, *Terminologie des universités au XIIIe siècle* (Rome, 1987), 14–26, 34–51.

law or medicine (see chapter 2). The students (often themselves called 'clerks' and distinguished by their tonsure), like clerics already in minor orders or monks or priests, were subject to certain restrictions, being forbidden to bear arms or wear 'secular' clothes, and usually to marry. But they also claimed to be answerable only to ecclesiastical courts and to enjoy the exemptions from taxation and military service allowed to the clergy. In comparison with ordinary clerics, indeed, members of universities enjoyed exceptional advantages. Their person and property were theoretically exempt from seizure or arbitrary summons (*ius non trahi*). To a great extent they were not subject to the jurisdiction of the local ecclesiastical authorities and could appeal directly to the pope or his representative. They were entitled to enjoy the income of ecclesiastical benefices without being resident in them.

By the end of the Middle Ages, university privileges, although not directly challenged, were less absolute. Civic authorities had begun to take the place of the church in guaranteeing university franchises, but also in restricting them. The personal privileges of students and masters, although not abolished, were subject to growing supervision. Their affairs were increasingly dealt with by lay officers and courts, which made it their business to hunt down persons posing as students.[2]

Such influences, together with factors such as the number of students, the founder's intention, or local pragmatic arrangements, contributed to the shaping of the organization and structure of the *studium generale*. University communities had subdivisions such as faculties, nations, and colleges, with similar corporative rights and organizations. The nature of these internal corporations determined the character of the whole university and requires some consideration at this point.[3]

FACULTIES

Besides its old meaning of a discipline or field study, from the mid-thirteenth century onwards *facultas* meant a body teaching a discipline, i.e. arts, law, medicine, or theology. Teachers and students were members of these faculties, and consequently also of the *studium generale*. Faculties were the most important divisions in the University of Paris, and in other institutions following the Parisian pattern.

The Bologna tradition was different. The *studium generale* of Bologna was, like its daughters, a cluster of universities, each for students of only one

[2] Kibre, *Privileges*; P. Classen, 'Libertas scolastica – Scholarenprivilegien – Akademische Freiheit im Mittelalter', in P. Classen, *Studium und Gesellschaft im Mittelalter*, ed. J. Fried, Schriften der MGH, 29 (Stuttgart, 1983), 238–84.

[3] Most of the data can be found in Rashdall, *Universities*; Cobban, *Medieval Universities*; Kibre, *Nations*; Kibre, *Privileges*; Weijers, *Terminologie* (note 1); Denifle, *Entstehung*; Kaufmann, *Deutsche Universitäten*. With a few exceptions, no further reference will be made to these publications.

discipline, and it was divided into two universities or 'nations' (*nationes*), each for students of a particular geographical origin. The teachers and the students born in Bologna did not belong to these *universitates*, because it was supposed that, as will be seen, students of Bolognese origin did not need a nation to protect them. Professors had their own corporation, the *collegium doctorum*, which was completely distinct from the students' corporation (see chapter 5).

Not all the Italian universities moulded on the Bologna archetype embodied this structure in its entirety. In the most elaborate form of the student university, which was limited to Bologna and Padua, the *studium generale* consisted of two universities, the *universitas legistarum*, which can be called the law faculty, and the *universitas artistarum et medicorum* (faculty of arts and medicine), *universitas* meaning the community of students. The faculty of theology was in the hands of the mendicant orders and existed on the fringe of the *studium generale*. Each faculty was divided into two 'universities', the *universitas citramontanorum* of students from the Italian peninsula, and the *universitas ultramontanorum* of students from beyond the Alps.

Each of these was further divided into nations for smaller geographic areas. The number and names of these nations constantly changed in the course of time, following and reflecting changes in the geographical recruitment of students. Both the law university and the arts university had a rector, who was a student member elected by the *consiliarii* or presidents of each nation. Although Padua most closely followed the Bologna pattern, it was only after two centuries of adaptation and reorganization. Padua was founded in 1222, but the *universitas legistarum* did not consist of two law faculties (as was the case in Bologna) until it was reorganized in 1260. A theological faculty arose there in 1363 on the fringe of the *studium*, and (as at Bologna) it was in the hands of the mendicants. The university of arts and medicine was originally subordinate to the jurists; it emancipated itself in 1399, although appeals were still addressed to the rector of the law faculty.

Other Italian *studia* attracted too few students from a wide area to justify so complex an organization as that of Bologna and Padua in its full form. Siena had a law university with ultramontane and cismontane universities, each with several nations, but its arts faculty did not have nations. In Ferrara the law university and the arts university were both divided into nations, but not into ultramontane and cismontane universities. Pisa and Perugia only had one *universitas* covering all disciplines, with one rector and only a few nations. The last group of universities had too few students, and certainly too few foreigners, to need nations. They are nearer to the northern pattern (e.g. Fermo, Parma). The Universities of Naples, founded by Frederick II in 1224,[4]

---

[4] *La Fondazione Fridericiana dell'Università di Napoli* (Naples, 1988).

and of the Roman court (*studium curiae* or *sacri palatii*), created in 1244–5 by Pope Innocent IV, were authoritarian establishments not fitting into the general pattern. Both universities started with a law and a theological faculty only, and were intended solely to educate the ruler's ecclesiastical and civil servants. After 1323 the *studium curiae* introduced oriental languages, and in the fifteenth century philosophy and medicine. About 1500, during the pontificate of Leo X, it merged with the *studium urbis*, the Roman urban university known as the Sapienza, whose structure was also simple.

In other countries, too, the influence of Bologna can be traced. The Spanish universities founded during the thirteenth century by the kings of Castile, and (more particularly) by those of Aragon, were modelled on Bologna although they also followed patterns of their own. They were student universities, but less independent than Bologna because more strictly controlled by the crown. Some other universities (those of Montpellier, Orléans, Angers, and Prague, for example) can also be related to the Bologna archetype, without having conformed closely to it. That at Montpellier arose spontaneously from local schools, in particular from the city's medical schools, well known since the first half the twelfth century. The papal legate granted it the status of a medical university in 1220, as a *universitas medicorum tam doctorum quam discipulorum*. An arts university came into existence in 1242, with statutes imposed by the bishop, and in about 1280 a law university, which after 1339 took the form of a students' university with a separate doctoral college. The University of Orléans arose from the twelfth-century arts schools and developed after a secession from Paris in 1229; but it taught only one discipline, law. Its organization combined elements from both archetypes, Bologna and Paris. Angers, another law university arising from the same secession, added faculties of theology, medicine, and arts to its law university in the fifteenth century.

The Prague *studium* is an interesting example of the flexibility of medieval institutions. This first university of the Holy Roman Empire was founded in 1346 by the Emperor Charles IV. It then consisted of four faculties, as at Paris. It was headed by a rector, who was not, however, connected with the arts faculty as in Paris. For political reasons (see chapter 3), the law faculty broke away in 1372 and founded an independent law university on Italian lines.

Besides this type of organization, in which university and faculty are more or less synonymous, there was another, that of the four faculties, the model which originated in Paris. It consisted of one lower faculty, arts, and three higher faculties, theology, law, and medicine. (After Pope Honorius III forbade the teaching of civil law in Paris in 1219, the law faculty taught only canon law – the University of Orléans can be considered as the civil law faculty of the Paris *studium*.) The masters, having quickly become aware of their own value, called these four faculties 'four rivers of paradise'. Saint

Bonaventure compared the arts to the foundations of a building, law and medicine to its walls, and theology to its roof and summit.

The Paris model was adopted by the *studia* of north-western and central Europe. The German universities, founded in the fourteenth and fifteenth centuries, were moulded on the Paris archetype and adopted its statutes. Sometimes, as at Louvain (founded in 1425), statutes were copied from Cologne, a daughter of Paris founded in 1388.[5] An ideal multidisciplinary university had four faculties, but in the thirteenth century some universities had only two or three. The Scottish universities offer an interesting example of difference between norm and reality. The *studium generale* consisted of the four traditional faculties, but until the end of the early modern period two of these (law and medicine), or perhaps three, were merely 'paper faculties'. Only arts students could follow a whole curriculum at a Scottish university.

One source of diversity of organization arose from the fact that, until the end of the thirteenth century, the popes protected the Parisian monopoly of theology and objected to the foundation of faculties of theology elsewhere. Another source of differentiation was that, although almost every university had a medical faculty, some of these could hardly survive, especially in the Holy Roman Empire or Denmark, and did not always have as many as 1 per cent of the total student population. The arts faculty inevitably had the most masters and students especially north of the Alps. Although it was regarded as preparing students for the three higher faculties, most of its alumni never entered a higher faculty. At the waning of the Middle Ages law faculties gained importance, and were increasingly attended by students attracted by the brilliant careers open to talented young graduates in law (see chapters 10 to 13).

Much of the administration of the university was done by the faculties, particularly in universities which had no nations, or in which nations were not important. They provided appropriate channels for active participation in the organization and management of the *studium generale*. As a corporation the faculty had its own head, usually called *decanus* (dean), a bursar (*receptor*), beadles, a common seal, and statutes. The dean first appears in the thirteenth century in Paris and Montpellier, and in the fourteenth century elsewhere. At first, he was the senior master still engaged in teaching. The dean was the chairman of the congregation constituted by the masters of the faculty; he was responsible for administration and teaching, disputations, and examinations. In Oxford, where the schools first appeared in 1208–9, the faculty of arts held a dominant position as in Paris, and the higher faculties did not have deans. In the Italian faculty-universities the rector had the same functions as the deans in the *studia* north of the Alps. The qualifications required to become a dean, the methods of election, and his term of office

---

[5] J. Goossens, 'De oudste algemene statuten van de universiteiten van Keulen en Leuven. Een vergelijkende tekstanalyse', *Archives et Bibliothèques de Belgique*, 48 (1977), 42–78.

varied from university to university. It is not always clear how a university or its subdivisions were organized.

STATUTES

One would think that statutes are far and away the best source of our knowledge of the structure and management of the medieval university. This, however, is not necessarily the case. Very few university statutes, in the strict sense of the term, have come down to us from the thirteenth century. The privileges granted by the papacy (as in 1215 and 1231 for Paris, 1214 for Oxford, 1219 for Bologna and 1220 for Montpellier) merely stated – and gave papal support in – certain matters of dispute between the university and the outside authorities, or within the university. Otherwise popes left universities to make their own regulations for programmes, curricula, examinations, salaries for master and beadles, mutual aid, university offices, student discipline, dress, and lodging.

These regulations were probably still fairly fluid and in some cases only a matter of unwritten custom. Even when written down, this was apparently done too informally for anything more than fragments (often incorporated into later codes) to have survived. The first university statutes (*strictu sensu*) still preserved are undoubtedly those of Cambridge, dating from between 1236 and 1254.[6] A text recently discovered in Bologna (a very incomplete one, for it relates to little else than the *puncta taxata* of teachers of law) has been ascribed to the year 1252.[7] Elsewhere, we do not find any really orderly sets of statutes before the fourteenth and fifteenth centuries. It is not easy to see how those were applied and it would be rash to assume, as a few commentators have done, that such rules were current in previous centuries.

In the older universities statutes sometimes introduced reforms to correct abuses, and this led to new regulations unknown in the thirteenth century. This is doubtless true of the Paris statutes of the 1360s and of the general reform of 1452. In Toulouse between 1309 and 1329, several important statutes stabilized the administration of a university already active for decades past. The law university at Montpellier received its statutes in 1339. In Bologna the first complete texts are not earlier than 1317 and 1432; in Salamanca they date from 1411. At Oxford the oldest collection of statutes was compiled in 1313, and incorporates older provisions.[8]

[6] R. K. Hannay, 'Early University Institutions at St Andrews and Glasgow, a Comparative Study' *Scottish Historical Review*, 11 (1914), 266–83; M. B. Hackett, *The Original Statutes of Cambridge University. The Text and its History* (Cambridge, 1970).

[7] D. Maffei, 'Un trattato di Bonaccorso degli Elisei e i più antichi statuti dello studio di Bologna nel manoscritto 22 della Robins Collection', *Bulletin of Medieval Canon Law*, new series, 5 (1975), 73–101. Concerning the *puncta taxata*, see chapter 12, p. 398.

[8] Rashdall, *Universities*, vol. I, 173–5, 443–7; vol. II, 83–5, 131–3, 168–70; *History of Oxford*, 53–4.

Many of the new universities founded at the end of the Middle Ages were given more or less complete statutes from the beginning (the oldest example appears to be that of Lérida in 1300).[9] These texts were, however, directly inspired by those of other universities, or even copied from them. We cannot therefore be sure that they were really suitable to local conditions or, therefore, that they were strictly applied.

In short, although there is always something to be learned from the statutes that have come down to us, it is wise to compare them with other sources, such as day-to-day administrative documents, masters' manuscripts, and reconstituted graduate courses. This often reveals great discrepancies.

NATIONS

The organization of the early medieval university was also shaped by another corporation, the nation already mentioned above. It first arose spontaneously, through the efforts of students or students and masters; later it was introduced into the organization of newly founded universities. In many universities the nations was an essential feature; often it was the heads of nations who elected the rectors and were members of the board of the *studium*.

In the student universities of Bologna and Padua the universities of law, arts, and medicine had each been divided into two *universitates* (*citramontana* and *ultramontana*), themselves divided into nations for smaller geographic areas (see p. 110 and chapter 9). The recruitment of other Italian universities was too regional to need this complex organization. It reflected their attraction for certain European countries or regions. For instance, in Perugia there were only three nations – German, French, and Catalan – for *ultramontani*. Nations in the Paris type of university were organized rather differently. To begin with, in Paris only the largest faculty, that of arts, had nations. These had constituted themselves soon after the university was founded, on the basis of a loose geographical classification; there were four, namely France, Picardy, Normandy, and England (the English nation included students from central and northern Europe). They comprised masters of arts from the arts faculty, and included professors of higher faculties with a degree in arts. The congregation of the nation was headed by a proctor (*procurator*) chosen for a period of one month by the masters and often re-elected several times. The nation had its own seal and registers, *libri nationis*, revenue, and expenditure, and became an important part of university life.[10]

Elsewhere in universities north of the Alps nations followed a variety of patterns. The law university of Orléans, one of the most international medi-

---

[9] Rashdall, *Universities*, vol. II, 93–4.
[10] See also G. C. Boyce, *The English–German Nation in the University of Paris during the Middle Ages* (Bruges, 1927).

eval institutions, had ten nations until 1532, being organized like the *universitas legistarum* of an Italian *studium*. At Oxford the border between the two nations, the northerners (*boreales*, who included the Scots) and southerners (*australes*, who included Irish and Welsh), was considered to be the river Trent, and masters of arts were headed by their respective proctors. As early as 1274, however, the nations were abolished because they were continually in conflict with each other. Later, the nation system was revived in the British Isles in the arts faculties of the three Scottish universities (St Andrews 1411, Glasgow 1450–1, and Aberdeen 1494), although the recruitment of these universities was purely Scottish. In this they followed the Iberian system. Spanish and Portuguese *studia generalia* were attended mainly by students from the Iberian peninsula. At Salamanca the four nations corresponded to the ecclesiastical provinces of Spain. In the Lérida *studium* only the law students were divided into nations; but there six of the twelve nations were foreigners (from Narbonne, Gascony and Provence, France and Burgundy, Italy, Germany, and the British Isles). In other Spanish universities nations were of minor importance.

In central Europe, the Paris model was at first followed in the nations system as in other respects. In Prague four nations (Czechs, Poles, Bavarians, and Saxons) included all the students. Their *consiliarii*, students or bachelors, were members of the university council together with the masters. In Vienna there were four nations covering all faculties; their student members took part in electing the proctors. The University of Leipzig also had four nations, but only professors were entitled to take part in the congregations. In Cracow, Erfurt and Cologne the division into nations was not authorized. Four nations were formed in Louvain, but never became important there.

At first nations were independent corporations. Their strength and influence in university matters varied from university to university, but they all had almost the same structure and organization. Proctors (*procuratores*) or *consiliarii* (in some Italian nations) headed the nations, and had administrative and financial powers, and to some extent jurisdiction; they took part in the university bodies as counsellors of the rector. The nations had sometimes their own bursars (*receptores*), and always their beadles (*bedelli*) as in Bologna. In Paris the nations elected every year one principal beadle (*bedellus maior*, the proctor's man) and a *subbedellus* or *bedellus minor* to assist him. The beadle's insignia were the verges. In Paris the proctors of the nations appointed, swore in, and paid the messengers (*nuntii volantes minores*, or *ordinarii*), who bore messages and money between members of the nations and their families. In the later Middle Ages the proctors also appointed principal messengers, *nuntii maiores*, functioning as financiers, bankers, and money-changers in the service of the university.

The books kept by proctors, bursars, librarians, and other officials of the nation are some of the most important sources of our knowledge of university life in the Middle Ages. They give information on the geographical and social origin and everyday life of members of the nation, and on its finances. College sources give similar information.

COLLEGES

As time passed, another university corporation, the college (*collegium* – not to be confused with the *collegium doctorum*, as is explained in chapter 5), came to surpass the nations in importance. In some universities of the later Middle Ages, collegiate establishments determined the structure and management of the university or faculty. The Collegium Artistarum (1390) of Heidelberg housed almost all the salaried masters of the faculty of arts, and the Louvain arts faculty was divided into four 'pedagogies' (colleges). The College of Glasgow for undergraduate students was always identified with the 'university' in the popular mind, since most of its students were arts undergraduates.

The college, or *domus scholarium* as it was first called, began as a boarding-house for poor students, then became an autonomous or semi-autonomous academic community of men living and studying together in an endowed building. These men, teachers and pupils, might come from a particular region or study the same discipline. In the twelfth and thirteenth centuries founders and benefactors of colleges especially promoted arts and theology, and in the fourteenth and fifteenth centuries canon and civil law. Colleges for physicians were always a rarity. (For more information on the college see chapter 7.)

At the University of Paris there were colleges almost from the beginning. They began as *hospitia*, boarding-houses for groups of students or fellows called *socii*. A few, including the first college, the Collège des Dix-huit, founded for eighteen needy students in 1180, and the College of St Thomas du Louvre founded in 1186, received endowments; there were even monastic colleges for students of theology. About 1257 Robert of Sorbon founded the college known as La Sorbonne, so that there should be a sufficient number of non-monastic students of theology. It housed first sixteen, then thirty fellowship holders (*bursarii*) and six young masters of arts working for a doctorate in theology. Louis IX endowed the college with a plot of land lying near the ancient Roman *thermae*. It was managed by a board of church and university dignitaries, and administered by a principal (*provisor*), who was appointed, a *prior* or *lator rotuli* elected every year by the fellows to record their duties, and four proctors. Other colleges such as the Collège de Navarre (1304), whose seventy students were divided into three classes – grammar, arts, and theology – remained basically student colleges. During the fourteenth and fifteenth centuries the founders' motives changed; willingness to aid poor young men was supplanted by the need to provide comfortable living conditions for an élite of monastic or noble students.[11] *Bursales* who studied with a grant had a stricter and less luxurious life in college than the *commensales* or commoners who paid for their own lodging (see chapter 7). As early as the fourteenth century lecturers were attracted by the houses, facilities, and libraries owned by the colleges. In the following century lectures began to be held in the colleges for external students as well as for the fellows (*bursarii*), the university retaining the right to control the colleges. By the end of the fifteenth century Paris had about seventy colleges, including monastic ones. Some were foundations for foreigners (Danes, Scots, Lombards, and Germans).

In Paris, the internal administration of the college was usually carried out by internal officers. External authorities appointed the head of the college, saw to it that vacant fellowships or *bursae* were filled, and so controlled college life. The managers of college properties often came from outside. In Oxford and Cambridge, on the contrary, colleges had little adminstrative connection with the governing bodies of the university; they organized their own endowment and benefited from the university's teaching and academic degrees; they elected their heads and co-opted the fellows, who governed them under their own charters and statutes. Thus colleges in England did not follow the course taken by Paris. In the twelfth and early thirteenth centuries undergraduate students of moderate means could get lodging and limited teaching facilities in halls and hostels. In the course of the thirteenth century the first colleges were founded to help less well-off bachelors of arts or masters of arts to continue their studies in the higher faculties. The first English 'graduate' college was Merton College, founded in 1264; Balliol College was established in 1261–6 but received its formal charter only in 1282; University College arose *c.* 1280. The first college at Cambridge, Peterhouse, was established in 1284, modelling itself on Merton. King's Hall College, Cambridge (founded in the early fourteenth century), and New College, Oxford (founded in 1379), were the first colleges to admit undergraduate students. Other colleges followed their lead. In 1550 or thereabouts many more college fellows than students lodged in halls or hostels. Oxford still had about eighty-nine halls in 1444, but in 1552 only eight, housing about 200 students in all. The thirteen colleges at that time had 450 students.[12] Increasingly, tuition at Oxford was given in the colleges rather than in the university, and consequently undergraduates were encouraged to apply for a college fellowship. As everywhere else, the regular orders had their own colleges with full accommodation and teaching facilities. On the continent, Louvain University (founded in 1425) had a flourishing collegiate life. To compare it with

---

[11] A. L. Gabriel, 'Motivation of the Founders of Medieval Colleges', in A. L. Gabriel, *Garlandia. Studies in the History of the Medieval University* (Notre Dame, 1969), 211–23.

[12] A. B. Cobban, *Medieval English Universities: Oxford and Cambridge to c. 1500* (Cambridge, 1988), 158.

Oxford, before 1500 most arts students were housed in the four *paedagogia* called after the houses where they were founded: Lily, Porc, Falcon, and Castle. These provided full accommodation and tuition, mainly for freshmen. There were also five residential colleges (without teaching) for students of theology and law. In 1526, 31.8 per cent of the 1,821 registered students lived in collegiate establishments (17.9 per cent in the four *paedagogia*, 11.6 per cent in colleges, and 2.3 per cent in religious houses), 52.2 per cent rented a room in a private house, and the rest lived at home.[13]

In central Europe, colleges were primarily or exclusively for masters. In Prague twelve *magistri* endowed with a prebend from the college chapel made up the Collegium Carolinum founded in 1361, and they co-opted their fellow members. The Collegium was important in that university meetings, and lectures, were held in the college building. Simultaneously, in Vienna there was the Collegium Ducale for endowed masters. In Cracow there were three colleges with living accommodation for professors: the Collegium Maius or Regium (1400) which had a flourishing library, and was headed by a provost; the Collegium Minus (1449); and the Collegium Juridicum (1403), which had a small adjacent student hostel, the Bursa Jerusalem. Cracow also had other hospices for poor students, such as the Bursa Pauperum (1417). In Erfurt, the earliest college, Collegium Maius, for masters of arts, probably dates from the official foundation of the university in 1379, and the Collegium Amplonianum or Porta Coeli for jurists was founded in 1412. In other German universities there were professors' colleges, and houses for poor scholars.

In southern Europe colleges were never as important as in north-western Europe – certainly not in the Middle Ages; until the Reformation and Counter-Reformation they did not acquire any such constitutional or educational significance. Italian students always had close ties with the towns. They lodged with the townspeople, and shared their living conditions and political preoccupations. The oldest colleges in Bologna were originally intended by their founders to supply lodging, board, and financial assistance only to a few needy students and provided no teaching. They were the College of Avignon, founded for eight poor students in 1267 by the bishop of Avignon, and the Collegium Brescianum founded in 1326; in 1436–7 both merged with the Collegium Gregorianum, a later foundation. The largest was the Spanish College (1367) with thirty students – eight of theology, eighteen of canon law, and four of medicine. They lived in the college for seven years, and theologians and medical students could stay longer after receiving their doctoral degree. The students came from Spanish dioceses chosen by the founder of the college, Cardinal Gil Albornoz. Candidates had to pass an

---

[13] E. De Maesschalck, 'De "goede" en de "eeuwige" student. Tucht en huisvesting te Leuven in de 15e en 16e eeuw', *Alumni Leuven*, 9 (1978), 11–15.

entrance examination. Poverty and competent grounding 'at least in grammar', and for theologians and medical students logic, were required. They were given a room and board, two suits of clothing a year, and a yearly stipend. The college was run on fairly democratic principles, but internal discipline was strict. Every year the scholars elected the rector and *consiliarii*. Important financial questions were settled by the general assembly. The patronage of the college was vested in the bishops and chapters of the above-mentioned dioceses, plus two members of the Albornoz family.[14] In Padua after 1363, the Collegium Tornacense and seven other colleges housed small numbers of students.

The Collegio di Spagna in Bologna was taken as a model for the Spanish colleges which emerged in Salamanca in the late fourteenth century. The most famous of the Spanish medieval colleges was the Colegio Viejo or Colegio Mayor de San Bartolomé, founded at Salamanca in 1401 for ten canonists and five theologians. Colleges in provincial France were primarily boarding-houses for needy students. Toulouse took the lead with the very early secular College of Vidal Gautier (1243) and the College of Montlezun (1391). The reason why so few colleges arose in Italy and in France south of the Loire is clear. Most of the wealthier and more mature students attended the law and medical faculties. They did not need cheap hostels, but preferred more comfortable rooms in private houses and freedom from the restraints of a college or cloister (for college life, see chapter 7). Moreover, the well-organized student nations offered students all kinds of assistance and financial and juridical help (as is shown by the minutes of the proctors of the German nations in Bologna, Padua, and Orléans). Theology was dominated by the mendicant orders, which had their own institutions. There were not many young grammar and arts students in those southern universities, and there was therefore no need for special accommodation for the few theologians or arts students of moderate means.

INTERNAL GOVERNMENT

Originally the bishop's representative was head of the *universitas*, with authority over students and masters. In the course of the thirteenth century different corporations were formed in the *studia generalia*. Most of the judicial powers of the bishop's representative passed to an elected head of the new institutions, the rector.[15] Except in England and Spain, as will be explained later, the role of the bishop's representative became, generally speaking, more formal. Depending on the constitution of the *studium* the rector was chosen from among the students, as in Bologna, or the masters, as in Paris. In

[14] B. M. Marti, *The Spanish College at Bologna in the Fourteenth Century* (Philadelphia, 1966).
[15] For a general review, see O. Eissfeldt, 'Rektor. Geschichte und Bedeutung des Universitätsamtes', *Studium Generale*, 5 (1952), 384–92.

universities with a mixed type of constitution, the rector was a master but chosen by masters and students. For instance, in Orléans the rector was a master chosen by the nations; in Angers, after the reform of 1398, the rector was elected from among the licentiates by electors nominated by the nations.

A would-be rector had to fulfil certain requirements for election. He had to be mature (usually aged twenty-five years or over), a *clericus* (to exercise judicial authority over clerical students), wealthy (the office entailed much expenditure), a graduate, and of irreproachable conduct. His term of office varied from one university to another. The rector was the administrative head of the university, the executor of resolutions adopted in the assemblies, and the supervisor of the observance of privileges and statutes; he administered the university's finances, presided at its meetings, sealed its documents, and represented it in official affairs. One of his important tasks in the Middle Ages was to keep discipline and to preside over the university court sitting to judge and punish offending *suppositi* (matriculated members of the university). Indeed, the judicial autonomy of the *studium generale* was guaranteed by several privileges starting with the *Authentica Habita* (1155) of Frederick I Barbarossa. Theoretically, all *suppositi* were exempt from civil jurisdiction and even, to a certain extent, from local ecclesiastical jurisdiction. *Suppositi* were regarded as comprising students and teachers, and their wives, families, and servants; the external officials appointed by the university; and persons engaged in the production and sale of books (booksellers, copiers, illumina-tors, preparers of parchment, suppliers of paper, etc).

At first, each of the law universities (civil and canon) in Bologna was headed by a rector chosen by the students from among themselves. Although both the town and the professors initially disapproved of the institution of a student rector, they were forced to comply with it in the course of the first half of the thirteenth century. The professors had to take an oath of obedience to the rector. This led to a particular form of student leadership within the university, except, to some extent, concerning the organization of studies. By the end of the thirteenth century the two law universities held common congregations; the two rectors deputized for each other when one was absent; they may even have had the same seal. Meanwhile the arts and medical university also elected a rector, but it was not until the early fourteenth century that he enjoyed the same legal recognition and privileges as his colleague of the law university. At Padua the rector of the medical university was subordinate to his counterpart of the law university until the fourteenth century. In Italian universities the rector generally had no authority over teaching and examinations; these matters belonged to the *collegia doctorum*, either of medicine or of law. In Bologna the rector was elected for a two-year period. He took precedence over archbishops and even over cardinals and legates, but not over the bishop of Bologna. His title was *dignissimus*; the title *magnificus* did not appear until the end of the fifteenth century.

The rector's stipend came from half the total income of legal fines; sometimes he received an additional subvention from the common treasury. By the end of the Middle Ages he was appointed to a special student professorship, financed by the town. He had to cover the cost of his official expenses and was obliged to keep two servants. The tightening grip of the towns or rulers on their universities, and the financial burden of the office, limited students' willingness to accept this dignity.

Although at Bologna the rector was a student, his jurisdiction in civil matters inside the university was recognized in the oath taken by all university members. He had to ensure that statutory decisions were enforced and fines for misdemeanours collected. He could fine keepers of lodgings who rented rooms to students, and craftsmen working on the production of books. Whether his sentences against members or servants of the university were executed depended on the agreement of the public authority (the *comune* of Bologna). Both universities demanded that the rector's jurisdiction should apply whether the student was the plaintiff or the defendant, but the city authorities repeatedly rejected this demand. The rector had no jurisdiction in criminal affairs until the fifteenth century, when it was conceded where both parties were scholars. However, canon law forbade any jurisdiction by a layman over a clerk; any student could therefore acquire the immunities of an ecclesiastic, and as the rector of a university of students was usually a beneficed ecclesiastic he was not subject to municipal law.

Universities modelled on Bologna had similar forms of rectorship, though its power tended to be more restricted by the influence of the external authorities. In Coimbra, the two rectors were chosen from among, and by, the students, but as in the Spanish universities the rector's influence was limited. Like Bologna, Salamanca was headed by a student rector elected by the students through their nations. As in Italy, teaching was the preserve of the faculties' *collegia doctorum*, not the rector. But unlike Bologna, Salamanca limited the rector's jurisdiction to violation of the statutes; it was the chancellor who possessed the real powers of jurisdiction and administration. In *studia* under strong urban influence, like those of Aragon, Lérida, Valencia, and Barcelona, the chancellor and civil government shared the rector's powers.

The origins of the rector's office in Paris are quite different. The four nations each had *rectores* or *procuratores*; in 1249 they decided to elect one rector – a master – as head of the faculty of arts and virtually of the whole university. In the beginning his authority was limited to his own faculty, but because of the great numbers of arts students, and because the rector collected money from all the faculties, and administered it on behalf of the entire university, often in defence of the rights of the corporation, he gradually gained authority over the whole institution, probably during the last quarter of the thirteenth century. The masters of theology opposed his influence and by the end of the century the chancellor of Notre-Dame retained only the power to appoint examiners in arts and the prerogative of conferring the licence.

At Paris, the rector had very limited judicial power; the statutes gave him jurisdiction only over members and servants of the university. The punishments he was allowed to impose were fines, suspension, and expulsion; the actions he tried were disputes about the rent of hostels, complaints against craftsmen and merchants supervised by the university, and personal matters between masters and scholars. The rector was assisted by the proctors in the permanent court of the arts faculty, but there was a right of appeal to the whole university, which was decided by special deputies. Where university members and parties from outside the university were involved, the autonomy of the university was limited by ecclesiastical and lay courts. Such disputes were settled – according to the sphere of competence – by the diocesan court (bishop's court) or by the Châtelet (the court of the provost of Paris, acting as conservator of royal prerogatives), or by the court of the apostolic conservator in Paris.

The Scottish universities closely followed the Paris model. The proctors of the nations, existing only in the arts faculty, held a conclave to elect the rector. According to the founding papal bull (1453), the bishop-chancellor was the chief authority of the University of Glasgow; he delegated his power to the rector chosen by the proctors of the nations. Many French universities with large nations, such as Montpellier, Orléans, or Angers, had, however, a different pattern. Even where the constitution of the University of Toulouse followed that of Paris, the students' rights were recognized to a greater extent. The rector had to be a doctor, but was elected by the professors of all faculties and the students in law. At Montpellier the rector of the law faculty was chosen from among the students; the faculty, or rather the university, of medicine was on the contrary presided over by the chancellor, nominated by the bishop and three masters. His post resembles the chancellorship of the English universities, where in Oxford and Cambridge, the chancellor, was the representative of the bishop in the university as elsewhere (see pp. 129–33, on external government), but his power was never handed over to a rector. He exercised the full rights and activities of a rector elsewhere. The reasons are clear: as early as the beginning of the thirteenth century the *studia* of Oxford and Cambridge had obtained from their respective bishops, those of Lincoln and Ely, the right to elect their chancellors. The selected candidate was chosen from among the doctors in theology or canon law and had to be a member of the faculty of theology. So the chancellor became an internal rather than an external officer, always taking the chair at congregations and acting as rector. In the course of the fifteenth century the chancellor, who as a prominent personality was usually absent on duties elsewhere, delegated his powers to a vice-chancellor who by the close of the Middle Ages had become the *de facto* head of an English university. He had wide civil and criminal jurisdiction and power to excommunicate and imprison. Originally his was a spiritual jurisdiction over scholars, but it was gradually extended to cover other groups, townsfolk included. By royal charter, the chancellor had criminal and civil jurisdiction in actions in which one party was a clerk. After quarrels and disputes with the burgesses, the university, victorious since the mid-fourteenth century, practically governed the town of Oxford; the chancellor's court, and the newly established university steward, with his jury half of privileged university persons and half of townsmen, controlled legal procedure in the extensive university precinct. The inquisitorial police of the universities' delegate judges supervised the morals of the inhabitants.[16]

The central European universities are generally believed to have been founded on the Paris model, but examination of their statutes shows that this is not altogether true. Firstly, unlike Paris, the arts faculties in this area never had a monopoly of the rectorship; the rector could be chosen from any faculty. The faculty of arts was headed by a dean, as were the three other faculties. Secondly, the two oldest universities – Prague and Vienna – had a mixed type of organization. After the secession of 1372 the jurists of Prague had a separate student university with a student rector, whereas the other faculties were dominated by the masters. The jurist rector had jurisdiction, in civil suits and actions for damages, over university members, who had the right of appeal to the chancellor-archbishop. In 1397 the court of the rector with the *consiliarii* of the nations obtained full jurisdiction, civil, criminal, and spiritual, over lawsuits in which one party was a scholar. But, in Vienna too, in the early period, masters and students through their nations participated in electing the rector.

The first University of Cracow (1364) was also headed by a student rector, but the royal chancellor controlled the examinations (although according to the papal bull this task was to be the bishop's). In the second university (1400) the bishop was chancellor and confirmed the statutes. His representative, the vice-chancellor, managed the university finances with the help of the dean of St Florian's chapter and the rector. The rector was elected by masters and bachelors for one year, by indirect representational suffrage. He had to be at least a master of arts or a graduate in law or theology, and usually had a church prebend. The rector convoked the general congregation of masters, sometimes with graduates.[17] The rector tried civil suits and minor offences, but from 1410 onwards the university conservators, the deans of three cathedral chapters, defended the university's claim to cite defendants from all dioceses. In other universities in this part of Europe it seems that the rector had a

---

[16] Cobban, *Medieval English Universities* (note 12), 259ff.
[17] J. Dąbrowski, Z. Kozłowska-Budkowa, and K. Pieradzka, *Dzieje Uniwersytetu Jagiellonskiego*, vol. I (Cracow, 1964), 15–20, 57–71, 127–38.

fairly wide jurisdiction, but no direct spiritual jurisdiction.[18] Everywhere student power waned at the end of the Middle Ages, as did the importance of the nations. Some German universities, such as Leipzig, continued to elect a student rector, a young man of noble, perhaps princely, birth, but he was controlled by a vice-rector or, as in Rostock, by a promotor or *superintendens*. The latter was a permanent executive officer discharging real rectorial powers as the representative of the (merely honorary) rector. The election of a rector gradually passed to a small group; in Tübingen it was dominated by the regent masters.

The University of Naples is rather an exception. It was a state university, founded by the emperor (1224) and completely subject to royal authority. The jurisdiction of the scholars therefore did not belong to the rector but to the king's officer, the *iusticiarius scholarium*. In the administration of justice in criminal cases the *iusticiarius* was assisted by three assessors chosen by the students. In civil cases the crown respected the imperial privilege, the *Authentica Habita*; thus the scholar might be tried by his own master or by the archbishop.

The real representative, legislative, and administrative authority of the *universitas*, of the corporation, lay with the general assembly (*congregatio generalis, plena congregatio, generale concilium, consilium*). Depending on the basic constitution of the *studium*, the general assembly was composed of masters, masters and students, or students alone, and presided over by the rector (or, in Oxford and Cambridge, the chancellor). Besides the general congregation there were assemblies (*convocatio, conventus, coetus, cetus*) on all levels of the university organization: faculties, nations, and colleges. Only slight differences in procedure are recorded in the statutes. In the course of time there was a general tendency to reduce the activities of a general assembly and to leave current affairs and decisions to a smaller council of leading officials.

In Paris in the early years of the university, regent masters of all the faculties formed the general congregation which, the rector being subject to it, managed the university. After the mid-fourteenth century the non-regent masters were frequently summoned by the rector to attend the congregation as highly placed persons in church and state. They voted, except at elections; their presence was probably not legally necessary to the acts of the university as it was at Oxford and Cambridge. The rector announced the time and place of the congregation and the agenda. The dean of the theological faculty was convened by the rector in his house or through a master of arts, the other

---

[18] F. Stein, *Die academische Gerichtsbarkeit in Deutschland* (Leipzig, 1891); P. Classen, 'Zur Geschichte der "akademischen Freiheit" vornehmend im Mittelalter', *Historische Zeitschrift*, 232 (1981), 278; 529–33; Dąbrowski, Z. Kozłowska-Budkowa, and Pieradzka, *Dzieje* (note 17); C. Vandenghoer, *De rectorale Rechtbank van de oude Leuvense universiteit 1425–1797*, Verhandelingen Koninklijke Academie, Letteren no. 124 (Brussels, 1987).

deans and proctors by letter. The deans and proctors summoned the master of faculties and nations by sending a beadle during morning lectures. The matters to be discussed were suggested by one of the component bodies and submitted to the assembly by the rector. One matter of importance was the statutes to be voted. Debates were conducted separately, by each faculty and nation. In the church of St Julien-le-Pauvre, one of the places in which the congregation was held, there were proctors' chairs in the four corners of the nave, and the nations used to retire to these corners. Three smaller bodies, the superior faculties, had their own places. The opinion or vote of a nation or faculty was announced by its proctor or dean. The rector then presented the conclusions of the whole university; where, as often, no conclusions were reached, he had no casting vote. But from the mid-fourteenth century there were some declarations of opinion by the majority, and before the end of the century the right of the majority to bind the minority was accepted in the nations of the faculty of arts, in the general congregation, and in the assemblies of the faculties. A dissenting body could obstruct the procedure by refusing its key to the chest containing the university seal, and on such occasions that chest could be broken open; another method was an appeal to the pope.

At Bologna, the rector and the councillors, *consiliarii* elected by nations, convoked the general congregation of the two universities. The consent of one rector and of a majority of the councillors was needed to call this assembly; at the demand of two councillors votes were taken by ballot with black and white beans. A majority of the congregation was necessary to pronounce the sentence of deprivation or declare a doctor or scholar perjured.It was compulsory for all students to take part; congregations were held in convents or churches, usually in the convent of St Dominic. Every member had the right to speak, but the rectors had the power to impose silence on the loquacious, as the statutes declare. Those statutes could not be altered more than once every twenty years; eight elected *statutarii* conducted the revision and published it without any confirmation. Amending them at any other time was not possible except by a unanimous resolution of the university upon a proposal accepted by the rectors and councillors, and then by twenty-four members of the university named by them; the consent of the doctors was also necessary.

Three separate congregations arose in Oxford. The first of them was the Black or Previous Congregation composed of the regent masters in arts. It was summoned in St Mildred's church (and, after 1437, in St Mary's) for inceptions in arts and for the preliminary discussion of proposed statutes. The second congregation, the Lesser Congregation of regents of all faculties, meeting in a building close to St Mary's church, controlled finances, lectures, studies, and graduation. The third congregation, the Full or Great Congregation of all the masters, regents and non-regents – later known as the convocation – voted upon the statutes according to a procedure of 1303 providing for a majority vote by faculties; the non-regents voted separately. This was the highest court of appeal in the university.

The universities of Spain were nearer to the Bologna model than to the Paris model. The students' congregation elected the rector; the doctors formed a college of their own, but were not excluded from votes in congregation as was the case at Bologna. But following the statutes of Salamanca in 1422 the general congregation of students was deprived of its rights, and management of the university passed to a body of *diffinitores*, a congregation consisting of a rector, the *scholasticus*, and twenty persons selected by the university from student nobles and holders of dignities, not being under twenty-five years of age, and by ten persons elected by and from the regents holding salaried chairs. A two-thirds majority was required for any proposal or matter to be laid before this body. The election of the *scholasticus* was entrusted to it, and finally confirmed by the pope.

At Prague the council or congregation of the university was composed of councillors, as heads of the nations, and of masters. Voting was by count of heads. Vienna, too, was a university of masters but the students had a vote in the election of proctors in the nations. In Cracow, the general congregation of the masters held its meetings, with the rector as chairman, in the Collegium Maius, but from 1464 the rector and the deans formed the real governing body of the university. In other universities of central Europe, in the fourteenth and fifteenth centuries, students are still mentioned as taking an indirect part in the election of the rector. But students' rights were curtailed everywhere. Nations were abolished or were deprived of the right to defend their interests other than by delegating representatives to the university councils, in which the masters gained a dominant and sometimes exclusive position.[19]

Besides the high officers of the university and the nations, faculties, and colleges, other permanent or temporary officials existed who had management duties but who did not belong to the body of masters and students. Their nature and number varied from university to university, depending on its size and wealth. At first their role was very limited, but with the growth of the *studia generalia* there was more need for sound administration by competent officials from outside the university.

The beadle (*bedellus*) and messenger (*nuntius*) were the first external administrators; their office is almost as old as the universities themselves. In French universities the office was often bought and sold – at Avignon in 1463 a beadle paid 200 guilders for his office.[20] Beadles preceded the rector and other higher officers during public appearances, in full ceremonial robes,

---

[19] A. Vetulani, 'Les origines et le sort des universités de l'Europe centrale et orientale fondées au cours du XIVe siècle', in *Universities in the Late Middle Ages*, 148–69.

[20] J. Verger, 'Dépenses universitaires à Avignon au XVe siècle (1455–1456)', in *Avignon au Moyen Age. Textes et Documents* (Avignon, 1988), 212.

carrying the decorated verge (*massa*) which was the emblem of their office; they collected the votes at meetings of the congregation and read lists of mandatory reading material and of books up for sale; they gave notice of disputations and kept the list of graduations; they read proclamations and the text of new statutes; they collected fees and fines, kept the names of those sentenced to imprisonment, and advertised the times of sittings in the academic court; as caretakers and porters they were responsible for the material care of the schools. Every *universitas* had a *bedellus maior* or *generalis* and usually several *bedelli minores* and/or *speciales*, who were attached to professors and to the faculties and nations. The beadles earned the respect of the academic community. They were citizens of the university town and they and their wives were granted the rights and privileges of the *studium*. They were paid out of special *collectae* (see p. 133). In many universities, the office of beadle became venal.

The *nuntii* or messengers appeared with the nations. They served as go-betweens for the students and their families, carrying money, goods, and letters. In international university towns *nuntii maiores* (as opposed to *nuntii minores* or *volantes*, the petty or flying messengers) operated as quasi-bankers who paid out the scholars' money advanced by their parents or lent money to scholars. At Padua money-changers (*mutuatores et feneratores*) loaned money to *suppositi*. Financial transactions of students were registered in the *libri memoriales* or notarial minute-books of the *comune* of Bologna. Students who were short of money often pawned books or even their horses to buy drink.

In the course of the Middle Ages other officials made their appearance in most of the universities, under different names. Thus the *notarius* in Bologna or Paris, and the *dictator* in Louvain, acted as secretary. He kept the *matricula*, recorded the official acts of the university, and wrote documents and letters. At Oxford a chancellor's scribe or clerk is mentioned for the first time in 1428. In 1447 the office of registrar was instituted; he was required to be an MA and public notary. A good knowledge of Latin and calligraphy became a requirement in the pre-humanistic and humanistic universities. Other salaried academic personnel were *syndici* or legal assessors and solicitors of the university or faculty; they looked after the *studium*'s legal affairs and its property. Litigation seems to have been very popular in medieval academic life, and permanent professional legal aid was therefore not a luxury. Officials were appointed to collect fees and keep accounts – two *massarii* (treasurers) in Bologna, the receiver-general in Paris or Orléans, and the proctors in Oxford and Cambridge. Of course other university corporations, such as faculties, nations, and colleges, also had receivers (*receptores* or *quaestores aerarii*), often from an earlier date than their university counterparts. The chaplain was usually a member of the community, sometimes a student, but usually somebody from the staff; his duty was to celebrate the statutory masses in the university calendar and to conduct masses for benefactors, and the funerals of deceased members. At Oxford University the chaplain also acquired the salaried function of librarian in 1412. Only with the expansion of university libraries after the invention of printing did librarians become important officials of the university, faculty, nation, and college.

Closely linked to the university were people dealing in books.[21] The book – the manuscript book, and from the last quarter of the fifteenth century the printed book – was vital to the intellectual life of the university. The publishers and librarians often belonged to the university, or were at least controlled and sworn in by it. The stationers (*stationarii*) and their workrooms and bookshops (*stationes*) in Bologna were subject to the town authority, but some of them, as *stationarii universitatis*, owed allegiance to the rector. The *stationarii peciarum* were mainly custodians of the original copies (*exemplaria*) of teaching texts, corrected and approved by the professors; those stationers copied them, and loaned them against payment to be copied by others. The official copies were unbound and delivered in fascicles called *peciae*; the *pecia* stationers were subject to inspection by the committee of *peciarii* named by the university. On the other hand, the book stationers (*stationarii, mercatores* or *venditores librorum*) were mainly merchants, sometimes involved in book production by loaning the *pecia* and giving it to professional copyists. At the end of the thirteenth century the university tried to limit the number of authorized stationers to five. At Paris, the stationers were the approximate equivalents of the first Bologna group, and the booksellers (*librarii*) of the second one, but sometimes both activities were practised by the same person. The booksellers sold books, served as brokers, and commissioned books for copying. Only a few were stationers empowered to lend out *peciae*. All this little world of books, and at the end of the fifteenth century of the printed book as well, was controlled by the university, but only in so far as its activities concerned the university; for the stationers and booksellers did not work only for the *studium*.

Besides being responsible for managing the exemplar-*pecia* system, as in Bologna or Paris, the stationers in Oxford were authorized university agents for conducting the book trade within the town, and for valuing books, manuscripts, and other articles offered as pledges. There is clear evidence that the *pecia* system was used in at least eleven medieval universities (Bologna, Padua, Vercelli, Perugia, Treviso, Florence, Naples, Salamanca, Paris, Toulouse, and Oxford).[22]

21 J. Destrez, *La pecia dans les manuscrits universitaires du XIIIe et du XIVe siècle* (Paris, 1935); G. Pollard, 'The "Pecia" System in the Medieval Universities' in M. B. Parkes and A. G. Watson (eds.), *Medieval Scribes, Manuscripts and Libraries: Essays Presented to N. R. Ker* (London, 1978), 145–61; L. J. Bataillon, B. G. Guyot, and R. H. Rouse (eds.), *La Production du livre universitaire au Moyen Age. Exemplar et pecia. Actes du Symposium tenu au Collegio San Bonaventura de Grottaferrata en mai 1983* (Paris, 1988).
22 Pollard, 'The "Pecia" System' (note 21), 148.

In central Europe, in the fourteenth and fifteenth centuries, the prevailing system was not the *pecia* but dictation of the texts (*pronunciatio*) to the students by the masters and bachelors in the university, as in Prague and Cracow, or in the schools. Even in Paris, students asked their teachers to dictate the courses, for financial reasons. Some professional copyists in towns worked for the universities, among them a specialized group of *cathedrales* (from the writing chair, *cathedra*) in Germany, Bohemia, Austria, and Poland, now and then approved by the university.[23] In addition, many universities mention various kinds of persons specializing in making books – *exemplatores, scriptores, correctores, miniatores, rasores librorum, ligatores* – all of them more or less subject to the rector or chancellor.

EXTERNAL GOVERNMENT

As explained in chapters 2 and 3, the history of the medieval university is dominated by its struggle for autonomy. It was a long time before church and state recognized the *studium generale* as an autonomous institution, and its relationship with the town was always precarious.

One of the first demands of the university corporation was the right to recruit its members. In the earlier medieval schools the right to confer the *licentia docendi* (permission to teach) belonged to the *scholasticus* or *magister scholarum*, and in a cathedral school to the chancellor of the chapter, who was in charge of the bishop's or archbishop's *scriptorium* or writing-office. In the course of the thirteenth century it became the practice for the chancellor also to supervise the university schools, which were under episcopal jurisdiction.

As early as 1212–13 the masters in Paris obtained the right to hold examinations and recommend candidates for the *licentia* to the chancellor of Notre-Dame, who was bound to confer the degree without requiring the candidates to pay money or swear individual oaths. In Bologna the archdeacon of the cathedral presided over the examinations committee and granted the teaching licence on the professors' recommendation. The archdeacon was sometimes called *cancellarius* and in the late Middle Ages it became usual to speak of the archdeacon of Bologna as chancellor of the university. In the Pisa *studium*, on the contrary, the archbishop figured as chancellor. The role of the chancellor thus tended to become formal rather than real, both in universities that arose *e consuetudine* and in those founded *e privilegio*. At Orléans, for instance, the flourishing cathedral school became a university; the *scholasticus* remained head of the masters until 1306, when the *studium* was officially recognized as a *studium generale* by papal bull; the masters were then allowed to elect a rector and the chancellor formally granted the degrees.

---

23 E. Potkowski, *Książka rękopiśmienna w kulturze Polski średniowiecznej* (Warsaw, 1984), 77–109.

This confronted universities created *ex privilegio* with a new situation. This is not to say that the pattern of development was everywhere the same. As already stated in the passages dealing with the rector, the chancellor retained more authority in the Spanish *studia* and in Glasgow. In the English universities the position of the chancellor evolved in a completely different way. There, the chancellor, being the official representative of the bishop, soon came to be elected by the masters' guild. From being an external officer set above the masters, he became one of them. (The rector–chancellor relationship in the English universities is mentioned on p. 122.)

The growth of the chancellor's power in Oxford was due to royal grants of privilege to the chancellor's court and the spiritual privileges, including even the power of excommunication, given to him by the archbishops of Canterbury. At the end of the thirteenth century, the chancellor was elected every two years by the university congregation. His appointment was submitted to the bishop of Lincoln, and finally to the archbishop of Canterbury for confirmation. In the fifteenth century, however, chancellors were not only re-elected, but non-resident. In spite of formal exemptions, the English universities were passing under greater crown control, with chancellors who were nominated for life and who appointed the vice-chancellor. In 1484 the bishop of Lincoln was appointed chancellor at Oxford. At Cambridge, from the early thirteenth century onwards the position of the chancellor was similar to that of his counterpart in Oxford. There is some parallel between the chancellor of the English universities and the chancellor of the university of medicine of Montpellier. The latter was a representative of the bishop and the head of the corporation; he was appointed by the bishop of Maguelone and chosen from among the masters. The chancellor's power was, however, somewhat limited; his jurisdiction was purely civil and the right to award the licence remained with the bishop. At other European universities there were still other differences in the method of appointment and the competence of the chancellor as the representative of episcopal authority. In many universities of central and eastern Europe the chancellor was the local bishop or archbishop, and delegated his authority to an officially elected member of the *studium*. At Tübingen (founded in 1477) the chancellor was a *commissarius perpetuus* of the bishop and his conservator. At Pozsony (Pressburg) in Hungary (founded 1465–7), on the contrary, the archbishop-chancellor chose the provost of the chapter of Pressburg as his vice-chancellor. The bishop of Cracow was chancellor of the university and also its general conservator. He did not preside over examinations, but awarded the licence in the higher faculties; he supervised finance and salaries, and intervened in university life to some considerable effect through his regulations (1422, 1433, etc.).[24]

---

[24] Dąbrowski, Kozłowska-Budkowa, and Pieradzka, *Dzieje* (note 17), 43–55.

As always, the situation was completely different in Naples; the university there was subject to the royal chancellor until 1497, when the king's grand chaplain became governor of the *studium*.

A second demand of the university corporation was for the right to make statutes regulating the internal organization of the *studium*. Consequently the university needed officers for the management of the *studium* and for dealings with the outside world. For instance, in almost every university town citizens and academics jointly appointed a committee of *taxatores* to fix and control the prices of rooms, food, and books and ensure an adequate supply in times of scarcity. At Padua there was more communal supervision: four citizens (*tractatores*) cooperated with the student rectors in a wide range of practical affairs. In Portugal the *almocatenes* or controllers of weights and measures were appointed by the students. In Salamanca the rent of lodgings was fixed by *conservatores privilegii*, who also exercised other supervisory functions. This privilege and others recognized by papal or royal authority were not always observed. Pope and king therefore appointed apostolic and royal conservators to safeguard the rights and privileges of the *studia generalia*. Members of the university could appeal to these conservators when their privileges and other rights were violated inside or outside the university. At Paris the system worked well: *suppositi* could appeal to the Châtelet – the court of the *prévôt* of Paris, who was the *conservateur des privilèges royaux* – or to the apostolic conservator in Paris, who was always one of three bishops, those of Meaux, Senlis, and Beauvais. At Oxford in the thirteenth century the pope nominated the bishops of London and Salisbury, and in the fourteenth century also the archbishop of Canterbury, as conservators of the apostolic privileges, but throughout those centuries the king's intercession was much more necessary to maintain the rights and privileges of the Oxford students. There was constant hostility between town and gown, and to avoid further violence against scholars the king made the sheriff and bailiff responsible for the preservation of the customary academic liberties and immunities. Moreover, in the course of the fourteenth century the king greatly reinforced the chancellor's authority over university members by giving him full jurisdiction over all *suppositi*, and the necessary power to keep the peace. In this the chancellor was in fact performing the same functions as the provost-*conservateur royal* of Paris.

In other universities the apostolic conservators were more powerful, as in Louvain where they were the archbishop of Trier, the abbot of the abbey of Tongerlo, and the dean of St Peter's chapter of Louvain. In Prague the pope designated other conservators: the provost of the chapter of Mainz and the deans of the chapters of Breslau and Prague, but, as the nation of Saxony complained that it did not have a conservator for its region, the dean of the chapter of Lübeck was also appointed (1396).[25] At Leipzig and Greifswald the bishop was recognized as *conservator jurium et privilegiorum*. Whereas in the German universities the apostolic conservators exercised spiritual jurisdiction over the university members, in Copenhagen the royal conservator had apparently unlimited jurisdiction over students. So did the *conservatores studii* named by the king from among the burghers in Portugal, where the royal authority was stronger than in Spain.[26] In Italy conservators of privileges played a minor role. The archdeacon of Bologna and a Dominican friar or another ecclesiastic were appointed to guard the apostolic privileges. In any event, the students seldom appealed to this papal jurisdiction for assistance in their conflicts and demands. The civic authorities, especially, the *comune*, approved this reticence. The Venetian rulers also tried to reduce ecclesiastical influence in the Padua *studium*.

The Italian cities were not only concerned to protect the rights of scholars; they also wanted to keep law and order inside the *studium*. In the fourteenth and fifteenth centuries more and more Italian communes paid *reformatores*, *gubernatores*, *tractatores*, or *tutores studii* to supervise student activities and to reduce student autonomy, and, with it, disorder in the *comune*. In 1391 at Ferrara a body of *reformatores*, appointed by the duke and municipality jointly, was entrusted with the general government of the university, including the appointment of professors. In Turin, in the fifteenth century, the duke appointed two canonists, four doctors of civil law, one of law and medicine combined, and one of theology. The government of Venice appointed *reformatores* to the University of Padua immediately after Padua came under its authority (1406). From 1517 onwards the Padua *studium* was governed by a body of *reformatores*. The princes of the Holy Roman Empire also tried to strengthen their influence on 'their' local university by appointing officials to supervise it or to carry out allegedly necessary reforms there. At Dole the duke of Burgundy appointed the three *distributores* (originally appointed to administer the public funds allocated to the university) as *reformatores studii*.

At the close of the Middle Ages French kings also tried to reduce academic autonomy, limit abuses of privileges, and restore order and discipline in the universities of Paris and the provinces by sending *reformatores studii*. These men were members of the *Parlement* of Paris, well known for their loyalty to the crown and their belief in a strongly centralized state. For the *réforme générale* of the University of Paris in 1452 the king also appealed to the papal legate, Cardinal d'Estouteville, whose family had long been devoted to the crown.[27] From the beginning papal legates took part in regulating consti-

---

25 P. Moraw, 'Die Universität Prag im Mittelalter. Grundzüge ihrer Geschichte im europäischen Zusammenhang', in P. Moraw (ed.), *Die Universität zu Prag* (Munich, 1986), 45.

26 A. García y García, 'Aspectos de la Universidad Portuguesa medieval', in *Universities in the Late Middle Ages*, 133–47.

27 J. Verger, 'Les libertés universitaires en France au Moyen Age', in *Les Libertés au Moyen Age*, Festival d'histoire de Montbrisson (Montbrisson, 1986), 426.

tutional matters. In Italy the influence of papal legates in university matters grew with the expansion of the papal state. When Bologna came under the direct control of Rome in 1506 the cardinal legate and sixteen *reformatores* became the real governors of the *studium*. Their power increased still more in the early modern period (see volume II, chapter 4).

The universities also had officials acting temporarily outside the university: solicitors represented the university in the ecclesiastical and civic courts, and the *studia* sent professors on embassy to popes, princes, and councils. How to pay for all this was a perpetual problem.

FINANCE

Every corporation within the university had its own budget, but medieval bookkeeping was primitive, and finance was kept to a minimum, as was material infrastructure. Financial resources and needs of course varied and became more and more important as time went on. The rather scanty remaining accounts of universities and nations give some insight into the way their finances functioned.

University income came from both internal and external sources. The internal sources were fees for matriculation and graduation, graces (dispensations from the statutory conditions for degrees) and other dispensations, money collected from the nations, and *collectae* (see below). External sources were ecclesiastical benefices, salaries paid by the king, duke, or town, gifts and legacies, and grants and endowments given for the permanent support of the university. Expenditure was modest. Much of the budget went to festivities, banquets, and entertainment, or on routine payments for administration or travel; lawsuits also cost money, and in the later Middle Ages the maintenace of buildings and other properties (e.g. insignia) burdened the academic budget. Teachers' salaries were not usually paid by the university (see chapter 5). Officials were not paid a salary but were entitled to a part of the *collectae*, a proportion of fines, and an allowance for expenses; gifts in kind could also be substantial.

Collectae were sums levied on the students once or twice a year, to pay some officials of the university (beadles and proctors) and the teachers, and some common expenses of the university. By the end of the Middle Ages *collectae* cost the students little, but examination and graduation fees, and gifts in kind to masters and beadles, were a burden to candidates. In the second half of the fifteenth century university statutes regulated and limited the fees demanded.[28]

The university coffers (*archa*) were fed by fines imposed by the university court for violation of the university statutes, disciplinary measures, neglect of

---

[28] M. Fletcher and C. A. Upton, 'Expenses at Admission and Determination in Fifteenth Century Oxford: New Evidence', *English Historical Review*, 100:395 (1985), 331–7.

duties, and so on. Some statutes exactly stipulate the scale of fines; thus the statutes of the Collegium Minus at Leipzig (1438) prescribe, for lifting a stone or similar missile with the intention of throwing it at a master, but not actually throwing it, a fine of 10 new groschen; for throwing but missing the fine was 8 florins, and still more for a successful throw. The fine for striking varied according to whether the victim was wounded by the blow and whether the wound produced mutilation.[29] In Vienna the poorest student offenders were flogged if they could not pay the fine. The statutes of Copenhagen, modelled on those of Cologne, are less explicit; they say only that fines are at the discretion of the rector and the four deans.[30]

Collectae and fines were collected by the beadles or receivers (*receptores* or *collectores*). Students could also pay the *collectae* direct to the masters, as in Toulouse, Montpellier, and Avignon, or in Bologna after some rather difficult negotiations between the professor and some of the students.[31]

At the English universities the proctors served as the principal financial officers. The earliest extant proctors' account dates from the middle of the fifteenth century. At Oxford the university's income came, in descending order, from degree fees, graces, rents of urban property, the payments by Eynsham and Oseney abbeys for the relief of poor scholars and regents in arts, fines, money from the keepers of grammar schools in Oxford, and small miscellaneous amounts. The university's expenditure

> embraced a lavish annual entertainment for graduates; an annual distribution of money to the regent masters; a feast for the auditors of the accounts; sundry expenses and allowances for the chancellor, proctors and bedels; the payment of a number of rents; salaries paid to the registrar and to the chaplain-librarian; payments to the parish clerk of St Mary's church; entertainment for visiting royalty; expenses in connection with the confirmation of the University's privileges; and payments towards the diverse building ventures.[32]

Cambridge's budget is similar to that of Oxford and in fact all the medieval universities' accounts were alike.

An example of central European financial management is Cracow University. After its renewal in about 1400 the funds were secured by the king, the bishop, and a group of lords. The income from the royal Cracow customs and salt-mines probably paid for seven to nine professorships. More important were fifteen ecclesiastical benefices for the masters in theology and law, and forty-six rather modest benefices distributed among the masters in arts

---

[29] Rashdall, *Universities*, vol. III, 363.

[30] J. Pinborg (ed.), *Universitas Studii Haffnensis. Stiftelsesdokumenter og Statutter 1479 Udgivet af Københavns Universitet*, English translation by B. P. McGuire (Copenhagen, 1979), 117, cap. 41.

[31] J. Verger, 'Le coût des grades: droits et frais d'examen dans les universités du Midi de la France au Moyen Age', in A. L. Gabriel (ed.), *The Economic and Material Frame of the Medieval University* (Notre Dame, 1977), 20.

[32] Quoted from Cobban, *Medieval English Universities* (note 12), 86.

(they had no more than ten to twelve *marcae* a year – bed and board in the Collegium Maius cost seven *marcae*); they also had an unknown proportion of the university funds. The central treasury received fees from students and graduates, rents from houses belonging to the university, incomes from financial operations with the foundations' estates, and cash payments by donors. The rector Thomas de Strzempino (1432) observed that 'the purpose of this institution is not to amass wealth'. Nevertheless, the university provided for about eighty masters, collected quite a good library, built a stately Collegium Maius at the end of the fifteenth century and even made loans to the crown and town.[33]

The extant accounts of the German nation at the Orléans *studium*, which start in 1444, and a variety of other source material, give some idea of the *studium*'s finances.[34] They show that the university derived its income mainly from part of the matriculation and graduation fees. Most of these fees went to the nation, for until 1532 matriculations and graduations were registered by the nation and not by the university. The professors had to pay a fee for permission to teach at the university, and were also urged to contribute to its extraordinary expenses. The university's other sources of income were, in order of importance, fines, legacies, and gifts. Its main items of expenditure, also in order of importance, were administration, the salaries of its few officials, the numerous lawsuits in which it was involved, and the growing cost of academic solemnities and religious feasts and of the maintenance of its few movable and immovable properties. For extra expenditure, such as a contribution to sums paid as security by, or for the ransom of, sovereigns (as, for instance, in 1529 for the French dauphin), the university appealed to its members' generosity. On other occasions too it might ask for special support. In 1506 the *studium* of Louvain contributed to the cost of restoring the city walls when a French invasion threatened.[35] Funds in the Orléans *studium* were always minimal, in the fifteenth century and later. Until 1532 they were managed by a *receptor generalis*, a graduate student chosen by roster among the *receptores* of the nations, who was paid a percentage of the income. As part of the reorganization (*reformatio*) of 1532, King Francis I ordered the financial management of the university and the nations to be centralized in the hands of a general *receptor* chosen by the burghers of the city. The

---

[33] A. Gieysztor, 'Aspects financiers de l'Université de Cracovie au XV siècle', in Gabriel (ed.), *Economic Frame* (note 31), 51–6; J. Michalewicz, 'Les bases économiques de l'Université Jagellonne et leurs aspects sociaux', and M. Michalewiczowa, 'Le bénéfice en tant qu'élément de la structure d'organisation de l'université Jagellonne', in *L'Histoire des universités. Problèmes et méthodes* (Warsaw, 1980), 25–104; J. Michalewicz, *Majatek kapitałowy Universytetu Jagiellońskiego XV–XVIII w.* (Cracow, 1984); J. Michalewicz and M. Michalewiczowa (eds.), *Liber beneficiorum et benefactorum Universitatis Jagellonicae in saec. XV–XVIII* (Cracow, 1978).

[34] H. de Ridder-Symoens, 'La vie et l'organisation matérielle de l'ancienne Université d'Orléans', in Gabriel (ed.), *Economic Frame* (note 31), 37–50.

[35] *De Universiteit te Leuven 1425–1985* (Louvain, 1986), 42.

finances of the University of Avignon are analogous. Its income came mainly from matriculation and graduation fees, and from letting academic rooms to bachelors giving 'extraordinary' lectures. Expenditure was principally for maintenance of the schools (seven classrooms in 1455), the clock, and the library; ceremonies, correspondence, and lawsuits also absorbed large sums. Extraordinary costs, such as those for building schools, had to be paid from external sources.[36]

In universities erected and strictly controlled by the crown, finance was somewhat different. A state university such as Naples had no financial independence. The universities of Castile were also financed by the crown, with the king appointing the *conservadores* charged with their administration and paying their salaries and those of the teachers, a librarian, and a pharmacist. The money was provided from the royal *tercias* (one-third of the ecclesiastical tithe). Salamanca, Valladolid, and other cities helped their *estudio* in times of crisis by levying special taxes on the burghers. The Castilian universities, like all the others, had financial privileges that helped them to survive. They were exempt from general taxation and from taxes on beer and wine and import duties on meat.[37] (The quantity of tax-free beer and wine to which universities were entitled was limited, as for instance by the Louvain city government, and abuse by the universities of their exemption from excise often led to tension and disputes between town and gown.) But in general, whatever the pattern of the university might be, the city was constantly aware of its university, and gave it financial assistance of various kinds. In return the universities often had to accept the financial control of the city government. In Prague two official *collectores* assisted the rector in managing the property of the university, but most of its possessions in Prague, as in German universities such as Cologne and Leipzig, were assigned to faculties and colleges, which ensured their own management. The rector had very little money at his disposal, and for every large item of expenditure he organized a *collecta*, or *bursa* as it was often called in German universities. In the course of the fifteenth century German princes became more and more involved in the finance of 'their' university in return for making it more allowances. Universities had no choice. Late medieval universities were not self-supporting. Their traditional income was completely insufficient to cover the high cost of acquiring and maintaining academic buildings.

UNIVERSITY BUILDINGS

In the late Middle Ages, as student populations grew and universities ceased to migrate, universities acquired buildings and movable property. For a long

---

[36] Verger, 'Dépenses universitaires' (note 20), 207–18.
[37] A. Rucquoi, 'Sociétés urbaines et universités en Castille au moyen Age', in D. Poirion (ed.), *Milieux universitaires et mentalité urbaine au Moyen Age* (Paris, 1987), 105–6.

time in Paris and Bologna the administration had not needed to take care of university buildings, because there were none. Lectures were held in houses rented by the masters, examinations and meetings in churches and convents. In Paris, however, both the theological faculty and the nations began renting property as early as the fourteenth century, and acquiring it in the fifteenth century. With lecture halls in the rue du Fouarre and many other places, with colleges and lodgings, and with churches (all of them on the left bank of the river), the Quartier Latin became the university quarter of Paris.[38] The young Bologna *studium*, too, contented itself with private houses and religious or public buildings for lectures, meetings, and ceremonies.

Growing numbers of students, some of them very young and needy, made housing facilities more necessary as time passed. College buildings arose everywhere, but especially in universities with large faculties of arts, such as Paris, Oxford, Cambridge, and later on the German universities. Italian *studia* also looked for lodgings for their students. The comparatively few colleges in northern Italy were founded in and after the fourteenth century, at first in converted private houses. After 1420 a special type of building appeared, the *domus sapientiae* (house of wisdom) or *sapienza*, a teaching college modelled on the Collegio de Spagna in Bologna, built in 1365-7. The rooms were grouped around an arcaded courtyard. Gradually the *sapienza* ceased to be dwellings and in early modern times became the official university buildings with lecture rooms, discussion rooms, a library, rooms for accommodation and administration, archives, and a graduation room. The *palazzo della sapienza* became the current name for these sumptuous university buildings.[39]

Besides the marvellous Collegio di Spagna in Bologna (which is still operating), there are outstanding examples of medieval building in Oxford and Cambridge. The English universities were also precocious in erecting official academic buildings. The first purpose-built building of this kind, the Congregation House at Oxford, dating from *c.* 1320, was the gift of Thomas Cobham, bishop of Worcester. The next important buildings, the Divinity School and schools of other faculties (all incorporated in the present Bodleian Library), were erected in the fifteenth century at the cost of individual benefactors and from university funds. Similarly, Cambridge's university building programme (the Schools Quadrangle) in the late fourteenth and the fifteenth century made inroads on the university's funds, benefactors' subscriptions being insufficient.[40]

The Schools in Salamanca (Las Escuelas), also a fifteenth-century quadran-

---

[38] A. Grabois, *La Génèse du Quartier Latin*, Studies in History, 23 (Jerusalem, 1972); L. E. Sullivan, 'The Burg of Sainte Geneviève: Development of the University Quarter of Paris in the Thirteenth and Fourteenth Centuries', Ph.D., Baltimore, 1975.

[39] M. Kiene, 'Der Palazzo della Sapienza – Zur italienischen Universitätsarchitektur des 15. und 16. Jahrhunderts', *Römisches Jahrbuch für Kunstgeschichte*, 23/24 (1988), 219-71.

[40] Cobban, *Medieval English Universities* (note 12), 86-8 and *passim*.

gle, conserve one room in its original state. The rude wooden benches and desks, and the *cathedra* in the Divinity School, were certainly an improvement for students used to sitting on straw on the floor.[41] The rue du Fouarre or Feurre (*vicus straminis* or street of straw) in the Quartier Latin of Paris is a reminder of this custom. The only remaining secular university building of the Middle Ages in France is the Gothic Salle des Thèses at Orléans. This two-storey building, having a big room for the library and another for meetings, dates from the first half of the fifteenth century. At the end of that century the university began to build its Grandes Ecoles, and bought a contiguous house for the Petites Ecoles.[42]

Because of the close ties between the German towns and their universities, the latter acquired housing facilities and an infrastructure from the date of their foundation onwards. At first schools were housed in converted private or religious houses, but as early as the fifteenth century special academic buildings were erected. Churches continued to be used for official ceremonies and festivities.[43] The local princes also saw to the upkeep of the buildings. At Heidelberg every year the rector, the dean of the faculty of arts, a master, and the beadle of the university were bound to inspect all the faculty buildings together with two workmen. Repairs were paid for from the university treasury.[44]

Their strong stone buildings encouraged universities, nations, and colleges to set up libraries. The Congregation House and Divinity School in Oxford, several buildings in Cambridge, the Schools in Salamanca, the Collegium Maius in Cracow,[45] and many others, housed book collections constantly added to from gifts, legacies, and fines, and to a lesser extent by purchase. In smaller institutions the library dates mainly from the early modern period. Some statutes laid down very detailed regulations for the upkeep of the library and the loan of books. In a decree of 1439 the rector of the University of Heidelberg took special and very strict measures for the collection of books left to the university by Louis III, count palatine of the Rhine.[46] Besides the libraries, located mainly in the colleges, the most treasured possessions of the academic institutions were archives kept in chests closed with a triple lock, as in Orléans, together with seals, maces, verges, and money. Nations and colleges had chalices, church ornaments, missals, utensils, banners, statutes,

---

41 J. A. Villar, *The University of Salamanca. Art and Traditions* (Salamanca, 1980), 49–50.
42 R. Boitel, 'La construction de la Salle des Thèses de l'ancienne université d'Orléans', *Bulletin de la société archéologique et historique de l'Orléanais*, new series, 1 (1960), 299–309.
43 H. Koller, 'Stadt und Universität im Spätmittelalter', and A.-D. von den Brincken, 'Die Stadt Köln und ihre Hohen Schulen', in E. Maschke and J. Sydow (eds.), *Stadt und Universität im Mittelalter und in der früheren Neuzeit* (Sigmaringen, 1977), 17–19, 34–6.
44 L. Thorndike, *University Records and Life in the Middle Ages*, 2nd edn (New York, 1949), 370–1.
45 K. Rückbrod, *Universität und Kollegium, Baugeschichte und Bautypen* (Darmstadt, 1977); K. Estreicher, *Collegium maius. Dzieje gmachu* (Cracow, 1968).
46 Thorndike, *University Records* (note 44), 315–17.

charters, and registers. Students and masters took good care of their valu-
ables. To open the chest of the Anglo-German nation at Paris, eight members
of the nation had to be present; to open the *archa exterior*, four members (the
procurator, the *receptor*, and two masters); and to open the *archa interior* or
scrinium, which contained the nation's money, four masters.[47]

By 1500 old and new universities alike possessed proper academic buildings
– lecture rooms, assembly rooms, a chapel, one or more libraries, lodgings for
students and teachers – and many articles of value. Throughout Europe,
faculty buildings, and particularly college buildings with libraries combining
functional needs with a show of magnificence, were visible signs that the
masters in the late medieval university were no longer footloose. No longer
could universities threaten to migrate, no longer could public authorities tol-
erate strikes or secessions; the monumental disposition and architecture of
the late medieval university showed how completely it had become a part of
society. University towns had acquired a character of their own.

ACADEMIC INSIGNIA

From the very beginning, the image and character of a *studium generale* were
expressed by its costumes, insignia, and festivities. The complex communication of university events required the symbolic ordering of ideas in rites and
ceremonies. Congregations, installations, examinations, inceptions, jurisdictional proceedings, lectures, divine services, and even meals and festivals
observed ritual sequences of words, gestures, objects, music, lights, and furni-
ture, and prescribed forms of dress. University insignia embraced a rather
large group of symbolic objects used in many ways and at different times by
the members of academic bodies: sceptres and verges, chains, rings, seals,
chalices, keys, registers and statute books, gowns and caps. Sceptres were the
visible signs of the autonomous and especially jurisdictional power of rectors:
Cracow University still has four rectorial sceptres dating from the fifteenth
and sixteenth centuries. Verges of different length were carried by beadles
before rectors and professors. Newly nominated doctors in Bologna received
gold rings with their *licentia docendi* (this custom still survives at Uppsala).

Academic costume originated in the dress[48] of the secular clergy, to which
masters and scholars at first belonged. The *cappa clausa*, a loose cape with a
hood and a hole for the head, was introduced in the thirteenth century as
clerical outdoor dress, and in Bologna, Paris, and Oxford was consequently

---

[47] A. L. Gabriel, 'Res Quaedam notatu dignae nationem Anglicanam (Alemanniae) Parisiensem
saeculo XV Spectantes', in A. L. Gabriel and G. Boyce (eds.), *Liber Receptorum Nationis
Alemanniae (1425–1494)*, vol. VI of *Auctarium Chartularii Universitatis Parisiensis* (Paris,
1964), 43–4.
[48] Rashdall, *Universities*, vol. III, 385–93; M. G. Houston, *Medieval Costume in England and
France* (London, 1939), 153–7; W. N. Hargreaves-Mawdsley, *A History of Academic Dress in
Europe until the End of the Eighteenth Century* (Oxford, 1963).

regarded as university dress, at least for doctors and masters. By the four-teenth century this costume had acquired a shape and cut of its own. The significance of colour was not recognized until later. In the fifteenth century the influence of lay fashion, as in hoods, birettas, bonnets, shoulder pieces, and scarves, is visible. From this fashion comes the wing-sleeved gown, used in Germany, the Low Countries, Oxford, and Cambridge. Some colleges recommended their fellows to wear a certain kind of dress. Occasionally we read of costume distinguishing between nations, as in Prague at the national festivals.

By the end of the Middle Ages each faculty wore robes of a distinguishing shape and colour. At Paris, Oxford, and Cambridge theologians wore black, and at Salamanca, Coimbra, and Perpignan white. Greenish-yellow or blood-red were the colours of the faculty of medicine. Blue at Perpignan, Coimbra, and Ingolstadt denoted the faculty of arts. Scarlet was for canonists. At Bologna, doctors of civil law appear to have taken to wearing scarlet cloth robes trimmed with ermine at an early date. Fourteenth-century doctors of canon law wore a blue ankle-length *cappa manicata* with elbow-length sleeves, and a cap (*pileus*) lined with miniver. The rector in 1432 was ordered to wear a black cloth *cappa manicata* buttoned up to the neck and a hood with miniver, and in summer it was to be made of thin cloth. In the four-teenth century the dress of Bologna doctors, except of theology, had come to consist of a round scarlet *pileus*, a *birretum*, and a long *supertunica* of the same colour trimmed with miniver or ermine. The costume of students was regulated; the statutes recommended them to wear the long black tabard (*tabardum*) and hood.

At Paris there are references to academic dress in the thirteenth century. In the fourteenth it became more or less regulated. The faculty of canon law wore a red *cappa* with miniver, and a lined scarlet *birretum*. The regents in medicine had a *cappa rotunda* of violet-brown colour. Masters of arts were to wear a *cappa* with shoulder piece (*épitoge*). Bachelors of arts were ordered to wear brown-black tabards, and after their *determinatio* a blue *cappa rotunda*, and a hood trimmed with miniver. Students had the *subtunica*, and for feast-days a *supertunica*. In the fifteenth century the rector wore a scarlet *supertunica* with a close hood.

At Oxford, the vice-chancellor was clad in a scarlet *supertunica* whose wide hanging sleeves were lined and edged with grey fur, and as head-dress a *pileus* with a small brim. In 1350 masters of theology were ordered to wear a *cappa clausa*, and a black *pileus rotundus*; full dress for doctors of canon law was the black *cappa clausa*, for doctors of civil law red, and for doctors of medicine crimson. Masters of arts wore a black *cappa clausa*, and later the sleeveless *roba* or *toga*; they were forbidden to wear the *pileus*, which was regarded as the preserve of doctors.

In central Europe, a long *supertunica* or tabard, with a small, low-crowned hat, seems to be the most common dress in the Middle Ages. Great latitude as to colour was allowed until the sixteenth century. In the faculty of theology, as in Cracow, the *cappa clausa* was preserved. Students seem to have been left to their own devices as long as their dress was decent and not over-costly.

Early universities devoted much thought to the design of their seals, which bore engraved emblems, figures, and words, since they were used to authenticate legal documents and were therefore a symbol of autonomy.[49] In the first half of the thirteenth century the right to possess a seal was contested, as at Paris where in 1246 the university regained its seal, which had been broken in 1225 by the decision of the pontifical legate. The great seal of the University of Paris from the thirteenth century until the Revolution bore the inscription 's. VNIVERSITATIS. MAGISTROR. [et]. SCOLARIV. PARISIVS', and in an architectural frame the Virgin with Jesus, Saint Nicholas and Saint Catherine, two doctors, and six students with books; and as the counter-seal the inscription '+ SECRETUM PHILOSOPHIE', with the figure of Sapientia (Wisdom). Besides the university seal, faculties and colleges in the fourteenth and fifteenth centuries had seals of their own.[50]

It was a far cry from the general emblems on a seal, whose principal feature was its inscription, to heraldic coats of arms on buildings and movable property as well as seals. In the fourteenth and fifteenth centuries university heraldry, with its armorial bearings of universities and colleges, was no less gorgeous than the coats of arms of cities, princes of the church, and the nobility. The chronicle of Ulrich Richental, written during the Council of Constance (1414–18), tried to present the European university community in a set of coats of arms of Paris, Avignon, Orléans, Cologne, Erfurt, Heildelberg, Vienna, Prague, Cambridge, Oxford, Cracow, Bologna, and Buda. The illuminator did not everywhere exactly follow the existing heraldic tradition, but added a book, sometimes held in the hand, as a collateral emblem in every shield. Indeed, the book served as a general symbol of learning, and a book of privileges and registration (*matricula*) was used, like a manuscript Bible, in swearing a solemn oath.[51] The international and national import of this heraldic set conveys a sense of the European intellectual community and conscious awareness of the ideal of a local academic

---

[49] *Corpus sceptrorum – Die akademischen Szepter und Stäbe in Europa*, vol. I, ed. G. Vorbrodt and I. Vorbrodt (Heidelberg, 1971); vol. II, ed. W. Paatz (Heidelberg, 1979); W. Maisel, *Archeologia prawna Europy* [Archéologie juridique Europe] (Warsaw, 1989), 264–6.

[50] *History of Oxford*, pl. nos. X, XI, text by J. R. L. Highfield, 225–63. For University of Paris: R. Gandilhon, *Sigillographie des universités de France* (Paris, 1952), 83–93.

[51] Anton Porg (ed.), *Conziliumbuch geschehener zu Constanz* (Augsburg, 1583); New York Public Library, Spencer Collection, MS 32 (about 1450—60): O. Neubecker, J. P. Broeked-Little, and R. Tobler, *Heraldry, Sources, Symbols and Meanings* (London, 1977), 240–1; A. L. Gabriel, 'The Significance of the Book in Medieval Coats of Arms', in Gabriel, *Garlandia* (note 11), 65–96.

body: *vivere socialiter et collegialiter, et moraliter, et scholariter* (Paris, 1454).[52]

The organization and administration of European universities during three centuries of the Middle Ages were moulded by forces both inside and outside the corporation itself. Universities therefore had many common features, but even more which were individual and particular. The legal status of university members and of the university as an institution varied greatly from place to place until the end of the Middle Ages and, indeed, until the end of the *ancien régime*. Although the present survey has aimed mainly at describing events and institutions, it has also made apparent an essential trend noticeable in other realms of university life; that is, the evolution from legal autonomy and privileged status for masters and scholars to a professorial caste system and growing dependence upon public authority, coupled with attempts to uphold corporative and professional prestige in contemporary society.

[52] A. L. Gabriel, 'The Foundation of Johannes Hueven of Arnheim for the College of Sorbonne (1452)', in Gabriel, *Garlandia* (note 11), 141.

SELECT BIBLIOGRAPHY

See also the select bibliography of chapter 7.

Álvarez, M. F., Robles Carcedo, L., and Rodríguez San Pedro, L. E. (eds.) *La Universidad de Salamanca*, 3 vols., Salamanca, 1990.

Bannenberg, G. *Organisatie en bestuur van de middeleeuwse universiteit*, Nijmegen, 1953.

Beltrán de Heredia, V. (ed.) *Bulgario de la Universidad de Salamanca*, 3 vols., Salamanca, 1966–7.

Beltrán de Heredia, V. (ed.) *Cartulario de la Universidad de Salamanca*, 6 vols., Salamanca, 1970–3.

Catto, J. I. (ed.) *The History of the University of Oxford*, vol. I, *The Early Schools*, Oxford, 1984.

Chartularium Studii Bononiensis. Documenti per la Storia dell'Università di Bologna dalle origini fino al sec. XV, 15 vols., Bologna, 1909–88.

Cobban, A. B. *The Medieval English Universities: Oxford and Cambridge, to c.1500*, Cambridge, 1988.

Cobban, A. B. *The Medieval Universities: Their Development and Organization*, London, 1975.

Denifle, H. *Die Entstehung der Universitäten des Mittelalters bis 1400*, Berlin, 1885; reprint, Graz, 1956.

Denifle, H. and Châtelain, E. (eds.) *Auctarium Chartularii Universitatis Parisiensis*, 6 vols., Paris, 1894–1964.

Denifle, H. and Châtelain, E. (eds.) *Chartularium Universitatis Parisiensis*, 4 vols., Paris, 1889–97.

Fournier, M. (ed.) *Les Statuts et privilèges des universités françaises depuis leur fondation jusqu'en 1789*, 4 vols., Paris, 1890–2.

Gibson, S. (ed.) *Statuta Antiqua Universitatis Oxoniensis*, Oxford, 1931.

Gloria, A. (ed.) *Monumenti della Università di Padova*, 2 vols., Venice/Padua, 1885–8.

Hargreaves-Mawdsley, W. N. *A History of Academic Dress in Europe until the End of the Eighteenth Century*, Oxford, 1963.

d'Irsay, S. *Histoire des universités françaises et étrangères des origines à nos jours*, 2 vols., Paris, 1933–5.

Ker, N. R. 'Oxford College Libraries before 1500', in J. IJsewÿn and J. Paquet (eds.), *Universities in the Late Middle Ages*, Mediaevalia Lovaniensia, series 1, studia 6, Louvain, 1978, 293–311.

Kibre, P. *The Nations in the Medieval Universities*, Mediaeval Academy of America, 49, Cambridge, Mass., 1948.

Kibre, P. *Scholarly Privileges in the Middle Ages. The Rights, Privileges and Immunities of Scholars and Universities at Bologna – Padua – Paris – Oxford*, Mediaeval Academy of America, 72, Cambridge, Mass., 1961.

Kiene, M. 'Die Grundlagen der europäischen Universitätsbaukunst', *Zeitschrift für Kunstgeschichte*, 46 (1983), 63–114.

Moreira de Sà, A. (ed.) *Auctarium Chartularii Universitatis Portugalensis*, 3 vols., Lisbon, 1973–9.

Moreira de Sà, A. (ed.) *Chartularium Universitatis Portugalensis*, 8 vols., Lisbon, 1966–81.

Rashdall, H. *The Universities of Europe in the Middle Ages*, 3 vols., ed. F. M. Powicke and A. B. Emden, Oxford, 1936; reprint, London, 1942–58; reprint, Oxford, 1988.

Verger, J. *Les Universités au Moyen Age*, Collection SUP, L'Historien 14, Paris, 1973.

Weijers, O. *Terminologie des universités au XIIIe siècle*, Rome, 1987.

CHAPTER 5

TEACHERS

JACQUES VERGER

It is self-evident that no university or school can exist without teachers. If a schooling differs from an apprenticeship, which is essentially practical, or from tutoring, which is in principle individual, it is because there is a teacher whose role involves him addressing himself collectively, as it were, to a given number of pupils. It is likewise the existence of a teacher that allows us to distinguish a school, even at the higher level, from the other cultural institutions familiar to the Middle Ages, such as the monastic *scriptoria*, the ecclesiastical or princely chancelleries or courts, academies, and so on, which tended to depend upon exchange between equals. Yet the fact that the function of teacher plainly existed in all historical periods should not be taken as an excuse for anachronism. The words describing this function have barely changed at all over the centuries, but does the teacher in medieval universities have anything in common with the teacher in present-day universities, as regards either his professional activity or his social profile – the image he receives or himself adopts?

THE DOCTORATE

The function of teacher is obviously much older than the medieval universities, as the borrowing of the key terms from classical Latin would suggest: *magister* (master), *doctor* (doctor), and *professor* (professor).[1] Although these three terms were not employed indiscriminately, they began by having a similar meaning, with the idea of teaching being associated with that of excellence in a given domain. It is this second aspect, in fact, which was most emphasized in the Middle Ages. A master or doctor could teach, but this was not indispensable. When affixed to a name, even when preceding it, the word

[1] Regarding all these questions of vocabulary, see O. Weijers, *Terminologie des universités au XIIIe siècle* (Rome, 1987).

simply meant that the holder of it had achieved total mastery of the discipline which he had studied. He was therefore equipped in his turn to teach it, but he was also equipped to fulfil all the other functions for which a recognized intellectual qualification prepared him. In a still broader sense, the general attitude at the end of the Middle Ages was that the title gave its bearer genuine social dignity, giving him access to the world of the privileged, indeed, to that of the nobility. So it was that those masters or doctors who actually taught were generally described as 'regent' masters or doctors, that is, *regens* or *actu regens*, a participle which soon became a substantive ('a regent'). This term is still employed at Cambridge.

How did one go about acquiring the title of 'master' or 'doctor'? It was already current in the twelfth century, if not earlier.[2] At that period, it would seem to have been merely a term in ordinary usage rather than an official title. Someone would call himself master if he ran a school (whether he was appointed or had founded it, upon his own initiative or with the authorization, the 'licence', of an authority, generally the representative of the bishop of the place in question) and, more broadly, the title might be used by anyone who had studied for a sufficient period of time and who had left a school with the more or less formal *satisfecit* of his own master, which seemed to guarantee the level of excellence achieved by his pupil. In the twelfth century, such *magistri* began to appear in the cathedral chapters, in the Roman curia, and in certain princely chancelleries, not to mention all those who founded new schools at Paris, Bologna, Montpellier, or Oxford.

When the universities first appeared, acquisition of the title of master ceased to be merely a matter of customary practice and involved instead a procedure which the universities claimed as their monopoly and which was meticulously described. Without going into details, it should simply be noted that the tests enabling one to use this title generally consisted of three elements.[3]

The first stage in the process involved the candidate, with the agreement of his master, who deemed him to have reached a sufficiently high level, presenting himself to the university authorities, the rector, and, above all, the chancellor. The latter, usually attended by a jury of masters, would check that the candidate had fulfilled the required conditions, that is, as regards both his morality and his previous studies. Had he studied for the requisite length of time? Had he, as bachelor, done the prescribed exercises, readings, and dispu-

---

[2] As C. Renardy, among others, has shown in *Le Monde des maîtres universitaires du diocèse de Liège 1140–1350. Recherches sur sa composition et ses activités* (Paris, 1979), especially 79–144.

[3] On procedures pertaining to the licence and the doctorate, see Rashdall, *Universities, passim*; one can find more detailed information regarding Bologna in M. Bellomo, *Saggio sull'università nell'età del dirito comune* (Catania, 1979), especially 239–63; regarding Paris, in P. Glorieux, 'L'enseignement au Moyen Age. Techniques et méthodes en usage à la Faculté de Théologie de Paris, au XIIIe siècle', *Archives d'histoire doctrinale et littéraire du Moyen Age*, 35 (1968), 65–186; regarding Oxford, *History of Oxford, passim*.

tations? There then followed the actual examination, often termed 'private' or 'rigorous' examination, which was also held in the presence of a jury of masters presided over by the chancellor. It ordinarily consisted of a disputation upheld by the candidate over a particular question, a 'point', which was drawn by lot the previous evening or in the morning. If he passed these first two tests, the candidate was regarded as having 'graduated' (*licentiatus*) but, paradoxically, this *licentia* granted by the chancellor, although it may have guaranteed his level of intellectual attainment, in no way entitled him to teach in the university. For this, he had to pass a third test, sometimes called a 'public' examination, which might take place fairly soon after the *licentia* had been granted. *Inceptio* or 'inauguration' was, significantly enough, the term used.

The public examination which resulted in a person being appointed a 'master' or a 'doctor' did not present any special difficulties, and there was no possibility of failing. It was in fact, a ceremony, which often took place in a church, and which involved prayers, solemn orations, and the bestowing upon the candidate of the emblems proper to a master, namely, biretta, gloves, and book. He would then perform his first magistral act, usually a disputation with students, on a theme of his choice. The meaning of the public examination was perfectly clear. It was simply a display of the competence which the previous examination and granting of the *licentia* had guaranteed. It was an act of corporate significance, which showed that the graduate was suited to teaching and which marked his solemn entrance into the body of doctors, his recognition and admission by his peers. Even if the chancellor were present at such ceremonies, he would not wield any authority, in the strict sense, over the awarding of masters' degrees and doctorates, for such awards were acts proper to the university, through which it declared one of the crucial aspects of its independence, namely its freedom to recruit whomsoever it wished.[4]

These, broadly speaking, were the statutory requirements. As far as terminology was concerned, it was customary to talk of a master's degree in the arts and of a doctorate in law; in theology and in medicine, there was more variation in the sorts of title bestowed upon graduates.

It is worth adding a few observations regarding the practical side of things. We should bear in mind, first of all, that only a minority of students ever actually graduated. This point is not in dispute, although it is hard to arrive at accurate percentages (save for the universities of the Holy Roman Empire in the fifteenth century, which kept records of matriculation and of examinations). These percentages varied a great deal from one university, faculty, or period to another. Why did so many students not last the full course? Apart

---

[4] A. E. Bernstein, 'Magisterium and License: Corporate Autonomy against Papal Authority in the Medieval University of Paris', *Viator*, 9 (1978), 291–307.

from the intrinsic difficulty of the studies involved, the time required, and the high cost, one should note the expense of the degree itself. It is reasonable to suppose that universities were more selective where the higher faculties were concerned, although the German arts faculties of the fifteenth century themselves recorded high failure rates, since accounts suggest that only three or four out of ten students were actually awarded their *baccalariatus*, and one out of ten their master's degree. On the other hand, there were instances of the more adroit or the richer managing, by fraud, corruption, or a special dispensation, to acquire degrees fairly easily.

Be this as it may, numerous students, whether they wished it or not, were never in a position to become teachers. But did all the *licentiati* themselves become masters or doctors? In some faculties, such as arts or theology, the two titles almost always went together and were awarded virtually simultaneously. On the other hand, in medicine, and more especially, in law, they would seem in the fourteenth and fifteenth centuries to have been wholly separate. Many *licentiati* did not petition for the doctorate, because this title was far more costly than an ordinary degree and, although it bestowed considerable prestige upon the holder, gave him no further intellectual competence and was only indispensable for those who, since they wished to teach, had to affiliate to the college of doctors.[5]

Finally, did all those who were awarded the highest title, whether a master's degree or a doctorate, teach? Originally, and especially in the great arts faculties, in Paris or in Oxford, the statutes made this compulsory. Every new master had to serve for two years, as an 'obligatory' (*necessarius*) regent. The advantage of this ruling was that it guaranteed that the teaching staff was renewed at regular intervals, but it did not necessarily satisfy those involved, since this obligatory regency could delay their professional advancement, nor did it please the masters who already held positions, since it was plainly in their interests to limit the number of schools and of chairs. For these reasons, the ruling was gradually set aside and, with the reform of 1452, it disappeared from the statutes of the University of Paris.

If all the masters or doctors did not teach, by whom were the teachers chosen? There were, generally speaking, two solutions to this problem. Firstly, co-option by the masters who already held positions, through the faculty assemblies (as in Paris), the 'general congregations' of the masters of the university (as in Oxford), or the college of doctors (as at Avignon); and, secondly, a contract drawn up between the candidate and either the university itself or an external authority (a town or a prince) which served as the university's protector. Generally annual and renewable, this contract speci-

---

[5] J. Verger, 'Le coût des grades: droits et frais d'examen dans les universités du Midi de la France à la fin du Moyen Age', in A. L. Gabriel (ed.), *The Economic and Material Frame of the Mediaeval University* (Notre Dame, 1977), 19–36.

fied very precisely both the teacher's duties and his remuneration.[6] The heartland of the contractual system was, to start with, Italy (Bologna, Padua), but it was then imitiated by those countries which followed, to a greater or lesser degree, the 'Bologna model', such as southern France or Spain. In thirteenth-century Bologna and Padua, it was the student universities which 'elected' the teachers and sealed a contract with them. From the fourteenth century, the appearance of teachers' salaries paid by the communes meant that the task of choosing teachers and negotiations regarding their contracts more and more became the responsibility of city magistrates, whose speciality, as *reformatores* or *tractatores studii*, this would be, although this did not rule out preliminary agreements with the university. At Coimbra, it was the king who appointed teachers, while at Salamanca, on the other hand, their appointment continued to be, for the whole of the Middle Ages, the prerogative of the student rector and his councillors.

TEACHERS' CAREERS

The body of teachers in a medieval university was not homogeneous.

If we set aside for a moment the mere *baccalarii* and *licentiati* (who were responsible, in fact, for a very significant part of the teaching), it should first be noted that, in the theology faculties, many teachers belonged to a religious order (mendicants, Cistercians). They taught in their monasteries and were subject to regulations regarding mobility, which were fixed by the general chapters of their orders, so that they only played a small part in the life and running of the universities and had quite specific careers. Yet the secular teachers were very various also. The main phenomenon, observable almost everywhere in Europe, but with a different term being applied in each case, was the gradual emergence of a group of genuinely professional regents.[7] They were often called 'ordinary', as opposed to 'extraordinary' teachers, the latter being a vaguer category.

The distinction was, first of all, a pedagogic one. For, in each discipline, there were the 'ordinary' texts, the most important ones, which were studied 'ordinarily' (*ordinarie*), i.e. more deeply, and the 'extraordinary' texts, which were not so fundamental and were often read in an 'extraordinary' or 'cursory' manner. The extraordinary readings were as a whole entrusted to the bachelors, but doctors could deliver them too. Given these circumstances, it was common enough to distinguish the ordinary regents, who claimed the

---

[6] At Bologna, these teaching obligations were strictly defined by the *taxatio punctorum*, that is, the precise calendar that the teacher had to observe, in order to study one after the other, without any omissions, all the *puncta* into which the texts of the *Corpus* had been divided (see Bellomo, *Saggio* (note 3), 205–8).

[7] As far as France is concerned, see J. Verger, 'Les professeurs des universités françaises à la fin du Moyen Age', in J. Le Goff and B. Köpeczi (eds.), *Intellectuels français, intellectuels hongrois, XIIIe–XXe siècles* (Budapest/Paris, 1985), 23–39.

right to give the ordinary readings, at the 'doctoral hour' or 'magistral hour' (first thing in the morning), from the extraordinary doctors, who were confined to the extraordinary readings, which generally took place in the afternoon, involved texts considered to be less important, and sometimes did not even feature on the examination syllabus.

But it was not only for pedagogic reasons that the ordinary doctors played a more important role. Financial and institutional considerations were also involved. These teachers tended, as we shall see, to earn the most. They claimed the right to exercise full authority over the students, believing that they alone were entitled to issue testimonials respecting their academic achievements and to sit on the board of examiners, since they were, as ordinary regents, the only ones fully in charge of the schools of the university. At Bologna, this exercise of authority was the main function of the 'colleges of doctors' of the various faculties. Being subject to a *numerus clausus* (sixteen in civil law, twelve in canon law, etc.), these colleges, which were co-opted, did not include all the regents but merely a select number of them. This élite, since it supervised the awarding of degrees and a large part of the relevant revenues, represented a genuine counter-weight to the power of the student universities.[8] This system was especially useful in those cases where the students participated to a greater or lesser degree in the running of the universities. But the ordinary regents were just as concerned to restrict their own numbers in the 'masters' universities'. This tendency was virtually as old as the universities themselves. In 1207, for example, Pope Innocent III had proposed restricting to eight the number of theology schools in Paris. Thus, there arose the notion of a university chair, in the sense of a secure teaching post, usually provided with a specific endowment, and sometimes tied to the teaching of a particular subject. However, chairs in the strict sense were rare in the medieval universities. Five were created in Bologna, alongside the traditional salaried regencies, in 1317.[9] Elsewhere, there were a few examples in the fifteenth century. On the other hand, one has the impression that almost everywhere the number of ordinary regents tended to be fixed at a low and stable number. This fixing of the number of ordinary teachers not only helped guarantee their incomes and their authority but also made it easier to reject undesirable candidates, especially the doctors from other universities[10] or, as was the case in Bologna, foreigners to the town, often in favour of the sons or nephews of the masters already in employment.

Yet the ordinary regents never enjoyed complete control over the university. Setting aside the power of the students in universities like Bologna, there

---

[8] A. Sorbelli (ed.), *Il 'Liber secretus iuris caesarei' dell'Università di Bologna*, vol. I, *1378–1420, con una introduzione sull'origine dei collegi dei dottori* (Bologna, 1938), ix–lxxvi.

[9] Bellomo, *Saggio* (note 3), 211–15.

[10] The large universities were especially concerned to keep out doctors from other universities, in spite of the fact that degrees were supposed to be universally valid. Small and new universities, on the other hand, sought to attract the doctors from prestigious universities.

remains the fact that those here designated extraordinary doctors, and, more generally, all the non-regent masters and doctors present in the university or in the university town (mainly masters of arts studying in a higher faculty) had generally won, sometimes after intense struggle, the right to participate more or less fully in the decision-making bodies of the university – and hence in the profits that might flow from them. This included the various assemblies and councils, the boards of examiners, and sometimes even the university offices. This challenge to the dominance of the ordinary regents was certainly accompanied by a critique, at least an implicit one, of their teaching, which was often marked by absenteeism and routine.

Developments such as those described above were especially evident in the faculties of law and medicine in southern Europe. There, teachers in such faculties were, at an early date, laymen and married; their family responsibilities made continuity in their careers a matter of particular importance. They often remained teachers all their lives, even if they had to move several times (depending upon the contracts which they were offered in the various universities). Those priests and monks who taught canon law or theology had more openings available to them, in that, after a few years as regent, they could opt for a strictly ecclesiastical career. From the thirteenth to the fifteenth century, many bishops, and even some cardinals and popes, were former teachers. In the thirteenth century, over 33 per cent of the recorded Parisian masters of theology became bishops, abbots, general ministers, or cardinals. In the fifteenth century, thirty-six of the seventy-nine English bishops (46 per cent) had taught at Oxford or at Cambridge.[11]

In the arts faculties, although there were a few 'professional' regents who taught grammar and logic, a large number of them, especially at Paris and Oxford, continued to be young masters, who completed their obligatory regency or, at any rate, only devoted a few years to this teaching, often going on to take up their studies in a higher faculty.

The late Middle Ages saw the emergence, especially in the arts, of a new type of regent, with a more stable position but with less dignity than the ordinary regent of the higher faculties. This was the college regent, who was most often to be found in universities with numerous colleges, such as Paris, Oxford, and Cambridge. Although they had first been conceived as lodgings for poor students, these colleges had gradually come to be entrusted with more and more teaching. This was also the case with more modest institutions, such as 'pedagogies' or 'halls'. These had begun by being no more than private lessons but, in the course of time, such forms of teaching were transformed, especially in the larger colleges, into complete exercises, which were

---

[11] R. Avi-Yonah, 'Career Trends of Parisian Masters of Theology, 1200–1320', *History of Universities*, 6 (1986–7), 47–64; J. T. Rosenthal, 'The Training of an Elite Group. English Bishops in the Fifteenth Century', *Transactions of the American Philosophical Society*, new series, 60:5 (1970), 5–54.

open not only to the bursars but also to an external audience, so that they were in direct competition with the faculties' lectures. The development of such activities led these colleges to recruit a body of salaried regents of their own. The colleges of the Sorbonne and Navarre at Paris and Magdalen College at Oxford (founded in 1448) were the first to develop such forms of instruction on a large scale.

PAYMENT OF TEACHERS

The form and scale of payment of the teachers was as various as their careers. In the 'private schools' of the twelfth century, both in Paris and in Bologna, the teachers lived off fees paid by pupils, which were very probably fixed on either an individual or a collective basis, by agreement, before the lectures began. But the church was not too favourably disposed towards this system, being of the view that 'science was a gift from God, which could not be sold'. The traditional cathedral schools therefore offered teaching that was, at least in theory, free, with masters generally being maintained by the granting of a prebend (canon 18 of the third Lateran Council, 1179).

The problem continued to arise in the universities. The teachers who were clerics often had ecclesiastical benefices, since the papacy favoured this solution to the problem and therefore granted them very freely and, with them, dispensations from being resident in these benefices, so that they might have the income and teach at the same time. Yet such incomes were not always adequate. In addition, many, especially among the younger masters of arts, were not granted benefices. This was also the case with lay teachers of law and medicine in the southern universities. The regents were therefore still fairly assiduous about collecting the money paid by the students, the *collecta*. The students were not always too happy about paying, and the *collecta*, which anyway varied from faculty to faculty, never amounted to very much. From the end of the thirteenth century, students also had to pay higher and higher fees when taking their examinations.

Teachers fought bitterly over access to the better benefices, and to the collection of the examination fees and the *collectae*, which shows just how crucial these funds were for the regents' livelihood. A theoretical debate served to justify these practices, with references to Aristotle, the Bible, and Roman law enabling jurists and theologians to admit both that knowledge, being a gift from God, could not be valued in terms of money, and that the labour of a teacher (especially if he had no other resources to call upon) deserved some recompense, it being understood that such recompense should not be taken from the poorer students.[12]

There was a third, and less hazardous, solution, namely the payment of a

---

[12] G. Post, K. Giocarinis, and R. Kay, 'The Medieval Heritage of a Humanistic Ideal: "Scientia donum Dei est, unde vendi non potest" ', *Traditio*, 11 (1955), 195–234.

salary (which anyway did not rule out the levying of *collectae* or of examination fees). Recourse was had to this measure from very early on, when new universities were founded, so as to guarantee a livelihood to those teachers they wished to attract. This happened at Naples (1224), Vercelli (1228), and Toulouse (1229). In Italy it became the custom to pay teachers a salary, and the first instances at Bologna date from 1280 and 1289; by 1381, there were twenty-three doctors of law whose wages were paid by the commune. Indeed, the latter managed, by this means, to extend greater control over the recruitment of teachers. The other Italian universities followed suit. A number (Perugia, Florence, Pavia) offered high salaries at the time of foundation, in order to try to attract famous teachers from Bologna or Padua. In the Iberian peninsula, too, salaries became usual; the kings of Castile and Portugal instituted them for the regents in the universities they founded at Salamanca, Valladolid, and Coimbra. The church covered the costs of this operation, since these salaries were based upon parts of the tithes and various other ecclesiastical revenues which these kings reserved for themselves.[13] On the other hand, in those universities which were founded in Aragon in the fourteenth century, such as Lérida and Huesca, the towns took responsibility for salaries.

In France, there were hardly any salaried teachers before the end of the Middle Ages (1479–93 at Avignon), if one excepts a number of new foundations, which enjoyed varying degrees of success (Orange in 1365, Poitiers in 1431) and which the towns tried to maintain.[14] At Oxford, it is worth mentioning the ephemeral chairs of philosophy, founded in 1437 by the duke of Gloucester, and, later, a chair of theology (1497). But one should bear in mind that, both in Paris and in Oxford, the college regents were paid by the college which employed them as holders of fellowships.

Finally, in the Empire, the founders and benefactors of universities created in the fourteenth and fifteenth centuries, whether by princes, towns, or private persons, provided a livelihood for the regents from the beginning. However, the solution of paying an annual salary, which was adopted at Louvain, for example, was something of a burden for the public finances. Universities therefore usually preferred to have recourse to perpetual foundations, while reserving for the masters, and for the masters of arts in particular, who were the most numerous and the most needy, prebends within the local chapters (from 1443, twenty-nine prebends at Louvain were reserved for the university, which considerably lightened the burden of wages shouldered by the town)[15]

[13] A. Barcala Muñoz, 'Las Universidades españolas durante la Edad media', *Anuario de estudios medievales*, 15 (1985), 83–126.

[14] For Orange: F. Gasparri, *La Principauté d'Orange au Moyen Age (fin XIIIe–XVe siècle)* (Paris, 1985), 235–9. For Poitiers: R. Favreau, *La Ville de Poitiers à la fin du Moyen Age. Une capitale régionale*, vol. II (Poitiers, 1978), 380–4.

[15] J. Paquet, *Salaires et prébendes des professeurs de l'université de Louvain au XVe siècle* (Léopoldville, 1958).

or places in the colleges (as was the case in Vienna, Heidelberg, Leipzig, Rostock, Greifswald, and so on), a system which was also to be adopted in Scotland (St Andrews, Glasgow).

Whatever the precise mode of payment in each university, there would seem to have been serious discrepancies. In general, those who taught in higher faculties seem to have had incomes that were patently larger (benefices, fees, examination fees, and salaries) than the regents of arts. But many other factors were involved, including the number of students and the wealth of the prince or of the town (which obviously varied greatly, as did the personal reputations of the teachers). At Pavia, for example, between 1387 and 1499, the number of salaried teachers ranged from nine to about seventy, depending upon the state of the duke of Milan's finances, whereas there were eventually huge discrepancies (in the ratio of 1 to 50) between the spectacular sums paid to a number of famous jurists and the miserable salaries, about as much as those paid to unskilled workers, paid to masters of grammar or of logic, who accounted for approximately half of the university's teaching staff.[16] Elsewhere, the discrepancies were not so great, but were nevertheless significant (in the ratio of 1 to 9 at Coimbra, according to a statute of 1323).

An exhaustive description would have to include some account of income earned by regents which derived from non-university sources. They might, for instance, have acquired, either through birth, marriage, or work, a personal fortune which guaranteed them an income. They might, on the other hand, have students lodge in their houses. Finally, they could, alongside their teaching, give legal or medical consultations, which were usually very costly.

To sum up, there were at least two kinds of teaching career possible in the medieval universities, with obviously a whole series of intermediate options. On the one hand, there were those young regents who only taught for a few years, generally beginning immediately after they had been promoted. They usually hoped to pursue an ecclesiastical or civil career outside the university. This does not imply that, after leaving, they ceased to be interested in their alma mater, for the oaths sworn at the time of their graduation, and when they took their examinations, bound them irrevocably to it. They would therefore sit at times on its councils, as non-regent doctors, and they might return to teach. Nor should their decision to leave after a few years be taken to mean that they were mediocre teachers. Indeed, being close to their own students in age, still unconfined by routine, they would seem in fact to have enjoyed real success. Less concerned with their own personal interests, they undoubtedly remained more sensitive to the collective aspects of the university as an institution, to the specific religious or political role that it could play.

Those whom we have called ordinary regents, and who were undoubtedly

16 D. Zanetti, 'A l'université de Pavie au XVe siècle: les salaires des professeurs', *Annales ESC*, 17 (1962), 421–33.

in the majority by the end of the Middle Ages, especially in the new universities, had quite different careers. Although it was rare for them to abandon all hope of a promotion outside the university, they tended to pass long years, or even the whole of their lives, in such places. Thus, of the sixteen professors of law at Orléans between 1378 and 1429 whose names are known to us, thirteen at least had taught for between twenty and forty years.[17] For such men, the university was not only a place for exchanges on the intellectual and the human plane; it also provided a frame for the whole of their lives, guaranteeing both their incomes and their social position. Less prone to engage in daring collective initiatives or to take radical decisions, they were prepared to sacrifice neither their personal or familial interests nor the image which they constructed of themselves, that of men of authority and experience or, if you like, that of notables. Both the modest regent of a college and the prestigious 'doctor in both the laws' sought to serve the university and to profit from it.

The advent of the ordinary regents obviously reduced teachers' geographical mobility. Admittedly, those who had graduated from the largest universities always managed to find themselves a good post. Thus, in the fourteenth and fifteenth centuries, doctors from Bologna and Padua were to be found in all the new Italian universities, which wrangled long and hard over such valuable catches. The masters or arts or of theology from the University of Paris were welcomed in southern France or, after 1378, in the Holy Roman Empire. If one adopts the larger view, however, it is fair to say that recruitment of teachers at the end of the Middle Ages tended to become more and more local.

Were such teachers necessarily mediocre and hidebound? A proper answer to this question demands that one first examines the concrete conditions governing their teaching.

TEACHING AS A PROFESSION

University statutes gave details of the teacher's teaching obligations. They varied from university to university, and from faculty to faculty, but were generally fairly constraining. In the end, they turned teaching into a full-time activity, a genuine profession. Rather than consider the formal and real content or teaching methods of the various disciplines (which are examined in a number of other chapters in this book), it is best to try to gauge just how onerous a teacher's duties might have been.

A regent's primary obligation was to 'read', that is, to deliver his magistral lectures on texts specified by the syllabus. These lectures were given in the morning and lasted one and a half to two hours. The regents had to read on every day upon which work was permitted (*dies legibiles*) but, in practice, if

---

[17] *Universités en France*, 101.

one set aside Sundays and religious festivals, days reserved for solemn disputations and examinations and summer holidays, there were barely more than between 130 and 150 *dies legibiles* a year. Some masters gave a second lecture in the afternoon, but the 'extraordinary', more specialized or optional lectures, which took place at the end of the morning or in the afternoon, were usually given by extraordinary regents or by bachelors. The doctors also had to arrange the disputations, generally in the afternoon, a duty which involved choosing the themes, presiding over them, and bringing them to a conclusion, through their own presentation, in the days that followed, of the 'determination' of the questions disputed. There was considerable variety in the number of disputations that were held. A great theologian such as Thomas Aquinas gave an average of two a week,[18] but in other contexts, especially in the law faculties, the rule was to have no more than one disputation per week. This stipulation helped to ensure that the ordinary teaching routine was not too much disturbed, for all the bachelors had to attend every disputation and therefore postpone their own lectures. Although circumstances varied with the size of the teaching staff, each master tended not to have personal responsibility for more than one disputation per month, per term, or per year (as was the case in Bologna).

To lecture and dispute, a teacher had to have copies of the essential books in his own library. In addition, he would have to devote a certain amount of time to preparation, even if he gave the same course year after year, for the statutes forbade, at any rate in theory, the dictation of a course that had been wholly written out in advance. The best teachers would also probably after the event, draft a version of their commentaries and entrust such texts to a stationer, who would circulate them among the students and the copyists.

University life entailed many obligations other than those that were strictly pedagogic. There were, for instance, religious ceremonies, both regular and occasional, examination boards, and the assemblies and councils of the university, the faculties, the doctors' colleges, etc. Teachers might have occasion to hold one or another of the many elective offices that the administration of the university required, namely rector, proctor, *taxator* (of the rents and prices in the university town), *receptor* and dean; even in the student universities of the Bologna type, there were the officers of the doctors' colleges (the priors). The mandates were generally short (a year at the maximum) but could subsequently be held again from time to time especially by the ordinary regents. During their period of office the university's officers had to be continuously present: they had to keep accounts and archives, resolve a thousand and one problems on a daily basis, and represent the university in all circumstances. Such offices, on the other hand, conferred authority and prestige. In Paris, the rector of the university marched at the head of official processions,

---

[18] Glorieux, 'Enseignement au Moyen Age' (note 3), 127.

next to the bishop. Finally, teachers were often summoned, as representatives of the university, to go on embassies (to the king or the pope) or to participate in commissions (for the purpose of examining a suspect book or of visiting a college).

These obligations were not the same for all. For jurists and doctors in medicine, it was the readings that were fundamental; the masters of arts, since they were addressing themselves to younger pupils, combined lectures with repetitions. On the other hand, the masters of theology very probably tended to accord more importance to disputations than to readings, a good proportion of which – indeed, virtually all of them – they handed over to the bachelors, the *sententiarii* and the *biblici*, whose task it was to give the students, regarding the two basic texts, Peter Lombard's *Sentences* and the Holy Scriptures, the basic knowledge required to tackle the great scholastic debates on the 'disputed questions'. As far as administrative duties were concerned, it is probable that particular men, either older or more influential within the university, were especially responsible for them.

By no means all teachers were equally zealous in the prosecution of their duties. Seriousness was a matter of personal capacity and temperament, and it would be quite mistaken to suppose that, even in the eyes of contemporaries, all ordinary regents were serious. The insistence of the university statutes and the penalties stipulated, especially at Bologna, where a number of students made it their business to watch over and denounce unsatisfactory teachers,[19] go to show, by their very frequency, that teachers almost everywhere 'read' only a part of their programme, dictated their courses, awarded degrees to unworthy candidates, absented themselves, and drafted in mere bachelors or *licentiati* in their place, ploys that the university regulations, it being impossible to prohibit them strove to limit, for example, to one month a year.

By 1317, Pope John XXII had begun to grow anxious: 'A number of regents [in law], who should have been devoting themselves to their lectures, are involving themselves in trials, pleadings, and other external activities.'[20] This absenteeism seems to have grown worse at the end of the Middle Ages, as so many teachers' biographies suggest (being famous, they were perhaps not representative). Periods spent in the service of a prince or the church, and extended visits to the Councils of Constance or of Basle kept many masters away from their chairs for months, sometimes years, disrupting the teaching schedule and leaving the way open for a whole number of different abuses (courses of study being curtailed and examinations a mere formality).

If we consider the case of a doctor who fulfilled his teaching obligations in accord with the statutes of his university, we may ask what the conditions were, practically speaking, under which he worked.

[19] Bellomo, *Saggio* (note 3), 208.   [20] *CUP*, vol. II, 200–1, no. 741.

A teacher's basic context was his school or *schola*. Materially, it consisted, first of all, of a room, whose features are familiar to us from the copious, though somewhat stereotyped, iconographic sources of the period. It had a magistral chair, students' benches, sometimes supplied with desks upon which books might be placed (often for the following of the master's lesson, usually without writing in them), a few cupboards along the walls, and the floor strewn with straw in winter. These rooms were generally hired by the regents, at their own expense. It was only belatedly that the universities themselves owned their own buildings, the University of Paris at the end of the fourteenth century, and those of Oxford, Cambridge, Coimbra, Salamanca, Avignon, Poitiers, etc. in the 1430s. In the universities of the empire and of eastern Europe, such as Prague, Leipzig, and of Cracow, lecture courses were often held in the colleges.

But schools also had a human and pedagogic dimension. They were sometimes likened, at any rate in the early days, to a 'society' (*societas*) consisting of the master and his pupils. What did this mean?

A student arriving at a university had to appear before the university authorities, but the crucial act, by which he became a genuine member of the university, was his registration as a member of a school, 'under' a given master. He would often have a few days in which to make up his mind. What were the criteria? One could apply to a compatriot or else opt for the most famous school. At any rate, as the first statutes of the University of Paris put it (1215), there could be 'no student without a master'. All medieval universities were in face obsessed by the struggle against the 'wandering', uncontrolled student, who went from one master to another.

The master was supposed to keep a register of those students who matriculated with him (if only in order to claim the *collecta* from them). He was responsible, to a certain extent, for their conduct, although the jurisdiction which the masters had originally held over their pupils would seem to have given way to that exercised by university officers (rector, chancellor). His main responsibility was to assure that they made good progress in their studies. It was he who decided (and the statutes often gave him some leeway here) when the student, having been for several years a virtually silent listener to lectures and disputations, could accede to the 'determination' or to the *baccalariatus*, which would one day entitle him to play a more active role, that of a kind of assistant. These assistants would provide answers in the disputations and deliver some of the extraordinary lectures, which knocked the rough edges off the novice students and prepared them for following the course of magistral lectures. The masters would also, at the appropriate moment, 'present' their 'formed' bachelor (*baccalarius formatus*) for the *licentia* and 'doctorate' examinations.

One can readily understand how very strong personal ties, of both an intellectual and an affective nature, could well have bound a master to his students (even if freshmen were sometimes a little disorientated at first by the lack of immediate constraints), especially if one bears in mind the duration of a course of studies, the onerous nature of the timetables, and the importance of oral examinations. A teacher's former pupils, particularly if he had subsequently been promoted to high office, were fond of talking of 'my master' (*dominus meus*) and of calling upon the good graces of him who had once formed and protected them.

This is of course a somewhat idealized picture. In practice, things might well pass less smoothly, with students proving critical of their master, judging him to have a difficult character, to be incompetent, or, conversely, to be the kind of person to indulge in vain subleties. It is rare for such protests to leave any trace,[21] but one can guess what the practical consequences might have been. Some students would switch schools in the hope of finding a more erudite master somewhere else or, conversely, a more accommodating one. Many students hesitated before taking so drastic a step but tended rather, in various ways, to display a manifest lack of enthusiasm for the official pedagogic formulae (as did a number of their masters), and on an ever-increasing scale in the fourteenth and fifteenth centuries.

Students were never shut up in their schools, with no contact with the outside world. Whenever a disputation was held, all the bachelors of a given faculty would meet in turn in each of the schools. Examinations were also held in the presence of juries upon which sat all or a part of the masters of the faculty. A master was therefore not free to do what he wished in his school, especially since the statutes bound him to particular syllabuses, timetables, and methods.

Nevertheless, the traditional forms of instruction seemed onerous and inappropriate to some. This is why many bachelors, especially in theology, tended to break free and to give a deeper and more personal form of teaching, especially in their reading of the *Sentences*. It also accounts for the sometimes bewildering proliferation of 'extraordinary' or optional exercises and courses, sometimes given privately or during the vacations, by *licentiati* or by bachelors, the success of which would seem to be explained by their more practical or more modern character (this was often how humanism, for example, found its way into the universities).

The proportion of these 'informal' teachings, only vaguely defined or even opposed in the official statutes, was certainly rising, especially where the most inquisitive and demanding students were concerned. Even if it is scarcely

[21] J. Leclercq, 'Lo sviluppo dell'atteggiamento critico degli allievi verso i maestri dal X al XIII secolo', in *Università e società*, which draws mainly, as regards the thirteenth century, upon some Parisian *quodlibeta*; these disputes may very well have served as an outlet for such a struggle.

possible for us to gauge their exact importance and their real efficacy, they plainly represent a new intellectual orientation. This same tendency may be held to account for the development of teaching within the colleges, where a new system for the allocation of pupils was emerging (with age being the criterion that determined their place in a particular class, each one of which had its own regent). In a somewhat analogous manner, the fifteenth century saw the masters of arts in a number of universities in Germany (Leipzig) and Scotland sharing out, through a system of yearly rotation, the various books on the syllabus, with the students passing from one teacher to the other. So it was that the restrictive framework of the school, in which year after year the students used to follow the same courses given by the same teacher, gradually gave way to more flexible and more progressive systems.

One would be better placed to understand the position of a medieval professor with regard to his students if one knew just how many of the latter there were. Obviously, numbers varied with the importance of the university, the size of the teaching staff, and the particular circumstances of the time. At Paris, where the number of regents was always high, the schools would probably have had on average, in the fifteenth century, only ten to twenty pupils, and still fewer in medicine.[22] But numbers of pupils tended in general to increase. In the big colleges, one would generally expect to find twenty to thirty pupils per regent.[23] Some famous jurists claimed that their reading drew dozens, if not hundreds, of listeners and, in those universities in which a small group of ordinary regents had managed to win a monopoly, they could count on having a substantial audience, which might perhaps vary from one school to another depending upon the reputation of the master.[24]

RELATIONS BETWEEN COLLEAGUES

If the relations between the master and his pupils, which were of a largely oral nature, often elude us, those of a master with his colleagues are somewhat better known. The documentation tells us for the most part of situations of tension and conflict. There were conflicts between immediate colleagues, involving accusations of the theft of their respective students (together with the associated profits, the *collectae* and the examination fees). There were conflicts between the masters of the various faculties. At Paris,

---

[22] I have used here the estimates given by J. Favier for the numbers of students of the University of Paris between 1400 and 1450, in *Paris au XVe siècle. 1380–1500* (Paris, 1974), 69–72.

[23] In the Collège de Navarre (Paris), there were three masters for, respectively, twenty pupils in grammar, thirty in logic, and twenty in theology; the colleges of the faculty of arts at Greifswald anticipated having ten regents and 340 students (Rashdall, *Universities*, vol. I, 511; vol. II, 272). One could give any number of other examples.

[24] At Avignon, in the fifteenth century, four ordinary regents in law were jointly responsible for, on average, 200 to 300 students (J. Verger, 'Le rôle social de l'université d'Avignon au XVe siècle', *Bibliothèque d'Humanisme et Renaissance*, 33 (1971), 489–504).

for example, the members of the arts faculties used to complain of the surveillance exercised by the theologians over their teaching, and in other places
the arrogance of the doctors of law was denounced. There were conflicts
between masters of different statuses, the most famous being those which
placed lay teachers and mendicants in opposed camps, as at Paris (especially
in 1250–39 and 1387–1403), at Oxford (1303–20), and at Cambridge (1303–6).
Conflicts of this latter kind were partly concerned with matters of doctrine
but the immediate causes were exclusively to do with questions of corporate
identity. Thus, the secular teachers, whether masters of arts or theologians,
having allowed the mendicant *studia* the same status as their theology
schools, charged the friars with exploiting their presence in the university (in
order to recruit new brothers or to win university degrees) without, at the
same time, submitting to the rules of the university community. They refused,
for example, to have anything to do with strikes in defence of the university's
freedoms, they founded new chairs without being authorized to do so, or they
disdained preliminary training in the arts faculty, on the grounds that they
had their own network of preparatory *studia*. These conflicts culminated in
various kinds of compromise, none of which ever posed any threat to the
dominant place that the mendicants had won in the teaching of theology.[25]
Finally, there were conflicts between masters of different origins, as at
Prague, where a feud between Czech and German masters only ended when
the latter were expelled, in 1409.[26]

These strictly professional conflicts were compounded by intellectual
clashes also. In almost all the theology faculties of the northern half of
Europe, the fourteenth and fifteenth centuries saw a confrontation between
the 'ancients' (Thomists, Scotists) and the 'moderns' ('nominalists'), with its
parade of invective, condemnation, and exclusion. A number of German
universities (Heidelberg, Freiburg, Ingolstadt, and Tübingen) withdrew from
this by establishing two separate paths (the *via antiqua* and the *via moderna*),
so that masters and students could opt for one or the other according to
choice.

Finally, the universities were not immune to political divisions either.
These were especially severe at Paris, where, at different periods, the supporters of Philip the Fair and those of Pope Boniface VIII, those of the pope and
those of the Council at the time of the Great Schism, and those of the Armag-
nacs and those of the Bourguignons at the end of the Hundred Years War

---

25 For information regarding the conflicts between secular masters and mendicants, one should
consult, as far as Paris is concerned, M.-M. Dufeil, *Guillaume de Saint-Amour et la polémique
universitaire parisienne, 1250–1259* (Paris, 1972); for Oxford: *History of Oxford*, 205–8; for
Cambridge: A. G. Little, 'The Friars versus the University of Cambridge', *English Historical
Review*, 50 (1935), 686–96.
26 F. Šmahel, 'The Kuttenberg Decree and the Withdrawal of the German Schools from Prague
in 1409: a Discussion', *History of Universities*, 4 (1984), 153–66.

struggled with one another. Sometimes this could lead to the exclusion of one party or another.

One should not conclude that members of universities lived in an atmosphere of underhand jealousies or of open quarrels. The great debates mentioned above mainly affected the arts and theology faculties of Paris and Oxford. Elsewhere, in the faculties of law and of medicine and in the smaller universities founded at the end of the Middle Ages, tensions seem to have been far less severe and the inevitable conflicts were quickly settled. Moreover, such quarrels were always counterbalanced by bonds linking the masters to each other, old ties of comradeship formed in student days, a shared awareness of the need to safeguard the independence of the university community by ensuring that it remained on an even keel, and the need to make a show of solidarity against outside threats. This collective feeling had undoubtedly grown weaker by the end of the Middle Ages, especially as a result of pressure from the state,[27] but the relations between teachers did not necessarily deteriorate as a consequence. It was simply that the age old solidarity of the first masters, mindful of the need to struggle for the emancipation of the *studium*, was replaced by a sociability of notables, the conformism of professional regents concerned to defend their common interests.

KNOWLEDGE AND AUTHORITY: THE TEACHER'S IMAGE

Finally, if we are to understand the medieval teacher, we need to consider his sense of his own identity and the image that he wished to project of himself. It is not easy to discern just what this image was, for medieval university teachers did not leave any autobiographical works. When teachers speak of their function, it is in glosses, scholarly tracts, and official texts (inaugural lectures (*proemia*) and harangues), and such sources only give us idealized portraits. Similarly, university statutes merely describe the norm. As for literature which was not directly connected to teaching, such as pedagogical treatises like the *De disciplina scolarium* or the various *De modo studendi*, the texts of moralists ('mirrors' or confessors' manuals), and sermons,[28] these might contain numerous allusions to masters and scholars, to their virtues and vices, but they were often pitched at so general a level that it would be difficult to relate them to the concrete realities of the time.

However, a number of themes in these texts serve to define the ideal that medieval teachers (allowing for variations with respect to discipline, country, and period concerned) sought to realize.[29]

[27] J. Verger, 'Université et communauté au Moyen Age', *CRE–Information*, 62 (1983), 21–44.
[28] P. Riché, 'Sources pédagogiques et traités d'éducation [au Moyen Age]', in 'Les entrées dans la vie. Initiations et apprentissages', *Annales de l'Est*, 34 (special issue) (1982), 15–29.
[29] In particular, Post, Giocarinis, and Kay, 'Medieval Heritage' (note 12); J. Leclercq, 'L'idéal du théologien au Moyen Age. Textes inédits', *Revue des sciences religieuses*, 21 (1947), 121–48; G. Le Bras, ' "Velut splendor firmamenti": le docteur dans le droit de l'Eglise médiévale', in

The crucial idea was that the teacher was a man of authority. The title of master or of doctor, guaranteed by his peers and by the church, was not merely a professional qualification to teach or a corporate rank. It defined a status, a dignity, and an order. It gave its holder access to a lofty social position which, naturally enough, many university members, especially if they were jurists, compared to that of the nobility. Like a noble, a doctor was 'illustrious'; in a city, he would be numbered among the 'greats' (*majores*). He had greater authority and power than did an ordinary knight, or so Simon of Borsano, a Bolognese doctor of the fourteenth century, claimed; he had, therefore, to be granted precedence, to enjoy privileges and immunities consonant with his dignity.[30]

This conception was not everywhere accepted, however. Theologians and moralists stressed the temptation of pride and reminded their audiences of the precept of the Gospel: 'But be not ye called Rabbi: for one is your Master ...' (Matthew 23.8). The ancient conception had generally involved counterposing the wisdom of the cleric to the violence of the knight but, in the society of orders which was consolidated at the end of the Middle Ages, each had to stick to his own place, and from then on the doctors seemed greedy to be assimilated into the ruling élites.

The authority which the masters and doctors assumed had two main aspects. First of all, it was intellectual. A doctor was a scholar, endowed with a science that was at once perfect and finished. His authority found its justification in the dignity of the knowledge he possessed. For the masters were also hired, on the whole with success, to sing the praises of their discipline, to defend scholastic theology against the attacks of the mystics, justifying their recourse to the liberal arts notwithstanding their pagan origins, just as the church fathers had done, exonerating law (which was a divine science, a *res sanctissima*, as Placentinus had declared as early as 1186) and medicine from the charge of being somewhat lucrative or mechanical affairs.

Was a doctor's science given, once and for all? Admittedly, people in the Middle Ages were ignorant of the modern notion of scientific progress. Nevertheless, many texts emphasized that a doctor should be zealous in his work and assiduous in his teaching. He should make progress or, at any rate, seek to make his formulations approximate ever more closely to the truth. It is in these terms that he would deserve not only glory, the respect of his contemporaries, and the admiration and the gratitude of his pupils, but also the salary he asked of them.

Yet a true doctor was also supposed to be humble. He was meant to be humble before God, the source of all knowledge, and before the providential

---

Mélanges offerts à Etienne Gilson (Toronto/Paris, 1959), 373–88; A. L. Gabriel, 'The Ideal Master of the Mediaeval University', *Catholic Historical Review*, 60 (1974), 1–40.

[30] D. Maffei, 'Dottori e studenti nel pensiero di Simone da Borsano', *Studia Gratiana*, 15 (1972), 230–47.

order of the creation, which the hierarchical arrangement of disciplines merely reproduced. He was therefore warned not to stray from his own domain, a warning which was especially aimed at the philosophers in the arts faculties, who were tempted to free themselves from the control of theology or, indeed, to invade its domain. This warning was to prove all the more necessary once certain regents of arts, especially at the time of the great 'Averroist' crisis in Paris in the 1270s, had openly criticized this conception. 'Is humility a virtue? No', Siger of Brabant had written. Through his knowledge, a teacher – or a 'philosopher', as the members of arts faculties termed him – attained to 'all the goods accessible to man', 'the best of all possible conditions'. In a world subject to the astral determinisms of Aristotelian cosmology, the sole wisdom was that of the philosopher, and the sole freedom was that offered by knowledge. Propositions such as these, in the formulations that were condemned in 1277, have a provocative aspect; they may, however, have served to express a new aspiration to a kind of 'laicization' of knowledge, of 'scholarly neutrality', and of the genuine social and intellectual emancipation of the teacher.[31]

These were not the dominant conceptions of the time, though, nor were they encouraged by the church. In its view, a doctor's authority was not only intellectual, but moral also. Science was indissociable, especially where teaching was concerned, from the uses to which it was put in the social world, and the teacher was eminently responsible for such uses. 'It is by his acts rather than his condition that a doctor earns his "aureola" [= his prestige]', stated Henry of Ghent in a question of 1277.[32]

A master should therefore be above reproach, in his life and in his morality, and he was scrutinized with this in mind when he was examined for his *licentia*. He was supposed to practise all the Christian virtues and, above all, those appropriate to his condition (impartiality, goodwill towards his colleagues and his pupils, keenness in work), and, conversely, to avoid those sins which directly threatened it (financial rapacity, negligence, vanity). The gravity of his deportment was meant to honour the science whose representative he was.

Above all, if we set this practical deontology aside, a teacher was supposed to be conscious of his social responsibility. Thus, 'vain curiosities' or 'useless subtleties' were of no value to students; doctrinal errors represented so great a risk that he should, under threat of revocation,[33] submit his teaching to the judgement and to the correction of his peers and of the church. A theologian was supposed to bear in mind that he was training priests and preachers,

---

[31] J. Le Goff, 'Quelle conscience l'université médiévale a-t-elle eue d'elle-même?', in J. Le Goff (ed.), *Pour un autre Moyen Age. Temps, travail et culture en Occident: 18 essais* (Paris, 1977), 181–97.

[32] Quoted in Leclercq, 'Idéal du théologien' (note 29), 146.

[33] There are in fact very few attested cases of a master falling into destitution; it is worth mentioning, however, the Parisian 'nominalist' Nicholas of Autrecourt, who, in 1346, was stripped of his degree of master of arts (*CUP*, vol. II, 576–87, no. 1124)

whose behaviour would influence the faithful; a jurist was supposed to be aware that his opinions contributed to 'common opinion', that is, to the elaboration of law, and therefore to all of social and political life. Masters in medicine had a still more immediate responsibility, for they were acknowledged to have a right of control over the legal exercise of their profession, and over the whole of public hygiene.

Concretely, such responsibilities were first of all exercised within the university itself, on examination boards and on the various committees, both permanent and occasional, which had to assess the orthodoxy of texts circulated by bookshops or to pass judgement respecting denunciations which were sometimes levelled against the teaching of one or other of their colleagues or of their bachelors. The many condemnations and censures which mark the doctrinal history of the medieval universities almost always had their origin in conflicts arising within the faculties themselves, between one or more teachers and the majority of masters.

Members of the universities were especially vehement in asserting their social and political responsibility in the more troubled periods, in particular at the beginning of the Great Schism, when they considered themselves entitled to proffer solutions to the crisis.[34] At times they also sought to play a role in affairs of state. Thus, the masters of the University of Prague played a major part in the revolt of Bohemia in 1419.[35] Likewise, the masters of Paris offered to collaborate with the king in promoting the 'reform of the kingdom' in Charles VI's reign, which provided ample justification for the chancellor John Gerson's explanation, in his great speech of 1405 (*Vivat rex*), as to how the university, through its four faculties, 'represented' the totality of accessible human knowledge, in both its theoretical and its practical dimension, and how, furthermore, through the recruitment of its members from every country and every state, it served as a microcosm of the whole society, and therefore the best of all interpreters of 'common utility'.[36]

'Of what value would science be', asked Gerson, 'if it was not put into operation? . . . One does not learn solely in order to know but also in order to demonstrate and to act.' There is some temptation, on the basis of this praise of political commitment, to define the teachers of medieval universities as 'intellectuals', but this would only be accurate if one specified that, in contrast with what nowadays would be regarded as normal for intellectuals, they never meant their interventions to be in the service of a will that was subversive or even merely critical of the established order. They were not, save for a few exceptions, men of violence, leading revolts or encouraging popular

[34] R. N. Swanson, *Universities, Academics and the Great Schism* (Cambridge, 1979).
[35] H. Kaminsky, 'The University of Prague in the Hussite Revolution: the Role of the Masters', in *Universities in Politics*, 79–106.
[36] J. Gerson, *Oeuvres complètes*, ed. P. Glorieux, vol. VII:1, *L'Oeuvre française. Sermons et discours* (Paris, 1968), 1137–85.

heresies. Being the bearers of a knowledge deemed stable and perfect, whose truth had been established once and for all at the creation, they simply wished to play their part, in face of all the disorders of their time, in healing the breach in this ideal order.

Of course, only the masters of the great universities (such as Paris, Oxford, or Prague) ever really had to play a role of this kind. But, even in universities that had been founded more recently or that were of only secondary importance, the teachers were undoubtedly aware that their social responsibility consisted in ensuring the best possible functioning of the civil and ecclesiastical institutions through the intellectual training of élites, at any rate local ones, élites to which they, as teachers, therefore felt themselves to belong. This does not mean that they invariably sought to obstruct every kind of social advancement through study, or that they tried in any systematic sense to discourage poor students. The significant point to note, rather, is that they henceforth considered, to a much greater degree than at the origins of the institution, the perfect accommodation of their work to the requirements of the existing social and political order to be one of the normal demands of their métier.

THE PLACE OF TEACHERS IN MEDIEVAL SOCIETY

The texts mentioned above all emanate, by and large, from the doctors themselves. But did their contemporaries really acknowledge the rightfulness of their claims?

Official texts were usually not sparing in their praises of the doctors. From the time that the universities had first emerged, popes had been in the habit of describing them as 'lights of the church, shining as brightly as stars in the firmament'. In spite of the reticence of urban populations, princes did not begrudge them honours and prerogatives either. Such authorities were anyway undoubtedly convinced of the usefulness of the universities, for they were tireless in their attempts to protect and to develop them, sometimes at great cost, and they were likewise convinced of the value to them of the masters, whose appointments they often supervised. Those outside the university who dared to criticize it were few and far between, and they were often disillusioned ex-university members. For example, Geert Groote (1340–84), the founder in the Low Countries of the movement of the Brothers and Sisters of the Common Life, which was a movement of popular and evangelical devotion, attacked the pride and stupidity of the Parisian masters, who were responsible, in his view, for the ruin of the church (he himself was a former master of arts at Paris): 'These men wreck all piety, make fun of ordinary folk, and deceive the people.'[37] Some humanists were just as harsh

---

[37] G. Epiney-Burgard, *Gérard Grote (1340–1384) et les débuts de la dévotion moderne* (Wiesbaden, 1970), 31.

in their condemnation. This was the case with, for example, Lorenzo Valla (1407–57), after his unfortunate experience at the University of Pavia, where he was the object of attacks by colleagues hostile to his new ideas. Yet the universities and the masters seem by and large to have enjoyed, up until the end of the Middle Ages, a real prestige, especially as far as the social and political élites were concerned.

One should note, however, that honorific titles and displays of generosity multiplied just when the universities' independence was rapidly being eroded by the increasing pressure from the state, and just when the latter was making it increasingly plain that it expected the universities not only to form the competent and devoted servants it needed but also, as a body, i.e. above all in the person of their teachers, to uphold and second its political actions.

How did such developments affect the social recruitment of the teachers? This is a problem that has not yet been very deeply studied, but it would seem that this recruitment did not differ fundamentally from that of the other graduates. However, even if the lesser nobility were fairly often recruited, especially in the case of teachers of law, students of the loftiest social origin do not seem to have been much attracted to the teaching profession. With the same degrees, other types of career, whether civil or ecclesiastic, would have seemed preferable to them, undoubtedly more remunerative, and more suited to their familial position.[38] They may have acknowledged the prestige of teaching as a profession, but this did not therefore mean that they desired to practise it.

Indeed, teachers seem to have been recruited in the main from among students whose social origins were lowly (this was the case with Wyclif, Gerson, and John Huss) or middle ranking. For such men, their wealth consisted, above all, in their intellectual gifts, and access to a regency was undoubtedly a form of social advancement. In addition, as time went on, regencies tended increasingly to be handed down to one's sons or nephews. Many special statutes, for example, dispensations concerning the duration of a course of study, exemptions from examination fees, or derogations to the *numerus clausus* imposed in the doctors' colleges, also did much in many universities, especially in the fifteenth century, to establish small teaching dynasties, in control of regencies which were anyway better and better established in their authority and their incomes. In 1317, the great Bolognese jurist, Johannes Andreae even went so far as to inscribe in the statutes that his descendents would enjoy, in perpetuity, a prior right to apply for the university's salaried chairs.[39]

---

[38] This would at any rate seem to be the case with the universities of the south of France; J. Verger, 'Noblesse et savoir: étudiants nobles aux universités d'Avignon, Cahors, Montpellier et Toulouse (fin du XIVe siècle)' in P. Contamine (ed.), *La Noblesse au Moyen Age. XIe–XVe siècles. Essai à la mémoire de Robert Boutruche* (Paris, 1976), 289–313, especially 311.

[39] Bellomo, *Saggio* (note 3), 212.

This tendency of regents to constitutue themselves as a caste, which went along with their professionalization, never resulted in a complete closure; teaching always remained, in the Middle Ages, a possible path to social advancement. The inheritance of offices was anyway everywhere on the increase among lawyers (who were for the most part graduates) during this period, and the case of regents is therefore not unique. But what position did they occupy, as caste or subcaste, within this social group as a whole? There have as yet been no studies comparing, in terms of prestige, income, and connections, regents with other categories of graduates (judges, the king's secretaries, etc.) However, one has the sense that, with only a few exceptions, such as the great Bologna jurists (Accursius in the thirteenth century, Johannes Andreae, Bartolus de Saxoferrato, and Baldus de Ubaldis in the fourteenth century), whom the universities quarrelled over and whom the princes deigned to greet and to consult, they tended to be situated at the lower end of the social scale. This factor also probably helped to renew the group from generation to generation.

In spite of the lofty conception they entertained of themselves, and in spite of the fulsome praises that were lavished upon them, the teachers in medieval universities, inasmuch as they constituted an identifiable group, only held a restricted and fairly modest place in the social and political élites of the time. The best and most ambitious of such men, if they really wanted to pursue a glittering career, whether in the church (which undoubtedly for a long time continued to offer the most possibilities to graduates) or in the service of a prince, were therefore compelled to desert the universities fairly rapidly. The teaching dynasties tended also to end fairly quickly, when the last heir, even though he had pursued the same course of studies as his predecessors, decided to give up teaching and to try for a more prestigious and more remunerative post.[40]

One certainly ought not to speak only in terms of social factors and of incomes. If teachers seemed disaffected, this was also because behind the regent's lassitude there lay an awareness of the crisis of traditional university pedagogy and, at the same time, of the difficulty of effecting a fundamental reform of the universities at a time when their ancient independence was being eroded. In such cases, the quest for alternative careers might also be a quest for more lively cultural activities and milieux (the courts and the chancelleries).

The Middle Ages thus witnessed, in its universities, the birth, or rebirth, of the profession of teacher, even if it was the case that, up until the fifteenth century, many courses of teaching were still provided by temporary or occasional teachers. Yet this profession remained a difficult one to define, for it was still marked, as the Middle Ages came to an end, by certain ambiguities.

---

[40] See chapter 8.

Jacques Verger

As a profession, its fate was bound up with the formation of social élites, yet those élites made sure that it was kept at arm's length. Moreover, for all its lofty claims about its intellectual and moral responsibilities, the teaching profession had in fact to serve ends which ultimately eluded it.

SELECT BIBLIOGRAPHY

Bataillon, L. J. 'Les conditions de travail des maîtres de l'université de Paris au XIIIe siècle', *Revue des sciences philosophiques et théologigues*, 67 (1983), 417–33.

Bernstein, A. E. 'Magisterium and License: Corporate Autonomy against Papal Authority in the Medieval University of Paris', *Viator*, 9 (1978), 291–307.

Gabriel, A. L. 'The Ideal Master of the Mediaeval University', *Catholic Historical Review*, 60 (1974), 1–40.

Grandi, R. *I monumenti dei dottori e la scultura a Bologna (1267–1348)*, Bologna, 1982.

Leader, D. R. *A History of the University of Cambridge*, vol. I *The University to 1546*, Cambridge, 1988, 242–63.

Le Bras, G. ' "Velut splendor firmamenti": le docteur dans le droit de l'Eglise médiévale', in *Mélanges offerts à Etienne Gilson*, Toronto/Paris, 1959, 373–88.

Leclercq, J. 'L'idéal du théologien au Moyen Age. Textes inédits', *Revue des sciences religieuses*, 21, (1947), 121–48.

Leclercq, J. 'Lo sviluppo dell'attegiamento critico degli allievi verso i maestri dal X al XIII secolo', in *Università e società nei secoli XII–XVI, Atti del nono convegno internazionale di studio tenuto a Pistoia nei giorni 20–25 settembre 1979*, Pistoia, 1982, 401–28.

Miethke, J. 'Die Welt der Professoren und Studenten an der Wende vom Mittelalter zur Neuzeit', in K. Andermann (ed.), *Historiographie am Oberrhein im späten Mittelalter und der frühen Neuzeit*, Oberrheinische Studien, 7, Sigmaringen, 1988, 11–33.

Paquet, J. *Salaires et prébendes des professeurs de l'université de Louvain au XVe siècle*, Léopoldville, 1958.

Post, G. 'Masters' Salaries and Student Fees in the Mediaeval Universities', *Speculum*, 7 (1932), 161–98.

Post, G. 'Parisian Masters as a Corporation, 1200–1246', *Speculum*, 9 (1934), 421–45.

Post, G., Giocarinis, K., and Kay, R. 'The Medieval Heritage of a Humanistic Ideal: "Scientia donum Dei est, unde vendi non potest" ', *Traditio*, 11 (1955), 195–234.

Verger, J. 'Les professeurs des universités françaises à la fin du Moyen Age', in J. Le Goff and B. Köpeczi (eds.), *Intellectuels français, intellectuels hongrois, XIIIe–XXe siècles*, Budapest/Paris, 1985, 23–39.

Zanetti, D. 'A l'université de Pavie au XVe siècle: les salaires des professeurs', *Annales ESC*, 17 (1962), 421–33.

PART III

STUDENTS

CHAPTER 6

ADMISSION

RAINER CHRISTOPH SCHWINGES

If one disregards the considerable distances and numerous obstacles and hardships involved in journeys in the Middle Ages, it was in fact relatively easy between the thirteenth and fifteenth centuries to attend university and become a student. European universities had no national, social, intellectual, or linguistic requirements for admission. The formal requirements were also relatively few and, in any case, they did not exceed requirements connected with matriculation. There were not even fixed periods for this or for commencing one's studies. Any day of the year was equally suitable. Even requirements for a minimum age did not exist. Minority was a problem only when taking the matriculation oath, not when being accepted at university, as numerous instances in the vast number of sources in university archives indicate.

The only criteria for admission, in addition to the self-evident one of being baptized as a Christian, seem to have been of a moral nature: they were criteria which everybody could, in principle, meet. The criterion of 'moral conduct' – which applied also in admission to the clergy, to citizenship, or to membership in a guild of a town – included proof of legitimacy of birth, but in practice this frequently amounted only to an affirmation that one believed oneself to be legitimate. Such affirmation was necessary only if one wished to acquire an academic degree, and, at some universities or arts faculties, it was required only before the conferring of the degree of *magister artium*.[1] Since, up to modern times, the award of a degree even at the lowest level of bachelor – *baccalaureus artium* – and thus admission to every type of examination – affected only a minority, the question of legitimacy of birth must never have been a particularly pressing issue for the majority of students.

[1] Kaufmann, *Deutsche Universitäten*, vol. II, 302, 310ff.

THE ACCESSIBILITY OF UNIVERSITIES

If on the one hand there were no particular requirements for admission and attendance at a university, so there were no particular rights of admission on the other hand. The universities accepted everyone wishing to become a *suppositum* or a *membrum universitatis*. Neither origin nor rank, neither proximity of residence nor distance, neither poverty nor wealth, neither health nor physical handicap influenced acceptance. Even blindness presented no obstacle. The case of the later *professor artium et juris*, Nicasius de Voerda from Mechelen in Brabant, who had been blind since the age of two, is perhaps only an especially prominent example of this: he attended the Universities of Louvain (1459) and Cologne (1489) and was awarded at the former a *magister artium* and a *licentiatus* of theology, and at the latter a *doctor decretorum.*[2]

Despite all the mania for statutory regulation, which often endeavoured to control university life down to the smallest and most petty detail, the important gateway to the *universitas* thus remained open to individuals who desired entry, provided that they had the necessary resources. This applied primarily in the case of the faculties of arts, but in principle it applied also to the higher faculties. In the latter case, however, after the late fourteenth century, preparatory study in the faculty of arts, regardless of where and in what manner the preparation had been obtained, had become established in practice.

There were essentially two reasons for this fundamental accessibility. The first reason has to do with the characteristic form of the pre-modern university as a community constituted primarily as an association of individuals. The second reason derived from the general system of education which prevailed in the Middle Ages.

Regarding the first, European universities were for long periods of their early history far from being the formally organized institutions and educational establishments which, with all their particular variations, are to be found today in European societies. They were dominated rather by those forms of communal corporate organization which were characteristic of collective life in guilds, confraternities, colleges, and families. Thus, the subsequent history of universities is the history of the progressive institutionalization, rationalization, and finally 'depersonalization' of the *universitas studii*. The process continued, of course, despite crises, fluctuations, and transformations, well into modern times, and can be traced both in the 'younger Europe' of the centre, north, and east of the continent, and the 'older Europe' of the north-west, west, and south (see chapter 8). Each part of

---

[2] J. Wils (ed.), *Matricule de l'Université de Louvain*, vol. II, 1 (Brussels, 1946), 67, no. 65; H. Keussen (ed.), *Die Matrikel der Universität Köln*, vol. II (Bonn, 1919), 255, no. 68.

the continent had its own distinctive cultural, social, economic, and political traditions.[3] In each, however, the same trend occurred.

The old universities consisted of quite fluid communities of individuals of the most varied hue. The association of students formed around a teacher, the *schola* or *familia* of the master, constituted the pattern of university life over the whole of Europe; and, in principle, whether based on the Paris or Bologna model, the university could be conceived as the aggregate of all *familiae* or schools formed around the individual *magistri*. There is, indeed, no pictorial or figurative representation of the medieval university other than that of the *familia* or the *schola* of the master teaching his students; and there are innumerable scenes of such teaching depicted in miniatures in manuscripts and in woodcuts in books. The well-known reliefs in Pistoia cathedral and the old university buildings in Siena and the University of Salamanca present the same pattern. There is also extensive official evidence in university seals, e.g. the seals of Paris, Oxford, Vienna, and Erfurt, which show the master surrounded by a circle of his pupils. A different image of the universities, for example, that of the main building as a symbol, belongs to a later stage in the history of universities; it was scarcely to be seen anywhere in Europe before the middle of the sixteenth century. Its appearance represented a large step away from the idea of a university as an association of individuals around a teacher towards that of an institution.

Within the medieval framework, attendance at a university and the pursuit of one's studies mean no more than associating oneself with the *magister* and his pupils, regardless of the particular part of the university involved, whether it was a faculty, a college, a hall (*bursa*), or a nation. Formal requirements for admission and attendance were secondary, therefore, to participation in an association of individuals. The latter had, however, been obligatory since earliest times. As early as 1215 it was said that nobody was a student of the University of Paris if he did not have a permanent teacher – *nullus sit scholaris Parisius qui certum magistrum non habeat*. There was no departure from this principle throughout the whole of the Middle Ages in any of the European universities, in so far as they conformed to the Paris model. By contrast, at those law universities which followed the pattern of the University of Bologna, the student *societates* and *nationes* were more prominent. Even then the teacher remained the central figure.[4]

[3] O. G. Oexle, 'Alteuropäische Voraussetzungen des Bildungsbürgertums – Universitäten, Gelehrte und Studierte', in W. Conze and J. Kocka (eds.), *Bildungsbürgertum im 19. Jahrhundert*, vol. I (Stuttgart, 1985), 29–78, 49ff.; Schwinges, *Universitätsbesucher*. Concerning inequality even in the European educational systems, see P. Moraw, 'Über Entwicklungsunterschiede und Entwicklungsausgleich im deutschen und europäischen Mittelalter, ein Versuch', in N. Bestmann (ed.), *Hochfinanz, Wirtschaftsräume, Innovationen. Festschrift für W. von Stromer*, vol. II (Trier, 1987), 607ff.

[4] *CUP*, vol. I, 79, no. 20. Similar cases occurred in Montpellier in 1220: Fournier (ed.), *Statuts*, vol. II, 5; in Oxford before 1231: S. Gibson (ed.), *Statuta Antiqua Universitatis Oxoniensis* (Oxford, 1931), 82; in Cambridge after 1236: M. B. Hackett, *The Original Statutes of Cam-*

The *magister* naturally played a prescribed role primarily in the exercise of discipline over generally very young students, who were thus under his protection, control, and power. In the main, relations between masters and students were not formally defined with quantitative specifications or purely intellectual criteria. Nor, however, were they established by chance. Rather, individuals were bound together in accordance with the traditional social norms which prevailed in European societies. The student, upon entrance to the university, selected his *magister* in accordance with the rules of local provenance, friendship, acquaintance, introductions, and patronage. In such *familiae*, prior affirmation of locality and region predominated. Thus, from the very outset, it was left to the individual university teacher, but not to the university as a whole, to assess his clients' capacity for study. Given the basic accessibility of the universities, the link with the *magister* was in the last analysis the sole, serious criterion by which every individual was admitted into the academic community; and this remained the basic pattern, even though regulations governing enrolment became more strict during the late Middle Ages.

Regarding the second reason for the fundamental accessibility of the universities, it should be pointed out that, if one thinks of admission in terms of certain standards of education, a certain level of substantive knowledge, and a certain extent of prior intellectual training, then such a concept of admission scarcely applies to the medieval university. There were no prerequisites. Previous attendance at school was not a precondition, nor was it absolutely necessary. This was just as true for the mastery of Latin, the universal lingua franca of the secondary world, as it was of academic instruction in general. It is not even certain, indeed, that all those attending university could actually read and write. The statutes of the University of Perpignan referred specifically to this.[5]

All this flowed from the fact that, although the medieval system of education, particularly in the later Middle Ages after the thirteenth century, was already differentiated, schools and universities were not directly linked in a functional way. Levels of education and educational tasks were not pursued through a series of stages in which each step invariably preceded the next. There was no orderly pattern of education which imparted a standardized body of basic knowledge. Rather, each part of the educational system – whether monastic schools, endowed schools, municipal Latin schools, parish schools, simple schools for teaching the written vernacular, private tutorial schools, or universities – was independent of all others. Moving from one to

---

bridge University. The Text and its History (Cambridge, 1970), 72, 211. Examples from universities in central Europe: R. C. Schwinges, 'Sozialgeschichtliche Aspekte spätmittelalterlicher Studentenbursen in Deutschland', in *Schulen und Studium*, 527–64, 535ff.

[5] Fournier (ed.), *Statuts*, vol. II, 660; § II.5; A. Wendehorst, 'Wer konnte im Mittelalter lesen und schreiben', in *Schulen und Studium*, 9–33; J. Coleman, *Medieval Readers and Writers 1350–1400* (New York, 1981).

another, including moving from university to school and back again, was quite common. It would be anachronistic to expect even the beginnings of the modern, hierarchically ordered educational system in the Middle Ages.

The fact that the terms pupil and student were scarcely distinguished from one another is evidence of the absence of clearly defined boundaries between universities and schools. Those attending both schools and universities were called *scholares*; this term referred primarily to the character of the relationship between the *magister* and his *schola* and to the status of the former. This was true even for the *scholares graduati* in the higher faculties of medicine, law, and theology. The terms *studens* and *studentes* were more likely to refer to the activity of studying than to a particular status in the university. Consequently, pupils at religious or municipal Latin schools could be *studentes*. This shows that the category of student in the modern sense of an individual having been admitted in accordance with formally stated criteria has no medieval equivalent. And this is even more true as far as the substance of knowledge is concerned.[6]

Furthermore, there were schools which were not merely equal to but superior to faculties of arts with respect to educational standards and educational achievement. This, too, was a result of the general development of schools, which led sooner or later – almost in parallel with each other – to the development of the universities. Schools such as these offered genuine alternatives to attendance at a university. Like universities, many of them had a high percentage of students who came from outside the locality and even from outside the region. The competence which they offered in the subjects that were taught in the faculties of arts sufficed for the majority of professions requiring the ability to write.

The schools and seminaries of the Brothers of the Common Life in the spirit of the *devotio moderna*, such as the schools at Zwolle in the Netherlands and at Liège in present-day Belgium, fall into this category. So, too, does the famous 'humanist school' at Schlettstadt (Selestat) in Alsace and the 'school-city' at Erfurt in Thuringia, where some of the schools were well known even before the founding of the university there in 1392. There were others in this category such as the cathedral schools and colleges, so rich in tradition, like Exeter and Winchester in England, Reims and Soissons in France, or the endowed school at Deventer in the Netherlands. (Towards the end of the Middle Ages the master of Deventer was the distinguished humanist educator, Alexander Hegius, whose students included Buschius, Erasmus, Murmellius, and Mutianus Rufus.) In Spain, too, some chapter and municipal schools enjoyed high status, among them those at Saragossa, Valencia, and

[6] J. A. H. Moran, *The Growth of English Schooling 1340–1548* (Princeton, 1985), 64ff.; G. A. von Mülverstedt, *Beiträge zur Kunde des Schulwesens im Mittelalter und über den Begriff scolaris* (Magdeburg, 1875), especially 21ff.; Kaufmann, *Deutsche Universitäten*, vol. II, 56f., 268ff., 315.

Huesca, the status of which was, for most of the Middle Ages, halfway between school and university. From the time of Dante, many schools in northern and central Italy, both within and outside university towns, were of high quality. Florence was probably only an especially outstanding centre, with Mantua, Milan, Verona, Urbino, and Genoa being of a very similar standing. Finally, the *studium generale* offered by the religious orders also provided a genuine alternative to study at a university, particularly those of the four great mendicant orders, i.e. the Dominicans, the Franciscans, the Augustinian Hermits, and the Carmelites.[7]

The decisive advantage that the universities enjoyed over all types of schools was their privileged position and their concomitant right to set examinations and to award academic degrees, *status in studio*. Those graduating from the best schools, such as the pupils of Hegius, also made sure of enjoying this advantage. Some individuals who were already teachers – teaching was by no means an academic profession in the thirteenth to fifteenth centuries, despite certain tendencies in that direction – matriculated in order to gain a bachelor's or master's degree in the faculty of arts at the end of the customary period of study. A Latin school comedy dealt with this subject in 1485, naturally in a disparaging manner, since the veteran schoolmaster, a veritable *codrus*, was striving too hard for academic distinction.[8] But even without an intention to graduate – this was the normal situation in western and central Europe around 1500 – the universities were sufficiently attractive because they enabled students to learn more at them than at the average endowed or municipal school, to say nothing of the much greater opportunities and social contacts which the universities offered.

Although it was, in principle, possible to attend university without any prior education, things were increasingly different in practice. Since the late twelfth century, towns had established their own 'municipal' schools, partly in intense competition with the educational system of the church. The process began in those areas of 'older Europe', the economies of which developed first in the towns of northern Italy, southern France, and the north-west, varying, as they did, in size and importance. Schools also sprang up sooner or later in the other parts of Europe, with greatest frequency – according to the available evidence – in the fourteenth and late fifteenth century. In about 1500, in the period prior to the Reformation, either an ecclesiastical or a 'municipal' school was to be found in almost every town, however small. Yet these schools are not to be thought of as being any more institutionalized than the universities. Educational continuity depended on the influence of

---

7 Concerning schools, see select bibliography.
8 W. Schulze, 'Codrus. Lateinische Schulkomödie aus dem Jahre 1485', *Archiv für Literaturgeschichte*, 11 (1882), 328–41. Other cases: Keussen (ed.), *Matrikel Köln* (note 2), vol. I, 277, no. 17, 285, no. 39; in England: N. Orme, 'Education and Learning at a Medieval English Cathedral, Exeter 1380–1548', *Journal of Ecclesiastical History*, 32 (1981), 265–83, especially 270ff.; Moran, *Growth* (note 6), 66.

individuals, and much still depended on the mobility of the school-teachers. Unfortunately, the state of the evidence does not permit us to say much about this.

General educational development was, of course, of exceptionally great significance for attendance at universities. Wherever this can be assessed quantitatively, i.e. wherever the location of schools can be related to the places of origin of students, as is demonstrable in the 'catchment areas' of the German universities, the evidence shows that, from the fourteenth century onward, schools formed the 'normal' precondition for university attendance. This is true, for example, of three-quarters of all students at the University of Cologne in the late Middle Ages.[9]

Whether or not particular formal academic requirements were met, the masters of the faculties of arts took it upon themselves to make up for the diverse amounts of knowledge initially possessed by their students, who came from the most heterogeneous national backgrounds. To become a member of a group formed around a *magister*, it was necessary to be able to do the most basic (Latin) exercises, and masters accordingly provided private tuition. Quite early on, so-called *paedagogia* were provided in the faculties of arts, where initial basic knowledge was necessary for successful participation in the *cursus* of the faculty. In some university towns, the Latin schools took over the functions of the *paedagogia*, partly still under the supervision of the local church, as in Cambridge, Coimbra (Santa Cruz), and Paris (Notre-Dame), and partly also under the supervision of the universities, as in Oxford, Salamanca, and Vienna (St Stephen). In Vienna, the schoolmasters themselves belonged to the university.[10]

MATRICULATION

Although the prospective student and the person attending the university became a member of the group through joining the association centred around a *magister*, it was only by matriculation under the authority of the rector that he also became a member of the legally defined community and thereby of the privileged community. Only by doing this did he become a *membrum universitatis*. Matriculation, which was one of the highest functions of the university authorities, was also the formal act which conferred a legally recognized status. This involved the student taking an oath of matriculation, paying a statutorily required matriculation fee, and registering his name in a specially provided register (*matricula album registrum*) which had

[9] Schwinges, *Universitätsbesucher*, 330–41. Concerning the development of schools, see select bibliography.
[10] Denifle, *Entstehung*; Rashdall, *Universities*; I. Hajnal, *L'Enseignement de l'écriture aux universités médiévales*, 2nd edn (Budapest, 1959); A. L. Gabriel, 'Preparatory Teaching in the Parisian Colleges during the Fourteenth Century', in A. L. Gabriel, *Garlandia. Studies in the History of the Medieval University* (Notre Dame, 1969), 97–124.

to record both the oath and the payment of fees of each matriculated individual. To distinguish such registration more clearly from other types of registration, including faculty, collegiate, or national registration, it might be described as the 'general university registration' or the 'rector's registration'. What was recorded in the register fully met with the formal requirements for attendance at university.

This was the situation at the end of the fourteenth century and throughout the fifteenth century in 'younger Europe', from Louvain to Cracow, from St Andrews or Copenhagen to Vienna and Basle. Matriculation in special documentary registers thus represented a relatively well-established procedure. The administrative arrangement associated with it through the rector marks a new stage in the development of the *universitas* as an institution. Particular national and territorial powers were increasingly displacing the earlier 'universalism' which, in the 'older' parts of Europe, was most enduringly embodied in the University of Paris. In the 'era of universalism', university rectors in Italy, France, the Iberian peninsula, and England had never kept their own general registers, although, in many university statutes since the early fourteenth century, the maintenance of the *inregistratio* fell within the scope of the rector's duties. Even their successors in the age of particularism did not do so until the threshold of modern times, undoubtedly because of the tenacious traditional patterns of organization of the *universitas* into *familiae*, colleges, and nations.[11]

In the universities of the 'era of universalism', particularly universities consisting of faculties of arts, theology, and medicine, at least north of the Alps, 'matriculation' was from the outset a responsibility of the individual *magister*. As student numbers increased, teachers in the large faculties of arts seem to have begun to register the names of their students. This occurred quite early in Oxford – prior to 1231 – and in Cambridge from 1236 to 1254, and also in Paris at a later date, when the faculty made a formal decision about registration in 1289. Since the number of students whose names were not known had obviously become a problem, there was a need for a 'master's registration book' (*rotulus, cedula, matricula magistri*) which would set out information enabling the master to survey and record the performance of participants at particular exercises and readings, and to distinguish genuine students from those spurious students who merely wished to enjoy the privileges of the university (Paris: *boni ac legitimi aut ficticii scholares discernere*).[12]

---

11 For a survey of matriculation lists in Europe: B. Schmalhaus, *Hochschulmatrikeln. Verzeichnis der Drucke nebst anderen Nachweisen* (Göttingen, 1937); E. Giessler-Wirsig, 'Universitäts- und Hochschulmatrikeln', in W. Ribbe and E. Henning (eds.), *Taschenbuch für Familiengeschichtsforschung*, 9th edn (Neustadt/Aisch, 1980), 141–80.

12 Oxford: Gibson (ed.), *Statuta* (note 4), lxxxii, lxxxix, 60f., 82, 107, 227. Cambridge: Hackett, *Statutes* (note 4), 72, 211, 330. Paris: *CUP*, vol. I, 35f., no. 561. A discussion of the problems

Thus, in accordance with the flexibility of the statutes, the *magistri* themselves verified the formal membership of their *scholae* in the university. Such appears to have been the prevailing situation throughout the Middle Ages. Soon *magistri* in other faculties began to draw up lists of names (*cedulae*), which they then turned over to the faculty, from which, sooner or later, but probably around the middle of the fourteenth century, genuine faculty registers emerged.[13] Understandably enough, practically none of these registrations has survived: they were private rather than official university documents. One manuscript, a collection of excerpts from Aristotle's logic, dating from before 1268 and belonging to Gonville and Caius College, Cambridge, has none the less survived. On its margin a *magister* had jotted down sixty names, and in each case the name is accompanied by numbers, which are presumably the number of years which each of the named students had studied.[14]

At those universities which had only law faculties – especially in Italy, Bologna, Padua, and Pavia amongst others, and, in France, Orléans and Angers – the student nations, faithful to their social conventions, undertook, perhaps from the outset, the matriculation of their prospective members. The procurators of the individual nations at the universities functioned like masters elsewhere and rectors later on; but in this instance, too, the general register was mentioned in the statutes, if sometimes only at a much later period. Apparently, the two types of registration were carried out concurrently in Prague and Vienna.[15] The oldest register of this kind – and one of the most significant for central, eastern, and northern Europe – was the Bologna *matricula nationis Germanicae*, which was kept from 1289. Such registers of nations ought not be confused, however, with those of Paris, which only recorded graduates by their particular nations.[16]

Thereafter, the most important – and as a rule the most complete – entries concerning university attendance and admission were to be found in the general registers of matriculation or in the rector's register. They were regularly kept only at the central European universities, beginning in about the second half of the fourteenth century. The first 'new' type of matriculation

can be found in J. Paquet, 'L'Immatriculation des étudiants dans les universités médiévales', *Pascua Mediaevalia. Studies for Prof. Dr. J. M. de Smet* (Louvain, 1983), 159–71.

[13] *CUP*, vol. I, 701, § 45, no. 1189; vol. IV, 703, no. 2671; Fournier (ed.), *Statuts*, vol. II, 70, § 36; 83. Cf. Paquet, 'Immatriculation' (note 12), 161f.

[14] Hackett, *Statutes* (note 4), 167.

[15] Fournier (ed.), *Statuts*, vol. I, 257, no. 356 (Orléans); 334, § 8 (Angers); F. Doelle, 'Ein Fragment der verlorengegangenen Prager Universitätsmatrikel aus dem 14. Jahrhundert', in *Miscellanea F. Ehrle*, vol. III, Studi e Testi, 39 (Rome, 1924), 88–102, probably only concerning the Saxon nation at Prague; P. Uiblein, 'Zur Quellenlage der Geschichte der Wiener Universität im Mittelalter', *Österreich in Geschichte und Literatur*, 7 (1963), 161–6.

[16] E. Friedländer and C. Malagola (eds.), *Acta Nationis Germanicae Universitatis Bononiensis (1289–1543)* (Berlin, 1887); H. Denifle and E. Châtelain (eds.), *Auctarium Chartularii Universitatis Parisiensis*, 6 vols. (Paris, 1894–1964).

register was the *matricula*, now lost, belonging to the arts, theological, and medical faculties of the University of Prague; this probably began before 1367. The matriculation register of the law university at Prague of 1372 has survived and may be considered the oldest rector's register in Europe.[17] The fact that both the universities in Prague kept the first general registers can hardly have been a coincidence. Indeed, the *studium Pragense* of 1348 constituted something of a turning-point in the transition from the universal to the national era of the history of European universities.

Although the traditional constitutional and social forms retained their force in central European universities as well, they were none the less being subjected to considerably stronger pressure for standardization and centralization than was the case in western and southern Europe. Vienna from 1377, Heidelberg from 1386, Cologne from 1388, Erfurt from 1392, Cracow from 1400, Leipzig from 1409, Rostock from 1419, and Louvain from 1426, to name only the oldest universities, followed Prague as universities maintaining matriculation registers. Finally, in the course of the sixteenth century, the rector's register spread throughout the whole of Europe as the central record of new arrivals. Probably the oldest surviving rector's register in Italy, the matriculation register at Perugia, is representative of this pattern. Although it was decreed in 1487, entries were made only from 1511. A comparison with the matriculation register for the German nation at Perugia, which contains a far more complete list of names than the central register of the university, shows how markedly and for how much longer the 'new' form was disregarded in favour of the 'old' one. This was a consequence of the persistence of the more traditional social patterns of society at large.[18]

Wherever the 'newer' form was taken up, the individual attending the university was obliged to be matriculated by the rector within a specific period, normally anything up to a month. This could be done on every day of the year, even on high holidays.[19] The general university statutes constantly stressed this obligation, especially in those passages which were to be read out regularly to the university public. Masters and doctors, too, were referred to the basic obligations to matriculate their students, while the heads of colleges and halls (*bursae*) were bound to accept only matriculated students who were genuine *membra universitatis* into their houses and teaching arrangements.

The ideal was set out in the 'information booklets' for new students, which were intended to provide introductory orientation, often in dialogue form, for those attending university. The new student presented himself to the

17 *Monumenta Historica Universitatis Carolo-Ferdinandeae Pragensis*, vol. II, *Album seu Matricula Facultatis Jurisdicae Universitatis Pragensis ab anno Christi 1372 usque ad annum 1418* (Prague, 1834).
18 F. Weigle, *Die Matrikel der Deutschen Nation in Perugia* (Tübingen, 1956), 7, 13ff.
19 Concerning the procedure, see the introduction in the matriculation lists of, for example, Heidelberg, Leipzig, Freiburg, Louvain, Cologne, and Vienna.

magister of his choice. His origins, parents, financial status, and academic interests and ambitions were discussed until finally, having concluded that the candidate had a serious intention to study, the *magister* requested his new pupil to accompany him to the rector to set the matriculation procedure in motion.[20] At the University of Louvain, new students belonging to the four main halls were regularly matriculated as a body in the register on the occasion of the inauguration of a new rector; this occurred on or about 26 February and 31 August.

The obligation to matriculate was a product of the university's legal or financial interests, or most frequently of both together. The legal interests of the university remained essentially the same as they had been in the thirteenth century in Oxford, Cambridge, or Paris: namely, to control the granting of privileges and to record the names of those granted the privileges in order to distinguish them from those who had not been granted such privileges. Through the listing of names and surnames, origin and status, day and year of matriculation, *veri scholares* could easily be identified should they require the protection and assistance of the university. They could also be distinguished from *falsi scholares*. At the Universities of Bordeaux and Valencia, it was declared to be absurd if a mother did not know her sons' names.[21]

In the course of the fifteenth century, it came to be less a matter of excluding the *falsi scholares* than of enforcing a universal registration. Anybody who disregarded this or even flouted it was in some places considered almost a rebel.[22] Finally, it was with the aid of the universal matriculation registers that the university was able to control its 'most sacred duty', which was the award of academic degrees, of doctorates, along with the grant of the *licentia docendi* to those who were regarded suitable for it.

Yet supervision by masters or administration by rectors did not necessarily work smoothly or even completely. It was not unusual for doctors and masters first and foremost to be entrepreneurs, especially if they taught in private houses or colleges and halls. Many made their livelihood exclusively from the fees of paying guests and 'auditors'. Here and there, they satisfied to their own advantage the demand for 'private' affiliation to a university. Many of those attending the university were able to enjoy exemptions from judicial proceedings and taxes while there. They were even able to study and to graduate 'unofficially', without complying with the legal and financial claims of the university as a whole. There were also students who dealt with the central authorities of the university by simply disregarding them. A comparison

---

[20] M. Bernhard, *Goswin Kempgyn de Nussia, Trivita studentium. Eine Einführung in das Universitätsstudium aus dem 15. Jahrhundert* (Munich, 1976), 61.

[21] Fournier (ed.), *Statuts*, vol. III, 352, § 47 (Bordeaux 1482); 394ff., § 15 (Valence 1490).

[22] Fournier (ed.), *Statuts*, vol. I, 492, § 39 (Toulouse 1314); vol. III, 103, § 9 (Dole 1424). Similar cases can be found also in Heidelberg 1442; E. Winkelmann (ed.), *Urkundenbuch der Universität Heidelberg*, vol. I (Heidelberg, 1886), 145, no. 100.

between the rectors' registers and the deans' registers or faculty registers at various central European universities provides evidence for this.

OATHS AND FEES

The oath (*juramentum*) was the symbol of all the legal grounds for the requirement of matriculation. Normally, taking the oath was the first and the most important act in the proceedings. Without the oath, the rector simply refused matriculation. Above and beyond the family-like relationship between the *magister* and his students, it was only the oath which sealed the voluntarily chosen bond with that corporation of individuals, the 'university', which was no different from other *universitates* and *corpora* in the 'older Europe' in being a corporation based on oaths. Students swore the oath to their university just as new townsfolk swore it to their town, or merchants and craftsmen to their respective guilds.

Naturally, the swearing of the oath varied in form and content from one European university to another. Four common features, however, can be identified as apparently indispensable elements. The newcomer swore obedience to the rector holding office at the time – in England, to the chancellor – often with the addendum *in licitis et honestis*, i.e. in so far as it was morally, legally, and socially permissible and honourable. He swore to abide by and to preserve the statutes of the university already enacted, as well as those to be promulgated in the future. He swore also to promote the welfare of the university to the best of his ability, regardless of the academic degree, status, or rank he might one day achieve. Finally, he swore to renounce any form of private vengeance for injustice which he might suffer, in favour of the rector's 'public order', by which was meant the maintenance of peace both within and outside the university.[23]

The sworn individual attending a university who had taken the oath and thus fulfilled his obligations could now rely on the rector to perform the obligations of his office, namely, to strive to defend the rights and freedoms of every individual *membrum universitatis*, to defend them tenaciously and rigorously when necessary, against everyone else. The history of universities offers innumerable examples of this.

It is not surprising that, in the national-territorial era of the fourteenth and fifteenth centuries, many forms of the oath created a bond between the person attending university and the prince. In this respect, too, the *studium generale* of the University of Prague appears to have been in the lead. All new arrivals, not merely native Bohemians, promised in the first instance loyalty to king and realm, *regi et regno fidelitatem*, and, then only, obedience to the rector. The situation at the University of Caen was similar, the oath of obedi-

---

[23] Examples in Paquet, 'Immatriculation' (note 12), 164f.

ence being sworn to the king of England as the ruler of that territory. In Freiburg im Breisgau, too, students bound themselves to do nothing during their stay at the university which might affront the honour of the house of Austria. This address of loyalty was understandably linked directly with the concern, attested by oath, for the well-being of the university, which had been the territorial university of '*Vorderösterreich*' since 1460.[24]

The taking of an oath presupposed the attainment of either the minimum age for swearing an oath or the age of majority. As a rule, canon law was followed, according to which the completion of the fourteenth year was sufficient. However, dates of the attainment of majority in the Middle Ages varied among the universities and, over a period of 200 years, ranged from ten years at Toulouse, to thirteen at Leipzig and sixteen at Oxford.[25] Accordingly, those who did not meet the minimum age or who were minors were not allowed to take the oath, although they could be in attendance in great numbers at universities which had no minumum age for admission. In Rostock, for example, in some years they constituted up to one-third of the enrolled students. In Cologne, during the fifteenth century, they amounted to between 2 and 3 per cent of all students. They were also quite common at the law universities in Italy, Spain, and France, where, however, youthfulness and high rank were closely correlated.[26] Since, for obvious legal reasons, there could be no exemption from the oath, there was no provision for such exemption in the university statutes; the rector therefore granted deferment on condition of a promise by a minor, although most commonly this was made by his father, relative, teacher, or preceptor, that the oath would be taken, once the age of majority had been attained.

Thus the individuals who swore the oath were normally aged fourteen or fifteen. The vast majority of new entrants to the university were of this age. Universities following the University of Paris pattern, predominantly made up of students in the faculties of arts, could be called 'juvenile universities'. The students of law, medicine, and theology were, as a rule, about four or five years older than those in the faculty of arts, apart from the exceptions made for those of high rank. The higher faculties and the law and medical univer-

---

[24] Prague (c. 1368): H. Jírecek (ed.), *Codex Juris Bohemici*, vol. II: 3 (Prague, 1889), 277, § 17; 281, § 29. Caen (1457): Fournier (ed.), *Statuts*, vol. III, 211, § 13. H. Mayer (ed.), *Die Matrikel der Universität Freiburg im Breisgau*, vol. I (Freiburg, 1907), 1ff.

[25] Fournier (ed.), *Statuts*, vol. I, 472, § 17 (1313); G. Erler (ed.), *Die Matrikel der Universität Leipzig*, vol. I (Leipzig 1895), lix (1543 and fifteenth century); Gibson, *Statuta* (note 4), 392ff. (1564–5); the statutes of 1581, Gibson (note 4), 421, leave a margin of twelve to sixteen years. In Cambridge fourteen years, but here too with a later document, see Hackett, *Statutes* (note 4), 167 n. 3.

[26] A. Hochmeister (ed.), *Die Matrikel der Universität Rostock*, vol. I (Rostock/Schwerin, 1899); Keussen (ed.), *Matrikel Köln* (note 2), vol. I, 35*ff.; 193*, table 3; S. Stelling-Michaud, *L'Université de Bologne et la pénétration des droits romain et canonique en Suisse aux XIIIe et XIVe siècles* (Geneva, 1955), 82; D. Illmer, 'Die Statuten der Deutschen Nation an der alten Universität Orléans von 1378 bis 1596', *Jus commune*, 6 (1977), 10–107, especially 79.

sities of the continent were, by contrast, 'adult universities'. For example, the 'novices' belonging to the German nation at the University of Orléans between 1444 and 1546 were almost exactly twenty years of age on admission to the university. In contrast with modern practices, the medieval concept of the student comprised a wider range of young age groups.[27]

In fact, however, the matriculation oath was not as unavoidable as it seems. Not only was it possible to postpone the taking of the oath, but dispensations and limitations were also allowed for legal or social reasons. The mere additional formulae *in licitis et honestis* and often also *pro posse* – concerning obedience to the rector and the statutes – reveal possibilities of evasion which the medieval casuists had little difficulty in elaborating. The status of the law university of Bologna, deriving from the first half of the fourteenth century, provided for a formal exception in the event of a *justa causa* – in other words, if there were good grounds for the exemption. Under the cover of the 'master's register' and of obedience towards 'one's *magister*', this was also possible in Cambridge at a quite early date, without in either case any legal reason being adduced.[28] Among the most important reasons for the practice were presumably conflicts of interest affecting persons who were simultaneously members of two groups legally defined as different. Thus, according to the fourteenth-century statutes, citizens of the municipality and the surrounding district of Bologna, Padua, Perugia, or Lérida in Aragon could not be forced to take the oath. They were, it is true, subject to the authority of the rector, but they were not, strictly speaking, members of the *corpus universitatis* and consequently could not be entered in any rectoral matriculation register. Political developments at the close of the fourteenth century led to change here, including a change in the matriculation itself – for which in Bologna, for example, a *liber specialis* was to be established.

In addition, there were special regulations for members of orders, who either took a limited oath, in so far as their religious and university obligations could be harmonized, or first required the permission of their abbot or superior before taking the oath in full.

In most European universities such exceptions were provided for without any formally enacted arrangment. There were special regulations, however, for the higher clergy and the higher nobility, especially for students who held the rank of prince, count, or nobleman and who were at universities in the Holy Roman Empire; the variety and social and legal status of the regional nobility were explicitly taken into account. Heidelberg was content with an

---

[27] See chapter 7, pp. 195–202. Concerning the age of students, see Rashdall, *Universities*, vol. III, 352ff.; Mayer (ed.), *Matrikel Freiburg* (note 24), vol. I, lxxxviff.; Moran, *Growth* (note 6), 64ff.; *Universités en France*, 93; R. L. Kagan, *Students and Society in Early Modern Spain* (Baltimore/London, 1974), 32; Illmer, 'Statuten' (note 26), 79; Cobban, *Medieval Universities*, 351ff..

[28] C. Malagola (ed.), *Statuti delle università e dei collegi dello studio Bolognese* (Bologna, 1888), 13; Hackett, *Statutes* (note 4), 211.

affirmation of honour, Cologne had a special 'nobleman's oath', while Tübingen and Basle always adapted the form of the oath to the status of each new entrant.[29] Thus, the matriculation oath adapted itself to the student's position. It was an oath which varied with status so that the concepts of *scholaris* and *membrum universitatis* had the most varied content. The newcomer did not divest himself of his status on entry to the university, but entered a university which was just as much defined by inequality as the surrounding society. It was only in the upper-class setting of Italian lawyers in Bologna, Padua, Florence, and Perugia that distinctions of status did not have to be emphasized. As a result of this, everyone had to take the oath except the legitimate sons and brothers of kings.[30]

The pecuniary interest in the matriculation of students was at least as important as the legal consideration. The admission fees laid down in the statutes were applicable *de jure* for all students, but *de facto* they applied primarily to the vast majority of 'middle-class' students, who faithfully fulfilled the obligations of matriculation; thanks to their numbers, their fees kept the *universitas* alive. They were generally called *divites*, i.e. the rich. As a rule, the obligatory fee was determined by the weekly charge for maintenance. Over the long run, the sums specified in the statutes could naturally only be fictitious.

In fact, the fees varied from one university to another, and, as a result, a distinction was drawn between 'more expensive' and 'less expensive' universities. Within the Holy Roman Empire, Rostock, Greifswald, and Erfurt belonged to the first category, while Leipzig, Cologne, and Vienna fell into the second category. In Italy, Padua and Florence were among the more expensive, while Bologna and Ferrara fell into the category of the less expensive.[31] In some respects, the social atmosphere of a university was affected by this difference.

Like the oath, the fees also had a social aspect. Depending on position and financial resources, the customary fee could exceed or fall short of the required fee, or it could also be waived. Many universities, particularly those in central Europe, had special paragraphs on fees in their statutes, in which fees subject to status were often dealt with in very differentiated fashion. According to rank and office, a particular fee above the average was required from the nobility and the senior clergy who were attached to cathedrals or collegiate churches. In addition, a donation over and above this was expected everywhere. Class behaviour and the practice of payment therefore caused

<hr />

[29] G. Toepke (ed.), *Die Matrikel der Universität Heidelberg*, vol. I (Heidelberg, 1884), 190 and n. 1; Schwinges, *Universitätsbesucher*, 378ff. and n. 19.

[30] H. Denifle, 'Die Statuten der Juristen-Universität Bologna vom J. 1317–1347, und deren Verhältnis zu jenen Paduas, Perugias, Florenz', *Archiv für Literatur- und Kirchengeschichte*, 3 (1887), 358; H. Denifle, 'Die Statuten der Juristen-Universität Padua vom Jahre 1331', *Archiv für Literatur- und Kirchengeschichte des Mittelalters*, 6 (1892), 410. See also chapter 7, p. 208.

[31] Schwinges, *Universitätsbesucher*, 424; Rashdall, *Universities*, vol. I, 226; vol. II, 54.

those concerned to enjoy special privileges at the university. However, everybody else could also manage to obtain those privileges if the required fees were paid *sub forma nobilis* – as if the student were from the nobility.[32]

The proceeds of matriculation fees made up one of the most important sources of revenue for medieval universities, as grants from the state were rather meagre. Indeed, the universities were in great measure dependent on fees. For this reason, particular attention was devoted everywhere to the matter of fees. At many universities, therefore, 'matriculation' or 'registration' was not the popular term; instead 'intitulate' and 'intitulation' were used in acknowledgement of the financial element of the act of admission (*intitulatura*). Evidently, this was considered so important at the law universities of Bologna and Parma, that the terms *matricula* and *liber solventium* were used synonymously.[33] Wherever possible, the rector and the treasurer were obliged to accept the payment of fees in cash and to record them with care in the register (*dedit* or *solvit totum*, for instance), or to note expressly deficient payments or the complete failure to pay the fees (for example, *nihil dedit, petivit dilationem tenatur dare*). On account of this, some of the registers kept by the rectors read like account books.

Some of the fees went into the university treasury, while some went to the rector and his assistants to compensate them for their 'expenses' in administering oaths and intitulation. This introduced a certain element of arbitrariness into the system of payment, in so far as the rector was allowed a certain latitude to allow the partial or total waiver of fees. However, in the course of the fifteenth century, the rectors tended to be encouraged to be strict in the enforcement of the university's scale of fees on every newcomer, for fiscal reasons.

The rector's discretionary power was limited to two groups of varying size, which can be categorized as belonging to the upper and lower ends of the student body. The group at the lower end were the *pauperes*, the poor students who wished to make use of the *privilegium paupertatis* of canon law to obtain a dispensation. At the other end, there were highly placed individuals and dignitaries belonging to the nobility and to the clergy, holders of the doctorate from foreign universities, as well as students enjoying special patronage, whose *reverentia* or testimonials conferred prestige and social benefits on the university; these were also granted dispensations.

Naturally, the two groups differed markedly from each another. What was conferred on one group as a formal honour on admission to the university was often a matter of urgent necessity for the other group.[34] Poverty was no obstacle to admission, but in general no particular consideration was shown

---

[32] Schwinges, *Universitätsbesucher*, 348–51.
[33] Malagola (ed.), *Statuti* (note 28), 74; Paquet, 'Immatriculation' (note 12), 166.
[34] Schwinges, *Universitätsbesucher*, 376.

as far as the payment of fees was concerned. Those who set the fees in each case had to examine the ability or inability of the student to pay. The poor students were urged to meet as far as they could the financial obligations connected with their matriculation. Strictly speaking, deferment of the payment of fees was to be allowed only *ad pinguiorem fortunam*, i.e. until the onset of better fortune.

As a rule, formal admission to university took place in the sequence swearing the oath, payment of fees, and registration. If, as mentioned at the outset, the new student was actually able to write, then he sometimes entered his own name in the register. This, however, was normally done by the rector or the *notarius* – the clerk – of the university. The important registers of the German universities have almost all been preserved more or less carefully by university staff. Detailed information about the students was first written down on slips of paper and later transferred partly in chronological order, partly in the order of social status, to the general register. Thus, an ordinary entry in the Cologne University register, dated 14 October 1478, reads as follows: *Conradus Pijckell de Swefordia, dioecesis Herbipolensis, artes, juravit et solvit.* The student subsequently became the famous humanist under the name Conrad Celtis, from near Schweinfurt in the diocese of Würzburg; born in 1459, he entered Cologne University at nineteen years of age to study the liberal arts, took the matriculation oath in its entirety, and paid the usual fees.[35]

THE FREQUENCY OF MATRICULATION

Wherever general registers were, in fact, kept by the rectorates of the universities, they reveal the bases and motives for the university taking an interest in the numbers of new students. Some universities, such as Leipzig, Erfurt, and Ingolstadt, tended to count up the total of all matriculations since their foundation, thus expressing a collective consciousness that had a historical reference; the matriculation or the oath created a permanent membership and legal relationship. Other universities, such as Heidelberg, Erfurt, Rostock, and Greifswald, drew up a *numerus intitulatorum* from the records of the rectorate; this was probably connected with calculation of income derived from matriculation fees. Fluctuations in student numbers could thus be kept in view, particularly if figures of attendance remained static or were decreasing; the latter was always critical, and on occasion it could be an event that threatened the very existence of the university as a whole. Perhaps this was why, at the Universities of Orléans and Paris, for example, something which resembled at times an inventory of the *universitas* at a particular moment was

---

[35] Keussen (ed.), *Matrikel Köln* (note 2), vol. II, 49, no. 18.

drawn up.[36] Until well into modern times, it was only the diminution and not the increases in attendance and matriculation which aroused a response.

However, one of the most interesting and most momentous features of attendance at medieval universities is the fact that, in the long run, the number of students who matriculated continuously increased. In central Europe alone, from the middle of the fourteenth century to the end of the Middle Ages, almost a quarter of a million individuals acquired the status of a student. A conservative calculation suggests approximately that three-quarters of a million students attended university in the whole of Europe over the same period.

These figures have to be judged, however, in the light of the growth of the population of Europe as a whole during this period. Disregarding national and regional variations, the population fell sharply all over Europe as a result of the recurrent plague epidemics between 1348 and 1450. Then it became stable, beginning to rise gradually only in the final quarter of the fifteenth century. Accordingly, the growth in university attendance and the growth of population moved in opposite directions for some decades.

In the Holy Roman Empire, where a precise account can be established because of the nature of the sources, the average rate of increase in the *Reichsfrequenz* (matriculations within the Holy Roman Empire) between 1385 and 1505 reached a high point of 1.75 per cent yearly, despite a concurrent decline in the population growth.[37] From the middle of the fifteenth century, between 2,500 and 3,000 students entered the universities of the Empire annually from Louvain to Vienna, from Rostock to Basle. The student body of the Polish University of Cracow also increased between 1400 and 1510, helped, however, by a high percentage of a mixture of foreign students who made up between 30 and 50 per cent of the total.[38] The supply of students, which was already high by medieval standards, was greater than the demand from the courts, the towns, the schools, the law courts, and the church. This was the first 'crisis of oversupply' in the German or central European university system. The crisis occurred after the 1480s, and it is possible that it occurred also in the western and southern European university

---

[36] Orléans 1412: Fournier (ed.), *Statuts*, vol. I, 194ff., no. 263 M. Spirgatis, *Personalverzeichnis der Pariser Universität von 1464* (Leipzig, 1888). A declaration of intent in Toulouse 1314: Fournier (ed.), *Statuts*, vol. I, 492, § 39.

[37] Schwinges, *Universitätsbesucher*, 30ff.; R. C. Schwinges, 'Universitätsbesuch im Reich vom 14. zum 16. Jahrhundert: Wachstum und Konjunkturen', *Geschichte und Gesellschaft*, 10 (1984), 5–30, especially 14ff. 'Reichsfrequenz' is the sum of matriculations of those universities of the Empire in the Middle Ages which kept registers: Vienna, Heidelberg, Cologne, Erfurt, Leipzig, Louvain, Rostock, Greifswald, Freiburg im Breisgau, Basle, Ingolstadt, and Tübingen.

[38] Z. Pauli, B. Ulanowski, and A. Chmiel (eds.), *Album studiosorum universitatis Cracoviensis*, vols. I–II (Cracow, 1887–1892). Cf. I. Kaniewska, 'Les étudiants de l'Université de Cracovie aux XVe et XVIe siècles (1433–1560)', in D. Julia, J. Revel, and R. Chartier (eds.), *Les Universités européennes du XVIe au XVIIIe siècle: Histoire sociale des populations étudiantes*, vol. I (Paris, 1986), 113–33.

regions. Furthermore, there are certain indications, at least, that the same occurred in England.[39]

The larger number – as many as 3,000 new students annually, which corresponded to a total capacity of more than 6,000 students anually[40] – was essentially the result of the closing of the gap between the central European universities and their established counterparts in 'older Europe'. In contrast with France, England, Spain, Portugal, and Italy, the countries of central, eastern, and northern Europe developed a comparable university life of their own only relatively late. There was a time-lag of between 100 and 200 years. Not only was the gap closed by the end of the Middle Ages, but, as far as the Holy Roman Empire was concerned, a stage of parity had been achieved both with respect to the number of universities – which did not necessarily progress at the same rate – and the total number of students. Some of the old universities which are still in existence today and which have grown into large-scale academic enterprises had their periods of greatest growth in student numbers in the fifteenth century. It was only in the nineteenth and twentieth centuries that expansion again occurred on a comparable scale.

However, there was no uniformity in the patterns of growth. As early as the late Middle Ages, an extraordinary variety emerged among the universities of Europe. Universities were of a wide range of sizes. It is extremely difficult, if not impossible, to draw on relatively reliable and comparable data for all of Europe. Nevertheless, the following can be stated:[41] universities which were large by medieval standards, that is, universities with capacity for a minimum of 1,000 students and with a frequency of matriculation of at least 400 to 500 students annually – in short, universities with a relatively high power of attraction for students – were on occasion to be found in Paris, Toulouse, Avignon, and Orléans, in Oxford and Cambridge, and in Bologna and possibly also other northern Italian universities such as Padua and Ferrara. From time to time, there were also large universities existing in Prague and, after the second half of the fifteenth century, in Salamanca, Vienna, Erfurt, Leipzig, Cologne, and Louvain. Beside them there were medium-sized universities with a frequency of matriculation of about 150 to 200 new students annually in almost every European country, and there was a substantial number of small universities, too, with sometimes barely 50 matriculations a year. Cracow, Rostock, Heidelberg, Ingolstadt, Siena, Perugia, Naples, Montpellier, Angers, Perpignan, Lérida, and perhaps

---

[39] Cf. G. F. Lytle, 'Patronage Patterns and Oxford Colleges *c.* 1300 – *c.* 1500', in L. Stone (ed.), *The University in Society*, vol. I (Princeton, 1974), 111–49, especially 123ff.; T. H. Aston, 'Oxford's Medieval Alumni', *Past and Present*, 74 (1977), 3–40, especially 30ff.

[40] For a stay of about two years.

[41] For the universities of central Europe, see note 37. See Schwinges, *Universitätsbesucher*, for problems relating to numbers in matriculation analysis. See also Cobban, *Medieval Universities*, 121–2; Kagan, *Students and Society* (note 27), 196ff; *Universités en France*, 8off; contributions in Julia *et al.* (eds.), *Universités européennes* (note 38), with further literature.

Lisbon-Coimbra belonged to the category of medium-sized universities, while Greifswald, Mainz, Freiburg, Basle, Tübingen, Cahors, Caen, and the city of Rome belonged to the category of the smaller universities, which flourished particularly in the post-universal, territorial epoch of the history of the European university. Piacenza, Pavia, Florence, and Pisa perhaps also fell into the same category, although here there are grounds for suggesting a larger estimate. There were undoubtedly many more smaller universities in France, Italy, and Spain, although at present there is no documentary evidence to support this.

St Andrews and Glasgow in Scotland and Copenhagen and Uppsala in Denmark and Sweden, as well as the Hungarian universities of Pécs, Buda, and Pozsony, were also small; they were never free from the danger of going out of existence in the Middle Ages. Even in the sixteenth century, Scots, Scandinavians, and Hungarians continued to attend foreign universities.[42]

These differences in size were, to some extent, affected by the quality of the university towns as towns, as well as the standing of the region for which they served as centres. With the sole exception of the two English universities, all the large universities of Europe were situated in medieval cities with a population of over 10,000. They were all important trading and handicraft centres, market-towns or sites where fairs were held, and were located within an economic and geographical network. Because of roads and other means of transportation, they were ideally situated and easily reached. They either belonged to old, already consolidated areas of princely or municipal government, or were surrounded by or part of the areas which, since the fourteenth century, had been successfully organized by governmental authority. This was true of a majority of the German regional universities. All these propositions apply also, if to a lesser extent, to those universities which exercised only average or small powers of attraction. Some Italian universities are exceptional because the number of their matriculated students bore no relation to the population of the cities in which they were located, e.g. Florence.

However, patterns were not rigid. There was no university in Europe which achieved a continuous increase in student numbers. The figures for matriculation, much affected by fluctuations in political, economic, and social conditions, often fluctuated several hundred per cent within a few successive years. Periods of growth alternated with periods of stagnation and the absolute size frequently changed. Paris, Orléans, and the universities of southern France, as well as those of Prague and Bologna, reached the height of their attractiveness in the fourteenth and early fifteenth centuries. At the time of

42 Schwinges, *Universitätsbesucher*, 234–44; J. M. Anderson, *Early Records of the University of St Andrews* (Edinburgh, 1926); J. Pinborg, 'Danish Students 1450–1535 and the University of Copenhagen', *Cahiers de l'Institut du Moyen Age Grec et Latin, Université de Copenhague*, 37 (1981), 70–122, especially 95ff.; S. Lindroth, *A History of Uppsala University, 1477–1977* (Stockholm, 1977), 10; A. L. Gabriel, *The Medieval Universities of Pécs and Pozsony* (Frankfurt, 1969).

the Council of Basle from 1431 to 1449, it was even feared that the University of Paris might lose all of its students. This was a matter of perspective, since Paris was probably the largest medieval university; the incomplete inventory of 1464 recorded almost 2,500 individuals, masters, students, and others connected with the university.[43] Prague, which in the 1380s had become possibly Europe's largest university, just after Paris, fell back to the status of a 'midget university' after 1409 and almost completely disappeared from the university pattern of central Europe with regard to the attraction it exercised on students from afar. By about the middle of the fifteenth century, after a growth of more than 100 per cent, Cambridge managed to approximate to the size of the student body at Oxford. In the course of the fifteenth century, Bologna's star waned while the stars of Padua, Pisa, Siena, and Perugia rose.

On the whole, the centre of concentration of matriculations in central Europe shifted greatly during the fifteenth century. It had moved from the south-east of the Holy Roman Empire in Vienna across central Germany – Erfurt and Leipzig – to the north-west, to the large region which embraced the Rhine and the Low Countries and which was, at this period, economically and demographically one of the leading regions in the empire. The figure for matriculations at Louvain and at Cologne must certainly have been equal to those at Cambridge, Oxford, Padua, Salamanca, or Paris towards the end of the Middle Ages. Underlying these shifts were the consolidation processes which occurred all over the European university system, and which were, as a rule, borne by the larger and mostly older universities of the continent.

The rise and fall in the number of matriculated students were not random phenomena. They were responses to events of fundamental importance which occurred outside the universities and which brought the universities and their students into very direct relationships with the surrounding society. These events followed a cyclical pattern; the many thousands of decisions made by individual students to attend university and to submit to matriculation were themselves cyclical in pattern. Although the process can be demonstrated only from German sources, it can be put forward plausibly as a hypothesis that can be applied to other universities.[44] The fluctuations were determined by economic factors, which were as relevant to the pattern of attendance at universities as the increase in the number of students, and there were both shorter and longer cycles within the pattern.

Even the cyclical process which underlay the growth of the numbers of students was variable, and was decisively altered on several occasions in the period between the fourteenth and sixteenth centuries. Structural variations in cycles of varying lengths in successive sequences of growth and stagnation are to be found in four different periods. There were two phases of growth, one between the late fourteenth century (around 1385) and approximately

---

[43] Spirgatis, *Personalverzeichnis* (note 36), 3f.
[44] Schwinges, *Universitätsbesucher*, 185–220.

Table 6.1   *Periodization of the history of university attendance*

I Cycles of 7–11 years	II Cycles of 3–5 years	III Cycles of 2–3 years
Louvain	Vienna	Erfurt
Cologne	Freiburg im Breisgau	Leipzig
Heidelberg	Rostock	Ingolstadt
Basle	Greifswald	
(Tübingen)		

1480; this may be regarded as the 'take-off stage' of matriculations in central Europe. Then there were two periods of stagnation, one between about 1430 and 1450. The second, which had more of the features of a grave crisis, ran from 1480 to about 1505. This was the period leading up to the 'crisis of oversupply' in the Holy Roman Empire.

These several cycles and their turning-points in about 1430, 1450, and 1480 may be viewed as constituting a periodization of the history of university attendance – granted, of course, that individual universities did not necessarily conform completely with the general pattern; no two universities 'enjoyed a boom' in matriculations at the same time. Given deviations, three distinct patterns may be distinguished in the second half of the fifteenth century, as shown in table 6.1.

These three groups disclose a coherent pattern. The longer cycles (I), which represent less severe fluctuations in numbers of students, were concentrated in places which were parts of the large western Rhine 'catchment area' along the main artery of traffic of the Holy Roman Empire. It was here, too, that the centre of gravity in the growth of student numbers was to be found in the late Middle Ages. There were pronounced economic fluctuations to a considerably greater degree in the numbers of matriculated students at the other universities; most intensively and most critically in a central region, more or less the 'heartland' of Germany (III), and somewhat less at the peripheries, in the Baltic sea region and in the south-east in the case of Vienna (II). The fact that Tübingen here was marginal (I) is less significant than the fact that the experience of Freiburg, in contrast with that of neighbouring Basle, does not belong to the category of Rhenish universities but is incorporated in category II, within a social and economic area under the dominion of the Habsburgs, which included Vienna.

The reasons underlying this very heterogeneous pattern of numbers of university students, including the long-term 'education explosion' and the cyclical pattern of matriculation, had little to do with the internal life of particular universities. They had little connection with the characteristics of the institutions, the content of their teaching, or the personal qualities of their teachers. This was also true in the case of humanism, an intellectual movement which might have been expected to have precipitated an increased attendance at the universities. Instead, the academic centres of humanism in the Holy Roman Empire – Erfurt, Basle, Ingolstadt, Tübingen, and Vienna – suffered several decreases in numbers of matriculation at the end of the fifteenth century. Such, according to the known figures, was also the case in Italy.[45]

The reasons for these cyclical patterns lay outside the universities, not so much in spectacular events, such as wars, revolts, and plagues, but in fluctuations in agricultural prices and, through them, in a cluster of variables affecting the level of other prices in medieval agrarian society. Within the context of regional and supraregional geography, attendance at university and the conditions prevailing in the market in the area where the university was located were closely related to each other. As a rule, the correlation was an inverse one. Upward movements in the number of matriculations corresponded to periods of low prices; and periods of stagnation in the number of matriculations were concurrent with periods of high prices. Depending on good or bad harvests, the prices of cereals determined the disposition to matriculate; they even determined the students' social status. Periods of high prices depressed the numbers matriculating, and they simultaneously allowed the number of students from poor families to increase beyond normal expectations. The long-term secular decline in grain prices, the so-called agrarian depression of the late Middle Ages, was, however, advantageous for the urban economy and hence for the long-term increase in the numbers of matriculations as well; hence the 'education explosion', which lasted from the fourteenth to the sixteenth centuries. Attendance at university was always largely an urban affair,[46] and the 'golden age of handicrafts' in the towns seemed to be also the golden age of admission to university.

---

[45] R. L. Kagan, 'Universities in Italy 1500–1700', in Julia *et al.* (eds.), *Universités européennes* (note 38), 155ff.
[46] See chapter 7.

SELECT BIBLIOGRAPHY

Bowen, J. *A History of Western Education* vol. II, *Civilization of Europe, Sixth to Sixteenth Century*, London, 1975.

Cantarino, V. 'Mediaeval Spanish Institutions of Learning: a Reappraisal', *Etudes Islamiques*, 44 (1976), 217–29.

Engelbrecht, H. *Geschichte des österreichischen Bildungswesens* vol. I, *Von den Anfängen bis in die Zeit des Humanismus*, Vienna, 1982.

Enseignement et vie intellectuelle (IXe–XVIe siècles). Actes du 95e Congrès National des Sociétés Savantes Reims 1970, vol. I, Paris, 1975.

Frank, I. *Die Bettelordensstudia im Gefüge des spätmittelalterlichen Universitätswesens*, Stuttgart, 1988.

Fried, J. (ed.) *Schulen und Studium im sozialen Wandel des hohen und späten Mittelalters*, Sigmaringen, 1986.

Garin, E. *L'educazione in Europa 1400–1600*, Rome/Bari, 1957, 3rd edn, Rome, 1967.

Julia, D., Revel, J., and Chartier, R. (eds.) *Les Universités européennes du XVIe au XVIIIe siècle: Histoire sociale des populations étudiantes*, Paris, 2 vols, 1986–89.

Manacorda, G. *Storia della scuola in Italia*, vol. I, *Il medioevo*, Palermo, 1913.

Moran, J.A.H. *The Growth of English Schooling 1340–1548*, Princeton, 1985.

Moraw, P. 'Über Entwicklungsunterschiede und Entwicklungsausgleich im deutschen und europäischen Mittelalter, ein Versuch', in U. Bestmann (ed.), *Hochfinanz, Wirtschaftsräume, Innovationen. Festschrift für W. von Stromer*, vol. II, Trier, 1987, 583–622.

Orme, N. *English Schools in the Middle Ages*, London, 1973.

Paré, G., Brunet, A., and Tremblay, P. *La Renaissance du XIIe siècle. Les écoles et l'enseignement*, Paris/Ottawa, 1933.

Parias, L.H. (ed.) *Histoire générale de l'enseignement et de l'éducation en France*, vol. I, Paris, 1981, esp. the article by M. Rouche.

Paul, J. *Histoire intellectuelle de l'Occident médiéval*, Paris, 1973.

Piltz, A. *The World of Medieval Learning*, Oxford, 1981.

Post, R.R. *Scholen en onderwijs in Nederland gedurende de Middeleeuwen*, Utrecht, 1954.

Schmid, K.A. *Geschichte der Erziehung vom Anfang bis auf unsere Zeit*, vol. II: 1–2, Stuttgart, 1889–92; reprint, Aalen, 1970.

Schwinges, R.C. *Deutsche Universitätsbesucher im 14. und 15. Jahrhundert: Studien zur Sozialgeschichte des alten Reiches*, Stuttgart, 1986.

Le scuole degli ordini Mendicanti (secoli XIII–XIV), Todi, 1978.

Verger, J. 'Universités et écoles médiévales de la fin du XIe à la fin du XVe siècle', in G. Mialaret and J. Vial (eds.), *Histoire mondiale de l'éducation*, vol. I, Paris, 1981, 281–309.

Wühr, W. *Das abendländische Bildungswesen im Mittelalter*, Munich, 1950.

CHAPTER 7

STUDENT EDUCATION, STUDENT LIFE

RAINER CHRISTOPH SCHWINGES

THE STUDENT: CONCEPT AND TYPOLOGY

At European universities and in European societies the concepts 'university', 'faculty', 'doctor', 'master', 'student', and the like have been in use for virtually 800 years. Despite this long usage, however, the realities behind the words have only ostensibly remained the same. In general, modern notions are of little help when it comes to understanding medieval phenomena, and this is particularly true of the social phenomena of universities organized around groups of individuals. Particularly in a chapter devoted to the 'medieval student', one must be aware from the outset that concepts can be no more than linguistic shells housing a great variety of different meanings, each dependent on its age. One should therefore approach the matter gingerly, seeking to find neutral terms like 'scholars', 'enrolled members', or 'matriculants' whenever – for reasons of historical fact or linguistic form – it is called for. For the sake of clarity, the term 'university attender' will be used in this chapter.

When one surveys the European scene, it is striking that there is not a single university in any country for which one can paint a generalized picture of the medieval student – and this irrespective of century. The mere issues of admission and matriculation serve to show how diffuse the concept is: there was no more or less uniform secondary education, school and university shading into one another, and no hard-and-fast distinction was made between the concepts 'pupil' and 'student'. Both were members of the university and of the school. Students were also members of a great variety of different age groups – from children under the age of fourteen to adults in their twenties or thirties. Such institutions as the 'oath appropriate to rank' and the 'rank fees' rendered at matriculation ensured that the status of students was not equal even on a legal plane, let alone socially.[1]

[1] Cf. chapter 6, pp. 177–86.

That, however, is not the end of the story. In contrast to today, there were substantial discrepancies in status between those studying in differing faculties or 'specialist' universities, notably in the universities of arts or of law – discrepancies which could occasionally break out into fullfledged discord. This was the case with the so-called secession in Prague in 1372 when, under the one roof of the *studium Pragense*, two universities with two rectors were established: on the one hand the *universitas* of the men of arts, theology, and medicine and on the other hand that of the men of law. The threat of such a development existed until the end of the Middle Ages and was even especially acute again in the opening phase of the University of Basle, when the students of law refused to make common cause with others attending the university. In the final analysis, the reason was always the mutual incompatibility of two social environments in one and the same *universitas*. Only with the emergence of the modern princely state and municipal government as bearers of the universities of the post-universal age could these dualistic tendencies be prevented. To keep up the old reserves and preserves it was sufficient to employ symbolic actions and exhibit a different life style.

Modern notions are equally unhelpful when one enquires into the objectives the students had in studying. From the perspective of today, the great proportion of medieval university attenders would have to be classified as drop-outs or even failures. As late as 1500, it was by no means normal to sit any form of examination. The vast majority were satisfied to attend and belong. The social possibilities opened up by the university did not yet require control by a special system of entitlement based on examinations and graduation.

Among those attending the medieval universities of Europe, at least five types of student can be detected. These types simultaneously make up a pyramid-shaped diagram of university attendance, the pyramid having a quantitatively broad base and relatively narrow apex.

The first type is to be found in the faculties of arts. The student is, in the vast majority of cases, a young man of between fourteen and sixteen years of age, who is, as a rule, matriculating at a university for the first time and who meets the prescribed legal and financial conditions of admission as well as he can. His social background is likely to be 'middle-class', with a broad range from rich to poor, corresponding to the spread among overall university attenders. In all probability, he has previously attended the Latin school in his home region and has acquired at least a basic knowledge of reading and writing as well as of Latin grammar. He attaches himself to a master of his choice and begins in school-like fashion under the latter's supervision to deepen his knowledge in the arts *cursus* or, if that is insufficient, to bring himself 'up to date' with the so-called *paedagogia*. This does not, however, make him the typical beginner. Such a perspective would be anachronistic since it is not his intention to achieve at university all that could be achieved there – up to a doctorate in medicine, theology, or law. His attendance is limited to an average duration of only 1.8 years (the estimate for German universities); the reality, however, is liable to have been below rather than above that figure. This type of student sits no examinations and acquires no academic title – and hence also no *status in studio*. The universities of the time called him the *scholaris simplex*. He is found most frequently in the developed four-faculty universities of 'younger Europe' as well as in 'older Europe' north of the Alps (see chapter 8), particularly in Paris and at the English universities. Not infrequently he accounts for 50 per cent or more of the total attendance and can therefore, with full justification, be described as the leading actor among students at medieval universities.

The second type of student is also to be encountered in the faculties of arts. His university attendance is, at first sight, not much different from that of the first type. In age, prior education, and social background there is little to distinguish them, except that the proportion of poor students – in German and central European universities the figures can be given with exactitude – rises as time goes by. This is presumably an indication of the fact that this second type represents, albeit on a very low level, hopes of social advancement via university and education. In contrast to the first type, this second types wishes to limit or – in the language of the time – to 'determine' his studies, i.e. to demonstrate the skills he has acquired. The goal is the degree of *baccalarius artium*, which can be gained after two to two-and-a-half years working with the *actus scholastici* under a chosen master. The student is then about sixteen to nineteen years old. If one wanted to employ a modern analogy, one could compare this graduation with the secondary school examination preceding the one for university entrance. The bachelors of arts account – between 1350 and 1500 – for approximately 20 to 40 per cent of university attendance and are thus the second largest grouping, with incidentally the same 'spread' as the first. For fully two-thirds of them, this is the only degree which they will obtain or wish to obtain at university; it is the precondition for acceptance as a fellow in most of the colleges in Spain, France, or England.

The third type, too, is associated with the faculties of arts, but has objectives which go beyond them. Starting as a rule with the *baccalarius*, this type of student acquires after two to three further years the degree of master of arts, analogous in the modern age to university entrance. By this stage he has usually reached the age of nineteen to twenty-one. The social background remains the same, although the proportion of poor students has gone down again substantially in comparison with the second type. If he does not leave the university with this degree – which is linked to a two-year teaching obligation in the *artes*, from which, however, dispensation is increasingly granted as the centuries pass – he then takes up studies in the higher faculties of medicine, theology, or canon or civil law. This 'master-student' is found throughout Europe, but most frequently at the universities which, by and large, followed the 'Paris model'. Only at first glance does he bear any resemblance to the freshman of today. The numbers themselves are markedly down when compared with the two preceding types. On average – though varying from university to university and from the thirteenth to the fifteenth century – he represents just 10–20 per cent of those in attendance. More decisive, however, is that, while still formally a student, he is simultaneously active in teaching, with the notions of student and professor being in many cases no longer clearly separable. The master-student, usually in theology or maybe medicine, teaches the younger members of the faculty of arts – those of the first or second type who have chosen him as their master. Around him congregates a clientèle, his *schola*, his *familia*. Many students of this type finance through this source alone their further studies, the next 'hurdle' being the bachelor's degree of one of the higher faculties. More fortunate colleagues have access in addition to paid professorships, college headships, scholarships, prebends, and university or church bursaries. Such a master-student can assume a series of official functions: he can become dean of the faculty of arts and even, if he is held in especially high regard, rector of the university. The best chance of achieving this was always to be found in Paris, where the rector was chosen solely from the arts faculty.

The fourth type of student is fundamentally different from the three previous ones. He encounters at university all the advantages of class and status which he has enjoyed elsewhere. He is already 'someone' before he ever crosses the university threshold. He is characterized by high rank, by high regard for his person and family of origin, by nobility, by the possession of church livings, or by 'middle-class' prosperity. If he is a member of the nobility or acts the nobleman, he arrives at university with a retinue of *familiares* – servants ranging from his private tutor to his groom. Socially, the typical and fitting place for him is not the faculty of arts, or the socially related environment of the students of medicine or theology, but the higher faculty or university of lawyers. His prior education to something approximating to master's level he acquires through private tutors rather than through schools for the public – or he attends arts courses 'alongside his main studies', without either having or desiring to demonstrate his knowledge in examinations. The teaching activity associated with graduation in the arts would be detrimental to his social status. The same holds even for degrees awarded by the higher faculties up to the level of doctor. Whether an academic title is appropriate to one's rank or – as usually the case with the higher nobility – unacceptable depends on one's social origins. Seeking social advancement through the university, as perhaps done by the average master-student, is something this type of 'student of rank' has no need of. He is found in all European universities, admittedly in greatly varying numbers. But he is to be found above all in the law universities or law faculties of older, southern Europe. Up to and into the fifteenth century, the 'international' centre for students of rank from Portugal to Scandinavia, from Hungary to the British Isles, is Bologna. Thereafter Padua, Pisa, Pavia, Perugia, Siena, and other Italian universities close the gap in reputation and attendance figures. The Bologna *matricula nationis Germanicae*, which despite its name contains law students from almost the whole of central, eastern, and northern Europe, documents the numerous figures of rank and name from 1289 on. Major centres for students of rank are also the universities of southern France and Spain, in Avignon and Toulouse, Salamanca and Lérida, where the law faculties seem by themselves to outstrip in numbers those for the arts. Orléans is a similar case. North of the Alps in younger Europe, however, the situation is quite different, with four-faculty universities in which students of the arts form around 80 per cent of those in attendance and seem to set the tone even in large institutions. Here too, however, it is social quality which is of greater importance. It is a matter of pride to admit the prestigious student and he is accorded the customary privileges as if this were a matter of course. Preferred universities in central Europe are, for example, Erfurt, Basle, Freiburg, and Ingolstadt, the three latter serving, as it were, as a springboard for the Italian journey. Just as the master-student is characteristic of the Paris model, so the student of rank is characteristic of the Bologna model. He is also similar to the master-student in that, in the universities (and faculties) of his choice with Bolognese privileges, he assumes similar functions and can, for example, with the agreement of his peers, become rector. In universities following the Parisian model, on the other hand, he would at most, assuming he had sufficient social standing, accept an honorary rectorship.

The fifth and last type would seem closest to the modern student, since it is his intention to conclude the major part of his studies with an examination – and perhaps with a doctorate, too. As a rule this 'specialist student' continues his studies after his *baccalarius* from one of the higher faculties and takes a licentiate in medicine, theology, or canon or civil law or both – a degree which also accords teaching rights (*licentia docendi*) in the faculties in question. If he so desires or is in a position to afford it, he subsequently takes a doctorate. Like the modern student he, too, is well into his twenties or thirties. There, however, all analogy ends. The very numbers tell a different story. Having arrived at the pinnacle of the 'attendance pyramid', one discovers this type to be only the few remaining per cent of the total. Very few are to be found in the universities of younger Europe north of the Alps (2–3 per cent of all those in attendance at German universities), and most in the classical university regions of older Europe, in the strongholds of medicine and law in Italy and France as well as in the theological faculties at Oxford and Cambridge, especially during the fourteenth century. In the universities of Italy, admittedly, the numbers of specialist students from abroad is particularly high; the majority of students and doctoral candidates come from what are called the German nations. This type is characterized by elevated social standing – knightly descent or membership of the urban 'upper class' or 'upper middle class'. For a poor student, it would take a mighty leap to reach this level, a leap hardly conceivable without intensive social support. What, however, notably distinguishes the medieval 'specialist student' from his modern counterpart is the fact that he is not out to find the crock of gold through university attendance and study, but has already found a firm footing in society well before or during his period of study: in municipal service, at the court, or most often in church offices. The licentiate and doctorate simply give him additional honours and prestige.

These five ideal types – the *scholaris simplex*, the *baccalarius*, the master-student, the student of rank, and the specialist student – never constituted a closed system. A number of mixed characteristics always existed in reality. 'Course-hoppers' – almost exclusively students of law and medicine – can be observed who had not first passed through the arts courses but who neverthe-less laid claim to a status akin to that of master, without necessarily being students of rank. Not infrequently, too, the social rules of old Europe could cut across the above categories. Social ties, friendships, kinship, patronage, and family structures could all influence status and study objectives. The individual ability of the 'student' and sound assistance from his teachers worked within these contexts. Special advantages, for instance, could be enjoyed by well-protected minors even if they were not members of the appropriate 'class'. Not capable of taking the oath but assuredly capable of study, they could – having as a rule attained the age of adjuration on com-pletion of their fourteenth year – immediately be graduated if, for example, they had done the prescribed courses for the *baccalarius artium*. One promi-nent example of this is Philip Melanchthon, who took up his studies of the arts as a twelve-year-old in his home town of Heidelberg and became a master of arts in Tübingen at the age of seventeen; being the nephew of Reuchlin, he had been well provided for and given every encouragement, but had nevertheless taken a completely normal length of time over his studies. In such contexts one should exercise caution when trying to interpret the sub-sequent significance of early academic honours.

There were, however, two common features which linked together all the student types. On the one hand, they were clerics – almost without exception in the early years of the universities and then in decreasing numbers, first in older, then in younger Europe. On the eve of the Reformation the cleric-student was probably already in the minority in Europe as a whole. This declericalization, however, should not be misinterpreted as being at the same time a secularization of the university or of university education. In the context of the developed university of the late Middle Ages, the term *clericus* is highly problematic. It denotes merely formal and legal membership of the *ordo clericalis*, the legal purview of the church; in terms of a typology or social history, however, the concept is diffuse and wholly unrevealing. It can be used only to describe categories – in a broader sense from the pope down to the ostiary, the holder of the lowest consecrated rank, and in a narrower sense the holders of the so-called minor holy orders below the subdiaconate. In addition, when dealing with matriculated *clerici* one encounters problems of source interpretation. The state of being a *clericus* was, at least until the mid-fifteenth century, so common in Europe as a whole that the rectors, deans, or procurators of nations in charge of the *matricula* set no great store on systematically registering clergy membership. To calculate the proportion of clerics in individual annual cohorts of matriculants is hence of little use. It is only over a longer period that the above-mentioned decline can be traced. Being a *clericus* at university, however, came to mean less and less in terms not only of statistics but also of a way of life. The roots of this development are to be traced back to the early Middle Ages, to the beginnings of university growth, when the educational monopoly of the clergy was still intact and the *litterati*, the men of learning, could be equated with the *clerici*. The term *clericus* finally became a synonym for anyone who knew how to write: the path towards modern usage – *clerc* in French or clerk in English – was open. Following the same trend, the term *laicus* took on, beside its connotations of the non-ecclesiastical, a dimension of ignorance. In German university towns at the close of the fifteenth century, it was common to distinguish between priests, students, and laymen, thus emphasizing the intermediate position of the student – an emphasis at times verified linguistically by the term 'half-priests'.[2]

Those 'half-priests' who had become *clerici*, moreover, in the strict legal sense of belonging to minor holy orders, had not thereby taken on any obligation towards the church. This is demonstrated by the occurrence of *clerici uxorati*, married clerics, among students of all types. Such a student would merely make use of certain rights, of his own legal status for example, although, in the already privileged university, this was not so important as the inestimable benefit of possibly being in receipt of a church living with its guarantee of life security, if not of life tenure. For the many, however, especially for the growing throng of students up to the master type, such a post was no more than a possibility. Nevertheless, all this did not mean immediate secularization. Many took holy orders only after matriculating, during their term of study or even later. Yet it would be anachronistic to believe that the church was no longer the partner of the university, and even more so of those attending the university. Though never an institution of the church, the university was always close to it. The church remained the largest subsequent employer and wage-payer of medieval students, often even when

[2] Rashdall, *Universities*, vol. III, 393ff.; Schwinges, *Universitätsbesucher*, 408ff.

they entered the service of kings, princes, lords, and municipalities; for powerful people of all kinds tried first of all to remunerate their graduate servants with church livings before reaching into their own pockets. At the end of the Middle Ages the secular world and the church were still not clear alternatives. The student-monks – mostly from the mendicant orders – who flourished in the thirteenth and fourteenth centuries in the strongholds of arts and theology (Paris, Oxford), and who accounted for most of the specialist students of theology at this time, are a special problem, to which this reference must here suffice.

The world of the medieval student was thoroughly masculine. For the girl or woman student this world had no place – a fact for which the ecclesiastical ties were not responsible: even with the increasing declericalization of the *universitas* nothing changed in this respect. Ostensible exceptions can, as a rule, be accounted for by a particular social background, sometimes even by the closeness of a prince or king. Leading families, noble and bourgeois alike, above all in southern Europe, had their sons and daughters educated in like manner by private tutors and partly even by renowned university scholars. In this way some women achieved a high level of knowledge in all subjects, even in law, and were able – in the Renaissance Italy of the fourteenth and fifteenth centuries this was apparently not uncommon – to enter into contact with university circles as if they were 'students of rank'. Magdalena Buonsignori, for example, or Novella d'Andrea, the daughter of the celebrated and wealthy Bologna professor Johannes Andreae, studied in accordance with their rank and became famed scholars of law. Or there was the Latin scholar Dona Beatriz Galindo, who had evidently been educated in Salamanca close to the university and who was from there summoned to the court of Isabella the Catholic to give the queen instruction in Latin.[3] Such exceptions, however, which seem, incidentally, to be restricted to the south of the continent, in the final analysis show only too clearly that the time was not yet ripe for the education of women within the universities. Nevertheless, women could legally be university members. As wives or maids of professors, as serving-maids, errand-girls, or cooks in colleges or student houses, they were considered university associates like the syndics and scribes, the apothecaries, the paper, and parchment-makers, or the book-printers. Consistent with this they were therefore also matriculated like the latter – the most meticulous instance seeming to be in the rector's *matricula* at the University of Louvain.

ORIGINS AND SOCIAL STRUCTURE

Whether one has in mind Salamanca or Bologna, Oxford or Paris, Cracow or Heidelberg, the medieval university was in every instance an organized

[3] W. Steffen, *Die studentische Autonomie im mittelalterlichen Bologna* (Berne, 1981), 173ff.; Rashdall, *Universities*, vol. II, 88.

grouping of individuals, a 'societal community'. As such it was the faithful reflection of its surrounding society, living like the latter by the traditional rules of old Europe. Yet, though standardized and privileged in legal terms, it was, like every other *universitas*, burghers' community, guild, or church, far from matching its togetherness in law with a social togetherness which might annul the status differences of those attending it. Of social integration, lifting the university out of its environment and transforming it into an egalitarian community based on shared 'academic activity', there was not a trace. Like every other group within society, the university, too, was subject to the prevailing social and economic criteria of stratification, including the conditions of economic growth already referred to in chapter 6 in the context of matriculation figures. Thus every student – in accordance, as it were, with his type – brought his personal and family rank with him to the university, seeking either to maintain and uphold it there or, within the realms of social acceptability, to improve it. His origins thus predetermined the social structure and social image of each and every university in a decisive manner. A high proportion of *simplices* or master-students or even students of rank made all the difference in prestige – between older and younger Europe in general, as already noted, but also within the individual university networks of Europe.

Origin had not only a social but invariably also a geographical dimension. The latter was fundamentally determined by what one might term the regional existence of a university community, the regionalism of a university being to a great extent governed by the regionalism of its university town. Just as the latter was the nodal point coordinating the social, economic, and cultural life of a region, so the university community equally laid claim to a heartland in which, as a social grouping, it could have its roots. Wherever a new university followed this rule it met with success and was, above all, ensured long-term survival. This held true both for the older universities with their informal origins and for the younger with their formal foundations. This underlying structure of regionalism has occasionally been misunderstood as narrowness; it should, however, be seen as propinquity, which has nothing to do with provinciality but a great deal to do with the functionality of the surrounding area. The dominant part played by propinquity was evident at all universities, both in central Europe and at its periphery. Even 'international centres' such as Paris, Avignon, and Bologna owed their century-long existence not to recruitment throughout Europe but first and foremost to their regional existence. The character of student origin naturally gave each university and indeed each of its parts – its faculties, nations, colleges, and students' hostels – a spatial identity of its own. This was true even in insular England, where Oxford and Cambridge each secured a distinct catchment area. In the final analysis, the upshot of all this is that, despite the numerous interchanges occurring over broad areas of the European university network, it hardly ever happened that one community prospered at the expense of another.

All kinds of factors, from the mere nature of a place of origin as a town, market-town, village, or monastic or castle domain, through the number of inhabitants, the economic circumstances, the travel facilities, the churches, and the schools, up to and including the complex character of circumstances of rule and land-ownership and the question of the stability and continuity of local power, left their mark on university attendance and on the composition of the student body in both geographical and social respects. The wealth of observations possible here forces one to be selective.

The background of all student types – and this is one of the most important findings concerning the universities of central Europe and the German lands – was essentially urban. At the end of the fifteenth century, one town in two in the Holy Roman Empire (if one proceeds on the basis of around 4,000 towns and market-towns in the overall Empire, including the Netherlands) sent students to one or more universities. Consequently, the extremely rapid growth in student matriculation in the Empire was accompanied by a continuous process, whereby places of origin came to be increasingly concentrated in the towns. With the exception of England, where there was apparently a rural majority, this was also true elsewhere, for example in Poland, France, Castile, and throughout the classic town networks of older, southern Europe. Urbanization and university education were closely connected in scale. One should not for all that, however, underestimate the village and rural element in university attendance. It is true that, in the university system of the Empire, one naturally has to cope with marked regional fluctuations in the proportion of 'village students', yet similar to the municipal process, there was also a process of village and rural concentration, especially in the immediate vicinity of the universities.

The university was peopled, according to the primitive polarizations of the general university statutes, by grand folk and small (*magni* and *parvi*) in a social sense, by rich and poor (*divites* and *pauperes*), by those of higher and of lesser rank (*superiores* and *inferiores*), and by especially marked illustrious, noble, honourable, and meritorious personages and dignitaries (*illustres, nobiles, honesti, meriti, tenentes statum honestum, habentes magnos status*), all of whom stood apart from the merely simple or common (*simplex* or *communis*). All, whether noble or not, rich or poor, had, it is true, in the event of any dispute, the right to the same statutory and duty-bound treatment by the rector or other leading university figures – yet students knew full well that their community, like any other social formation, was governed by an 'order of difference'. Meticulous and fitting regard for the personal rank of university members was seen as one guarantee of the continuing existence of the university, because no community could sensibly exist without such regulations of distinction. What was meant by this was by no means only the internal differentiation in terms of faculties and graduates, but even – and sometimes especially – in terms of such public matters as the regulation of positioning for the public and non-public acts of the university at sessions, disputations, quodlibets, or church services, orders of procession for when the community presented itself to the outside world, even orders of enrolment for supplications to the pope, which in many universities even served as general ordinances, and not least even orders of graduation. Universities responded to the pronounced need of noble and bourgeois, clerical and lay people of the day to think in terms of rank and standing; as succinctly expressed at Oxford in the year 1432, all were always to be accorded the accustomed honours (*consueti honores*).[4]

Particular care was, of course, called for when, at the start of a procession, an order of seating according to graduation or social status had to be transformed into a moving column with university members aligned alongside and after one another. The university proctors and 'protocol officals' specially appointed for the task had to supervise both seating and marching order. One can be sure that, within the formal framework of statutory orders, there were informal wrangles about the placement of individuals. University servants were threatened with severe fines if they ushered somebody *ad locum sibi non competentem* – to a place not fitting for him. After the rector were placed students of rank and specialists, both thus coming before, or at least alongside, the doctors at the apex of the graduate hierarchy; then came the master-students on a par with the lower students of rank – the university also thus demonstrating the reality of social inequality in nobility and church; and finally, the baccalaureate students and the throng of *simplices*, who in theory came from all faculties but in practice tended to be from the arts. The world of the university and the world outside were deliberately interlaced – *racione gradus aut status*, as it was put in Vienna, according to academic rank or social position.[5]

This can be seen in more or less distinct form at all the universities of Europe. Many of them had rigid, formal ordinances which read almost like administrative regulations – for example, those in Prague, Vienna, and Heidelberg, in Erfurt and its entire 'statute family', in Oxford and Avignon, Toulouse, Aix, Bordeaux, Cahors, Valence, Dole, Orléans, and Caen, and in Coimbra, Salamanca, and Huesca as well as in Perpignan, which at that time belonged to Aragon. For many universities – for example at Paris, at Cologne, and at its 'daughters' Louvain and Copenhagen as well as at most Italian institutions, for example Bologna, Perugia, Pavia, and Florence – informal rules were clearly sufficient, without the *differencia* to be regulated for ever being forgotten on either side of the Alps. The ordinances listed, which covered a period of around 200 years, from the early fourteenth century

---

4 Schwinges, *Universitätsbesucher*, 343ff.; S. Gibson (ed.), *Statuta Antiqua Universitatis Oxoniensis* (Oxford, 1931), 239.
5 R. Kink, *Geschichte der kaiserlichen Universität zu Wien*, vol. II (Vienna, 1854; reprint, Frankfurt-am-Main, 1969), 91, no. 14.

(Toulouse 1313) to the close of the Middle Ages (Valence 1490/1513), were – compared with each other – certainly stable over a period of time, as is to be expected from statutes, but nevertheless sometimes becoming more severe and exact as time passed (though it was not until the fifteenth century that some universities put in written form what they had presumably always practised).

Besides placement, other visible tokens of rank were differing fees, tied to faculty and status, paid on entering the university and its subdivisions. Noble birth, high standing in church and society, and the readiness to pay high fees were always convertible into privileges that could be exploited throughout the university. During teaching, prelates, and the sons of the aristocracy and monied aristocracy naturally sat in the front rows. As in the university churches during meetings, services, and disputations, so in the lecture halls as well, the seats at the front were reserved for the *nobiles, honesti,* and *notabiles* – the noble, honourable, and high-ranking. In Aix-en-Provence, such 'separate seating arrangements' were explicitly justified in the new statues of 1420–40 by the argument that it was not seemly to place high-ranking people on the same level as lesser mortals. Always, however, students of (urban) bourgeois origin had the possibility of buying themselves a *statum honestum* on the 'noble bench'. For the universities of medieval Europe were from the outset urban phenomena, responsive to the economic power and culture of the bourgeois majority. It was even possible, as at the Prague law university after 1372, to acquire higher social prestige after the event and as it were, in instalment payments, by subsequently adding to the normal seating price first paid the price difference for the noble bench. In the 'refined milieu' of Orléans, a gradation in seat prices was fixed as early as in the statutes of 1307: for a place in the first row ten shillings were payable, for one in the second six shillings, for the third four, and for the fourth and every subsequent row two, unless one were excused by poverty – which, however, amounted only to saying that the poor student had virtually no chance of ever getting farther forward than row four.[6]

Roughly speaking, the student body normally consisted of three strata: the large central stratum of the rich (*divites*) was flanked on either side by more or less broad peripheral groups against which it stood out: above, the nobility, church dignitaries, and other people of status (*nobiles statum tenentes*), and, below, the poor students (*pauperes*). This division into *nobiles, divites,* and *pauperes* was to be found throughout Europe, occasionally expressed in different terms – for example in the Iberian peninsula where the corresponding distinction was between *ricos, medianos,* and *pobres*.[7] In addition, there was a

---

[6] Aix: Fournier (ed.), *Statuts*, vol. III, 12. § 32. Prague: *Monumenta Historica Universitatis Carolo-Ferdinandeae Pragensis*, vol. II, *Album seu Matricula Facultatis Juridicae Universitatis Pragensis (1372–1418)* (Prague, 1834), 162. Orléans: Fournier (ed.), *Statuts*, vol. I, 23, § 30.

[7] C. M. Ajo González de Rapariegos y Sáinz de Zúñiga, *Historia de las Universidades Hispánicas*, vol. I, *Medievo y Renacimiento Universitario* (Madrid, 1957), 387 (Lisbon–Coimbra).

plethora of intermediate forms from half-rich to half-poor, which reveal awareness of the fact that none of the social strata could be socially homogeneous and that there were grey areas in both the upper and lower regions. It goes without saying that, quite apart from the European north–south divide, all these things were also subject to temporal change.

University attendance was neither a matter of course for the nobility of the Middle Ages nor at all necessary. The host of privileges which the universities granted, especially to the students of noble rank, bore no relation to their numbers. Probably, they nowhere exceeded the proportion of the nobility in the population at large. The lay nobility, whose political and military functions were still dominant, had no need of a university background. The case was somewhat different for the noble clergy, who came via their benefices at cathedral and collegiate chapters to the university, even if only to do the prescribed *biennium*, the two-year training course within the framework of the basic arts or, mostly, the basic law programme. Yet even clerical nobles remained relatively few. It is true that the universities of older Europe had, almost as one might expect, somewhat higher numbers of student-noblemen than those of younger Europe, above all in the fourteenth century in the vicinity of the French or papal courts at the law universities of the Midi, but also those of Italy and Spain (Salamanca, Lérida) – and this irrespective of the fact that many of these universities, such as Avignon, Montpellier, Bologna, and Padua (Orléans should also be added), were centres of international rank, goals for the educational journeys of the European aristocracy. In the Holy Roman Empire, but also in Poland and England, the attendance figures for students of noble rank rose only in the last decades of the fifteenth century at the dawn of the modern period, when the nobility of Europe as a whole set about regaining lost ground in state and church in the only way open to them, in view of the severe competition from a bourgeoisie now self-confident in the social and economic spheres and increasingly well educated at school and university. In order to counter education and training with more than just honourable birth, they likewise decided to embark on university education – a step which was all the easier to take as they did not have to forgo their accustomed privileges.

Apart from the aristocracy and high ecclesiastical dignitaries, who as a rule sought to be near popes, kings, princes, or high-ranking churches, the overwhelming majority of students all came from within the vicinity of the universities. A tightly spun web of social geography comprising *familiae*, table companionship, and patronage groups, mostly based on kinship, friendship, or compatriotism, surrounded the university. In the medical university at Bologna, for example, brothers, sons, and nephews were given preference over others as a matter of course and in 'full knowledge of the statutes'. High-ranking men in the church and at court, members of parliament in England, university professors, legal scholars and practitioners, merchants, and burghers (especially town councillors) – such was the family background of the protégés. Admittedly, they often arrived at university without office or title and hence were 'not yet anybody', but this was more than compensated for by their origins and connections. And yet, for all this, this exclusive group, exempted from the normal fees even at matriculation on account of their 'wealth of connections', were only the tip of the proverbial iceberg; *familia* structures for the most part permeated the entire student body.

Of all the strata in the student body it is precisely the most numerous whose composition is the most difficult to grasp. If one follows the sources, above all the *matriculae*, one can characterize this broad central stratum of the rich (*divites, solventes*) only from outside, from what it is not. Its members were neither of rank, nor already in office, nor again linked to a clientèle, nor finally dependent on remission of fees like the poor. About where they came from, about the standing and profession of their fathers or other relatives, medieval sources – the named excepted – rarely give any information. The members of this central stratum have only one thing in common: on their path through university, faculty, nation, and college, they always and everywhere paid the fees and *honoraria* demanded. Small wonder that they were described as *divites* pure and simple. Through all the economic, political, and demographic fluctuations of the age, the universities of older and younger Europe alike, the strongholds of law and of the arts in equal measure were continually concerned to attract a sufficiently large number of rich students to ensure their continuing viability. *Divites* were the representatives of almost all the collective characteristics of university attenders from the *simplex* to the specialist student. The patterns of living and studying were geared to them, above all. After all, they were the ones who really carried the university in a social and financial sense, thus helping substantially to guarantee its regional existence.

Like every stratum, that of the *divites* was rich in social gradations. Doubtless there was little difference from the social stratification in the place of origin, since every person who matriculated brought with him his rank and that of his family. An analysis of stratification would hence have to be transferred from the university to the place of origin, where the students' families and their position in the local social matrix could be traced. Here, however, there is a lack of local research into the correlation between university attendance, education, and stratification in towns and villages, both on a regional and, even more so, on a national and international level. In addition, in most European countries, the very prerequisites in terms of university sources, which would make such an undertaking feasible, are absent. And so one must rely on conjecture. For the Holy Roman Empire, one fact can be established by way of comparison: in the course of the late Middle Ages, and with special impetus in the second half of the fifteenth century, there was a push to university education by a group from the leading political and economic echelons of towns great and small – a group restricted in rather large numbers but largish relative to the population as a whole. In the university towns of Cologne, Heidelberg, and Vienna these people were members of merchant, commercial, and often burgher families with entrepreneurial tendencies and the capital to match. Their activity and comparatively higher incomes were paralleled by higher matriculation numbers. In contrast, although the 'golden age of the craftsmen' did admittedly bring the greater number of their sons to university, they were less strongly represented in comparison with their presence in the population at large. This did not, however, prevent the majority of them from joining the broad circle of students of adequate means in the central stratum. It seems as if the merchant and craftsman professions characteristic of the many different towns – in conjunction for the most part with generally higher incomes – displayed the greater attraction to university education. Among the families of origin in the crafts, the armourers of Cologne were matched by the shoemakers of Heidelberg and the pewterers of Vienna. Within the Holy Roman Empire, all the above holds equally true for those of village and country origin.

The poor (*pauperes*) – without means, often without name (family name), and above all without connections – formed a problem group at the lower end of the community, in many respects disadvantaged, to a large extent separated from the other student groupings, and even lacking in cohesion among themselves. The medieval university had no social commitment to improve their lot. On the contrary: the path through the university held far more obstacles for them than for others, all the more so since social attitudes towards poverty took a turn for the negative in the period 1200 to 1500, the old idealization of voluntary poverty becoming a thing of the past. The universities – i.e. the rectors, treasurers, and accountants, the doctors, masters or master-students, and specialist students, who often lived, as it were, as educational entrepreneurs from the revenue from fees and *honoraria* – were increasingly demanding: individual solvency or insolvency was appraised from the standpoint of total self-interest. Only thereafter did they accept or grant a certificate of poverty. The University of Freiburg im Breisgau kept a special book, the *liber taxatorum*, to keep a check on the recognized poor. *Nulli parcere* – to spare no one – was the strictly kept precept in Erfurt.[8] There existed all kinds of facilities for the poor: dispensation from fees, special lectures, or the awarding of doctorates by the pope – *in forma pauperum*. However, these facilities had connotations of social lowering and were, at best, commitment through passive encouragement, which, in the final analysis, helped only to cement the marginal position of the poor. Moreover, scholarships and special places for *pauperes* were a rarity, particularly at the end of the Middle Ages. Nor were they to be expected accord-

---

[8] H. Weissenborn (ed.), *Acten der Erfurter Universität*, vol. I (Halle, 1881), 12.

ing to the traditional rules of community in medieval societies. A pauper's living or a place in a hostel for poor students (*domus pauperum*) was allocated not according to proven want and actual need but often according to the quality of the social ties between the usufructuaries and the benefactors, who were invariably private individuals and who everywhere gave preference to relatives, friends, and compatriots. Scholarships in English colleges, as Rashdall remarked, 'were filled with men whose parents were quite well able to pay for the support of their sons',[9] and elsewhere in Europe things were no different. Among the first institutions to break through this kind of social conditioning, at the close of the fifteenth and the outset of the sixteenth century, were the Standonck Colleges. The theologian John Standonck from Mechelen, who, though himself the son of a poor cobbler, had attended university in Louvain and Paris, knew the situation of the *pauperes* at first hand. Colleges named after him appeared first in Paris at the Collegium Montaigu in 1490 and later in Louvain – whose statutes explicitly admitted only the genuine poor and not the sons of the rich and mighty, as improperly occurred everywhere. If, however, one believes Erasmus of Rotterdam, then the poorhouse of Montaigu seems to have been a pretty wretched place with a repressive style of management.[10] Nevertheless, between 15 and 20 per cent of the students attending the universities of both older and younger Europe – at least north of the Alps – were poor, though the exact figure depended on the economic cycle.

Indeed, the poor were not easily shaken off their university attendance by external influences (e.g. wars and plagues) – with, of course, the exception of rising prices. There was no sharply defined boundary between 'rich' and 'poor' at the universities but rather a fluctuating border crossed and recrossed by 'commuters on the economic cycle'; in the *matriculae* they were fittingly described as *semidivites* or *semipauperes*. Poor students often ignored the universities close at hand, preferring the large and above all cheap universities with less social prestige in the big cities of easy access (in the Holy Roman Empire: Vienna, Leipzig, Cologne, and Louvain; and the Anglo-German nation in Paris). Here they could still live relatively cheaply even in periods of crisis and perhaps had a better chance of finding occasional jobs or of begging. In this environment of poverty, the only ones who could attend university according to the social rules were those who successfully managed to acquire a social partner by acting as a live-in servant (*famulus*). Such positions – mostly within the framework of the university and far removed from mere occasional jobs – were obtained by patronage. Recommendations from acquaintances, friends, and relatives and often also the same place of origin as the master proved more decisive than the 'free market'. The social advantage

[9] Rashdall, *Universities*, vol. III, 412.
[10] M. Godet, *La Congrégation de Montaigu (1490–1580)* (Paris, 1912), 31ff., 144. Erasmus: C. Dupille, *Les Enragés du XVe siècle. Les étudiants au Moyen Age* (Paris, 1969), 113ff.

of belonging to the *familia* of a university teacher (of as high a rank as possible) perhaps made up for the onerousness of service. At least, this form of student support seems to have been the type most suited to the Middle Ages.

STUDENT ASSOCIATIONS

Although the medieval university was organized in individual bond groups, it was not organized hierarchically. Faculties, nations, colleges, student hostels, and other groups were, for all the variety of the respect in which they were held, relatively independent units on a shared organizational level. They were sectional parts with many areas of overlap, though linked together like the cells of one organism drawn from among the individual families of doctors and masters.

The oldest and at the same time the most significant groups to which those attending universities belonged were the 'nations'.[11] Their heyday, admittedly, was limited by and large to the universal phase of European university history before the schism of the papal church in 1378 and was hence necessarily confined to the universities of older Europe in the west and south. Largely independent of linguistic, political, and geographical boundaries, university nations were anything but nationally-minded constellations or even agents of national ideology as the term 'nation' might suggest. Nations were rather organizations of convenience based on like interests ranging from the welfare of members to a share in the government of the overall university. Accordingly, wherever they sprang up, the nations defined themselves as *fraternitates*, *societates*, *congregationes*, *corpora*, or *collegia* – as brotherhoods, associations, congregations, corporations, or colleges; they were the living communities in the university towns and cities, which for most students constituted an unknown, alien environment. Their significance and weight varied greatly from one university and country to another, depending on the influence of their representatives (procurators or councillors) or on the political and social government of the university (for example, in the election of the rector). It also depended – a factor directly connected with the above – on the student group from which the majority of their members were typically drawn. Here one can observe a substantial disparity between the older and the younger social forms: in Bologna and other law universities, where the administration tended to be decentralized, the students of rank and specialist students were in preponderance; in Paris, it was the baccalaureates of arts and the master-students who dominated, to the complete exclusion of the *simplices*, who were not even registered in the *matriculae* of the nations and gained entry only through being linked to a master; and in the younger universities, which already had a central admin-

---

[11] Kibre, *Nations*, 137 ff. See chapter 4, pp. 114–16 and chapter 9, pp. 282–4.

istration – such as Prague, Vienna, or Leipzig – all student types were represented, but in proportions which meant that precisely the *simplices* were the overwhelming majority of the 'regular' members. The latter were thus the social linchpins of the nations there but they did not have a parallel political function and were hence of only subordinate importance. In the jobs they performed for the communities, however, all nations more or less resembled one another: they all had their own leaders and administrators, procurators, proctors, money-receivers, and notaries; they all had their own seals, *matriculae*, and budgets; they took care of discipline and organized supervision and training courses; they had their own celebrations and special church services, thus honouring their own patron saint; and the longer the Middle Ages continued the more they saw it as their paramount task to support their members away from home and in any situation of danger, to give them succour in times of need and illness, and, in the event of death, to arrange a worthy funeral.

Alongside nations, colleges, halls, and *bursae*, there was also a wide variety of completely free student associations, of which, however, little is known. Many ostensibly had organizations like the then customary brotherhoods of merchants, craftsmen, and priests. One of the rare examples hails from Avignon, where in 1441 more than 200 students of law founded a Sebastian's Brotherhood. Under the leadership of a prior and twelve-strong advisory council it was to organize common divine service and processions, to foster communal and harmonious living among its members, to care for them in times of illness and want, to support them in conflicts with outsiders, and, if need be, to give deceased brethren a decent burial. These were the same tasks as were otherwise performed by nations, only here the origin of the brethren was of no significance. Elsewhere, student brotherhoods with a regional or local emphasis were formed. One of these was the Brotherhood of 'Our Dear Lady' for Paris students (mainly of arts) from Ypres, which received official approval in 1331; in Paris it had links with the Picardian nation. The special thing about this kind of community was that it brought together in their place of origin students and non-students, present and former students, clergy and laity, men and women, and, beside the usual functions of a brotherhood, also concerned itself with the financial support of students. In Italian university towns, students, craftsmen, and merchants from north of the Alps came together in unique *societates* which pursued common religious and cultural but also economic interests. Thus, in Perugia, there was from 1441 a documented Franco-German *Confraternitá* or *Compagnia degli Ultramontani ciò theodeschi e franciosi*. In the course of the fifteenth to sixteenth century, its organization was taken over by the students (mostly lawyers), who then gradually forced the others out. Eventually, the two nationalities also separated.[12]

---

[12] Fournier (ed.), *Statuts*, vol. II, 417–20, 440ff.: P. Trio, 'A Medieval Students' Confraternity at Ypres: the Notre Dame Confraternity of Paris Students', *History of Universities*, 5 (1985),

Below the formal level of the university and its sectional units, table companionships, and brotherhoods, students of all types met in small groups which had often coalesced on the journey to the university town and had been continued during the time of study. Forming groups and joining motley travelling associations were nothing uncommon, given the general hazards of medieval travel; these small groups, however, were something special. They were entered by the university rector in the general *matriculae* and thus received a good deal of attention from university officialdom. On account of the sources, admittedly, these small groups can be observed only in the universities of central Europe, from Louvain to Cracow and from Rostock to Vienna; there, however, they are so omnipresent on the scale of 15 to 30 per cent that – not least in the light of the 'Italian journey' phenomenon – one can probably view their existence as the general state of affairs.[13] The composition of the groups and the number of their members varied. There were groups of masters and students, groups of monks, groups of noblemen with their retinues, groups of relatives, and, as the substantial majority, open groups of compatriots. The close identity of home region, which obtained so often, defined all five types. Numerically, the type found most frequently at German universities was the 'cluster of two' or *Paargruppe* (70 per cent). This was clearly the most appropriate type of group formation, both on the journey to university and at university, in the *bursa* and the *familia* of the master: quite apart from the student world, it was a basic pattern of medieval mobility in general, affecting other social forces as well, such as the journeyman-craftsman. It was, above all, the equal rank of the members that gave these small groups – with the exception of the lord-and-servant groups – their stability. Poor and rich students mostly kept company with their peers.

LODGINGS

Over a long period of time, nations and faculties employed for themselves the term *collegium*, as befitted their character as individual bond groups. Alongside them there had existed since the thirteenth century a further sectional unit of the university, for which the term *collegium* was also used, denoting a more rigid form (more of an institution, a specific form of organization and living for students of all types). This institution was – it could hardly have been otherwise – close to the church, in part even down to its architectural shape, being comparable in form both to the monastery and to the colle-

15–53; F. Weigle, *Die Matrikel der deutschen Nation in Perugia (1579–1727)* (Tübingen, 1956), 8. See also chapter 9, p. 285.
[13] R. C. Schwinges, 'Studentische Kleingruppen im späten Mittelalter', in H. Ludat and R. C. Schwinges (eds.), *Politik–Gesellschaft–Geschichtsschreibung. Giessener Festgabe für Frantisek Graus* (Cologne/Vienna, 1982), 319–61. S. Stelling-Michaud, *L'Université de Bologne et la pénétration des droits romain et canonique en Suisse aux XIIIe et XIVe siècles* (Geneva, 1955), 82ff.

giate church. The architectural configuration of the college, that is to say, buildings grouped in a square around a central court and generally including a dining-hall, living-rooms and bedrooms, a kitchen and cellar, a lecture hall, a library, and a chapel, was in its developed form to leave a decisive mark on the institutional self-understanding of the university, first in older and then in younger Europe.

One of the very first, the renowned college of La Sorbonne in Paris, founded in 1257 by the chaplain of Louis IX, Robert of Sorbon, formulated the central idea of the future college system in exemplary fashion: *vivere socialiter et collegialiter, et moraliter, et scholariter* – a formulation which implies the existence of a study community organized in the form of a brotherhood and living together in regulated and moral fashion.[14] As opposed to mere hostel foundations and elementary forms of collegial living, such as the Collège des Dix-huit with beds for eighteen 'poor clerics' in the hospital of Notre-Dame (1180), or the Collège des Bons Enfants de St Honoré (1208–9), the 'Sorbonne type' brought with it two novelties, above all.

On the one hand, such institutions were endowed with at times substantial holdings in land, property, and fixed-interest capital, which could be considerably increased during the course of the Middle Ages by the acquisition of benefactions and by ground-rent. In addition, they could have special privileges which, for example, facilitated cheap housekeeping by granting the right to produce or to import duty-free commodities such as bread, meat, beer, and wine. The college fellows benefited from all this, as if they were holders of a scholarship. They received free board and lodging and a weekly allowance – the *bursa* (purse) – and, not infrequently, even a contribution towards their summer and winter clothing or academic dress. The number of college members (*bursarii, collegiati, socii*) corresponded to the financial strength of the individual foundation. The length of stay in the college was in principle limited: in practice, however, it was extremely flexible even within one and the same institution.

On the other hand, there was a new pattern to the day, regulated by the college's own statutes, with most of the time taken up by disciplined studying. The latter was, it is true, still strongly indebted to church models, but it can be seen as the first pedagogical scenario for communally organized study outside the educational world of the church and monastery. At first, this activity was restricted to repetition of an exercise in material encountered outside. During the later Middle Ages, however, university courses in all subjects, but especially in the arts and in theology, were transferred into the colleges themselves. At the end of our period, the situation over much of Europe was dominated by the colleges, above all in England and France; in Paris, in 1445, it was baldly said that the entire university was situated in its

---

[14] P. Glorieux, *Les Origines du collège de Sorbon* (Notre Dame, Ind., 1959), 17.

colleges, and this statement held equally true for Oxford and Cambridge.[15] By then, even non-college members were attending the college courses. The faculties did little but organize examinations and award degrees. In this form, the college system also exerted influence on other spheres of education, for example on the famous English public schools of Winchester (1382) and Eton (1440), on the arts and grammar schools in Languedoc, instituted by Pope Urban V (1362–70), and also on the extra-university study foundations in Spain, from which subsequently, through papal grants of privileges and the right to award doctorates, the new type of 'college university' could emerge – first in Sigüenza (1476–89), and then also in Alcalá (1499) and Seville (1502–5).

The constitution of the colleges was essentially no different from that of the other sectional parts of the university. They took care of their own privileges and statutes, and ran their own administration over a varying range of affairs. Just as nations and faculties were under the proctor and dean, so all college members and their associates, servants, and chaplains came under a principal (a dean, rector, regent, or warden), who was himself more or less stringently responsible for his college to the university governing body, to the chancellor or the diocesan bishop concerned, to superintendents appointed by princes or municipalities, or to especially instituted visitors.

The colleges were clearly moulded by the social milieu of their age. This was due in part to their founders and conditions of foundation. The benefactors were usually the great figures of the land: kings and queens, princes and princesses, together with the remaining aristocracy, the pope, cardinals, bishops, and canons of major churches, councillors to kings and princes, municipal authorities, and even professors, who admittedly had habitually earned their foundation capital through some characteristic dual role as men of the church, personal physicians, law scholars, or court theologians. Bourgeois foundations were still rare in comparison, even if behind not a few royal or princely names (e.g. Queen's College Cambridge, 1448) there was a good deal of bourgeois money. Those most likely – qualitatively and quantitatively speaking – to emerge as benefactors were personages in high offices of state, court, or church. This was the case in Paris with Robert of Sorbon, the royal chaplain and canon of the cathedral of Notre-Dame and – to name but a few instances – in Bologna (Collegio di Spagna 1364) with Cardinal Gil Albornoz, dubbed the second founder of the church state, in Valladolid (Colegio Mayor de Santa Cruz 1479) with Cardinal Pedro Gonzáles de Mendoza, the chancellor of Castile, and, it would seem, especially in England with English prelates: all the larger English colleges were founded by bishops who were or had been lord chancellor of England, as for example was the first, Merton, founded by Walter de Merton, bishop of Rochester, in 1264. The selection is, at least in geographical terms, not entirely arbitrary, for such benefaction

[15] Rashdall, *Universities*, vol. I, 519.

was, until the close of the Middle Ages, a phenomenon more of the west and south than of the remainder of Europe.

Whatever the rank and size of the foundations, the motives of the founders were usually similar. However much they changed in the course of the later Middle Ages or were complemented by charitable, educational, intellectual, or political factors, two fundamental motives – one religious and one social – remained relatively continuous. The first was a formal religious motivation, in that the foundation arose out of concern for the founder's own soul and that of his family (*donatio pro anima*). College members, as beneficiaries, had the duty of rendering perpetual prayer and divine service for the founder's salvation. Closely connected with this as part and parcel of the life pattern of traditional societies were social motives. It was not that the founders had social engineering at heart. In the Spanish College in Bologna, even high-ranking members received *elemoysinas* – alms – but the reality of the allocation of places allegedly reserved for *pauperes* belied the name.[16]

The social motivation had instead a *familia* character; naturally, this was first and foremost true of secular foundations and less of those of monastic orders. The chance of college membership was closely linked to the local and regional network of the founder's *familia*, be it that of a prince, of the church, of a municipality, or of a private individual. In most cases, preference was given, in hierarchical order, to relatives, family and friends, and family associates, the inhabitants of the founder's town of birth or town of origin, compatriots, or diocesan members. The patronage of the founder was disseminated through the administrators of the foundation and the visitors to the college members, who had family connections of their own and could accordingly co-opt further members. Links between regions and foundations could be numerous: in Paris, for example there were the Collèges des Daces, d'Uppsala (des Sueses), de Skara, des Ecossais, des Lombards, and des Allemands. The Spanish College in Bologna admitted by statute first and foremost Castilians, then Aragonese, then Portuguese, and lastly Italians, on the condition that these 'foreigners' would have to withdraw if further Spanish applicants were to come forward. New College, Oxford, was, by the founder's stipulation, reserved primarily for students from the bishopric of Winchester; the family connections of the fellows allowed additional emphases to emerge, with several areas and even small townships receiving special preference. In Germany, the professor of medicine Amplonius Ratingk had designated his Erfurt college foundation Zur Himmelspforte (Porta Coeli 1412) to be almost exclusively for the students from his home region in the electorate of Cologne and, above all, for inhabitants of his small native town, Rheinberg am Niederrhein. In the fifteenth century the latter thus became, on a head count, one of the leading 'graduate towns' of the Holy Roman Empire. In

---

[16] See p. 118. B. M. Marti, *The Spanish College at Bologna in the Fourteenth Century* (Philadelphia, 1966), 17ff.

comparison with these widespread social–geographic factors, all other admission criteria were of lesser importance.

Among those attending the universities of Europe, college members were thus a privileged and protected minority, though they were not a socially homogeneous group or a closed-circle élite. The differing rank and capital of the founder, the personal rank of the college member, and not least the faculties attended ensured this. Many colleges were modest and small, catering for the young arts student of the *simplex* or baccalaureate type and for his social background. Others again were open almost exclusively to students of the higher faculties, to master-students and specialist students, or solely to graduates, with bachelors of arts being the least frequently accepted unless non-graduates had sufficient prestige or prior education. For a long time, students of theology or of arts and theology were in the majority – and not only in the institutions of the various monastic orders. From the fourteenth century on, however, students of law – both canon and civil – gained more and more college places and began to push back the arts and theology predominance. The arts colleges founded at the University of Cahors in the second half of the fourteenth century were clearly so uncommon in the 'law area' of southern France by that time that they were transformed into colleges of law in the following century. Kings and princes and men of court and of church increasingly used their foundations of those entrusted to them to strengthen their staffs, recruiting the next generation of legal scholars for the church and the civil service. Older Europe, especially Oxford and the universities of the south, were in the vanguard here. One should, however, beware of overestimating things. The majority of students of law, being as a rule specialist students and students of rank, had no need of college places. Thus, at a decidedly legal university such as Orléans there were no such foundations; and it was not by chance that Italy and the Iberian peninsula had relatively few colleges; only in the sixteenth century, under different conditions, did the situation change. The situation may have been similar for the medical scholars, who did, it is true, receive individual places at colleges, but rarely – with the exception of Montpellier – had entire colleges founded for them.

The colleges of the Holy Roman Empire followed a path of their own. The members of the Prague Carolinum, the Vienna Collegium Ducale, or the Major and Minor Colleges in Leipzig were, admittedly, in the majority of cases, master-students and specialist students like many of their European fellows; yet, from the very outset, they were employed to teach in the faculty of arts by the university founders, who – territorial rulers, princes, and municipalities alike – were also the founders of most of the colleges. The college member who had at least the master of arts degree was a *magister regens* and hence a professor for the arts students; his position was the forerunner of a chair in this faculty and his scholarship money consequently a remuneration of his teaching. This 'German model', which incidentally had its imitators elsewhere in younger Europe, in Scotland and Poland and probably in Sweden also, had little to do with the ancient and widespread practice of younger students receiving teaching and guidance from older students – the tutors of the English colleges. In the German case, the student element always had a professorial overlay.

Despite their contemporaries' alacrity in establishing new colleges, the great majority of students of whatever type and whether graduate or not had to look around for accommodation, even in richly endowed Paris, where during the fifteenth century at most 15 per cent of university attenders had the benefit of college membership.[17] Basically, there were from the outset only two possibilities: either one lived alone or with others in rented or subrented private accommodation, or one lived in communal fashion in a student house licensed or supervised by the university, for which there were several different terms current: *domus, hospicium, paedagogium, contubernium, regentia, bursa, aula,* or in English 'hall' or 'hostel'. As a rule, the house was run by a master of the arts, who likewise had to have a licence for the job, or by a specialist student with a higher degree.

The former possibility was the habitual state of affairs in the lawyer-dominated universities of western and southern Europe, from Orléans to Bologna and Salamanca. Students of almost all types resided as lodgers (*cameristae*) in the houses of townsfolk, in student boarding-houses or in the households of their professors, arranging to be fed and looked after either there or elsewhere as table companions (*commensales*) or paying guests for meals (*portionistae*; in Spain, *pupilos*). In the arts-and-theology environment north of the Alps, with its large numbers of young arts undergraduates, private lodging was largely restricted to masters and specialist students and to groups on the margin of the student body: on the one hand the high-ranking students from the nobility, the upper reaches of the clergy, and the rich bourgeois class, who often took up accommodation with their servants and private tutors, and on the other hand the poor students, who could neither afford the hostels nor obtain places there or elsewhere as servants. Not everywhere were there, as in Vienna, special *Bettelkotter* (*coderie*) – cheap and lowly digs where the poor rubbed shoulders with the poor.

The second possibility, which the universities always encouraged, had economic good sense and social behaviour patterns on its side: when away from home, students and masters of the same language and origin naturally tended to come together to live in communities suitable to them; this met the need of a connection with the master and his *familia* and in addition fulfilled the desire of the university administration and of other secular and ecclesi-

---

[17] J. Verger, 'Collegium', in *Lexikon des Mittelalters*, vol. III (Munich, 1986), 41. In Oxford and Cambridge 10–20 per cent also: T. H. Aston, G. D. Duncan, and T. A. R. Evans, 'The Medieval Alumni of the University of Cambridge', *Past and Present*, 86 (1980), 14. In the Empire the estimation is lower than 5 per cent.

astical bodies to oversee housing. From the fourteenth century on, this latter desire led to a general residence requirement. Around 1410, for example, and again – with royal support – in 1420, Oxford impressed upon all attending the university, even young students of law, the obligation of residence either in the colleges or in the authorized halls. The hope was that this would put a check on the 'chamberdeacons' – students living at large in the town without permission or ties, allegedly sleeping by day and by night leading a shocking life of plunder and murder in the taverns and brothels. The general tenor of such ordinances, which acquired the rank of statutes, can also be found throughout the northern part of the continent – in 1410 in Vienna against the outside students (*extra bursas stantes*), and in 1452–7 in Paris against the so-called *Martinets* (swallows). Nowhere, however, were such efforts very successful in practice. As the modern period approached, private lodgings proved more and more attractive, even north of the Alps: the many *cameristae* in Louvain were one good example.[18]

Like the colleges, the English halls (Oxford) or hostels (Cambridge), the Parisian hospices or *paedagogia*, and the *bursae* of the Holy Roman Empire were genuine sectional parts of the university. For the majority of their inmates, the *hospites* or *bursales* (from which is derived the later German term for a student, *Bursche*), to attend a university was often no more than to be linked to such an institution, in the geographical, social, and intellectual sense. The head of the 'house', the principal (rector, *regens*, *conventor*) accredited by the university, was himself – or with the help of further masters – responsible for the appropriate furnishing of the building he had bought or rented, as well as for board, lodging, and academic teaching and learning. In return, his student *familia* paid him the weekly purse, the fee for board, lodging, and study, customarily calculated on a weekly basis.

The communal life naturally gave such student houses their own unique regional and social characteristics. In general, these resembled those of the colleges (and in part also of the nations), since both were based on a *familia* or compatriot footing as well as on the rules of social propinquity. The will of the college founder was merely supplanted by the pull of the ruling master. And so, according to the origin of their principals, the student houses represented particular spectra of the university catchment area – spectra which could of course shift in the course of time – or were downright exclusive, such as St Edmund Hall for the Welsh in Oxford, the Olavsbursa in Rostock largely preserved for the Norwegians, the Swabian Bursa in Heidelberg or the Hungarian Bursa in Cracow, which, however, by no means accepted all Hungarians but only those from certain towns, especially Szeged, Pest, and

---

[18] Gibson (ed.), *Statuta* (note 4), 208ff., 226ff.; Kink, *Geschichte* (note 5), 234ff; Rashdall, *Universities*, vol. II, 526; E. De Maesschalck, 'De "goede" en de "eeuwige student". Tucht en huisvesting te Leuven in de 15e en 16e eeuw', *Alumni Leuven*, 9: 1 (1978), 11–15. For the figures see chapter 4, p. 118.

Ofen.[19] The social character of the institutions, all too closely linked to particular regions, depended solely on the status and financial means of the inmates. *Bursae*, halls, and hospices were anything but charitable foundations, even if, in certain cases, there were a few free places. The poor were, as a rule, granted admittance only as servants, and thus worked to pay all or part of their weekly fee. Student hostels, one presumes, ranked the higher the more favourable was the proportion of *communarii* to *semi-communarii* (in Oxford, 'battelers'), or, in more general terms, of rich to poor. The weekly prices were staggered accordingly: at the bottom of the list, in Vienna – if one ignores the special houses for the poor – were the 'twopenny halls' (*Zwei-Groschen-Bursen*); in Erfurt the sum would have just sufficed to obtain a midday meal at table in one of the big colleges. There followed 'threepenny halls' and perhaps halls in upward gradations of a penny a time. Presumably, there were similar subdivisions in many other university towns; in general, at any event, from Portugal to England, universities sought to control rents.

The number of self-supporting student houses in the various university towns depended on demand and on the degree of institutionalization. It thus went up and down over the years with the economy, the fluctuations being far greater than in the case of the colleges. As a result, the number of houses can rarely be ascertained with any accuracy. Numerous hospices, halls, and *bursae* must have been so small and have had so short a life that they left no trace in the sources. In Paris, there was no doubt a thoroughgoing 'school industry', but without it being at any time quantifiable. Things were similar in Italy, Spain, and the lands on the periphery of the European university system. A point of reference can be found in Oxford, where, around the year 1313, the names of 123 halls were recorded; in the first half of the fifteenth century, however, they numbered around seventy and in the second half approximately fifty, with a mere eight remaining in 1530. In mid-fifteenth-century Cambridge, probably no more than seventeen hostels were being run. At the University of St Andrews in Scotland, there was only one *paedagogium* and one college, with students from 1506 onwards being entered in the *matricula* as belonging to the one or the other. As early as before 1400, there were 'many houses' (and six mentioned by name) in Prague. In 1413, Vienna had twenty-nine *bursae*, and thirty years later still eleven with six *coderie* for the poor. In Basle, there were seven *bursae* before 1496 and thereafter only four. The remaining universities of the Holy Roman Empire registered fluctuating figures; two to four institutions would seem, however, to have been generally sufficient.

These figures, of course, are not directly comparable – and not only on account of the completely haphazard nature of the sources: a further problem is that the individual institutions had vast differences of capacity. To establish

---

[19] K. Schrauf, *Regestrum Bursae Hungarorum Cracoviensis* (Vienna, 1893), xixff.

a recognized community, the *bursa integra* of a master-principle, it was adequate in Vienna to have three to four students; elsewhere, six would generally suffice. The upper limit was bounded only by the room facilities available and by student attendance figures. Thus, in the main *bursae* at the major German universities, several hundred persons could be accommodated; around 1450, for example, 294 and 246 students of the arts, respectively, were living and working in the two *bursae* of the Majus and Porta Coeli colleges at Erfurt; the building complex of the latter contained twenty rooms (*commoda*), each thus housing on average twelve persons. In Paris around the same time, hospices such as the Sainte-Barbe are likely to have had seventy and more places on offer, a figure similar to the big *collèges*. In Cracow, the Jerusalem Bursa was set up in 1454 for a hundred inmates. On the other hand, the many halls at Oxford housed in mid-century an average of eighteen students, of arts and law alike; the approximately eleven arts hostels at Cambridge, meanwhile, accommodated from twenty-five to thirty on average, and the six law hostels, eighty. In contrast to Oxford, where the 'single-hall' type predominated, the hostels at Cambridge were larger and more ambitious in their facilities, having more rooms and buildings and, not least, more continuity. In this, they resembled a number of large *bursae* and *paedagogia* on the continent.

A phenomenon common throughout Europe was the decline in student houses in the course of the fifteenth century, a decline quite evident in the cases of Oxford and Vienna. One can perceive here a process of concentration in which many of the smaller units failed to stay the course or were annexed by larger units, or eventually became outdated as forms of community. In western Europe, as the modern period approached, this process favoured the colleges or the emerging 'college-universities' as a whole. Parallel to this came a rise in the latter's capacity for foundation. For some time now, there had been an ever stronger flow of inmates from the hospices, halls, and hostels moving as paying guests into those colleges which had already taken up the full business of academic teaching; independent units were being transformed into places of residence which, though not incorporated, were affiliated to the colleges and thus came under their supervision. Even before the century came to an end, for example, Merton College, Oxford, had acquired a ring of satellite halls – St John's, St Alban's, Colishalle, Knyght, and Nunn Hall; as a rule, they were overseen by older fellows, who became their principals. In Paris, too, masters and students gradually left the *paedagogia* and schools on the rue du Fouarre in favour of that good third of the colleges (some eighteen in number) which, around 1500, were already organizing all of the teaching (*collèges de plein exercice*).

In the universities of central Europe, the colleges also profited from the demise of the student houses and indeed helped to bring it about. From the very outset, 'college professors' ran *bursae* of their own, which were, in some cases, integrated into their colleges to the extent of forming part of the building itself. Such college *bursae*, in which the *bursales* had to pay rent and board but did not have to contribute to the upkeep of their *magister regens*, must have been an unparalleled attraction in the university towns. In their shadow, the private entrepreneurial *bursae* had little chance of establishing themselves. This was undoubtedly the general run of events, true also in the case of halls, hostels, and hospices. Where the entrepreneurial *bursae* had to compete with the – mostly larger – college *bursae*, the course of the fifteenth century regularly saw the former squeezed out, all the more so since they also suffered keen competition from one another. Only 'specialist institutions' – grammar schools and humanist circles with special syllabuses and teaching styles, which at the same time often betokened a higher social level – were able to hold their own. The competitive situation is underlined by the repeated ban on soliciting freshmen, the often cheap-jack-like advertisement of individual *bursae* to freshmen – in Basle, for example, when their Rhine ships had just moored and they were in the process of disembarking.

The entrepreneurial *bursa* was able to come into its own only when there was no competition from college foundations, as was, remarkably, the case in Louvain and Cologne, the two most westerly universities in the Holy Roman Empire. Here, the entrepreneurs and their employees, who were employed as it were as 'drillers' (*magistri exercentes*), represented almost the entire arts faculty. In contrast to the college *bursae*, which in actual fact offered only exercises to accompany a course of study elsewhere, the attempt was made from the middle of the fifteenth century onwards to concentrate the entire training of arts students in these *bursae*, thus largely extinguishing the minor competition from four principals' *bursae* in Cologne and four *paedagogia* in Louvain. This was a close approximation to the western forms of college education. In Louvain, the *paedagogia* came in part under strong influence from foundations and colleges even before the Middle Ages had drawn to a close; in Cologne, on the other hand, the principals' *bursae* evolved in the sixteenth century into grammar schools (*Gymnasien*), thus successfully surviving in type, albeit in different circumstances, whilst the rest of the *bursae* network in the Holy Roman Empire gradually disappeared. In western and now also in southern Europe, the great age of the college-universities was now dawning, while, under the influence of the sectarian age, and universities of the Holy Roman Empire and of its northern and eastern neighbours began to follow a logical course of development into professorial universities; the old masters' or professors' colleges of arts dissolved together with the student *bursae*. At the end of the day, there were professors with a bourgeois position and students with freedom to move and choose.

STUDENT LIFE

None of the five types of European student seems to have enjoyed a good reputation. From the thirteenth to the fifteenth century the same laments are heard again and again from all quarters. Students are bawling and brawling, carousing and whoring, singing and dancing, playing cards and chess, are addicted to dice and other games of chance, are up and about town day and night, are swanking around in inappropriate, fashionable clothing, are behaving provocatively to burghers, guild members, and town law-and-order forces, are carrying arms, and are even making use of them. It is not the university and knowledge which attract them but the diversions and seductations of town life.

The University of Paris, preached Cardinal Jacques de Vitry (d. 1240), was an international parliament of sin, a rendezvous for vice-ridden souls the world over. The students of Paris – the cardinal continued – studied only in winter and spent the summer roaming far and wide; they went from one teacher to the next, attending no course to its conclusion, just doing the bare minimum to avoid losing their student privileges; they would, if need be, attend lectures in canon law solely because they took place at an hour when they had awoken from their slumbers, but they were nevertheless foolish enough to give themselves scholarly airs by the demonstrative carting around of ponderous folios.[20] The chorus of the churchmen was taken up by the professors, who (in a stereotyped reaction which has held until today) were dissatisfied with the lifestyle and the work of their students. Odofredus de Denariis (*c.* 1200–65), one of the renowned glossators in Bologna, observed and commented forthrightly on the student's excesses, penchant for luxury and pleasures, liking for fine clothes and amorous adventures, and predilection for dice, dance, and drink. The cardinal had in mind, above all, the young students of the arts, the *simplices* and *baccalarii*: the learned jurist, on the other hand, was referring to the elevated clientèle of the students of rank and the older students of law. The tenor, however, was the same. In the Italy of the thirteenth and fourteenth centuries, the professors – lawyers and grammarians alike – issued warnings in unison against idleness, upholding themselves and their profession as an example: the famed Azzo dei Porci of Bologna, they claimed, had lived so conscientiously that he had been ill only in the holidays and had even died when on vacation. In the late Middle Ages, such criticism took on an admixture of derision at the human failures which eventually resulted: risible, dissolute creatures – known in the Holy Roman Empire as *henselini* (nincompoops) – who had frittered away their youth at university, squandered their father's money, learnt nothing but how to bring in the wine, and finally taken back home only shame. Such was the vision of

---

[20] Rashdall, *Universities*, vol. III, 439ff.

the professor of canon law in Basle, Sebastian Brant, who found room for students in *Das Narrenschiff* (*The Ship of Fools*), his great social satire of 1494.[21]

Many such remarks and assessments, if taken together, would amount to an unmitigated *histoire scandaleuse*. Yet it would be no more true than the opposite tale of the diligent student fulfilling equally the academic and religious tasks of the age and dividing his university day between chapel and study, meal-times, and sleep. Both the vice-ridden and the dutiful student were, in most cases, the distorted products of cautionary tales. Literary confirmations could be collected without difficulty, from the *carmina burana* of the twelfth-century *vagantes* through the *Canterbury Tales* of Geoffrey Chaucer (b. 1440), to the ballads of François Villon (b. c. 1465). For the historian, the situation is a wretched one. Before the sixteenth century there are virtually no personal accounts from students which could offer a contemporary challenge to the anecdotal and rather haphazard source material which is available. Student letters were, as a rule, 'SOS' entreaties to parents, uncles, or patrons, full of woe at the deprivations of life, now in prose now in verse, but forever pleading for release from problems of finance and apparel – so much so that one is tempted to believe that the letters must often be based on models in widespread circulation.[22]

Student behaviour was least felt to need regulation in the older law universities, above all in southern Europe, and most in the younger universities of central Europe. Judging by the number of pertinent statutes, it was here that university life was most closely superintended. One cannot, however, deduce from this that those attending the universities of central Europe were wilder than those elsewhere. It is true that the vast majority of them were young arts and masters students between the ages of fourteen and twenty; yet this was the case in, say, Paris as well, or at the English universities, without producing similar administrative measures there. It was also a constitutional question: whilst elsewhere the overseeing of students remained to a greater extent and longer in the hands of the old sectional associations – the nations, faculties, and colleges – in the universities of the Holy Roman Empire, which were from the outset centrally administered, student life was also centrally regulated to a far greater extent and in a substantial number of ways. A comparable state of affairs was not brought about elsewhere until the Paris reform of 1452 and the Oxford *statuta aularia* of 1489; in the remainder of Europe, however, such steps were not taken. One can see here a parallel to the rectoral *matriculae*, which are exlusively to be found in younger Europe.[23]

---

[21] Steffen, *Studentische Autonomie* (note 3), 122–6; Sebastian Brant, *Narrenschiff*, ed. F. Zarncke (Leipzig, 1854), cap. 27, 29, 356ff.
[22] C. H. Haskins, *Studies in Mediaeval Culture* (New York, 1929), 1–35 ('The Life of Mediaeval Students as Illustrated by Their Letters').
[23] Cf. chapter 6, p. 179.

The general statutes established norms for all matriculated members of the university from the doctor of theology to the beginner in grammar. In the medieval world there was nothing special about this and it should not only be associated with monastic rigours. Strict rules and regulations were ubiquitous: there were guild regulations, regulations for craftsmen and apprentices, regulations for burghers' clothing, regulations for patrician community houses, regulations for princes' courts, and more besides – all of them governing many different human groups and differing classes in their day-to-day dealings, leisure time, and social gatherings. In the statutorily governed colleges and student hostels it was not only knowledge, methods, and other standards of academic life that were purveyed but also social skills and patterns of behaviour, whose function was to facilitate the way the entire community dealt both with its own members and with the less privileged world outside. The often elaborate commandments and prohibitions, which might well seem to be grotesque coercion when viewed against the backdrop of modern academic freedom, had beyond doubt their stabilizing function. There was a general concern – the earliest documentary evidence of which can be found in Cambridge (1236–54) – for the preservation of the public peace.[24]

Honeste se gerrere, decent behaviour, meant – from Lisbon–Coimbra to St Andrews – above all else, four things. First, it meant avoiding contact with women of all kinds, both outside and even more so inside the hospices, *bursae*, and colleges. In a close-knit, exclusively male society, which produced a surplus of men in every university town, thus disturbing the balance of the sexes and for that reason alone sowing the seeds of conflict, this was an understandable ban. Married doctors, masters, and students were relatively few north of the Alps even around 1500. In the south, on the other hand, they could be found more frequently. This different attitude towards women in the south is, moreover, documented by statutes.[25] The second ban was on bearing arms, above all at night and on principle in any gathering or lesson of the university – *calamitatibus provideri*, as the phrase went at Bologna and at related Italian universities, to obviate misfortunes among the students and between them and townsfolk.[26] Apart from the battles of the Paris nations among themselves and the continual frictions between town and gown, there were nevertheless occasional armed conflicts and serious 'student wars': in 1278 in Paris, for example, in 1332 in Toulouse, in 1355 in Oxford, in 1387 in

[24] M. B. Hackett, *The Original Statutes of Cambridge University. The Text and its History* (Cambridge, 1979), 211ff. Oxford: Gibson (ed.), *Statuta* (note 4), 81.

[25] For example, Fournier (ed.), *Statuts*, vol. III, 13ff., § 36 (Aix 1420–40). On married medical students and masters, see chapter 11.

[26] H. Denifle, 'Die Statuten der Juristenuniversität Bologna vom Jahre 1317–1347 und deren Verhältnis zu jenen Paduas, Perugias, Florenz', *Archiv für Literatur- und Kirchengeschichte*, 3 (1887), 363, § 71 (also Perugia and Padua). U. Gualazzini (ed.), *Corpus Statutorum almi Studii Parmensis*, 2nd edn (Milan, 1978), 151, § 64.

Orléans, in 1410–11 in Salamanca, and in 1422 in Heidelberg. The third prohibition concerned the wearing of fashionable clothes and above all the display made of them. Unobtrusive and simple apparel, a *habitus honestus*, was demanded. This 'academic dress', however, which developed only gradually from its clerical origins, was so varied in its forms that it is impossible to determine its shape and colour even in individual countries and periods (see chapter 4). The fourth thing to be prohibited throughout Europe was insults in word and deed against fellow students and professors. What was at stake here was personal honour – but also, and more so, the avoidance of internal conflict. In Prague, which was so to speak the bridge between the older and younger university forms in Europe, there is even a list of the most common forms of verbal insult employed: *ribaldus*, *nequam*, and *mendax* – 'scallywag', 'good-for-nothing', and 'liar' – were the relatively harmless and received milder punishment than *filius meretricis*, *spurius*, *fur*, and *traditor*, 'son of a whore', 'bastard', 'villain', and 'traitor'. It was also from Prague that the curious 'hurling paragraph' on bodily injuries reached the statutes of some German universities, a paragraph in which the vary facts of intent behind each object cast – an unaimed throw, an aimed throw, a hit, and finally an injury – were treated with textbook casuistry as deserving increasingly severe punishment.[27]

Alongside these absolute commandments and prohibitions there was a welter of further regulations, which were given varying degrees of emphasis at the individual universities, thus revealing the social rank of the student bodies in the various university regions. In the law citadels of the *domini studentes* in southern France and Italy and, in part also, on the Iberian peninsula, special emphasis was laid on restraining the extravagant 'aristocratic life style': luxurious clothing, the number of scribes and servants, the games of chance such as dicing for money (*ludus taxillorum*), which was denounced in Perugia and Florence ahead of all other misdemeanours, and in addition the keeping and equipping of horses, dogs, and birds for hunting (which in Coimbra and Salamanca were expressly forbidden except for the high nobility). In Lérida, riding to courses was forbidden except in cases of necessity. The ban on weapons, on the other hand, was somewhat relaxed in Italy: it was no longer valid when their lordships the lawyers of Bologna, Padua, Perugia, or Parma needed to display themselves to the world at funerals, in processions, and on other ceremonious occasions.[28] In the universities north of the Alps, with their habitual predominance of arts and theology students, however, other problems were more pressing. Here there was a need to regu-

[27] H. Jírecek (ed.), *Codex Juris Bohemici*, vol. II: 3 (Prague, 1889), 278ff., § 21.

[28] A. Gomes da Rocha Mahadil (ed.), *Livro verde da Universidade de Coimbra* (Cartulario do século XV) (Coimbra, 1940), 13; P. U. González de la Calle and A. Huarte y Echenique (eds.), *Constituciones de la Universidad de Salamanca (1422)* (Madrid, 1927), 73ff. Lérida: Liber constitutionum, J. Villanueva, *Viaje Literario a las iglesias de España*, vol. XVI (Madrid, 1851), 230; Denifle, 'Statuten' (note 26), 363, § 71: Gualazzini (ed.), *Corpus* (note 26), 151, § 64.

late the large numbers of *simplices*, the normal, young students, the majority of whom had no degree and left relatively soon. Consequently, the bulk of time and effort was devoted to the overseeing of student hostels, with the aim of ensuring that students were in the hostels at the appointed times and not roaming the streets and squares or frequenting ale-houses and other 'suspect places'. Colleges, hospices, halls, or *bursae* were to be locked after the ringing of the evening curfew – in summer between 8 and 10 p.m., in winter between 7 and 9 p.m., or, as in Paris and Oxford, at 9 p.m. the whole year through – and to remain locked until 5 or 6 a.m.

It goes without saying that many regulations were frequently breached and that many *bursa* entrepreneurs turned a blind eye. The universities reacted with sanctions which, in the long term, probably did have a stabilizing and educative effect. Each single statute was accompanied by a specially formulated threat of punishment. Repeated recitations of the statutes – for example, whenever a new rector took office – were intended to impress both on the mind. Official university *denunciantes*, proctors, and other watch-dogs had the task of ensuring that the rules were everywhere kept and that those in breach of them were brought to book. One of these overseers was the notorious *lupus* (wolf), whose duty it was to watch over the use of Latin in the student hostels and colleges. His activities were no doubt not restricted to the universities of central Europe alone. Speaking Latin was understandably a chore for the many young people whose intention it was, after all, to live in the social environment of their home country and native tongue even when in their university town. From the Heidelberg *Manuale scholarium*, a kind of introduction to student life from the late fifteenth century, one can learn how frequently speaking in the vernacular was prosecuted and thus how successful the *lupus* was, but also how furious the students were about this.[29] The means of sanction employed by the universities were fines, graded according to the number of repetitions and the severity of the offences; in severe cases the culprit landed in the detention cell or was even 'excluded', thus losing the important protection of university privileges. With the exception of a few individual cases very late in the day, corporal punishment was unknown throughout the Europe of the Middle Ages. Fines were extremely repressive instruments: from Copenhagen to Padua and Salamanca they hit all culprits where it hurt most – their purse – naturally hurting those most who had the least to spare. In Paris and at the German universities at least, the *pauperes* would seem, by and large, to have received severer punishments and to have been more often criminalized and expelled than others.

Life was probably at its most strict in the colleges and the student hostels affiliated to them. By way of example, one can study the regulations of the Collegium Sapientiae in Freiburg im Breisgau, a foundation of the Freiburg

---

[29] *Manuale* in F. Zarncke, *Die deutschen Universitäten im Mittelalter* (Leipzig, 1857), 28ff.

theologian and suffragan bishop of Augsburg, Johannes Kerer von Wertheim (1497).[30] The twelve college members could be made up of students from all levels; they lived communally under a head who had to be a specialist student, that is, at least a baccalaureate of a higher faculty. Women and girls were not allowed to visit college members or set foot on the premises, except as washerwomen or night-nurses in the event of severe illness – and even then only on condition that they were of blameless character. The college members themselves were responsible for board on a weekly rota basis: each week, one of them served at table, both bringing in and carrying away the dishes, cleaned the dining hall, and presumably also did the cooking himself, either alone or with assistants. Going by the bill of fare prescribed by the founder, this can have been none too difficult:

> Since wisdom is not found in the countries of those who live in sumptuousness, and since our house bears the title 'Home of Wisdom', and it being our wish that wise men be educated there in reverence of God, the true wisdom, it follows that sumptuous feasting and all creaturely pleasures are, like wanton sirens, to be kept distant from it.

Each day for the midday or evening meal there was half a pound of cooked meat per person with root vegetables, cabbage, pease-pudding, or other vegetables. The meal was usually accompanied by wine. Roast meat was served only on high feast-days, on the admission of new members, or on the anniversaries of the founder and his brother. The procurement of specialities or special rations was explicitly prohibited; the kitchen and cellar were under watch. Exemption from table service could be granted to graduates. All slept in the same dormitory, which, however, was subdivided into separate sleeping-compartments to be entered by no one but the owner; there was normally no heating; during the hours of sleeping a lamp was to remain lit, the charge of the rota man of the week, who also cleaned the dormitories; the compartments were cleaned by their individual owners, 'so that the dirts is not a burden to the soul'. In other ways too, care of the soul was an essential part of the household regulations. Mass was celebrated daily, a sermon was delivered once a week, and, at least on all feast-days, confession was to be made. The concern for physical well-being may seem rather summary. Yet, among the smaller foundations in Germany and beyond, the Collegium Sapientiae was relatively richly endowed. It had substantial holdings of land and perpetuities, its own chapel and library, simple furnishings but copious and valuable kitchen-ware and table-ware – in part even of silver, which was in the safe-keeping of the college head. As everywhere, however, discipline was strict: punishment was threatened, especially for those breaching the peace of the college (breaches included the playing of musical instruments, cards, and

---

[30] H. Beckmann, *Johannes Kerer, Statuta Collegii Sapientiae 1497*, facsimile (Lindau/Constance, 1957).

dice, with only the clavichord and chess being permitted); equally liable to punishment were leaving the premises with impure motives, and insults in word or deed, which had to be atoned for on the same day. In severe cases – for example, concerning whether a culprit was to be excluded temporarily or permanently from a living – the decision was taken by the university rector, but in all other cases punishment was meted out by the college head, in the form of the denial of food and especially wine on one or more days. In the circle of dining comrades such punishments may have been even harder to bear than others. Above all other injunctions – in Freiburg as much as elsewhere – was the commandment to attend courses and the admonition to acquire an academic degree.

As for free time and holidays, there were enough of these to make the business of teaching and learning bearable. Here, admittedly, extreme variations existed between universities and even between faculties: each organized its own calendar. The cause of this was that the universities were basically operational the whole year through and many offered courses – the extraordinary lectures and revision exercises – during the vacations and on Sundays and holidays (but never on a Sunday in Salamanca). Right into the fifteenth century the 'ordinary books' determined the rhythm of the academic year (which began on 1 October): the longer period from the beginning of October to the end of June was known as the *magnus ordinarius* and the shorter from July to the end of September as the *parvus ordinarius*. A different subdivision of the year was into semesters, trimesters, or four terms (at Oxford), interrupted by the Christmas, Easter, and Whitsun holidays as well as by the two-month-long 'great vacation' stretching, with differences from faculty to faculty, from the Feast of St Peter and St Paul (29 June) to Michaelmas (29 September). Many would travel home in these periods, returning with money and foodstuffs.

The good number of teaching-free days alongside the official Sundays and holidays were meant for relaxation – something for which there was little room in day-to-day life as determined by statute. Of Bologna it was mockingly quipped that the number of vacations almost exceeded the number of working-days. The anniversaries of the patron saints of the faculties, nations, brotherhoods, or particular university regions were commemorated with great ceremonies, church services, processions, and various amusements. Especial fun for the many young students of arts was in prospect on St Nicholas's Day, which was commemorated with processions and games – such as the Bishop's Game in Paris or the Christmas King Game in Oxford – and by all kinds of mummery. In Aragonese Perpignan in 1381, the authorities felt compelled to prohibit what was clearly an established tradition among the students of arts (and practised in Lérida, too) of dressing up and running around, on St Nicholas's Day and the days of the popular St Catherine and St Eulalia into the bargain, as Jews, Saracens, and women – something which was felt to bring hurt and shame upon the aped parties.[31] These 'spare-time activities' were augmented by carnivals, May-time, and excursions 'into nature', and presumably by many things done in nations, colleges, halls, and *bursae* or in private groups – from the free days which the Scottish universities set aside for cockfighting to the 'Feast of the First Snow' and the banquets on each month in Bologna. Assuredly, the vacations were also taken up with all that the statutes forbade or restricted; with 'wine, women, and song', with raucous behaviour and music-making in the streets, houses and taverns, with quarrels with the townsfolk, with sauntering about, with dancing, chess, and games of chance, with ball-games, fencing, jousting, and hunting – all, of course, depending on the age and rank of the students. The extent to which the customary social order also affected such shared free time and festivities is demonstrated *pars pro toto* by the 'Snow Festival' in Bologna: first, the high-up students of law were allowed to offer the citizens snowballs in exchange for money, wine, or food for their evening festivity, and only then was it the turn of the common students of medicine and arts.[32]

A welcome occasion for celebration on any day was provided again and again by the admission of freshmen – *bejauni*, *beani* (greenhorns) – into the community of older students, a procedure which involved all kinds of pranks, to some extent rough treatment, and of course a redeeming drinking session at the newcomer's expense.[33] With the exception of the Italian law area, this custom seems to have been, with various nuances, widespread throughout Europe since time immemorial. In western Europe, from southern France to the British Isles (of Spain we know only that the custom as such existed), various forms of purification (*purgatio*) were known, in which water or beating played a part. The latter form was found, for example, in Aix-en-Provence, even in lofty social circles, although noble ladies present could put in a plea for leniency; elsewhere, the freshmen were put 'in dock' before the 'students' abbot', where they had to display humble and servile behaviour towards the older students until being cleansed with water from the taint of newness (Avignon, Paris). In central Europe, on the other hand – above all in the Holy Roman Empire – there developed the *depositio cornuum*, the striking-off of the horns, whereby the 'wild beast' of the freshman was to be transformed into a 'civilized student creature'. As early as around 1400 – and not only towards the beginning of the modern age, when the process of striking-off became an obligatory part of the academic ceremonies in Germany – it was not uncommon for a good deal of rough-and-tumble to be

31 Fournier (ed.), *Statuts*, vol. II, 674, § 35; Villanueva, *Viaje* (note 28), 231; Ajo González de Rapariegos y Sáinz de Zúñiga, *Historia* (note 7), 246.

32 Steffen, *Studentische Autonomie* (note 3), 122ff.

33 Derived from the French *bec jaune* (in German *Gelbschnabel*); CUP, vol. II, 523 ff. (Paris, 1342); Fournier (ed.), *Statuts*, vol. I, 121–6 (Orléans 1366–8); vol. II, 238 (Montpellier 1465); vol. II, 440 (Avignon *c*. 1450): vol. III, 12ff. (Aix 1420–40). Summarized in Rashdall, *Universities*, vol. III, 376–85.

involved. From the fourteenth century on – earlier in France, later in the Holy Roman Empire – the statute-making powers of the universities hence tried to regulate this practice of *bejaunium* or *beanium*, which they could not suppress, in order to avoid excesses, extortions, bullying, and above all robbery – with, however, only limited success. In line with the character of the medieval student and professorial bodies, above all in the arts-and-theology centres, the guardians of the peace were *baccalarii*, master-students, or specialist students, and as such 'merely students' – that is, they were all too often themselves involved.

LEARNING

No student at any university between Salamanca and Copenhagen would have had any difficulty in complying with the admonition to attend courses and acquire an academic degree. For at the universities of medieval Europe and in their four faculties nothing was so uniform and relatively stable over time as the content and form of academic teaching.[34] True, there were differing emphases, concerning for example the full programme of the *artes* in the *trivium* and *quadrivium*, which in the absence of sufficiently large numbers of teachers and students could not everywhere be carried through as in, say, Oxford, or concerning also the position taken in the philosophical *querelle* on the old or new way, realism or nominalism. Certainly, grammar teaching in Renaissance Florence, Bologna, or Padua was qualitatively different from the teaching dispensed in Greifswald, Uppsala, or Aberdeen, the names of universities north of the Alps naturally being interchangeable. Nowhere, however, would one have found the Holy Scripture, the writings of Aristotle, Euclid, and Ptolemy, the books of canon and civil law, the writings of Hippocrates and Galen together with their systematizing *sententiae, summae*, glosses, and commentaries being taught and learnt any differently than in the originally established manner, which was valid everywhere.

This, of course, was the view of the fully developed fourteenth-century university, whose faculties had already cast their syllabuses into statutes. What dynamic potential there may have been in the thought and methodology of scholastic rationalism in the period prior to and in the early years of the European university, from the eleventh century to the thirteenth, was now ensconced in an almost immutable doctrinal structure. The student of whatever level did not receive a 'scientific' education, but was rather introduced to a tradition of knowledge accumulated and commented on by recognized authorities. To acquire, absorb, and transmit this knowledge as a firm, secure stock of insight were the tasks of teacher and student alike.

It was not the 'academic personality' of the teacher that was important but

[34] See part IV: 'Learning' (chapters 10–13).

the content and its transmission. In such a system, teachers were interchange-able – especially the all-rounder arts men, who, unlike the lawyers, theo-logians, medical students, and humanist *poetae*, could not develop into specialists for particular books. At the beginning of each academic year, the heritage of knowledge and commentary was shared out among the teaching masters of the faculty in packages of books or chapters, following a particular rota by choice or by the drawing of lots, or simply according to time already spent *in studio*. At the universities of younger and older Europe, it was thus established which teacher had to teach which texts in which sequence at which time per day and per course and for what fee. Theoretically, each teacher was sometimes to benefit from having the well-attended courses and the remunerative books: in practice, however, the principals and the 'govern-ing masters' ensured that it was they who had first choice. A key factor here was the categorization of books – practised in all faculties – according to their importance in the syllabus, a distinction being drawn between ordinary and extraordinary books (*libri ordinarii, extraordinarii*). Over the course of time, these distinctions became linked to questions of remuneration and status, all the more so as the presentation of extraordinary texts was, until well into the fifteenth century, left to *baccalarii*.

The material was conveyed to the students of all faculties in the every-where identical forms of the lecture (*lectio*) and the disputation (*disputatio*), the two forms being closely related. In the lecture, the master read out the canonical text ascribed to him and explained it in segments. The audience followed the lecture in their own copies of the text and made notes. In order to remedy the lack of expensive, handwritten texts there were also dictation sessions (*pronunciare*); the main task of the lecture, however, was always explanation. In line with the importance of the books, the lectures were also divided into ordinary and extraordinary; as a rule, the one type of lecture was delivered in the morning, the other in the afternoon. While the function of the lecture was to acquaint students with material and to ensure that it passed down from one generation to the next, the disputation was concerned with the material's application. Here, scholasticism was in its element. Teachers and pupils practised the solution of contentious *quaestiones* of philosophy, theology, and medicine or the resolution of *casus*, (disputed) cases in the two kinds of law. For the arts and, in principle, for the other faculties as well there were three types. On the one hand, there was the *disputatio ordinaria*, the big weekly disputation, which in small universities would probably be attended by the entire faculty. One of the masters presided and posed the *quaestio*; other masters and *baccalarii* argued and opposed, while the beginners, the *simplices*, probably tended to restrict themselves to listening; if necessary, the presiding master intervened in a guiding capacity and would finally put an end to – or determine – the disputing of theses and counter-theses on the solution of the problem posed by means of his magisterial synthesis. On the other hand, once or twice a year the *disputatio de quodlibet* was held, a public demonstration of the scholastic method as applied to any questions what-soever, freely chosen. This form of disputation, which in the early period of the university – say, in the Paris of the thirteenth century – could freely tackle difficult issues of the moment, even delicate religious and political problems, became in the course of the later Middle Ages diluted into, at worst, a forma-listic nonsense-event. The notorious question as to how many angels could stand on the point of a needle has its origins here. It was from the third type that students benefited most, the *simplices* and baccalaureate students as much as their teachers, the master-students and specialist students. In exer-cises and repetition work (*exercitia, repetitiones, resumptiones*), which took place in the afternoons and partly also in the evenings following the lectures – mostly within the circle of one's own master's family in colleges, at the master's house, or in student hostels – they memorized the material and the technique of school-like distinguishing and arguing. Practice was gained in the use of authorities, commentaries, and rational proofs – and not least in the continual employment of scholarly Latin. This form of collective intel-lectual training was probably the medieval university's most creative contri-bution to European education.

For all this, the extent of the written element should not be overestimated. On the one hand, 'oracy' was a natural goal of education: the aim was to keep texts and arguments readily available for a wide variety of occasions – some of them beyond the bounds of the universities, in courts of law, in administra-tive offices, and in the church, for instance while preaching. And, on the other hand, it could not be presupposed that expensive manuscripts and law-books were in everyone's possession. Right into the modern period, until the tech-nology of book-printing had been able to take widespread effect, there was a great difference between the purchasing power of 'their lordships' the students of law and that of the medical students and theologians, not to mention the mass of arts students. The major factors behind this were age and differences in status. Swiss students of law in thirteenth and fourteenth-century Bologna – most of them students of rank, who already 'were some-body' before they went to university – are said by the end of their studies to have owned between ten and thirty manuscripts each.[35] Given a comparable social background, these figures can presumably be generalized and also applied to the last century of the Middle Ages, all the more so as Bologna and related law universities, together with Paris and Orléans, had developed a special system of issue and reproduction of books (the *pecia* system) operated by university *stationarii* – 'booksellers' – who also issued texts to be copied. Yet even in this system the completion of a legal manuscript took ten to fifteen months and, depending on the quality of its production, was still a

[35] Stelling-Michaud, *Université de Bologne* (note 13), 100–14.

dear purchase costing from twenty to sixty pounds of Bologna pennies. The overwhelming majority of the students, even among law students, would have owned substantially fewer writings, as a rule perhaps no more than a few 'study books' containing lecture transcripts, text excerpts (*peciae*), and personal notes. The universities of the thirteenth century still had no public libraries. University libraries emerged only from the fourteenth and fifteenth centuries onwards, with the usual time-lag between older and younger Europe; the pioneers were the libraries of the colleges, whose basic stocks were mostly made up of their founder's book collections. Important examples were the libraries of the Sorbonne in Paris, of Merton and New College in Oxford, and of the Amplonianum (Zur Himmelspforte) in Erfurt.

The minority of students who embarked on the by no means usual course of setting out to acquire a degree were systematically guided to success by the formalized syllabus. The study or *cursus* of arts normally lasted four to five years and consisted of approximately half of material from the baccalaureate and half of material from the master's course. For each part a certain quantity of knowledge and skills were prescribed, and evidence of attending the compulsory number of lectures and disputations had to be provided. This was done in most cases by the affidavit of the student's own teacher or, if the student had changed university, by a formal certificate of study sealed by the rector of the other university. Latin grammar and the logical writings and parts of the *Physics* of Aristotle were compulsory in the first stage; in the second came the remaining writings of 'the philosopher', the rest of the *Physics*, *Metaphysics*, *Ethics*, *Politics*, and – depending on the capacities of the faculty – mathematics, astronomy, and music. If everything was in line with the statutes, and if the candidate proved to be a matriculated member of the university and had paid all the required fees, then he was allowed to proceed to examination. In the presence of the chosen examiners of the faculty, he 'determined' under his master and acquired the degree of *baccalarius/baccalaureus artium*. For by far the greatest proportion of students this meant the end of the course and of their days at university; only a small minority took the next step and received – formally, through the chancellor – the following degree of *licentiatus artium*, which concluded academic training in the arts and was linked to permission to teach a course of one's own (*licentia docendi*). The *inceptio magistri* – the so-called inaugural lecture of the new master to the assembled faculty – was only the ceremonious conclusion to the procedure, in which the master's biretta, the symbol of the *status in studio* acquired, was also presented. According to the statutes, the new master should be between twenty and twenty-one years of age; like the length of the course itself, this was naturally only a guideline.

Depending on the size of the university, the examinations of the baccalaureate students took place two to four times a year, those of the master-students usually only once. For each examination date a group of candidates was gathered together, each individual receiving a certain ranking (*locus*) according to his 'qualities in examination'. These results, which were recorded in the faculty *matriculae* or the dean's books, were by no means wholly, and not even mainly, determined by actual examination performance. The students in the top places were not necessarily the best in their year; ranking order, which could certainly have consequences for the timing of a candidate's subsequent rise in the academic hierarchy, was instead decided by age, date of matriculation, duration of study, patronage, and not least by personal and family status. Even in the university province *par excellence*, the awarding of degrees, regard had to be paid to particular and social considerations: noblemen and holders of church livings were given preference. The fact that passing the examination, even if at times *cum difficultate*, was the absolute rule fits into this picture. Rejections of candidates on grounds of crassly poor performance were (if one goes by German sources) extremely rare: failure tended to be justified rather by the reproach of immoral conduct.[36]

The sequence of degrees in the higher faculties – baccalaureate, licentiate, master, or doctor – resembled that in the faculties of arts, with the sole difference that the courses of study took longer from degree to degree, so that the master-students and specialist students (with the exception of students of high rank) were substantially older – or, to put it another way, the age qualifications for the various graduations were higher. In both types of law and in medicine, six to eight years were required before proceeding to the licentiate; in theology, even fifteen years, the doctorate there being unobtainable before one's thirty-fifth year. These particulars were no more than guidelines, however: they could – as usual under the dictate of social or economic circumstances – be shifted both downwards and upwards.

COSTS OF LIVING AND LEARNING

For all students, attendance at university was relatively expensive, but the pressure to pay for study and living costs naturally varied from one university town to the next across the spectrum of poor to rich. Most students had to meet two sets of needs – their actual studying costs and the cost of living. Only those taking degrees had increasing costs from level to level consisting of fees for admission and examination and, as a rule, of the often high costs of the graduation ceremonies and celebrations. Studying costs included one-off and ongoing expenses. A typical one-off payment was the matriculation charge. Depending on the university, up to three different fees could be payable: fees for registration in the general rectoral *matricula*, in the faculty *matricula*, and, if there were university nations, in their *matriculae* as well –

---

[36] Schwinges, *Universitätsbesucher*, 355 ff.

this being payment for the documentary and social act of admission to the university and its sectional parts. In addition, at many universities there was the so-called *bejaunium* or *beanium*, a kind of 'entrance fee' into the student body demanded by older students from the freshman (*beanus*) and without upper limit, even if universities did try by statute to avoid abuses and hardship.

Among the ongoing costs were the doctors' and masters' fees for their courses (*collectae pastus*). These fixed costs, the admission fees and the tuition fees, which were relatively inflexible even over longer periods of time and economic change, were everywhere linked to personal status within and outside the university. Graduates paid more than undergraduates, the 'rich' more than the 'poor'. In Lisbon–Coimbra, for example, following a decree of King Juan I in 1392, the rich students of law had to give their professors a lecture fee of forty pounds (*libre*); the 'middle-class student's (*medianos*) were to pay twenty pounds and the poor ten.[37] What was here ordained by the king was elsewhere organized by the authorities themselves: the burden the poor had to bear was eased, but nowhere – apart from totally exceptional cases – was it removed completely. Ongoing costs were incurred further – and relatively regardless of status – for texts and books, parchment, paper and ink, quills and penknives, and for the purchase and care of or the hiring of the student's habit. Quite frequently, too, there was the cost of borrowing texts which one could copy (or have copied, thus incurring further costs for a public or private scribe). To be added to the general costs of study were fees for writing out and certifying study documents and various testimonials, as well as fees for the proctor and occasional special expenditure, for example for university ceremonies, for the kitting out of university envoys, or for being listed on a papal supplication *rotulus*.

Among the costs of living were a lump sum for board and lodging, for clothing, footwear, bed-linen, laundry, and repairs, for creature comforts (baths, barber, and doctor), for fuel and lighting (candles), for journeys between university and home, for messengers, for leisure-time activities of all kinds, for fines, and, not least, presumably for interest on borrowed money. Lodging and credit costs were, of all burdens, those most prey to arbitrary interpretation. From early times, therefore, the universities sought to regulate the conditions of rents and loans. In the lawyer citadels of older Europe, accommodation committees of (law) students and citizens were formed, first in Vercelli in 1228, then in Naples, Salamanca, Lérida and Orléans; the Bolognese regulations of 1317/47, according to which the committees of the so-called *taxatores hospiciorum* determined the rent of the accommodation (*pensio*), agreed annual or half-yearly payments and fixed the price for three years, became standard for the entire southern region. In Paris, Oxford, and

---

37 Ajo González de Rapariegos y Sáinz de Zúñiga, *Historia* (note 7), 387.

Cambridge, masters and citizens likewise assessed the rentable value of suitable student dwellings jointly. In the centrally administered universities of younger Europe, on the other hand, where from the very outset the emphasis was on collective living in *bursae*, the cost of boarding-houses was also centrally dictated and supervised.[38] Regulated and favourable terms of credit and pawnbroking were equally in the interest of the universities, especially in the big 'international' university towns such as Bologna, Padua, or Paris. The statutes in Bologna and Padua demanded the annual re-election of suitable merchants and money-lenders for whom, in an official and controlled way, credit could be received and money borrowed on pledges of books. In addition, professors sometimes made their students loans – something which proved a highly successful side-line. As a rule, however, it was always a question of short-term credits (with Swiss law students, three to four months on average), which ensured that the interest-rate burden (up to 20 per cent) did not grow too forbidding before parental assistance arrived via courier or bank. In Oxford, from 1240 on, several loan chests emerged – five between 1293 and 1323 alone – where students could obtain advances to the tune of their status; around 1375 there were sixteen such loan chests and around 1500 twenty. Paris also had an institutionalized system of money-lending; selected citizens under oath to the university, the so-called 'grand messengers' (*nuntii maiores*), agreed to supply creditworthy students with money within the framework of the nations. The demand can best be gauged by the fact that, at one time, the Gallic nation was employing 164, the Anglo-German nation 60, the Norman 16, and the Picardian 14 *nuntii maiores*.[39]

All of this was naturally conditional on subjective needs and possibilities, on the changing level of prices in large or small university towns – a level which was itself a factor of the economic cycle – and on the readiness to adapt to a different setting. Though many had a *familia* to support beside grooms and horses, others had quite enough problems on their own. Europe's 'normal students', the mass of the *mediani* in the south and of the *divites* in the north, could, it is true, normally bear the costs accruing, but they tended all to be of modest means. In the arts-and-theology enclaves of the Holy Roman Empire, this meant that their minimum annual budget, above all for board and lodging, amounted between *c.* 1368 and 1500 to something above the twelve and later above the twenty florin mark. These two amounts

---

[38] Denifle, 'Statuten' (note 26), 346–55, §§ 64–74; González de la Calle and Huarte y Echenique (eds.), *Constitutiones* (note 28), 74ff., § 25; Villanueva, *Viage* (note 28), 231; K. A. Schmid (ed.), *Geschichte der Erziehung*, vol. II: 1 (Stuttgart, 1892), 510ff; D. Illmer, 'Die Rechtsschule von Orléans und ihre deutschen Studenten im späten Mittelalter', in *Schulen und Studium*, 423; *CUP*, vol. I, 597ff., no. 511; Gibson (ed.), *Statuta* (note 4), 71; Hackett, *Original Statutes* (note 24), 317.

[39] Denifle, 'Statuten' (note 26), 283ff., § 21 with Padua; Stelling-Michaud, *Université de Bologne* (note 13), 92; A. Budinszky, *Die Universität Paris und die Fremden an derselben im Mittelalter* (Berlin, 1876; reprint, Aalen, 1970), 42; Schmid (ed.), *Geschichte* (note 38), vol. II: 1, 528; J. I. Catto, 'Citizens, Scholars and Masters', in *History of Oxford*, 172.

delineated, as it were, the 'official' boundaries between poor and rich, which on account of the decline in purchasing power of the Rhenish florin (fl.), especially in the second half of the fifteenth century, shifted from 12 fl. at the outset (Prague, Vienna, Heidelberg, Cologne, etc.) through 16 fl. (Tübingen 1478) up to 20 fl. (Louvain 1500). Anyone whose income was below these levels – irrespective of his goods and chattels, his clothes and books – could be recognized as a pauper. There was a certain band of tolerance for the many semi-poor or – depending on one's perspective – semi-rich: for example, the 1452 statutes of the Heidelberg Dionysianum house for the poor decreed that an inmate should have to leave not, as hitherto, if his annual income rose above 12 fl. but only if it exceeded 20 fl.[40] This amount, the approximate equivalent of the income of urban craftsmen and service people of the 'lower middle class', seems to have enabled a student to manage more or less well at German universities, depending on their 'tone'. At any event, the sum of 20 fl. was widely accepted as the lower standard, whereas the minimum allowance for noble students of the arts and for really rich students from the bourgeoisie was 50 fl.[41]

In the opinion of Amerbach, the renowned Basle book-printer, this should also have been the case in Paris, where he sent his two sons to study the arts from 1501 to 1506 as *magni portionistae* (paying members) of a college. For three years he paid them an allowance of 50 fl. per head, but then decided to reduce the sum to 21 or, at most, to 27 fl. The higher rate may have been offered in view of the cosmopolitan nature of Paris, but would nevertheless not have been appropriate. For the fifteenth and early sixteenth centuries the overall costs of a simple Paris arts scholar originating from elsewhere have been estimated at about 75 *livres*, or some 45 fl.; 12 to 36 *livres* are the amount reckoned for academic matters and 50 for suitable board and lodging in a *collège*. For Parisians who lived with their parents the costs were reduced to a good third. In Oxford the lower limit in the thirteenth century seems to have been around two to two-and-half pounds sterling per year: loans or money against security from the loan chests was given only to such as could give proof of an annual income of at least two pounds. The normal annual loans made by the colleges to undergraduates and junior fellows were on the same scale. From 1264, Merton College was to pay two pounds to each – admittedly without lodging; in 1266 Balliol College paid two pounds five shillings, and in 1340 two pounds seven shillings and sixpence with free lodging. With the development of purchasing power, the lower limit probably shifted upwards by about one pound by the end of the Middle Ages. At New College, members had to leave if their annual budgets exceeded five silver

---

40 E. Winkelmann (ed.), *Urkundenbuch der Universität Heidelberg*, vol. I (Heidelberg, 1886), 167, no. 111.
41 E. De Maesschalck, 'De criteria van de armoede aan de middeleeuwse universiteit te Leuven', *Revue belge de philologie et d'histoire*, 58 (1980), 337–54.

marks (three pounds six shillings and eightpence). Around 1424 Merton College granted two pounds five shillings and sixpence for three terms – that is, nine months, the holidays not being included – and towards the end of the fifteenth century for the same period two pounds twelve shillings and sixpence. For a whole year that would have been three pounds and eightpence or three pounds ten shillings, respectively. If one goes by the college bills, these sums seem to have covered the entire cost of undergraduate education in Oxford from the tuition fees through food and drink, paper, ink and candles, clothing and footwear to the cost of the journey home during the vacation. Admittedly, the students so favoured were members of the founder's kinship, so that they were perhaps a little better provided for than others.[42]

The expenses of the – generally older – masters and specialist students in the higher faculties or universities were naturally greater than such threshold values. Higher tuition fees and, above all, the cost of obtaining degrees had now to be met. More so than among students of the arts one can find among theologians, medical students, and lawyers extraordinary differences in costs over the European university network as a whole: there are discrepancies within the individual regions, let alone between south and north, between the 'rich' universities of Italy, the Iberian peninsula, the Midi, and Orléans and the more modest establishments of central Europe. The information available, however, often gives only individual items, fragments, or exceptions and little 'normality'. Even within Italy, Bologna was the most expensive university town for ultramontane students of law. The 'poor' among the high-ranking students were those members of the lofty Spanish College, whose incomes could by statute not amount to more than 50 Bolognese gold florins (= 75 lire). In the thirteenth and fourteenth centuries, however, 100 lire were called for: 20 to 50 went on lodging and board, the remainder on sundry other requirements and on tuition. At least as much again was required for doctorates, examinations, celebrations, and gifts (of money and gloves) for the examiners and doctors, and the proctors, servants, and notaries. The level of these outgoings may have been a contributory factor in the decline in matriculations in the course of the fifteenth century in favour of other Italian universities. Not infrequently, students would merely attend the University of Bologna and acquire their doctoral biretta elsewhere, in Ferrara, Siena, Perugia, Pavia, or Padua, where the degree could simply be had more cheaply.[43]

---

[42] Schmid (ed.), *Geschichte* (note 38), vol. II: 1, 523ff.; L. W. B. Brockliss, 'Patterns of Attendance at the University of Paris, 1400–1800', *Historical Journal*, 21 (1978), 529ff.: Catto, 'Citizens' (note 39), 171; J. M. Fletcher and C. A. Upton, 'The Cost of Undergraduate Study at Oxford in the Fifteenth Century: the Evidence of Merton College "Founder's Kin" ', *History of Education*, 14 (1985), 1–20.

[43] J. Paquet, 'Coût des études, pauvreté et labeur: fonctions et métiers d'étudiants au Moyen Age', *History of Universities*, 2 (1982), 17, with n. 4 (literature concerning individuals); G.

We know little about the way in which studies were financed.[44] First and foremost it was probably – entirely or in part – a matter for parents and relations, the ecclesiastical uncle supporting his nephew becoming already a kind of institution. Beside this, there was a series of other sources, not infrequently interwoven with the parental, though available in Europe's different university regions in varying developmental stages, emphases, and amounts; for many they took on increasing relevance only with advancing *status in studio*. Among these were the college foundations already mentioned above. With their college places they offered a broad spectrum of sufficiency scholarships. Church livings, for simple altar benefices to important canonships in a cathedral church, were a further way of supporting students. The universities, especially the French on account of the nearby papal court in Avignon, furthered this form themselves by their own supplication scrolls, in which the Pope was asked to grant benefices to the University members listed. Admittedly, one can hardly draw a line here between the scholarship character of such livings and their character as a remuneration for a church office which could, in certain circumstances, be for life, even if the residence requirement at the place of office was lifted for the duration of the stay at university. The papal church was here benefactor and employer at one and the same time. Priests, canons, and prelates often enough returned to offices after attending university (or continued to enjoy their livings). Only in the second half of the fifteenth century, in the wake of a certain professionalization of church vocations and parallel to the almost complete demise of the practice of supplication in Europe, did the sequence gradually change: increasingly, tenure of an office presupposed university study. Pious benefactions, wills, and legacies in favour of one or several students were a further form of financing, albeit one hardly researched and the extent of which it is hard to estimate. In line with the traditional rules, these boons again favoured relatives and compatriots first and foremost. Such benefactions, known in western Europe as *bursae volantes* – 'flying' because they were not tied to a college or other institution – could be found in Paris as early as the first decades of the thirteenth century. The benefactors were at first high members of the clergy, but subsequently well-to-do burghers, merchants, widows, and professors joined them. Older Europe naturally had a lead here, whilst in younger Europe noteworthy funds from private donation came into evidence only on the threshold of the modern period and especially after the Reformation. The same holds true for the brotherhood-like organizations which gave students support and particularly for measures of support undertaken by

---

Pardi, *Lo studio di Ferrara nei secoli XV e XVI* (Ferrara, 1903), 206ff; Stelling-Michaud, *Université de Bologne* (note 13), 88ff.; Steffen, *Studentische Autonomie* (note 3), 185ff., 202ff.
[44] See, in particular: Paquet, 'Coût des études' (note 43), 15–52, and P. Trio, 'Financing of University Students in the Middle Ages: A New Orientation', *History of Universities*, 4 (1984), 1–24.

princes and states. The kings and ruling houses of western Europe and Spain and the aristocracy also patronized students from the thirteenth century on, even beyond their own college foundations, while the Holy Roman Empire lagged behind in this area. One of the major reasons for this lay in the differing ways in which the respective constitutions and statehoods developed. Before the time of Maximilian I, the Holy Roman (or Roman–German) Emperor was not involved at all in the foundation of universities. Universities were founded by the territorial rulers, but their interest was directed less at the students than at subsequently employable graduates. Among the few exceptions were the comparatively modern Netherlands and the German Order in Prussia, which systematically gave grants to suitable young people.

Finally, students of all types covered a substantial part of the costs by work, mostly through teaching and other services rendered. For baccalaureates, master-students, and specialist students, teaching was done on the one hand within the framework of normal university education, instructing younger students in the subject in question on an individual fee basis, and on the other hand privately, working as teachers in schools or rich houses, giving coaching (*ruminare*) in colleges and student hostels, or accompanying prosperous wandering students through their studies in the capacity of *paedagogi* and *praeceptores*. The possible services to be rendered, from which the *pauperes* could profit above all, were many and various. They could be found as scribes and secretaries, as copiers of manuscripts and text books, as personal servants (*famuli, servitores*) to professors, rectors, deans, college principals, and other university officials, as servants to church dignitaries or to noble or well-to-do fellow students, as serving staff and porters, as cooks, kitchen hands, and table-servants in colleges, hospices, halls, and *bursae*, as chancel assistants and choristers in town churches, as street singers like the *Bons-Enfants* in Paris or the *Litaneibuben* in Vienna, as occasional workers in trade and commerce, as salesmen of, for example, foodstuffs from their home region (which, in theory, they could bring in free of customs duty only for their own consumption), and – last but not least – as beggars. In the university towns of Europe, of course, the service-sector market was not always the same. It depended substantially on the type of the university, on its law or arts-and-theology atmosphere, on the size of the town, and on its economic importance. Thus in the universities most heavily frequented by noblemen and the sons of the rich bourgeoisie, above all in the south from Orléans to Bologna and Salamanca, it was not service in houses but primarily personal services that understandably found a larger market than in the college or *bursae* universities located north of the Alps.

It is thus clear that the medieval student as such does not exist in reality. Various types of student can be differentiated, depending on geographical and social origins. It is even more true to say that the university in the Middle Ages was less democratic than has been stated in a number of older works on medieval university history. In the next chapter, the career possibilities of these different types of student will be examined.

SELECT BIBLIOGRAPHY

See also the select bibliography of chapter 4.

Aston, T. H. 'Oxford's Medieval Alumni', *Past and Present*, 74 (1977), 3–40.

Aston, T. H., Duncan, G. D., and Evans, T. A. R. 'The Medieval Alumni of the University of Cambridge', *Past and Present*, 86 (1980), 9–86.

Boiraud, H. *Contribution à l'étude historique des congés et des vacances scolaires en France du Moyen Age à 1914*, Paris, 1971.

Brizzi, G. P. 'I collegi per borsisti e lo studio Bolognese. Caratteri ed evoluzione di un'istituzione educativo-assistenzialo fra XIII e XVIII secolo', *Studi e memorie per la storia dell'università di Bologna*, new series, 4 (1984).

Cabanes, D. *Moeurs intimes du passé, vol. IV, La Vie d'étudiant*, Paris, 1949.

Di Fazio, C. *Collegi Universitari Italiani*, Rome, 1975.

Dulieu, L. *La Médecine à Montpellier, vol. I, Le Moyen Age*, Avignon, 1975.

Dunlop, A. I. 'Scottish Student Life in the Fifteenth Century', *Scottish Historical Review*, 26 (1947), 47–63.

Dupille, C. *Les Enragés du XVe siècle. Les étudiants au Moyen Age*, Paris, 1969.

Fletcher, J. M. *The Liber Taxatorum of Poor Students at the University of Freiburg im Breisgau*, Notre Dame, Ind., 1969.

Gabriel, A. L. 'The College System in the 14th Century Universities', in F. L. Utley (ed.), *The Forward Movement of the 14th Century*, Columbus, Ohio, 1961, 79–124.

Gabriel, A. L. 'Motivations of the Founders of Medieval Colleges', in P. Wilpert (ed.), *Beiträge zum Berufsbewusstsein des mittelalterlichen Menschen*, Berlin, 1964, 61–72.

García Mercadal, J. *Estudiantes, Sophistas y Picaros*, Buenos Aires, 1954.

Hajnal, I. *L'Enseignement de l'écriture aux universités médiévales*, 2nd edn, Budapest, 1959.

Hargreaves-Mawdsley, W. N. *A History of Academic Dress in Europe until the End of the Eighteenth Century*, Oxford, 1963.

Haskins, C. H. *Studies in Mediaeval Culture*, New York, 1929. ('The University of Paris in the Sermons of the Thirteenth Century', 36–71; 'The Life of Mediaeval Students as Illustrated by Their Letters', 1–35.)

Kagan, R. L. *Students and Society in Early Modern Spain*, Baltimore, 1974.

Kibre, P. *The Nations in the Medieval Universities*, Cambridge, Mass., 1948.

Kiene, M. 'Die Grundlagen der europäischen Universitätsbaukunst', *Zeitschrift für Kunstgeschichte*, 46 (1983), 63–114.

Kuhn, W. *Die Studenten der Universität Tübingen zwischen 1477 und 1534*, 2 vols., Göppingen, 1971.

Lytle, G. F. 'Oxford Students and English Society c. 1300–c. 1510', Ph.D. dissertation, Princeton, 1975.

Müller, R. A. *Universität und Adel. Eine soziostrukturelle Studie zur Geschichte der bayerischen Landesuniversität Ingolstadt 1472–1648*, Berlin, 1974.

Paquet, J. 'Coût des études, pauvreté et labeur: fonctions et métiers d'étudiants au Moyen Age', *History of Universities*, 2 (1982), 15–52.

Paquet, J. 'Recherches sur l'universitaire "Pauvre" au Moyen Age', *Revue belge de philologie et d'histoire*, 56 (1978), 301–53.

Paulsen. F. 'Organisation und Lebensordnung der deutschen Universitäten im Mittel-alter', *Historische Zeitschrift*, 45 (1881), 385–440.

Post, G. 'Master's Salaries and Student Fees' in the Mediaeval Universities', *Speculum.* 7 (1932), 161–98.

Rait, R. S. *Life in the Medieval University*, Cambridge, 1912.

Reynier. G. *La Vie universitaire dans l'ancienne Espagne*, Paris/Toulouse, 1902.

de Ridder-Symoens, H. 'Adel en universiteiten in de zestiende eeuw. Humanistisch ideaal of bittere noodzaak', *Tijdschrift voor Geschiedenis*, 93 (1980), 410–32.

de Ridder-Symoens, H. 'L'aristocratisation des universités au XVI siècle', in *Les Grandes Réformes des universités européennes du XVI au XXe siècle*. Zeszyty Naukowe Uniwersytetu Jagiellonskiego DCCLXI, Prace Historyczne, Z. 79, Warsaw/Cracow, 1985, 37–64.

Rosenthal, J. T. 'The Universities and the Medieval English Nobility', *History of Education Quarterly*, 9 (1969), 415–37.

Rückbrod, K. *Universität und Kollegium, Baugeschichte und Bautyp*, Darmstadt, 1977.

Samaran, Ch. 'La vie estudiantine à Paris au Moyen Age', in *Aspects de l'université de Paris*, Paris, 1949, 103–32.

Schulze, F. and Ssymank, P. *Das deutsche Studententum von den ältesten Zeiten bis zur Gegenwart*, 2nd edn, Leipzig, 1910.

Schwinges, R. C. *Deutsche Universitätsbesucher im 14. und 15. Jahrhundert. Studien zur Sozialgeschichte des alten Reiches*, Stuttgart, 1986.

Schwinges. R. C. 'Migration und Austausch: Studentenwanderungen im deutschen Reich des späten Mittelalters', in G. Jaritz and A. Müller (eds.), *Migration in der Feudalgesellschaft*, Frankfurt-am-Main/New York, 1988, 141–55.

Schwinges, R. C. 'Sozialgeschichtliche Aspekte spätmittelalterlicher Studentenbursen in Deutschland', in J. Fried (ed.), *Schulen und Studium im sozialen Wandel des hohen und späten Mittelalters*, Sigmaringen, 1986, 527–64.

Seifert. A. 'Die Universitätkollegien – Eine historisch-typologische Übersicht', *Lebens-bilder deutscher Stiftungen*, 3 (1974), 355–72.

Trio, P. 'Financing of University Students in the Middle Ages: a New Orientation'. *History of Universities*, 4 (1984), 1–24.

Verger. J. 'Prosopographie et cursus universitaires', in N. Bulst and J.-P. Genet (eds.), *Medieval Lives and the Historian*, Kalamazoo, 1986, 313–32.

Wieruszowski, H. *The Medieval University: Masters, Students, Learning*, Princeton, N.J., 1966.

CHAPTER 8

CAREERS OF GRADUATES

PETER MORAW

THE INTERACTION BETWEEN UNIVERSITY AND SOCIETY

The university is anchored in society by those who attend it and those who leave it. The word 'university' denotes a social body for its members. The nature of this anchorage in society is difficult enough to see in our own day, despite the fact that modern industrial societies, and, so it often seems, modern universities, have become very much alike. The question is more difficult for the very diverse societies and universities in the long stretch of time from the twelfth to the fifteenth centuries. Of no aspect of early university history is less known. The number of universities which came into existence in Europe in that period is known, but who knows how many different societies there were and how many local and regional élites within them?

This also explains the lack of a complete social history of medieval Europe and a comprehensive theory of its social history.[1] To the question of the role of the university graduate in medieval society, only provisional and simplified answers are possible and even these apply only to limited areas. The present state of research permits us, however, to discern certain uniformities, particularly in those features which were important for the implantation of universities in society: a minimum of freedom and mobility for many and a minimum of legal stability for most social orders, which though hierarchical, were seldom static or impermeable; demographically, economically, and socially concentrated centres, i.e. cities; a gradual mutual differentiation between churches and states; respect for education and culture; special groups of agents servicing these and other demanding social functions.

To this inchoate mass of actual situations, the social data of the universities

---

[1] Cf., for example, R. Fossier, *Histoire sociale de l'Occident médiéval* (Paris, 1970); *Handbuch der europäischen Wirtschafts- und Sozialgeschichte*, vol. II, ed. J. A. van Houtte (Stuttgart, 1980), vol. III, ed. H. Kellenbenz (Stuttgart, 1986); O. Brunner, *Neue Wege der Verfassungs- und Sozialgeschichte*, 2nd edn (Göttingen, 1968).

and their members can only be related intelligibly if certain emphases are accepted, specific aspects brought out, and a number of interpretative principles assumed which are partly hypothetical and require further research.

Yet, as long as certain precautions are taken, and despite geographical and historical differences, non-synchronic economic fluctuations, crises, intervals, and delays, the social history of Europe can be seen as a comparatively advancing process. It was undoubtedly a process of increasing differentiation and complexity, i.e. of 'modernization' in the broad sense.

If the social history of Europe, for all its geographical and historical diversity, is to be understood in this relatively unitary way, a model is required which interprets these differences wherever possible as shifting phases. Such a model appears to be available.[2] It begins by distinguishing between an 'older' and a 'younger' Europe. 'Older' Europe consisted, on the one hand, of Italy and southern France, together with parts of Spain perhaps, and, on the other hand, of northern France and the imperial territories west of the Rhine, together with England. To some extent, this 'older' Europe was the direct heir to Roman antiquity, which still influenced and found expression in urban culture and in relatively less feudalized churches, for example. 'Younger' Europe – in the centre, east, and north – was able to assimilate this heritage only belatedly and never completely during the Middle Ages, by laborious processes of equalization.

Before the beginning of the university era and well into it, the church was culturally and socially the *prima causa* and chief base of the groups and concerns which were important for the social history of the universities. Throughout the whole medieval period, the world of the universities was in the main that of the church. The city, with its social and economic consolidation, complexity, division of labour, mobility, and accumulation of resources, became increasingly, and soon decisively, the milieu and *sine qua non* of the history and social development of the university and its graduates.

The interaction between university and society is also quantitative. Unfortunately, reliable statistics are almost completely lacking for the period up to the late fourteenth century and, where they exist, apply only to a part of Europe. Only from this time, moreover, can we estimate the economic and cyclical fluctuations connecting the overall impression of a long-term numerical growth with reality. The proportion of graduates among the total of university students may, by and large, have increased, but the proportion of both graduates and non-graduates in the whole population at any given time remains uncertain throughout the whole period. In any case, only a minority of students graduated and only a proportion of these can be traced from successful careers.

[2] P. Moraw, 'Über Entwicklungsunterschiede und Entwicklungsausgleich im deutschen und europäischen Mittelalter', in U. Bestmann (ed.), *Hochfinanz, Wirtschaftsräume, Innovationen. Festschrift für W. von Stromer*, vol. II (Trier, 1987), 583–622.

Contemporaries were never in a position to analyse either the development of society as a whole or even basic aspects of this development. While the universities were being founded or expanded, there was no conscious intention of influencing social conditions generally. Far more important were the 'prestige' and the practical, economic, and administrative benefits accruing to communities and rulers. Many of the social changes produced by university men must be regarded as an unintended 'spin-off' of quite different concerns. We should thus be chary of speaking of a 'labour market' and its supply and demand, and can only speak about specific instances.

Mere attendance at university and even graduation were not automatically respected and welcomed as new qualifications for the furtherance of a career. The traditional qualifications of birth and property put up a stiff resistance to such newcomers. Graduation was seldom more than just another qualification among those a person possessed or lacked. Its function within a set of qualifications varied widely and depended on a graduate's birth or property qualifications. Only gradually did the newcomer gain a foothold and establish himself within the old conditions or even create quite new ones, though much became established practice without leaving any identifiable trace. Yet there could be no question of monopolistic claims on the part of graduates prior to the end of the medieval period.

One of the paradoxes of the universities and their components is that they tried to claim social autonomy in many detailed respects without being socially autonomous at all, let alone socially powerful. In fact, in order to maintain their position, they strove to conform to the regional milieu. Students brought with them the social rules of their personal background and tried to maintain and develop their particular position. Before and after the start of a career, both within the university and outside it, the governing principles were patronage, privilege, and inheritance. A family's wealth was put to use in the promotion of certain expectations. The expense of a chosen course of study and the faculty and university selected varied considerably, and the career was meant to prove that this investment had been worth while. Universities and faculties differed in status and this affected the social value of the degrees they conferred. In 'younger' Europe, at all events, the social cachet attached to graduation diminished with the passage of time, chiefly because of the growing number of graduates. No less far-reaching in its effects on the same milieu was the relative equalization of the four faculties within the increasingly narrow structure of the territorial university. All this brought graduation closer to our modern view of it as a certificate of achievement. Up until then, however, the important thing was the diversity of 'graduation' as a social starting-point.

Despite all this, the universities enjoyed a certain autonomy and even had an inherent dynamic, which became, in time, a social factor. This is already shown simply, yet decisively, by their longevity; they gradually assumed new social roles unimaginable at the outset. The relative autonomy of the university system was due mainly to those who, after graduating, continued their careers in the university and so fulfilled the basic function of that graduation. The autonomy of the university is also recognizable from the spatial structure which developed around a college or university location and which, in due course, also began to influence careers. The medieval university can already count it as an outstanding achievement to have gradually clawed its way into and increasingly merged with its regional milieu, with all this implied for careers.

THE BEGINNINGS IN ITALY AND FRANCE (TWELFTH CENTURY UNTIL AROUND 1200)

The social position of university-leavers is most difficult to establish for the early period of the universities and, above all, for their prehistory. What we call 'graduation' existed only in a rudimentary form. Many accounts refer only to a small group of university men or even to a single individual. At best, what emerges are the worlds these people inhabited: the towns, churches, and courts of 'older' Europe. The lead established by the northern Italian towns is clearly visible in the eleventh century. They were bigger, more prosperous and more 'aristocratic', more active politically and economically, more diverse and mobile socially, more effectively laicized, and more interested in education and culture than all other contemporary communities. It was here rather than in the rest of Europe that an independent and literate laity first appeared and developed with surprising speed. This was connected with early rationalism, and the development of law and 'modern' constitutional forms. Out of these there gradually developed the professions of the jurist, the notary, and the physician.

The law schools of Bologna were the focal point for the jurists. These schools had existed on a private basis since the second half of the eleventh century, and were united to form a 'university' after 1180. They made possible the emergence of groups of persons who, as legal experts, occupied posts of growing importance for the life of society. The communities needed these specialists for their domestic administration and legal system, in the quest for increasing autonomy and in the competitive struggle with their neighbours. Already in this early period, the general point made above applied: it was a question of introducing something new. Here the high social, aristocratic position of the *causidicus* (advocate) or *iudex* (judge) was primary, whereas the exploitation of legal knowledge must be seen at first as only a secondary concern. Two legal experts from Bologna appeared in this capacity before the Emperor Henry V in the year 1116. Judicial practice having paved the way, the practice of law as an urban profession emerged during the twelfth century. The persons concerned were laymen, who have to be seen against the background of a steadily growing literate urban laity. The posts now being gradually opened to those trained in the law schools had formerly been occupied by persons well versed in customary law. In the second half of the twelfth century and connected with this phenomenon, a constitutional and social change took place from an aristocratic to a *podestà* constitution. As leaders of the cities, *podestà* appointed for one year took over from the old aristocratic families. Although themselves of noble birth, these *podestà* were above all professional administrators, having studied law at Bologna. They went from one city to another, accompanied by a small group of judges, notaries, and secretaries, who also had had some legal training. The specialist qualification thus increased in importance compared with evidence of birth. Moreover, more posts were available. The speed but also the sporadic character of this development must be stressed. Only in this qualified way can we speak here of the emergence, for the first time, of an academically trained class. In contrast to the situation in Paris during the same period, in Bologna well-to-do persons normally studied jurisprudence and soon began to do so with a fairly clear professional interest focused on the community.

Law graduates were at work from a very early date in one or two courts, beginning with that of the countess of Tuscany (before 1100) and continuing under the emperor (1112). After the middle of the century, a first high-water mark was reached at the time of Frederick I Barbarossa (1155 *et seq.*). Clerics also studied in Bologna, especially canon law. Increasing numbers of canons, archdeacons, and bishops were trained in law schools. From 1153, a canonist headed the papal chancellery. The great Pope Innocent III (1198–1216) was a former student of Bologna. Finally, aside from all community employment, we can also discern in early Bologna – as, too, at Paris, though fewer in number – the figure of the intellectual, who was socially and professionally an ambiguous 'outsider'. The cultivation of the *artes* in Bologna indicates a less strict professional attachment and this, too, had its roots in the eleventh century. Masters of arts (especially of grammar and *dictamen*, the art of letter-writing) were often trained notaries as well, the most widespread semi-legal professional class of medieval Italy.[3]

Paris, along with its very advanced and differentiated urban society, was at the centre of the early history of the university in the northern half of 'older' Europe in the twelfth and thirteenth centuries. Despite numerous personal contacts, however, the world of its studies was basically different from that of northern Italy. The surrounding city, despite its considerable size and many-

---

[3] J. Fried, *Die Entstehung des Juristenstandes im 12. Jahrhundert* (Cologne, 1974); M. Bellomo, *Saggio sull'università nell'età del diritto comune* (Catania, 1979); *I ceti dirigenti dell'età comunale nei secoli XII e XIII* (Pisa, 1982); P. Classen, 'Richterstand und Rechtswissenschaft in italienischen Kommunen des 12. Jahrhunderts', in P. Classen, *Studium und Gesellschaft im Mittelalter*, ed. J. Fried (Stuttgart, 1983), 27–126.

sided importance, was an indispensable soil rather than a formative factor in the social life of the university. The church milieu in the broadest sense was more important. From the forties of the twelfth century, former Paris students achieved pre-eminence in the papal court, in the college of cardinals, and then in the papacy itself. One in six of the cardinals appointed by Innocent III had studied or taught in Paris, one in two of those appointed by Gregory IX (1227–41).[4]

The University of Paris came into existence as a social factor almost anonymously. The only way to evaluate its social influences is to analyse the available information about the group of masters. In many respects, beginning with age, the active masters were like the law students of Italy, in contrast to the young students of the arts. Here we must bear in mind the basic twofold division, which is important in any assessment of the universities in the Parisian tradition. As has been shown in chapter 5, they fulfilled at one and the same time the role of present-day colleges (for many pupils) and that of present-day universities (for a small minority). As teachers of the arts, masters could also be students in a higher faculty. Our knowledge of the Paris masters and those of other schools prior to and around 1200 is slight. Certainly, the master's career was more fluid and uncertain than that of the law student, at least the urban Italian law student. But we know virtually nothing of the masters' social origin. In most cases we do not even know exactly where they had studied. The most plausible hypothesis about employment is that there was a steady increase in the proportion of those actively engaged in the court life of the French and English kings or of French and English bishops, for example, in the emergent office of the 'official'. One possible periodization for France would be: first traces, 1140 to 1180; discernible growth, 1180 to 1220; finally, a fairly clear increase from 1220 onwards. The percentage of masters who were also bishops confirms this evolution: 3 per cent in the royal bishoprics in France under Louis VII (1137–80), 20 per cent under Philip II Augustus (1180–1223) – whereas the English percentage was already approaching 30 per cent – and 41 per cent under Louis IX (1226–70). On average, the English kings employed at least twice as many masters as the French sovereigns.[5] As will be explained later, the leading position of the English administration can be documented almost a century before 1200 and the gap was hardly made good before 1250. Conditions in the imperial diocese of Liège (including Aix-la-Chapelle, the imperial city), which was part of 'older' Europe, fit smoothly into this chronology. The existence of some

---

4 P. Weimar (ed.), *Die Renaissance der Wissenschaften im 12. Jahrhundert* (Zürich/Munich, 1981); P. Classen, 'Die Hohen Schulen und die Gesellschaft im 12. Jahrhundert', in Classen, *Studium und Gesellschaft* (note 3), 1–26; J. W. Baldwin, *Masters, Princes, and Merchants*, 2 vols. (Princeton, 1970).

5 J. W. Baldwin, 'Studium et Regnum. The Penetration of University Personnel into the French and English Administration at the Turn of the Twelfth and Thirteenth Centuries', *Revue des études islamiques*, 44 (1976), 199–215.

thirty 'masters' in the twelfth century has been traced, almost all after 1170. They were employed in the churches of Aix-la-Chapelle and Liège, or formed part of the retinue of important lay lords.[6] The extent to which the process of equalization had at that time prospered in 'younger Europe' east of the Rhine is dicussed below.

Finally, no account of the masters would be complete without reference to the fact that very little is known of the lives and careers of the vast majority of those Paris students around 1200 who did not graduate. A wide social range and an infinite diversity of individual circumstances can be assumed.

THE BEGINNINGS IN ENGLAND, IN THE IBERIAN PENINSULA, AND IN 'YOUNGER' EUROPE

The University of Oxford (before 1214) was only a few years younger than the University of Paris and, in many respects, was very similar to it, in the range of disciplines, for example. Not surprisingly under an Angevin monarchy, conditions in state and church were also similar, except for England's less direct involvement with the papacy. Yet it was a decisive century later than in Italy or France that potentially rival school activities were established in Oxford, clearly not earlier than around 1185. The careers of the English students and teachers provide the best explanation of this.[7] Prior to 1190, those who attained onerous ecclesiastical dignities and court offices, or who wrote important works or even merely became schoolmasters, always spent a longer time on the continent, especially in Paris or Bologna. Foreign students did not come to England. On the other hand, we find a great many Englishmen among those Parisian masters around 1200 of whom a little more is known. In the second half of the twelfth century, a loose association of English scholars existed, which, not long after 1200, became the 'English nation' in Paris. All this was despite the fact that the island monarchy was more modern and disposed of an élite in the shape of a group of educated experts, the royal clerks, as well as the fact that well-educated laymen already cultivated law very actively and independently within the royal court, and the fact that literature and culture were highly regarded in the royal entourage. In this respect, England counted as part of 'older' Europe, even if no urban milieu capable of assuming responsibility for higher education yet existed. An important university came into existence in Oxford, even though the town itself could by no stretch of the imagination be compared with Paris or Bologna.

[6] C. Renardy, *Le Monde des maîtres universitaires du diocèse de Liège 1140–1350* (Paris, 1979); C. Renardy, *Les Maîtres universitaires dans le diocèse de Liège. Répertoire biographique 1140–1350* (Paris, 1981).

[7] G. Stollberg, *Die soziale Stellung der intellektuellen Oberschicht im England des 12. Jahrhunderts* (Lübeck, 1973); Baldwin, 'Studium et regnum' (note 5), 199–215; J. Dunbabin, 'Careers and Vocations', in *History of Oxford*, 565–605.

As for the Iberian peninsula, there is little known for sure about the University of Palencia (1180?–1243/63) in Castile. We should therefore stress the presence of Spanish and Portuguese students in Italy and France. Most of these probably were or became canons.[8]

When we turn from 'older' to 'younger' Europe, it is possible, on the whole, to envisage the latter as divided into two parts. On the one hand, there was the centre of the continent, open to and in some measure comparable to the west, widely dominated economically and socially by the Rhineland (part of 'older' Europe). On the other hand, there was the periphery in the east and north where conditions were still retarded: density of population, the urban milieu, and the superstructure of church and state are taken here as the indicators. These conditions did not favour interest in the new knowledge. Quite apart from this, however, the new could even appear alien from the standpoint of the traditional Ottonian and Salic educational system of the centre. Nevertheless, the new was in fact received. Broadly speaking, however, it was not yet supported by any general demand; its reception remained, therefore, the outcome of individual decisions taken against the background of an already customary mobility of students and teachers.

When the situation of the English in Paris is compared with that of the Germans, Danes, or Hungarians, typical differences can be noted. The number of visiting students who subsequently distinguished themselves by their careers (and are therefore the only ones of whom we have any knowledge) was clearly smaller in the case of those from the periphery. The arrival date of those from the periphery is later than that of those from the centre; the success of students from a distance was less than that of those whose homes were closer. On the other hand, to the extent that it is known, the social rank of the students from far away was above the average. This was natural enough, since those advantaged by birth and property were enabled to continue even in difficult circumstances and were undeterred by failure. A centuries-old wind was blowing through Europe in the new-style educational system, mostly from west to east but also from south to north. It was not easy for anyone without special advantages to resist this trend. Even two centuries later, the two eastern 'nations' of the jurists' university in Prague were plainly more aristocratic than the two western ones. In other words, the further west we look, the more modern the social world we find and the more chances someone with fewer or no advantages of birth and property had than in the east. The differences could be glaring, moreover. We have already mentioned the somewhat better-known Paris masters around 1200. The geographical origin of forty-two of them is known. Sixteen were English and only one – a Dane – came from 'younger' Europe. It is no accident, of course, that the latter was far and away the highest-born of the whole group. Among the

---

[8] J. Veríssimo Serrão, *Les Portugais à l'Université de Montpellier* (Paris, 1971); A. García y García, *Iglesia, Sociedad e Derecho* (Salamanca, 1985).

seven identifiable teachers singled out for mention by John of Salisbury (d. 1180), only one was not from 'older' Europe.[9]

In 'younger' Europe, the situation best known is that of Germany.[10] Almost simultaneously (between 1153 and 1156), university men became leading figures at the papal, English, and imperial courts; yet the only aristocrat among them (and certainly the least educated) was the imperial chancellor, Rainald of Dassel. If measured by the title of master of the western pattern, the imperial court was not behind the times compared with the papal court and was even in advance numerically of the French court. What Frederick I Barbarossa (1123–90) already had, only Philip II Augustus (1165–1223) attained. The data about German dioceses in the forties of the twelfth century point in the same direction as in the west. But whether the title of master meant academic studies or the old-fashioned dignity of the *scholasticus* of a cathedral or collegiate church becomes increasingly uncertain the further the distance from the new educational institution.

Yet study does not appear as an effective motor for promoting a career or even as a factor in the establishment of 'professional groups'. We have evidence that, of the German bishops between 1002 and 1197, only 4 per cent attended foreign education centres (25 out of a total of 646), fifteen of whom spent some time in Paris in the twelfth century. In this group, which into the thirteenth century included a majority unable to write, aristocratic birth and influential patrons were more important than a period of study. If the social conditions of 'younger' Europe in the twelfth century are considered, successful careers which included university studies could only end up in church posts. If this was already true for Germany, it was even truer for the east and north of the continent, with sharply diminishing numbers.

Together with the introduction of Christianity in the northern countries (eleventh till early thirteenth centuries), a well-educated higher clergy had to be established. Pope Gregory VII proposed in 1079 to the kings of Norway and Denmark that they send some well-born young men to the curia to be instructed in canon law. In the second half of the twelfth century, Paris was the educational centre for the Norwegian and, to a lesser extent, for the Danish and Icelandic higher clergy. Indeed, after the introduction of Christianity in Iceland in the year 1000, this island showed a remarkable interest in learning and education. Sweden and Finland followed the same pattern, but

[9] P. Riché, 'Jean de Salisbury et le monde scolaire du XIIe siècle', in M. Wilks (ed.), *The World of John of Salisbury* (Oxford, 1984), 39–61.

[10] J. Ehlers, 'Verfassungs- und sozialgeschichtliche Studien zum Bildungsgang Erzbischof Adalberts II. von Mainz', *Rheinische Vierteljahrsblätter*, 42 (1978), 161–84; R. M. Herkenrath, 'Studien zum Magistertitel in der frühen Stauferzeit', *Mitteilungen des Instituts für Oesterreichische Geschichtsforschung*, 87 (1979), 3–35.

also with a time-lag of one (Sweden) or two (Finland) centuries, compared with central European countries.[11]

THE UNIVERSAL AGE (1200–1380)

The 'universality' of the age 1200–1380 was due to the existence and influence of the papal church. The universities were primarily and essentially clerical institutions, even when the university's pathway slowly began to lead out of and away from the shelter of the church, or even – in the communal universities of northern Italy and southern France – to bypass it to a large extent. Outside Italy, their members were for the most part clerics. The 'younger' a surrounding society was by the yardstick of European development, the more clearly was this the case. The universal age of university history ended with the Great Schism of 1378, the division of the papacy between Rome and Avignon, with its consequent exposure to the pressure of regional powers. Until then, the increase in the number of university students in the individual medieval societies can be estimated roughly and compared with their advance in church administration. Of the 134 cardinals in the Avignon curia (1309–78), 66 were university graduates. The social status of the various disciplines is, on the whole, reliably reflected in the fact that, of these 66 cardinals, 71 per cent had graduated in law, 28 per cent in theology, and 1 per cent in the arts.[12]

Everywhere and at every level, a church emerged in the thirteenth and fourteenth centuries which was, in general, legalist in emphasis. The synodal system, fiscalization, and transactions between local churches and the curia all contributed to this general trend and to a growing demand for university graduates. Avignon became a main centre of the university's social success, one of the most important focal points for the establishment of personal contacts and a whole network of personal relationships. To be close to an important personage in the curia was an advantage for a graduate's career.

However, a sober assessment is necessary when the situation is viewed from the angle of the career-hungry individual. He was no more aware of how many people like him were studying in Paris or Bologna, still less of the state of the 'employment market' in his profession, than were the responsible contemporary leaders then or are the historians today. The social range of students at university may have been very wide and the geographical area from which they were drawn extremely vast, but this is not to be misinterpreted as an ideal come true. It was indicative, on the contrary, of

---

[11] S. Bagge, 'Nordic Students at Foreign Universities until 1660', *Scandinavian Journal of History*, 9 (1984), 1–29.
[12] B. Guillemain, *La Cour pontificale d'Avignon 1309–1376. Etude d'une société* (Paris, 1962), 277–356.

uncertainties and incalculable risks. Yet the individual needed some predictability, and this only existed in the regions.

This regional emphasis was thus a prevalent feature already of the universal era. The catchment area of a whole series of universities was never other than regional in character; indeed, the importance attached to the 'nation' reflected the need for regional anchorage. We would completely misunderstand the nature of university studies and careers in this period if we were to link them with complete freedom of movement throughout Europe. A person who lost the permanent link with his region was rootless and socially handicapped. If it were impossible to assume that this anchorage in the (often modest) home society with the aid of non-academic qualifications was seen as the primary and essential element, the picture we should have to paint of the early universities would be a very sombre one, considering the relative paucity of outstanding posts available in churches, courts, and cities – with the possible exception of northern Italy. This anchorage was either modified positively by university studies or, in the event of failure, not modified at all. Since attendance at university without graduation was regarded as quite normal, however, the notion of 'failure' was far from clear. In the case of the successful and the unsuccessful, a career was normally pursued in the individual's home milieu. Central career posts, which now appear as supraregional (in papal or royal courts), were no less controlled by certain pressure groups than minor career posts, and in this way localized.

Nor should the choice of a specific university be seen as the exercise of a preference, since, here again, the career was normally the determining factor in the choice. For the end of this era, this is confirmed by the precise data from the only university of 'younger' Europe which was for a time 'universal', i.e. that of Prague. Many scholars were drawn there from the disadvantaged half of the continent, some of them from great distances. But, despite the common use of the Latin tongue, hardly a single student came from 'older' Europe outside the German-speaking area. Such a student would have compromised his position socially.

Finally, broad interactions between the university and society can be illustrated by careers within the university itself. The case of the university teacher is examined in chapter 5. But the churches, lords, and communes also claimed the services of professors for their own ends. The extent of these services in comparison with teaching provides a reliable test of the social value of the university as a whole. The churches and the courts were obviously the stronger parties, so that professors came to have second or 'under-the-counter' careers and the most successful left the university altogether. The most important of these social developments was established in the thirteenth century, namely, the separation of graduation from the replenishment of the ranks of university teachers. Still fundamental even today, this decision, by which graduation was left to the university and the majority of grad-

uates were sent out into the world, was accepted by society. It was an acceptance all over Europe which only the church could have brought about. The
opportunity of having a qualification which was largely or to some extent
independent of birth and property was important everywhere, but supremely
important in the modernization of less advanced societies.

THE UNIVERSAL AGE IN 'OLDER' EUROPE

The urban societies of northern Italy in the thirteenth and fourteenth centuries were the most developed in Europe. Strongly expansive forces were
operating there, to which, as elsewhere – by 1350 at the latest – the brake was
suddenly applied. Given the endless variety of detail and the lack of representative statistics, all we can attempt here is a brief outline of the general
developments.[13]

In the first place, alongside the usual social classes, certain factors dependent on 'market mechanisms' should be noted. Mobility between aristocratic
and common birth was nowhere greater than in Italy. An aristocracy which
had lost most of its resources came to terms with the wealthy bourgeoisie,
which felt the attraction of the courts. Knowledge and culture as administered by the universities were hardly less helpful here than the already tried
and tested field of law. In the communes, minimum standards were established for active jurists in the thirteenth century, and this meant not so much
graduation as a minimum period of study. Only two centuries later was this
the case in France. To a far greater degree than elsewhere in Europe, the
Italian university also lived off the city in the cultural area of rhetoric and
dictamen as part of political and administrative life. A developed educational
system offered further opportunities for arts graduates, not only as teachers
but also as secretaries in the chancelleries of princes or towns. Physicians
appeared as practitioners, scholars, and members of the urban élite. More
properly here than elsewhere we can thus speak of 'professions'.

For France in the thirteenth and fourteenth centuries, the view from the
south is instructive, especially if, out of the wealth of facts, we emphasize
only the historically very important role of the jurists, who implemented the
royal policy of establishing a strong, expansive, and unifying monarchy. For
the beginning of the period, however, the difference between north and south
and the latter's connection with northern Italy should be stressed. A relatively
uniform north-western Mediterranean area, including parts of Catalonia, is
evidenced later on as a largely urbanized and laicized region through trade,

---

[13] C. Lefebvre, 'Juges et savants en Europe (13e–16e s.)', *Ephemerides iuris canonici*, 22 (1966),
76–202; 23 (1967), 9–61; T. Pesenti Marangon, 'Università, giudici e notai a Padova nei primi
anni de dominio Ezzeliniano (1237–1241)', *Quaderni per la storia dell'Università di Padova*, 12
(1979), 1–61; W. M. Bowsky, *A Medieval Italian Commune. Siena under the Nine, 1287–1355*
(Berkeley, 1981).

communications, and the legal system. The Italian influence on the spread of the consulate system, the notariate, and even jurisprudence in southern France can be traced step by step. Bologna influenced legal culture from the beginning of the twelfth century. Many Frenchmen from the south had studied there, but most of these returned home for their careers. Since Bologna was so easily accessible, effective law teaching was not established in the Midi earlier than around 1260–70 – in Toulouse a generation later, in Montpellier earlier than the official foundation of the university (1229, 1289). An almost 'Italian-style' legal landscape, with written law even in the private sphere, already existed at that time.

Here it is possible for the first time to gain a more precise idea of academic careers. In the five *sénéchaussées* of the south between 1280 and 1320, 189 jurists are named as being in royal service, 131 of them as judges, and 58 as advocates and procurators, with 54 of them bearing the title of doctor.[14] This is a figure which would have to be regarded as unimaginable in 'younger' Europe even centuries later. Work for private or public employers in the towns of the region was regarded as normal. Service in the royal entourage was not eagerly sought; it was poorly rewarded and only on a short-term basis. No more than ten or eleven jurists found their way to the king or parliament in Paris. The jurists outside the royal service created a legal climate which kept the acts of the monarchy under constant surveillance, in the formal expert way at least. As a result, the king's servants also had to be sufficient in number and of good enough quality to avoid wasting time in parliament. For the king's opponents employed advocates, too. The cities in particular hired them in growing numbers, and, from the fourteenth century, an increasing number of jurists also figured among their *consules*, with the exception of Montpellier. The new legal culture thus spread in terms of both 'style' and personnel, providing employment for other colleagues. Even the offspring of aristocratic families became *doctores*, though most of the latter were bourgeois. Most of them continued to be interested solely in the problems of the regions to which they returned after university. There were exceptions, of course, such as Guillaume de Nogaret, professor of Roman law in Montpellier, and Pierre Flote, well known as royal ministers with few scruples. At home, hopes of rising into the patriciate were cherished. As examples of careers from Lyon show, it was necessary to invest a considerable sum of money and this the family had first to find. Without it, success was hard to come by.[15]

In the north, which gradually gained the upper hand politically, we have

---

14 J. R. Strayer, *Les Gens de justice du Languedoc sous Philippe le Bel* (Toulouse, 1970), 20ff.
15 *Universités en France*, 95–108; J. Verger, 'Les rapports entre universités italiennes et universités françaises méridionales (XIIe–XVe siècles)', in *Università e società*, 145–72; A. Gouron, Le rôle social des juristes dans les villes méridionales au Moyen Age', *Annales de la Faculté des Lettres et Sciences Humaines de Nice*, 9–10 (1969), 55–67; R. Fedou, *Les Hommes de loi lyonnais à la fin du Moyen Age. Etude sur les origines de la classe de robe* (Lyon, 1964).

documentation of conditions from the royal court and the churches. Jurists from both the south and (more numerous) the north were in royal service. However, after 1285 and with the advent of Philip IV the Fair, one finds above all jurists from the northern part of the kingdom trained at Orléans working in the parliament, the public accounting office, and the chancellery.[16] As everywhere in Europe, compared with the knightly aristocracy on which every ruler continued to be dependent, they constituted a minority in the royal court. There were, however, posts which only jurists could fill competently, and these were growing in number. After a preliminary stage under Philip II Augustus and Louis IX (1214–70), jurists were regularly present. Around 1300, an era matured. Careers began to emerge which had originated in the *bailliages* and *sénéchaussées*. Self-recruitment in social groups became a familiar phenomenon. From around 1280, jurists are to be found among the counts of Flanders, who were particularly dangerous vassals; twenty or forty years before this, there were *magistri* who may have been jurists.[17]

Under Pope John XXII (1316–34), the entire world of the French church can be surveyed in terms of the system of benefices.[18] Numbers which command respect clearly show the superiority of France, at all events on the continent north of the Alps. Of 16,773 papal interventions in the French and Burgundian churches, 4,879 were concerned with graduates. If the accumulation of benefices is considered, 14,000 persons were involved, of whom around 4,000 were graduates. More than half of these, i.e. 2,836 clerics, had studied jurisprudence. We find the amazing figure of 1,255 doctorates and licentiates in civil law, to which figure must be added 252 canon law titles and 329 from both disciplines. Finally, of the 556 who graduated in more than one faculty, another 403 were jurists of all grades. This leaves a total of 381 arts men, 359 physicians, and 305 theologians. Only 442 figure as non-graduates. The best individual example in the long run is the royally connected cathedral chapter of Laon.[19] From 1272 to 1412, 48 per cent of 850 canons were masters or held a higher degree. Prior to 1200, the proportion was 15 per cent, rising to 22 per cent between 1200 and 1220 and then, from 1240 to 1280 and thereafter until 1378, already to 45 per cent and 43 per cent, respectively. After 1378, the proportion was 65.5 per cent. One hundred and sixty canons were jurists, 110 of them doctors or licentiates. Not more than 15 per cent of the

---

[16] R. Cazelles, *Société politique, noblesse et couronne sous Jean le Bon et Charles V* (Geneva, 1982); R. Cazelles, 'Une chancellerie priviligiée: celle de Philippe VI de Valois', *Bibliothèque de l'Ecole des Chartes*, 124 (1966), 355–81.

[17] B. Guenée, *Tribunaux et gens de justice dans le bailliage de Senlis à la fin du Moyen Age (vers 1380–vers 1550)* (Strasburg, 1963); J. Gilissen, 'Les légistes en Flandre aux XIIIe et XIVe siècles', *Bulletin de la Commission royale des anciennes lois et ordonnances de Belgique*, 15 (1939), 117–231.

[18] L. Caillet, *La Papauté d'Avignon et l'église de France* (Paris, 1975). See also note 12.

[19] H. Millet, *Les Chanoines du chapitre cathédral de Laon 1272–1412* (Rome, 1982).

canons were of noble descent, though most of the rest were not really bourgeois in the broad sense but – as befitted a church with royal and papal
connections – members of a bourgeois church officialdom. Since statistics of
this kind must mostly do service for general social conditions, even in large
nations, another of the few still known groups of data is added here. If the
names of all known French health specialists (physicians in the strict sense, as
well as barbers and surgeons) are arranged chronologically, the resultant
picture is of a fairly clear increase from the first half of the twelfth to the
second half of the fifteenth century, though at different rates, of course. The
largest increase occurred in the second half of the thirteenth century and the
smallest in the fourteenth century. The numbers for the first half of the
twelfth century are related to those of the second half of the fifteenth century
in the proportion of one to five.[20]

It is difficult to obtain more than an accidental glimpse into less lucrative
professions than those of jurists and physicians. This is the case, for example,
when an attempt is made to demonstrate the difficult position in which
masters of arts, no less than other arts men, found themselves. Even at an
advanced age, 'ordinary' masters found themselves badly provided for in the
way of benefices attached to teaching posts for permanent servants of the
university. That makes sense since, in this respect, the pre-state university fell
between all possible stools. In the first instance, secular and ecclesiastical
patrons were obliged to provide for closely connected persons, so that there
was rarely anything left over for the 'free enterprise' of the masters. The
simple masters of arts, if they did not obtain a sufficient ecclesiastical benefice, often had to resort to modest employment as schoolmasters. Although
masters of theology had better chances, either in high offices of the church or
in better endowed professorships, they suffered from the competition of the
jurists in their careers. The luckiest were those who belonged to mendicant
orders and who generally attained high posts in their respective orders.[21]

The Iberian peninsula's part in the universal age of university history was
more passive than active. The most valuable input came from the Universities
of Salamanca (from 1218–19), and Lisbon–Coimbra (from 1288–89). Particularly in the thirteenth century, however, the migration to Italy and southern France, and also to Paris and even to Oxford (in both instances for theology, which was lacking at home before the Great Schism), seems to be more
important. This was true, above all, for canon law, though the Iberian universities followed the Bologna model. But there was no urban milieu, as in Italy,
nor was there any early laicization; rather the dominant role of monarchies
and churches prevailed. In Castile, however, the two universities – Salamanca

---

[20] D. Jacquart, *Le Milieu médical en France du XIIe au XVe siècle* (Geneva, 1981).

[21] T. Schmidt, 'Pariser Magister des 14. Jahrhunderts und ihre Pfründen', *Francia*, 14 (1987),
103–38; J. Verger, 'Pour une histoire de la maîtrise-ès-arts au Moyen Age: quelques jalons',
Médiévales: Langue, Textes, Histoire, 13 (1987), 117–30.

and Valladolid – which were both protected and financed by the king and the towns, trained a not insignificant number (though inferior to the numbers trained in France or England) of *letrados*, masters of arts and law graduates, who subsequently found employment in the royal, ecclesiastical, or municipal administrations and tribunals. However, given the 'feudal' structure of the country, which was still predominant, the group of *letrados*, while becoming increasingly important during the course of the fourteenth century, never really became autonomous; many graduates entered the entourage of the aristocracy.[22] This situation already announced that of the countries belonging to the Holy Roman Empire.

Of English bishops between 1216 and 1499, 57 per cent studied at Oxford and another 10 per cent at Cambridge. The numbers increased from century to century, so that in the fifteenth century, for example, the proportion of bishops having attended one of the two universities rose to 91 per cent; under Henry III (1207–72) the figure was 51 per cent and under Edward III (1326–77) it was 70 per cent. The proportion of theology to law, which in the beginning was surprisingly high, declined to what was still a high level, i.e. around 40 per cent. At a very rough estimate, a fifth of all Oxford students in this period attended a higher faculty. Given the overall situation, it is not surprising that graduates not only followed the customary road into cathedral and collegiate chapters but also, to an internationally exceptional degree perhaps, into the parish clergy. Already between 1280 and 1317, the highest figures in some dioceses were 26 per cent and the lowest 7 per cent.[23]

Again, we have no comparable statistics for the secular field, that is to say for judges and other civil servants of the crown. As in France, the erasure of the boundary between clergy and laity within the group of 'clerks' in the thirteenth century was an important factor. In point of fact this accelerated the laicization of society.[24] The discernible trends are, as expected, in the direction of really 'modern' conditions. Among the graduates, for example, the success of arts men continued to diminish. Despite the fact that judicial careers were still pursued in the field of customary law far from the universities, the most effective way of entering administration of all kinds was to have studied civil law or, at a pinch, canon law, at the university.

[22] A. Rucquoi, 'Sociétés urbaines et universités en Castille au Moyen Age', in D. Poirion (ed.), *Milieux universitaires et mentalité urbaine au Moyen Age* (Paris, 1987), 103–17.

[23] T. H. Aston, 'Oxford's Medieval Alumni', *Past and Present*, 74 (1977), 3–40; T. H. Aston, G. D. Duncan, and T. A. R. Evans, 'The Medieval Alumni of the University of Cambridge', *Past and Present*, 86 (1980), 9–87; R. B. Dobson, 'Recent Prosopographical Research in Late Medieval English History: University Graduates, Durham Monks, and York Canons', in N. Bulst and J. P. Genet (eds.), *Medieval Lives and the Historian. Studies in Medieval Prosopography* (Kalamazoo, 1986), 181–200.

[24] Cf. J. R. Strayer, 'The Laicization of French and English Society in the Thirteenth Century', *Speculum*, 15 (1940), 76–86.

THE UNIVERSAL AGE IN 'YOUNGER' EUROPE

Only from the last period of the universal era of university history did a university also exist in 'younger' Europe. What does this imply for the period before 1348 and what changed after that date?

Despite considerable regional differences, central Europe is to be seen as a unity. From the thirteenth to the fifteenth century, a significant acceleration and equalization took place in medieval university history, once this central area had, in some measure, reached the demographic and urban level of the west (but not of the south), and once the clerical monopoly of literacy had begun to be broken. The chronology of this process is still insufficiently known. At all events it was characterized, as normally happens in historical developments, by speedy accommodation at the summit and a slower effort, intensively and qualitatively speaking, on a broad front. Studies and careers were more clearly separated than in 'older' Europe. There was less social mobility; usually it was more a matter of redistributing existing resources than of securing fresh ones. The decisive change in the direction of an academic 'competitive society', already existing in the northern Italian cities to a great extent, did not take place here until the late fifteenth century.

Although there were a number of quasi-university institutions – the result of efforts mostly in the first half of the thirteenth century – studies in 'younger' Europe relied on migration to the 'older' European centres, since the domestic educational institutions did not offer graduation. For the many who subsequently occupied leading posts, the experience abroad was of supreme importance, particularly for the Germans. Unfortunately, we have more or less precise knowledge only of the 'upper class', comprising those who followed successful careers. They probably numbered altogether several thousands in the thirteenth and fourteenth centuries. Round about 1300, the German nation of the University of Bologna regularly totalled more than 200 students.[25] From the very beginning, however, there must also have been a migration of poor students, often in the wake of the powerful, though it is still hardly possible for poor people to be identified as individuals. Even in Germany, the university, once it existed, was mainly an urban phenomenon. In the measure that university study was followed by a successful career, it was for the Germans, none the less, an aristocratic privilege. Only in the lower Rhineland was the situation somewhat different; the behaviour pattern there was part of 'older' Europe. Moreover, in many areas it is not easy to distinguish between the lesser nobility and early urban leadership groups. Only in the later fourteenth century do we find the vital social changes

---

[25] S. Stelling-Michaud, *L'Université de Bologne et la pénétration des droits romain et canonique en Suisse aux XIIIe et XIVe siècles* (Geneva, 1955); A. I. Pini, ' "Discere turba volens". Studenti e vita studentesca a Bologna dalle origini dello Studio alla metà del trecento', *Studi e Memorie per la Storia dell'Università di Bologna*, new series, 7 (1988), 62–9.

taking place, with the participation of many from the bourgeois class as well as with the beginnings of laicization.

A second mark of the first successful students was their church connection. In contrast to the situation in 'older' Europe, here the study of canon law was the main discipline for politics and higher administration. Except in the lower Rhineland, Roman law remained a luxury discipline up to the fifteenth century, until the emperor finally made this an option for Germany as well, and not exclusively one for his Italian subjects (as during the Salian and Staufer period already). The élite usually pursued their studies after having first secured a canonry or similar benefice on the basis of birth. This led to attitudes of superiority and even arrogance in centres such as Bologna, Padua, and Orléans. At first, therefore, there was a tendency in Germany to stress rather than ignore the old differences in development. Most of the benefices in cathedral and collegiate churches were in the west and south, since the north and east were often poorly provided for in this respect. An aristocratic student or jurist still belonged to a minority in his own aristocratic society, which continued to fill posts by regional family alliance. Noble birth made successful study possible, but successful study was not a typical sign of nobility. Even up until about 1350, there were many noble canons able, at a pinch, to read, but unable to write. The attitude of a collegiate chapter to study largely depended on regional and social conditions. It was in the fifteenth century that the sudden change came about. Whereas 29 per cent of the canons in the cathedral chapter of Breslau (1341–1417) and 21 per cent of those in the cathedral chapter of Bressanone (Brixen) (1300–1400) were students, the percentage soon after increased sharply, to 60 per cent in Bressanone, for instance.[26]

A third characteristic of aristocratic study was its markedly minority role at the moment when it became possible for the masses to enter the arts faculties. Even in the fifteenth century, less than 3 per cent of all German university students managed to obtain a degree in a higher faculty. The opportunity of becoming a graduate in this way was good for someone of noble birth or – from the fourteenth century – of wealthy urban origin. In other words, the division between the haves and have-nots was fairly clearly reflected in the faculties. Jurisprudence was the science for the élite even in the church, which, in Germany, was still largely 'feudal' in the higher ranks. The arts and theology faculties were bastions of the middle class and poorer classes, particularly of social climbers – though mostly only up to a stage below the really important posts. One reason why the faculties of medicine were the smallest among the higher faculties north of the Alps (see chapter 11), and enjoyed less esteem than the others, was due to the fact that, of all the graduates, medical doctors frequently received the lowest recognition in

---

[26] L. Santifaller, *Das Brixner Domkapitel in seiner persönlichen Zusammensetzung im Mittelalter*, 2 vols. (Innsbruck, 1924–25), especially vol. I, 114ff.

medieval society. *Doctores medicinae* or *physici*, as they were also called, were few and originated from the middle or artisan classes (often surgeons' sons). Medical education and the medical profession were often tied to certain families.[27]

As for jurists, what happened in the courts of the king and princes is this time better known than in 'older' Europe. The numbers were fewer in comparison, the degrees more modest, and social relationships more old-fashioned. Just as clearly observable as in the west and south of the continent, however, is the evidently irresistible tendency for all higher administration to be brought under the control of the jurists and the increasing range of career possibilities accompanying this process. The number of jurists who had business with the ruler multiplied sixfold from King Rudolf I (1273–91) to the Emperor Frederick III (1440–93) – 230 persons in all. The princes of the Holy Roman Empire followed suit with their legal staff (some 700 persons from 1250 to 1440), depending on the challenges facing the princes and the situation of their country's development. As usual, the west and south of the empire were favoured.[28]

Despite the relatively homogeneous social background of the jurists, there was no uniform recruitment pattern for the Holy Roman Empire as a whole. Decisions were made regionally depending on the situation at the centre of government. Until the fifteenth century, study abroad continued to be a socially more valuable qualification and here, apart from west of the Rhine, Italy was the clear favourite. From around 1370, jurists would appear to occupy posts on the basis of their training at German universities, with the result that those with an urban background became increasingly important.

Although the university founded in Prague in 1348 closed down after two generations it was of fundamental importance for the relation between higher education and society in 'younger' Europe. There were fewer possibilities for careers, and the accessibility of less modern societies was more limited, given the practically irreparable backlog of a century or more. Prague could never become Paris or Bologna, any more than could Vienna or Heidelberg. These and other 'daughter' institutions of Prague were implanted by the authorities, as in Prague itself; there was no development in stages. Because of their poverty, they were subject to the pressure of the need for constitutional and social unity and, later on, to the pressure of the regional lord in favour of 'rationalization'. The rectorial register, henceforth the most important source for the social history of universities, since it enables us to replace guesses by

---

27 E. T. Nauck, 'Die Zahl der Medizinstudenten deutscher Hochschulen im 14.–18 Jahrhundert', *Sudhoffs Archiv für die Geschichte der Medizin und der Naturwissenschaften*, 38 (1954), 175–86; Schwinges, *Universitätsbesucher*, 468–70.

28 P. Moraw, 'Gelehrte Juristen im Dienst der deutschen Könige des späten Mittelalters (1273–1493)', in R. Schnur (ed.), *Die Rolle der Juristen bei der Entstehung des modernen Staates* (Berlin, 1986), 77–147; I. Männl, 'Die gelehrten Juristen im Dienst der deutschen Fürsten im späten Mittelalter (1250–1440)', dissertation, Giessen, 1986.

statistics, was itself the product of such straitened conditions. It is no accident that the oldest one we have is that of the jurists' University of Prague (1372–1418).

The social situation of Prague can be seen as a continuation and development of the two-stage study pattern of the migration period. Over and against the 3,563 inscribed jurists, there were at least five times as many arts students, the vast majority of whom did not even obtain the lowest degree. University attendance thus meant very different things. The first signs of the social modernization processes (of which we shall speak later) began to appear towards the end of the century, for example, in the remarkable devotion to the study of arts and theology in Bohemia. There seemed to be too few suitable posts in churches and administration, however. The university crisis, which, after 1400, culminated in the Hussite question, was also connected with the over production of masters or arts who wished to prolong their stay at university.[29]

Prague University initiated for future leaders experiences of the kind that had previously been provided by the south and west of Europe for the benefit of central Europe. But this 'international' role of Prague concerned only 'younger' Europe in a surprisingly strict way. The Scandinavians soon switched from Paris to Prague and, after Prague's demise, mostly to Leipzig (from 1409) and Rostock (from 1419), so that a part of Europe was reoriented. The same principle applied in other eastern European countries, such as Poland and Hungary. The highest input of students was from Poland. The fact that the leading urban groups were often of German origin made it easier for students from Poland and Hungary, and perhaps also from Sweden, to pursue their studies in Germany.[30] The main social attributes of German students can be found some time later in Scandinavia, firstly in Denmark, then in Sweden and Norway, and finally in Finland. Studying in Italy continued to be important because of the high social rank of students and the corresponding likelihood of their subsequently occupying high positions, mostly in the churches.

From the fourteenth century, nearly all the Nordic bishops had studied and about half of the canons of the cathedral and collegiate chapters, including those from Finland. The number of educated clergymen increased constantly until the Reformation in all the northern countries. Lay graduates from the upper social strata could also follow a career in the king's service. The Norwegian royal administration had more educated non-noble laymen than the Swedish or Danish. Both Denmark and Sweden had a wealthier and more

[29] P. Moraw, 'Die Universität Prag im Mittelalter', in *Die Universität zu Prag* (Munich, 1986), 9–134.

[30] G. Bonis, 'La pénétration du droit romain dans les pays slaves et hongrois', *Recueil de Mémoires et Travaux publié par la Société d'Histoire du Droit et des Institutions des Anciens Pays de Droit Ecrit*, 6 (1967), 75–83.

privileged aristocracy, whose education conformed more to the normal pattern of aristocratic families in central Europe.[31] All in all, there were enough career opportunities for wealthy students coming home after having spent some years at a foreign university. It is, however, difficult to know to what extent an academic education stimulated social mobility.

THE NATIONAL AND REGIONAL ERA IN 'OLDER' EUROPE (1380–1500)

The third phase of European university history may be described as one of concentration i.e. of both intensification and narrowing, as with many other contemporary developments. The concrete event which serves as the caesura here – the Great Schism of 1378 – points both to the decline of the universal church and the growth of the individual state. Equally important, at a time when the total population was sharply decreasing, was the relative and somtimes absolute increase in the number of university students. From around 1450, this was once again offset by a general increase in population. Instead of small groups of students, as was the case prior to and around 1200, we are now able to envisage totals running into hundreds of thousands, even when some of the older universities encountered a period of difficulties during the course of the fifteenth century (Avignon, Montpellier).

In this phase, urban northern Italy, still the most modern of the four main contexts of medieval universities, also offers the least clear profile. It would be presumptuous to venture any summary. We can, however, consider the dozen or so more or less successful Italian universities existing around 1500 as a single system in which students often moved from one place to another. This was independent of the fact that these universities, too, were increasingly being pressed into the service of the states. At the same time, throughout the fifteenth century, the social mobility within these universities remained considerable.

When we compare its jurists and educated physicians, certain features of the leading and also most attractive community, namely Florence, are characteristic of the wider picture.[32] These are significant groups (163 individuals from 1380 to 1530, 150 individuals from 1350 to 1450) with radically different social patterns. On the basis of a far better quality of biographical material than exists for all the above-mentioned groups, one common feature which could previously be presumed but is now demonstrable was that a career did not depend solely on the study pursued. Both career and study are part of a long-term and broad-based ensemble of social connections, which have to be interpreted in terms of the family destiny at their centre. The decision to

31 Bagge, 'Nordic Students' (note 11), 8–13; H. Holma and A. Maliniema, *Les Etudiants finlandais au moyen âge* (Helsinki, 1937), 13–15.
32 L. Martines, *Lawyers and Statecraft in Renaissance Florence* (Princeton, 1985).

study and the choice of discipline were not just autonomous options marking a fresh start, but were often determined by factors which continued to affect the career beyond the study period.

For the groups of Florentine patricians and leading social climbers whose success was already evident, a period of legal studies was, in the first place, the consequence of a successful family history, now consolidated after generations of risky trading: one's son and grandson would study jurisprudence. This pattern reminds us of capable upper middle-class merchants north of the Alps and their efforts to establish themselves in their more traditional milieu by 'old-fashioned' land ownership and noble rank. Those jurists practised their profession but it was not a profession of the kind familiar to us in the modern struggle for existence. It was only the third group of Florentine jurists that came close to assimilating this active model, since those who belonged to it had to offset their foreign origin; but they were of respectable status, too, otherwise they would have had no chance of success at all. To achieve success, hard work was indispensable. There was no fourth group worth speaking of. Not surprisingly, in view of the increasing complexity of conditions both at home and abroad, the commune recruited from these subgroups on the basis of individual achievement, with opportunities diminishing proportionately from the first to the third of them, those jurists who served as political leaders in Florence – and, all in all, they were an impressive number. A similar process has also been established in the case of Milan and Venice, here with political conditions of an even pricklier kind. Even smaller towns like Pistoia increased the number of posts to be filled by jurists.[33] In Florence, if nowhere else, it was an élite of a kind rarely encountered with such a clear profile.

To be a physician on the Arno, on the contrary, was much more 'modern' and also more uncertain and the prospects were poorer, not to mention the dangers of the profession in times of major epidemics. This may have been a major reason why the group of 'incomers' from the rural districts and from beyond the frontiers was the largest; this was already the occasion of much unrest in the social history of the medical doctors. But even among the Florentines, who found themselves increasingly in a minority, the study of medicine and the careers to which it led were, from the angle of family history, only a first and usually the only step upwards for secondary health agents, minor traders, and notaries, and even artisans (but very seldom – only three cases have been identified). Three doctors came from the aristocracy, fifteen were recognized social climbers. Medical studies were very expensive and subsequently extremely rewarding financially. The mercenary factor was much more prevalent than among the jurists. The medical profession had no powerful tradition, received less support from family connections, and had

[33] D. Herlihy, *Medieval and Renaissance Pistoia* (New Haven/London, 1967).

less traditional influence on sons than was the case with the jurists. When, as in three instances, a doctor broke into the limited circle of those with some political influence, this was certainly an individual achievement of some weight by comparison with the fifty jurists who did likewise.

The better-known French conditions none the less need to be commented upon in any attempted survey, even if it is only possible to speak of trends rather than quantities.[34] One fundamental feature of what also happened here was the process of regionalization, characteristic of the world into which the eight universities founded in the fifteenth century were born (on the whole, these remained relatively small). This regionalization affected even Paris and, to an increasing extent, the 'customers' of the universities, even the royal institutions. The French law faculties developed into almost exclusively professional and largely laicized training schools. By 'professional' here we mean not so much immediate applicability but a general training in legal thinking and, even more, the process of socialization among one's peers. At all events, the universities established very concrete contacts with the families which sent them their sons, ties which even tended to transform the social structures of the university. The heavy fees typical of the system meant that the profession was restricted almost completely to well-off families. All this was hardly possible except on the basis of an expensive and private preparatory education at school or at home. It was a far cry from the traditional Parisian 'general' arts courses open to all and which, judged from the standpoint of social success now (and probably earlier), turned out to be vague and ineffectual. A second Paris was never established in France. It remains unclear how large arts faculties should be judged, whether as more advanced philosophical schools or as training grounds for beginners, differing little from the school milieu. Even the higher level of the lawyers was full of uncertainties. It is astonishing, or perhaps indicative of fluctuations in social life, which must be assumed to have been widespread, that the pool of French jurists studying at one and the same time (estimated as from 3,000 to 3,300 in all) changed its proportions within a few years (1393/94–1403): a two-thirds majority from the south was changed into a two-thirds majority from the north, with the total figure remaining unchanged.

For canonists, the churches were the main employers. Yet graduates in Roman law enjoyed greater prestige; even in the church, they often occupied the highest positions. But it was obviously the king, important princes (duke of Burgundy, duke of Brittany, count of Provence), or the cities which nor-

[34] In addition to references in notes 15–17: J. Favier, 'Les légistes et le gouvernement de Philippe le Bel', *Journal des Savants* (1969), 92–108; J. Verger, 'Sul ruolo sociale delle università: La Francia tra Medioevo e Rinascimento', *Quaderni storici*, 23 (1973), 313–58; A. Gouron, 'Le recrutement des juristes dans les universités méridionales à la fin du XIVe siècle: Pays de canonistes et pays de civilistes?', in *Universities in the Late Middle Ages*, 524–48; A. Rigaudière, 'Hiérarchie socioprofessionnelle et gestion municipale dans les villes du midi français au bas Moyen Age', *Revue historique*, 269 (1983), 25–68.

mally made use of their competence. Compared with Italy and the south of France, the laicization of northern lawyers and the advance of northern jurists in the cities was clearly belated, not occurring until the second half of the fourteenth century. Once again, this advance had a twofold thrust; it served the ambitions of newcomers who wished to rise in the world and, later, the further consolidation of existing leading families or those still of secondary rank. Examples from Lyon, Poitiers, or smaller towns show that here, though a start was made later than in Florence, the success was greater. This was probably due to the fewer political demands made under the cloak of the monarchy and to a more restrained political climate. In the leading cities, at all events, after earlier beginnings, roughly between 1430 and 1456–60, jurists became so firmly established in the ranks of lay assessors and councillors that it became possible to speak in superficial terms of a pre-dominance of doctors and licentiates. What this amounted to, however, was not only a dissolution of the old aristocracy but also a new legitimacy of hitherto leading families. The result was a transformed urban world. At the same time, graduates were well represented amongst the clergy, especially in the cathedral chapters; many canon lawyers served both the state and the church. The spread of Gallicanism and the retreat of papal intervention in the fifteenth century did not permanently exclude graduates from ecclesiastical benefices; they were too numerous and too indispensable.[35]

In the fifteenth century, the development of the power of the monarchy was also dependent on leading groups of various kinds and was seriously hindered by fickle political fortunes. However, the social factors proved the most difficult to master. A group of jurists on whose expertise every monarch increasingly depended reacted with temporary changes rather than with a really fresh start. The Paris parliament – the supreme royal court – and the central administration outside the court were two groups each consisting of roughly a hundred persons with very extensive structures by European stan-dards. The parliament (we have details of 678 of its members between 1345 and 1450) was undoubtedly the more compact group. Perhaps with the excep-tion of the papal court, this parliament contained more legal expertise in an increasingly concentrated social form than anywhere else in Europe. The data on graduation show the expected increase, but it is generally agreed, with more reason here than elsewhere, that possession of a degree is already to be assumed as normal practice around 1350. During the latter part of the fifteenth century, the practice of handing down an office in the family, which as a widespread normal practice hardly raised an eyebrow any longer, also existed in the group of members of parliament. However, the hereditary nature of an office did not imply abandoning one's law studies, as the act of studying had become a family tradition.

35 H. Millet, 'Quels furent les bénéficiaires de la soustraction d'obédience de 1398 dans les chapitres cathédraux français?', in Bulst and Genet (eds.), *Medieval Lives* (note 23), 123–37.

The extent of the legal complexion of the teams of twenty-seven bailiffs and twelve seneschals was clearly less than the number of posts available, i.e. two or three in each case. Here, again, an increase was possible, but hardly prior to 1500. At the end of the fifteenth century, as illustrated by the case of the small *bailliage* of Senlis, north of Paris, not only the two or three royal judges of the tribunal but also the advocates and even the mere attorneys were increasingly university graduates.

From 1434, five new provincial parliaments were created. This made it possible for advocates, who were now – with increasing frequency – licentiates and doctors, to establish a permanent place in administrative and judicial circles. In many cases the way was opened to wealth and nobility. All these posts, however, lacked any supreme decision-making authority. Posts with such authority were still reserved for the ruler's aristocratic ministers, although, before the end of the fifteenth century, hardly any thought was given to supplementing their training with legal education. There were never more than a few jurists in the royal council.

The year 1450 is the rough boundary between the earlier stagnation and the extension of possibilities. Henceforth we can reasonably speak of a legally educated leading stratum independent of the church. The next step, which appears logical but which was only tentatively taken prior to 1500, was to establish conditions for controlling admissions to the legal 'professions', too. As dates, 1490 may be indicated for advocates and 1499 for the *lieutenants généraux* of the bailiffs and seneschals. This was not so much the creation of something entirely new, but rather the confirmation of customary practice in written form. Correspondingly, perhaps also as the result of an oversupply, the importance of graduation to some extent declined. The same thing is found in other countries as well, so that licentiates and doctors are now found occupying posts which previously seemed inappropriate. This reversal applied still more to graduation in the arts. Apart from individual cases, however, we still do not know which professions the masters and students of the large Paris faculty entered before and after 1450. Certain masters of arts became attorneys, others schoolmasters; many remained in the lower ranks of the urban clergy.

There was little change in the main features of English university history in the fifteenth century. The first interesting point is that, with an estimated 2,000 persons studying contemporaneously at Oxford and Cambridge prior to 1400, and with the increase in this figure to roughly 3,000 around the year 1450, the student population was very large in proportion to the population as a whole. It was certainly higher than in France and far higher than in central Europe. 'Older' than in France or Italy, however, was the fact that in England all this was closely connected with the church. Here again, we must remember the gradual blurring of the boundaries between clergy and laity. The situation was not greatly altered by the Reformation.

The registers of New College, Oxford (founded in 1379), enable us for once to cite original 'statistical' data for medieval England. An analysis of the background of students (937 in all, excluding unclear cases), which presents a rather more 'conservative' picture than the university average, shows that, from 1380 to 1500, 63.2 per cent of the students came from the rural areas; the majority of them may have belonged to families of 'smallholders'. Only 21.8 per cent were urban residents, and one in seven of them from the urban 'aristocracy'. The proportion of gentry (including state officials in this group) amounted to 12.5 per cent. Only six persons were nobles in the narrower sense and only two from the lower class. A very remarkable fact is that 45 per cent of the 'smallholders' lived on college land.[36] A study of the careers of 2,040 persons (42.5 per cent of these are unclarified cases or early deaths) demonstrates the overwhelming predominance of church posts, also for the period from 1451 to 1500: 39 per cent joined the ranks of the parish clergy, a further 5 per cent of clergymen went into church administration and the courts, another 2.5 per cent into an amalgam of church and secular administration and justice, and finally 7.5 per cent into other clerical posts. For only 2.5 per cent is there evidence of posts exclusively in the lay world (officials, judges, schoolmasters). If we examine the same source material for the longer but less uniform period from 1380 to 1520 (with 44 per cent of unclarified cases or early deaths), we find that at least 46 per cent entered the ecclesiastical sphere and only 5.5 per cent that of the laity.[37]

As everywhere in 'older' Europe, in England civil and canon law stood side by side and even attracted increasing numbers of students from around 1460, but both were primarily in the service of the church. In contrast to the situation in highly urbanized northern Italy, the laity may well have represented the more modest part. In these circumstances, the benefice situation was hardly less fundamental than in Germany. Fluctuations in the attitude of those with disposal rights became vital questions for the university – a situation very different from the one prevailing in the Mediterranean area. Clerical activities to a large extent overlapped with secular ones. Equally 'medieval' was the open rivalry between graduates and otherwise qualified persons for posts outside cathedral chapters and large collegiate churches. This, of course, was another aspect of the continuing relatively high social mobility, even into the rank of bishop. On the other hand, the element of 'self-recruitment' was not absent in official circles. As for the career opportunities of the

---

[36] G. F. Lytle, 'The Social Origins of Oxford Students in the Late Middle Ages: New College, *c.* 1380–*c.* 1510', in *Universities in the Late Middle Ages*, 426–54.

[37] In addition to references in note 23: J. T. Rosenthal, 'The Fifteenth-Century Episcopate: Careers and Bequests', in D. Baker (ed.), *Sanctity and Secularity* (Oxford, 1973), 117–27; R. N. Swanson, 'Universities, Graduates and Benefices in Later Mediaeval England', *Past and Present*, 106 (1985), 28–61; R. N. Swanson, 'Learning and Living: University Study and Clerical Careers in Later Medieval England', *History of Universities*, 6 (1986–7), 81–103.

poor, nothing can be said with certainty.[38] Yet the fairly high proportion of *pauperes* in the combined English–German 'nation' in Paris (1425–94: 17.6 per cent) will probably not have been the situation of the continentals only. In short, though we may know little of the social history of the English universities, the distinctive position of the kingdom of England between the main landscapes of Europe emerges very clearly.

The most important general change in the career of Spanish students took place not long before 1500.[39] In a period of rapid economic growth, 'modern' monarchies needed far more good-quality officials than before. The number of holders of higher offices with academic titles thus steadily increased, by as much as 11.7 per cent in the reign of Ferdinand and Isabella (1474–1516). The first appearance of these *letrados* can be traced back to the late fourteenth century. The new foundations were state universities, to promote jurisprudence in the first instance. In the kingdom of Castile, the *letrados* trained at the Universities of Salamanca and Valladolid continued to obtain high clerical posts – in the fifteenth century, they represented almost half of the members of the chapters of Valladolid – and offices in the royal administration. Barcelona, the capital of Catalonia, with its characteristics of Italian and southern French communes, demonstrated from the late fourteenth century considerable participation and influence of jurists in its municipal and private affairs.[40]

THE NATIONAL AND REGIONAL ERA IN 'YOUNGER' EUROPE

Between 1348 and 1505, there were 200,000 German university students. This figure is the first and only statement based on a reliable overall estimate. For the generation prior to 1380 we have only to subtract a few thousands. For 1470–80, the number is reckoned as five times that for 1390–1400; there were at the end of the period easily 2,500 new students each year. Around 1480, the number becomes more or less fixed at this level. The total population of Germany in 1500 can be estimated as roughly 15 million or more. A comparison between these two sets of figures brings out quantitatively what could already be gathered from previous less accurate considerations: the 'student

---

38 N. Orme, 'Schoolmasters, 1309–1509', in C. H. Clough (ed.), *Profession, Vocation, and Culture in Later Medieval England* (Liverpool, 1982), 218–41; R. S. Gottfried, *Doctors and Medicine in Medieval England 1340–1530* (Princeton, 1986).

39 R. L. Kagan, *Lawsuits and Litigants in Castile 1500–1700* (Raleigh, 1981); W. D. Phillips Jr, 'University Graduates in Castilian Royal Service in the Fifteenth Century', in *Estudios en homenaje a Don Claudio Sánchez Albornoz en sus 90 años* (Buenos Aires, 1986), vol. IV, 475–90; M. Lunenfeld, *Keepers of the City. The Corregidores of Isabel I of Castile (1474–1504)* (Cambridge, 1987), 73–106.

40 Rucquoi, 'Sociétés urbaines', (note 22); C. Carrère, 'Refus d'une création universitaire et niveaux de culture à Barcelone: hypothèses d'explication', *Moyen Age*, 85 (1979), 245–73; J. S. Amelang, 'Barristers and Judges in Early Modern Barcelona: The Rise of a Legal Elite', *American Historical Review*, 89 (1984), 1264–84.

density' in the centre of Europe was considerably less than in the west but, despite the simultaneous decline and halt in population figures (between 1348 and 1450–70), the gap was in the end reduced. This was the result of the work of fifteen new universities (founded before 1506).[41]

What is true of the Holy Roman Empire can be taken on the whole to apply also to the north and east of the continent, but with considerable delay and quantitatively on a smaller scale. Compared with the preceding period, some essential changes took place in northern Europe. Since the Norwegian king and his administration had moved to Denmark, the career opportunities for the Norwegian aristocracy and bourgeoisie had considerably diminished. For Norwegian students, mostly of middle-class origin, only the church could henceforth provide comfortable positions. The impoverished nobility showed very little interest in higher education. In Denmark the number of students from aristocratic or upper middle-class origin grew constantly. The increasing centralization and bureaucratization which occurred during the period of the Nordic Unions produced a demand for educated administrators (lawyers). From the fifteenth century onwards, laymen gradually replaced clerics in the central and local administrations. The Swedish part of Finland followed the Swedish pattern of education. The cathedral and collegiate chapters were filled with rather well-educated aristocrats. In contrast with Sweden, however, the Finnish élites continued to visit Paris and perhaps not German universities so frequently as their Swedish counterparts.[42]

An important difference between continental 'older' Europe (with the exception of Paris) and 'younger' Europe is the higher proportion of arts students in the latter. This could be as much as 75–80 per cent. Among law students, the central Europe increase in numbers, at least around 1400, appears to have been minimal, if there was any increase at all. The crisis and disappearance of the Prague law university (1409–17) was a setback. Whereas before and around 1400 the number of French jurists studying contemporaneously was 3,000, the German figures may have amounted to only 10–20 per cent of that figure, even in the Prague 'springtime' (1380–90).

Another essential condition of academic career opportunities in Germany is the tendency to a levelling-down of the faculties in the four-faculty universities under the influence of the territorial state. With few exceptions, the new universities were small and poor. They put down roots in the neighbourhood and mostly lacked munificent bequests and foundations. In contrast to Paris and Bologna, we have here a new, third, combined type of European university, with different implications for the careers of the students. There was, therefore, a fairly clear twofold division between a student type continuing in

---

[41] Schwinges, *Universitätsbesucher, passim*; P. Moraw, 'Aspekte und Dimensionen älterer deutscher Universitätsgeschichte', in P. Moraw, and V. Press (eds.), *Academia Gissensis* (Marburg, 1982), 1–43.

[42] Bagge, 'Nordic Students' (note 11), 13–17.

the aristocratic and propertied tradition and the 'exclusively' arts student type now emerging into view, for the most part lacking in financial resources. The career possibilities open to these two student types differed considerably. The former type of student was recognizable among the Germans long before their own universities emerged; they were relatively few in number and tended to study law. They could also, if they wished, travel abroad in the fifteenth century. That the main recruiting places were small towns and, not infrequently, villages was mainly true of the second student type. The middle classes and artisans supplied the majority of these students. Most of them returned to their regional towns, since a high value was attached to the link with the home region. They appear to have been particularly affected by the oversupply crisis after 1480.[43]

As individuals, the better-situated students were less affected by the level of development in their own region than the poorer students, as illustrated by their status and number. The conditions in Brabant were probably the most modern in the empire – whether in law studies in aristocratic, 'elitist' Orléans or in participation in communal and territorial decision-making bodies at home. Of the Brabant students in Orléans (from 1444) – and thus outside the area of the new four-faculty universities – only 20 per cent came from noble families, the majority being from prosperous bourgeois families, especially from the large cities. The behaviour pattern was aristocratic to begin with, but in the long run the aristocrat was introduced to the 'modern', urban style of life. What emerges clearly here, too, is something that was true quite generally for the final phase of the medieval period: the social history of students continued uninterrupted into the sixteenth and seventeenth centuries. Only in the modern period does it turn out that the Brabant way produced a fairly uniform group of 'jurist officials' from good backgrounds, who gradually became qualified through their specialist and professional achievement.[44] The more or less parallel influence of Nuremberg and Augsburg can be traced among the southern Germans, in Pavia, in smaller numbers and in a milieu which was even more 'feudal'. If we look beyond into the sixteenth century, the same was true in the long run for the 'aristocratic' University of Ingolstadt, which began functioning in 1472.[45]

It is in the church milieu that we can best approach the difficult question of the temporal course of the most important changes. Increased participation in study – though with a clear time-lag compared with western Europe – is observable everywhere, even in whole dioceses, but most clearly perhaps in a

43 Schwinges, *Universitätsbesucher*, passim.

44 H. de Ridder-Symoens, 'Brabanders aan de rechtsuniversiteit van Orleans (1444–1546). Een socioprofessionele studie', *Bijdragen tot de Geschiedenis*, 609 (1978), 195–347.

45 R. A. Müller, *Universität und Adel. Eine soziostrukturelle Studie zur Geschichte der bayerischen Landesuniversität Ingolstadt, 1472–1648* (Berlin, 1974). A. Sottili, 'La Natio Germanica dell'università di Pavia nella storia dell'Umanesimo', in *Universities in the Late Middle Ages*, 347–64.

'recent' case like that of the cathedral chapter of Roskilde.[46] Until 1430, 55 per cent of the members of the Roskilde chapter had been former students; then, until 1493, the percentage was 76.1 per cent. Only a small proportion of these were graduates, with a steep decline in the proportion of jurists in the early fifteenth century, due doubtless to the collapse of Prague. This shows how flimsy the network of study connections was at the periphery. From 1418 onwards, conciliar decrees encouraged this development towards a growing emphasis on study in the church, more or less successfully. A less easily discernible change was far more important, however: the transition from study based on an already acquired canonry to study with a view to securing a benefice thereby. In this second more 'modern' case, all that was at first offered was the chance to qualify by performance. In 'younger' Europe, this was a change which began only in the fifteenth century.

Even in this century, study and careers in 'younger' Europe were still related primarily to churches. But laicizing trends of the sort which were already visible further south or even west in the thirteenth century are unmistakable. In general, certainly in the second half of the fifteenth century as far as the most modern careers were concerned, leadership passed to the secular authorities. It was in the lower Rhineland that this succeeded the earliest and also the most. Here, there was something like a legal, secular, administrative and judicial 'career path' which it was possible to choose on the basis of appropriate study. For the earliest successes of lay jurists in territorial administrations and judicial systems, reference is made once again to Brabant, which itself was half a century late on the scene compared with Flanders. Of the members of the Raad van Brabant (court of justice) in the second quarter of the fifteenth century, 40 per cent were graduates; during the next fifty years this proportion rose to almost 70 per cent.[47] The urban career involved entry into the administration and, finally, advance to the executive decision-making bodies. Certainly caution is needed with respect to this final stage, since it is possible that the existing ruling oligarchy – mostly trained in economics – sought to keep jurists at a safe distance from its affairs. In this case, it was necessary to wait until sons from the leading families were sent to university, and this could take a long time. In Germany, Nuremberg employed jurists early on (from 1366) with the title of doctor, on a permanent basis and not just as 'lucky flukes', but for centuries it kept them at a distance from the *Rat*. In the north-west, in Antwerp and Louvain, there was a more

---

[46] E. Mornet, 'Préliminaires à une prosopographie du haut clergé scandinave: le chapitre cathédral de Roskilde 1367–1493', in Bulst and Genet (eds.), *Medieval Lives* (note 23), 159–62.

[47] H. de Ridder-Symoens, 'Milieu social, études universitaires et carrière des conseillers au Conseil de Brabant, 1430–1600', in *Recht en Instellingen in de Oude Nederlanden tijdens de Middeleeuwen en de Nieuwe Tijd, Liber Amicorum J. Buntinx* (Louvain, 1981), 257–301. H. de Ridder-Symoens, 'Internationalismus versus Nationalismus an Universitäten um 1500 nach zumeist südniederländischen Quellen', in F. Seibt and W. Eberhard (eds.), *Europa 1500* (Stuttgart, 1987), 397–414.

open attitude; jurists appear there in 1431 and 1451 as lay assessors for the first time, and the law qualification soon became a standard requirement. The first graduate jurist in the Lübeck court of justice dates from 1460, in Hamburg from 1465; the first doctor sat in the Cologne *Rat* in 1484. The whole development lasted well into the sixteenth century. In the fifteenth century, roughly three-quarters of the chief posts in the city administration of Antwerp and Louvain were occupied by graduate jurists, and in the sixteenth century practically all of them were. For the Holy Roman Empire, that was a very modern attitude.[48]

From the fourteenth century in the Mediterranean area and from the fifteenth to sixteenth century in the rest of Europe, medical doctors became more important in society. The great plague of 1348–50 not only stimulated the activities of the medical faculties, particularly in the field of *consilia* or medical advice, but gradually persuaded city councils to appoint *doctores medicinae* as town physicians. Before that time, medical doctors could mainly find a position in the service of high-ranking people or hospitals, or they could start up a private practice in a large city for well-to-do citizens. The majority of the medieval population never saw a doctor who had graduated. The barber-surgeon or quack doctor was their only succour.[49]

It continues to be difficult to obtain a clear picture of the careers of students of lesser rank in Germany and the whole of 'younger Europe', and still more of the 30,000 or so German *pauperes*. What happened to the students of a whole university offers a fairly useful cross-section, but a study of this kind exists only for the university founded in Tübingen in 1477.[50] At that time, this university occupied ninth place in the German university system, with roughly a hundred new students annually. Until 1534, the number of persons attending the institution was 5,800. It has proved possible to quarry information about the careers of 28 per cent of them. Of the 1,627 students about whom we have more precise information, no fewer than 1,097 entered clerical professions; 314 are to be found in administrative and judicial posts and 110 in the university itself or in posts closely connected with it. There were 33 physicians, 23 schoolmasters, and 13 notaries or advocates. A

48 F. W. Ellinger, 'Die Juristen der Reichsstadt Nürnberg vom 15. bis 17. Jahrhundert', in *Reichsstadt Nürnberg, Altdorf und Hersbruck* (Nuremberg, 1954), 130ff. H. de Ridder-Symoens, 'De universitaire vorming van de Brabantse stadsmagistraat en stadsfunktionarissen. Leuven en Antwerpen, 1430–1580', *Varia Historica Brabantica*, 6–7 (1978), 21–126; K. Wriedt, 'Das gelehrte Personal in der Verwaltung und Diplomatie der Hansestädte', *Hansische Geschichtsblätter*, 96 (1978), 15–37; B. Moeller, H. Patze, and K. Stackmann (eds.), *Studien zum städtischen Bildungswesen des späten Mittelalters und der frühen Neuzeit* (Göttingen, 1983).

49 A. W. Russel (ed.), *The Town and State Physician in Europe from the Middle Ages to the Enlightenment* (Wolfenbüttel, 1981).

50 W. Kuhn, *Die Studenten der Universität Tübingen zwischen 1477 und 1534*, 2 vols. (Göppingen, 1971). Cf. comparative data in F. Smahel, 'L'université de Prague de 1433 à 1622: recrutement géographique, carrières et mobilité sociale des étudiants gradués', in D. Julia, J. Revel, and R. Chartier (eds.), *Les Universités européennes du XVIe au XVIIIe siècle. Histoire sociale des populations étudiantes*, vol. I (Paris, 1986), 65–88.

comparable number were involved in the book trade in the broadest sense and in the armed forces. Given the weakness of the higher faculties, what is reflected here is the arts milieu as it appears to have been generally in 'younger' Europe, and therefore, for the most part, the middle and lower levels of social life. The quota of graduates was highest among the clergy and administrative and legal personnel. Existing family status and newly acquired qualifications were here mixed in a way which now defies disentanglement. Despite all provincialism, the tide of innovation also reached Tübingen. That important trends won the day is evidenced by, among other things, the advance of Roman law as the basis of a 'civil' career, which, around 1500, was evidently the most respected one.

Further details serve to show that this whole situation is fairly typical of the provincial milieu in central Europe. One basic fact was that so many returned without discernible social change to their domestic urban life. It is in the university towns that we can see most clearly that, for many, the university was a basic educational institution rather than a social one. Although, up to the bachelorship of arts, the poor were more than averagely diligent, from that point on, or at latest from their graduation as masters, they remained practically without further possibilities; at this point a quite clear barrier to social advance traversed the country, a fact which helps to explain the lot of so many. From this angle, there were in fact two universities in one. The pathway from being an artisan, which was the social background of many scholars at the end of the medieval period, hardly led anywhere beyond the lower clerical and scribal posts, where these existed at all. The 'better' families in the many small towns are typical of the background of many students, but this status had little value in a faraway place or in the larger cities. Study made little difference to the direction of the lives of numerous sons of patricians, still less in the case of the sons of artisans. They remained what they were and, like their fathers before them, had to assert themselves on the basis of qualifications other than those acquired by study. Is it cynical to say that all that was achieved in this way was merely an enrichment of intellectual life? Not altogether! The world was already being changed by the mere fact that it became possible for almost everyone to meet people who had been to a university and had thereby caught at least a glimpse of the world of letters and felt in some measure, at least, the power of the word. The university thus came closer to everyday life. That, too, was a social fact.

It has been impossible until now to date in any consistent way the transition whereby study became a mass phenomenon in Germany and a changed social and cultural situation emerged, without which the Reformation, among other things, would have been inconceivable. Something decisive happened around 1470. This was chronologically connected, surely not accidentally, with the general economic change from a long period of stagnation to a new upsurge which inaugurated the 'long' sixteenth century. With the increase in the number of students, a period began in which civil authorities exercised more control over society and the social classes closed ranks. The fragile social body of those who had attended university was unable to breach this situation but had to accommodate itself to it. The pressure of supply which undoubtedly existed in the last quarter of the century could find no other outlet than in the increasingly muscular struggle for existing posts; the holders of higher degrees contented themselves with posts which had previously been filled by those of more modest rank. Changes in the power to dispose of church benefices seem, at the same time, to have come about in the shape of a retreat of the papacy. Perhaps they had important repercussions on the German 'employment system' for university students. An unregulated social system, left to shape itself painfully and unconsciously, tried – as in every previous generation – to achieve some sort of balance at the expense of the weak. It was to be a long time before the strongest arguments would be those of university students and graduates.

After the (re-)foundation of the University of Cracow (1400) and the foundation of the Scottish universities from 1412, Poland and Scotland were the only countries of 'younger' Europe besides Germany that were in a position to replace the migration of their sons to foreign countries by studies of their own. Because of the attraction of Italian, French, and German universities, however, these studies remained no more than a complement. Foundations in Sweden and Denmark were too late and too small to have any remarkable effects, while Norway and Finland had no universities. Again, the social context of careers is quite comparable with earlier contexts, as in Germany, for instance. Numbers were small, the role of the churches as employers was always important, and laicization was late. In Hungary, for example, it did not occur before the sixteenth century. But the general direction of 'modernization' remained the same.[51]

This first attempt to understand the social history of the European universities in the medieval period as the history of those who attended the universities and as a more or less integrated process leaves many questions unanswered. Not surprisingly, therefore, the briefest conclusions sound paradoxical. Born in social interstices and very fragile as a structure, the universities nevertheless survived and became one of the phenomena treasured by leaders of societies. That is an astonishing fact in itself. The products of the university, both its graduates and those who failed to grad-

---

[51] A. Kubinyi, 'Städtische Bürger und Universitätsstudien in Ungarn am Ende des Mittelalters', in E. Maschke and J. Sydow (eds.), *Stadt und Universität im Mittelalter und in der früheren Neuzeit* (Sigmaringen, 1977), 161–5; J. Durkan and J. Kirk, *The University of Glasgow 1451–1577* (Glasgow, 1977); J. Pinborg, 'Danish Students 1450–1535 and the University of Copenhagen', *Université de Copenhague, Cahiers de l'Institut du Moyen Age grec et latin*, 37 (1981), 70–122; I. Kaniewska, 'Les étudiants de l'université de Cracovie aux XVe et XVIe siècles (1433–1560)', in Julia, Revel, and Chartier (eds.), *Universités européennes* (note 50), 113–33.

uate, emerged from that fragile structure, forced their way into numerous societies, and, not without success, opposed their new qualifications to the old traditional qualifications of these societies. The process of education and training of people through universities was, as a whole, unplanned and unpiloted, only partly canalized and finally instrumentalized. Much remained a spin-off of quite diverse individual intentions. Yet the university definitely helped to modernize the medieval world, even if it only remained mobile by adapting itself to external social rules and by willingly accepting the changes taking place in the societies around it. It was a question of mobilization rather than of mobility – in other words, more a case of oscillating movements in different directions than of a straight path ahead.

Rapid advancement on the basis of university qualifications alone was rare, however. From the standpoint of all the societies taken together, the influence of the universities was in stabilizing systems rather than disturbing or even shattering them; the changes they brought about helped to make the 'feudal' or communal worlds capable of adaptation and survival. It was therefore an appropriate price to pay for this when, as the new technicians of power, the jurists pushed their way forward into positions of second or third importance. This served to stabilize the posts of first importance, which continued to be occupied on the basis of birth and often of property and influence. Graduation was, in the main, only one qualification among others on the road to securing a post. The greatest success could be expected by young men who combined the largest number of qualifications. Only in a long-term perspective does it become clear that all this was, at the same time, the first step on the way to the modern goal of making the principle of achievement the determining factor.

SELECT BIBLIOGRAPHY

Autrand, F. *Naissance d'un grand corps de l'Etat: les gens du Parlement de Paris 1345–1454*, Paris, 1981.
Autrand, F. (ed.) *Prosopographie et genèse de l'Etat moderne*, Paris, 1986.
Baldwin, J. W. *Masters, Princes, and Merchants*, 2 vols., Princeton, 1970.
Bartier, J. *Légistes et gens de finances au 15e siècle. Les counseillers des Ducs de Bourgogne sous Philippe le Bon et Charles le Téméraire*, Brussels, 1955–7.
Benvenuti, A. and Cardini, F. (eds.) *Storia della società italiana, parte seconda*, vols. VI and VII, Milan, 1982, 1986.
Bullough, V. L. 'Achievement, Professionalization, and the University', in J. IJsewijn and J. Paquet (eds.), *Universities in the Late Middle Ages*, Louvain, 1978, 497–510.
Bullough, V. L. *The Development of Medicine as a Profession*, New York, 1966.
Bulst, N. and Genet, J.-P. (eds.) *Medieval Lives and the Historian. Studies in Medieval Prosopography*, Kalamazoo, 1986.
Burke, P. *The Italian Renaissance: Culture and Society in Italy, 1420–1540*, Cambridge/Oxford, 1987.
van Caenegem, R. C. *Judges, Legislators, and Professors*, Cambridge, 1987.

Cazelles, R. *La Société politique et la crise de la royauté sous Philippe de Valois*, Paris, 1958.

I ceti dirigenti nella Toscana del Quattrocento, Monte Oriolo, 1987.

Classen, P. *Studium und Gesellschaft im Mittelalter*, ed. J. Fried, Stuttgart, 1983.

Clough, C. (ed.) *Profession, Vocation and Culture in Later Medieval England*, Liverpool, 1981.

Dotzauer, W. 'Deutsche in westeuropäischen Hochschul- und Handelsstädten, vornehmlich in Frankreich, bis zum Ende des alten Reiches', *Geschichtliche Landeskunde*, 5:2 (1969), 89–159.

Dotzauer, W. 'Deutsches Studium in Italien unter besonderer Berücksichtigung der Universität Bologna', *Geschichtliche Landeskunde*, 14 (1976), 84–130.

Ehbrecht, W. (ed.) *Städtische Führungsgruppen und Gemeinde in der werdenden Neuzeit*, Cologne/Vienna, 1980.

Fried, J. *Die Entstehung des Juristenstandes im 12. Jahrhundert*, Cologne, 1974.

Fried, J. (ed.) *Schulen und Studium im sozialen Wandel des hohen und späten Mittelalters*, Sigmaringen, 1986.

García y García, A. *Iglesia, Sociedad y Derecho*, Salamanca, 1985.

Gottfried, R. S. *Doctors and Medicine in Medieval England 1340–1530*, Princeton, 1986.

Gouron, A. *La Science de droit dans le Midi de la France au Moyen Age*, London, 1984.

Hattenhauer, H. *Geschichte des Beamtentums*, Handbuch des öffentlichen Dienstes, 1, Cologne, 1980.

Jacquart, D. *Le Milieu médical en France du XIIe au XVe siècle*, Geneva, 1981.

Kagan, R. L. *Students and Society in Early Modern Spain*, Baltimore/London, 1974.

Lytle, G. F. 'Oxford Students and English Society, *c.* 1300 – *c.* 1510', Ph.D., Princeton, 1975.

Martines, L. *The Social World of the Florentine Humanists 1390–1460*, London, 1963.

Meuthen, F. *Die alte Universität*, Kölner Universitätsgeschichte 1, Cologne/Vienna, 1988.

Moraw, P. 'Organisation und Funktion von Verwaltung im ausgehenden Mittelalter (*ca.* 1300–1500)'. in K. G. A. Jeserich, H. Pohl, and G.-C. von Unruh (eds.), *Deutsche Verwaltungsgeschichte*, vol. I, Stuttgart, 1983, 21–65.

Peset, M. 'Universidades Españolas y Universidades Europeas', *Ius comune*, 12 (1984), 71–89.

Poirion, D. (ed.) *Milieux universitaires et mentalité urbaine au Moyen Age*, Paris, 1987.

de Ridder-Symoens, H. *Tot nut of onnut van 't algemeen. De functie van de universiteit in de middeleeuwen*, Inaugural Lecture, Vrije University, Amsterdam, 1987.

de Ridder-Symoens, H. 'Possibilités de carrière et de mobilité sociale des intellectuels-universitaires au moyen âge', in N. Bulst and J.-P. Genet (eds.), *Medieval Lives and the Historian. Studies in Medieval Prosopography*, Kalamazoo, 1986, 343–56.

Schilling, H. and Diederiks, H. (eds.) *Bürgerliche Eliten in den Niederlanden und in Nordwestdeutschland*, Cologne/Vienna, 1985.

Schnur, R. (ed.) *Die Rolle der Juristen bei der Entstehung des modernen Staates*, Berlin, 1986.

Schuchard, C. *Die Deutschen an der päpstlichen Kurie im späten Mittelalter (1378–1447)*, Tübingen, 1987.

Storia della cultura veneta, vol. III:1, Vicenza, 1980.

Ullmann, W. *The Growth of Papal Government in the Middle Ages*, London, 1955.

Université et cité: à la recherche du passé – Town and Gown: the University in search of its origins, *CRE–Information*, new series, 62 (1983).

Verger, J. 'L'histoire sociale des universités à la fin du Moyen Age: problèmes, sources, méthodes (à propos des universités du Midi de la France)', in S. Hoyer and W. Fläschendräger (eds.), *Die Geschichte der Universitäten und ihre Erforschung*, Leipzig, 1984, 37–53.

Verger, J. 'Les universités médiévales: intérêt et limites d'une histoire quantitative. Notes à propos d'une enquête sur les universités du Midi de la France à la fin du Moyen Age', in D. Julia, J. Revel, and R. Chartier (eds.), *Les Universités euro-péennes du XVIe au XVIIIe siècle. Histoire sociale des populations étudiantes*, vol. II, Paris, 1989, 9–24.

CHAPTER 9

MOBILITY

HILDE DE RIDDER-SYMOENS

Medieval men loved travel. It mattered little that roads were few and that they could go only on foot or on horseback, by cart or by boat. The twentieth century thinks of the travellers thronging the roads of Europe in the Middle Ages as the ubiquitous armies, merchants going from town to town, and pilgrims. Especially pilgrims, for thousands and thousands of the faithful went on pilgrimage to the holy places of Jerusalem, Rome, or Santiago de Compostela, or to shrines nearer home. There was no lack of these in medieval Christendom, or of hostels, boarding-houses, inns, hospitals, and refuges along the pilgrimage routes.

Until the end of the eighteenth century pilgrims or travellers (*peregrini*) of another kind were also a familiar sight on the roads of Europe. These were the university students and professors. Their pilgrimage (*peregrinatio*) was not to Christ's or a saint's tomb, but to a university city where they hoped to find learning, friends, and leisure.

Literary tradition represents medieval students as undisciplined, unprincipled, bohemian, violent, footloose, all for wine, women, and song. Among the goliards there were of course real students, seekers for an alternative culture, members of a medieval intelligentsia; in their critical attitude to society they were at one with the motley crowd of clerical debauchees, ribalds, jugglers, jesters, singers, and sham students who peopled the fringes of society. Any study of wandering students must distinguish between writers and singers of *carmina burana* and students bent on learning and a university degree, with whom this chapter is concerned.

The European 'academic pilgrimage' (*peregrinatio academica*) merits definition. We mean by this a journey by students and teachers made in a European country or countries for the purpose of study. Until the seventeenth century all universities taught in Latin and curricula and degrees were the same. A student could therefore begin his course at one university, usually the nearest, and continue it at another, or at several others.

In the twelfth and thirteenth centuries, when there were not many universities and they were not widely distributed over Europe, the 'happy few' who aspired to higher education had to leave home and travel long distances to the *studium* of their (rather limited) choice. Towards 1500, however, nearly every territory in Europe had its own centre of higher education, and at all of them the teaching methods, the subjects taught, and the degrees awarded were much the same. From that time onwards one has to distinguish between what could be called external migration – of students to a foreign country – and internal migration, in the course of which a student attended several *studia* in his own country. For Spain and France there is no difficulty. By the end of the Middle Ages many universities had been founded there, and both countries were so far consolidated territorially and politically that 'internal migration' is no misnomer. In Britain, however, there was so much difference between English, Scottish, Irish, and Welsh students that 'internal migration' hardly seems the appropriate term. The situation is still more complicated in Italy and the Holy Roman Empire, where from the fourteenth century onwards local rulers founded universities in their own dominions to train officials for their absolutist bureaucracy. Whether travel between their virtually independent states was internal or external migration becomes a matter of opinion; we believe that, in the European context, 'academic pilgrimage' within the Holy Roman Empire was internal migration rather than external. Our information on student migration comes mainly from university rolls of students, and therefore includes student drop-outs as well as the earnest students whose doctorate was the reward for long years of study. Partly for this reason, no special attention has been paid to itinerant teachers; they have been dealt with in chapter 5.

'Academic pilgrimage' did not come into being with the twelfth-century university. Long before that, masters and scholars had set out for renowned centres of learning, either a monastic or episcopal school (the most important of these were between the Loire and the Moselle at Bec, Chartres, Laon, Reims, Paris, and Liège) or a more specialized centre on the border of Christendom like the school of medicine in Salerno or the translators' school in Toledo, one of the main centres for the transmission of Arabic science and learning to Christendom. Their masters attracted students from all parts – from Germany, Britain, and Italy. A well-known early example is Gerbert of Aurillac, the future Pope Sylvester II, in the tenth century. Dissatisfied with his education as an oblate at the monastery of Saint-Gérault d'Aurillac, in 967 he accompanied the count of Barcelona to Vich in Catalonia, where he studied mathematics, geometry, astronomy, and music (the *quadrivium*), disciplines then hardly known in the west. Later he lived in Rome and at the court of the Emperor Otto I, and continued his studies of dialectics in Reims, where he became an eminent professor before taking up his political career in the church.

Mobility among clerics – at that time all intellectuals were clerics – eroded the European monastic ideal of *stabilitas loci* (stable residence), but the intellectual enthusiasm of the twelfth-century renaissance paid scant attention to this. Twelfth-century intellectuals did not feel bound to any particular school or curriculum; they freely chose their discipline and teacher (the autobiographical works of Abelard and his pupil John of Salisbury vividly portray this international world of masters and scholars), and the first universities arose in Paris and Bologna from the influx of students from the four corners of Europe.

NATIONS, COLLEGES, AND FRATERNITIES

Lonely students in a foreign, sometimes hostile city formed associations whose members spoke the same language or shared the same tastes. As a group they could look after themselves better and cope more easily with the difficulties of a long stay abroad. They hired houses in common, met at church or at an inn to celebrate their national days, and organized postal services between the university city and their homeland so as to keep in touch with their family and receive from them money, letters, and parcels. In Paris, Jacques de Vitry (1160/70–1240), a famous preacher who had studied theology at the university there, listed twelve nations differing widely in their character and customs, and particularly in their vices. Foreign university students, declared this eminent moralist, were responsible for the debauchery and drunkenness afflicting the Latin Quarter.

> The English are drunken cowards, the French proud, soft and effeminate; the Germans are quarrelsome and foul-mouthed, the Normans vain and haughty, the men of Poitou treacherous and miserly, the Burgundians stupid brutes, the Bretons frivolous and flighty, the Lombards miserly, spiteful and evil-minded, the Romans vicious and violent, the Sicilians tyrannical and cruel, the men of Brabant are thieves and the Flemings are debauched.[1]

These *de facto* associations quickly became publicly recognized corporations. Under the name of 'nations' (*nationes*) they were the mainstay of the oldest universities; medieval university organization is founded on its nations (see chapter 4).[2]

The nation to which scholars belonged depended primarily on their mother-tongue, and secondarily on their birthplace, cultural community, or

---

[1] Jacobus de Vitry, *Historia occidentalis. 7, de statu Parisiensis civitatis*, ed. J. F. Hinnebusch (Fribourg, 1972), 92 (Latin); English translation: D. C. Munro, *Translations and Reprints*, vol. II:3 (University of Pennsylvania, Philadelphia, n.d.), 19–20.

[2] General survey: Kibre, *Nations*.

shared history. Universities such as those of Bologna and Padua, which took in a steady stream of students from elsewhere, could follow this practice fairly strictly and form more than a dozen ultramontane and cismontane nations covering most European regions or provinces. Other Italian universities had to make do with only a few nations covering much larger (and therefore more arbitrary) geographical areas; the Perugia *studium*, for example, had three ultramontane nations, those of France, Germany, and Catalonia, and four cismontane nations, those of Rome, Tuscany, Ancona, and Sicily. These universities were nearer in organization to the University of Paris and its imitators (Prague, Leipzig, Vienna, and Louvain), which had only four nations, whose catchment area was somewhat fanciful or highly inconsistent. In Paris only the well-attended arts faculty had nations. The French nation comprised the masters and students of the Ile de France, the south of France, the Iberian peninsula, and Italy, Greece, and Asia Minor. The Norman nation drew its members from the geographical province of Rouen, and the Picard nation from north-eastern France and the old Low Countries as far as the Meuse. The English–German nation was a medley of students from all the other countries of Europe. Each nation had its 'provinces' of members from a particular region, but was of such mixed composition that there were never-ending conflicts and 'nationalist' frictions in that nominally international, not to say universal, institution, the university. It is hard to say how far nations within a university were instrumental in forging a common identity and 'nationalist' feeling, but clearly there was an *esprit de corps* among fellow-countrymen and the growth of nationalism had political repercussions. In the late Middle Ages political loyalties were often stronger than linguistic or ethnic ones, as is shown by the Burgundian and Armagnac factions at the end of the Hundred Years War. In 1470 400 subjects of the Burgundian Low Countries were ordered to leave the University of Paris although they were duly inscribed members of the German or Picard nation.[3] S. Stelling-Michaud has written that, from the fifteenth century onwards, Swiss national feeling was fostered by prolonged contact in universities between confederates from different cantons and walks of life.[4] In the first decades of the fifteenth century, the University of Prague was a hotbed of Czech nationalism and Hussite politics. Students from Bohemia, Moravia, and Hungary formed the Bohemian nation, which included both Czechs and students of German origin. All other students, the *extranei*, mainly from the Holy Roman Empire, formed the Bavarian, Saxon, and Polish nations (very loosely defined). Rivalry between the Czech and the German communities in Bohemia came to a head in the student nations of Prague. The Bohemian

---

[3] J. Verger, 'The University of Paris at the End of the Hundred Years' War', in *Universities in Politics*, 47–78.

[4] S. Stelling-Michaud, 'La Suisse et les universités européennes du XIIIe au XIVe siècle', *Revue universitaire suisse* (Sept. 1938), 160.

nation demanded three votes in the university council as against a single vote for the three other nations, and this demand was granted in 1409 by the Decree of Kutná Hora. The Germans refused to accept the decision and left Prague to found a new university in Leipzig, modelled on the University of Prague.[5] By then the attachment to nations had lost most of its meaning, for university recruiting was becoming regionalized, as will be shown below. The new universities of Heidelberg (1385) and Cologne (1388) did not adopt the system of nations.

Scotland, however, respected that tradition. The Universities of St Andrews (founded 1411), Glasgow (founded 1451), and Aberdeen (founded 1495) kept the four nations in the arts faculty but named them after Scottish districts – logically enough, as these universities recruited no foreigners before the Scottish Enlightenment of the eighteenth century (see volume II, chapter 10). Generally speaking, the names given to the nations are a pointer to university catchment areas. By analogy with Scotland, the nations of the Spanish *studia*, founded on the model of the University of Bologna, were named after those regions of the Iberian peninsula from which nearly all their students came. Oxford and Cambridge were a special case: there, division into nations was still more arbitrary than elsewhere, and indeed meant nothing, since more than 94 per cent of the students were English. The river Trent divided the northerners (*boreales*) from the southerners (*australes*). Scots had to register with the northerners, and the Irish, Welsh, and continentals with the southerners. The 'nationalities' in the two nations quarrelled so bitterly that as early as the end of the thirteenth century the government of the university took away all power and functions from the two nations.

Foreign students were also admitted to colleges reserved for natives of a particular region, province, or diocese. As in all colleges, entrance was at first restricted to poor students, but later well-off students were accepted against payment. In the thirteenth century the 'College of Constantinople' was founded in Paris on papal initiative, to house twenty or so young students from Greece and Asia Minor who were to train as missionaries to evangelize unbelievers in their home countries. This kind of 'national' college prospered most in the sixteenth and seventeenth centuries, at the time of the Reformation and Counter-Reformation. There were, however, very few students from regions under Byzantine or Turkish domination in the universities of medieval Europe. With rare exceptions they were in the Italian *studia*, particularly that of Padua, because this was the university of the Venetian republic, which had a thriving trade with the Byzantines and Turks.

In Paris the Germans, Swedes, Danes, Scots, Lombards, and other nationalities had their own colleges. In the Middle Ages only the Spaniards, the men of Avignon, and poor students from the dioceses of Limoges and Toul had

[5] S. Schumann, 'Die "nationes" an den Universitäten Prag, Leipzig und Wien. Ein Beitrag zur älteren Universitätsgeschichte', Ph.D., Berlin, 1974.

colleges in Bologna, and they were equally rare in other Italian university cities. In the fifteenth century regionalization and social change caused the colleges to decline.

A less known and less common form of student's association is the confraternity for nationals of a particular country. At the end of the thirteenth century a confraternity of clerics and students of the University of Paris called the 'Confraternity of Our Lady of Douai', composed of students and former students of the University of Paris who were natives of Douai, was formed to support young fellow-townsmen in their studies and forge permanent links between alumni of the University of Paris who came from Douai. In the fifteenth century the confraternity became a literary society. In 1331 the statutes of a similar association for alumni of the University of Paris and other universities were drawn up in Ypres. The list of members for the years 1330–1600 shows that five members of the confraternity studied in Paris (between 1330 and 1450), two in Cologne (between 1400 and 1450), one in Orléans (between 1330 and 1400), one in Montpellier (between 1400 and 1450), and twenty-two in Louvain (between 1425 and 1600).[6] The confraternity was founded to support natives of Ypres studying abroad, but when the first regional university was founded it lost this function and became merely an association of academics from Ypres.

FROM INTERNATIONALISM TO REGIONALISM

Preference for a regional university or for the nearest university became general at the end of the fourteenth century, and most marked in the fifteenth century, when every state and political or ecclesiastical unit tried to found a *studium* so that its citizens should study there instead of abroad. In this way it kept their intellectual and ideological training under observation and prevented the flight of capital abroad, detrimental to local traders and craftsmen.

This policy succeeded by enacting laws forbidding students from frequenting foreign universities on penalty of exclusion from public office. When the emperor Frederick II founded the Naples *studium* in 1224, to ensure its survivial he forbade his subjects to frequent any other *studium*. Similar protective measures were taken to benefit the University of Pavia in 1361, 1392, and 1412, and the University of Padua in 1407 and 1468. To revive the declining *studium* at Aix, the counts of Provence tried to oblige their subjects throughout the fifteenth century to study there and take their degrees there. Danes were allowed to study abroad after spending at least two years at the

---

[6] G. Espinas, *Les Origines de l'association*, vol. I, *Les Origines du droit d'association dans les villes de l'Artois et de la Flandre Française jusqu'au début du XVIe siècle* (Lille, 1942), 590–9; P. Trio, 'A Medieval Students' Confraternity at Ypres: the Notre Dame Confraternity of Paris Students', *History of Universities*, 5 (1985), 15–53. See also chapter 7, pp. 211–13.

recently founded University of Copenhagen (1498 and 1522).[7] For political and religious reaons, such regulations became more common in modern times.

Indifference to the plight of poor students was widespread in the fifteenth century (see chapter 7), and hindered academic mobility. Students were now predominantly laymen, and universities were becoming predominantly aristocratic institutions. The time was long past when a goliard, vagabond, or social outcast could expect any sympathy, or even understanding, from public opinion. Poor students (*pauperes*) now stayed at home, or made do with internal migration to a less expensive centre of learning, many of which were well endowed with colleges and scholarships, as in Cologne, Vienna, Leipzig, and Louvain. The 'academic pilgrimage' was now the preserve of the happy few, the sons of intellectual and financial élites. It is significant that as late as the sixteenth century 25 per cent of students in the Holy Roman Empire (9 per cent of them poor students) went to at least two universities. The second was usually another popular *studium* in the Holy Roman Empire.[8]

In the first centuries of the universities' existence, rulers encouraged the less wealthy to undergo dangers and fatigue to acquire a thorough intellectual and professional training in a distant *studium* in preparation for an honourable and lucrative career in the church or state. As the number of students – lay and clerical – from the upper reaches of society grew larger, such encouragement became less common. Poor students could still live abroad by taking service under a rich student and following him in his foreign studies. This procedure was especially popular at the time of the modern Grand Tour (see volume II, chapter 10).

Thirteenth-century students did not have a great choice of universities. Centres of higher education were few and far between, and fairly specialized. For the study of canon and civil law the best university was Bologna; then came a few other schools in Italy or Spain, or Montpellier or Orléans. The only famous schools of medicine were at Bologna, Padua, Montpellier, and Paris. For arts and theology the choice was theoretically wider, but in practice the most important schools were at Paris and Oxford. There are all too few exhaustive studies of university attendance by any one population in the twelfth and thirteenth centuries, and it is therefore not easy to say which were the preferred universities. One of the few studies of this kind is C. Renardy's work on the diocese of Liège between 1140 and 1350.[9] Only for 85 of the 700

---

[7] d'Irsay, *Histoire des universités*, vol. I, 201–2, 220, 238; Rashdall, *Universities*, vol. II, 21, 23, 189; Denifle, *Entstehung*, 71: E. Mornet, 'Le voyage d'études des jeunes nobles danois du XIVe siècle à la Réforme', *Journal des Savants* (1983), 299.

[8] Schwinges, *Universitätsbesucher*, 463–4; E. Schubert, 'Motive und Probleme deutscher Universitätsgründungen des 15. Jahrhunderts', in P. Baumgart and N. Hammerstein (eds.), *Beiträge zu Problemen deutscher Universitätsgrundungen der frühen Neuzeit* (Nendeln, 1978), 29, 34.

[9] C. Renardy, *Le Monde des maîtres universitaires du diocèse de Liège 1140–1350. Recherches sur sa composition et ses activités* (Paris, 1979), 175, 182.

university students from Liège who were listed was she able to identify the university they attended; 50 of them went to Paris (25 studied arts, 15 theology, 6 canon law, and 4 medicine); 14 to Bologna (canon or civil law 9, arts and medicine 1, not known 4); 7 to Orléans (civil law): 6 to Montpellier (canon and civil law 3, medicine 1, not known 2); 5 to Avignon (theology 3, canon and civil law 2); 3 to Toulouse (canon and civil law), and 1 to Angers (law). In the twelfth and thirteenth centuries, intellectuals from the Vaud attended university in Paris and Bologna, as far as can be ascertained from the few available sources. After the year 1300 they preferred the nearer and more accessible French law faculties in Orléans, Montpellier, and Avignon.[10]

With every new university foundation in the fourteenth and fifteenth centuries university recruitment became more regionalized, so much so that in the fifteenth century external migration actually came to a halt. Only under the influence of Italian humanism did the academic pilgrimage regain its old popularity. The statistics available for this period suggest that three-quarters of all students at the end of the Middle Ages were content to go to a regional university, usually the one nearest their homes. The journeys of the remainder, especially the English, Spaniards, French, and Italians, and to a lesser extent the Germans, were nearly always within their country of origin. As will be seen later, circumstances in the smaller countries were different. The real itinerant scholars – those who crossed Europe – were few, most of them young people keen to continue their studies in an internationally renowned university and in disciplines not taught in their own schools.

For example, at the start of the fourteenth century 301 doctors were registered in France; 57.8 per cent of them had studied in Paris, 35.2 per cent in Montpellier, 2.7 per cent in other French faculties of medicine, and 4.3 per cent abroad. At the end of the fifteenth century, of a total of 436 graduate physicians, the alumni of Montpellier formed only 6.3 per cent and those of Paris 47.5 per cent; other French universities now accounted for 27.6 per cent and foreign faculties for 8.5 per cent. Paris, and even more Montpellier, lost ground to Caen, Toulouse, and Avignon, or to Perpignan, Cahors, Angers, Dole, Nantes, Poitiers, Bordeaux, and Bourges. The graduates of foreign universities were nearly all foreigners who, after finishing their studies, practised in France. The nearby Louvain University was the most frequented foreign *studium* (17 graduates); then came Salerno and Bologna, each with 10 graduates. Other Italian *studia* produced only a few graduates.[11] W. Frijhoff has identified 5 inhabitants of the town of Zutphen in Gelderland who studied at university before 1350 (3 of them in Paris, 1 in Bologna, and 1 in

[10] J.-D. Morerod, 'Le Pays de Vaud et les Universités aux XIIe et XIIIe siècles', in A. Paravicini Bagliani (ed.), *Ecoles et vie intellectuelle à Lausanne au moyen âge* (Lausanne, 1987), 27–52, 63–71.

[11] D. Jacquart, *Le Milieu médical en France du XIIe au XVe siècle. En annexe second supplément au 'Dictionnaire' d'Ernest Wickersheimer* (Geneva, 1981), 75–6, 365–6.

Montpellier). Between 1350 and 1399 the number of university students identified rose to 18, of whom 8 went to Paris and 1 to Bologna; the others chose the new German universities nearer to their homes: Prague (1), Erfurt (2), Heidelberg (3), and Cologne (3). In the fifteenth century students from Zutphen showed a decided preference for German-speaking countries and for the arts faculty (in the case of 132 of the 142 university students). Four men of Zutphen registered with Louvain University, 1 with Bologna University, 1 with Orléans University, and 4 with the University of Paris; these were the few doctors and jurists produced by the town of Zutphen.[12] The pattern is much the same among graduates from Reichstadt Schweinfurt in Franconia. The first university student is reported in 1395. In the fifteenth century, with a few exceptions (Padua 2 students and Cracow 3 students), all the students of Schweinfurt went to German universities, preferring those nearest their homes: Erfurt (35 per cent of the 247 university students), Leipzig (30.8 per cent), and Vienna (17 per cent). In the sixteenth century some of them went to Bologna and Ferrara Universities, and to the new humanist universities such as Wittenberg; none yet went to a French university.[13]

By the fifteenth century, when large numbers of universities flourished in Europe, there might be several reasons for choosing a foreign *studium*: firstly, the discipline taught and the renown of the university; then came the geographical reasons of proximity and easy access, the economic tie of commercial links between towns and regions, and the political attractions (scholarships offered by the university, and political and dynastic relations). Some universities thrived for a time, not because they were famous as centres of learning or for the quality of their teaching, but for extraneous reasons. A notable example of this is the University of Avignon.

For political and religious reasons the *studium* at Avignon drew its students from many more nations than its intellectual worth warranted. As long as the popes were in Avignon (1309–78), despite the counter-attraction of the *studium* of the Roman curia the University of Avignon thrived on papal encouragement and the influx of student-clerics hoping for a fat papal benefice. Unfortunately, the first *rotulus* of any substance dates only from 1378, the last year of the 'second Babylonian Captivity' and the beginning of the Great Schism of 1378–1417. In 1378 Christendom split into two opposing camps, one of them supporting the pope in Rome, Urban VI, the other the pope in Avignon, Clement VII. States and universities supported one or the other; France, Spain, and Scotland gave their unqualified support to the pope in Avignon; Italy, the Holy Roman Empire, England, and the Nordic coun-

[12] W. Frijhoff, 'Le rôle des études universitaires dans une société locale: la ville de Zutphen en Gueldre du moyen âge au début du XIXe siècle. Premier bilan d'une recherche', in *Actes de la VIème session scientifique internationale, Cracovie mai 1987*, Zeszyty Naukowe Uniwersytetu Jagiellońskiego, Prace Historyczne (Cracow, in press).

[13] M. Mahr, 'Bildungs- und sozialstruktur der Reichstadt Schweinfurt', dissertation, Würzburg, 1978, 217–22.

tries no less vigorously supported the pope in Rome. Some countries – Portugal, Iceland, Sicily, and some dioceses in the empire – wavered and changed their allegiance. The General Councils of Constance and Basle only made the rivalry worse by introducing voting by nation and not by diocese. The *rotuli* for the years 1378–9 and 1393–4 mention students at the University of Avignon as coming from 194 French dioceses on the western borders of the Holy Roman Empire, and from the Iberian peninsula, but hardly any from dioceses professing obedience to the popes of Rome.[14] When the Great Schism ended, Avignon lost its international attraction and the *studium* became a centre training local jurists, like other universities in the south of France at that time.

The Schism nevertheless had serious consequences for European universities, which had been obliged to trim their sails to suit the policy of their dioceses. Paris was one of the principal sufferers from the rift in the church. The nations of France and Normandy, and the three superior faculties, rallied to Clement VII, whereas most members of the English–German and Picard nations opted for Urban VI. Disputes in the German nation reached such a point that in 1383 its masters and students left Paris for the German universities of Prague, Vienna, Heidelberg, Erfurt, and Cologne; among them were Marsilius of Inghen and Henry of Langenstein, to whom Heidelberg and Vienna respectively owe their brilliant reputation of that time (see p. 436). Fewer German and Scandinavian scholars went to other French universities or to the Urbanist Italian *studia*. Instead they attended the German universities that came into being all over the empire. As these schools usually taught only arts, canon law, and theology, students of medicine and civil law who wanted first-class teaching still had to make their academic pilgrimage abroad to study – in Italy, and after 1417 in France – after preliminary studies at the nearest university in their homeland.

To take as an example law students of the Teutonic Order in the fifteenth century, 22 of the 44 university students studied in the empire, most of them in Leipzig and Vienna, 27 or 28 in Italy (Bologna 11, Padua 7, Perugia 4, Rome 4, Siena 1 or 2), and 1 at Orléans. They were simultaneously representatives of the Order and carried out diplomatic missions.[15] Nearly all the Carmelites of the German province, however, most of them students of arts or theology, attended only *studia* in the empire (of 3,349 registered students, 2,364 of them attended the *studia* in Vienna, Cologne, Louvain, Trier and Mainz between 1281 and 1555). They ceased to attend French universities at the beginning of

---

[14] J. Verger, 'L'université d'Avignon au temps de Clément VII', in *Genèse et débuts du Grand Schisme d'Occident* (Paris, 1978), 4–5.

[15] H. Boockmann, 'Die Rechtsstudenten des deutschen Ordens', in *Festschrift H. Heimpel*, vol. II (Göttingen, 1972), 364–5. The total number of registrations is higher than the total number of students because several students went to more than one university.

the Great Schism, and did not return to them later. Italian faculties of theology were not popular with ultramontane students.[16]

THE HOLY ROMAN EMPIRE

Nevertheless, the subjects of the Holy Roman Empire were the greatest academic pilgrims of the Middle Ages and modern times. Before the first university was founded in the Empire, would-be university students had no choice but to leave their own country. The *Authentica Habita* constitution of 1155 (see chapter 3) reflects the German emperor's anxiety to have the services of experts in imperial Roman law, then recently rediscovered. From the end of the twelfth century until the second half of the seventeenth century, the *iter italicum* was popular with subjects of the Empire. Bologna was their first choice in the Middle Ages, followed by Padua and in the fifteenth century by Ferrara and Pavia; Pisa and Siena did not become really popular until the second half of the sixteenth century. German students attended these universities mainly to study canon and civil law and medicine (the German universities specialized more in arts and theology, and some of them in canon law). As will be shown later, English students flocked to Paris in the twelfth and thirteenth centuries; but in the fifteenth century the Germans began to oust the English in the English–German nation. The foundation of the first university in the Empire, at Prague in 1347, did not at first much change the pattern of academic pilgrimage, which remained unchanged until the Great Schism, but the newly founded German universities were popular with less affluent or more stay-at-home students, for whom foreign travel was not possible but who wanted to study at university. Our figures for Bologna are eloquent of this. In Bologna 3,230 law students registered as members of the German nation of the university between 1289 and 1499. Before 1300 their average number was 45; in the fourteenth and more particular in the fifteenth century the average fell to below 10 a year and at the beginning of the sixteenth century rose to about 30.[17] These figures are roughly equal to those of the English–German or German nation of the arts faculty in Paris. Between 1333 and 1494 approximately 3,300 members of the German nation sat for examinations at the arts faculty in Paris. According to M. Tanaka's meticulous research,[18] 1,806 bachelors were admitted to that nation between 1333 and 1452; 1,116 of them (61.8 per cent) were natives of the Holy Roman Empire, and 42 per cent of the ecclesiastical province of Cologne (759 of the 1,116, one-quarter of whom came from the diocese of Utrecht). The Scots sent 229

[16] F.-B. Lickteig, *The German Carmelites at the Medieval Universities* (Rome, 1981), 416–17.
[17] A. Luschin von Ebengreuth, 'Vorläufige Mitteilungen über die Geschichte deutscher Rechtshörer in Italien', *Sitzungsberichte der Wiener Akademie der Wissenschaften, Phil.-Hist. Klasse*, 127 (1892), 19–21.
[18] M. Tanaka, 'La nation anglo-allemande de l'université de Paris à la fin du moyen âge', thesis, Paris, 1983, 30ff.

students (12.6 per cent), the province of Denmark–Sweden 79 (4.3 per cent), the province of Bohemia 18, the province of Hungary 11, and the province of Poland 4 bachelors. As these figures show, and as J. Verger and L. W. Brockliss have shown from other calculations, the University of Paris was not particularly international in the fifteenth century, when only 12 per cent of all the bachelors in canon law came from other than French dioceses.[19]

Foreigners regarded the law university of Orléans as the faculty of civil law of the University of Paris. The two cities were closely associated and very many alumni of Orléans University had previously studied in Paris, without necessarily following an entire university curriculum there. The German nation in Orléans attracted fairly large numbers of young aristocrats, most of them laymen intending a career in provincial and central government. Between 1444 and 1499 that nation had 225 members, most of them from the old Low Countries; between 1500 and 1546 their number rose to 1,040, among them a growing proportion of Germans.[20] A number of Germans were also to be found in the Roman law *studia* of Angers and Poitiers, the canon law and medical *studia* at Montpellier, the canon and civil law *studia* at Avignon, and the Burgundian (later Habsburg) University at Dole. Other French universities attracted Germans only occasionally.

From 1370 onwards, most students from the Swiss cantons attended the universities of the Holy Roman Empire, particularly those of Vienna, Heidelberg, and Erfurt. In the fifteenth century many Swiss students also went to Cracow University because of the close trade links of the time between eastern Switzerland (especially the city of St Gallen) and Poland. Students from French-speaking Switzerland still went in large numbers to French universities. Until the mid-fourteenth century Bologna enjoyed a virtual monopoly in the teaching of civil law; next in importance came Paris, and then Montpellier. After 1460 Basle took over. S. Stelling-Michaud notes that, between 1370 and 1470, 1,488 Swiss students attended foreign universities and 400 attended Basle University. Between 1470 and 1525 Swiss students at Basle University numbered 1,100 and those at other *studia* 1,900.[21]

THE NORDIC COUNTRIES AND EASTERN EUROPE

Students from Scandinavian countries, Iceland, Ireland, and Scotland had to go abroad for university training because they had no *studia* in their own country, at least until the end of the Middle Ages. Even then, if their country

[19] J. Verger, 'Le recrutement géographique des universités françaises au début du XVe siècle d'après les suppliques de 1403', *Mélanges d'Archéologie et d'Histoire publiés par l'Ecole Française de Rome*, 82 (1970), 895; L. W. Brockliss, 'Patterns of Attendance at the University of Paris 1400–1800', *Historical Journal*, 3 (1978), 527.

[20] H. de Ridder-Symoens, 'Les origines géographique et sociale des étudiants de la nation germanique de l'ancienne université d'Orléans (1444–1546). Aperçu général', in *Universities in the Late Middle Ages*, 455–74.

[21] Stelling-Michaud, 'Suisse et universités' (note 4), 148–60.

possessed a university it did not keep young people at home. In most cases they were content with a general training in their own arts faculties – the only efficient faculties there before the sixteenth century. Historians of those countries, particularly the northern countries, have thoroughly investigated their ancestors' academic pilgrimage.[22]

Once the Nordic countries were converted to Christianity between the early eleventh century (in Denmark, Iceland, and Norway) and the mid-twelfth century (Sweden in the early twelfth century and Finland in the mid-twelfth century), the newly installed church needed ecclesiastical dignitaries learned in Roman law – to administer it, for the cure of souls, and to found an educational system. In 1219 Pope Honorius III encouraged them to study abroad. Their academic pilgrimage falls into two main stages, one from 1200 to 1350, and the other from 1350 to 1530, the beginning of the Reformation.

In the first period the University of Paris, followed by the University of Bologna, attracted by far the most students, three-quarters of them going to Paris and the other quarter to Bologna. Fourteenth-century records show the names of 128 alumni in Paris and 36 in Bologna. There are some traces – but until the seventeenth century no continuous flow – of Scandinavian students in Oxford and Cambridge in the thirteenth century. It would be misleading to judge by the few Scandinavian scholars abroad, for the Scandinavian countries were thinly populated and those scholars were the entire ecclesiastical élite – bishops, canons, and clerics in the king's service – almost without exception members of the wealthier classes, that is, of the aristocracy.

Once the universities of the Holy Roman Empire were founded, academic pilgrimage patterns underwent great changes. Prague, founded in 1348, supplanted Paris, just as Leipzig, founded in 1409, supplanted Prague, the Scandinavians having followed the Germans in their exodus from Prague to Leipzig. From 1419 onwards Rostock, being nearer, was the favourite *studium*, then in order of preference came Greifswald, founded in 1456, and Cologne, founded in 1388. The importance of the Universities of Rostock and Greifswald in the Hanseatic League will be enlarged on below (p. 301). Orléans took the place of Bologna in training experts in civil law, and few northern students went to Paris any more. The foundation of the Universities of Uppsala in 1477 and Copenhagen in 1479 did little to disturb established habit; both universities probably met the growing demand for academic training among the lower classes, for at that time the demand for university graduates, lay or ecclesiastical, far exceeded supply. Social élites continued to prefer study abroad. Figures of registered students in Uppsala and Copen-

---

[22] S. Bagge, 'Nordic Students at Foreign Universities until 1660', *Scandinavian Journal of History*, 9 (1983), 287–318; J. Pinborg, 'Danish Students 1450–1535 and the University of Copenhagen', *Cahiers de l'Institut du moyen âge grec et latin de l'université de Copenhague*, 37 (1981), 74–81.

hagen Universities at that time are not available, but there is ample information on the number of students at foreign universities between 1350 and 1530. Denmark had 2,146 students abroad, Sweden 724, Norway 219, and Finland 97. Some indication of the large numbers of Scandinavians studying at foreign universities, and of the importance of their studies, is that nearly all bishops of Nordic dioceses were graduates of a foreign university, usually Paris and, rather less often, Bologna. More than half the canons in cathedral chapters appear to have been at least masters of arts, who before the latter half of the fourteenth century graduated in Paris, and later in the schools of north-east Germany. These alumni helped to extend European culture to the Nordic countries, and the jurists among them introduced Roman–canon law into the church and state.

The *studiosi* of eastern Europe had similar academic difficulties and overcame them in the same way. Until Cracow University was founded in 1364, Prague University, at that time not a flourishing one, was the nearest *studium* for Lithuanians, Poles, and Hungarians. Until the seventeenth century Hungarians and Lithuanians had for all but a short time (1389 – c. 1450 at the University of Buda, Budapest, 1367 – c. 1400 at the University of Pécs, and 1465 – c. 1492 at the University of Pozsony, Bratislava) to go to a foreign university for their degree. Like the Scots, northerners, and Germans, young east Europeans were fervent academic pilgrims. Neither Prague nor Cracow, nor other more ephemeral centres, sufficed to keep ambitious students in their home country. Available information shows that, throughout the Middle Ages, the Universities of Bologna, Padua, and Paris took in a steady trickle of students from those countries, even though many of them were isolated individuals. In Bologna and Padua there was a nation of Bohemians, Hungarians, and Poles; in Paris the English–German nation numbered several provinces, one of them for students of Upper Germany. In the fourteenth century a few Bohemians even crossed the Channel to study philosophy and theology in Oxford. 'The high reputation which Oxford then enjoyed at the Bohemia University is illustrated by a Statute of Prague passed in 1367, providing that students who dictated books to their fellow-students were to dictate only works compiled by masters from the illustrious universities of Prague, Paris or Oxford.'[23] The condemnation of Wyclif's works and the suppression of the Lollard movement severed the ties between Prague and Oxford. Towards the end of the fifteenth century eastern Europeans went in greater numbers to study in Paris and Italy. Towards 1500 seven messengers were employed in maintaining contacts between Hungarians studying in Paris and their families in Hungary. Most Hungarian students at that time went, however, only to the Universities of Vienna and Cracow. Astonishingly few

---

[23] R. F. Young, 'Bohemian Scholars and Students at the English Universities from 1347 to 1750', *English Historical Review*, 38 (1923), 72.

Hungarians managed to graduate, but according to A. Kubinyi[24] there was little demand for graduates in Hungarian public services in the Middle Ages, even in the church. Licentiates and doctors of law were to be found principally in the more important posts. University studies were regarded as intellectual training for the sons of the urban bourgeoisie, as a means of learning foreign languages, making contacts, and cultivating group loyalties. Kubinyi believes that is why the Hungarian universities could not survive until the Hungarian establishment came to prefer graduates to patricians.

In Poland young people began their studies in Cracow or in a neighbouring university before going abroad to graduate. They were few in number, because in Poland too there was no real progress in professionalizing the public services until the sixteenth century (see chapter 8).

GREAT BRITAIN

The Scots are known as great travellers. Diplomats, mercenaries, priests and pilgrims, merchants, craftsmen, and students, all went to the continent.

> Mark you what the proverb says
> Of Scotsmen, rats and lice;
> The whole world over take your ways
> You'll find them still, I guess.[25]

Dr Watt has traced about 1,100 Scottish graduates between 1150 and 1410, when the first Scottish university was founded in St Andrews.[26] Available sources are so incomplete that this figure is certainly less than the real number. The foundation of national universities did nothing to reduce Scottish migration and even seems to have had the opposite effect. The universities most frequented by Scotsmen were those of Paris (260 names between 1340 and 1410), Orléans (60 alumni), and Avignon (34 alumni). The first traces of Scots, as of Scandinavians, at the University of Paris date from the beginning of the university. Contacts between France and Scotland were confirmed by the 'Auld Alliance', the treaty of peace and mutual aid against the common enemy, England, concluded in 1295 and several times renewed until 1560. At all costs, Scots avoided going to Oxford and Cambridge *studia* – their numbers there did not exceed 1 per cent of all the students – and they therefore had to cross the Channel. They preferred Paris for arts, theology, and canon law and Orléans for canon and civil law. The Scots had a college

---

24 A. Kubinyi, 'Städische Bürger und Universitätsstudien in Ungarn am Ende des Mittelalters', in E. Maschke and J. Sydow (eds.), *Stadt und Universität im Mittelalter und in der früheren Neuzeit* (Sigmaringen, 1977), 161–5.
25 Quoted in A. I. Dunlop, *Scots Abroad in the Fifteenth Century*, Historical Association Pamphlet, 124 (London, 1942), 3; English translation of a French rhyme published in Pierre le Jolle, *Description de la ville d'Amsterdam, etc.* (Amsterdam, 1666), 25.
26 D. E. R. Watt, *A Biographical Dictionary of Scottish Graduates to A.D. 1410* (Oxford, 1977).

in Paris, founded in 1325, which was far from sufficient for their growing numbers. That they formed part of the English–German nation did little to make them less uncomfortable bedfellows. According to the chronicles of the English–German nation,

> The root and origin of almost all the scandals committed by [the Scottish] students was vagabondage. There was no adequate provision of residential colleges for Scottish scholars, who were thus the more prone to remove from one master's house to another, to the obvious loosening of academic disciplines. In 1469, therefore, certain masters of the province of Scotland were empowered to choose an inquisitor to visit and examine the morals of the scholars.[27]

The Scots flocked to Paris before and after their exodus when the English occupied the city in 1411. Between 1466 and 1500 approximately 350 candidates for the arts examinations appear in the registers of the English–German nation.[28] In Orléans the Scots had a nation of their own; the few English scholars formed part of the German nation. The Scottish nation was in decline because of the political situation in the early fifteenth century. As stated above, the fillip given to the *studium* of Avignon by the presence of the popes did not last.

The Hundred Years War brought about great changes in the Scots' *iter gallicum*. When Paris fell into English hands in 1411 the Scots left Paris for Cologne, and from 1425 onwards for Louvain, and continued to attend these universities until the Reformation. In Cologne, 91 Scottish students registered between 1400 and 1449 and 257 between 1450 and 1499; in Louvain 160 Scottish students registered between 1426 and 1484, and 182 between 1485 and 1527.[29] There were economic reasons for their preference for these universities; the most important Scottish commercial bank in Europe was at Bruges, and that city allowed Scottish merchants to send goods tax-free to their sons, near relatives, and friends studying in Paris, Louvain, or Cologne.[30] There had been an English nation in Bologna and Padua since the thirteenth century, but there were few Scottish scholars in Italy in the Middle Ages. The English conquests in France had driven some Scots farther south, where, however, their numbers did not much increase until the sixteenth century. Only a few dozen names have been found in the archives for the Middle Ages

[27] D. E. R. Watt, 'Scottish Student Life Abroad in the Fourteenth Century', *Scottish Historical Review*, 59 (1980), 7.

[28] J.-B. Coissac, 'Les étudiants écossais à l'université de Paris', *Revue internationale de l'enseignement*, 71 (1917), 26–7.

[29] J. H. Baxter, 'Scottish Students at Louvain University 1425–1484', *Scottish Historical Review*, 25 (1928), 327–34; A. Schillings, *Matricule de l'Université de Louvain, III. 1485–1527*, 2 vols. (Brussels, 1958, 1962), vol. II, tables, s.v.; H. Keussen, *Die Matrikel der Universität Köln* (Cologne, 1928, 1919, 1931), vol. III, tables, s.v.; Schwinges, *Universitätsbesucher*, 236–8.

[30] 'excepto eo quod predicti mercatores poterunt mittere suis filiis aut parentibus et amicis studentibus in universitatibus Parisiensi, Coloniensi et Lovaniensi', d.d. 1–4–1470 n.s.: L. Gilliodts-Van Severen, *Inventaire des archives de la ville de Bruges. Section première. Inventaire des Chartes*, vol. I (Bruges, 1876), 39.

for the Universities of Bologna, Padua, Pavia, and Ferrara.[31] It is noteworthy that from the fourteenth century onwards, and particularly in the fifteenth century, many Scottish graduates stayed on the continent as teachers or members of religious orders. Frisian graduates too, like the Scots, were more numerous than their national population and the backward state of their urban economy would suggest, and had to seek a career abroad once they had their university degree.

The Irish appear to have taken much less interest in university education. For the whole of the Middle Ages, only thirty names of students from *Hibernia* (Ireland) have been found in documents pertaining to the University of Paris, and hardly any such names in other continental universities. M. H. Somers has identified forty-seven students from Ireland at Oxford University in the thirteenth century, fifty-seven in the fourteenth, and eighty-three in the fifteenth century, most of them of Anglo-Norman extraction.[32] Few Irishmen took part in the European academic pilgrimage.

Throughout the Middle Ages, English students studied mainly at the Universities of Oxford and Cambridge, but towards 1200 there were large numbers of English students in the French schools. Until 1215, 38 per cent of all masters of arts in Paris were of English origin;[33] thereafter, for political reasons, their number so far declined that the English nation had to change its name to English–German nation and then to German nation. In the Middle Ages the universities of the Holy Roman Empire had little attraction for English and Irish students, of whom there were not more than a dozen in the various *studia*. Not many Englishmen went as far as Italy either; there were only 20 English names in the thirteenth century, 55 in the fourteenth, 125 in the fifteenth, and 55 names between 1500 and 1525.[34] These English alumni of the Italian universities were, however, of remarkable calibre. At an early date they (William Grey, Robert Flemmyng, Thomas Linacre, William Grocyn, William Lily, John Colet, Cuthbert Tunstall) introduced Italian humanism and the teaching of Greek into England. Something similar happened in other European countries, such as Portugal, Poland, and the Low Countries, where a few graduates of Italian universities introduced humanism into their native land in the fifteenth century.

Similarly, continental students showed little interest in the English *studia*. Only 2 per cent of the students at Oxford and Cambridge came from the Continent, and only 4 per cent were Welsh, Irish, and Scottish. Most of these

---

[31] R. J. Mitchell, 'Scottish Law Students in Italy in the Later Middle Ages', *Juridical Review*, 49 (1937), 19–24.

[32] M. H. Somers, 'Irish Scholars in the Universities of Paris and Oxford before 1500', Ph.D., City University of New York, 1979.

[33] J. W. Baldwin, 'Masters of Paris from 1179 to 1215. A Social Perspective', in *Renaissance and Renewal*, 148–51.

[34] G. B. Parks, *The English Traveller to Italy*, vol. I, *The Middle Ages (to 1525)* (Rome, 1954), 423–7.

foreigners were members of the mendicant orders studying for a degree in theology. The policy of those orders was to place monks as students in all university cities of Europe where they had a cloister and/or *studium* of their own.

THE IBERIAN PENINSULA

Intellectual relations between England and Spain were close in the twelfth and thirteenth centuries because of the Toledo translators' school, where Englishmen like Adelard of Bath, Robert of Chester, Alfred the Great, and Michael Scot were active, but intellectual and academic relations between the Iberian schools and those of north-western Europe did not endure. Few Spaniards or Portuguese went beyond Paris, where they were inscribed in the French nation; university lists from German-speaking countries mention no more than five Spaniards or Portuguese. Although Spain did not lack *studia generalia* teaching civil and canon law on the model of Bologna, Spaniards – mostly Catalans – and Portuguese went on to continue their studies at the universities of the south of France (Avignon, Toulouse, and Montpellier), often using them as stages on their way to Italy. Bologna was the most important university city outside the Iberian peninsula – so important, indeed, that in 1364 one of the few colleges for foreigners, the Collegio di Spagna (which is still in operation), was founded there, and served as a model for the many colleges founded in the Spanish *studia* in the fifteenth and sixteenth centuries. Siena, too, attracted the Portuguese. Around 1500 the other Italian schools were also popular with Spaniards and Portuguese. Available figures suggest that hundreds of Iberian students attended the Italian *studia* before 1500, and that about one hundred attended the French schools. For the thirteenth century alone, more than a hundred references to Catalans in Bologna have been found.[35] Of course there were intensive contacts between the Spanish and Portuguese universities. Salamanca had so many Portuguese students in the Middle Ages that it could almost be considered a Portuguese university.[36]

Apart from Catalans and Basques, hardly any *studiosi* living east of the Pyrenees attended Spanish universities.

[35] R. Kagan, *Students and Society in Early Modern Spain* (Baltimore/London, 1975), 63, 65; J. B. Pérez, 'La Tradición española en Bolonia', *Revista de Archivos, Bibliotecas y Museos*, 3rd series, 33 (1929), 174–84; J. Miret y Sans, 'Escolares catalans al estudi de Bolonia en la XIIIe centuria', *Boletin de la real Academia de Buenas Letras de Barcelona*, 59 (1915), 154; V. Rau, 'Studenti ed eruditi portoghesi in Italia nel secolo XV', *Estudos italianos em Portugal*, 36 (1973), 7–73; M. Peset, 'Estudiantes hispanos en las Universidades francesas, siglo XIV', in *Estudios dedicados a Juan Peset Aleixandre*, vol. III (Valencia, 1982), 273–94.

[36] M. Peset, *Interrelaciones entre las universidades españolas y portuguesas en los primeros siglos de su historia* (Coimbra, 1983).

ITALY AND FRANCE

The Italians were more stay-at-home than the Spaniards, but as is clear throughout this chapter their schools attracted hosts of young scholars. Internal migration in Italy was intense. The Alps certainly formed a frontier, academic if not political. The Sicilians congregated mainly in Bologna and Padua, in numbers little affected by the foundation of the University of Catania in 1434 (1444). Available sources record 53 Sicilian students at Bologna between 1400 and 1442, 68 there between 1434 and 1499, and 101 and 109 at Padua for the same periods.[37] The few Italian students to be found beyond the Alps were in a few universities in frontier regions, in Basle and Ingolstadt and in the Mediterranean region. The republic of Venice obliged its students to study at Padua, except for those wanting to go *ultramontes*, i.e. north of the Alps; but this did not stimulate Venetian youth to go abroad.[38] Many of the Italian itinerant scholars belonged to religious orders. Before the latter half of the fourteenth century regular and secular clergy wishing to take a degree in theology had no choice but to cross the Alps, and were naturally drawn to Paris by the renown as teachers of Albertus Magnus and Thomas Aquinas.

Conversely, Italian teachers were much sought after by ultramontane universities in the fifteenth century. Certainly the spread of humanism in the fifteenth and sixteenth centuries would have been impossible but for the *iter italicum* of hundreds or thousands of students and learned men from all over Europe. Disciples of humanism sought to introduce the new culture into their own country by all possible means. By offering attractive conditions they attracted Italian humanists – second-rate in Italy but first-rate elsewhere – to teach in their universities – at Salamanca and Lérida, Cracow, Paris, Orléans and the south of France, Oxford and Cambridge, Erfurt, Leipzig, Strasburg, Basle, Louvain, and Vienna.[39]

Academic relations between Italy and the south of France date from the earliest times. In the twelfth century several Italian jurists trained in Bologna worked and taught in the universities of southern France. In the thirteenth century the influx was mainly of students from southern France into Bologna, where the two ultramontane nations of Provence and Gascony/Auvergne were there to welcome them. In the fifteenth century Italy lost its attraction for scholars from southern France and for Frenchmen in general, for the Great Schism hindered contacts with Italian intellectual centres. Moreover,

37 N. Rodolico, 'Siciliani nello studio di Bologna nel medio evo', *Archivio Storico Siciliano*, new series, 20 (1895), 89–228; F. Marletta, 'I Siciliani nello Studio di Padova nel Quattrocento', *Archivio Storico per la Sicilia*, 2–3 (1936–7), 147–211.

38 R. E. Ohl, 'The University of Padua, 1405–1509: an International Community of Students and Professors', Ph.D., University of Pennsylvania, 1980, 39, 53.

39 Many examples in R. Weiss, 'Italian Humanism in Western Europe 1460–1520', in F. J. Jacobs (ed.), *Italian Renaissance Studies* (London, 1960), 69–93.

the growth of French national unity, and consequently of government administration and royal justice, encouraged and indeed obliged future officials to take their degrees at a local university. Only in the last years of the fifteenth century and the first half of the sixteenth century did Italian humanism bring the *iter italicum* again into fashion (for this pan-European phenomenon see volume II, chapter 10).

Students from central and northern France had no particular liking for travel. If they did go abroad to study they generally chose a not-to-distant *studium* – Cologne, for the men of Champagne and Louvain for students from the border regions of the Low Countries. Occasionally young French scholars were encouraged to study abroad for circumstantial reasons – large numbers of French students came to Pavia because of French political influence in the duchy of Milan at the beginning of the sixteenth century, and also because Pavia was the first university in Italian territory for travellers entering Italy from the Riviera. Dynastic relations between two countries could also temporarily affect the influx of scholars – large numbers of Spanish students came to Louvain in the first half of the sixteenth century, not only because of the success of the humanist College of the Three Languages (Latin, Greek, and Hebrew), founded in 1517 at the suggestion of Erasmus. The joint rulers, Philip the Handsome and Charles V, improved relations between the Low Countries, Spain and Portugal (only 5 Iberian students were registered at Louvain between 1426 and 1485, but 46 between 1486 and 1527, and 180 between 1527 and 1559);[40] but dynastic ties were not reciprocal; few subjects of the Habsburgs from the Low Countries ventured beyond the Pyrenees to study. The Dole *studium*, which all Burgundian subjects regarded as 'their' university, attracted more students, and was often a transit university on the road to Italy.

TRAVELLING CONDITIONS

Academic pilgrimage was very dependent on roads. When international trade revived in the eleventh and twelfth centuries, a network of roads was made. Tracks were given a hard surface and sometimes metalled, and bridges were built at the busiest fords.[41] Nevertheless, the poor quality of roads, bridges, lodgings, and vehicles remained a major problem for travellers until the eighteenth century. Robbers on land or water, undisciplined soldiery, prostitutes, vagabonds, and bad weather or other natural disasters added to the dangers of travel. In populous areas travellers arrived every evening at a town

---

[40] H. de Ridder-Symoens, 'Internationalismus versus Nationalismus an Universitäten um 1500 nach zumeist südniederländischen Quellen', in F. Seibt and W. Eberhardt (eds.), *Europa 1500* (Munich, 1986), 408.

[41] There is an abundant literature on travel in the Middle Ages. Some examples: N. Ohler, *Reisen im Mittelalter* (Munich/Zurich, 1986); A. Newton (ed.), *Travel and Travellers of the Middle Ages* (London, 1968); M. N. Boyer, 'Travel in Medieval France (1300–1450)' Ph.D., Columbia University, 1958.

or village offering adequate lodging and food – Avignon at the time of the popes had some sixty inns with beds. The most frequented universities of Europe in the Middle Ages were all in thickly inhabited and easily accessible areas. Travellers on foot could do 30 to 40 km (20 to 25 miles) a day and horsemen 50 to 60 km (30 to 40 miles). Couriers managed 100 km (60 miles) a day.

The most accessible roads were the Roman ones, disused in the early Middle Ages but restored when international trade revived.[42] Several Italian universities were connected by the Aurelian, Aemilian, and Flaminian Ways. To reach Italy a traveller could travel via France or follow the 'Dutche road' or 'merchandese road' through Germany. For Englishmen and continentals living west of the Schelde, the best route – military operations permitting – was from Paris to Dijon and thence to Lausanne and the Mont Cenis or the Great Saint Bernard Pass, and then along the Aemilian Way to Pavia or Bologna. Another easy road was from Paris to Orléans (the first paved highway in France) and then to Lyon, whence travellers could continue towards the Mont Cenis or follow the Rhône valley to Avignon, and then take the road along the coast before picking up the Aurelian Way in Genoa for Pisa, Siena, or Rome. As the Po was navigable as far as Ferrara, which was connected by canal to Venice, students could easily reach the Universities of Padua and Ferrara by following the French itinerary. Sir Richard Guylforde, an English pilgrim, noted in his diary in 1506 that his journey from Rye (near Hastings on the English coast) to Venice took him 37 days: 26 days overland, 6 by water, and 5 days' rest. The journey via Germany took about as long, as Richard Torkyngton, also a pilgrim to Jerusalem, recorded in 1517. He reached Venice in 38½ days (23 days overland, 8 by water and 7½ days' rest).[43] From the Channel the Rhine road went to the university cities of Louvain, Cologne, Heidelberg, Strasburg, and Basle before reaching Milan and the Aemilian Way by the Saint Gotthard Pass. Farther east the Venetian trade route crossed the Brenner to join the Hanseatic roads.

The Hanseatic League vastly improved the road system[44] by building and maintaining roads linking the towns that were members of the League. Transport by the North Sea and the Baltic and on inland waterways was no less important. Rivers were made navigable by locks and similar facilities, and by building canals between natural waterways. There were no special arrangements for passenger transport; travellers had to make do with what little comfort they could get. Nevertheless, travel by barge had its advantages, being less tiring than walking, more comfortable than an unsprung cart or

[42] W. Götz, *Die Verkehrswege im Altertum und Mittelalter. Die Verkehrswege im Dienst des Welthandels* (Stuttgart, 1888; reprint, Amsterdam, 1969).

[43] Parks, *English Traveller* (note 34), 495–501.

[44] F. Bruns and H. Weczerka, *Hansische Handelsstrassen*, 2 vols., vol. I, Text, vol. II, Atlas (Cologne/Graz, 1962), maps A and B; P. Dollinger, *The German Hansa* (London, 1970).

carriage, and fairly cheap. In moderately flat country travel was quicker downstream. Many students reached their university by the Hanseatic trade routes. From London to Bruges they could follow a trading caravan along the Rhine to Basle (as stated above), or bear east to Frankfurt-on-Main and the Brenner and then direct to Padua and Ferrara. Crossing the Alps was arduous even in the summer. Pero Tafur, a Portuguese pilgrim, wrote in 1438:

> The next day I arrived at the foot of the St Gotthard Pass, high in the Alps. It was the end of August when the snow melts in the great heat, making the crossing very perilous. An ox, accustomed to the ways, goes in front drawing a long rope. To this a trailer is attached, on which the passenger sits, holding his horse behind him by the reins. In this way, if any accident happens, only the ox is imperilled.[45]

From Cologne several roads led direct to Rostock, Leipzig, Erfurt, Prague, or Cracow. Northerners could travel down the Elbe to Leipzig or Prague or take the road from Stralsund or Danzig to Cracow. Rostock University, founded in 1419, is the only university that can be called Hanseatic. Its students were nearly all from the area of the Hanseatic League – the Baltic and Scandinavian countries and the Low Countries. The Greifswald *studium*, founded in 1456, was especially popular with Scandinavians, but was never as popular as Rostock with students from the western Hanseatic cities, who at one time in the fifteenth century accounted for one-quarter of all the students registered there.

Students going to Italy or Spain could perhaps follow in the train of a personage of high rank – a sovereign, nobleman, dignitary of the church, or diplomat – or join a merchants' caravan or group of pilgrims bound for Rome, Jerusalem, or Santiago de Compostela. Four great itineraries crossed France towards the holy shrine of Santiago de Compostela on the western edge of Christendom, taking in the university cities of Paris, Orléans, Bourges, Poitiers, Bordeaux, and Cahors. From the fifteenth century onwards, travel guides became popular, written mainly for pilgrims but of course equally useful to students. There is evidence to show that students travelled in groups for safety and comfort: university registers show that several scholars from the same town or region registered at the same time on the university rolls. Other *studiosi* joined the group in its journey. University messengers used the same routes, and where there was no messenger service students resorted to merchants, fellow students, or visiting fellow-countrymen. From the thirteenth century onwards, young people studying in university cities that were also busy trading centres had money sent to them through bankers with offices and correspondents in the big European trading centres.

Travellers had to face not only the dangers of the road but also customs

[45] Quoted in M. Rowling, *Everyday Life of Medieval Travellers* (London/New York, 1971), 38.

dues, tolls, and other taxes, levies, and exactions. Centuries before, the Emperor Frederick I Barbarossa had tried to spare them all these in his *Authentica Habita* constitution, and later sovereigns had granted many privileges protecting foreign students in many different ways. Even in time of political tension or military operations, sovereigns from the Emperor Frederick I onwards protected itinerant students and their messengers, granting them safe-conducts to cross territories in a state of war and exempting them from customs dues on food and clothing. Sometimes, however, scholars were imprisoned or molested while crossing an enemy country, or even expelled if their host country was at war with their home country. In 1419 the French regent Charles granted a safe-conduct to the members of the Burgundian nation in Montpellier, who were subjects of his rival the duke of Burgundy, granting them permission to live 'seurement et sauvement en ladite étude de Montpellier sans que on puisse aucune chose demander, supposé qu'ils soient dudit pays de Bourgogne ou d'autre qui ne nous soit pas si obéissant comme il deust' (safe and sound in the said *studium* of Montpellier without anything being required of them should they be of the said country of Burgundy or any other country that is not as obedient to us as it should be).[46] This precedent did not deter King Louis XI from expelling 400 students from Paris in 1470 because they were subjects of Charles the Bold, duke of Burgundy. In 1524 the procurator of the German nation in Orléans noted in the Book of Procurators that he himself and William Cupreus of Flushing were made prisoners in Châteauneuf-sur-Loire by the duke of Luneberg, an ally of Francis I in his war against the emperor Charles V. The procurator added that, although his predecessor had omitted to mention it, he recorded this event as a warning to his colleague to take due care in time of war, and not to leave the city of Orléans without good reason in time of military operations.[47]

Other privileges relating to foreign currency, and the especially important privilege of exemption from the right of escheat, were everywhere recognized. Exemption from the right of escheat meant that the property of students dying abroad was not confiscated by the local ruler but was returned to their heirs. If they did not claim the property it was sold and the proceeds were spent on prayers for the dead man's soul, or for charitable purposes.

These privileges, and more general ones relating to justice or control of rents or food prices (see chapter 4), made it possible for itinerant students to survive. The use of Latin as a common language, and of a uniform programme of study and system of examinations, enabled itinerant students to continue their studies in one *studium* after another, and ensured recognition

---

[46] Fournier (ed.), *Statuts*, vol. II, 183, quoted in M. Waxin, *Statut de l'étudiant étranger dans son développement historique* (Amiens, 1939), 67–8.

[47] C. M. Ridderikhoff and H. de Ridder-Symoens (eds.), *Premier Livre des Procurateurs de la nation germanique de l'ancienne Université d'Orléans 1444–1546. Première partie: Texte des rapports des procurateurs* (Leiden, 1971), 263–4.

of their degrees throughout Christendom. Besides their academic knowledge they took home with them a host of new experiences, ideas, opinions, and political principles and views. Also – and this is important – they brought back manuscripts and, later on, printed books. They had become familiar with new schools of artistic expression, and with living conditions, customs, ways of life, and eating and drinking habits all previously unknown to them. As most itinerant scholars belonged to the élite of their country and later held high office, they were well placed to apply and propagate their newly acquired knowledge. The consequences of academic pilgrimage were, indeed, out of all proportion to the numerically insignificant number of migrant students.

SELECT BIBLIOGRAPHY

Aston, T. H. 'Oxford's Medieval Alumni', *Past and Present*, 74 (1977), 3–40.

Aston, T. H., Duncan, G. D., and Evans, T. A. R. 'The Medieval Alumni of the University of Cambridge', *Past and Present*, 86 (1980), 9–86.

Boyce, G. *The English–German Nation in the University of Paris during the Middle Ages*, Bruges, 1927.

Budinsky, A. *Die Universität Paris und die Fremden an derselben im Mittelalter*, Berlin, 1876; reprint, Aalen, 1970.

Dotzauer, W. 'Deutsche in westeuropäischen Hochschul- und Handelsstädten, vornehmlich in Frankreich, bis zum Ende des alten Reiches. Nation, Bruderschaft, Landmannschaft', *Festschrift L. Petry, Geschichtliche Landeskunde*, 5 (1969), 89–159.

Dotzauer, W. 'Deutsches Studium und deutsche Studenten an europäischen Hochschulen (Frankreich, Italien) und die nachfolgende Tätigkeit in Stadt, Kirche und Territorium in Deutschland', in E. Maschke and J. Sydow (eds.), *Stadt und Universität im Mittelalter und in der frühen Neuzeit*, Sigmaringen, 1977, 112–41.

Kibre, P., *The Nations in the Mediaeval Universities*, Cambridge, Mass., 1948.

Miethke, J. 'Die Studenten', in R. Schultz (ed.), 'Unterwegssein im Spätmittelalter', *Zeitschrift für Historische Forschung*, (special issue) (1985), 49–70.

Pini, A. I. '"Discere turba volens". Studenti e vita studentesca a Bologna dalle origini dello studio alla metà del trecento', in G. P. Brizzi and A. I. Pini (eds.), *Studenti e Università degli studenti del XII al XIX secolo*, Bologna, 1988, 45–136.

Schwinges, R. C. 'Zur Prosopographie studentischer Reisegruppen im fünfzehnten Jahrhundert', in N. Bulst and J. P. Genet (eds.), *Medieval Lives and the Historian. Studies in Medieval Prosopography*, Kalamazoo, 1986, 333–41.

Simák, J. V. 'Studenti z Cech, Moravy a Slezska na nemeck ch universitách v XV.–XVIII. st.' (Students of Bohemia, Moravia, and Silesia at the German Universities in the Fifteenth – Eighteenth Century), *Časopis Ceského Musea*, 79 (1905), 290–7; 80 (1906), 300–5, 510–39.

Trombetti Budriesi, A. L. 'L'esame di Laurea presso lo studio bolognese, Laureati in diritto civile nel secolo XV', in G. P. Brizzi and A. I. Pini (eds.), *Studenti e Università degli studenti del XII al XIX secolo*, Bologna, 1988, 137–91.

Verger, J. 'Géographie universitaire et mobilité étudiante au moyen âge: quelques remarques', in A. Paravicini Bagliani (ed.), *Ecoles et vie intellectuelle à Lausanne au moyen âge*, Lausanne, 1987, 9–24.

Veríssimo Serrão, J. *Les Portugais à l'Université de Toulouse, XIIIe–XVIIe siècles*, Memórias e documentos para a história luso-francesa, 5, Paris, 1970.

Veríssimo Serrão, J. *Les Portugais à l'Université de Montpellier, XIIe–XVIIe siècles*, Memórias e documentos para a história luso-francesa, 8, Paris, 1971.

Veríssimo Serrão, J. *Portugueses no Estudo de Salamanca*, vol. I, *1250–1550*, Lisbon, 1962.

Waxin, M. *Statut de l'étudiant étranger dans son développement historique*, Amiens, 1939.

PART IV

LEARNING

THE FACULTY OF ARTS

CHAPTER 10.1

THE *TRIVIUM* AND THE THREE PHILOSOPHIES

GORDON LEFF

THE LIBERAL ARTS IN MEDIEVAL EDUCATION

Medieval universities gave institutional form to a hierarchical notion of knowledge which they inherited from antiquity. Both Plato (*Republic* II, III, VII) and Aristotle (*Politics* VII, VIII) described a basic education which comprised a grounding in elementary grammar, literature, music, and arithmetic, and which prepared the way for the advanced study of mathematics and finally philosophy, whose object was wisdom, the supreme end of knowledge. That view of the propaedeutic role of the 'liberal arts', as they were called, arts for the free, as opposed to the servile, man passed into Roman education, where they had the directly practical end of preparing for a training in law and public life. It was in turn inherited by the Middle Ages and adapted, above all by Saint Augustine, to Christian objects of mastering the meaning of Scripture as the repository of Christian wisdom founded upon faith and the love of God. By the time of the emergence of universities in the twelfth century, theology, as the end of profane knowledge, had been joined by the more practical ends of law and medicine.

The arts were therefore distinguished from the higher subjects in a number of important ways. In the first place they were a heterogeneous grouping without any unity other than their common introductory function. From antiquity they were divided between the three verbal disciplines of grammar, rhetoric, and logic (the *trivium* or threefold way to wisdom), and the four mathematical disciplines, of arithmetic, geometry, astronomy, and music (the *quadrivium* or fourfold way). But, although the notion of the liberal arts was usually retained (as in Oxford), by the middle of the thirteenth century they no longer corresponded to the content of the arts course and were supplemented or superseded by other classifications, notably the addition of the three philosophies, natural, moral, and metaphysical, which were not covered by the older divisions of the *trivium* and *quadrivium*.[1]

In the second place, because of the heterogeneity of the arts, there was an uneven development both within the subjects of the *trivium* and the *quadrivium* and between the two groups. Generally speaking, until the 1230s the *trivium* was more studied than the *quadrivium*; that remained true especially of Paris. At the same time, certainly in the two leading northern universities of Paris and Oxford, within the *trivium* grammar and logic largely ousted rhetoric, which became an adjunct of grammar, while grammar itself largely came to be governed by logical considerations. South of the Alps, at Bologna especially and at Padua, rhetoric was dominant and was for a time, during the first part of the thirteenth century, almost autonomous at Bologna.

In the third place different emphases among the arts subjects were due primarily to the relation between the arts and the higher faculties. Here we can distinguish between the northern and the southern universities. Until the middle of the fourteenth century, Paris and to a lesser extent Oxford and Cambridge were the theological universities; outside the cathedral schools and the schools of the mendicant orders they had a virtual monopoly of the teaching of theology, a monopoly which seems to have been jealously guarded by the papacy, which for a long time refused to grant a faculty of theology to other universities. Since entry to the theological faculty, as to the other higher faculties, could until the fourteenth century normally come only after passing through the arts faculty (except for the mendicants who were permitted to study arts in their own schools), there was a close connection between the two faculties. And at all three northern universities, above all

---

[1] For the liberal arts, see the select bibliography. For the history of the three philosophies: J. A. Weisheipl, 'The Classification of the Sciences in Medieval Thought', *Mediaeval Studies*, 27 (1965), 54–60.

Paris, the arts course had a strongly philosophical character, with logic as the dominant subject in the old *trivium* and the three philosophies supplementing the old *quadrivium* in different proportions; at Paris greater attention was given to practical and metaphysical philosophy than at Oxford, where the emphasis was on natural philosophy.

In southern France, Italy, and Spain law ruled supreme, with medicine as the other main study, to which, at Bologna and Padua, the arts were subordinated and did not necessarily have the same preparatory role. The character of the arts course was correspondingly more practical, with rhetoric the main ancillary to the law, and logic and the natural sciences were regarded as instrumental to the study of medicine with less independent scope for speculation, grammatical, logical, or metaphysical. That did not prevent developments in both the literary and scientific subjects, but it limited the autonomy of the arts within the university. That was even more true institutionally in the student universities of Bologna and Padua, where the universities of the law students preponderated. For much of the thirteenth century and into the fourteenth century their rectors claimed jurisdiction over the more recent student universities, and masters' colleges, of arts and medicine. It took a prolonged struggle before the latter were able to exercise their own jurisdiction in the fourteenth century.

The effect of these different developments within the northern and southern universities was that the arts faculties of the southern universities never attained a comparable status with those in Paris and Oxford, where they were the dominant element both numerically and juridically; they also had the youngest and most volatile membership. On the other hand, the absence of a theological faculty or professors of theology in such universities as Bologna, Padua, and Salamanca until the second half of the fourteenth century meant a corresponding absence of the tensions between the naturalistic disciplines of the arts faculty, especially those connected with the three philosophies, and the Christian presuppositions involved in the study of theology and the Bible. As will be seen elsewhere, the tensions were greatest at Paris, the undisputed centre of theological studies in the thirteenth and fourteenth centuries.

The differences between the arts in the northern and southern universities derived from different educational traditions. North of the Alps education until the eleventh century had developed within the almost exclusively religious framework of the earlier monastic and cathedral schools and along the lines prescribed in Saint Augustine's *De doctrina christiana*: it involved the acquisition of profane or natural knowledge to serve Christian ends. The effect was to consider the arts directly subordinate to theology, having as their *raison d'être* the putting of worldly wisdom at the service of the Christian wisdom to be found in the Bible. If in practical terms that often meant little more than meeting the utilitarian requirements of elementary literacy and numeracy needed in the performance of monastic and priestly duties, it nevertheless also meant conceiving the arts in a wider context. That can be seen in the continuation of the Greek and Roman classificatory schemes of knowledge, transmitted to the Middle Ages by Boethius, Cassiodorus, and Isidore of Seville, of which the division into the three philosophies in the thirteenth century was one outcome.[2]

The connection between the arts and theology was given an institutional foundation in Charlemagne's educational reforms under Alcuin at the end of the eighth century and the beginning of the ninth century: these made the monasteries and the cathedrals responsible for providing instruction for the purpose of comprehending the Bible, and indirectly for educating a class of clerks capable of carrying out the administration of the new empire.[3] Such schools remained the main foci of higher education and learning until the middle of the twelfth century, and they continued to exist until the end of the Middle Ages. Although intellectually the universities gave their stamp to higher education, numerically they were only one component in the network of *studia*, and, as late as 1400, they numbered only some forty. Both north and south of the Alps and Pyrenees, therefore, other kinds of institutions preceded and co-existed with the universities, both providing a preparation for them, as the grammar schools and individual masters did, and supplementing them, as the cathedral schools and the houses of study of the different religious orders did.

Where the schools and masters and universities, above all of Italy, differed from those elsewhere was in their retaining the lay and civic character of Roman education.[4] Rhetoric was the dominant subject in the arts, studied as a preparation for a career in law and public life; and teaching was in the hands of the urban schools and masters of rhetoric, who taught the elements of the other liberal arts, particularly grammar and logic, as a foundation for it. As the cities began to recover and expand in the tenth and eleventh centuries, so did the range of civic activities, both in connection with the revival of law and the development of notarial skills, and in the emergence of medicine as a discipline and a career. Concomitantly, theology, as already said, was the preserve of the religious orders.

Although that lay and civic ambience was peculiar to Italy, to be seen in the emergence of its distinctive literary culture in the thirteenth and fourteenth centuries, the same predominantly non-theological orientation of the arts was shared by the Spanish universities despite their being, as at Salamanca and Valladolid, under the religious authorities, and also by southern French

[2] Weisheipl, 'Classification', (note 1), 55–6.
[3] F. L. Ganshof, *The Carolingian and Frankish Monarchy* (London, 1971), 20, 28–9; H. R. Loyn and J. Percival, *The Reign of Charlemagne* (London, 1975), 63–4.
[4] For the history of classical education: H. I. Marrou, *Histoire de l'Education dans l'Antiquité* (Paris, 1948; English transl. by G. Lamb, New York, 1956); J. Bowen, *A History of Western Education*, vol. I, *The Ancient World* (London, 1972).

universities, such as Montpellier. Even the university originally founded at Toulouse in 1229 by papal decree, to consolidate the recent victory over the Cathar heretics, was a century later, in 1335, forbidden by Pope Benedict XII to allow graduation in theology, while the university at Avignon only received a theological faculty in 1413, granted papal immunity by John XXIII.[5] The ban upon the teaching of theology outside Paris – and Oxford and Cambridge – until the 1360s was designed to keep the monopoly of it at Paris, where it was jealously protected by periodic papal interventions against what were regarded as subversive doctrines arising from the study of pagan authors in the arts faculty. In consequence of that close association with theology, the arts at Paris and at Oxford and Cambridge evolved in a different milieu from that in almost every other university until around the middle of the fourteenth century. Far from being subservient to theology, the arts in those universities continued to follow their own autonomous development, as they had in the eleventh and twelfth centuries, as well as being the dominant faculty.

All such divergences nevertheless arose from within a common scheme of knowledge, which, apart from its particular modes of treatment and organization, provided the universally accepted foundation of education and learning in the Middle Ages. It emerged in two stages. The first, as already indicated, was, by more or less direct inheritance from ancient educational theory and practice, based on the liberal arts, which became divided into the two groupings of the *trivium* and *quadrivium*. The second was through a series of translations into Latin, extending from the middle of the eleventh century to well into the thirteenth century, and reaching its height in the second two-thirds of the twelfth century, of an almost completely new corpus of philosophical, medical, and scientific works, principally of Greek and Arabian origin, hitherto unknown to the medieval West. This new body of knowledge had a transforming effect upon the existing state of knowledge, of which the emergent universities were the direct recipients. It not only radically changed the content and enlarged the structure of the liberal arts, as it did of medicine, the two subjects chiefly affected by the new accessions: it also challenged many Christian conceptions about the nature of the world and of man, and accordingly involved a redefinition of Christian belief in relation to philosophy, particularly the three philosophies, which were principally those of Aristotle, accompanied and mediated by Arabic interpretations. Christian thinkers were therefore faced with what at first often appeared a bewildering task of assimilation, which for the most part was achieved in the different faculties of the universities, and, in the case of arts and theology, occupied the greater part of the hundred years between the 1230s and 1330s.

[5] Rashdall, *Universities*, vol. II, 166–7, 176.

THE EARLY STAGE

In the first stage the absence of an independent body of Greek and Arabic sources was the accompaniment of a Latin-based culture, which the Middle Ages inherited from the Roman Empire in the West. It was confined not only to one language – that broadly remained true of the whole of the Middle Ages until the late fourteenth century – but to what was accessible in that language. By the sixth century, after the Roman Empire had politically ceased to exist in western and central Europe, the cultural base consisted principally of handbooks and encyclopedias of the liberal arts together with the writings of the main Latin authors and poets.[6] Apart from law, which was Rome's chief intellectual legacy to medieval and European culture but did not start to take effect before the eleventh century, it was pre-eminently a literary culture, with rhetoric the dominant member of the arts, to which grammar and logic were subordinate. There was no first-hand knowledge of the subjects of the *quadrivium* at all, as there had not been any in Roman education; from the first they had always been studied in popularized versions through handbooks and digests, a practice taken from the contemporary Hellenistic world and leading to the progressive adulteration of their contents, as ever more convenient, and superficially intelligible, versions succeeded one another. It was on this slender and incomplete foundation that the arts were transmitted to the Middle Ages and were continued, with growing additions, until, in the eleventh and twelfth centuries, they directly encountered for the first time the previously unknown world of Greek science and philosophy, greatly enriched, and often preceded chronologically, by a further body of Islamic science and philosophy. Together the old and the new combined to provide the base for the arts faculties. We must now consider its constituents.

First, there was grammar, which was always regarded as the preliminary study among the arts, in giving knowledge of the forms of language on which the other arts of expression depended. In fact, grammar involved elements of both logic and rhetoric as well as extending to literature.[7] It was therefore interconnected with the rest of the *trivium* and was not simply a separate adjunct. Until the twelfth century the main texts were the two primers of Donatus, the *Ars minor* and *Ars major*, and Priscian's *Institutiones grammaticae*. Composed in the fourth and sixth centuries respectively, they at once summarized classical grammar and virtually constituted medieval grammar as the elementary and advanced textbooks; they continued to be such after the coming of the new verse grammars of Alexander of Villedieu

[6] For a brief survey of these developments: D. L. Wagner, 'The Seven Liberal Arts and Classical Scholarship', in D. L. Wagner (ed.), *The Seven Liberal Arts in the Middle Ages* (Bloomington, Ind., 1984), 10–22; R. R. Bolgar, *The Classical Heritage and Its Beneficiaries* (Cambridge, 1954), chs. 1 and 3.

[7] For a résumé and bibliography: J. F. Huntsman, 'Grammar', in Wagner (ed.), *Seven Liberal Arts* (note 6), 59–95; J. J. Murphy, *Rhetoric in the Middle Ages* (Berkeley, 1974).

and Eberhard of Béthune at the end of the twelfth century and the beginning of the thirteenth century, passing into the curriculum of the arts faculty and, in the case of Donatus's *Ars minor* in particular, surviving the Middle Ages. Both Donatus and Priscian and the later verse grammars, which acquired great popularity, represented literary or practical grammar concerned with the parts of speech and syntax. Donatus's two books treated the former, descriptively in the *Ars minor*, more elaborately in the *Ars major*, which in book III (often called the *Barbarismus* from its first word) extended to figures of speech. It came to be taken as a separate text both at Oxford and at Paris. So did the last two of the eighteen books of Priscian's *Institutiones*, known as *Priscianus minor* or *De constructionibus*, from their subject-matter, which was syntax; they, too, were specified separately under that title, as the first sixteen books were under the title of *Priscianus major*.

Priscian's was a much more substantial work than the two books of Donatus; it was written at Constantinople, the capital of the surviving eastern part of the Roman Empire, whose culture was Greek. Priscian therefore had access to a much richer cultural tradition than his western counterparts, although he also refers to them, including Donatus. He also included classical (Latin) texts as illustration, making the *Institutiones* a repository for classical sources, especially Virgil (whose standing was doubtless further increased by Priscian's separate grammatical study of the first twelve lines of the *Aeneid*). At Oxford officially, at least in the regulations, Priscian appears to have remained in use longer than Donatus, well into the sixteenth century. The reason may well have been his strongly semantic approach to grammar, treating the parts of speech for their meaning, as a noun denotes a substance and quality, and a verb action or being acted upon. His approach was based upon the so-called grammar of Apollonius, in which simple elements combine into more complex elements, beginning with letters which are joined to form syllables, which in turn form words, and words sentences, which owe their meaning to the meaning of the words composing them.

That helped to stimulate a philosophical, or, more strictly in its first phase, logical, approach to grammar, directed to its general characteristics, especially the analysis of meaning.[8] It had its beginnings in the mid-eleventh century, emerging as a separate field of enquiry in the second half of the twelfth century under Peter Helias and Peter of Spain (not to be confused with the thirteenth-century logician Petrus Hispanus, who became Pope John XXI in 1276). Although Aristotle's so-called 'old logic', of the *Categories* and *Interpretation*, pointed to the close connection between grammar and logic, the developments in grammar were indigenous. So, too, was the concurrent development of terminist logic, also going back to the eleventh century and having a similar concern with the meaning of words, particularly indefinite,

---

[8] S. Ebbesen, 'Ancient Scholastic Logic', in N. Kretzmann, A. Kenny, and J. Pinborg (eds.), *The Cambridge History of Later Medieval Philosophy* (Cambridge, 1982), 110.

or syncategorematic, words like 'any' and 'not' which could not stand alone in propositions. They each antedated, therefore, the rediscovery of Aristotle's new logic, or the *Prior* and *Posterior Analytics*, *Topics*, and *Sophistical Refutations*, in the twelfth century. Apart from the *Sophistical Refutations*, these works were only systematically studied, like the rest of Aristotle's newly translated writings, in the thirteenth century. Their main influence upon grammar was through the *Posterior Analytics*, *Soul* (*De anima*), and *Metaphysics*, and they helped to produce a new genre of speculative grammar, principally in the arts faculty at Paris, between about 1270 and 1300; it consisted in the systematization of the different modes of signification which words could receive into something like a universal grammar of word forms.[9] It had close affinities with terminist logic and was the furthest to which the logical treatment of grammar was taken in the Middle Ages.

Turning next to logic, Aristotle's logical works were divided into the old and the new logic because, although Boethius had translated all Aristotle's main works on logic, apart from the *Posterior Analytics*, only those of the so-called 'old logic' had continued to be known before the twelfth century. The old logic, in addition to Aristotle's *Categories* and *Interpretation*, also included Boethius's translation of the *Introduction* of Porphyry, the third-century Neoplatonist, to the Categories, accompanied by Boethius's commentaries (two for the *Categories* and Porphyry) on each of those works, together with a commentary on Cicero's *Topics* and his own treatises on division, categorical and hypothetical syllogisms, and topics (*De differentiis topicis*).

The last-named work was especially important in stimulating a new interest in dialectical reasoning in the eleventh and twelfth centuries, and only came to be displaced by Aristotle's *Topics* in the thirteenth century, while the commentaries on Porphyry were responsible for initiating the debate on universals, over the independent existence or non-existence of universal natures, such as animal or man. Boethius's translations of Aristotle's other logical writings remained unknown until the 1120s, when they became the foundation of the 'new logic'. They were again translated in the twelfth century, the *Posterior Analytics* for the first time by James of Venice, then the foremost translator of Aristotle, who also translated the *Sophistical Refutations*. His translations, all from the Greek, were made between about 1125 and 1150.[10] Until the middle of the twelfth century, Aristotle was known to the West only by his logical writings. They therefore stand in a category of their own, in giving him a purely logical identity, and one which was to have a far-reaching effect when his more or less complete philosophical works

9 J. Pinborg, 'Speculative Grammar', in Kretzmann, Kenny, and Pinborg (eds.), *Cambridge Medieval Philosophy* (note 8), 254–69.
10 B. Dod, 'Aristoteles Latinus', in Kretzmann, Kenny, and Pinborg (eds.), *Cambridge Medieval Philosophy* (note 8), 54–5, and table of translations 74–5.

became known by the first quarter of the thirteenth century. Although his *Physics, Metaphysics,* and *De anima* were also translated by James of Venice before 1150, they only began to have an impact at the beginning of the thirteenth century. For most of the twelfth century Aristotle was regarded as a logician. Plato, on the strength of the surviving first half of Chalcidius' commentary on the *Timaeus,* and Boethius, through his *Consolation of Philosophy* and theological as well as logical and other works, were still the chief philosophers. As we shall discuss later, the introduction of the main body of Aristotle's philosophical writings into the arts faculty largely transformed the arts course in the thirteenth century.

In the case of logic, we can conclude that, like grammar, its progress until the thirteenth century was largely indigenous, from within the existing stock of texts, which had come down principally through Boethius. Then, under the influence of the new logic, as well as important non-Aristotelian Stoic and Galenic elements, especially those contained in the so-called Alexander's commentaries on the *Sophistical Refutations* and *Posterior Analytics* (mistakenly taken for those of the second-century commentator, Alexander of Aphrodisias), translated by James of Venice,[11] its ramifications, in contrast to grammar, extended to every aspect of Aristotelian and terminist logic, producing new forms as well as directly bearing upon the three philosophies and theology.

The third element of the *trivium,* rhetoric, remained the most indigenous of all; apart from its application to the practical activities of letter-writing, in the *ars dictaminis* and *ars notaria,* and, in the thirteenth century, preaching, the *ars predicandi,* it underwent no internal development comparable to that in speculative grammar or logic. It remained from the beginning governed by Cicero, directly through his early *De inventione,* with its stress upon forensic argument, giving it a legal bias, and indirectly through the pseudo-Ciceronian *Ad Herrenium* from the ninth century onwards, with its emphasis upon ornamentation of style.[12] Although in the twelfth century the popularity of *Ad Herrenium* came to challenge that of *De inventione,* the latter remained the undisputed source of rhetorical principles, resisting the attempts of Boncompagno da Signa in the first part of the thirteenth century to displace the Ciceronian five-part letter by a letter in three parts.[13] It was at Bologna in the thirteenth century that the *ars dictaminis* became for a time a separate faculty before being supplanted by the *ars notaria* as a separate skill.

Of all the subjects of the liberal arts, rhetoric never established a separate identity and had to wait until the fifteenth century in Italy before it fully gained one. In the Middle Ages it was the most anomalous of the arts because

---

[11] Ebbesen, 'Ancient Scholastic Logic', (note 8), 108–10.
[12] M. Carmago, 'Rhetoric', with bibliography, in Wagner (ed.), *Seven Liberal Arts* (note 6), 97–124; Murphy, *Rhetoric* (note 7).
[13] Murphy, *Rhetoric* (note 7).

the very conditions of public life and the central importance of the law-courts, which had fostered it in Roman times, ceased to exist, and never properly returned in their classical or post-medieval forms. Hence rhetoric became subordinated to a written culture, to grammar in the earlier Middle Ages and, in Italy, as the ancillary of law from the eleventh century, gradually broadening its influence to letter-writing and later preaching.

What had doubtless helped to ensure its preservation north of the Alps was the rhetorical training which the early Christian fathers, including Saint Augustine, had received, and the need, recognized by him in his *De doctrina christiana*, to use persuasion in preaching Christian wisdom. That was given fullest expression by the new mendicant orders in the thirteenth and four-teenth centuries. But it is noteworthy that the argument made no difference to the status of rhetoric north of the Alps, for all the importance of the mendicants at Paris and Oxford and the other universities. Nor did the com-paratively late translation of Aristotle's *Rhetoric* around the middle of the thirteenth century. Rhetoric remained subsidiary to the other two members of the *trivium*, overlapping with grammar as in the new verse grammars or subsumed under dialectic as in effect it was in Boethius's treatise on topics. It was a set text for rhetoric at Oxford, while at Paris study was initially con-fined to the fourth and last book, and relegated, with the *quadrivium*, and philosophy, to public holidays, in the first statutes given by the papal legate, Robert of Courson, in 1215. Although Cicero had always to be read, and the *dictamen* had flourished at Orléans and Tours in the twelfth century and was in general use in northern Europe, as well as in Italy, to serve the needs of law and administration, it was in Italy that the *ars dictaminis* was most advanced, and even there the creative period of the *ars dictaminis* was over by the middle of the thirteenth century and rhetoric took an increasingly civic course. Allowing for the far-reaching developments to come in logic in the thirteenth and fourteenth centuries, and the more restricted development in grammar and rhetoric, it can be said that the main components of the subject of the *trivium* were in place by the middle of the twelfth century with little further outside addition and that they entered the curriculum of the arts faculty at the beginning of the thirteenth century largely in that form. That can also be said of music as an academic subject, for which Boethius's treatise on music (*De musica*) and the passage on music in Martianus Capella were the main sources.[14]

THE IMPACT OF THE TRANSLATIONS

The translations, which were to transform the arts course in the thirteenth century, began in the tenth century in Spain, from where Gerbert of Aurillac, the future Pope Sylvester II (999–1003), who had studied earlier in Catalonia,

[14] T. C. Karp, 'Music', with bibliography, in Wagner (ed.), *Seven Liberal Arts* (note 6), 169–217.

almost certainly gained his knowledge of Arabic numerals and astronomy, which he was among the first to employ in the medieval West.[15] Spain, however, only became the main source for Arabic texts after the reconquest from the Muslims in the twelfth century. The other main areas were southern Italy, especially Monte Cassino and Salerno, the meeting point of Arabic, Greek, and Latin culture, where the first translations of Arabic and Greek medical texts, including those of Galen, were made; Sicily; and Constantinople. Broadly speaking, Spain was the main source of the translations from the Arabic, Constantinople and Italy of the Greek texts, and Sicily of both Arabic and Greek. Contrary to earlier long-held belief, the chronological sequence of the translations was not from Arabic to Greek; they proceeded concurrently; and, in the case of those of Aristotle's works,[16] the earliest translations were by James of Venice, between *c.* 1125 and 1150, direct from the Greek. They included the new logic, the *Physics*, the *Soul*, part of the *Metaphysics* (to book IV, chapter 4), and a number of the smaller biological treatises. Other works of Aristotle taken from the Greek, in the twelfth century, included an almost complete translation of the *Metaphysics* (except for book XI), which remained unknown until the middle of the thirteenth century, the *Generation and Corruption*, books II and III of the *Nicomachean Ethics* (the only one of Aristotle's two works on ethics known, apart from a single chapter from the *Eudemian Ethics* in a compilation called *De bona fortuna*, translated in the thirteenth century), and new translations of some of the works translated by James. In Spain, somewhat later during the twelfth century, Gerard of Cremona, the century's most prolific translator from the Arabic, before 1187 also translated the *Posterior Analytics*, *Physics*, and *Generation and Corruption*, the only translations of new texts of Aristotle being his *Meteors* and *The Heavens*, which were also the only ones to circulate widely.

By the later twelfth century, then, the main body of Aristotle's works had been translated into Latin, the majority of them from Greek. Of the remainder still untranslated, the *Ethics* was translated in full by Robert Grosseteste around 1246 and 1247, and re-done, in a revised version of Grosseteste, between 1250 and 1260, perhaps by William of Moerbeke, who was responsible for revised translations of virtually all Aristotle's works from the Greek in the middle decades of the thirteenth century. He also translated for the first time the *Politics* in about 1260 and the *Poetics* in 1278. The former was of the first importance for subsequent political theory; the latter

---

[15] The pioneering studies are by C. H. Haskins, *Studies in Mediaeval Science* (Cambridge, Mass., 1924; 2nd edn, 1927; reprint, New York, 1960); C. H. Haskins, *The Renaissance of the Twelfth Century* (Cambridge, Mass, 1927; reprint, New York, 1957), 278–302. The most recent authoritative revision is by M.T. d'Alverny, 'Translations and Translators', in *Renaissance and Renewal*, 421–62. For the Arabian contribution: G. Beaujouan, 'The Transformation of the Quadrivium', in *Renaissance and Renewal*, 463–8.

[16] For a comprehensive survey: Dod, 'Aristoteles Latinus' (note 10), 45–79.

had to wait until the fifteenth century to take effect. Hardly less significant were his translations of some of Aristotle's early Greek commentators, Simplicius of Cilicia on the *Categories*, John Philoponus and Themistius, both on the *Soul*, but perhaps most important of all, Proclus' *Elements of Theology*, a reworked epitome of which had been taken by Gerard of Cremona from the Arabic in the twelfth century, becoming generally known in the thirteenth century as the *Book of Causes*. In the first half of the century this work was generally attributed to Aristotle and entered the prescribed books for the arts faculty at Paris. Numerous commentaries were made on it during the thirteenth century, including that of Thomas Aquinas, who identified its true derivation from William of Moerbeke's translation, and that of Siger of Brabant, the main protagonist of philosophical autonomy in the arts faculty at Paris, and for a time Aquinas's opponent. The full ramifications of the influence of the *Book of Causes*, including its influence upon Aquinas, and its role in associating Aristotle's thought with a quite alien Neoplatonism, remain to be investigated.

The *Book of Causes* is only the most egregious example of the early association of Aristotle with non-Aristotelian works, many of them of Arabic origin and of a different intellectual cast. It must also be recognized that Aristotle's works were only one element, even if in due course a decisive element, in a much wider, heterogeneous collection of texts. They included not only a great body of non-Aristotelian science, Hippocratic and Galenic medicine, Ptolemaic and Arabic astronomy, and Arabic mathematics; they also presented the Christian West with independent philosophical systems in the writings of al-Farabi, Avicenna (Ibn Sina), Ibn Gabirol, and Maimonides, to mention only some of the most prominent, which were in varying degrees syncretisms of Platonism and Aristotelianism and thereby affected the interpretation of Aristotle's own system. The combination no doubt helps to account for the slow reception of Aristotle's ideas, particularly at Paris.[17] Although his philosophical works, as opposed simply to his logical works, were being read in the arts faculty during the 1230s, the influence of Avicenna's metaphysics, cosmology, and psychology is far more apparent, especially upon those who had graduated in arts and included philosophical issues in their theological commentaries, an inclusion which became the universal practice in the thirteenth century.

The influence of Averroës (Ibn Rushd), Aristotle's commentator *par excellence*, is even more apparent, especially in relation to the arts faculty at Paris in the 1260s and 1270s. Many of his series of commentaries on Aristotle's works were translated, probably by Michael Scot, in Sicily in the 1220s and 1230s, often, as in the case of Aristotle's *Metaphysics*, with an accompanying translation of the text which was being commented on. Averroës'

---

[17] For the main stages: F. van Steenberghen, *Aristotle in the West* (Louvain, 1955).

determination to restore the true Aristotle from what he castigated as the misrepresentations of his predecessors, especially Avicenna, merely presented those at the receiving end in the West with one more Arabic version of Aristotle, interpreted in terms of Arabic philosophy. It could be accepted as authoritative, as it was for the greater part of Aristotle's philosophy in the later thirteenth and fourteenth centuries, because of the mastery and completeness of Averroës' treatment, which had no parallel among Latin commentators, certainly not before the second half of the thirteenth century. Or it could be rejected for its non-Christian implications, which is what happened in the condemnations at Paris, in the 1270s, of purported doctrines being taught in the arts faculty, and applied to Greek and Arabic philosophy generally as it had come through the translations. But that was only one extreme – and theologically directed – response to them; and, for all the importance attached to it at the time, it involved only a minority. The greater part of the new complex of knowledge and philosophical concepts was gradually assimilated into the arts; and that occurred principally in the arts faculties at Paris and Oxford, to which we must now turn.

THE PERIOD OF ASSIMILATION (THIRTEENTH CENTURY)

The history of the arts faculty in the thirteenth century is largely that of the gradual broadening of the curriculum and the range of studies and writings to accommodate the new knowledge.[18] The gradual absorption of Aristotle's philosophy and its differentiation from that of his Arabian accompaniments, including some of the pseudo-Aristotelian writings, like the *Book of Causes*, was only one part of that process, which extended to the whole range of non-Aristotelian science. What Aristotle did was to provide a common theoretical framework in a common vocabulary, the notion of a science as an organized body of knowledge with its own defining principles and conclusions, and a comprehensive natural philosophy and cosmology based upon a metaphysics of form and matter, producing a qualitative non-mathematical conception of being, which, to the detriment of the subsequent development of the natural sciences, displaced the predominantly Platonist Timaean cosmology of the twelfth century based upon quantity. At the same time Aristotle supplied the substantive knowledge to go with that framework for each of the recognized branches of knowledge. One individual could hardly do more; and, once encountered, his influence upon the intellectual life of the high and later Middle Ages became as pervasive as it had been in Islam. Even so, much remained effectively outside it, including the very subjects of the *quadrivium*, to say nothing of medicine, while, as we have seen, of the *trivium*, grammar and rhetoric derived from other sources, and logic in its

[18] E. Gilson, *History of Christian Philosophy in the Middle Ages* (London, 1955), especially 250ff.

most formative aspects followed an independent development that owed much to Stoic and other non-Aristotelian influences, such as that of Porphyry transmitted through Boethius.[19]

In approaching the arts faculty we must accordingly distinguish between official responses to the new knowledge, in the reactions of the ecclesiastical authorities and in the prescribed subjects of the curriculum, on the one hand, and what was actually being studied and written, on the other hand. The distinction applies particularly to Paris as the main confluence of arts and theology. The first of a series of official reactions there to the new knowledge was at the Council of Sens in 1210, which, among other things, banned the public and private lecturing on Aristotle's works of natural philosophy and, probably with Avicenna in mind, the commentaries on them.[20] The ban was repeated in 1215 by the papal legate, Robert of Courson, in his regulations for the arts faculty, which will be considered presently.[21] It was again renewed in 1228[22] and in 1231[23] by Pope Gregory IX, but on the latter occasion pending the examination and purging of all the errors from the books so that they could be studied without delay. Whether or not that was taken as the signal for studying them, the first evidence of their study in the arts course at Paris comes from around that time in an anonymous student guide to the examination questions and books to be read in logic, grammar, and ethics in descending order of importance, with logic by far the most important.[24] But it also briefly included, as non-examination subjects, metaphysics and natural philosophy; and there the books mentioned were Aristotle's *Metaphysics*, with the *Book of Causes* as its third part, *Physics* and other works on natural philosophy, the first three books of his *Ethics*, Euclid's *Elements*, and Ptolemy's *Almagest*, all part of the new accessions to the arts, together with Boethius's *Consolation of Philosophy* and the *Timaeus* representing the older practical and natural philosophies. It also contained a general introduction to philosophy classified according to Boethius's divisions into rational, natural, and moral, which, although not new, may have indicated an awareness of the need for a broader scheme to accommodate the new developments.

Whether one chooses to interpret this brief excursus into natural philosophy as a sign of its insignificance at Paris in the 1230s or as denoting that it had gained a foothold there, the guide undeniably shows that it was being read and studied. Corroboration is to be found in the writings of the masters

---

[19] Examples in Ebbesen, 'Ancient Scholastic Logic' (note 8), 124–7.

[20] *CUP*, vol. I, 70, no. 11.

[21] *CUP*, vol. I, 78, no. 20. [22] *CUP*, vol. I, 114–15, no. 59.

[23] *CUP*, vol. I, 136–9, no. 79.

[24] Described in M. Grabmann, *Mittelalterliches Geistesleben*, vol. II (Munich, 1936), 183–99. A parallel case for Oxford a century later is to be found in the early fourteenth-century catalogue of philosophical texts in Merton College library, which has eighty-five entries, going far beyond the number of books prescribed by the arts faculty. J. Fletcher, 'The Faculty of Arts', in *History of Oxford*, 376; P. Kibre, 'The "Quadrivium" in the Thirteenth Century Universities', in P. Kibre, *Studies in Medieval Science* (London, 1984), 175–91.

in the faculty of theology, William of Auxerre, Philip the Chancellor, and William of Auvergne, at the same period; they all refer to some of Aristotle's works of natural philosophy as well as, and in the case of William of Auvergne's extensively, to Avicenna. That inclusion of philosophy in works of theology is a feature of both Oxford and Paris. The secular masters of theology, who were not members of a religious order, learned their philosophy in the arts faculty. The theological commentaries on the *Sentences*, as one of the two main components of the theological course, became the main repository of metaphysics and moral philosophy; hence the very close involvement of the theological faculty in arts, above all at Paris.

That involvement is apparent in the patterns of bans and proscriptions set by the Council at Sens in 1210, which was presided over by Peter of Corbeil, who had been a master at Paris in the faculties of theology and canon law in the last decade of the twelfth century. Successive former masters in theology continued in that role, notably Stephen Tempier, who, as bishop of Paris, was responsible for the later condemnations of heterodox propositions in 1270 and 1277, an action repeated on a smaller scale at Oxford, in 1277 by Robert Kilwardby and John Pecham, in 1284, previous members of the theological faculty there and at Paris, in their capacity as archbishops at Canterbury. Yet it has to be recognized that the bans of 1210, 1215, 1228, and 1231 applied only to Paris; the public study of Aristotle and the other new texts was uninterrupted at Oxford; and at Toulouse, founded in 1229 by Gregory IX, such study was actively canvassed as one of its attractions.[25]

The beginnings of the study of these texts at Paris and Oxford and of the arts generally before the middle of the thirteenth century are obscure. In the first regulations of Robert of Courson for Paris in 1215 the prescribed texts were confined to the old and new logic and all of Priscian for grammar, with Donatus's third book deemed optional; the unspecified quadrivial subjects (the only time that the term was used at Paris) were, as already said, reserved for holidays, when there was no other teaching or disputing, together with the fourth book of Boethius's *Topics* and the known part of the *Ethics* of Aristotle. Taken in conjunction with the renewal of the ban on the study of natural philosophy, the narrow range and conservative nature of the first formal curriculum probably reflects the still inchoate state of the new knowledge at Paris, as at Oxford, in the early years of the thirteenth century.

Officially that remained true of the next extant syllabus, that of the English–German nation at Paris in 1252;[26] the only addition was that of Aristotle's treatise on the *Soul* (*De anima*). Too much weight should not be put on its appearance, since by then the more or less full complement of the works of natural philosophy was known and being read. Nevertheless, *De anima* was probably the single most important source of the disputes between

---

[25] *CUP*, vol. I, 129–31, no. 72.   [26] *CUP*, vol. I, 227–8, no. 201.

the theologians and the philosophers in the arts faculty during the 1260s and 1270s, culminating in the condemnations of 1270 and 1277, because it was from Averroës' 'Great [i.e. line by line] Commentary' on its text that the issue of one intellect for all mankind, perhaps the most burning issue of all, arose.

The official change at Paris came three years later in 1255 with the new curriculum promulgated for the whole arts faculty by the masters of arts, as part of a general reform of the syllabus designed to remedy overhasty reading of the texts leading to inadequate preparation.[27] Virtually all Aristotle's main works on natural philosophy, together with his metaphysics and a number of pseudo-Aristotelian writings, among them the *Book of Causes*, were now included among the set books, and their study was now integrated into a strict timetable, which, even if it only permitted a few weeks' acquaintance, marked the final acceptance of the new knowledge at Paris. In contrast, rhetoric was confined, as it had been in the first statutes of Courson, to Boethius's *Topics*, but now the first three books instead of only the fourth book. From the second half of the thirteenth century the study of Aristotle emerged from obscurity and the number of texts multiplied.

That is also true of Oxford, where there was none of the inhibiting effect of the bans on natural philosophy at Paris. The earliest surviving syllabus of texts, from 1268, displays a comparable position, with a corresponding paucity of identifiable works on Aristotelian philosophy or references to them in the first part of the thirteenth century. The best known are a commentary on *De anima* by John Blund, who was a master of arts, first at Paris in about 1205 and then at Oxford between 1207 and 1209, which also draws upon the Arabic writings of Algazel (al Ghazāli) and Avicenna, and above all Robert Grosseteste's commentary on the *Posterior Analytics*, containing Grosseteste's theory of scientific demonstration.[28] Together with his other works on light and optics, it helped to inaugurate a mathematically inspired scientific tradition at Oxford which reached its fullest development in the fourteenth century. Among Grosseteste's polymathic activities, which, as already mentioned, included the first complete translation of Aristotle's *Nicomachean Ethics*, he also wrote biblical and theological works which were closer to the exegetical spirit of the twelfth century than to the emerging speculative attitude of the thirteenth century.[29] That spirit extended to the liberal arts, which Grosseteste still saw as the attendants to natural and moral philosophy. It was maintained by Grosseteste's pupils, especially Roger Bacon, who went further than Grosseteste, and almost all of his contemporaries, in giving mathematics primacy over logic as the condition of all knowledge as well as theological understanding.[30]

---

[27] *CUP*, vol. I, 277–8, no. 246.
[28] A. C. Crombie, *Robert Grosseteste and the Origins of Experimental Science* (Oxford, 1953).
[29] J. McEvoy, *The Philosophy of Robert Grosseteste* (Oxford, 1982).
[30] Kibre, ' "Quadrivium" ' (note 24), 177–9.

The unbroken line running through the thirteenth century from Grosseteste, as first teacher to the Franciscans at Oxford as well as probably the first chancellor of the university in 1214, to Bacon, who lived into its last decade, helped to imbue Oxford with its distinctive approach to the natural sciences, extending to all the subjects of the old *quadrivium* as well as to physics and cosmology. Correspondingly the emphasis in logic was more upon the contextual meaning of terms, for what they signified, than upon their purely formal features, which were the focus of concentration at Paris, in keeping with the more abstract, speculative character of the arts there.[31] While logic was always the dominant pursuit in the arts faculty generally, at Oxford its main accompaniment was natural philosophy, in its wider associations with mathematics and astronomy, rather than moral philosophy, psychology, and metaphysics, which were more strongly represented at Paris.

Those differences are hinted at in the official curricula of the two universities. At Paris, the only existing reference to mathematics and astronomy before 1350 is contained in the regulations on the oaths to be taken in the Anglo-German nation. Neither the set books on mathematics, nor the mathematics to be studied is specified; and the book on astronomy, John of Sacrobosco's *Sphere*, which is named, can be dispensed with if a hundred hours of lectures on mathematics have been heard.[32] They were therefore treated as alternatives. At Oxford there is no mention of Aristotle's *Metaphysics* before 1407.[33] On the other hand, there is very much more on mathematics and astronomy before 1350. John of Sacrobosco's three treatises, Euclid's *Elements* for geometry, and Boethius's *Arithmetic*, in addition to Aristotle's works, which now included the *Politics*, and the other standard authorities, like Donatus and Priscian, are specified in the regulations of 1340.[34] By 1431, almost a century later, Ptolemy's work, now usually known as the *Almagest*, and the anonymous thirteenth-century exposition of planetary theory, the *Theorica planetarum*,[35] as well as the treatises on optics by Alhazen (Ibn al-Haitham), whose work was translated from the Arabic in the twelfth century, and Witelo, the thirteenth-century Polish scientist, had been added.[36] Witelo's name is especially instructive in pointing to a distinctive Oxford scientific tradition, since he was a direct continuator of the investigations of Grosseteste and Bacon into the properties and effects of light.

---

[31] See the respective chapters on science and logic at Oxford in the thirteenth century by J. A. Weisheipl and O. Lewry in *History of Oxford*.

[32] *CUP*, vol. II, 678, no. 1185.

[33] S. Gibson (ed.), *Statuta Antiqua Universitatis Oxoniensis* (Oxford, 1931), 193.

[34] Gibson (ed.), *Statuta* (note 33), 33–4.

[35] For an account of the development of astronomy during the Middle Ages: O. Pedersen, 'The Corpus Astronomicum and the Traditions of Medieval Latin Astronomy', *Colloquia Copernicana*, 3 (1975), 57–96.

[36] Gibson (ed.), *Statuta* (note 33), 234–5.

The statutes do not, however, reveal anything of that tradition, as they do not of the different emphases at Paris or of the developments in the different branches of the arts, for they were directed to the official requirements of the course; they were therefore concerned only with the teaching and study of those texts needed to qualify for admission to the degrees of bachelor and master. They accordingly represented the official minimum, which, as we have seen from the anonymous guide to the subjects of the arts faculty at Paris, was far from being the full range.[37] To mention only the examples of Euclid's *Elements* and Ptolemy's *Almagest*, among the works named there, they had still not officially appeared at Paris in the century and two centuries respectively which it took for them to appear officially at Oxford. None the less, the regulations themselves do sometimes indicate the existence of additional texts, either as optional, like Boethius's *Consolation of Philosophy* in those same statutes of the English–German nation at Paris, or as alternatives, like a hundred hours of lectures on mathematics and Sacrobosco's *Sphere*. At Oxford provision was made for those who had not participated in the requisite disputations to spend extra time hearing further lectures.[38]

Above all, however, there were the indigenous products of the arts faculty, the great mass of textbooks, treatises, commentaries, and disputed questions which arose from the arts course itself at every level and mostly remain unedited in thousands of manuscripts. They turned from a trickle in the earlier part of the thirteenth century into an unbroken stream by the end of it, continuing into the fifteenth century. They were at once the means of assimilating the new Graeco-Arabic corpus which came with translations and the means of providing the diverse responses to it. They thereby largely shaped the subsequent development of the arts, as their counterparts in the higher faculties shaped their subjects, in being the vehicle for studying and interpreting them. Since the arts faculty was predominantly the faculty of the absolute beginners, a high proportion of its output was of the most elementary nature, particularly in logic, in the quadrivial subjects, and in natural philosophy, its main foci, in which the great majority of entrants would have had no previous grounding. But they were also the point of departure for the most advanced works, which became increasingly formative as well as numerous in the second part of the thirteenth century and reached their fullest development in the fourteenth century. An outstanding illustration of that progression is to be seen in the role played in astronomy and mathematics by the works of Sacrobosco and similar elementary texts with which they were usually associated in the curriculum.

There was a comparable evolution in the other disciplines, even if not so clear-cut as it was in astronomy, which, unlike logic, was a minority subject; and its newly acquired mathematical character demarcated it from cosmo-

---

[37] A. C. Crombie, *Medieval and Early Modern Science*, vol. I, (New York, 1959), 99–111.
[38] Gibson, (ed.), *Statuta* (note 33), 26, 34.

logy, governed by Aristotle's physics, on which everyone could have an opinion without having a knowledge of mathematics. What the main disciplines all had in common was the gradual formation of an established body of texts and authorities, and the growth of a repertory of topics and doctrines with their divergent interpretations and schools, not only within universities but between them, as we have already noticed in the case of Paris and Oxford. Among the two universities' divergences were significantly different attitudes towards non-Aristotelian knowledge, which can be seen from their contrasting responses to Sacrobosco and Grosseteste. At Paris, Sacrobosco's name is not to be found officially among the prevailing Aristotelian texts which were promulgated in the arts faculty by 1250, and his influence belonged as much outside Paris as within it; at Oxford Grosseteste's name and influence were pre-eminent both in his own lifetime and especially beyond it through the distinctive scientific tradition which he inaugurated. It was from such diverse responses, individual and collective, that the arts, as the other branches of knowledge, evolved.

THE COURSE OF STUDIES

This evolution was connected with the very structure of the course of studies within the faculty. Its two main components were the degrees of bachelor and master, each with its own separate requirements. There is no evidence of any formal requirement for entry into an arts faculty, beyond presumably evidence of elementary proficiency in Latin and some grasp of numeracy in order to be able to cope with the course. At Paris the minimum age for graduation as a master was fixed at twenty years by Robert of Courson's statutes of 1215, a provision repeated in the 1252 regulations of the Anglo-German nation; and the prescribed length of the course was six years with a minimum age of fourteen or fifteen for admission. That probably remained fairly constant, but the length of the course could vary according to individual circumstances, leading to the subtraction or addition of a year. At Oxford the standard length seems normally to have been seven years, and remained so throughout the Middle Ages, while almost everywhere else the tendency was for the length of the course to decrease.

At Paris the first official provisions for the bachelor's degree are contained in the English–German nation's regulations for 1252.[39] Those of Oxford date from not long afterwards,[40] although the distinction between master and bachelor antedates them and can already be identified in Robert of Courson's Paris statutes of 1215.[41] At both universities the status of bachelor was reached after four years of study, the first two spent listening to lectures

[39] *CUP*, vol. I, 227–32, nos. 201, 202.   [40] Gibson (ed.), *Statuta* (note 33), 25.
[41] G. Leff, *Paris and Oxford Universities in the Thirteenth and Fourteenth Centuries* (New York, 1968), 147.

and attending disputations and the next two also participating in disputations under the supervision of a master, with whom the student had to enrol for the arts course and in whose house he might live, in contrast to the student universities of Italy where the masters had their own separate existence as members of their own college or guild.

Lectures and disputations were the two official modes of instruction and training, although there were also unofficial ones, such as revision classes and private tuition, and probably increasingly formal ones in the halls and colleges during the later Middle Ages.[42]

Lectures in the arts faculty, as in the other faculties, were all on prescribed texts. They were divided into masters' lectures (ordinary lectures) and bachelors' lectures (cursory lectures). Ordinary lectures were more detailed and analytical. They involved the master first reading the text to be lectured on and explaining it, then considering any noteworthy points, and finally, if necessary, raising any questions which arose from it without digressing from the text.[43] Cursory lectures were closer to paraphrases to supplement the ordinary lectures (which were always given at set times in the morning) and were part of the bachelors' own training as apprentice masters; they might also be given by masters, as extraordinary lectures, as a means of extending the range of texts.

There were correspondingly masters' and bachelors' disputations, in which set questions were debated, and objections and replies presented by successive opponents and respondents, ending with a final resolution or determination, which always seems to have been the prerogative of masters, except during the bachelors' period of determining or disputing during Lent. The disputations themselves were of two kinds, on logic and on mathematical subjects or those taken from the three philosophies, the branches of real knowledge as opposed to knowledge of signs; but in practice, especially at Oxford, they tended to be on natural philosophy.

At Paris and Oxford, students for the bachelor's degree, in addition to having to hear the ordinary lectures of their own masters daily, had also to attend his weekly disputations, and after about two years to engage in disputations themselves. At both universities that included the obligation to respond to objections in logical disputations and to what was called the question. In the statutes of the English–German nation the first was to be for two years and the second for one year; at Oxford a full year had to be taken over logical disputations before 'responding to the question' – responsion – could begin; hence they could not run concurrently, as it seems they could at Paris, where there was no such stipulation. But at Oxford, on the other hand, the

42 Fletcher, 'Faculty of Arts' (note 24), 378.
43 Gibson, (ed.), *Statuta* (note 33), 236, gives a later description dating from 1431, and, more briefly, 192, dating from 1407 or before.

need to respond in logical disputations could also be obviated by spending longer time listening to lectures, including those on the *Posterior Analytics*.[44]

There could, however, be no dispensation from responding to the question, which had to be reached by a certain time (which varied at different periods) in order to qualify for admission to determine. The precise nature and status of responding to the question remain a matter of dispute. At Oxford responding to the question carried with it the title of questionist, as that of sophister was given to those responding in logic in their third year, and so would normally describe undergraduate students in their fourth and final year.[45] It may have involved disputing with bachelors during their determination exercises at Oxford; and at Paris it ran from Lent to Lent, when determination occurred; it also, a little later, entailed responding publicly there in a master's disputation before Christmas in order to be admitted to determine in the following Lent.[46] At the same time responsion had its own ceremony of admission at Oxford, with the swearing of oaths and payment of fees which accompanied the conferment of all degrees. But whether that constituted a separate status[47] or represented the granting of bachelor status[48] is less clear. What is apparent is that responding to the question acted as a preliminary examination for admission to determine, and that those admitted were regarded as bachelors when they determined, having thereby been granted their application to lecture on some book of the arts faculty, one of the main functions of a bachelor. Moreover, at Oxford they appear to have exercised that function during determination.[49]

Admission at Oxford to determine was decided by four regent masters, appointed by the faculty of arts, immediately before the beginning of Lent; it marked the point of entry into the second and higher part of the course, of preparation for the master's degree. The candidates had to swear that they had attended all the prescribed lectures and disputations and engaged in the necessary exercises, including responsion, supported by the testimonies of masters and bachelors, with any extenuating circumstances taken into account. Those accepted then had to dispute daily in logic during the afternoons of Lent, except on Fridays, which were reserved for grammar. The disputations formed a preparation for the mastership and were only taken by a minority who stayed on in the arts faculty after the completion of the first part of the course; for, as their name indicates, the determiners were exercising the masters' role of determining or resolving the questions being disputed, which also involved putting the initial objections to the question, to which the respondent – another bachelor or student – replied.

After completing determination in his fifth year the bachelor spent the

[44] Gibson (ed.), *Statuta* (note 33), 26.   [45] Gibson (ed.), *Statuta* (note 33), lxxxix.
[46] Rashdall, *Universities*, vol. I, no. 4, 452, citing *CUP*, vol. I, 530–2, no. 461.
[47] Gibson (ed.), *Statuta* (note 33), lxxxix.   [48] Fletcher, 'Faculty of Arts' (note 24), 380–1.
[49] Gibson (ed.), *Statuta Antiqua* (note 33), 28.

remainder of that year and the next two years taking part in masters' and bachelors' disputations as well as lecturing cursorily in the afternoons on set texts assigned by his master, two of logic and one of natural philosophy selected from Aristotle's books on nature. The disputations were correspondingly on logic and natural philosophy, and, although there is also a reference in the Oxford statutes to free – quodlibetal – questions,[50] no traces of any have yet been found, in contrast to the faculty of theology, where they form a separate literature. At the end of seven years – or eight for those who had not determined – the bachelor could be presented by his master to the chancellor for a licence to incept for the mastership. That initiated a much more elaborate series of depositions by a much greater number of regent masters concerning the candidate's fitness in morals and learning, as well as requiring the performance of tests by him; in addition to the statutory payments and oaths that he had completed all the necessary parts of the course, which included having lectured cursorily, he had also to undertake that he would give ordinary lectures in the faculty of arts and hold disputations for the following two years (necessary regency), a provision peculiar to the arts faculty because of its far greater numbers and the transience of its membership.

The successful candidate then received the licence to incept and had formally to be admitted as a master at the ceremony of inception, to which he personally invited all the regent masters. It was in two stages. The first was at vespers on a day when lectures could be held and consisted of a solemn disputation at which the candidate master had the usual part of respondent to the presiding master. The second stage was on the following day, when the candidate was invested with the insignia of his office and exercised his new status, first by delivering a short inaugural lecture (*principium*) and then by presiding at a disputation, when two questions were debated, putting the questions and raising the objections in each, and finally determining them.[51] He had thereby performed his first magisterial acts of lecturing and disputing. He then entered into his role as a full member of the arts faculty.

LATE MEDIEVAL DEVELOPMENTS

The products of the arts faculty reflected its logical and physical emphases as the principal sources of its commentaries, questions, and treatises. Logic was always predominant, but in the fourteenth and fifteenth centuries natural philosophy became increasingly prominent. For both subjects the first two-thirds of the fourteenth century were the culmination of their medieval devel-

---

[50] Gibson (ed.), *Statuta*, 32.
[51] J. A. Weisheipl, 'The Curriculum of the Faculty of Arts at Oxford in the Early Fourteenth Century', *Mediaeval Studies*, 26 (1964), 164–5; see also J. A. Weisheipl, 'Developments in the Arts Curriculum at Oxford in the Early Fourteenth Century', *Mediaeval Studies*, 28 (1966), 151–75.

opment; and in each case the direction was from Oxford to Paris, in contrast to the other main activity of speculative grammar, in which progress largely ceased after 1300, although its influence remained strong at Paris for another fifty years. In logic the range of topics extended from the earlier indigenous ones of paradoxes, properties of terms, and syncategorematic terms, often combined, to the more recent ones of obligations and consequences (conditional propositions), together with the assimilation of Aristotle's new logic, of syllogisms, demonstrations, and fallacies, the last of which, with modal propositions and future contingents (principally in connection with the theological problem of God's knowledge), received growing attention in the fourteenth and fifteenth centuries. These different areas were both treated separately and incorporated into more general works on logic, usually to serve as introductions and textbooks, such as those by William of Sherwood and Petrus Hispanus (Pope John XXI), the author of the most popular textbook on logic in the Middle Ages, in the thirteenth century, and very differently nearly a century later by William of Ockham and Walter of Burley. The contrast between them indicates how far the earlier indigenous logic of terms, as the main non-Aristotelian component in the thirteenth-century compendia, had been taken beyond Aristotle and expanded to include propositions by the first part of the fourteenth century.[52]

There was a comparable indigenous evolution in natural philosophy, initially at Oxford, in the first half of the fourteenth century, which was a continuation of the mathematical and scientific tradition of Grosseteste and his pupils. It was associated with the so-called Oxford calculators, mainly at Merton College, in the second and third quarters of the fourteenth century. They had their beginning in the *Treatise on Proportions*, by Thomas Bradwardine, who attempted to develop Aristotle's idea of the velocity of a moving body as proportional to the moving force, and inversely proportional to the resistance of the median, by means of a new mathematical technique. Bradwardine's example inspired the Mertonians to formulate mathematical rules for the different kinds of motion and changes in the speeds of moving bodies,[53] and also to measure the alterations in the degrees of intensity of physical qualities, such as heat or cold in bodies, and the first and last instances in which they occurred. As with developments in logic, they took their point of departure from Aristotle's definitions, here principally contained in his *Physics*, and for the first time gave his qualitative explanations a quantitative formulation. For this purpose a graphical method was invented by Nicholas of Oresme at Paris in the 1350s, as the outstanding member of a comparable group of logicians and natural scientists in the arts faculty there, between the 1340s and the 1360s, who utilized most of the concepts of the

[52] For those developments: Kretzmann, Kenny, and Pinborg (eds.), *Cambridge Medieval Philosophy* (note 8), parts IV and V.
[53] M. Clagett, *The Science of Mechanics in the Middle Ages* (Madison, 1961).

Oxford calculators. Their founder, John Buridan, a leading figure in the arts faculty for over thirty years, from the 1320s to at least the end of 1350s, was among the first to employ the terminist logic of the Oxford logicians, to which he made important contributions; he also, in his theory of *impetus*, gave a lasting definition to the recently revived explanation of violent or projectile motion as due to an impressed force, and not, as Aristotle held, to the air through which it passed – a notion adopted with modifications by Nicholas of Oresme and his contemporaries at Paris.

The Mertonians and Parisians together created a set of mathematical tools and mechanical terms, some of which were later employed by Galileo and his contemporaries in the sixteenth century. Although still bound by Aristotle's qualitative classifications, their medieval predecessors took the first steps towards a physics founded on measurement and calculation, even if they lacked empirical application. During the fourteenth and fifteenth centuries their influence both as logicians and as natural philosophers spread through the arts faculties of Italy and Spain and also the new foundations of northern Europe, to which some of the most prominent members of the arts faculty went, among them Albert of Saxony and Marsilius of Inghen, as the first rectors of Vienna and Heidelberg.

In addition to their separate treatises, questions, and commentaries on logic and natural philosophy, one of the most common forms which their logical and calculatory activities took was as *sophismata*, independent logical questions on some problematic statement or paradox, usually containing a syncategorematic term such as 'besides' or 'begin' or 'end', which could be treated both logically and mathematically.[54] As the subject of logical disputations in which all undergraduates had to engage, their freedom from any set texts made *sophismata* the most universal means of debating physical problems, such as the first and last instants of change in physical qualities, like heat or cold or colour. The vast output of *sophismata* literature provides probably the fullest record of the main intellectual and academic trends in the arts faculties of the last two centuries of the Middle Ages, a source which had only begun to be investigated. But they remained predominantly logical questions.[55] As often the work of mature scholars – such as *The Rules* for solving *sophismata* by William of Heytesbury, one of the Mertonians, written in about 1335 for first-year students in logic – they point to another feature of the arts faculty in the later Middle Ages: the tendency to make a career in arts, even though those who did so, as for example William of Heytesbury and Nicholas of Oresme, had frequently graduated in theology. The ability to continue to pursue the arts – although in no way unprecedented in the earlier

54 N. Kretzmann, 'Syncategoremata, exponibilia, sophismata', in Kretzmann, Kenny, and Pinborg (eds.), *Cambridge Medieval Philosophy* (note 8), 211–53.

55 E. D. Sylla, 'The Oxford Calculators', in Kretzmann, Kenny, and Pinborg (eds.), *Cambridge Medieval Philosophy* (note 8), 540–63.

centuries – probably owed something to the establishment of autonomous colleges at Paris, Oxford, and Cambridge; at the two English universities certain colleges, such as Merton, New College, and King's, made provision for the study of arts. In Italy in the fourteenth and fifteenth centuries the arts became incorporated into the educational programme of the humanists, extending northwards to Paris and Cambridge and other universities at the end of the fifteenth and the beginning of the sixteenth century.

Beyond the particular developments in logic and natural philosophy, there were the wider doctrinal and philosophical issues with which they were connected. Here, too, there was a discernible change in the first third of the fourteenth century, again coming initially from Oxford or from individuals associated with it, and reaching Paris during the 1330s. Although, however, the main areas – metaphysics, moral philosophy, cosmology, psychology, epistemology – belonged to the arts, their treatment was not confined to the arts faculty in virtue of their close connection with theology. Not only were they the inseparable constituents of any theological outlook, included in the commentaries on the *Sentences*, the standard theological textbook in the theological faculty (see chapter 13, 'The faculty of theology'), as well as in numerous other kinds of works; theologians, especially members of the religious orders who studied arts in their own religious houses, were in the forefront of their evolution throughout the thirteenth, fourteenth, and fifteenth centuries. Hence it is artificial to separate philosophical from theological issues; and many of the most formative ones, such as the nature of being, the eternity of the world, the powers of the heavenly bodies, free-will, knowledge through inner illumination versus abstraction through the senses, and the relation of the body to the soul, were at the centre of the controversies which led to and succeeded the condemnations of suspect doctrines in the arts faculties at Paris and Oxford in the 1270s (see chapter 13), because of their theological implications.

The shift that came in the fourteenth century was away from those broader philosophical concerns to a more restricted view of epistemology, bounded by more strictly defined notions of evidence and demonstration, and closely connected with terminism and natural philosophy in substituting a logical and physical for a metaphysical approach to both knowledge and reality. It was accompanied by a new emphasis upon contingency, both in nature and in the economy of grace and salvation, leading to a comparable overlapping of philosophy and theology over such issues as merit and free-will and the relation of human actions to God's omnipotence, foreknowledge and predestination, and the scope of natural knowledge in matters of faith. Although many of these questions received their currency from Duns Scotus (d. 1308) and William of Ockham (d. 1349), both Franciscans who studied at Oxford, it was not until the early fifteenth century, contrary to what used to be thought, that their divergent outlooks became associated with the old and new ways (*via antiqua* and *via moderna*), and then as part of a wider spectrum of schools.[56] The fourteenth century was marked by an absence of schools; instead there was a complex of doctrines on which different individuals drew in different combinations: nominalism in the rejection of common natures, such as humanity; logical terminism in the different meanings which terms can have according to what they stand for; opposing interpretations of the status of Aristotle's ten categories as either independent realities or merely describing individual states of existence; epistemological questions of whether objects are known directly or by means of species or images in the senses or intellect. None of these was answered consistently in the same manner by defined groups of thinkers; that applies particularly to the distinction between nominalism and terminism. By the 1340s the majority of thinkers at Oxford and increasingly at Paris – though not without opposition from the older conservative adherents to speculative grammar, expressed in a series of decrees against the new logical doctrines in the arts faculty between 1339 and 1341[57] – were terminists but not necessarily nominalists, as Ockham was but Buridan and Walter of Burley were not.

Correspondingly there was no need to be a nominalist or terminist to be a calculator, as the example of Bradwardine, a conservative theologian, shows, and no basis at all for the belief that Ockham was the cause of the new developments in natural science. His own position of reducing concepts to a minimum was directly at variance with their multiplication by the calculators in their imaginary experiments, as well as with Buridan's theory of impetus, which involved the introduction of an additional concept of an impressed force, beyond that of a moving body to which Ockham reduced movement, in keeping with his denial of real status to any of Aristotle's ten categories other than substance and quality. There was a similar diversity over theological questions concerning free-will, grace, merit, and predestination, as well as God's power to dispense with intermediaries (see chapter 13).

It was only in the later fourteenth century that the followers of Ockham, or nominalists, came to be identified with the moderns and by the beginning of the fifteenth century opposed to the ancients, or realists, variously identified with the revived schools of Thomism, Scotism, and Albertism, as the most important. The division between the old and the new ways was therefore theological as well as philosophical and logical, involving not only different approaches to questions of logic and natural philosophy with their own authorities, but different outlooks. In certain universities, such as Heidelberg and Ingolstadt, the division led to separate arts faculties,[58] and at most

---

[56] W. J. Courtenay, 'Antiqui and Moderni in Late Medieval Thought', *Journal of the History of Ideas*, 48 (1987), 3–10.

[57] W. J. Courtenay and K. H. Tachau, 'Ockham, Ockhamists and the English–German Nation at Paris, 1339–1341', *History of Universities*, 2 (1982), 53–96.

[58] Rashdall, *Universities*, vol. II, 253–4, 277.

universities both north and south of the Alps to separate chairs for the different ways, a process which continued into the sixteenth century. Only in England, at Oxford and Cambridge, was there no such division, and realism, principally that of Scotism, reigned unchallenged.[59]

THE FACULTY OF ARTS AND THE UNIVERSITY

The organization and role of the arts faculty varied with the different kinds of universities. In the older, northern foundations of Paris and Oxford, and also Cambridge, the arts faculty was preponderant. It was, like the rest of their institutions and faculties, a masters' organization. But only at Paris was there a defined faculty structure, where each of the faculties was in effect a corporation within the greater corporation of the university, having its own assembly, elected head, officers, statutes, seal, chest, schools, meeting place, and patron saints. Those features were reproduced in the four nations into which the arts faculty, as by far the largest and most heterogeneous faculty, was divided. They were the French, the Normans, the Picards, and the English, later English–German. None of them strictly corresponded to their names; the French nation extended to Italy and Spain, and the English–German nation included the rest of the British Isles, the German empire, eastern Europe, and Scandinavia. The nations were the basic units of the arts faculty; it was in them that the teaching, disputing, and examining, leading to the licence, were conducted under the recognized regent masters, who administered the nation and in whose schools the students enrolled. The nation was responsible for overseeing the schools, appointing the masters annually, and fixing their stipends, paid from the fees which were the main source of its income; and the nations collectively decided on the curriculum and organization of the course after deliberating separately. At the head of each nation was a proctor, elected in rotation from among the regent masters, usually for one month, and assisted by other officers, to conduct its affairs, including its finances, to maintain its statutes, and to enforce discipline. The four proctors from the four nations in turn elected the rector as head of the arts faculty, who held office for a period of six weeks, later becoming three months, and presided over its assembly. Together with the proctors he governed it between assemblies and formed the tribunal of the faculty. In the middle of the thirteenth century the rector became head of the whole university, not without opposition from the higher faculties.[60]

That combination of headship of the arts faculty with headship of the university was peculiar to Paris; it arose from the earlier rejection by the masters at the beginning of the thirteenth century of the claims of the

---

[59] D. R. Leader, 'Philosophy at Oxford and Cambridge in the Fifteenth Century', *History of Universities*, 4 (1984), 25–46.

[60] Leff, *Paris and Oxford Universities* (note 41), 51–67.

chancellor to be head of the university. Henceforth the chancellor's power was reduced to the formality of granting the licence to candidates approved by the examining masters in the faculty concerned. At Oxford and Cambridge, on the other hand, where there had been no such struggle, the chancellor was accepted as head of the university, drawn from the regent masters as one of themselves. Although at most other universities, both those in Italy, southern France, and Spain, and the new universities founded in northern Europe in the fourteenth and fifteenth centuries, the rector was head, he did not represent the arts faculty. Nor did the nations have the same constitutional place elsewhere as at Paris. At Oxford the university persistently refused to recognize the earlier groupings of northerners and southerners, although it did unofficially recognize a north–south division as the basis of appointing the two proctors, one from each region, and the other main officers, except the chancellor.[61] Correspondingly the two proctors were representatives of the whole university, as they were at Cambridge. The two English universities therefore lacked the federal elements of Paris, as they lacked its size and international character. Nevertheless in all three universities constitutional power – as well as numbers – was heavily weighted in favour of the arts faculty. At Paris it was maintained in the general congregation of the university by a permanent majority of four votes, one for each of the nations, to three votes by the higher faculties; at Oxford it lay in the provision that any majority must include the arts faculty as a whole, which also alone of the faculties had its own separate congregation, enabling it to meet and decide policy before the university congregation met. In addition members of the higher faculties, who had graduated from the arts faculty, continued to be bound by their oath of obedience to its statutes. In Paris that obligation came to extend to whatever future state its graduates might reach,[62] while at Oxford the claim of the arts faculty to be the fount and origin of the other faculties was never challenged.[63]

The dominance of the arts faculties at Paris, Oxford, and Cambridge was not paralleled elsewhere, even though the arts faculty was by far the most numerous element in the new northern universities of the later Middle Ages, often, as in the Scottish and some of the smaller German universities, to the virtual exclusion of the higher faculties. For, as the creation of secular rulers, they were much more directly under the control of the local powers than the three older universities, which originated more or less independently and, Paris especially, owed more to papal recognition, which was no longer of the same account in the fifteenth century, after the Great Schism.

That control went together with a second development in the later Middle Ages, the emergence of a system of salaried teachers, which began in the

[61] M. B. Hackett, 'The University as a Corporate Body', in *History of Oxford*, 65–7.
[62] Rashdall, *Universities*, vol. I, 328–9; in *CUP*, vol. I, 586–8, no. 501.
[63] Hackett, 'University as Corporate Body' (note 61), 66.

Italian universities in the thirteenth and fourteenth centuries and was adopted by the newer universities in northern Europe. Such payment obviated the need for a period of necessary regency, which also ceased to be obligatory at Paris after 1452.[64] Hence both externally and internally there was no longer the same scope for autonomy by the members of any faculty.

The role of the faculties was further diminished in two other directions. One was the almost universal reduction of the length of the arts course from six or seven years to four and sometimes three years by the later fourteenth century. The other was the growing importance of colleges as places of teaching at the expense of university teaching in the faculties and, at Paris, the nations.[65] That was equally true of the three older northern universities. Before the end of the fifteenth century, while only at Oxford and Cambridge were there still unsalaried regent masters and the arts course alone still took seven years, the colleges there were providing a full range of instruction. In Paris college lecturers were recognized by the university and were appointed by the faculty. At Oxford and Cambridge, where the colleges had much greater autonomy as independent foundations, college teaching was being extended to undergraduates. During the sixteenth century colleges at all three universities virtually replaced the older faculties as the centres of teaching; and they were an integral part of the newer northern universities, although they never had the same importance in southern European universities.

---

[64] Rashdall, *Universities*, vol. I, 447; in *CUP*, vol. IV, 733, no. 2690.
[65] For a general account: Cobban, *Medieval Universities*, ch. 6.

SELECT BIBLIOGRAPHY

See also the select bibliography of chapter 10.2.
Benson, R. B. and Constable, G. (eds.) *Renaissance and Renewal in the Twelfth Century*, Cambridge, Mass., 1982, and Oxford, 1985.
Clagett, M. *The Science of Mechanics in the Middle Ages*, Madison, 1961.
Courtenay, W. J. '*Antiqui* and *Moderni* in Late Medieval Thought', *Journal of the History of Ideas*, 48 (1987), 3–10.
Courtenay, W. J. and Tachau, K. H. 'Ockham, Ockhamists, and the English–German Nation at Paris, 1339–1341', *History of Universities*, 2 (1982), 53–96.
Crombie, A. C. *Medieval and Early Modern Science*, 2 vols., New York, 1959.
Crombie, A. C. *Robert Grosseteste and the Origins of Experimental Science 1100–1700*, 2nd edn, Oxford, 1961.
Emden, A. B. 'Northerners and Southerners in the Organisation of the University', in *Oxford Studies Presented to Daniel Callus*, Oxford, 1963, 1–30.
Gibson, M. (ed.) *Boethius: his Life, Thought and Influence*, Oxford, 1981.
Gibson, S. (ed.) *Statuta Antiqua Universitatis Oxoniensis*, Oxford, 1931.
Gilson, E. *History of Christian Philosophy in the Middle Ages*, London, 1955.

Haskins, C. H. *Studies in the History of Medieval Science*, 1st edn, Cambridge, Mass., 1924; 2nd edn, Cambridge, Mass., 1927; reprint, New York, 1960.

Hudson, A. and Wilks, M. (eds.) *From Ockham to Wyclif*, Oxford, 1987.

Kibre, P. *Studies in Medieval Science*, London, 1984.

Koch, J. (ed.) *Artes Liberales vom den Antiken Bildung zur Wissenschaft des Mittelalters*, Studien und Texte zur Geistesgeschichte des Mittelalters, 5, Leiden/Cologne, 1959.

Koch, J. (ed.) *Arts libéraux et philosophie au Moyen Age. Actes du IVe Congrès internationale de philosophie médiévale 1967*, Montreal/Paris, 1969.

Kretzmann, N., Kenny, A., and Pinborg, J. (eds.) *The Cambridge History of Later Medieval Philosophy*, Cambridge, 1982.

Leader, D. L. 'Philosophy at Oxford and Cambridge in the Fifteenth Century', *History of Universities*, 4 (1984), 25–46.

Leff, G. *Paris and Oxford Universities in the Thirteenth and Fourteenth Centuries* New York, 1968.

Murphy, J. J. *Rhetoric in the Middle Ages*, Berkeley, 1974.

van Steenberghen, F. *Aristotle in the West*, Louvain, 1955.

Verger, J. 'Remarques sur l'enseignement des arts dans les universités du Midi à la fin du Moyen Age', *Annales du Midi*, 91 (1979), 355–81.

Wagner, D. L. (ed.) *The Seven Liberal Arts in the Middle Ages*, Bloomington, Ind., 1984.

Weisheipl, J. A. 'The Classification of the Sciences in Medieval Thought', *Mediaeval Studies*, 27 (1965), 54–90.

Weisheipl, J. A. 'The Place of the Liberal Arts in the University "Curriculum" during the XIVth and XVth Centuries', in J. Koch (ed.), *Arts libéraux et philosophie au Moyen Age. Actes du IVe Congrès internationale de philosophie médiévale*, Montreal/Paris, 1969, 209–13.

Weisheipl, J. A. 'The Structure of the Arts Faculty in the Mediaeval University', *British Journal of Educational Studies*, 19 (1971), 263–71.

Weisheipl, J. A. 'Developments in the Arts Curriculum at Oxford in the Early Fourteenth Century', *Mediaeval Studies*, 28 (1966), 151–75.

CHAPTER 10.2

THE QUADRIVIUM

JOHN NORTH

SOURCES OF UNIVERSITY LEARNING

One of the most conspicuous purposes of the medieval university was that of providing an élite with the knowledge and skill needed to serve society, whether in an ecclesiastical or a secular role. When we examine the careers of university masters of theology, we are left in no doubt that this purpose was well fulfilled, and theological attitudes no doubt coloured attitudes to knowledge generally. The general medieval paradigm of knowledge was an inheritance, to be jealously purified of alien accretions and misunderstandings, and then commented on and passed on. This paradigm, however, fits the sciences of the quadrivium less well than it fits the 'arts of expression' (*artes sermonicales*) of the *trivium*. Even at the elementary level of the arts curriculum, there are signs of somewhat less rigidity in the teaching of arithmetic, music, geometry, and astronomy. Perhaps this was a consequence of the fact that, being more advanced, the *quadrivium* was in the hands of more experienced masters in the schools. Certainly it seems to have often depended on the initiative of individuals – in Paris, as we shall mention later, teaching in mathematics was mainly on feast-days – and we know from the writings of many of those individuals that they were often infected with the excitement of discovery, discovery not only of new texts, but of new ways of elaborating on the contents of those texts. There was, in other words, an element of 'research', as distinct from teaching. Sometimes it was pursued in the pure spirit of the original text. More often, it was heavily constrained by the intellectual protocols of the time – those stemming from logic and rhetoric – that governed commentary and debate throughout the university. At the same time it took some benefit from them.

The curriculum of the *quadrivium*, like that of the *trivium*, was in direct descent from Greek philosophy, which Pliny and Varro followed.

With the elimination of architecture and medicine, what had been nine arts in Varro became the seven liberal arts of the Middle Ages. It was Martianus Capella (*fl.* 410–39) who finally canonized the sevenfold division, in his *The Marriage of Mercury and Philology*. The first three of the twenty books of *Etymologies* of Isidore of Seville (d. 636) dealt with those seven liberal arts, and both Hrabanus Maurus and Bede made compilations with comparable structures.

Medieval Greek and Hebrew encyclopedias are of less relevance than the Latin to the European university tradition. Encyclopedias produced in the Islamic world, on the other hand, with their roots in the scientific traditions of Hellenistic Alexandria, were to become central to that tradition. In organization, the sciences were arranged by the lights of Aristotelian philosophy, with some Neoplatonic rearrangement. Among the greatest of writers in the Islamic encyclopedic tradition we have al-Kindi, who in the ninth century surveyed almost all of ancient Greek science, Avicenna (Ibn Sina), in the eleventh century, with his great medical *Canon*, and Averroës (Ibn Rushd) ('Commentator'), in the twelfth, with his numerous commentaries on Aristotle. When such works as these were eventually absorbed in the West, they tended to be crammed into the categories of the Latin encyclopedias around which the schools were already organized.

For the later Middle Ages, we know more or less what textbooks were in use, primarily from university statutes. Unfortunately, however, these statutes arrived on the scene only after a number of important changes in the curriculum had taken place, notably in connection with the influx of translations from the Arabic. C. H. Haskins has given us an older list, from the end of the twelfth century, that seems to presuppose something like the university organization of four faculties. The list is arranged in the order of the seven liberal arts, and the professional studies of medicine, civil and canon law, and theology. The list is perhaps due to Alexander Neckam.[1]

Neckam (1157–1217) was one of those who had promoted natural science in its older, popular, and rather uncritical, encyclopedic form, through his *De naturis rerum*. Even in that work we find references to Arabic and Hebrew writers. When we read such authors now, we tend to seize upon such references, and upon such textual discoveries as the 'first European reference to a magnetic compass for navigational use', and overlook the sad truth of the matter: we cannot honestly claim to find in them the seeds of a self-sufficient scientific discipline. What is true of Neckam is true of other writers in this genre. We have, for instance, the *De natura rerum* of Thomas of Cantimpré (*c.* 1186 – *c.* 1294), the extremely popular and much-translated *De proprietatibus rerum* of Bartholomeus Anglicus (*fl.* 1220–50), the *Speculum maius* of

---

[1] For this book list, and reference to several sets of statutes (Paris 1255, 1270, etc., Oxford 1267, and later Naples, Salerno, Bologna, and Montpellier): C. H. Haskins, *Studies in the History of Medieval Science* (Cambridge, Mass., 1927), ch. 18.

Vincent of Beauvais (*c.* 1190–1264), a work that acquired a supplement in the first quarter of the fourteenth century, and Brunetto Latini's French encyclopedia, *Li Livres dou trésor* (1260–7). Their continuing popularity – which lasted well beyond the Middle Ages – is not in question, but they ceased to reflect university practice in anything but their outward forms and occasional bibliographical lists. They were outwardly systematic, but they simply failed to lend themselves to the truly systematic development of any of the sciences of the *quadrivium*. For the works that did so, we must look elsewhere.

Alexander Neckam himself helps us out for the early Parisian period. (After an education at St Albans, he had studied in Paris.) Boethius was to be used, he said, for arithmetic and music, and Euclid for geometry.[2] Euclid's *Elements* had been translated by Adelard of Bath early in the twelfth century. It was also translated by Hermann of Carinthia, and later by Gerard of Cremona. As for astronomy, Alexander Neckam mentions the *canones* of Ptolemy, and the compendious introduction to Ptolemy by Alfraganus (d. after 861). Whether by 'canons' he meant Ptolemy's *Almagest*, or canons (explanatory principles) for Ptolemaic astronomical tables, is hard to say.[3] The magisterial *Almagest* became widely known in western Europe through Gerard of Cremona's Latin translation from the Arabic, dated 1175, although a little-known Latin version had been made from the Greek in Sicily perhaps even more than twenty years earlier.[4] The work of Alfraganus (it is known by various titles,[5] but we shall refer to it as the *Elementa*) had been twice translated in the same century, once by John of Spain in 1135 and again by Gerard of Cremona before 1175. Apart from the opening chapter, which dealt with the various calendars of the world, it was based on Ptolemy's *Almagest*. The *Elementa* of Alfraganus was even so of far greater direct medieval influence than its prototype, for it was the sort of digest with which students could – with difficulty – cope. It was to be largely but not entirely replaced in the thirteenth century by John of Sacrobosco's *De sphera*, and yet that later work still owed much to it.[6]

Here we have the makings of the curriculum of the arts student of the *quadrivium* for the whole of the Middle Ages, as seen through northern European eyes. How much and how little its ingredients were later supplemented and modified we shall explain in due course. From the perspective of the Iberian peninsula, however, the picture so far given must seem a distorted

---

[2] P. Glorieux, *La Faculté des Arts et ses maîtres au XIIIe siècle* (Paris, 1971), 33.

[3] There is a third possibility: a work known as the 'canon of Ptolemy and Pythagoras' survives in a manuscript from a later period (*incipit* 'Inventum Ptolomei ...'; see MS Budapest 59, 14c., fols. 19 v-20).

[4] The precise circumstances of the Sicilian translation have recently become a subject of keen controversy. R. Lemay, in *La Diffusione delle scienze islamiche nel medio evo Europe (Convegno Internazionale)* (Rome, 1987), 399–535, argues against Haskins, *Studies* (note 1), 53–4, that Hermann of Carinthia was responsible (*c.* 1150).

[5] Typical are *De scientia astrorum* (John of Seville) and *De aggregationibus scientie stellarum* (Gerard of Cremona).

[6] See p. 348.

one, for there the technicalities of Aristotelian natural philosophy and Greek and Arabic mathematics and astronomy were well established, and this at a time when the monastic teaching of the *quadrivium* elsewhere meant little more than the abacus, the ecclesiastical calendar, the practice of plainsong, and a little practical geometry.

The first translations from Arabic into Latin in Spain were done in the Catalonian marches, in about the middle of the tenth century, as a consequence of the immigration of Mozarabs from Muslim Spain into Catalonia. There were, of course, scholars from other parts of Europe who were aware of the relative deficiencies of their own scientific culture: witness such notable visitors to Spain as Gerbert of Aurillac (later Pope Sylvester II, *c.* 945–1003), Plato of Tivoli (active in Barcelona, 1134–45), Adelard of Bath (*fl.* 1116–42), Hermann of Carinthia (*fl.* 1140–50), Robert of Ketton (friend and literary collaborator of Hermann), and Rudolf of Bruges (a disciple of Hermann).

It will suffice to take two of these men to illustrate changing styles. It is not easy to ascertain how much Muslim science was available to Gerbert in his Catalonian centre (Vich): he appears to have learned how to use an abacus different from the old Roman version, and how to construct an armillary sphere and a sundial, and conceivably an astrolabe. Any eastern influence on his work is unremarkable, but, after his return, he kept up a correspondence with the translator Llobet. Adelard, on the other hand, made his own translations from the Arabic, particularly noteworthy being that of the astronomical table of al-Khwarizmi from the revision done by the Cordoban astronomer al-Majriti (d. *c.* 1007). Evidence for his visit to Spain is admittedly only indirect, but he speaks of visits to Syria and southern Italy, and a Spanish interlude is not improbable, in view of his acceptance of the tables for Cordoba.[7] His translation of the *Elements* of Euclid, the first significant version into Latin, was based on the Arabic of al-Hajjaj ibn Yusuf ibn Matar (ninth century).[8] Adelard produced a polished treatise on the astrolabe (*c.* 1149) for the future Henry II, but this was done in England.

The reputation of the Peninsula as a centre of learning continued to draw others thither, and Iberian learning was even exported far and wide in person, for example through the travels of the Jewish scholar Abraham ibn Ezra (*c.* 1090 – *c.* 1164), who journeyed as far as London. This twelfth-century activity preceded the establishment of any *studium generale* in Spain. (That in Salamanca was founded by Alfonso IX of León in 1218, and that in Seville by his son in 1254.) The translations of the twelfth century were done in many places – Barcelona, Tarazona, Segovia, León, Pamplona, and beyond the Pyrenees at Toulouse, Béziers, Narbonne, Montpellier, Marseille, and so on.

---

[7] J. D. North, *Horoscopes and History* (London, 1986), 96–107.

[8] For a general account of Spanish activity: J. Vernet, *Ce que la culture doit aux Arabes d'Espagne* (Paris, 1985). On the complex interrelations of the various translations of the supremely important text of Euclid, see the scheme in ibid., 133, for example.

Later, Toledo achieved some sort of pre-eminence, and it was to Toledo that Gerard of Cremona, the most assiduous of all translators, was drawn, expressly by the lure of Ptolemy's work.[9]

Jewish scholars played an important part in all this work. To take one example: the Jew Abraham bar Hiyya (Savasorda, *fl.* 1136) acted as intermediary in the translating activities of Plato of Tivoli. Besides translations into Hebrew, and Hebrew works based on Arabic models, there are manuscripts in Arabic written in Hebrew characters. Most of the works that were in common use in Spain became available in Hebrew, notably in southern France, in the thirteenth and fourteenth centuries, and there was a modest two-way traffic in ideas between Jewish scholars and Christian universities in the rest of Europe throughout the Middle Ages.[10]

The scientific curricula of the universities of Europe owed to Spain much more than translations from the Arabic, however. Averroës (Ibn Rushd), the great Cordoban natural philosopher, stands over the late European Middle Ages almost as a proxy for Aristotle, but does not have much immediate bearing on the introductory courses in the arts faculty. Many other Iberian writers, however, were of great importance to the coming educational explosion: from Spanish translations of the key text of al-Khwarizmi on arithmetic (with sections on what was effectively algebra), and Arabic reworkings of it, a series of texts emerged that were to serve the universities for three centuries and more, in the teaching, among other things, of vulgar fractions, the system of Hindu–Arabic numerals, and the sexagesimal arithmetic used in astronomy. This is the tradition in which Sacrobosco's *Algorismus* stands – to name but one key text of the thirteenth century and after.

Another vital text for European scientific learning contained the collection of astronomical tables usually associated with the name of Arzachel (Ibn az-Zarqellu, d. 1100). These, the Toledan tables, translated and supplemented with some Christian material by Gerard of Cremona, took Europe by storm. They were issued from various European centres (Marseille, Paris, London, and so on) in appropriate redactions, and were even translated into Greek, around the year 1340.[11] The canons written for the tables by Arzachel were an important source of trigonometrical and astronomical theory for the better student, although they would not have been enough for the best – for the canons taught the subject only by rote, rather than from first principles. Arzachel, like so many others around him, gave much time to the study of

[9] For a short but detailed account of the great wave of translations in Spain: J. Millás, 'Translations of Oriental Scientific Works (to the End of the Thirteenth Century)', in G. S. Metraux and F. Crouzet (eds.), *The Evolution of Science* (London, 1963). For a wide cultural survey: Vernet, *Ce que la culture* (note 8), especially ch. 3–9.

[10] For recent surveys of the Jewish contribution: B. R. Goldstein, *Theory and Observation in Ancient and Medieval Astronomy* (London, 1985), especially chs. 20–24.

[11] G. J. Toomer, 'A Survey of the Toledan Tables', *Osiris*, 15 (1968), 1–174; J. M. Millás, *Estudios sobre Azarquiel* (Madrid/Granada, 1943–50).

astronomical instruments, and in particular to new astrolabe projections, and to the instrument known as an *equatorium*, for evaluating planetary positions.

In the last quarter of the thirteenth century, under the patronage of Alfonso X the Wise of León and Castile, a new and even more important set of tables was prepared, with the help of Muslim and Jewish scholars. The canons written for them were now in the Castilian vernacular, which might explain in part the fact that several decades passed before the work was accepted into the Latin tradition. When this finally happened, the version that obtained most currency – it was printed in 1483 – was that of John of Saxony (*c.* 1327). His was not the first Latin version, however: his fellow Parisians Johannes de Muris and John of Lignères had produced others in 1321 and 1322, and they were to follow with yet further alternatives. The tables also reached England at much the same time, via Paris. We find them early associated with Glasgow, Northampton, and London, and they were developed in important ways in Oxford, as we shall see later. There remains the mystery of the fact that they evidently lay dormant in the Latin world outside Spain for half a century after their first composition.[12]

Spain was not, of course, the only port of entry of ancient Greek and Arabic learning into the schools of Europe. We have already mentioned Sicily as a source of translations. By the time Leonardo of Pisa (Fibonacci, *c.* 1170 – *post* 1240), the greatest European mathematician of his age, became imperial mathematician to Frederick II, he had travelled extensively in north Africa and the Mediterranean, and had absorbed Muslim learning in a very direct way. Even he, however, had important Spanish contacts – for example, with the Toledan Jewish scholar Judas ben Salomon Cohen, and through translations by Adelard of Bath, Robert of Ketton, and Gerard of Cremona. Fibonacci is in a historical sense a lonely figure, too great for his contemporaries to appreciate properly.[13] They sensed his genius, but one suspects that they put a greater value on Michael Scot, the imperial astrologer whom Dante thought it proper to place in hell. It should not be overlooked, however, that the motivation of so many of those who studied the arts of the *quadrivium* was undoubtedly astrological. Astrology was a system of belief that was at the same time in a very real sense 'rational', and that required a thorough mathematical training for its mastery. The rules whereby scholars predicted

[12] For a general survey of their history, and the English treatment of them: J. D. North, 'The Alfonsine Tables in England', in Y. Maeyama and W. G. Saltzer (eds.), *Prismata* (Hildesheim, 1977), 269–301. For the John of Saxony version: E. Poulle, *Les Tables alphonsines, avec les canons de Jean de Saxe* (Paris, 1984). Later printed versions – the last of which was as late as 1641 (Madrid) – have the canons of Santritter or Gaurico. For much useful material on Alfonsine astronomy as a whole: J. Samsó (ed.) *De astronomia Alphonsi regis (Proceedings of a Berkeley symposium on Alfonsine astronomy, 1985)* (Barcelona, 1987).

[13] K. Vogel, 'Fibonacci', in C. C. Gillispie (ed.), *Dictionary of Scientific Biography*, vol. IV (New York, 1971), 604–13.

the fortunes of individuals, of princes, of nations, of the weather, and so forth, on the basis of the configurations of the heavens, have a markedly arbitrary element in them. They were nevertheless accepted and acted upon, and for this purpose very precise astronomical calculation was required, to determine the exact state of the heavens. It was undoubtedly the feeling that Spain was a centre of excellence in astrological education, and in the ancillary mathematics it demanded, that caused so many scholars to cross the Pyrenees.

MUSIC

In the period before the rise of the universities, of the four branches of the *quadrivium*, music – by virtue of its importance in Christian worship – took pride of place. It was, said Brunetto Latini later, the second mathematical science, 'which serves for our delight and for the service of the Lord'. It offered – shades of Pythagoras – a means to the perfection of the spirit, a point that Boethius made strongly. It had, of course, its practical side – vocal and instrumental – but in the context of the schools a strongly theoretical element predominated, based largely on the theory of the monochord, with which almost all important works on music began. (Even practical music seems to have been taught in a strictly analytical fashion, although by the nature of things much less is known about practice than about bookish theory.) There are well over a hundred medieval texts on this one theme, but the most important of all remained Boethius's synthesis of ancient traditions, *De institutione musica*.[14]

The Pythagorean theory of music purveyed by Boethius in this work, which is really a continuation of his *Arithmetica*, rested on the arithmetical, geometrical, and harmonic ratios of the numbers, 6, 8, 9, and 12. He catalogued, at what one might consider unnecessary length, the numerical relations that seemed to him most important, with a technical terminology that seems now more designed to mystify than to enlighten. By the use of letters in place of numerical ratios, a musical notation was gradually evolved and improved, by such scholars as Philippe de Vitry and Guillaume de Machaut. Greatest musical progress was made where the subject was taught in association with some great church or cathedral, such as the chapel of Notre-Dame de Paris, or the monasteries of Saint-Victor or Sainte-Geneviève. Léonin and Pérotin were both chapel-masters.[15] There was perhaps no comparable university city in Europe offering the same sort of opportunities as Paris –

[14] *Patrologia Latina*, vol. LXIII (Paris, 1847; reprint, Turnhout, 1977). For further bibliography: Glorieux *Faculté des Arts*, (note 2), 35.
[15] J. Smits van Waesberghe, *Musikerziehung: Lehre und Theorie der Musik im Mittelalter* (Leipzig, 1969). On Boethius: M. Gibson (ed.), *Boethius: his Life, Thought and Influence* (Oxford, 1981).

although Salamanca offered degrees in music – and one suspects that else-where the teaching of Boethius was a relatively dry and theoretical affair, concentrating on memorizing the ratios, and drawing consolation from the fact that music was not only instrumental but (following Boethius) universal and human. The concept of *musica humana* concerned the supposed harmony of psychical and bodily function. That of *musica mundana*, with each of the heavens having its own chord, would have reminded the student of astronomical pleasures in store.

Boethius seems to have been at the core of teaching in every university where music was a part of the arts curriculum, and to have remained there throughout the Middle Ages, wherever music survived as a part of the course. The place of music is somewhat obscure in early Oxford history, but Boethius is stipulated in 1431, and still finds a place in the Elizabethan statutes of 1564–5. He survived in the Oxford statutes, indeed, until the nineteenth century.[16] In view of the arithmetical component in the subject it is hardly surprising that figures famous in astronomy or mathematics should have contributed to music, and conversely. The Parisian Johannes de Muris wrote extremely important works on both astronomy and music, for example, while Walter of Evesham (Walter of Odington), who was probably at Oxford, and who is certainly more famous for his music, made not insig-nificant contributions to astronomy.

ARITHMETIC

For arithmetic, most statutes – and, where they are not available, the testi-mony of biographies and numbers of surviving manuscripts – make it clear that Boethius (*De institutione arithmetica*) was again the staple diet of the young arts student. Euclid was often a supplement: we recall that the *Elements* contains much arithmetic. Other works in use were Alexander of Villedieu's *Massa compoti* (on the principles underlying calendar compu-tation) and Sacrobosco's *Algorismus*, which we mentioned earlier. This was Parisian practice, and in the earliest known Oxford requirements (of the early fourteenth century), in stipulating simply '*Compotus*' and '*Algorismus*', Oxford was probably following suit.[17] There were other texts, to be sure: a summary of Boethius by Oxford's Thomas Bradwardine (*c.* 1290–1349: or was it Simon Bredon's?) was probably used there, and, judging by its avail-ability in manuscripts in Munich, Erfurt, Berne, and Vienna, was also found a

---

[16] J. Caldwell, 'Music in the Faculty of Arts', in J. McConica (ed.), *The History of the University of Oxford*, vol. III (Oxford, 1986), 201–12.

[17] See Glorieux, *Faculté des Arts* (note 2). For Oxford: J. A. Weisheipl, 'Curriculum of the Faculty of Arts at Oxford in the early Fourteenth Century', *Medieval Studies*, 26 (1964), 161, 170.

use in some central European universities.[18] One may indeed take almost any text from a typical arts curriculum and, by searching manuscript catalogues, unearth a handful of different summaries or commentaries on it. Such commentaries testify to a style of teaching, but also to the intrinsic difficulty that some students had with material that to us looks painfully simple, for example the rules of simple addition, subtraction, multiplication, and long division.

In order to sweeten the pill of arithmetic, and provide practice, a curious arithmetical game called *rithmomachia* was devised. It is a sort of draughts, with pieces numbered with selected odd and even integers. The numbers in question are simple quadratic functions of numbers less than 10, and may be as large as 289 and 361 (the squares of $2n + 1$, for $n = 8$ or 9). The rules of the game, which had a long history, are complicated enough to make one wonder whether the unadorned Boethius was not preferable.[19] There were other games and pedagogical aids for the arts student, in astronomy and in the *computus*. The 'manual *computus*', representing calendar letters and numbers by the joints of the fingers, was a technique no doubt familiar to almost every student. There were similar manual systems in music, and some survive to this day; but the calendar, in the life of the cleric, was especially important, in particular because it was organized around Easter, the celebration of the most important event in Christian history.

The rules of the calendar are simple, to the extent that, once the astronomy behind them is agreed, they depend on cycles of counting. Unfortunately, the astronomical element gave the more perspicacious scholars cause for concern, and there were recurrent attempts at reform. These were not to meet with success until the Gregorian reform of 1582. It is doubtful whether many ordinary students in arts were aware of the problem or concerned by it, yet Robert Grosseteste (*c.* 1170–1253) and Roger Bacon (*c.* 1219 – *c.* 1292), both of them significant names in the history of western science, considered the problem a serious one. When Bacon sang the praises of the mathematical sciences, and spoke of them as a potential weapon for the defence of Christendom, he was thinking of their geographical use – of the missionary value of latitudes and longitudes of place, and the whereabouts of the ten tribes and the Antichrist – but also of the calendar. Among other things, he feared the derision of the Jews, who seemed to have the Passover calculation under better control than his co-religionists.[20]

[18] L. Thorndike and P. A. Kibre, *Catalogue of Incipits of Mediaeval Scientific Writings in Latin*, The Mediaeval Academy of America (London, 1963), cols. 641, 783, 1175, 1401.

[19] G. Beaujouan, 'L'enseignement du quadrivium', in *Settimane di studio del Centro italiano di studi sull'alto medioevo*, vol. XIX (Spoleto, 1972), 679–723.

[20] M. A. Hoskin, and O. Pedersen (eds.), *Gregorian Reform of the Calendar. Proceedings of the Vatican Conference to Commemorate its 400th Anniversary, 1582–1982* (Vatican City, 1983). An especially useful work on calendars in the present context is C. Wordsworth, *The Ancient Calendar of the University of Oxford* (Oxford, 1903–4).

GEOMETRY

Such practical considerations were never far from view in any part of the arts curriculum. Consider Brunetto Latini on geometry:

> par qui nous savons les mesures et les proportions des choses, par lonc et par lé et par hautece; c'est la science par quoi li anchien sage s'effochierent par soutill-ite de geometrie de trover la grandeur dou ciel et de la tiere, et de la hautece entre l'un et l'autre, et maintes autres proportions ki a mervillier font.

> [by which we know the sizes and proportions of things in length, breadth, and height; it is the science by which the wise ancients – through their geometrical expertise – were able to find the size of the heavens and of the earth, and the distance separating them, not to mention other proportions that are a source of wonder.][21]

The same reservations about geometry apply as those made about the canons to astronomical tables: more attention was given to the rehearsal of rules than to the logical structure of the science by which those rules had been obtained in the first place. Euclid's *Elements* was the universally accepted prime text. How far the student went depended to some extent on the length of the arts course, which varied between wide limits; but even at Oxford, with its long course, only the first six books were required pro forma.[22] Translations available were, as already mentioned, by Adelard of Bath, Hermann of Carinthia, and Gerard of Cremona. Other works of 'speculative' geometry were a pseudo-Boethian commentary on the *Elements*, Euclid's *De quantitatibus datis* (as Bacon informs us), and Jordanus Nemorarius' *De triangulis*.

On the side of 'practical' geometry, we find a variety of styles. The distinction between speculative and practical goes back to Plato and Aristotle, but in the twelfth and thirteenth centuries it was no mere classificatory rhetoric. There is abundant evidence that Euclid was studied by many in order to prepare the way for a study of *Almagest* – 'which is the principal goal of our study', as Robert of Ketton said.[23] The quotation from Brunetto Latini sounds as though it might echo Hugh of Saint Victor's *Didascalion* (Hugh died in 1141), with its subdivisions *planimetria*, *altimetria*, and *cosmimetria*. A treatise on one of the various sorts of quadrant could have been expounded under any of these headings. The most famous early treatise was perhaps the *Tractatus quadrantis* (twelfth century?), ascribable either to Robertus Anglicus or Johannes Anglicus of Montpellier.[24] It describes a small, hand-held,

---

[21] Glorieux, *Faculté des Arts* (note 2), 36, from which I also take the following information about the curriculum.

[22] Weisheipl, 'Curriculum' (note 17), 171.

[23] Burnett, in *Diffusione delle scienze* (note 4), 25n. 45.

[24] S. K. Victor, *Practical Geometry in the High Middle Ages: 'Artis cuiuslibet consummatio' and 'Pratike de geometrie'* (Philadelphia, 1979), 22–3; F. Maddison, 'Early Astronomical and

quadrant, usually made of brass and engraved with scales, over which a cursor could be moved. Sighting vanes on the quadrant itself allowed the altitudes of celestial bodies and buildings to be taken, and made time calculations possible.

Other texts of practical geometry commonly expounded were those on statics (for example, the *De ponderibus* of Jordanus) and those on optics. Optics is especially interesting, for it is a subject not only in which progress was made in the Middle Ages – this is true of every branch of the *quadrivium* – but in which that progress was taken into account in teaching, which was seldom true elsewhere, so far as one can tell. Studies by Euclid, Ptolemy, and Alhazen (Ibn al-Haitham) of the reflection and refraction of light were unknown in the West before the thirteenth century, and the encyclopedic tradition (Alexander Neckam, Bartholomeus Anglicus, and so on) was a poor substitute, drawing as it did on impressionistic materials from such writers as Plato, Pliny, Saint Augustine, and Chalcidius. The entire subject was revivified, however, by Robert Grosseteste, who had available to him Euclid's *Optica* and *Catoptrica*, Aristotle's *Meteorologica*, al-Kindi's *De aspectibus*, and possibly Ptolemy's *Optica*.[25]

Optics was concerned with general metaphysical and physical problems, such as modes of transmission, the 'multiplication of species' and so forth, and with such geometrical problems as those of refraction and reflections, colour, the eye, and the rainbow. Grosseteste considered all of these. He was in some respects obsessed with light, which was important to his entire philosophy. His short *On Light or the Beginning of Forms* (*De luce seu de inchoatione formarum*), a product of his later years, and memorable for its style of scientific argument, explains the creation of the entire material universe as due to the activity of light. While not of direct concern to those who studied the *quadrivium*, the overall metaphysical views of Oxford's first chancellor could not have been entirely absent from the minds of those who taught the more mundane aspects of optics to their charges. Grosseteste had a very great influence on subsequent generations, especially through his connection with the Oxford Franciscans, to whom he was first lector. His most influential follower was Roger Bacon, but through the Franciscans generally he had a very strong European influence, and this makes his work of more than common interest. And he was driven by his theology, especially his theology of creation.

Grosseteste was unfortunate not to have had access to the masterly *Optica* of Alhazen (Ibn al-Haitham), which was translated in the early thirteenth

---

Mathematical Instruments. A Brief Summary of Sources and Modern Studies', *History of Science*, 2 (1963), 17–50.

[25] A. C. Crombie, *Robert Grosseteste and the Origins of Experimental Science, 1100–1700* (Oxford, 1961); R. W. Southern, *Robert Grosseteste: the Growth of an English Mind in Medieval Europe* (Oxford, 1986). Excerpts from many of the fundamental writings on optics are to be found in E. Grant, *A Source Book in Medieval Science* (Cambridge, 1974).

century or late twelfth century. Roger Bacon and the two writers of the most widely used university texts, John Pecham (*c.* 1230–92) and the Silesian scholar Witelo (*c.* 1235 – *post* 1274), did have access to this, as well as to several useful works of Avicenna and the *Optica* of Ptolemy. The writings of all three were very much the products of thirteenth-century university learning: all were at various times in Paris; and Bacon and Pecham were also at Oxford, both as Franciscans, and almost inevitably, therefore, coloured with Grosseteste's Augustinianism. Bacon was about forty when he entered the order (*c.* 1257), while Pecham, a far more career-conscious individual, became eleventh lector to the Franciscans in Oxford in 1271–2, moving from there to become provincial of the order, then to the papal curia as master in theology, and finally to the archbishopric of Canterbury.

Sources continued to accumulate. We can say, for example, that Witelo's principal text in optics, the *Perspectiva*, must have been written after 1270, since it makes use of William of Moerbeke's translation of Hero of Alexandria's *Catoptrica*, dated the last day of 1269. Grosseteste, Bacon, Pecham, and Witelo all advanced the science of optics in the thirteenth century, but more than that: they virtually exhausted medieval capabilities. It is an odd fact, hard to explain, that the fourteenth century, for all its growing mathematical expertise, could add very little to what they had done; and the texts written by Pecham and Witelo continued in university use until well into the seventeenth century. The influence of their texts throughout the whole of Europe was enormous, and copious references to them will be found in such authors as Nicholas of Oresme, Regiomontanus, Leonardo da Vinci, Francesco Maurolico, Thomas Harriot, Johannes Kepler, and René Descartes – to name seven men who played a significant part in the later history of optics.

ASTRONOMY

A grossly oversimplified Aristotelian scheme – with concentric spheres carrying the planets, and a sublunar set of spheres of the elements at its centre – lay at the heart of medieval cosmological teaching. Although Ptolemy's *Almagest* lay behind the curriculum, it was rarely used, but was replaced by digests such as that by Alfraganus already mentioned, or by one of several derivative works with the generic title *De sphera*. Of these, Sacrobosco's was by far the most famous, although another by Grosseteste and a more ambitious anonymous *Almagestum abbreviatum* were among the alternatives. Sacrobosco's work, in use until at least the seventeenth century, was one of the most widely used of all textbooks in the Middle Ages, and it is hard to see why, unless its slow pace and abundant classical literary ornament were considered virtues. It deals with spherical astronomy and some corresponding geography. For all its simplicity, it was the object of commentary, almost as though it were a sacred text. The best-known medieval example was perhaps that of Robertus

Anglicus (1271); even the highly intelligent Christopher Clavius (1537–1612) wrote a commentary on it, running to some 800 pages in the later editions.[26] There are some hundreds of surviving manuscripts, and they are found in libraries throughout all of Europe. There were thirty-five Venice printings, and others from Bologna, Milan, Avignon, Dijon, Louvain, Frankfurt-on-Main, Cracow, Vienna, Augsburg, and Antwerp. If one may speak of a European experience, Sacrobosco was certainly a part of it.

Sacrobosco's much longer *Computus* was in some universities (Oxford, for instance) set under astronomy, rather than under arithmetic. It was widely diffused, although less so than *De sphera*, and unlike that work does not seem to have been put into the vernacular. Both of his works – despite their antiquated character – were promoted by Philip Melanchthon, in an effort to provide the reformed University of Wittenberg with textbooks.[27] (Many other Lutheran universities were strongly influenced by Melanchthon.) Grosseteste's *Computus* had been an alternative to Sacrobosco's in the thirteenth century, but had soon yielded place to Sacrobosco's thereafter.

The *De sphera* scarcely touched on planetary motions, and it is probable that few arts graduates before the late thirteenth century knew much about that subject, which was nevertheless of the very essence of medieval astronomy. We have already seen how canons to the Toledan and Alfonsine tables could convey a modicum of information on this theme, albeit information implicit in computing routines. To fill the obvious gap, a type of work was produced under the generic name *Theorica planetarum*. John of Seville's version of Alfraganus falls under this heading, as does another twelfth-century work by Roger of Hereford, but, without doubt, the most widely diffused text with this name was one that opened with the words '*Circulus eccentricus vel egresse cuspidis*'.[28]

The first five chapters of the anonymous *Theorica* are concerned with the motions in longitude of the sun, moon, lunar nodes, and superior and inferior planets. They give a competent account of the Ptolemaic eccentrics and equants, complete with interpolation methods for the so-called equations. Ptolemaic – in some respects pre-Ptolemaic – though the doctrine is, no mention is made of *Almagest*. In a sense, the *Theorica* did something for western astronomy that the translations of Ptolemy's *magnum opus* could not easily do: it provided a fairly stable, unambiguous, astronomical vocabulary. In some of its later chapters, the writer's touch is unsure. There are technical misunderstandings, later to be criticized by Peurbach and Regiomontanus. It was singularly uninformative when it came to giving numerical parameters,

---

[26] L. Thorndike, *The Sphere of Sacrobosco and its Commentators* (Chicago/London, 1949). On Sacrobosco and his *oeuvre*, see the comprehensive O. Pedersen, 'In Quest of Sacrobosco', *Journal of the History of Astronomy*, 12 (1981), 113–23.

[27] Pedersen, 'Sacrobosco' (note 26), 184.

[28] For further details of literature of the *Theorica planetarum* type: O. Pedersen, 'The origins of the Theorica Planetarum', *Journal of the History of Astronomy*, 16 (1985), 175–221.

whether geometrical or kinematic, but these were implicit in (and could in principle have been deduced from) whatever astronomical tables the reader used. The real value of the *Theorica* was that it gave an understanding of what the student was about, when computing planetary positions, the movement of the eighth sphere (the precession of the equinoxes, in our language), or whatever.[29] It gave no real understanding of the ways in which planetary theories had been, or could be, developed. It long outlived in the universities the Copernican system that replaced the Ptolemaic implicit in it. It is a sad measure of European university conservatism that many university handbooks of the seventeenth century simply set these and other systems side by side, as though they were of equal value. Astronomy was probably never handled in a truly practical way in the *quadrivium*, in the sense of requiring that observations be made, recorded, and reduced. The quadrants that must have been used by many students in one form or another, and examples of that ubiquitous instrument the astrolabe – which a few dedicated scholars would have made for their own use – were no doubt used primarily for time-telling, where at a lower place on the socio-intellectual scale a man might have used a simple portable cylinder dial, or a monumental dial; but one suspects that such instruments were more often used for pedagogical purposes, like the armillary sphere that encapsulated the image of the Aristotelian universe, and that we so often find used as a symbol of university learning.

Another astronomical instrument, this time for purely computational use, was the *equatorium*. In its simplest form, this was a series of graduated scales on circular discs that could simulate the movements of the circles of Ptolemaic astronomy, and so shorten the otherwise lengthy and tedious Ptolemaic calculations. Other *equatoria* were constructed on less intuitively obvious principles, and the most sophisticated of all, the *albion* (1327) of Richard of Wallingford (*c.* 1292–1336), would have been well beyond the understanding of the average arts student. It travelled Europe, nevertheless, and we find references to it in manuscript sources connected with such universities as Paris, Vienna, Erfurt, and Ingolstadt.[30]

THE TRANSMISSION OF TEXTS

To take the *albion* as a typical case of a new idea: it spread over Europe, but how exactly it was transmitted is an important question that cannot be answered with confidence. Were *albion* manuscripts simply copied by itinerant university scholars, or was Richard's Benedictine connection of more

---

[29] An outline of the essentials of the methods used for calculating longitudes is given in J. D. North, *Richard of Wallingford*, vol. III (Oxford, 1976), appendix 29.

[30] North, *Richard of Wallingford* (note 29), vol. II 127–287 *passim*.

significance? (He became abbot of St Albans after determining as B.Th. at Oxford in 1327.) The symbiosis of monastic Europe and university Europe is a subject about which we have much to learn.

Among the many scientific works appearing in the lists of lectures given at Vienna in 1399 was the *Proportiones* of Bradwardine – presumably the *Tractatus de proportionibus velocitatum in motibus*. There are today at least three copies of the same work in the Jagiellonian Library in Cracow, one of them copied by a certain Sandivogius de Czechel, but none giving any clue as to how precisely the text travelled from Oxford. One can only guess that it was first taken there by a master who had been nurtured on it in Oxford or Paris: but the movement of texts and ideas was certainly not always as simple as this.

This can be seen from one example, Cracow, where the *studium generale* had been founded on the Bologna model in 1364. There are strong associations with the Universities of Paris and Oxford for several manuscripts now in Cracow.[31] They seem never to have been studied from the point of view of university migration. One of them (R. 82) is an astrological compilation explicitly signed by '*frater Augustinus de Tridente*, lector Parisii'. One dated 1436 (R. 1383) lists star coordinates obtained by observation with the 'Paris armillary'. While in the *studium* at Perugia, Johannes Zmora of Leznicz in 1453 made a copy of the *equatorium* treatise of John of Lignères, the fourteenth-century Parisian master; three years later he made a second copy whilst in Cracow. Some manuscripts with astronomical tables would not strictly have been useful outside Paris or Oxford, their towns of origin (tables of houses; solar altitudes; eclipses), while others have had their tables recalculated, for Cracow, Prague, or wherever (e.g. R. 1306, with a note by Nicolaus of Grabostow). One gets a strong sense of intellectual community when coming across a volume giving distances between cities – mainly universities, that is – for astronomical purposes, these being needed so that astronomers in one may make use of the calculations or observations of those in another. One Cracow manuscript (R. 1562), with a note by Henry of Munsterberg, so relates Paris with Vienna, Toruń, and Malbork.

Just how much remains to be uncovered of such intellectual movements as are evident here it is impossible to judge accurately: that is the nature of uncharted territory. Much surely remains to be discovered. In the case of the Alfonsine astronomical tables, for example, it used to be assumed that the various Oxford versions produced in the fourteenth and fifteenth centuries were all relatively trivial variants of what had gone before, modified for

---

[31] That is, in the Jagiellonian Library. I use G. Rosinska, *Scientific Writing and Astronomical Tables in Cracow* (Wrocław, 1984), here denoted by 'R'.

geographical place, but in few other very significant ways. This is now known to be mistaken.[32]

THE *QUADRIVIUM* IN CONTEXT

The information we can glean from official documents about the curriculum clearly leaves much to be said about subjects such as astrology, geomancy, even magic. Even if they were not immediately catered for, these must have figured in the ambitions of many students in arts. Some universities – Orléans in the fourteenth century was a case in point, perhaps without justification – acquired a reputation for doctrinally dangerous forms of divination, and yet there were large tracts of astrology that did not properly fall under that heading, and that were more or less universally studied as an extension of astronomy.[33] The evidence is in the form of texts written and manuscripts copied. Among extant manuscripts, the numbers of copies of treatises by such astrological authors as Albumazar and Alchabitius are numerous, even though they fall short of those of *Theorica planetarum* literature. (Geomancy and magic are relatively much scarcer than astrology.) One or two crucial and difficult astrological ideas would in any case have been transmitted as a matter of course in books on the astrolabe, which must have played a part in the arts curriculum, but which are only occasionally explicitly mentioned in that connection. (The first treatise on the astrolabe in the English vernacular

---

[32] Ten years ago, or so, I showed that there were two extremely important revisions done in Oxford, one in 1348 by an unknown astronomer, possibly one Batecombe, and the other by John Killingworth, fellow of Merton College, around 1442. Within a few years Professor J. Dobrzycki had found the 1348 tables, described simply as '*tabulae Anglicanae*', in Cracow – once in a Silesian manuscript (fifteenth century), and once in a manuscript from Prague (fourteenth century). I then recalled how Henry Arnaut of Zwolle, a fifteenth-century Parisian master, had referred to '*tabulae Anglicanae*'; presumably again these were the 1348 tables. Professor B. R. Goldstein (see his *Theory and Observation* (note 10)), working on Hebrew astronomical texts, then found a Hebrew version of the 1348 Oxford tables, done by Mordecai Finzi of Mantua, a fifteenth-century scholar. Finzi refers to a 1360 glossator of the Latin manuscript, and to an anonymous Christian who helped him in Mantua. Finzi was also known as 'Angelo'. In Pico della Mirandola's *Disputationes adversus astrologiam* there are references to Angelus Mantuanus as well as to the '*Oxonienses tabulae*'. Those tables are as severely intellectual as one could wish to find – beyond the reach of the ordinary arts student – and yet we find that their surprisingly wide diffusion was in part a university phenomenon, and in part not. Ten years ago no one had paid any attention to them, and now they are seen to have been esteemed throughout Europe. One cannot help wondering how many similar cases there are.

[33] For textual traditions of magic, see D. Pingree, 'The Diffusion of Arabic Magical Texts in Western Europe', in *Diffusione delle scienze* (note 4), 57–102. The reputation of Orléans seems to rest on Chaucer's reference to it in the 'Franklin's Tale', and is evidently unsupported in the records of the university there. See D. Mackay Quynn, 'The medieval extracurriculum: the Orléans example', *Mississippi Quarterly*, 10:3 (1957), cols. 120–34; cols. 129–34 relate to magic.

was written by the poet Geoffrey Chaucer for his ten-year-old son, around the year 1393.[34])

Wherever music was used by the educated clergy as a part of the liturgy, wherever in large churches astrological imagery was visible in glass and in the astrolabe dials of clocks, wherever – with his blend of Dionysian and Aristotelian cosmology – Dante was read, wherever princes coupled with their wives to the sound of music under selected stellar configurations, in all those cases the influences of the *quadrivium* were in evidence. There is in Geoffrey Chaucer's *Canterbury Tales* – in 'The Miller's Tale', in fact – a young Oxford scholar Nicholas, at the head of whose bed there was a shelf containing a copy of Ptolemy's *Almagest*, an astrolabe, a set of augrim stones for arithmetical calculation, and a musical instrument, a psaltery. That shelf symbolizes well the *quadrivium*, with its geometry, astronomy, arithmetic, and music (we can stretch a point, and find geometry in the *Almagest*). The augrim stones (for the abacus table) and psaltery remind us of the practical side to the *quadrivium*. They remind us, too, of the question of the relative cost of different sorts of study. The neurotic Roger Bacon complained bitterly about the vast sums of his own money that he had been obliged to spend on his experiments. At a more mundane level, though, how many students of astronomy could afford an astrolabe, or an armillary sphere, or even the metal from which to make such things? Augrim stones were cheap enough, and a psaltery was probably easy to come by, but what about books? We may be certain that not one in a hundred ever owned a copy of the *Almagest*, and that Nicholas of 'The Miller's Tale' was a very unusual student.

Reference to chapter 11 on medical education will underline the pragmatic value of astronomy, showing as it does that in Padua and Bologna astrology teaching was encouraged by the need to instruct medical students in the subject. (The medieval presumption was that the heavens influenced the progression of disease, and could be made an ally in its cure only by those who could calculate their motions.) Those medical students of course became the élite of their profession. Mention is made in chapter 11 of Cecco d'Ascoli's justification of the value of astrology to medical studies, and of the classic examples of a man truly expert in both subjects, Giovanni de Dondi; but we are reminded, too, that medical astrology was not confined to a university milieu. The universities, one imagines, set standards for the world outside their walls, but one should not be too complacent about university standards, or condescending about the outsiders. To take Chaucer, again: he had no university education, and yet there were in England in his day probably fewer than a dozen university men who could match his expertise in astronomical calculation. We do not know enough about his biography to call him an autodidact, and yet there are very few scholars about whom we know a tenth

---

[34] There was a vernacular version in French, by Pèlerin de Prusse, before Chaucer's, but less complete: J. D. North, *Chaucer's Universe* (Oxford, 1988).

as much as we know of him. We still know far too little of the *alternatives* to university education to be able to set a true value on the arts curriculum.

The case of Leonardo da Vinci offers another example of the sort of interactions worth exploring. Paul of Venice and Thomas de Vio (Cardinal Cajetanus) argued Aristotelian physics and chopped logic far into the night within the traditions introduced by the Ockhamists, Parisians, and Oxonians, but science has roots, too, in craft traditions. Leonardo was above all a practical man, but he focused attention on numerous rich veins of importance to theory – to take a single example, he threw a spotlight on the sorts of practical geometry that Tartaglia later made academically respectable.

In view of the astrological determinism that was so often thought to threaten the souls of those who practised astronomy, one imagines that the absence of the theological faculty or of professors of theology in such universities as Bologna, Padua and Salamanca (until the second half of the fourteenth century) must have meant a corresponding absence of at least some of the tensions implicit in an arts faculty. Those tensions seem a priori likely to have been greatest in Paris, and after that in Oxford and Cambridge, all great theological universities. Did such tensions affect in any way the development of the mathematical sciences? Did they, for example, deter scholars from pursuing these subjects, replete with so much pagan literature? Thomas Bradwardine, doyen of natural philosophy at Merton College, but also writer on the freedom of the will, turned away from the natural sciences and towards theology; and Richard of Wallingford, the best English astronomer and mathematician of his century, said that he regretted having wasted his time on those subjects and having ignored theology. Perhaps such feelings of guilt were typical, but were they rarer in Bologna and Padua? Perhaps they acted as a kind of hurdle that only the dedicated few would cross.

Much remains to be learned of the relation of the religious orders to quadrivial studies. We know, for example, that Bologna (1364), Salamanca (1411), and Toulouse (1360), in setting up theology faculties, drew graduates almost entirely from the religious orders. One might suppose as a corollary that, since friars and monks had their preliminary training in arts within the walls of their own houses, not necessarily in university centres, encouraging theology would have weakened the arts faculties. What sorts of expertise – for example in the practical arts – did such monks, coming into the universities from outside, whether in southern or northern Europe, bring with them and with what did they return? Richard of Wallingford is one example of a Benedictine who managed to combine the speculative astronomy of the university with the real estate of his abbey, and he produced an astronomical clock of a cost and complexity never before seen and rarely matched at any subsequent date before the sixteenth century.

One should not overlook the fact that scientific writings of a good, even original, quality continued to originate in non-university centres, throughout the entire Middle Ages. Even in university towns, the different orders often tried to insulate their students from the temptations of the world of the scholars, and presumably therefore developed ideas of a characteristically private colour. From an analysis of scientific texts produced by members of the various Oxford colleges and other houses, it appears that Merton College – as was to be expected – reaches much the highest score; those of unknown affiliation come next; but after that it is the Franciscans, the Carmelites, and the Benedictines, before any other college.[35] This is as judged by scientific writing – just about the only reasonable gauge. (Judging by casual scientific reference – ownership of a lens, use of an astrolabe, loan of a book, and so forth – the results are virtually the same.) Is a similar phenomenon to be detected in other universities, and what are the strengths and weaknesses of the different religious orders in different subjects at different periods? Why, for example, do the Oxford Dominicans produce so little in the exact sciences, when they were in Oxford in larger numbers than the Franciscans and Carmelites, at least in the most vital period of Oxford science, the early fourteenth century? (Their numbers were in the ratio of, say, 100 to 75 to 45, at any one time.) A part – but only a part – of the Oxford answer must be the influence of Grosseteste, lector to the Franciscans, and the heritage of Bacon. The scientific bias of Oxford is in contrast with Paris, 'the seat of theology and dialectic', where mathematics seems not to have been the subject of regular compulsory teaching. In Paris, this led to lessons being given by young masters in their homes, with the result that the practice had to be officially controlled, for there was a fear of furtive Averroism.[36] In 1276, therefore, rules were drawn up to control private meetings, partly to stem Averroism. The tradition of teaching on feast-days in private went back at least to the 1215 statutes, in which rhetoric, the *quadrivium*, and ethics received the same treatment.[37] Later the tradition strengthened the hand of the colleges, with their private libraries and bursaries. Two scholarships founded in 1378 by Charles V of France, at the College of Master Gervaise in Paris, were specifically to encourage the study of astrology. This is a symptom of what was happening elsewhere: in many centres – Bologna, Salamanca, and Cracow are important examples – mathematics was gradually becoming an auxiliary to the study of astrology, and the *quadrivium* was beginning to look decidedly unbalanced.[38]

Cracow had a strong tradition of astronomy – a separate chair in the subject was inaugurated as early as 1394 – but the relative weakness of theol-

[35] J. D. North, '1348 and All That: Science in Late Medieval Oxford', in J. L. Berggren and B. R. Goldstein (eds.), *From Ancient Omens to Statistical Mechanics* (Copenhagen 1987), 155–65.
[36] G. Beaujouan, 'Motives and Opportunities for Science in the Medieval Universities', in A. C. Crombie (ed.), *Scientific Change* (London, 1963), 219–36.
[37] S. C. Ferruolo, 'The Parish Statutes of 1215 Reconsidered', *History of Universities*, 5 (1985), 1–14.
[38] Beaujouan, 'Motives and Opportunities' (note 36), 223.

ogy and the higher faculties there and in Vienna undoubtedly goes some way towards explaining why they earned reputations for the fostering of scientific work. At Vienna there is an element of illusion created by the presence there of four famous masters: Henry of Langenstein (1325–97), John of Gmunden (c. 1380–1442), George of Peurbach (1423–61), and Regiomontanus (1436–76). It has been shown that, with the exception of John of Gmunden, none of these men had anything to do with teaching in the arts faculty, and that the number of lectures on astronomy by Vienna regents over the period investigated (1390–1460) was always small, and at an advanced level positively meagre. The old texts continued in use, despite the occasional set of *lectiones* on new themes (such as the *albion*, newly edited by John of Gmunden).[39] The conservatism of lecturers and the dependence of scientific reputation on the researches of a few individuals are of course phenomena not unknown today.

From the proven tenacity of such works as those of Boethius and Sacrobosco, one might be inclined to suppose that textbook writing in the *quadrivium* stagnated. This is not entirely true, even overlooking the many commentaries produced. There was a whole genre of *Theorica planetarum* texts, of which one of the most famous examples was by George of Peurbach. The circumstances of its production are these: Cardinal Bessarion asked Peurbach to write an abridgement of the *Almagest*, which was about half-finished when he died, aged not yet thirty-eight. His assistant in Vienna, Regiomontanus, completed the work in Italy. The work, *Theoricae novae planetarum*, was exactly what the universities of Europe needed, an authoritative text by someone who knew the *Almagest* backwards, and one that was illustrated with very good figures that the printing-press could reproduce so much more accurately than the average professional scribe or limner. Between its first printing (1473) and the middle of the seventeenth century, at least fifty-six editions of this 'new theory of the planets' appeared, many printings containing also Sacrobosco on the sphere. It is safe to say that virtually every important astronomer in the period was indebted to it. It was the product of a humanist initiative and the astronomical knowledge of a man trained entirely in the medieval university tradition, but one with a strong feeling for getting back to the original text. Peurbach knew no Greek, although of course Regiomontanus did. According to Regiomontanus, Peurbach held the *Almagest* in his memory '*quasi ad litteram*'. To emphasize once more the point that the *Almagest* was not widely read: there were seven printed editions of Ptolemy's *Geography* before 1500, but no single edition of the *Almagest* before 1515.

We do not know of Peurbach's itinerary, but when he was in his twenties he travelled through Germany, France and Italy, lectured in Padua, and was

---

[39] C. Kren, 'Astronomical Teaching at the Late Medieval University of Vienna', *History of Universities*, 3 (1983), 15–30. For the John of Gmunden edition of Albion: North, *Richard of Wallingford* (note 29) vol. II, 130–248.

offered university positions there and in Bologna. He was rather like those academics who today manage to work in the university but have lucrative civil contracts outside. Having returned to Vienna and become court astrologer to the Emperor Frederick III, he continued to perform some duties within the University of Vienna: surprisingly, they seem to have been mostly in the humanities (he lectured on Virgil, Juvenal, and Horace, in different years, for example).[40]

The case of Vienna illustrates the point made in the section on the *trivium* (chapter 10.1) that in approaching the arts faculty we must distinguish carefully between official attitudes and what was actually being studied and written. It might be worth considering alternative sorts of 'official' attitudes and responses. Astrology, for example, was under pressure from three or more distinct directions. There were those – especially ecclesiastics – who mistrusted its pagan associations. Then there were scholars who launched a scientific attack on basic astrological premises. Although their motives were in most cases moral or theological, they did not really depend on any specifically theological point of view. One finds both sorts of attack in the ancient world as well as the medieval. The third prong of the attack, however, is more or less peculiar to the context of the medieval university, and was a blend of arguments concerning free-will and future contingents. This sort of argument often came from an 'official' group of theologians and philosophers, but they were, after all, merely trying to preserve what most of mankind thinks it necessary to preserve, that is, a feeling of personal responsibility for one's actions. Although attacked in some or all of these ways throughout most of its history, judicial astrology seems to have steadily increased in popularity throughout the Middle Ages, and to have continued in the same direction well into the seventeenth century. It is dangerous to make rough generalizations, but for the sake of brevity let it be said that Italian scholars seem to have pursued the more dangerous, personal varieties of astrology with abandon, especially before the counter-Reformation: the Parisians were much more hesitant; and the English before the fifteenth century spent most of their time in prognostication on meteorological problems, but made up for lost time at a later date. In the German universities, astrology seems to have gone from strength to strength, especially from the mid-fourteenth century onwards.

One brand of astrology that seems to have been everywhere practised, and to have been virtually above reproach, was that which associates great conjunctions with historical events, in particular the rise and fall of religious sects. This, like meteorology, was respectable university material. University men did not have a monopoly of astrology – to imagine so would be to commit a fallacy. They certainly provided its back-bone, but texts that were

[40] C. D. Hellman and N. M. Swerdlow, 'Peurbach, Georg', in C. C. Gillispie (ed.), *Dictionary of Scientific Biography*, vol. XV (New York, 1978), 473–9.

being copied and doctrines that were being learned do not bring us down to grass-roots level. What was really being practised in astrology can only be accurately judged by analysing as many materials as possible, especially of the horoscopic type – whether nativities, elections, or whatever. As an example, we have the horoscopes of twenty-nine Wittenberg students of the mid-sixteenth century, used in a recent study to determine ages at matriculation, and certainly not unusual for the period in question. Such horoscopes were in some ways the student photographs of the time.[41] The burgeoning numbers of personal horoscopes over the period from the twelfth to the seventeenth centuries tell us a great deal about seriousness of purpose. Indeed, they tell us far more than any university statutes or any theological polemic can do.

[41] M. Gingerich and O. Gingerich, 'Matriculation Ages in Sixteenth Century Wittenberg', *History of Universities*, 6 (1986–7), 135–7.

SELECT BIBLIOGRAPHY

See also the select bibliography of chapter 10.1.

Beaujouan, G. 'L'enseignement du quadrivium', in *Settimane di studio del Centro italiano di studi sull'alto medioevo*, vol. XIX, Spoleto, 1972, 639–723.

Coyne, G. V., Hoskin, M. A., and Pedersen, O. (eds.) *Gregorian Reform of the Calendar. Proceedings of the Vatican Conference to Commemorate its 400th Anniversary, 1582–1982*, Vatican City, 1983.

Crombie, A. C. *Robert Grosseteste and the Origins of Experimental Science, 1100–1700*, 2nd edn, Oxford, 1961.

La Diffusione delle scienze islamiche nel medio evo Europeo, Convegno Internazionale, Rome 1984, Academia Nazionale dei Lincei, Rome, 1987.

Gibson, M. (ed.) *Boethius: his Life, Thought, and Influence*, Oxford, 1981.

Glorieux, P. *La Faculté des arts et ses maîtres au XIIIe siècle*, Paris, 1971.

Goldstein, B. R. *Theory and Observation in Ancient and Medieval Astronomy*, London, 1985.

Grant, E. *A Source Book in Medieval Science*, Cambridge, Mass., 1974.

Haskins, C. H. *Studies in the History of Medieval Science*, 1st edn, Cambridge, Mass., 1924; 2nd edn, Cambridge, Mass., 1927; reprint, New York, 1960.

Kretzmann, N., Kenny, A. and Pinborg, J. (eds.) *The Cambridge History of Later Medieval Philosophy: From the Rediscovery of Aristotle to the Disintegration of Scholasticism, 1100–1600*, Cambridge, 1982.

Lindberg, D. C. (ed.) *Science in the Middle Ages*, Chicago/London, 1978.

Maddison, F. 'Early Astronomical and Mathematical Instruments. A Brief Summary of Sources and Modern Studies', *History of Science*, 2 (1963), 17–50.

Millás, J. M. *Estudios sobre Azarquiel*, Madrid/Granada, 1943–50.

Millás, J. M. 'Translations of Oriental Scientific works (to the End of the Thirteenth Century)', in G. S. Metraux and F. Crouzet (eds.), *The Evolution of Science*, London, 1963.

North, J. D. '1348 and All That: Science in Late Medieval Oxford', in J. L. Berggren and B. R. Goldstein (eds.), *From Ancient Omens to Statistical Mechanics. Essays in the Exact Sciences Presented to Asger Aaboe*, Copenhagen, 1987, 155–65; reprinted in J. D. North, *Stars, Minds and Fate*, London, 1989, 361–71.

North, J. D. *Chaucer's Universe*, Oxford, 1988.

North, J. D. *Horoscopes and History*, London, 1986.

Poulle, E. *Les Tables alphonsines, avec les canons de Jean de Saxe*, Paris, 1984.

Samsó, J. (ed.) *De astronomia Alphonsi regis. Proceedings of a Berkeley Symposium on Alfonsine Astronomy, 1985*, Barcelona, 1987.

Smits van Waesberghe, J. *Musikerziehung: Lehre und Theorie der Musik im Mittelalter*, Leipzig, 1969.

Southern, E. W. *Robert Grosseteste: the Growth of an English Mind in Medieval Europe*, Oxford, 1986.

Thorndike, L. and Kibre, P. A. *Catalogue of Incipits of Mediaeval Scientific Writings in Latin*, London, 1963.

Vernet, J. *Ce que la culture doit aux Arabes d'Espagne*, Paris, 1985 (tr. from *La Cultura hispanoárabe en Oriente y Occidente*, Barcelona, 1978).

Victor, S. K. *Practical Geometry in the High Middle Ages. 'Artis cuiuslibet consummatio' and 'Pratike de geometrie'*, Philadelphia, 1979.

Weisheipl, J. A. 'Curriculum of the Faculty of Arts at Oxford in the early Fourteenth Century', *Mediaeval Studies*, 26 (1964), 143–85.

Weisheipl, J. A. 'Development in the Arts Curriculum at Oxford in the Early Fourteenth Century', *Mediaeval Studies*, 28 (1966), 151–75.

Wordsworth, C. *The Ancient Kalendar of the University of Oxford*, Oxford, 1903–4.

CHAPTER 11

THE FACULTY OF MEDICINE

NANCY SIRAISI

The establishment of university faculties of medicine provided a distinct type of professional and intellectual formation that shaped a new medical élite. Yet the content of the medicine studied and practised by those trained in the medieval universities of western Europe was neither the creation nor the exclusive property of the university milieu. The medicine of learned university physicians was at once an intellectual enterprise grounded in the medicine of classical antiquity and the Islamic world and an activity that had much in common with that of the numerous contemporary medical and surgical practitioners who received their formation outside the universities.

The intellectual preparation for the rise of university medicine, as for other aspects of the learning of the high and later Middle Ages, was provided by the translations of Greek and Arabic texts which began to proliferate in the late eleventh century. For medicine, the results included not only the availability of more of the medical heritage of antiquity, but also an enlargement of the theoretical component in contemporary medical writing, along with an increased stress on the connections between medicine and natural philosophy and the expansion of the role of dialectic in medical discourse. And the general intellectual revival that accompanied the reception of the new translations produced a great expansion in quantity and increase in diversity of all kinds of Latin medical writing, whether commentaries, works containing recommendations for practice, books on surgery, or *consilia* (that is, advice for individual cases or conditions).

Also fundamental to the successful establishment of medicine as a university discipline, as to the university movement in general, was the economic, demographic, and urban growth of western Europe in the twelfth and thirteenth centuries. More specifically, academic medicine grew up and flourished in a context of the multiplication of schools providing Latin literacy, the proliferation of healers of all kinds who practised their art for pay, and the spread through many levels of society of willingness and ability to purchase medical intervention – a willingness exemplified not only by the patronage of famous surgeons or learned physicians by monarchs, nobles, and prelates, but also by the retention of medical or surgical practitioners by civic authorities, and the livelihoods (or partial livelihoods) gained by barber-surgeons, pharmacists, herbalists, midwives, and wise men and women. Yet the religious and cultural context of academic medicine throughout the Middle Ages always included powerful traditions linking healing with religious charity and/or miraculous intervention, and the imperative that gave at least lip-service to the priority of the healing of the soul over the healing of the body.[1]

Throughout the thirteenth to fifteenth centuries, and thereafter, the university-trained physicians who are the subject of this chapter were a minority of those who practised healing. Of a total of more than 4,000 medical practitioners – excluding surgeons and barber-surgeons – known to have been active in France between the twelfth and the fifteenth century, fewer than 2,000 appear to have studied medicine at (not necessarily obtained a doctorate in medicine from) a university. The situation was similar in Florence, where the proximity of Bologna presumably ensured a large regional supply of university-educated practitioners.[2] In the century following the black death, between a third and a little over a half, depending on the decade, of those who practised medicine or surgery in Florence probably had some university education. And, among university-trained physicians, those who made teaching in the milieu of the faculties of medicine their main activity were yet a further minority. For example, of the almost 2,000 practitioners in medieval France known to have attended a university, 417 are known to have been regent masters or professors.[3]

Thus, the physician who had studied medicine at a university faced constant competition both from non-university-trained practitioners of medicine and surgery and from those who offered various types of spiritual or supernatural remedy for physical afflictions – the latter category of healers including deceased saints.[4] Moreover, in the thirteenth to fifteenth centuries those medical and surgical practitioners who were not educated in the universities

[1] Regarding religious attitudes to the body and medicine: J. Agrimi and C. Crisciani, *Medicina del corpo e medicina dell'anima: Note sur sapere dal medico fino all'inizio del secolo XIII* (Milan, 1978).
[2] K. Park, *Doctors and Medicine in Early Renaissance Florence* (Princeton, N.J., 1985); D. Jacquart, *Le Milieu médical en France du XIIe au XVe siècle* (Paris, 1981).
[3] Jacquart, *Milieu médical*, 363, table 1:1; 364, table 2; Park, *Doctors and Medicine*, 75.
[4] Examples in E. C. Gordon, 'Child Health in the Middle Ages as Seen in the Miracles of Five English Saints. AD 1150–1220', *Bulletin of the History of Medicine*, 60 (1986), 502–22.

were by no means all unlearned empirics or illiterate village healers. No doubt there were many who could be so described; many, too, for whom the boundaries between medical or surgical practice to gain a living (or a partial living) and the provision of informal and occasional assistance to neighbours, family, and friends were by no means clearly defined; and many others who combined the practice of medicine or minor surgery with one or more of a variety of other petty trades or crafts.[5] Some of these lesser practitioners of medicine probably did not so much compete with the possessors of medical degrees as serve a different clientèle (one for whom both the fees and the social and intellectual pretensions of university-educated physicians would have constituted an insurmountable barrier).

But between the modest forms of medical or surgical activity just outlined and the learned medicine of the universities was a broad range of intermediate categories. The latter included practitioners of surgery as a skilled and organized art or craft, and literate (and in some cases literate in Latin) surgeons and *medici*. In the thirteenth, fourteenth, and fifteenth centuries, important attributes of university students and professors of medicine were shared by some *medici* and surgeons outside university circles – notably knowledge of both ancient and recent medical books (either in Latin or via the vernacular translations that multiplied in the late Middle Ages) and traditions, and the ability to form or participate in professional associations (in the shape of guilds and urban medical colleges). And the medical learning cultivated by numerous practitioners among the Jewish communities of Spain, Provence, and Italy in the thirteenth and fourteenth centuries also drew upon many of the same classical and Islamic sources as the medicine of the universities.[6] Thus, although, in terms of both wealth and social status, university-educated physicians always stood at the top of the medical profession as a whole,[7] medical and surgical practitioners formed outside the universities included some who had access to considerable educational, economic, and social resources. Such practitioners were in many respects well equipped to compete with university-educated physicians for prosperous, and even noble or royal, patients.

One contemporary comment illustrates both the overlap between some aspects of the training provided in some of the faculties of medicine and the kind of knowledge possessed by literate *medici* and surgeons without university training, and the wide social range of those who involved themselves in

[5] M. Pelling, 'Occupational Diversity: Barbersurgeons and the Trades of Norwich', *Bulletin of the History of Medicine*, 56 (1982), 484–511 (referring to the sixteenth century).

[6] J. Shatzmiller, 'Livres médicaux et éducation médicale: à propos d'un contrat de Marseille en 1316', *Mediaeval Studies*, 42 (1980), 463–70; B. Richler, 'Manuscripts of Avicenna's Kanon in Hebrew Translation; a Revised and Up-to-date List', *Koroth*, 8 (1982), 145*–68*, lists 106 manuscripts of medieval Hebrew translations of a major Arabic medical work; Jacquart, *Milieu médical* (note 2), 380, has identified 331 Jewish *medici* and 57 Jewish surgeons.

[7] For example, Park, *Doctors and Medicine* (note 2), 152–8.

healing activity broadly considered. Writing in 1363, and recalling the ancient medical sects described by Galen, the 'surgeon and master of medicine' Guy de Chauliac expressed the opinion that the people willing to undertake the care of surgical cases in his own day could be divided into no fewer than five sects. The first three Guy divided simply on the basis of differences of opinion on a technical issue: they were the followers of different surgical authors of the twelfth and thirteenth centuries (all of whom wrote in Latin), and were divided over the proper treatment of wounds. As the reader will see (p. 381) some of those among his contemporaries whom Guy placed in these three categories could have received their training in southern European universities; but other members of these same categories would have been found among literate, but not university-trained, surgeons. These divisions of surgical opinion are indeed something like sects in the Galenic sense of the term (although the differences Galen had in mind had philosophical foundations). However, Guy's fourth and fifth categories invoke social and occupational differences, as well as differences of opinion: the fourth consisted of German military men, who placed their confidence in the idea that God had imparted powers to words, herbs, and stones, and accordingly used incantations as well as physical care for battle wounds; and in the fifth Guy placed women and the unlettered, who, according to him, simply invoked God and the saints.[8]

Moreover, it is, of course, unlikely that in the period under consideration the possessors of medical degrees could ever have been consistently more successful than any of their various competitors in effecting cures (although it is equally unlikely that the contrary was the case). It seems probable, too, that a good many remedies were more or less common to several categories of practitioner. And, as a practical matter, a measure of mutual accommodation or cooperation was often unavoidable; for example, in some cities different categories of practitioners were united in a common medical guild.[9] Furthermore, the university-educated physician was not exempt from, indeed perhaps was especially likely to be the object of, criticisms or judgemental evaluations of medicine from outside the medical profession. Such criticisms were sometimes made on the grounds of ineptitude but more usually for such moral failings as concern for the body rather than the soul, intellectual pretentiousness, and greed.[10]

[8] I cite Guy's remarks from G. de Chauliac, *La Grande Chirurgie*, ed. E. Nicaise (Paris, 1890), 15–16.

[9] Such was the case in Florence: Park, *Doctors and Medicine* (note 2), ch. 1.

[10] For example, F. Petrarca, *Invectiva contra medicum: Testo latino e volgarizzamento di Ser Domenico Silvestri*, ed. P. G. Ricci (Rome, 1950). There is, however, a long antecedent tradition. Furthermore, moral issues relating to medicine were frequently discussed by theologians and the authors of *summae* for confessors. These issues included, for example, the maintenance of adequate standards of professional competence considered as a moral responsibility, the sinfulness of fee-gouging (once agreement as to the legitimacy of charging any fee had been established, itself a matter of much debate), and the responsibility to treat the poor gratis. For

The foregoing considerations may explain if they do not excuse the emphasis laid by university-educated physicians on the distinctiveness and superiority of their own learning, and their frequent expressions of hostility and contempt for other categories of practitioner.

In this context, and under these pressures, the medical faculties of European universities acquired between the thirteenth and the fifteenth centuries institutional and intellectual characteristics that would continue to influence medical education well into the early modern period. Not all of those characteristics were positive. The university faculties contributed to the creation of a medical élite that was on occasion arrogant and self-serving, and to the devaluation of other healers, especially Jews and women.[11] Some historians of medicine would add to the debits needless elaboration of fundamentally simple and largely untestable physiological theories and the proliferation of confused and ill-understood pharmacological terminology.

But the positive accomplishments of medieval academic medicine were substantial. They included the establishment of durable institutions for providing formal medical education; an insistence upon the validity and status of human physiology, health, and disease as objects of intellectual enquiry; the production of a rich, variegated, and complex medical literature; the refinement of a technical vocabulary; the identification of topics of physiological debate (usually discrepancies among ancient authors), which continued to be the focus of attention until the time of Harvey; and the creation of an environment in which the bold innovation of the public dissection of human cadavers could be legitimized.

ORIGINS, DISTRIBUTION, AND ORGANIZATION OF THE MEDICAL FACULTIES

A faculty of medicine was provided in most of the *studia generalia* established before 1500, but major centres of academic medical education were always few in number. In terms of the chronological and geographical distribution of such centres the salient facts are the early emergence and early decline of Salerno (late eleventh to early thirteenth century), and the subsequent pre-

details and citations: D. W. Amundsen, 'Casuistry and Professional Obligations: the Regulation of Physicians by the Court of Conscience in the Late Middle Ages', Parts I and II, *Transactions and Studies of the College of Physicians of Philadelphia*, 3 (1981), 22–39, 93–112. In addition, certain obligations were laid directly on secular physicians by canon law. These were contained in canon 22 of the fourth Lateran Council of 1215, which was subsequently incorporated in the *Decretales*: it required practitioners, before providing physical treatment, to urge their patients to call a priest, and forbade them to recommend any means of recovering physical health that involved sin – for example, eating meat on a fast-day or illicit sexual intercourse (for citations and discussion. ibid., 96–7).

11 J. Agrimi and C. Crisciani, 'Medici e "vetulae" dal Duecento al Quattrocento: Problemi di una ricerca', in *Cultura popolare e cultura dotta nel seicento. Atti del Convegno di Studio di Genova, 23–25 novembre 1982* (Milan, 1983), 144–59.

dominance of just three *studia*: Bologna, Montpellier, and Paris. A fourth, Padua, the home of medical studies from the thirteenth century, increased in size and importance in the course of the fifteenth.[12] The leading position of these medical schools (as measured by reputation among contemporaries, ability to attract students from far away, output of medical writings, presence of numerous or famous teachers, and, where known, numbers of graduates with medical degrees) was not challenged in the period before 1500. Additional *studia* of medieval foundation attained more than local renown for medical teaching in the course of the sixteenth century, but they were not major centres for the study of medicine at an earlier date. This applies as much to Salamanca, an important university since the thirteenth century, as to the regional educational centre of Tübingen, still small, struggling, and recently founded when the fifteenth century ended.[13]

The difference between the various faculties of medicine lay more in numbers, reputation, and institutional position than in curriculum. In the latter, the common heritage of Greek and Islamic medical learning and Aristotelian natural philosophy ensured a good deal of uniformity throughout Europe. But the intellectual as well as the professional and collegial ambiance of the various medical faculties varied widely. In all these respects, the experience of the four otherwise obscure doctors of medicine who taught at Poitiers in the fifteenth century must have been very different from that of the more than 125 professors (including a number of well-known medical authors) and promoters of candidates for medical degrees at Padua during the same period.[14] Moreover, the sources of information are richer for the larger and more celebrated medical faculties and have been combed with more diligence by historians. Hence, despite the existence of some valuable studies of medical faculties that were chiefly of local importance,[15] medieval university medicine outside the major centres of medical learning remains relatively little known. But, although future research on the smaller faculties will round

---

12 N. G. Siraisi, *Arts and Sciences at Padua* (Toronto, 1973), ch. 5; T. Pesenti, *Professori e promotori di medicina nello studio di Padova dal 1405 al 1509: Repertorio bio-bibliografico* (Padua/Trieste, 1984).

13 Regarding Salamanca: G. Beaujouan, *Manuscrits scientifiques médiévaux de l'université de Salamanque et de ses 'Colegios Mayores'*, Bibliothèque de l'Ecole des Hautes Etudes Hispaniques, 32 (Bordeaux, 1962), 3, 59–60. Regarding Tübingen: W. Kuhn, *Die Studenten der Universität Tübingen zwischen 1477 und 1534*, 2 vols. (Göppingen, 1971); G. Fichtner, 'Padova e Tübingen: La formazione medica nei secoli XVI e XVII', *Acta medicae historiae patavina*, 19 (1972–3), 43–62.

14 R. Favreau, 'L'université de Poitiers et la société poitevine à la fin du Moyen Age', in *Universities in the Late Middle Ages*, 578, no. 71; 580, no. 102; 582, nos. 120 and 121; Pesenti, *Professori* (note 12). *passim.*

15 Examples are F. M. Getz, 'Medicine at Medieval Oxford', in J. I. Catto (ed.), *The History of the University of Oxford*, vol. II, *Late Medieval Oxford* (Oxford, in press); M. Fuiano, *Maestri di medicina e filosofia a Napoli nel Quattrocento* (Naples, 1973); faculty of Turin: I. Naso, *Medici e strutture sanitarie nella società tardo-medievale: Il Piemonte dei secoli XIV e XV* (Milan, 1982), 111–22.

out the picture of academic medicine and of the careers of university-educated physicians, understanding of the goals, methodology, and limitations of medical teaching is best gained from consideration of the most successful schools. These will be the main, though not the exclusive, focus of the following account.

In one sense, Salerno does not belong in a discussion of the principal medieval university faculties of medicine: formal university organization was not introduced at Salerno until after the end of the period of its predominance as a centre of medical education. Yet important features of medieval university medical teaching took shape at Salerno between the later eleventh and the early thirteenth century.[16]

By the eleventh century Salerno was already a place where medical practitioners (apparently both male and female) gathered and no doubt taught their successors, informally, orally, and by practical demonstration. The introduction of an academic and book-oriented emphasis in Salernitan medicine was the result of a confluence of factors. Access to some of the medical writings in Latin available in the early Middle Ages no doubt played a part. This body of material was not negligible, and it should be stressed that early medieval medicine in western Europe retained, in however truncated and simplified a form, some textual and pedagogical elements inherited from classical antiquity.[17] Secondly, the geographical situation and early medieval history of the southern part of the Italian peninsula provided opportunities for intellectual contact with both the Greek- and Arabic-speaking worlds. Among the Salernitan clergy, Archbishop Alfanus (d. 1095) actively participated in the adaptation of Greek medical learning. And the medical translations of Constantinus Africanus (d. 1087), a monk at nearby Monte Cassino, provided early access to medical texts by Muslim authors.

In addition to writing various guides to medical practice, twelfth- and early thirteenth-century Salernitan authors brought together a collection (subsequently known as the *articella*) of short treatises conveying the rudiments of Hippocratic and Galenic medicine to serve as a basic curriculum, and established the practice of teaching by commentary on these texts. The collection as put together in the twelfth century (later other texts were added) consisted of two Hippocratic treatises, the *Aphorisms* and the *Prognostics*, a brief Galenic treatise known under various titles – *Ars medica*, *Ars parva*, *Tegni*, or *Microtechne* – an Arabic introduction to Galenic medicine known in the Latin West as the *Isagoge* of Johannitius and short tracts on the main diagnostic tools of the medieval physician, namely pulse and urine.

[16] P. O. Kristeller, *Studi sulla Scuola medica salernitana* (Naples, 1986).
[17] A. Beccaria, *I codici di medicina del periodo presalernitana* (Rome, 1956); A. Beccaria, 'Sulle trace di un antico canone latino di Ippocrate e Galeno', Part I, *Italia medioevale e umanistica*, 1 (1959), 1–56; Part II, ibid., 4 (1961), 1–75; Part III, ibid., 14 (1971), 1–23.

The association of medicine with natural philosophy was also emphasized at Salerno; Salernitan masters were among the earliest Latin writers to reflect Aristotelian influence; and the well-known 'Salernitan questions' mingled medical and general scientific topics.[18]

Salernitan, Arab, and Jewish influences have at various times each been posited by historians as sources of the early development of medicine at Montpellier.[19] Giles of Corbeil (*c.* 1140 – *c.* 1224), who was born in northern France, studied in Salerno, spent some time in Montpellier (where he became involved in acrimonious controversy with the Montpellier masters), and at the end of his life taught medicine and served as a royal physician in Paris, provides one example of personal, if infelicitous, contact between Salernitan academic medicine and the schools of Montpellier.[20] In general, however, evidence of knowledge of Salernitan and Arab medicine among Montpellier masters is to be ascribed to their study of written works. And, although, as already noted, Jewish practitioners played a significant role in medieval European medicine, at Montpellier as elsewhere members of the Jewish medical community were excluded from teaching in the faculty of medicine, once this took institutional shape.

Montpellier seems to have become known as a centre of medical activity by about the middle of the twelfth century. Medical teaching was being carried on there before the century's end. Medical masters and students at Montpellier were already organized into a university in 1220, when they were the recipients of a set of statutes granted by the papal legate. The earliest surviving written exposition of a medical textbook by a Montpellier master appears to be the commentary on the medical *Isagoge* of Johannitius (one of the works included in the *articella*) by Henry of Winchester, who flourished in 1239–40. A papal bull of 1289 recognized Montpellier as a *studium generale*, where a licence conveying the *ius ubique docendi* might be obtained in canon and civil law, in arts, and in medicine.[21]

Medicine emerged as a major discipline at Paris in approximately the same period as at Montpellier. A list of medical books read at Paris has been

[18] R. M. Thomson, '"Liber Marii de elementis": The Work of a Hitherto Unknown Salernitan Master?' *Viator*, 3 (1972), 179–89; Marius, *On the Elements*, ed. and trans. R. C. Dales (Philadelphia, 1973); A. Birkenmajer, 'Le rôle joué par les médicins et les naturalistes dans la réception d'Aristote au XIIe et XIIIe siècles', in A. Birkenmajer, *Etudes d'histoire des sciences et de la philosophie du Moyen Age*. Studie Copernicana 1 (Wroclaw/Warsaw/Cracow, 1970), 73–87; B. Lawn (ed.) *The Prose Salernitan Questions* (London, 1979).

[19] L. Dulieu, *La Médicine à Montpellier*, vol. I, *Le Moyen Age* (n.p., n.d. [1976]) provides a narrative history; there are numerous documents pertaining to the faculty of medicine in *Cartulaire de l'Université de Montpellier* . . . , vol. I, *1181–1400* (Montpellier, 1890).

[20] For a summary of his career, and bibliography: E. Wickersheimer, *Dictionnaire biographique des médicins en France au moyen age*, vol. I (Paris, 1936), 196–7, and its *Supplément*, ed. D. Jacquart (Geneva, 1979), 90–1

[21] *Cartulaire* (note 19), 180–223, doc. 2; 210–13, doc. 20. M. R. McVaugh, 'An Early Discussion of Medicinal Degrees at Montpellier by Henry of Winchester', *Bulletin of the History of Medicine*, 49 (1975), 57–71.

ascribed to Alexander Neckam, who studied there from about 1175 until about 1182.[22] The oldest traces of medical teaching in an organized faculty date from 1213; statutes listing books to be studied by candidates for a Parisian licence in medicine were issued between 1270 and 1274.[23]

The presence of physicians, surgeons, and medical students at Bologna is attested during the first two decades of the thirteenth century. In the second half of the thirteenth century, several notable Latin treatises on surgery were written by surgeons who practised at Bologna, but who were not, as far as is known, part of an organized medical faculty engaged in public teaching. The organization of medical masters and students into academic corporations had probably taken place by the 1260s. The first recorded public *laurea* (degree) in medicine, following examination by a group of masters, was awarded in 1268. Tax and other privileges were extended to medical masters and students by the city government between 1274 and 1288.[24] Among Bologna, Padua, and other less celebrated centres of medical learning that multiplied in northern Italy from about the mid-thirteenth century, there developed a fairly constant circulation of medical faculty, so that it is probably unwise to attribute ideas exclusively to any one of these schools. However, there appear to have been real differences of opinion between the medical teachers of Salerno and those of Bologna (for example, as regards the proper treatment of wounds).

The development of philosophical and Aristotelian aspects (already present, as we have seen, in the medicine of Salerno to some extent) in north Italian academic medicine was of course stimulated by the general growth of philosophical studies in Italian schools; however, in the context of the nascent faculties of medicine such interests may to some extent have been fostered by influences from Paris as well as by local factors. It is at any rate worth noting that Petrus Hispanus (Pope John XXI, d. 1277), a major logical as well as medical author, studied at Paris and subsequently taught medicine in Siena from 1245 to 1250. The almost equally celebrated Peter of Abano (d. 1316) returned to teach medicine, philosophy, and astrology at Padua after some years at Paris. Perhaps more importantly Peter of Abano incorporated the fruits of his Parisian study and, apparently, teaching of those subjects into a work that retained an influence in the Italian schools for centuries, namely his

[22] C. H. Haskins, 'A List of Text-books from the Close of the Twelfth Century', in C.H. Haskins, *Studies in the History of Mediaeval Science*, 2nd edn (Cambridge, Mass., 1927), 356–76, with medical books listed on 374–5. The dates given for Neckam's stay in Paris are, however, those suggested in R. W. Hunt, *The Schools and the Cloister: the life and Writings of Alexander Nequam (1156–1217)*, ed. and rev. M. Gibson (Oxford, 1984).

[23] Jacquart, *Milieu médical* (note 2), 68; *CUP*, vol. I, 517, no. 416; D. Jacquart, 'La réception du *Canon* d'Avicenne: Comparaison entre Montpellier et Paris au XIIIe et XIVe siècles', in *Histoire de l'école médicale de Montpellier. Actes du 110e Congrès National des Sociétés Savantes (Montpellier, 1985)*, vol. II (Paris, 1985), 69–77.

[24] N. G. Siraisi, *Taddeo Alderotti and His Pupils* (Princeton, N.J., 1981), 13–24.

Conciliator of the Differences of the Philosophers and, Especially, the Physicians.[25]

As with other aspects of academic institutionalization, the organization of the faculty of medicine differed at Paris, Montpellier, and Bologna. At Paris, the faculty of medicine consisted of a group of teaching masters. At Montpellier, the separate university of medicine seems in the thirteenth century to have included both professors and students.[26] The arrangements at Bologna, and similarly at Padua and other southern European *studia*, consisted of a doctoral college and a student university, each of which conjoined arts and medicine. The doctoral college was an association, restricted in number and limited to Bolognese citizens, which included both senior professors of medicine in the *studium* and physicians practising in the town. By contrast, the university of arts and medicine was an association of students who were not of Bolognese origin.

SOCIAL AND
ECONOMIC ASPECTS

Regardless of the differences in their internal organization, the medical professoriates of Paris, Bologna, and Montpellier all represented the summit of the medical profession. Although the social origins of this medical élite were as a rule more modest than those of lawyers of equivalent achievement or professors of theology, senior professors of medicine in the great centres of medical education were citizens of substance. Frequently, they either came from or established families whose members included other successful practitioners and/or medical professors. Their incomes came primarily from practice (particularly the patronage of wealthy individuals) and to a lesser extent from student fees, but also from public sources, including in some cases ecclesiastical benefices.[27]

In Italy, where medical teaching in the universities was an occupation in which married laymen predominated, a few publicly salaried medical professorships were provided at an early date. At Bologna a professor of *physica* (medicine) was on the public pay-roll in 1305; and a professor of medical

---

[25] For the development of Aristotelian philosophy in Italy: P. Marangon, *Alle origini dell'Aristotelismo padovano (sec. XII–XIII)* (Padua, 1973). On Petrus Hispanus (John XXI) as a medical author and influence: Jacquart (ed.) (note 20), 232–6; E. Paschetto, *Pietro d'Abano, medico e filosofo* (Florence, 1984), for Peter's biography, and bibliography of manuscripts and editions of the *Conciliator differentiarum philosophorum et precipue medicorum.*

[26] '... de communi consensu et consilio ... Universitatis medicorum, tam doctorum quam discipulorum, Montispessulani ...,' In *Cartulaire* (note 19), 181, doc. 2, medical statutes (1220).

[27] For example, a good many of the documents pertaining to medical masters in A. Moreira de Sá (ed.), *Chartularium universitatis portugalensis (1288–1537)*, vols. I–VIII (Lisbon, 1966–81), either request or confer benefices: see vol. I, 151, doc. 134 (1345); vol. II, 80–2, docs. 663–4 (1415): vol. II, 125–6, doc. 689 (1418); vol. II, 154–6, docs. 713–15 (1418); and many others similar.

practica was receiving a municipal salary in 1324. At Cologne and the other newer universities of northern Europe, salaries for medical as for other professors were provided at the time of or very soon after foundation.[28] In medicine as in other faculties, the provision of salaried professorial chairs by local municipalities or territorial rulers tended to strengthen both the ties of the professors to authorities outside the *studium* and the control of those authorities over the academic community. At Bologna the medical professoriate was an integral part of the same citizen class which, at different times, either controlled a communal government, or retained much influence at the lower levels of signorial administration. The senior teaching position in medicine were reserved for Bolognese citizens, a privilege jealously guarded by the college of medical doctors (who also legislated favourable terms of admission to the college for relatives of members). Non-Bolognese graduates in medicine at Bologna were obliged to swear not to attempt to lecture in the morning hours when the principal or 'ordinary' lectures were given.[29] In *studia* in regions under the rule of territorial princes or *signori*, ties between an academic faculty of medicine and a princely court sometimes developed, in that a physician who was in personal attendance on a ruler might also occupy a professorial chair. Princely patronage, was, for example, probably a major factor in the development of the *studium* of Ferrara as a centre of medical humanism in the late fifteenth and early sixteenth century. And the provision of a medical teacher for the University of Aberdeen in the early sixteenth century was possible only when the position was combined with that of royal physician.[30]

The principal medical faculties occupied positions of importance in the public sphere, as well as within the academic community. They were used by public authorities (royal, noble, ecclesiastical, or municipal) as guarantors of medical standards, sources of medical information, and a reservoir of reliable practitioners. Thus, at Paris, Montpellier, and elsewhere, the faculty of medicine acquired the right and responsibility of examining and licensing all medical practitioners in the city.[31] At Bologna, where a surgeon was already maintained on the municipal pay-roll in 1214, the public provision of medical or surgical treatment for the citizens antedated the appearance of academic medical corporations. But, shortly after a formally organized faculty of medi-

[28] Siraisi, *Alderotti* (note 24), 21, and bibliography there cited; Rashdall, *Universities*, vol. II, 255–6, 282.

[29] C. Malagola (ed.), *Statuti delle Università e dei Collegi dello Studio bolognese* (Bologna, 1880), 430–2, 466 (doctoral college statutes of 1378).

[30] G. Pardi, *Lo studio di Ferrara nei secoli XVe e XVIe* (Ferrara, 1903), 85, referring to the 1530s to 1550s, notes the close association between the principal medical professors and the ducal court. R. French, 'Medical Teaching in Aberdeen: From the Foundation of the University to the Middle of the Seventeenth Century', *History of Universities*, 3 (1983), 127–8.

[31] P. Kibre, 'The Faculty of Medicine at Paris, Charlatanism and Unlicensed Medical Practice in the Later Middle Ages', *Bulletin of the History of Medicine*, 27 (1953), 1–20 *Cartulaire* (note 19), 185–6, doc. 4 (1239); 234–5, doc. 33 (1316).

cine appeared, professors of medicine from the *studium* were being called upon to provide expert medico-legal opinions for the civic authorities; by the first decade of the fourteenth century the public service asked of these professors on occasion included the performance of autopsies.[32] The most famous example of a request by a governmental authority for the expert opinion of a medical faculty is doubtless the solicitation of a report on the causes of the Black Death from the Paris faculty by King Philip VI in 1348.[33]

Medical students at each of the major centres of medical education came primarily from the surrounding region, but also from all over Europe. For example, of the university men active in the diocese of Liège before 1350, those known to have studied medicine and whose place of study is known all went to Paris, Bologna, or Montpellier.[34] Moreover, the establishment of universities in the German lands in the fourteenth and fifteenth centuries did not diminish the ability of Bologna and Padua to attract German medical students in significant numbers. If anything, the foundation of German and eastern European universities may have widened the pool from which the Italian medical schools drew. Ambitious medical students could now complete the necessary preliminaries in arts and the first part of their medical studies locally (and inexpensively), and then cross the Alps to a more prestigious institution for the final stages of medical education and graduation.[35]

Some medical students (like some masters) were at least partially supported by ecclesiastical benefices, since a significant proportion of university-educated medical practitioners were members of the secular clergy, especially in northern Europe.[36] It is perhaps necessary to state that the existence of clerical medical practitioners, professors, and students did not contravene ecclesiastical law. A canon promulgated in 1163 merely prohibited monks and canons regular from leaving their religious communities in order to travel to study in secular medical schools (in 1219 the ban on forsaking religious obligations in favour of secular medical studies was extended to certain other

---

[32] M. Sarti and M. Fattorini, *De claris archigymnassii bononiensis professoribus*, ed. C. Malagola, vol. II (Bologna, 1888–96f), 214–15; L. Munster, 'La medicina legale in Bologna dai suoi albori fino alla fine del secolo XIV', *Bollettino dell'Accademia Medica Pistoiese Filippo Pacini*, 26 (1955), 257–71; L. Munster, 'Alcuni episodi sconosciuti o poco noti sulla vita e sull'attività di Bartolomeo da Varignana', *Castalia: Rivista di storia della medicina*, 10 (1954), 207–15.

[33] Described in A. M. Campbell, *The Black Death and Men of Learning* (New York, 1966; facsimile of original 1931 edition), 14–17.

[34] C. Renardy, *Le Monde des Maîtres universitaires du diocèse de Liège 1140–1350* (Paris, 1979), 182.

[35] Ultramontane scholars earned 30–40 per cent of all the degrees awarded at Padua for much of the fifteenth century: R. Ohl, 'The University of Padua 1405–1509: an International Community of Students and Professors', Ph.D., University of Pennsylvania, 1980, 59–61.

[36] For France: Jacquart, *Milieu médical* (note 2), 380, table 15, shows that, of 342 medical students or masters whose status can be identified, 128 were married, 13 were regular clergy, and 201 were secular clergy. These figures include Montpellier, which had many married laity in the medical community.

categories of clergy). Medical knowledge and practice as such were never forbidden to the clergy, and expertise in these areas was no bar to a highly successful clerical career (Petrus Hispanus being a notable case in point). In any case, in 1298 the canons in question were in part rescinded and in part modified into the reasonable requirement that members of religious orders seek permission before leaving their communities to study medicine.[37]

Practitioners trained at the most prestigious *studia* for medicine found positions all over Europe. One example is provided by Master Pancius of Lucca. In his homeland, Master Pancius was modestly successful. Probably educated in medicine at Bologna, as a young man he became personal physician there to his compatriot the bishop and surgical writer Theodoric of Lucca, a Dominican. He also took some part in academic medical debate, since one of his opinions was subsequently quoted by the well-known medical commentator Gentile da Foligno (d. 1348). In England, however, Pancius was able to translate this respectable but hardly distinguished record into a richly rewarded position as household physician, general factotum, and money-lender to King Edward II and King Edward III, which he held from 1317 until his death in 1340.[38] In the later fourteenth and the fifteenth centuries faculties of medicine in the new universities provided teaching opportunities in their homelands for northern European graduates of Paris, Montpellier, and the Italian *studia*.

The total number of those who taught and studied medicine at Paris, Bologna, Montpellier, and Padua between the thirteenth and the fifteenth century cannot be recovered. Moreover, although it is clear that levels of population in the medical faculties were from time to time affected by general demographic trends, by local or regional political crises, and by the attraction of a famous teacher, the effect of these factors and their interaction on either numbers or quality was seldom simple or obvious.

One can, however, arrive at some idea of the relative size of the student body in these medical faculties at different times, as compared with one another, with other faculties in the same *studium*, and with other *studia*. Thus of 1,681 practitioners in France before 1500 whose university affiliation is known, 1,008 went to Paris, 376 to Montpellier, and 297 to other *studia*. In France, the number of university medical students seems to have peaked in the second half of the fourteenth and first half of the fifteenth century, a fact which suggests that generalizations about the effect of the Black Death on the medical profession should be approached with caution. At Bologna, between 1419 and 1434, sixty-five degrees in medicine and one in surgery were

---

[37] For citations and discussion: D. W. Amundsen, 'Medieval Canon Law on Medical and Surgical Practice by the Clergy', *Bulletin of the History of Medicine*, 52 (1978), 22–44.

[38] Sarti and Fattorini, *De professoribus* (note 32), 235 (will of Theodoric of Lucca); Gentile da Foligno, *Questions et tractatus extravagantes* ... (Venice, 1520), question 46, fol. 63r; C. H. Talbot and E. A. Hammond, *The Medical Practitioners in Medieval England: a Biographical Register* (London, 1965), 234–7.

awarded (figures that cannot necessarily be extrapolated to other periods of that *studium*'s medieval history). By contrast, Turin (founded 1404) granted only thirteen medical degrees between 1426 and 1462, while in the entire period from its foundation in 1477 until 1534 the University of Tübingen granted thirty-five doctorates in medicine.[39]

These figures clearly imply that even in schools such as Montpellier and Bologna, which were famous for their medical teaching the number of medical students present at any one time was not very large. None the less, it deserves to be emphasized that the ratio of medical students to medical degrees awarded was probably always high. A full medical course took four or five years; but it is also necessary to allow for those – and they were apparently numerous – who abandoned their medical studies before graduation or completed them at another *studium*. And the population attending medical lectures may have been swelled by students or teachers in other faculties who had a secondary interest in medicine.

Similar uncertainties prevail with regard to the numbers of teaching masters and distribution of courses. For example, the names of numerous medical masters who taught at Bologna during the thirteenth and first half of the fourteenth century are, of course, known from their writings, and from scattered university documents and other records. But systematic records of teaching positions held and courses offered started to appear only with the introduction of the practice of issuing an official *rotulus*, or list of professors and courses, for each academic year; this practice began in the latter part of the fourteenth century, but only scattered examples survive from before the fifteenth century.[40] And, even for the period after the practice of issuing *rotuli* became customary, it seems likely that, in addition to the professors recorded in the *rotuli* who lectured publicly on the books in the official medical curriculum, some others may from time to time have taught medicine or surgery briefly, informally, or privately.

The largest community (and probably one unprecedented in size) of medical students and professors in Europe before 1500 may have been that in mid-fifteenth-century Padua. At Padua, the number of medical degrees awarded rose from four in 1407 to eight in 1434, to nine (two of these being in surgery) in 1450. The award of eight or nine degrees in medicine in a given year may imply a medical student body of around one hundred. This estimate is roughly confirmed by the facts that in 1457 the total number of students in all faculties at Padua is known to have been 800, and that in 1450, when nine

---

[39] Jacquart, *Milieu médical* (note 2), 364, table 3; 365, table 4. C. Piana, 'Lauree in arti e medicina conferite a Bologna negli anni 1419–1434', in C. Piana, *Nuove ricerche sulle Università di Bologna e di Parma* (Florence, 1966), 110–74; Kuhn, *Studenten der Universität Tübingen* (note 13), 35; Naso, *Medici e strutture sanitarie* (note 15), 114.

[40] The Bologna *rotuli* are edited in U. Dallari (ed.), *I rotuli dei lettori e artisti dello Studio Bolognese dal 1384 al 1799*, 3 vols. (Bologna, 1889).

medical and surgical degrees were awarded, the total number of degrees was ninety-three.[41]

Light of a different kind is thrown on the relative position of the major centres of university medical education if one attempts to compare not numbers of degrees or of students but contributions to medical learning. Collectively, the faculties of medicine contributed a large proportion of the written output of late medieval medicine since university-educated physicians, and, in particular, professors of medicine, were naturally far more likely than other medical or surgical practitioners to write books. Montpellier, which apparently trained many fewer practitioners than Paris, was the affiliation of a larger number of medical authors.[42] Medical writers associated with the north Italian *studia*, collectively considered, probably outnumbered authors from Montpellier. At any rate, this is the case if one uses as a measure commentaries on the Hippocratic works most widely studied in the universities, namely the *Aphorisms*, *Prognostics*, and *De regimine acutorum*. Moreover, Montpellier authors were most productive of these commentaries in about the half-century turning on the year 1300, whereas the output by Italian medical writers continued in the later fourteenth and the fifteenth century.[43]

RELATIONS BETWEEN THE MEDICAL FACULTY AND OTHER FACULTIES

Yet another difference among *studia* lay in relations between the medical faculty and other faculties. The relations with the faculty of law chiefly involved institutional organization and rivalries in the southern European *studia* (see chapter 12). In Paris and other northern *studia*, the presence of faculties of theology facilitated the combination of studies in medicine and in theology by some scholars,[44] but otherwise seems to have affected medicine only indirectly, via the influence of the faculty of theology on the faculty of arts. It is also sometimes suggested that the absence of theological faculties in the north Italian *studia* during the formative years of the faculties of medicine had the effect of leaving arts and philosophy free to develop in particularly close association with medicine, and that this state of affairs may have fostered the development of particular attitudes and interests within those disciplines.

Unquestionably, the most important relation of the faculty of medicine was

---

[41] Ohl, *University of Padua* (note 35), 46; G. Zonta and G. Bronto (eds.), *Acta graduum academicorum gymnasii patavini ab anno 1406 ad annum 1450*, 2nd edn (Padua, 1970), vol. I, 3–4, 312–28; vol. II, 312–34.

[42] Jacquart, *Milieu médical* (note 2), 390, table 28.

[43] Based on a survey of the commentaries on these works by known authors of the thirteenth to the fifteenth centuries in P. Kibre, *Hippocrates latinus: Repertorium of Hippocratic Writings in the Latin Middle Ages* (New York, 1985).

[44] Jacquart, *Milieu médical* (note 2), 393, table 32.

with the faculty of arts. This relation, unlike those with the other higher faculties, had to do with the content as well as the institutional context of medical learning. And the contrary may also have sometimes been the case, in the sense that concepts or information from medical sources were from time to time adopted in philosophical arguments.

Venerable truisms, repeated by university medical writers, asserted that all the liberal arts and natural philosophy were necessary for medicine.[45] This belief, as well as institutional history and convenience, underlay the arrangements linking arts and medicine in a single university and a single doctoral college at Bologna, Padua, and elsewhere. At Montpellier, the expectation that a medical student should be competent in arts was made explicit by a provision in the statutes of 1240, and the papal bull of 1309 to the effect that students already proficient in arts could complete their medical studies in a shorter period than those lacking such preparation.[46]

Moreover, competence in Latin and some command of logic, astrology, and natural philosophy were a practical preparation for the kind of medical education provided in the universities. The study of medical authorities demanded Latin literacy. The substantiation of the frequently reiterated claims that medicine was rational and could offer some certain knowledge required, in the context of contemporary notions of reasoning and of scientific certitude, the ability to handle logical demonstrations. The stars were universally believed to influence human health and sickness. And a knowledge of natural philosophy was pertinent to medicine considered as descriptive of a natural entity, namely the human body.[47] Furthermore, among the principal medical *studia*, not only Paris, but also Bologna and Padua flourished as centres of advanced teaching in arts and philosophy.

There can be no question that the leading medical writers, particularly those who produced commentaries, had extensive training in logic, astrology, and natural philosophy. A few of them – Peter of Abano (d. *c.* 1316) is a celebrated example – had a command of these subjects equal to that of any of their colleagues in other faculties, along with a pronounced interest in philosophical questions. Many others whose treatment of philosophical issues was abbreviated or routine none the less displayed in their writings extensive familiarity with the *libri naturales* of Aristotle and competence in handling syllogistic reasoning.[48]

---

[45] For example, Peter of Abano, *Conciliator* (Padua, 1985; facsimile reprint of the edition of Venice, 1565), fols. 3v–4r; C. B. Schmitt, 'Aristotle Among the Physicians', in A. Wear, R. K. French, and I. M. Lonie (ed.) *The Medical Renaissance of the Sixteenth Century* (Cambridge, 1985), 1–15.

[46] *Cartulaire* (note 19), 187, doc. 5: 357, doc. 68, section 51.

[47] P. Kibre, 'Arts and Medicine in the Universities of the Later Middle Ages', in *Universities in the Late Middle Ages*, 213–27.

[48] N. G. Siraisi, 'Pietro d'Abano and Taddeo Alderotti: Two Models of Medical Culture', *Medioevo*, 2 (1985), 139–62.

When one turns to look at the teaching careers of medical masters in the major *studia*, a similar picture emerges. Of fourteen doctors involved in drawing up a set of statutes for the medical branch of the Bologna College of Doctors of Arts and Medicine in 1378, seven are recorded as having degrees in philosophy as well as medicine, and five are known to have taught logic and natural philosophy as well as medicine. Indeed, a common career pattern in the Italian schools was to teach arts while studying medicine. Furthermore, it is evident that a substantial proportion of the graduates in medicine from Italian *studia* also obtained degrees in arts. Thus of the sixty-five medical graduates at Bologna between 1419 and 1434, thirty-one already had degrees in arts at the time of their graduation in medicine, and two more took arts and medical degrees simultaneously.[49]

It by no means follows either that individuals always or even customarily obtained their arts and medical degrees from the same institution, or that, in *studia* organized with a university and doctoral college of arts and medicine, arts and medical studies were integrated. On the contrary, students often moved from one *studium* to another, and the importance in their own right of the philosophy schools of early fourteenth-century Bologna and fifteenth-century Padua is well known.[50] But the medical and the arts faculties in these centres evidently supported one another in terms of attracting and providing for students and teachers. In particular, the provision of astrology teaching was probably encouraged by the need to instruct medical students in this subject. Thus, the lectures on the *Sphere* of Sacrobosco, an elementary text-book of cosmology, given at Bologna in the early 1320s by the famous (and unfortunate) astrologer Cecco d'Ascoli were prefaced by a justification of the value of astrology for medical studies.[51]

Further evidence for the arts studies of university-educated physicians is provided by the facts that a number of them wrote on subjects other than medicine, served as general (not exclusively medical) advisers to rulers or nobles, or associated with literary or humanistic authors. Some famous examples are the Montpellier medical master Arnald of Villanova (d. 1311), who wrote extensively on spiritual and ecclesiastical reform and served the crown of Aragon in a political as well as a medical capacity; Giovanni de Dondi, professor of medicine at Padua, designer and builder of a celebrated astronomical clock, and friend and correspondent of Petrarch; and Michele Savonarola (d. after 1466), one time professor of medicine at Padua, author of a humanistic work in praise of that city and its outstanding citizens, and

---

[49] Malagola (ed.), *Statuti* (note 29), 425, 448; Piana, 'Lauree in arti e medicina' (note 39). A similar pattern is suggested by the writings of some northern authors, for example, Bartholomaeus of Bruges (on whom see Jacquart (ed.), *Supplément* (note 20), 38).

[50] A. Poppi (ed.), *Scienza e filosofia all'università di Padova nel Quattrocento* (Padua/Trieste, 1983).

[51] Cecco d'Ascoli, proem to *In spheram mundi enarratio*, in L. Thorndike, *The Sphere of Sacrobosco and Its Commentators* (Chicago, 1949), 344–6.

subsequently physician and education adviser to Leonello and thereafter to Borso d'Este, rulers of Ferrara.[52]

In sum, membership of the élite among university-trained physicians implied substantial preparation in arts. Nevertheless, a modest grounding in arts disciplines and a minimal interest in them probably characterized other university-trained medical practitioners. For example, those who received their entire education at one of the small German universities presumably took only an arts course taught at an elementary level to very young students. Doubtless, too, many university-trained practitioners studied arts or philosophy only to the minimum extent necessary for medical professional purposes, and retained no interest in those subjects once their education was finished.

MEDICAL CURRICULA AND THE CONTENT OF MEDICAL LEARNING

By the time medical faculties were established in *studia generalia*, the corpus of medical texts of Greek and Islamic origin available for study in Latin was substantial. To the various early medieval translations and the output of Constantinus Africanus already referred to had been added in the twelfth century the translations of medical books from Arabic produced by Gerard of Cremona and his circle and from Greek by Burgundio of Pisa. Hence, Latin versions existed of more than forty treatises circulating under the name of Hippocrates and of a considerably large body of material attributed to Galen, as well as of Dioscorides' *Materia medica*.[53] Major works of Islamic origin (to a considerable extent Galenic in their content) included, in addition to the *Canon* of Avicenna (al-Husain b. Abdallah Ibn Sina), other encyclopedic treatments of medicine by Haly Abbas (Ali b. al-Abbas al-Magusi), and Rasis (ar-Razi), as well as a work on surgery by Albucasis (Abu al-Qasim Halaf b. Abbas az-Zahrawi).[54]

The Hippocratic and Galenic material in circulation included treatises attri-

---

[52] Arnald's career is summarized in M. R. McVaugh (ed.), *Arnaldi de Villanova opera medica omnia*, vol. II, *Aphorismi de gradibus* (Granada/Barcelona, 1975), 76–7. F. Petrarca, *Seniles*, book XII: Pesenti, *Professori e promotori* (note 12), 186–96, provides a bio-bibliography of Michele Savonarola.

[53] Kibre, *Hippocrates latinus* (note 43), which, however, includes but does not usually distinguish medieval *spuria*. No comprehensive list of medieval Latin Galenic manuscripts has yet been published, but much information is found in R. J. Durling, 'Corrigenda and Addenda to Diels' Galenica', parts 1 and 2, *Traditio*, 23 (1967), 463–76, and 37 (1981), 461–76, and in index entries s.v. Galen in L. Thorndike and P. Kibre, *A Catalogue of Incipits of Medieval Scientific Writings in Latin*, 2nd edn. (Cambridge, Mass., 1963). J. M. Riddle, 'Dioscorides', in P. O. Kristeller and F. E. Cranz (eds.), in *Catalogus translationum et commentariorum: Medieval and Renaissance Latin Translations and Commentaries*, vol. IV (Washington, DC, 1980), 1–143.

[54] H. Schipperges, 'Die Assimilation der arabischen Medizin durch das lateinische Mittelalter', *Sudhoffs Archiv für Geschichte der Medizin und der Naturwissenschaften*, 3 (special issue) (1964).

buted to Hippocrates in antiquity and a number of authentic works of Galen. Access to an additional important treatise of Galen was provided by the translation into Latin of *De usu partium* directly from Greek in the early fourteenth century; and, at the very end of the period with which we are concerned, the endeavours of medical humanists opened a new phase of translation of ancient medical works. But the medieval Latin Hippocrates and Galen were incomplete, especially as regards Galen's major anatomical treatises (for example, *De anatomicis administrationibus* was first translated into Latin in the sixteenth century), and were contaminated by late *spuria*, such as the allegedly Hippocratic work on medical astrology. Furthermore, students of medicine learned ancient medical ideas only partially through direct consultation of the longer treatises of ancient authors; a large role was also played by highly abbreviated or aphoristic treatises, by compendia, and by the mediation of the Arabic medical encyclopedias. Arabic medical works were valued not only for their synthesis of ancient medicine, but also for their independent contributions to treatment and to herbal pharmacology. However, the Arabo-Latin translations both of works of Greek origin from Arabic versions, and of works originally written in Arabic, sometimes presented problems as regards the comprehension of pharmacological vocabulary, problems only partially solved by the compilation of volumes of medical *synonima*.[55]

Although learned medical writers were familiar with material in all the categories mentioned above, and with much else besides, not all of it was the subject of regular lectures in the *studia*. Lists of books officially prescribed for medical lectures at Montpellier and Bologna show a curriculum of courses on works in the *articella* collection, which continued to supply the pedagogical need for brief statements of fundamental concepts; on up to a dozen or more longer works of Galen; and on selections from Arabic writers, notably Avicenna.[56] The cycle of lectures does not appear to have been arranged in order of ascending difficulty, but certain books none the less functioned as basic texts. These were the brief Galenic compendium known as the *Tegni*, *Microtechne*, or *Ars parva*, the Hippocratic *Aphorisms*, and sections of the *Canon*. The parts of the *Canon* regularly used as textbooks for university lectures contained a synopsis of physiology (book I, part 1), a treatise on fevers (book IV, part 1), principles of disease and treatment (book I, part 4),

---

[55] G. Beaujouan, 'Fautes et obscurités dans les traductions médicales du Moyen Age', *Revue de synthèse*, 3rd series, 89 (1968), 145–52; D. Goltz, 'Studien zur Geschichte der Mineralnamen in Pharmazie, Chemie und Medizin von den Anfängen bis Paracelsus', *Sudhoffs Archiv für Geschichte der Medizin und der Naturwissenschaften*, 14 (special issue) (1972), 323–33.

[56] *Cartulaire* (note 29), 220, doc. 25 (1309); 347–8, doc. 68, sections 20 and 21 (1340); Malagola (ed.), *Statuti* (note 29), 274–7 (1405). Siraisi, *Alderotti* (note 24), 96–106, shows that most of the works listed in the 1405 statutes were already being studied at Bologna in the late thirteenth or early fourteenth century.

and diseases from head to toe (book III). The writings of Rasis on diseases also frequently served as the basis of lectures.[57]

The exposition of the *Ars*, the *Aphorisms*, and the *Canon* was hence a major task of late medieval medical masters; its central role explains the prevalence of written commentaries on these works, although it is difficult to determine how closely such commentaries resemble the original lectures. The commentary tradition also suggests that university lectures on the longer and more specialized works of Galen assigned by statute were given most frequently during the half-century divided by 1300, and less often thereafter. Yet patterns of citation in other works leave no doubt that these books continued to be studied.

As the last example shows, statutory lists of books and lectures tell only part of the story of academic medical education. The prescribed public lectures and other exercises were supplemented by 'extraordinary' lectures on works chosen by the master, and by private teaching and study. Moreover, antedating and surviving the information of relatively impersonal and sometimes mutually adversarial academic corporations of medical teachers and students was another kind of relationship: that of an individual practitioner and a younger *socius* who was his master's pupil, assistant, apprentice, and potential successor. At Bologna, the surgeon Ugo of Lucca (*fl.* 1214) passed on his skill to a select, closed circle of younger relatives or apprentices; at Montpellier, the oldest regulations referring to a medical university (1220) required each student to choose a master, and penalized attempts to lure a scholar away from his master.[58]

The length of the medical course varied: at Montpellier the statutes of 1240 provided that the status of bachelor of medicine should be attained by a student not already proficient in arts after three and a half years of study and six months of practice outside Montpellier; the papal bull of 1309 fixed the entire course of study at six years for students not previously proficient in arts (five years for those who were), and extended the practice to eight months or two summers. At Bologna, the statutes of the university of arts and medicine, issued in 1405, provided for three years each of philosophy and *astrologia* and four years each of *medicina* and (medical) *practica*, that is, lectures on books about particulars of disease and treatment.[59] All these subjects are treated under a single rubric of the statutes, all presumably being regarded as pertaining to medical students. No doubt at least some of the courses in the different subjects could be taken concurrently. In medicine as in other disciplines, the

---

[57] This and following remarks about the distribution of commentaries on different medical works are based on the manuscript listings in Thorndike and Kibre, *Catalogue of Incipits* (note 53).

[58] Siraisi, *Alderotti* (note 24), 14–15; *Cartulaire* (note 19), 181–2, doc. 2.

[59] *Cartulaire* (note 19), 187, doc. 5 (1240); 220, doc. 25 (1309); Malagola (ed.), *Statuti* (note 29), 274–7.

requirements for graduation were hearing lectures on prescribed books, participation in disputation, and success in oral examination.

The curriculum was geared toward training practitioners, for practice was the acknowledged goal of university medical education. All university teachers of medicine trained students who would practise, and most professors were also practitioners themselves – often successful and highly rewarded ones. It is doubtless true, however, that the practice of some leading professors of medicine was largely consultative, and that those university-trained physicians who could afford to do so tended to delegate some forms of physical intervention to assistants. But for lay physicians, including university professors, practice of some kind was an economic necessity, since it was their most lucrative source of legitimate income. The frank admission of Taddeo Alderotti (d. 1295), one of the most celebrated medical professors of Bologna, that he had temporarily suspended writing commentaries in favour of *lucrative operatio* merely made explicit the main source of the substantial wealth revealed by his will. The term *operatio* is especially revealing, as Taddeo distinguished carefully between *practica*, or knowledge about practice, and *operatio*, actual treatment.[60] The topics most frequently treated in the medical writings produced in the ambience of the *studia* were regimen, symptoms, disease, and remedies (chiefly medication and phlebotomy).

Moreover, university education in practical medicine involved not merely the study of texts about diseases, remedies, and so on, but also such requirements and opportunities as a period spent in actual practice before graduation (as already noted, obligatory at Montpellier from 1240), the study of collections of *consilia* describing individual cases, and attendance upon a senior professor and practitioner when he visited patients. As is well known, medieval university medical students also attended anatomical demonstrations on the human cadaver. At Bologna, dissections were openly held by 1316; at Montpellier annual or biennial dissections were provided for by statute in 1340. Infrequent official dissections were on occasion supplemented by clandestine private dissection.[61] In university medical education, the object of dissection was to familiarize the student with the gross anatomy of the internal organs, rather than to teach him either how to dissect (although in at least one fourteenth-century private dissection the students actually participated) or how to perform surgical operations.

The position of surgery differed in different *studia*. As is well known, surgeons were excluded from the faculty of medicine at Paris, where relations between physicians and surgeons were marked by mutual rivalry and denigration. Henry de Mondeville (d. after 1316), a learned surgeon who served the French royal court, taught in Paris, but not in the faculty of medicine of

---

[60] Siraisi, *Alderotti* (note 24), 27–39, 121–2, and bibliography there cited.
[61] *Cartulaire* (note 19), 334, doc. 68, section 13. Siraisi, *Alderotti* (note 24), 110–13, summarizes the early history of anatomical dissection at Bologna and indicates bibliography.

the *studium*. Henry was the author of a Latin book on surgery, which, although it owed much to his own studies of school medical authors, was as dismissive of learned physicians as of ignorant surgeons. His attitude to the former is summed up in his remark that God himself had frequently acted as a surgeon (when he made Eve from Adam's rib, and when Jesus made clay to anoint the eyes of a blind man), but that the Scripture nowhere recorded that the Lord engaged in the characteristic medical activities of feeling the pulse and inspecting urine.[62] Yet Henry himself had studied and given lectures (not necessarily publicly in the *studium*) at Montpellier, with medical students among his audience.

As Guy de Chauliac, the author of the most celebrated Latin surgical work of the Middle Ages, explained, surgery fell within Galen's definition of therapy and was one of the three instruments of medicine (the other two being medication and diet). The formulation was in no way peculiar to Guy or to surgeons, since the same list of the three instruments of medicine was also presented by numerous school medical authors. Guy called himself *magister in medicina* and had presumably graduated in medicine as well as studying surgical books at Montpellier. He dedicated his own work on surgery to the physicians of Montpellier, Bologna and Paris – the three chief centres of medical learning – and of the papal court of Avignon, where he made his own career. His book is distinguished both by a Galenic learning that resembles but goes beyond that of many contemporary university medical authors (he was one of the first to make extensive use of Galen's lengthy and detailed anatomical physiology entitled *On the Uses of the Parts*) and by its claim that surgery itself is a science – 'as if one were to say a science of manual operation'. That claim was bold, given the usual reservation of the term *scientia* for disciplines that proceeded by syllogistic demonstration.[63]

At Bologna and other Italian *studia*, a few degrees were granted in surgery. A curriculum of books to be read in surgery was, moreover, included in the statutes of the Bologna University of Arts and Medicine of 1405; it consisted of one of the Latin surgical compendia produced in Italy during the thirteenth century and appropriate sections of school authors – a work attributed to Galen, a portion of the *Canon* of Avicenna, and a work of Rasis.[64] Furthermore, academic authors commented on surgical works; for example, Dino del Garbo (d. 1327, professor of medicine at Bologna and elsewhere) wrote on a section of the *Canon* dealing with skull fractures.[65] As far as books were

62 J. L. Pagel (ed.), *Die Chirurgie des Heinrich von Mondeville (Hermondaville)* (Berlin, 1892), 79–80.

63 de Chauliac, *La Grande Chirurgie* (note 8), 4–8; M. S. Ogden, 'The Galenic Works Cited in Guy de Chauliac's "chirurgia magna"', *Journal of the History of Medicine and Allied Sciences*, 29 (1973), 24–33.

64 Malagola (ed.), *Statuti* (note 29), 247–8.

65 *Expositio super III, IV et parte V Fen Avicenne* (Ferrara, 1489); there are other early editions.

concerned, the reading of surgeons who obtained a university degree was probably not very different from that of their literate colleagues outside the schools; how much practical training in surgery was provided in the university setting is unknown. Surgeons treated fractures, wounds, ulcers, and skin problems, using medication as well as actual surgery.

Nevertheless, in the *studia* medicine was primarily a body of knowledge about the natural world grasped through the study and exposition of authoritative texts. Hence, *lectio* and *disputatio* were central to medical instruction, as to other academic disciplines, notably natural philosophy, and were used to teach both the courses in *theoria* and the courses in *practica* into which university curricula in medicine came to be divided. And, although academic medical writings of the thirteenth to fifteenth century show that the introduction of content drawn from speculative natural philosophy was a rule restricted to a few topics, scholastic Aristotelianism influenced the organization of discourse in a great deal of academic medical exposition. In university lectures, books on essentially practical topics were treated to full scholastic analysis by means of *quaestiones*, objections, and so on, as may be seen, for example, from the commentary by Dino del Garbo on the surgical portions of Avicenna's *Canon*.[66] The resultant medical scholasticism belonged to the same intellectual universe as medieval natural philosophy, in which analysis, comparison, and reconciliation of texts was the normal task, and syllogistic reasoning the normal way of arriving at conclusions.

Moreover, there were powerful pragmatic incentives for medical teachers and students in the university milieu to emphasize those aspects of medical learning that could be linked to or paralleled with natural philosophy. The intellectual priorities of the age ensured that such an emphasis provided the strongest support for the claim of medicine to a place among the higher branches of learning, and hence to a respected position in the hierarchy of academic faculties. And university physicians could hope for social and economic advantages in their practice by calling attention to the way in which their book-learning and consequent possession of explanatory theory distinguished them from other medical practitioners.

No brief summary of the actual teachings of academic medicine can easily be given. In essence, what was conveyed to students was usually a Galenism that was at once simplified, in the sense that it was shorn of Galen's polemical context, breadth of knowledge of ancient medicine, and attention to anatomical and clinical detail, and greatly elaborated by the pharmacological additions, efforts at systematization, and theoretical complications introduced by later authors.

A central concept was *complexio* (*krasis* or temperament), the balance of the elementary qualities of hot, wet, cold, and dry both in the human body,

[66] See note 65.

especially its humours (blood, two biles, and phlegm), and in substances used for therapeutic purposes. As a physiological theory, *complexio* lent itself to elaboration since not only each species, and among human beings each individual, was considered to have its own *complexio*, but also each body parts. Furthermore, *complexio* was simultaneously conceived of as an essential characteristic of human individuals (medical men discussed whether it was to be equated with the substantial form of the philosophers), and as varying with sex, age, climate, and regimen. Illness was normally attributed either to *solutio continuitatis*, meaning, essentially, trauma, or to complexional imbalance. 'Rational' therapy involved determining the proper balance of qualities between medicine and patient. The *complexio* assigned to various medicinal substances (mostly herbal) was determined, either by manifest characteristics (the hotness of pepper) or by tradition; the intensity of the qualities was supposed to differ in different substances. Arnald of Villanova grasped the difficulties for compound medicines posed by this last idea, and devised a quasi-mathematical system for compounding medicines of a determined degree of complexional intensity from ingredients each of which had its own degree of complexional intensity.[67] Other learned physicians seem to have relied on intuition and tradition in identifying the complexion or complexional intensity of patients and medicines. In addition, the notion that certain substances owed their medicinal action to 'specific form', that is to an otherwise unidentifiable characteristic peculiar to the species, provided a convenient explanation in cases where it appeared difficult to apply the theory of complexion. Moreover, a number of the substances used as medicines had properties (for example, as opiates or laxatives) with which physicians were fully familiar from experience, whatever theoretical explanation was adopted for them.

A second fundamental concept was that of the influence of the heavenly bodies on terrestrial events, including health and disease. Medical astrology permeated all of late medieval medicine, and was not confined to the university milieu. But in the fourteenth and fifteenth centuries the faculties of medicine were closely associated with the cultivation and development of astrology.[68] Yet, among university professors of medicine, interest in the stars varied widely in both degree and kind. Some paid minimal attention to the whole subject; others drew on astrological material when composing theoretical explanations or practical prescriptions, but made no contribution to the development of the subject; yet others produced works of their own on medical astrology, such as the two commentaries on the pseudo-Hippocratic

---

[67] This is the subject-matter of the *Aphorismi de gradibus*: see McVaugh (ed.), *Arnaldi de Villanova* (note 52).

[68] G. Zanier, 'Ricerche sull'occultismo a Padova nel secolo XV', in Poppi (ed.), *Scienza e filosofia* (note 50), 345–72; see also M. Markowski, 'Astronomie an der Krakauer Universität im XV. Jahrhundert', in *Universities in the Late Middle Ages*, 266.

treatise; and a few – and those the most learned – wrote on or otherwise contributed to astrology in a more general context or to astronomy. The last group includes Peter of Abano whose astronomical and astrological works include a treatise on the motion of the eighth sphere, and Giovanni de Dondi (d. 1370), whose astronomical clock has already been mentioned.[69]

The intellectual enterprise of academic medicine was thus complex and demanding. In the context of medieval science, the endeavour to assimilate ancient and Islamic medical and biological ideas and texts was a worthy contribution. Furthermore, the introduction of scholastic methods of disputation and reconciliation into medicine led to the useful result that learned physicians isolated clearly the discrepancies among ancient authors (most notably, between Galen and Aristotle). But scholastic medicine like scholastic natural philosophy, is criticized not only for the premium it set on honing disputational skills, but also for providing only tenuous connections between theory and the data of experience. Yet it is hard to see how learned physicians could have developed any system of relating theory and experience different from that of the contemporary Aristotelian natural philosophers whose ideas about the nature of, and means of arriving at, scientific knowledge they shared. Moreover, it seems likely that their experience of medical practice familiarized professors of medicine to a greater extent than their colleagues in philosophy with the need to take account of the empirical and the particular. Certainly, learned physicians were very conscious of the dual nature of medicine as craft and learning and devoted considerable discussion to the ambiguous relations between its two aspects.[70] And, to the extent that their actual therapeutic activities can be known (the large medieval prescriptive literature about medical practice is not necessarily always an accurate guide to what was acually done), their practice was at least in part governed by their theory. Furthermore, a few instances can be cited in which theoretical conclusions were criticized or modified on the grounds of practical experience.[71]

The characteristics indicated above probably did not vary much from one of the principal centres of medical education to the other. For example, a recent examination of the use of and attitudes toward sections of the *Canon* of Avicenna as medical textbooks at Paris and Montpellier in the thirteenth and early fourteenth centuries has shown that there appears to be little basis for the idea that the teaching of Montpellier was more 'practical' or more 'Hippocratic' than that of Paris.[72] Moreover, some important developments in medical teaching were not confined to any one *studium*, but affected major

---

[69] Details are provided in Paschetto, *Pietro d'Abano* (note 25); S. A. Bedini and F. R. Maddison, *Mechanical Universe: the Astrarium of Giovanni Dondi* (Philadelphia, 1966).

[70] Usually under the rubric of the question 'whether medicine is an art or a science', frequently discussed at the beginning of general treatises or commentaries. The usual solution of scholastic medical authors was that medicine is in some sense both art and science.

[71] This issue is dealt with by M. R. McVaugh (see select bibliography).

[72] Jacquart, 'Réception du *Canon*' (note 23).

centres at about the same time. Thus, for example, the *Canon* of Avicenna (d. 1037), one of the most influential of medieval medical textbooks, was translated into Latin from Arabic before 1187. But its introduction into medical studies at Paris took place probably around 1230, and at Montpellier around 1240.[73] Similarly, in the decade round 1300, an expansion of interest in direct study of works of Galen seems to have occurred at both Bologna and Montpellier.[74]

As the foregoing examples suggest, the formative period for the faculty of medicine extends from the mid-thirteenth to the early fourteenth century. Soon afterwards the outbreak of the Black Death killed learned physicians, among them Gentile da Foligno, as it killed many others; produced a new genre of medical writing, the plague tractate; and perhaps made members of established Florentine families somewhat reluctant to go into medicine, thereby opening up opportunities for 'new men' of more modest background.[75] But, by the mid-fourteenth century, academic medical faculties were so securely established that even this medical calamity of unprecedented magnitude did not undermine their institutional position or invalidate their teaching. On the contrary, some of the most celebrated scholastic medical commentators – Giacomo da Forlì (d. 1414), Ugo Benzi (d. 1439), Jacques Despars (d. 1458)[76] – belong to the late fourteenth and the early fifteenth century. Moreover, recent studies of late medieval vernacular medical writing and of the books owned by practitioners suggest a growing influence of Latinate academic medicine on practitioners not trained in the *studia*.[77] Thus school medicine played a major part in shaping the scientific understanding, the approach to ancient scientific texts, and the healing practices of the period.

[73] Jacquart, 'Réception du *Canon*' (note 23), 69, 73. L. G. Ballester, 'Arnau de Vilanova (*c.* 1240–1311) y la reforma de los estudios médicos en Montpellier (1309): El Hipócrates latino y la introducción del nuevo Galeno', *Dynamis*, 2 (1982), 101–4.

[74] Ballester, 'Arnau de Vilanova' (note 73), 97–158; Siraisi, *Alderotti* (note 24), 100–5.

[75] Campbell, *Black Death* (note 33), 6–33, lists plague tractates written 1348–50; Park, *Doctors and Medicine* (note 2), 150–1 (and elsewhere).

[76] On Giacomo and Ugo: Pesenti, *Professori e promotori* (note 12), 53–8, 103–12, and bibliography there cited; D. Jacquart, 'Le regard d'un médicin sur son temps: J. Despars (1380?–1458)', *Bibliothèque de l'Ecole des Chartes*, 138 (1980), 35–86.

[77] For example, F. M. Getz, 'Gilbertus Anglicus Anglicized', *Medical History*, 26 (1982), 436–42; L. E. Voigts, 'Editing Middle English Medical Texts: Needs and Issues', in T. H. Levere (ed.), *Editing Texts in the History of Science and Medicine* (New York/London, 1982), 39–66; and, although the author stresses the absence of participation in practical obstetrics by academic physicians, A. Delva, *Vrouwengeneeskunde in Vlaanderen tijdens de late middeleeuwen* (Bruges, 1983), 203–6, notes the relation of the Flemish *Trotula* to a Latin text presumably produced in academic circles.

SELECT BIBLIOGRAPHY

Agrimi, J. and Crisciani, C. *Medicina del corpo e medicina dell'anima. Note sul sapere del medico fino all'inizio del secolo XIII. Episteme*, Milan, 1976.

Amundsen, D. W. 'Casuistry and Professional Obligations: the Regulation of Physicians by the Court of Conscience in the Late Middle Ages', Parts I, II, *Transactions and Studies of the College of Physicians of Philadelphia*, 3 (1981), 22–39, 93–112.

Bullough, V. L. *The Development of Medicine as a Profession: the Contribution of the Medieval University to Modern Medicine*, Basle/New York, 1966.

Campbell, A. M. *The Black Death and Men of Learning*, New York, 1931; reprint, 1966.

Dulieu, L. *La Médecine à Montpellier*, vol. I, *Le Moyen Age*, Avignon, 1975.

Fuiano, M. *Maestri di medicina e filosofia a Napoli nel Quattrocento*, Naples, 1973.

Garcio Ballester, L. 'Arnau de Vilanova (*c.* 1240–1311) y la reforma de los estudios médicos en Montpellier (1309): El Hipócrates latino y la introducción del nuevo Galeno', *Dynamis*, 2 (1982), 97–158.

Getz, F. M. 'Medicine at Medieval Oxford', in J. I. Catto (ed.), *The History of the University of Oxford*, vol. II, *Late Medieval Oxford*, Oxford, in press.

Jacquart, D. *Le Milieu médical en France du XIIe au XVe siècle*, Paris, 1981.

Jacquart, D. 'La question disputée dans les facultés de médecine', in B. C. Bàzan, J. F. Wippel, G. Fransen, and D. Jacquart, *Les Questions disputées et les questions quodlibétiques dans les facultés de théologie, de droit et de médecine*, Typologie des sources du Moyen Age occidental, ed. L. Génicot, fasc. 44–45, Turnhout, 1985.

Jacquart, D. 'La réception du *Canon* d'Avicenne: Comparaison entre Montpellier et Paris au XIIIe et XIVe siècles', in *Histoire de l'école médicale de Montpellier. Actes du 110e Congrès National des Sociétés Savantes tenu à Montpellier en 1985*, vol. II Paris, 1985, 69–77.

Kibre, P. 'The Faculty of Medicine at Paris, Charlatanism and Unlicensed Medical Practices in the Later Middle Ages', *Bulletin of the History of Medicine*, 27 (1953), 1–20.

Kibre, P. *Hippocrates latinus: Repertorium of Hippocratic Writings in the Latin Middle Ages*, New York, 1985.

Kristeller, P. O. *Studi sulla Scuola medica salernitana*, Naples, 1986.

McVaugh, M. R. 'The Development of Medieval Pharmaceutical Theory', in R. McVaugh (ed.), *Arnaldi de Villanova Opera medica omnia*, vol. II, *Aphorismi de gradibus*, Granada/Barcelona, 1975.

McVaugh, M. R. 'The Two Faces of a Medical Career: Jordanus de Turre of Montpellier', in E. Grant and J. E. Murdoch (eds.), *Mathematics and Its Applications to Science and Natural Philosophy in the Middle Ages*, Cambridge, 1987.

Ottosson, P.-G. *Scholastic Medicine and Philosophy*, Naples, 1984.

Park, K. *Doctors and Medicine in Early Renaissance Florence*, Princeton, N. J., 1985.

Paschetto, E. *Pietro d'Abano, medico e filosofo*, Florence, 1984.

Pesenti, T. *Professori e promotori di medicina nello Studio di Padova dal 1405 al 1509: Repertorio bio-bibliografico*, Padua/Trieste, 1984.

Premuda, L. 'Le conquiste metodologiche e tecno-operative della medicina nella scuola padovana del sec. XV', in A. Poppi (ed.), *Scienza e filosofia all'Università di Padova nel Quattrocento*, Padua/Trieste, 1983.

Schipperges, H. 'Die Assimilation der arabischen Medizin durch das lateinische Mittelalter', Sudhoffs Archiv für Geschichte der Medizin und der Naturwissenschaften, (special issue) (1964).

Siraisi, N. G. *Medieval and Early Renaissance Medicine: An Introduction to Knowledge and Practice*, Chicago, 1990.

Siraisi, N. G. *Taddeo Alderotti and His Pupils: Two Generations of Italian Medical Learning*, Princeton, N. J., 1981.

CHAPTER 12

THE FACULTIES OF LAW

ANTONIO GARCÍA Y GARCÍA

THE ORIGINS AND EARLY HISTORY OF LAW FACULTIES

The University of Bologna is first heard of at the end of the eleventh century, when it was probably a private secular institution. Its faculty of law, the first in Europe, was to be the prototype and model of all others until the end of the old regime. Bologna, a city of perhaps no more than 10,000 souls in the eleventh and twelfth centuries, did not absorb the *studium* there but took on a distinctive character from its presence. And the *studium*, wooed by the spiritual and temporal powers alike, sided with neither and received the favours of both.

The privileges known as the *Authentica Habita* conferred on the *studium* by the Emperor Frederick I Barbarossa are evidence of the lively imperial interest in Bologna. Although referring explicitly to the students coming to Italy (most of them to study civil and canon law), they implicitly grant the Bologna *studium* a measure of independence and support against the *comune* or municipal authorities.[1] The papacy, on the other hand, supported the students as a means of exerting indirect influence on the *comune*, and implicitly on the German emperors' policy towards Italy, in the feud between Guelphs and Ghibellines. That was the purpose of the bull of 1217 in which Pope Honorius III took the students' part against the *comune*. The teaching of ecclesiastical subjects in Bologna, such as canon law from the time of Gratian onwards, gave the popes a doctrinal interest, so to speak, in the masters and students there. In 1219 Honorius III granted the archdeacon of Bologna cathedral the power to confer the right of teaching everywhere (*licentia ubique docendi*), so making the university a dependency of the Holy See.[2]

---

[1] Cf. chapter 3 (P. Nardi).
[2] G. Cencetti, 'Sulle origini dello Studio di Bologna', *Rivista storica italiana*, series 3, 5 (1940), 248–58; G. Cencetti, 'Studium fuit Bononiae', *Studi medievali*, 7 (1966), 781–833; G. Cencetti,

Among the most distinguished of the many Italian faculties founded in the image of Bologna were those of Padua, Pavia, Perugia, and Siena. Whatever the quality of their teaching at any particular time, the Italian faculties always attracted large numbers of foreign students. These scholars were responsible for the spread of the Bolognese model in and outside Italy. Indeed, in general the law schools followed the Bologna model, but adapted it sometimes drastically to suit local conditions.[3] Only in this sense can it be said that there were different schools of medieval law.

The principal faculties in France were those of Montpellier (which came into being largely because Piacentino the Bologna jurist taught there), Orléans, Toulouse, and Avignon. Paris had a high reputation, but only for canon law since Honorius III prohibited the teaching of civil law in Paris in 1219 (bull *Super specula*).[4] After the Italian faculties, the French faculties attracted many scholars from all over Europe from the eleventh century onwards. The leading faculties in the Iberian peninsula were those of Salamanca, Lérida, and Coimbra–Lisbon, none of which attracted students from outside the peninsula. The foundation in 1367 of the Spanish College of Saint Clement in Bologna was a signal event for Spain and Portugal, about 600 of whose scholars, most of them law students, attended it between then and the year 1500. The fact that another legal system was still firmly entrenched in England had repercussions on the attitude to Roman law and on law teaching in England. Thus in the London law schools (the Inns of Court), which did not rank as full-fledged law faculties, it was forbidden to teach Roman law because the law in force was common law. The law faculties were founded in Oxford, one for civil law and one for canon law, but civil law was never regarded there as more than a necessary addition to canon law, and Oxford's avowed aim was to train good and effective canonists. No restrictions were placed on the teaching of Roman law in Scotland, or elsewhere in Europe except in Paris. The Scottish faculties of St Andrews, Glasgow, and Aberdeen were

'L'Università di Bologna ai tempi di Accursio', in G. Rossi (ed.), *Atti del Convegno internazionale di studi accursiani*, vol. I (Milan, 1968), 55–70.

3 On the spread of the Bologna model in Europe: M. Fournier, *Histoire de la science du droit en France*, vol. III, *Les Universités françaises et l'enseignement du droit en France au moyen âge* (Paris, 1892; reprint, Aalen, 1970); *Ius romanum medii aevi*, ed. under the supervision of the Société d'Histoire des Droits de l'Antiquité, part I (Milan, 1961), in which there are one or more fascicles for each country; R. Feenstra, 'Influence de l'enseignement du droit romain sur les nations étrangères', in *Actes du congrès sur l'ancienne université d'Orléans (XIIIe–XVIIIe siècles)* (Orléans, 1962), 45–62; A. Gouron, *La Science du droit dans le midi de la France au moyen âge* (London, 1984); H. Coing, 'Die juristische Fakultät und ihr Lehrprogramm', in H. Coing (ed.), *Handbuch der Quellen und Literatur der neueren europäischen Privatrechtsgeschichte*, vol. I, *Mittelalter (1100–1500)* (Munich, 1973), 39–128; S. Kuttner, 'The Revival of Jurisprudence', in *Renaissance and Renewal*, 299–323.

4 A. Potthast, *Bibliotheca historica medii aevi. Wegweiser durch die Geschichtswerke des europäischen Mittelalters bis 1500* (Berlin, 1896; reprint, 1954), 539–40, no. 6165 (*Decretals of Gregory IX 5.5.5*). Cf. S. Kuttner, 'Papst Honorius III. und das Studium des Zivilrechts', in *Festschrift für Martin Wolf* (Tübingen, 1952), 79–101.

founded in the fifteenth century, but languished for two centuries, as the Scots continued to go to the continent for their law studies. Finally, canon law was also the main subject of law teaching in the Holy Roman Empire in the Middle Ages. The leading faculties were in Prague, Vienna, Heidelberg, Cologne, Erfurt, Leipzig, Würzburg, Rostock, Greifswald, Freiburg, Ingolstadt, Trier, Tübingen, Mainz, Louvain, and Basle; all but the first two are foundations of the late fourteenth or the fifteenth century. They attracted scholars from Scandinavia (which had no effective law faculties in the Middle Ages), the Low Countries, and eastern Europe (e.g. Poland and Hungary).

The Padua school paid more attention than Bologna to Lombard law and other local statutes of Italian cities. The north of France was governed by customary law, the south of France by written law, and French jurists consequently showed a preference for the study of one or the other; thus in Orléans there was some lack of appreciation of the *glossa ordinaria* written by Accursius of Bologna in the thirteenth century, but lively interest in local customary law. In Spain, with the adoption of Castilian as the normal vehicle for cultured thinking, a galaxy of legal works in the vernacular – the *Setenario*, Partidas, Fuero real, and *Espéculo* – appeared in the reign (1254–84) of Alfonso X (Alfonso the Wise).

Bologna's teaching of canon law quickly spread to other countries. Its offshoot was the Anglo-Norman and Rhineland school, whose more rhetorical style derives mainly from the two flourishing Paris faculties of arts and theology; its masters of canon law were slow to use the papal decretals that so powerfully stimulated the school of Bologna. Texts of canon law of this school appeared in northern France and the Rhineland in the 1260s. There were hardly any other schools of canon law worth mentioning in the rest of Europe.[5]

There are three schools of modes of comment on legal texts: the glossators' school, the post-glossators' school or *mos italicus*, and the *mos gallicus*.

The characteristic methods of the glossators were their use of the complete Justinian collections, not anthologies or fragments of them as in the high Middle Ages, and concentration on the letter of the law-books, on word-by-word exegesis. Not that they were uninterested in the sense of the law; contrary to the criticism sometimes made, understanding the letter of the text, or its exegesis, was not their goal but merely a starting-point. Their goal was the sense of the text and the legislator's intention, and as time goes on the litera-

[5] On the legal schools: H. Kantorowicz, *Rechtshistorische Schriften*, ed. H. Coing, and G. Immel (Karlsruhe, 1970); D. Maffei, 'Qualche postilla alle ricerche di E. M. Meijers sulle scuole di Orléans, Tolosa e Montpellier', *Tijdschrift voor Rechtsgeschiedenis*, 36 (1968), 387–400; A. García y García, 'Aspectos de la universidad portuguesa medieval', in *Universities in the Late Middle Ages*, 133–47; E. Cortese, 'Scienza di giudici e scienza di professori tra XII e XIII secolo', in *Legge, giudici, giuristi. Atti del Convegno tenuto a Cagliari nei giorni 18–21 Maggio 1981* (Milan, 1982), 93–148; H. Schlosser, 'Rechtsgewalt und Rechtsbildung im ausgehenden Mittelalter', *Zeitschrift der Savigny Stiftung für Rechtsgeschichte, Germ. Abt.*, 100 (1983), 53–74.

ture of glosses becomes increasingly concerned with the sense of the law. As indicated below, this literature began with mere interlinear or marginal glosses elucidating the meaning of words, and in its final stage produced great critical apparatuses or commentaries, consisting of extensive and continuous glosses on an entire collection of laws, which strive to capture not only the meaning of each word but the sense of the text and the legislator's intention.

Among the innumerable glosses on the various collections of civil and canon law, the *glossa ordinaria* or *glossa magna* on each one of these collections is outstanding by its mass and by the very extensive use made of it for centuries. The principal *glossae ordinariae* were those of Accursius (d. *c.* 1263), on the entire *Corpus iuris civilis*, consisting of more than 96,000 glosses; Johannes Teutonicus (*c.* 1216) on the *Decretum* of Gratian (with minor alterations by Bartholomeus Brixiensis between 1238 and 1245), Bernard (Parmensis) of Botone (d. 1263) on the Decretals of Gregory IX, and Johannes Andreae and other authors on the remaining collections of the *Corpus iuris canonici*. There are also *glossae ordinariae* on various collections of law, which although not forming part of a *Corpus iuris* were usually edited with it or were closely connected with it: thus Jacobus Colombi on the Lombard laws of 1227–40, Carlo de Tocco on the *Libri feudorum*, and Odofredus on the Peace of Constance of 1183.

The post-glossators or commentators of both the *Corpus iuris civilis* and the *Corpus iuris canonici* used the new methods introduced in other branches of knowledge by the discovery of the works of Aristotle, all of which reached Europe through Spain and Italy in the form of translations from the Arabic, and through direct contacts with Greece made in the crusades. Those methods, as used by jurists, consisted in investigating the sense of the law by a dialectic process. For the glossators the touchstone was authority, for the post-glossators reason – which meant greater freedom in the study of law. This dialectic or scholastic method was also applied to philosophy and theology.

The most important members of this school were the Italians Cino da Pistoia, Bartolus de Saxoferrato, and Baldus de Ubaldis, and among their ultramontane colleagues the French masters Jacques de Révigny and Pierre de Belleperche. For these and innumerable other authors the chosen genre of legal writing was not the gloss but the treatise, an exhaustive monograph that could deal with a particular subject or be a commentary on an entire collection of laws and even on the whole of the *Corpus iuris canonici* or *Corpus iuris civilis*. Collectively, their work founded a legal system that in the work of the glossators was much more scattered. The greatest of the many post-glossators or commentators on canon law were Henry of Susa (Cardinal Hostiense), Goffredo of Trani, Guillaume Durand, Johannes Andreae and Niccolò dei Tudeschi (Abbas Panormitanus).

Glossators and post-glossators alike knew nothing of history or philology, a lacuna they attempted to fill by stretching the sense of old legal texts to fit medieval conditions.

The post-glossators' method is known as *mos italicus* because it was widely followed in Italy in the fourteenth and fifteenth centuries. *Mos gallicus* is the name given to a school of legal humanists who adopted a philological and historical approach in their study of books of law. This school began in Italy with Petrarch, Ambrose of Camaldoli, Filelfo, Maffeo Vegio, Lorenzo Valla, Angelo Poliziano, Ludovico Bolognini, and others, but was raised to its greatest splendour by French authors like Andreas Alciatus and Jacques Cujas. These authors did not regard Roman law as still current, but as matter for historical and philological research. Antonio Agustín, archbishop of Tarragona, is the most illustrious of the commentators on canon law. The *mos gallicus* was most influential in the Netherlands; in the Holy Roman Empire the *mos italicus* was the usual one until the rationalist movement of the end of the seventeenth century and the eighteenth century. In Spain the Salamanca school used both the *mos gallicus* and the *mos italicus*, but mainly the latter, in the revival of interest in medieval philosophical and theological thinking, especially in its Thomist version. Nineteenth-century historians, however, overestimated the importance of legal humanism in the development of legal knowledge at the end of the Middle Ages and in early modern times, and thereby unduly belittled the *mos italicus*.

GENERAL CHARACTERISTICS

In university law schools the language of instruction was Latin; but from the thirteenth century onwards important legal works were written in the vernacular. Legal teaching and writing in Latin and in the vernacular were not mutually exclusive; they stimulated each other to such an extent that they became interdependent, as jurists writing in the vernacular had studied at university and perhaps taught there. Thus, for example, the *Siete partidas* of Alfonso X the Wise were written in Castilian, and commentaries on them in Latin or Castilian.

Clerical as well as lay ignorance of Latin was often given as a reason for translating legal source-books and commentaries into vernacular languages. Such translations circulated freely; so did works written directly in the vernacular, such as those that appeared in Castile in the time of King Alfonso X the Wise. The translations include much of the *Corpus iuris* (*canonici* and *civilis*), commentaries by the fourteenth-century Italian jurist Bartolus de Saxoferrato, the French thirteenth-century jurist Neveu de Montauban (Nepos de Montealbano), and a host of canon law texts and comments.

Medieval teaching, and most medieval writing, used a few legal texts (the same in all universities), basically those contained in the *Corpus iuris canonici* or the *Corpus iuris civilis*. To these were added the commentary on the constitutions of the German emperors (*Libri* or *Consuetudines feudorum*), which appear in old editions of the *Corpus iuris civilis* as the *Collatio decima* (Tenth Collation), and other isolated texts finally incorporated in the *Corpus iuris* (*canonici* and *civilis*), such as the Old Compilations, the collections of Pope Innocent IV and a number of isolated papal decrees or papal letters. These legal texts and their commentaries are known as Roman–canon law (*ius commune*), a name signifying that this code of laws was in principle considered to be valid throughout the whole of medieval Christendom, although co-existing with many statutes and other local regulations forming exceptions from it. With rare exceptions, the only law taught in European universities until the seventeenth century was Roman–canon law. This, it was considered, also equipped jurists to interpret adequately any other legal system peculiar to a given kingdom, local church, or other community.

Roman–canon law being current everywhere in the Christendom of that day, there was what we should now call European ordinary law. Masters, students, and books circulated freely throughout the length and breadth of Christendom, from Poland to Portugal and from Scandinavia to Sicily, attracted or repelled only by the reputation of each text, master, or faculty, and the law of supply and demand. Professors and students from all the kingdoms of Europe went from one centre of learning to another, drawn only by its reputation or prevented only by lack of money.

LEGAL SOURCE-BOOKS

It has just been said that the basic legal texts studied at medieval universities were the *Corpus iuris canonici* and the *Corpus iuris civilis*. The former comprised Gratian's *Decretum* of the mid-twelfth century, summarizing the legislation of the first millennium of the church; the Decretals of Gregory IX, or *Liber extra*, of 1234; the *Liber sextus* of Pope Boniface VIII (1298); the Clementine Decretals (with legislation by Clement V from 1305 onwards and of the Council of Vienna of 1311–12), approved as a collection of canon law by Pope John XXII in 1317; the *Extravagantes Ioannis XXII* (1325); and the *Extravagantes comunes* (1501, 1503) with legislation by other medieval popes collected in the Paris edition of 1500 and 1503 of the *Corpus iuris canonici*. Thus the canonists concerned themselves partly with laws several centuries old but still in force, and partly with laws of the twelfth to the fifteenth centuries.

The civil law schools taught Roman law from Justinian's collections of the first third of the sixth century, which incorporated a great volume of much older law. Medieval jurists divided the collections into the Digest, the Code, the Institutes, and the Novels. In the Digest they distinguished three parts: the Old Digest (*Digestum vetus* from book 1 to book 24.2), the *Inforciatum* (from book 25 up to and including book 38), and the New Digest (the remainder up to and including book 50). They divided the Code of Justinian into the Code (*Codex*) itself (books 1–9), and the Little Volume (*Volumen parvum* or *Tres libri* – books 10–12), at times using the title *Volumen parvum* to mean the *Tres libri*, the Institutes, and the *Novellae*. The *Novellae* (Novels) are a collection of 134 imperial constitutions done into Latin in the sixth century, with later small alterations, and were widely known in the west from the eleventh century onwards under the name of *Authenticum* or *Authenticae* or *Liber authenticorum*. The medieval glossators gave the collection a 'new look' by grouping ninety-seven of the Novels into nine collations. A number of summaries or recapitulations of the Novels were inserted in the Code of Justinian in the Middle Ages where there was held to be some similarity in the subject-matter. As just mentioned, the Middle Ages enlarged the *Corpus iuris civilis* by adding to the Justinian collections various constitutions of the German emperors (the *Libri feudorum* or *Consuetudines feudorum*) known in old editions of the *Corpus iuris civilis* as the *Collatio decima*.

LITERARY GENRES IN LEGAL WRITING AND QUESTIONS OF NOMENCLATURE

It is useful to know the terminology used in legal literary genres, as it gives some indication of content.[6] Here are some introductory headings: *prooemium* (proem), *materia* (subject), *accessus* (approach or entry), *principium* (beginning), *praefatio* (preface), *praeludium* (prelude), *introitus* (entry), *exordium* (exordium), *praeparatoria* (preparations). The modern equivalents are unknown because the words no longer have the technical meaning they had in the Middle Ages. All these terms were explanations placed before legal or other works to tell the reader, in conformity with the rules of rhetoric, who wrote the text and why, the method followed, and the aim in view. All this is signified by the Latin words *nomen* (name), *materia* (subject), *intentio* (intention), *utilitas* or *finis* (use or purpose). It was customary also to specify the division of philosophy (*quaenam pars philosophiae*) to which the work belonged, philosophy then being regarded as comprising logic, physics, and ethics, and law as part of ethics.

Whereas the terms just explained refer to a work as a whole, *intro-*

---

[6] M. Ascheri and E. Brizio, *Index repetitionum iuris canonici et civilis*, Quaderni di informatica e bene culturali, 8 (Siena, 1985); F. Martino, *Richerche sull'opera di Guido de Suzzara. Le Supleciones* (Catania, 1981); L. Fowler-Magerl, *Ordo iudiciorum vel ordo iudiciarius, Begriff und Literaturgattung*, Ius commune, 19 (Frankfurt-on-Main, 1984); G. Fransen, 'Les questions disputées dans les facultés de droit' in B. C. Bazàn, J. F. Wippel, G. Fransen, and D. Jacquart, *Les Questions disputées et les questions quodlibétiques dans les facultés de théologie, de droit et de médecine*. Typologie des sources du moyen âge occidental, 44–5 (Turnhout, 1985), 225–77; G. Fransen, 'Les gloses des canonistes et des civilistes', in *Les Genres littéraires dans les sources théologiques et philosophiques médiévales* (Louvain-la-Neuve, 1982), 133–49; A. Bernal Palacios, *La Concordia utriusque iuris de Pascipoverus* (Valencia, 1980), 39–53, which gives a description of the bibliographical information on this literary genre.

ductiones or *declarationes titulorum* relate to each one of the titles into which legal texts were divided, and attempt to explain the significance of the text, its relations with other titles (*continuationes titulorum*), and the divisions or partitions of the subject within each title. They may give a synopsis of the subject-matter of several titles or of an entire legal collection, and are then called *summulae* (summaries or little summaries). Such texts either are inserted in a legal text or commentary, or exist separately and independently of it.

So much for introductory terms; the following are the names of the principal remaining genres.

Casus is an introduction to each law, canon or chapter, and paragraph, summarizing its text.

Glossae (glosses) are commentaries, usually short, on words in a legal text. The earliest in date are the 'isolated glosses', short glosses explaining the significance of a difficult word, giving cross-references to other legal texts, or pointing out the most important parts of the text, in which case they are called *notabilia* (noteworthy), from their opening words *Nota quod*. Alternatively, they may be *allegationes pro et contra* (arguments for or against) a question raised in a legal text. The name *apparatus glossarum* is given to the most numerous, extensive, and continuous compositions of glosses, which attempt an exegesis – a word-for-word commentary – of an entire legal text.

Lectura is the name given to an *apparatus glossarum* composed by a professor.

In the course of time one of the various *apparatus glossarum* in each legal collection comes to be recognized as the most authoritative, and is then styled the *glossa ordinaria*. All other versions are then *glossae extraordinariae*.

Summae are concise but systematic commentaries on a legal text, without the word-for-word exegesis of the *apparatus glossarum*; *commentum* or *commentarium* (commentary) is sometimes used to mean such a *summa*.

Dictinctiones or *divisiones*, a genre derived from logic, are basically definitions of all the meanings contained in the idea, fact, words, or concepts used by the legal text.

Argumenta, brocarda (brocardica), generalia, singularia, and *solutiones contrarietatum* are similar but not identical variants of a literary genre consisting in enunciating general principles of law, quoting the passages in the legal text said to be for and against each principle enunciated. Comparison of possible decisions for or against is typical of scholastic reasoning and medieval law-courts. From the end of the twelfth century onwards *brocarda* are also called *solutiones contrarietatum*. They were usually resolved by means of *distinctiones* (distinctions). A certain kind of *quaestiones legales* (*quaestiones legitimae*, described below) was used to demonstrate contradictions between legal sources.

Insolubilia (unsolvables) are the fallacies of Aristotelian derivation which occupied the attention of logicians of the late twelfth and early thirteenth centuries, when jurists began to use them, as a new genre on its own, for exegesis or dialectic. This may have something to do with the reform of dialectic methods that took place at this time.

The general principles of law are called *argumenta* or *generalia*. When applied to a category of cases they are known as *specialia*, and when applied to an individual case as *singularia*.

Notabilia, mentioned on p. 395, when used to indicate where the *argumenta* relating to particular subjects are to be found in a legal text, generally begin with the word *Argumentum* followed by the name of the subject.

Quaestiones legitimae, which explore or consider contradictions in a legal text and try to reconcile them, are usually in the form of a question beginning with the Latin word *Quare* (Why). Questions of this kind are therefore called *quaestiones legitimae 'Quare'*, and appear independently of the legal text to which they refer. There were also the *quaestiones legitimae* implicit in the *solutiones contrarietatum* just mentioned.

Quaestiones de facto, known to some scholars as *quaestiones disputatae* are those arising not from the law but from a fact or *species facti* (component elements of a fact determining what law is applicable). The fact could be taken from real life, or be imagined without necessarily referring to real life. One way of treating these *quaestiones* for didactic purposes was a *disputatio* – a debate between two students under the guidance of a master, who gave judgement as if in a court of law. This practice was called *quaestiones scholasticae* or *quaternales*, which were named after the day of the week on which they were held – *mercuriales* after Wednesday, *veneriales* after Friday, *sabbatinae* after Saturday, and so on.

Consilia or *consilia sapientum* (expert opinion) are terms taken from the conduct of legal proceedings, when the judge called for expert opinion on the case. The purpose of *allegationes* was to clear up doubts raised by the judge regarding the conduct of the lawsuit; in this context, they were a reply to the adverse party's *resolutiones*. They were also called *allegationes* or *responsa pro parte*. *Consilia* were also given by private jurists, that is, jurists consulted not by the judge but by a party to a lawsuit anxious to know what case could be made out for him at law.

Rules for the conduct of lawsuits were scattered throughout Justinian's corpus of laws. Twelfth-century jurists therefore compiled handbooks called *ordines iudiciarii* or *ordines iudiciorum*, giving an orderly and systematic description of each part of lawsuit from beginning to end. The canonists, learning from the jurists, brought out even better *ordines iudiciarii* of their own, based on Gratian's *Decretum*. There are numerous adaptations and translations into vernacular languages of some of the *ordines iudiciarii*.

Abbreviationes are texts selected from a collection of laws and transcribed literally or with few changes, eliminating the rest as irrelevant to the abbreviator's purposes. Selected texts whose order is changed are *trans-*

formationes. Excerpta, exceptiones, breviariam, or *flores* are texts selected from a collection of laws but not transcribed verbatim, the abbreviator redrafting them to include his own ideas as well as those of the text.

Alphabetum, tabula, repertorium, vocabularium, dictionarium, lexicon, margarita, summarium, registrum, etc. are aids to the study of legal sources and occasionally of legal literature. They vary in form and style with the author's purpose, but are usually in alphabetical order of concepts. Their subject may be a legal text or a work by a famous author.

Concordia, concordantia, concordantiae, contrarietates, and *diversitates iuris* compare civil and canon law, pointing out similarities and trying to reconcile differences between them; or they compare canon law and the Bible in a similar spirit; or they try to find agreement or concordance between Gratian's *Decretum* and the Decretals of Gregory IX. Occcasionally they assemble disagreements between different *apparatus glossarum*.

Recollectiones, recollecta, reportata, reportationes, additiones, and *suppletiones* are names given to the copies or notes taken by students at lectures or *disputationes*. The *reportator* quotes the words of the text, *additiones* contain other people's additions to the original, and when a professor takes another author's text in class and adds to it whatever he sees fit the result is *suppletiones*.

In the arts faculties at Bologna, Padua, Perugia, and some other universities there was a chair for the teaching of the notary's art. The *ars notaria* was a development – given a legal slant – of the *ars dictandi* or *ars dictaminis* (a manual on letter-writing) of the cathedral schools or other non-university centres. The most famous works of this genre were written in Italy.

Summae confessorum, Summae casuum, Summae casuum conscientiae, Tractatus de matrimonio, Arbores consanguinitatis et affinitatis, Arbores actionum, etc. are titles that designate collections, arranged in alphabetical or systematic order, of canonic rules and moral standards for administration of the sacrament of penance. This kind of literature comes to the fore particularly from the time of the fourth Lateran Council of 1215, chapter 21 of which requires the faithful to confess themselves, and receive communion, annually. Some works of this kind are in the vernacular and some in Latin. The most important vernacular work is the *Libro de las confesiones* by Martín Pérez (*c.* 1316). Chapter 51 of the Lateran Council of 1215 revived interest in the *Arbores consanguinitatis et affinitatis*, which contain rules and diagrams for reckoning consanguinity and affinity. The *Arbores actionum* dealt with legal procedure in lawsuits; they classified and gave legal rules for every possible kind of legal action.[7]

---

[7] A. García y García, 'Glosas de Juan Teutónico, Vicente Hispano y Dámaso Húngaro a los "arbores consanguinitatis et affinitatis"', *Zeitschrift der Savigny Stiftung für Rechtsgeschichte, Kan. Abt.*, 58 (1982), 153–85.

METHODS OF TEACHING LAW

Until the humanists came along, law was taught by dialectical methods, with virtually no reference to history or philosophy.[8] Teachers of civil law, and to some extent teachers of canon law, worked on legal texts whose origins went back many centuries, yet these texts were still considered to be in force in the Middle Ages, in spite of all the difficulties of applying them to medieval society; and civil law was regarded as subsidiary to canon law, in spite of the differences or *contrarietates* which certainly existed between them.

In order that no part of a legal text should be unexplained in class, the system was introduced of *puncta* (points) – divisions of a book of law into a number of parts, stating the days on which each part was to be explained, which parts belonged to the *lectio ordinaria* – a lesson read out and explained by a master – and which to the *lectio extraordinaria* (or *lectio cursatoria*) – a lesson read out and explained by a bachelor. The earliest *puncta* are those of Bologna dating from 1252.[9] Other important ones are those of Bologna (1317–47), Toulouse (prior to the fifteenth century), and Bologna (mid-fourteenth century).[10]

According to Henry of Susa (Cardinal Hostiensis) (*c.* 1253),[11] the *lectura* of a legal text in class comprised: (1) a summary of the text (the *casus*); (2) reading out the text (*littera*) and explaining difficulties; (3) showing parallels (*similia*) with other legal texts; (4) quoting arguments against it (*contraria*) and disposing of them generally by means of *distinctiones* (defined on p. 395); (5) stating and answering the questions arising from the text read out; (6) pointing out *notabilia* – the most noteworthy topics or associated ideas to be inferred from the text read out.

In *disputationes* or *quaestiones disputatae*, the practice of the University of Bologna was followed, with local variations, in all other universities. In Bologna disputations were held in spring and summer. They were, basically,

---

8 M. Fournier, 'Méthodes de l'enseignement du droit du moyen âge à nos jours', *Annales d'histoire des facultés de droit et de science juridique*, 2 (1985), 11–152; G. Le Bras, ' "Velut splendor firmamenti"; le docteur dans le droit de l'Eglise médiévale', *Mélanges offerts à Etienne Gilson* (Toronto/Paris, 1959), 373–88; A. García y García, *Estudios sobre la canonística portuguesa medieval*, Publicacions de la Fundación Universitaria Española Monografías, 29 (Madrid, 1972), 17–65; G. Fransen and D. Maffei, 'Harangues universitaires du XIV siècle', *Studi senesi*, 83 (1981), 7–22.

9 D. Maffei, 'Un trattato di Bonacurso degli Elisei e i più antichi statuti dello Studio di Bologna nel manoscritto 22 della Robbins Collection', *Bulletin of Medieval Canon Law*, new series, 5 (1975), 73–111 (especially 91, n. 80).

10 B. Kurtscheid, 'De utriusque iuris studio saec. XIII', in *Acta Congressus Iuridici Internationalis*, vol. II (Rome, 1935), 309–42; A. García y García, 'El decretista Fernando Alvarez de Albornoz y la fundación del Colegio de España', in *El Cardenal Albornoz y el Colegio de España*, vol. II, Studia Albornotiana, 12 (Bologna, 1972), 131ff., 145–50, 154–7; G. Rabotti, 'Elenco descrittivo di codici del Decretum in archivi et biblioteche italiane e straniere', *Studia Gratiana*, 7 (1959), 78ff.

11 Henricus de Segusia (Card. Hostiensis), *Summa aurea* lib. 5, tit. (Augustae Taurinorum, 1579), 291.

public discussion of a legal subject chosen at random or taken from real life or the courts. In Bologna the only persons allowed to make these disputations were the doctors of the university, but it was open to any member of the audience to raise objections (*oppositiones*); objectors appointed for the purpose were called *concurrentes*.

In Bologna *repetitiones* (dissertations) were held from the beginning of the course until Christmas. All salaried professors, starting with the youngest, were obliged to perform them. Elsewhere, as in Salamanca, doctors who were professors of the university were obliged to hold *repetitiones* only for twenty consecutive years. There was also in Bologna another kind of *repetitiones* consisting of daily revision or summary of the matters taught.[12]

As for examinations and academic degrees, the University of Bologna did not hold a separate examination for each academic course. The only title it conferred was that of doctor or master, later called the *laurea*, and all studies and examinations were in preparation for that title. The statutes of the University of Bologna prescribed five courses to 'read', that is, explain, a 'title' (part of a book of law) and six courses to 'read' an entire legal work. In canon law four years were required to 'read' a 'title' and five to 'read' a complete work. There was no examination for the title of bachelor, but students who had taught a complete book for one year as bachelors were considered qualified to take the examination for the licentiate. At first there may possibly have been only one examination, that for the doctorate, but before long there were two, the first by a committee of professors and the second by the College of Doctors. From the end of the thirteenth century onwards both examinations were by the College of Doctors. The first led to the grant of the *licentia docendi*, and was the more substantial one, which really showed how much the candidate knew. The second examination, the *conventus* or *conventatio*, was little more than a formality – in effect the ceremony of the award of a doctorate – but the title of doctor could not be granted without it. At the licentiate examination candidates had to explain two subjects, taken from the *Decretum* and the Decretals for students of canon law, and from the Old Digest and the Code of Justinian for students of civil law, and reply to objections on them. The ceremonial award of the doctorate usually followed in the same year, sometimes only a few days after the licentiate examination.

The College of Doctors just mentioned was a dual one in Bologna – there was one college for canon law and another for civil law – but some of its members formed part of both. It was not essential for each member to teach in the university, but in practice they were usually professors on the active list. The origin of these colleges is not precisely known, but they are first mentioned in the latter half of the thirteenth century. There was a *numerus clausus*: the college of doctors of civil law had sixteen members and the

---

[12] Juan Alfonso de Benavente, *Ars et doctrina studendi et docendi*, ed. B. Alonso Rodríguez, Bibliotheca Salmanticensis, vol. II (Salamanca, 1972), 93.

college of doctors of canon law twelve. There were also three supernumerary members. Famous men were admitted to the colleges as extraordinary members, supernumerary or otherwise. They were presided over by a prior, who recorded their meetings in the *Liber secretus*, a register now of extraordinary historic value. Besides examining candidates for the licentiate and doctorate, the colleges gave opinions to all kinds of applicants. Conservative, nepotist, and formalist though they were, their prestige remained intact over the centuries; indeed, their clientèle included the kings of Portugal and England and other notables able to pay their high fees.[13]

STUDENTS AND SCHOLARS

Statistics giving a complete idea of the total number of the scholars for whose training law faculties existed, their distribution over faculties, their geographical and social origins, their average age, their previous studies, the percentage studying in their own country or abroad, the proportion of scholars attaining a degree, and the career prospects open to graduates in law are usually lacking. None the less, it is believed that between 6,000 and 7,000 scholars studied at German universities in the second half of the fifteenth century, most of them in the arts faculty. Next in numerical importance, it seems, came students of civil and canon law, of whom there were about 1,000 (15.3 per cent of the total number of scholars) in the second half of the fifteenth century. Between 1386 and 1540 there were 504 students in Leipzig, 427 in Erfurt, 388 in Cologne, 219 in Heidelberg, 161 in Tübingen, and 147 in Freiburg. In 1389 the number of students matriculated at the University of Cologne was 759, of whom 156 (20.5 per cent) were jurists. Leipzig had on average 100 law students during the fifteenth century; at Erfurt their number varied from 80 to 350.[14] Bologna is believed to have had between 500 and 1,000 scholars in the thirteenth century; in 1269 it had as many as 1,464. In 1339 Perugia had 119 law students.[15]

The number of scholars in each faculty is somewhat better known. In the *colegios mayores* of Salamanca there were 76 statutory places in the fifteenth century; 27 of them (36 per cent) were reserved for students of canon law, 22 (29 per cent) for theologians, 12 (16 per cent) for law students, whether of canon or civil law was immaterial, 2 (2.6 per cent) for students of civil law, and 2 (2.6 per cent) for medical students. This dominant tendency is confirmed by lists of students at Salamanca during the Great Schism and by the registers of other universities: a list of 331 students at Salamanca in 1381

[13] A. Pérez Martín, 'Los colegios de doctores de Bolonia y su relación con España', *Anuario de Historia del Derecho Español*, 48 (1978), 5–90; C. Piana, *Il 'Liber Secretus iuris caesarei' dell'Università de Bologna*, 1 (Milan, 1984), 1*–109*; 2 (Milan, 1989), 3*–33*.
[14] Schwinges, *Universitätsbesucher*.
[15] S. Stelling-Michaud, *L'Université de Bologne et la pénétration des droits romain et canonique en Suisse aux XIIIe et XIVe siècles* (Geneva, 1955).

shows 166 students of canon law (50.1 per cent), 63 students of unspecified disciplines (19 per cent), 66 students of grammar (19.9 per cent), 20 of civil law (6 per cent), 12 of logic (3.6 per cent), 2 of arts (0.6 per cent), 1 of theology (0.3 per cent), and 1 of music (0.3 per cent).[16] Of some 15,000 students recorded in England in the last three centuries of the Middle Ages, 4,614 studied in the superior faculties – those of law (2,359 or 51.1 per cent), theology (2,104 or 45.6 per cent), and medicine (the remaining 151 or 3.2 per cent).[17] Of the 598 scholars of the Spanish College in Bologna between 1368 and 1500, 120 studied canon law (20 per cent), 61 theology (10.2 per cent), 35 medicine (5.8 per cent), and 2 civil law (0.3 per cent).[18] It was usual to obtain dispensation to assign to one faculty places statutorily reserved for another, and in this way many places for the study of theology were made over to the study of civil law. The large number of places reserved for canon law is not surprising, as most of the scholars were clerics.

The student's geographical or national origins varied with political, economic, and cultural conditions: since Roman law was more acceptable in Scotland than in England, there were more Scots than English scholars in certain foreign universities of civil law. Available records for the Iberian peninsula show that there were more scholars in Bologna from the eastern Iberian peninsula (the territories subject to the crown of Aragon) than from the western part (Portugal and Castile).[19] Throughout the Middle Ages the most numerous and the largest faculties in Italian universities, and in the principal Iberian ones, were the law faculties, partly because these were the most Romanized countries but mainly because the faculties of theology and arts were founded there, and flourished, later than in, say, Paris or Oxford. In France the leading law faculties were at Angers and Montpellier, and at Orléans, which had no other faculty. At Paris, Oxford, and the universities of the Holy Roman Empire theology attracted more students than law.

Canon law faculties usually had more students than civil law faculties, primarily because more clerics than laymen studied law at university (the papal bull forbidding clerics to study civil law affected some clerics, but only very slightly). Also, clerics generally had more (but not always better) opportunities of finding employment in church service than under a secular authority; and, so that they could study abroad without forfeiting the emoluments of their benefice, they were granted dispensation from the requirement to live in its area. Laymen too could obtain minor ecclesiastical benefices by taking

---

[16] A. M. Carabias Torres, *Colegios Mayores: Centros de poder*, vols. I–III, Acta Salmanticensia, Historia de la Universidad, 46 (Salamanca, 1986), vol. II, 247–85, 490.

[17] T. H. Aston, 'Oxford's Medieval Alumni', *Past and Present*, 74 (1977), 6–10, 22–3; T. H. Aston, G. D. Duncan, and T. A. R. Evans, 'The Medieval Alumni of the University of Cambridge', *Past and Present*, 86 (1980), 35, 74–5.

[18] A. Pérez Martín, 'Collegiales de S. Clemente de los Españoles en Bolonia (1368–1500)', *Salmanticensis*, 20 (1973), 69–84.

[19] Cf. chapter 9 (H. de Ridder-Symoens).

the tonsure, even though they might give up a clerical career later; but clerics, particularly those in major orders, always had more and better opportunities than laymen of ecclesiastical benefices.

Nevertheless, at some universities the civil law faculty was more important than that of canon law; thus at the University of Bologna in its first few decades the teaching of canon law was modelled on that of civil law. By the end of the Middle Ages the gap between the number of students of civil and canon law had narrowed in some universities, but in others students of canon law were still in the majority. None the less, in the Middle Ages it was inconceivable that anyone versed in canon law should not know civil law, and vice versa. Each faculty gave some training in both, and in addition many students studied civil law as well as canon law – *utrumque ius* – in separate faculties. In this event they followed a somewhat shorter course of study, in consideration of their having already learned in one faculty something of the subject taught in the other.

The social origins of law students are mainly, in descending numerical order, chapters of canons, clerics with cure of souls, bourgeoisie, and gentry. Of the 220 scholars of the German 'nation' in Bologna between 1265 and 1300, 151 were ecclesiastics, 32 laymen, 34 of unknown status, and 3 seculaorized ecclesiastics. Their numbers of course vary according to time and place, but university cartularies show this to be the general trend.[20]

The average age of scholars in Bologna is thought by Stelling-Michaud to have been twenty-three to thirty. There were of course one or two scholars outside this age bracket; for instance one Portuguese scholar in the Spanish College was aged only fifteen, and another was aged forty.

University statutes are not usually very explicit about the previous studies required. In Bologna they are not specified. At the University of Salamanca and other universities candidates had already to be '*in grammaticalibus competenter instructus*' (proficient in grammar).[21] The University of Lisbon–Coimbra required candidates to be '*ad minus grammaticus vel logicus*' (at least a grammarian or logician).[22] The biographies of a number of jurists and the foregoing statistics mention law students who had previously studied in the arts faculty, but they are always fewer than those who previously trained in institutions not of university rank.

University students, except the minority with means of their own, usually financed their studies by obtaining an ecclesiastical benefice of some kind. Scholars of all faculties were eligible for these, but the many known records of applications show that most, and the best, benefices went to jurists. Clerics

---

[20] Cf. chapter 8 (P. Moraw).
[21] V. Beltrán de Heredia, *Bulario de la Universidad de Salamanca, 1219–1549*, vol. II (Salamanca, 1966), 187, N.647.15.
[22] A. Moreira de Sà (ed.), *Chartularium Universitatis Portugalensis, 1288–1537*, vol. IV, *1288–1377* (Lisbon, 1970), 15–19, no. 949.

holding residential benefices could always get a dispensation from residence for seven years to study at university; this was confirmed by the decretal *Cum ex eo* of Boniface VIII.[23]

Such records as survive of the numbers of law students graduating show that, then as now, their proportion was low. Even in as rigorously selected a group as the 598 scholars of the Spanish College of Bologna, there were only 3 licentiates in civil law, 25 in canon law, and 1 in theology; 47 masters of arts and medicine, and 25 masters of theology; 7 doctors in civil law, and 51 doctors in canon law – in all 159 graduates, or 26.5 per cent of the 598 scholars appearing in the records consulted. Like all statistics, especially historical ones, these figures should not be accepted without reserve, for the information available is not exhaustive, and some scholars graduated not in the university but by special papal concession (*per bullam*) or in other universities;[24] many others came to grief because they neglected their studies.

Considerable opportunities were open to law graduates. A small but significant and influential élite went on to teach at the university at which they had studied, or at other universities – the number of foreign professors in Bologna in the late twelfth and early thirteenth centuries is impressive. But most law graduates filled important administrative posts in church or state. In the church they included popes, bishops, officials of the papal or diocesan curia or members of chapters, and to a lesser extent members of monastic or other religious orders (most of the surviving legal manuscripts of the Middle Ages belong, or used to belong, to chapters of canons). Something similar happened in secular administration; law graduates, both clerics and laymen, held official posts with various authorities, from the imperial and royal chanceries downwards. Both in the church and in civilian employment men of law held economic as well as administrative posts. Their legal training gave jurists a chance to rise in the world by occupying important positions where they rubbed elbows with the nobility, or if they were laymen by marrying above their station.

In the twelfth and thirteenth centuries all but a few university professors were clerics. Fourteenth-century records mention rather more lay professors, and in general laicization proceeded in the fifteenth century. There were no women students or practitioners of law in the Middle Ages. For the sake of completeness it should be added that legal disciplines were also taught at centres of lesser standing, such as monastic, cathedral, or municipal schools or schools of the mendicant orders. At all such centres law was taught by a single professor. *Studia* – some of them even ranking as *studia generalia* – sprang up all over Europe without attaining university status, either because they laid no claim to it or claimed it in vain. Law was also taught at schools of notaries not forming part of university faculties, and sometimes a king com-

---

[23] *Liber Sextus*, 1.6.34.   [24] García y García, *Estudios* (note 8), 54.

missioned great legal works, such as those sponsored by Alfonso X of Castile (Alfonso the Wise) or by the French court; most of these teachers of law or writers of legal works were trained at university.[25]

LAW, THE CHURCH, AND SOCIETY

The extent to which law affected Western political theory and practice is an important and interesting topic. In the early Middle Ages the Western nations were on the verge of relapsing into barbarism. It was the task, first of the church and later of the empire and the kingdoms, to make right prevail over might. In this they were helped by the rediscovery and study of Roman law in the twelfth century and by the birth of canon law at almost the same time. Especially in the twelfth and thirteenth centuries, the constitution and government of the medieval church and state followed a model fashioned largely by jurists, who were helped by the rediscovery of Aristotle's political works. That model is predominantly authoritarian, being drawn mainly from the law of the Roman Empire, but it is only fair to add that medieval law contains the seeds of modern democracy. Corporations – chapters of canons, and religious orders, especially the mendicant orders – which ascertained the will of the *maior et sanior pars* (the greater and sounder part) by voting functioned in a collegial, democratic way within the macrocosm of the church. The Middle Ages took over some Romanic institutions or principles, giving them a more democratic content: in Roman law, for instance, the formula *Quod omnibus tangit ab omnibus approbari debet* (What affects everybody must be approved by everybody) belonged to private law; in medieval (especially canon) law it applies even in political and constitutional law.

The conciliarism of the late fourteenth and early fifteenth centuries, following the Great Schism, was deeply rooted in twelfth-century canonistic thought and precedent. It established for the church, and implicitly for the state, principles (such as that of limited monarchy) which were adopted by seventeenth-century thinkers, and in later versions still influence modern thought. Sixteenth-century Protestant and Catholic reform (grounded on medieval theory of a theocratic bent) became the firm supporter of absolute monarchy. The legal tradition inherited from Rome, the Aristotelian tradition from Greece, and Christian thought together produced a model for

---

[25] C. Lefevbre, 'Juges et savants en Europe (13e–16e siècle)', *Ephemerides iuris canonici*, 22 (1966), 76–202; 23 (1967), 9–61; M. Bellomo (ed.), *Scuola, diritto e società nel mezzogiorno medievale d'Italia*, especially the articles by D. Maffei (9–29), E. Cortese (31–134), and A. Romano (237–58); G. Santini, ' "Legis doctores et sapientes civitatis" di età preirneraria', *Archivio giuridico*, 169, 6th series, 38 (1965), 114–71; E. Cortese, 'Intorno agli antichi *iudices* toscani e ai caratteri di un ceto medievale', in *Scritti in memoria di Domenico Barillaro* (Milan, 1982); J. Sánchez Herrero, 'Centros de enseñanza y estudiantes de Sevilla durante los siglos XIII al XV', in *En la España medieval: Estudios dedicados al Prof. D. Angel Ferrari Nuñez*, vol. IV (Madrid, 1984), 875–98.

Western society that is different from, and irreconcilable with, that of any other culture of the past, whether Islamic, Inca, Aztec, Chinese, or Japanese. On the other hand, and at a different level, imperial claims, which had their supporters throughout the Middle Ages, urged that kingdoms were in some ways subordinate to the empire. Not only kings but most jurists never accepted this, and in practice the church supported the anti-imperial view. To some extent, therefore, law was a restraint on absolute power whether civil or ecclesiastic, and made for more relaxed relations between church and empire, between the spiritual power and the temporal power.[26]

Twelfth- and thirteenth-century changes in the government of church and state also profoundly influenced ecclesiology, that is, theological thinking on the church. Canonistic thought strongly influenced ecclesiology and the attitude of the church to the sacraments and to its pastoral duties. The sacraments received at least as much attention from canonists as from theologians. Medieval canon law is more zealous than theology itself in regulating the pastoral duties of the church, that is, its spiritual guidance of believers.[27] In ecclesiology, medieval canonists from the twelfth century onwards refused in particular to admit the pope's claim to absolute power and tried to reconcile his divine right with the rights of the Christian community, holding that these were no less divine, having been, like his, instituted by Christ. At the time of the conciliarism of the late fourteenth and early fifteenth centuries these ideas were given new life. They were so much amplified that some people came to regard the ecumenic council as a higher authority than the pope. Such canonistic theories, upheld by some theologians and rejected by others, have continued deeply to influence even modern ecclesiology.[28]

Notoriously, throughout the history of Christianity there have been two schools of thought, one accepting and the other rejecting the humanities as part of clerical training. Acceptance is personified by Saint Augustine and rejection by Saint Jerome. These are doubtless oversimplifications, but the epigones in both camps have quoted these two fathers of the church. It is all too easy, and unnecessary, to enlarge on this well-known controversy. It is mentioned here only to explain why in the mid-twelfth century Gratian's *Decretum* brings together the most authoritative texts of the first millennium of Christianity, some of which inevitably contradict each other on this subject. Gratian juxtaposes them to reconcile their underlying contradictions, in the spirit of the original title of his work, *Concordia discordantium*

---

[26] B. Tierney, *Religion, Law and the Growth of Constitutional Thought, 1150–1650* (Cambridge, 1982) with the bibliography quoted therein.

[27] P. Anciaux, *La théologie du Sacrement de Pénitence au XII siècle* (Louvain, 1949); J. M. Soto Rábanos, 'Derecho canónico y praxis pastoral en la España bajomedieval', in *Proceedings of the Sixth International Congress of Medieval Canon Law, Berkeley, California, 28 July – 2 August 1980*, Monumenta iuris canonici, Series C, Subsidia 7 (Vatican City, 1985), 595–617.

[28] K. Pennington, *Pope and Bishops. The Papal Monarchy in the Twelfth and Thirteenth Centuries* (Pennsylvania, 1984) with the bibliography quoted therein.

canonum. The fathers of the church and other writers of the first millennium furnished him with texts that accept or reject, praise or revile the humanities of their time. Gratian's use of dialectics to reconcile the contradictions in these texts enabled his successors to consider them in a comparatively thoughtful and responsible spirit. Medieval canonists regarded the humanities with less disfavour than some of their contemporaries, who rather than consider whether it was fitting for clerics to study the humanities went witchhunting among the philosophers. Gautier de Saint Victor, for example, calls Peter Abelard, Peter Lombard, Peter of Poitiers, and Gilbert de la Porrée, 'the four labyrinths, or Minotaurs of France', and Saint Peter Damian affirms that the first professor of grammar was the Devil, when he taught Adam to decline the noun 'God' in the plural. Lanfranc, Saint Anselm, and Saint Bernard are similarly critical of human reason. The canonists, however, did not generally bother with other humanities; nor did the legists, except some who practised them, such as Cino da Pistoia, no less eminent as poet than as legist, who enjoyed the friendship and admiration of Dante Alighieri, and Clemente Sánchez, a prolific writer on canon law and author of the *Libro de los exemplos*,[29] one of the great literary works of fifteenth-century Spain. Canonist ambivalence towards the humanities is, however, well shown in a thirteenth-century introduction to Gratian's *Decretum*, of French origin, known by its opening words as *Vidit Iacob*.

As for the relation of law to literature, in primitive societies law, religion, and literature were one. Only later did they become separate entities, and even in the late Middle Ages the *Sachsenspiegel* still affirms that God is law.[30] No wonder, then, that even in the Middle Ages poetry still exalted obedience to God, emperor, or king. Law in its entirety was not only positive law but also natural; law, divine law, *ratio*, *ordo*, *lex aeterna*; and naturally enough all these were of interest to theologians, as is clear from Saint Augustine's *De civitate Dei* and Saint Thomas Aquinas's *Summa theologica*. The people too regarded law as expressing God's will in human affairs. Among the lawyers and men of letters there were many clerics, some of them expert both in literature and law, like the Archpriest of Hita (Juan Ruiz), author of the *Libro del buen amor*.[31] Another and doubtless better-known example of this dual expertise is Dante Alighieri.[32] It is therefore not surprising that in the Middle Ages, and even later, some law faculties followed just behind or even took precedence over the faculty of theology.

---

[29] A. García y García, *Iglesia, Sociedad y Derecho*, vol. I, Bibliotheca Salmanticensis Estudios, 74 (Salamanca, 1985), 143–67.

[30] G. Kirsch, 'Biblical Spirit in Medieval German Law', *Speculum*, 14 (1939), 38–55.

[31] H. A. Kelly, *Canon Law and the Archpriest of Hita*, Medieval and Renaissance Texts and Studies, 27 (New York, 1984).

[32] G. Zanetti, 'Le dottrine giuspubblicistiche delle *Questiones de iuris subtilitatibus* e il pensiero politico di Dante', *Proceedings of the Fourth International Congress of Medieval Canon Law*,

Parallel to this view of literature as the handmaid of law is the complementary one of law as the handmaid of literature; men of letters drew inspiration from codes of law, borrowing some of their terms and imitating legal construction; and methods of investigating and studying literary texts inspired methods of studying and investigating legal texts, and vice versa, whether the texts were in Latin or almost any of the vernacular – Old and Middle English, German, Icelandic, French and Provençal, the Hispanic languages (Castilian, Catalan, Portuguese, and Galician), Italian, and so on.

Such, in brief, were the organization and intellectual horizons of the medieval law faculties, and their potent influence on the society of their times.

Toronto, 21–25 August 1972, Monumenta iuris canonici, Series C, Subsidia 5 (Vatican City, 1976), 351–82, with the bibliography quoted therein.

SELECT BIBLIOGRAPHY

Alford, J. A. and Seniff, D. P. *Literature and Law in the Middle Ages, A Bibliography of Scholarship*, New York/London, 1984.

Burmeister, K. *Das Studium der Rechte im Zeitalter des Humanismus im deutschen Reichsbereich*, Wiesbaden, 1974.

Calasso, F. *Medio Evo del Diritto*, vol. I, *Le fonti*, Milan, 1954.

Coing, H. (ed.) *Handbuch der Quellen und Literatur der neueren europäischen Privatrechtsgeschichte*, vol. I, *Mittelalter, 1100–1500*, Munich, 1973.

Cortese, E. 'Scienza di giudici e scienze di professori tra XII e XIII secolo', in *Legge, giudici, giuristi. Atti del Convegno tenuto a Cagliari nei giorni 18–21 Maggio 1981*, Milan, 1982, 93–148.

Feenstra, R. 'L'enseignement du droit à Orléans. Etat des recherches menées depuis Meijers', *Bulletin de la Société archéologique et historique de l'Orléannais*, new series, 9 (1985), 13–29.

Fournier, M., *Histoire de la science du droit en France*, vol. III (only volume published), *Les Universités françaises et l'enseignement du droit en France au moyen âge*, Paris, 1892; reprint, Aalen, 1970.

García y García, A. 'Los estudios jurídicos en la Universidad medieval', in *Lex Ecclesiae. Estudios en honor del profesor Dr. Marcelino Cabreros de Anta, Bibliotheca Salmanticensis*, vol. I, Salamanca, 1972, 143–69; republished in A. García y García, *Estudios sobre la canonística portuguesa medieval*, Publicaciones de la Fundación Universitaria Española, Monografías 29, Madrid, 1976, 17–65.

García y García, A. *Iglesia, Sociedad y Derecho*, vol. I, Bibliotheca Salmanticensis, Estudios 74, Salamanca, 1985.

Gouron, A. *La Science du droit dans le Midi de la France au Moyen Age*, Variorum Reprints, London, 1984.

Grundmann, H. 'Sacerdotium, Regnum, Studium', *Archiv für Kulturgeschichte*, 34 (1952), 3–21.

van Hove, A. *Prolegomena ad Codicem iuris canonici*, 2nd edn, Malines/Rome, 1945.

Ius Romanum Medii Aevi, 5 vols., Milan, 1961–8.

Koschaker, P. *Europa und das römische Recht*, 4th edn, Berlin, 1966.

Kuttner, S. *The History of Ideas and Doctrines of Canon Law in the Middle Ages*, London, 1980.

Kuttner, S. *Medieval Councils, Decretals, and Collections of Canon Law*, London, 1980.

Kuttner, S. *Repertorium der Kanonistik. Prodromus Corporis glossarum*, Studi e Testi, 71, Vatican City, 1937; reprint, 1983.

Le Bras, G., Lefebvre, H., and Rambaud, J. *L'Age classique, 1140–1378. Sources et théorie du droit*, Histoire du droit et des institutions de l'Eglise en Occident, 7, Paris, 1965.

Maffei, D. 'Dottori e e studenti nel pensiero di Simone da Borsano', *Studia Gratiana*, 15 (1972), 229–49.

Maffei, D. *Gli inizi dell'umanesimo giuridico*, Milan, 1956–60.

Meijers, E. M. *Etudes d'histoire du droit*, ed. R. Feenstra and H. F. W. Fischer, vols. I, III, IV, Leiden, 1956–66.

Ourliac, P. and Giles, H. *La Période postclassique, 1378–1500*, vol. I, *La Problématique de l'époque. Les sources*, Histoire du droit et des institutions de l'Eglise en Occident, 13, Paris, 1971.

Pérez Martín, A. 'Los colegios de doctores de Bolonia y su relación con España', *Anuario de Historia del Derecho Espanol*, 48 (1978), 5–90.

Pérez Martín, A. (ed.) *España y Europa, un pasado jurídico común. Actas del I simposio Internacional del Instituto de Derecho Común. Murcia 26–28 Marzo 1985*, Murcia, 1986.

Savigny, F. C. *Geschichte der römischen Rechts im Mittelalter*, 7 vols., 2nd edn, Heidelberg, 1834–51; reprint, Bad Homburg, 1961.

von Schulte, J. F. *Die Geschichte der Quellen und Literatur des canonischen Rechtes von Gratian bis auf die Gegenwart*, vols. I–II, Stuttgart, 1875–77; reprint, Graz, 1956.

Stelling-Michaud, S. *Les Juristes suisses à Bologne, 1255–1330. Notices biographiques et regestes des actes bolonais*. Travaux d'Humanisme et Renaissance, 38, Geneva, 1960.

Stelling-Michaud, S. *L'Université de Bologne et la pénétration des droits romain et canonique en Suisse aux XIIIe et XIVe siècles*, Travaux d'Humanisme et Renaissance, 17, Geneva, 1955.

Troje, H. E. 'Die Literatur des gemeinen Rechts unter den Einfluss des Humanismus', in H. Coing (ed.), *Handbuch der Quellen und Literatur der neueren europäischen Privatrechtsgeschichte*, vol. II, Munich, 1977, 615–795.

CHAPTER 13

THE FACULTY OF THEOLOGY

MONIKA ASZTALOS

FROM BIBLICAL EXEGESIS TOWARDS SCHOLASTIC THEOLOGY

One of the main characteristics of medieval university teaching was the stability of a set of doctrinal textbooks such as those of Aristotle in the faculty of arts, of Justinian in the faculty of law, and of Galen in the faculty of medicine. For theology the authority was the Bible, but its lack of doctrinal coherence made it insufficient as a textbook alone. It needed interpretation, and from the beginning of the Christian era theology was essentially the exegesis of sacred Scripture, hence its name *sacra pagina*.[1]

This hermeneutic activity had been carried on since antiquity by the fathers of the church and by monks in the monasteries, the centres of learning before the rise of the universities. A most important patristic contribution which influenced all later medieval exegesis was Saint Augustine's (d. 430) *De doctrina christiana*. The first three books contain rules for interpreting Scripture, while book four is a treatise on how to preach the doctrine built up by the methods established in the previous books. Saint Augustine vindicates the pagan liberal arts and moral precepts on the grounds that they rightly belong to those who preach the gospel. The insistence on the usefulness of secular learning for Christian speculation, at least on a moderate scale, is only to be expected in one who, like Saint Augustine, was well trained in Roman rhetoric and spent his youth reading Virgil and Cicero.

In the sixth century, when barbaric invasions had reduced ancient culture in western Europe to a few scattered remnants, Boethius (d. *c.* 524) not only preserved some of what was left of the Greek and Roman heritage, but also composed works that later became influential on theology. Through his

---

[1] The following account of the development of theology in the schools before the rise of the universities is mainly based on G. Paré, A. Brunet, and P. Tremblay, *La Renaissance du XIIe siècle. Les écoles et l'enseignement* (Paris/Ottawa, 1933); J. De Ghellinck, *Le Mouvement théologique du XIIe siècle* (Bruges/Brussels, 1948; reprint, 1969).

translations of and commentaries on Aristotle's works on logic, Boethius developed an interest that is documented not only in his own philosophical writings, but also in his *Theological Tractates*. The entry of logic into matters of faith did not, however, have any real following until the eleventh and, especially, the twelfth centuries. The initiator of this movement is usually held to be Gerbert of Aurillac (d. 1003), later Pope Sylvester II, who in the *De rationali et de ratione uti* stressed the importance of definition and classification.

The use of logic in theology found its adversaries, an often quoted instance of whom is Peter Damian (d. 1072) who, in his treatise *De Dei omnipotentia*, criticized those who applied philosophical notions of necessity and impossibility to God's power, thereby restricting God's omnipotence. Problems of this nature, which concern the reconcilability of the articles of faith, such as God's omnipotence, with reason, would later become central issues in the theological faculties of the medieval universities.

The first person to attempt a synthesis of reason and faith was Anselm of Canterbury (d. 1109). With his *Monologion* and *Proslogion* – the original title of which was *Fides quaerens intellectum* (Faith in search of understanding) – he established himself as the 'father of scholasticism'. In demonstrating the truths of faith Anselm relied more on reason than on authority.

By this time the cathedral schools had become more important than their monastic counterparts. The secular students and masters were not bound by any *stabilitas loci*, but could move from town to town according to their intellectual tastes. Teachers like Anselm of Laon (d. 1117) could even attract students from Italy, Germany, and England. This increased the prestige of individual masters, a tendency which is evident in the development of teaching methods.[2] The most important product of the Laon school was the *Glossa ordinaria*, a commentary on the Bible in the form of interlinear and marginal annotations. In addition to traditional patristic sources the *Glossa ordinaria* quoted more recent masters, thereby raising the latter to the status of *auctoritates*. The recognition of their teachings as authoritative has been described as the most characteristic feature of early scholasticism.[3]

This new role of the masters is apparent in the introduction of *quaestiones* into the biblical commentaries, a method practised already by Anselm of Laon.[4] The intensified use of *quaestiones* in the twelfth century reflects a changed attitude towards biblical studies: the traditional exegesis had been

---

[2] For an account of this development: B. Smalley, *The Study of the Bible in the Middle Ages* (Oxford, 1983), 49–77.

[3] A. M. Landgraf, *Introduction à l'histoire de la littérature théologique de la scolastique naissante* (Montreal/Paris, 1973), 24–5.

[4] For the origins of this teaching method and literary genre: B.C. Bazàn, 'Les questions disputées, principalement dans les facultés de théologie', in B. C. Bazàn, J. F. Wippel, G. Fransen, and D. Jacquart, *Les Questions disputées et les questions quodlibétiques dans les facultés de théologie, de droit et de médecine*, Typologie des sources du Moyen Age occidental, ed. L. Genicot, fasc. 44–5 (Turnhout, 1985), 25–40.

the unfolding of the different senses hidden in the sacred text – the literal or historical, allegorical, tropological or moral, and anagogical or eschatological senses – and the commentary was confined to the margins of the text expounded; by introducing *quaestiones* into the commentary, the masters merely used the text as a starting-point for theological discussions set out in dialectical form.

The work that has been singled out as a manifesto of this shift in theology is the *Sic et non* of Peter Abelard (d. 1142), Anselm of Laon's contemptuous pupil. In the prologue of this work Abelard acknowledges the fact that biblical and patristic sources sometimes contradict each other, and suggests methods for explaining these contradictions on the assumption that the authors in question never lie. In fact, the absolute truth of the biblical and patristic sources makes the investigation into the causes of apparent contradiction so much the more challenging. The truth of the Bible, which cannot be called into question, provides an excellent starting-point for rational questioning, which is according to Abelard the key to wisdom.

The use of *quaestiones* in biblical commentaries was a decisive step towards scholastic theology. Another important innovation was the collecting of *sententiae*, the origin of theological *summae*, in which different topics were presented in a systematic order.[5] The school of Laon proved itself pioneering once more through the compilation of *sententiae* from modern masters as well as church fathers, collections that also included *quaestiones*.

One of the earliest theological *summae* was the *Theologia scholarium* by Peter Abelard, who is also said to have established the use of the word *theologia* instead of the traditional *sacra pagina* or *sacra doctrina*. Another influential work of doctrinal systematization from the same period was Hugh of Saint Victor's (d. 1142) *De sacramentis christianae fidei*. Gilbert of Poitiers (d. 1154), another pupil of Anselm of Laon, learned the importance of the liberal arts, both in and of themselves and as a preparation for theology, in the school of Chartres. He also became familiar with Boethius, whose writings were highly esteemed in Chartres, and, like other theologians of that school, applied grammar and logic to theological topics. Gilbert was one of the first who attempted to give a scientific structure to theology, and in his commentary on Boethius's *De Trinitate* he introduced the word *facultas*, 'faculty', in the sense of scientific discipline. In theology, he held, faith comes before reason, whereas in the other 'faculties' faith follows upon reason.[6] Such rationalization of theology met with fervent opposition from traditional theologians such as Bernard of Clairvaux (d. 1153), but the efforts to bring scholastic theology back to its monastic fold were vain.

About the middle of the twelfth century there arose a tendency toward

5 Landgraf, *Introduction* (note 3), 44–7, 50–4.
6 N. M. Häring (ed.), *Expositio in Boecii Librum secundum De Trinitate*, vol. I: 7–9, Studies and Texts, 13 (Toronto, 1966), 164.

codification of knowledge both in canon law (*Decretum Gratiani*) and theology (the *Glossa ordinaria* and the theological *summae* of Hugh of Saint Victor and Abelard). In theology this movement culminated in the *Sentences* of Peter Lombard (d. 1160), which consist of questions systematically arranged around central doctrinal topics: God and the Trinity (book 1), creation (book 2), the incarnation and the virtues (book 3), the sacraments and the Last Judgment (book 4). It almost immediately became an object of commentary in the schools, and was recognized as a school-book by the Lateran Council of 1215. The lasting success of this work of compilation has been ascribed to its lack of originality, its relative orthodoxy, its complete coverage of the debated issues of the day, and the author's unwillingness to give final solutions to difficult questions. By the middle of the twelfth century theology was thus being taught in the schools as a separate science related to other sciences. New teaching methods were being used by masters, who formulated problems in a dialectical way and solved them with rational arguments. The Bible was still the indisputable written authority, but to compensate for its unsystematic character it was now accompanied by a standard textbook, Peter Lombard's *Sentences*.

Towards the end of the twelfth century, Paris had more renowned masters of theology than any other school. Among the most productive and influential theologians were Peter of Poitiers (d. 1161), Praepositinus of Cremona (d. 1210), Alan of Lille (d. 1202–3), Peter the Chanter (d. 1197), and, above all, Stephen Langton (d. 1228). A corporation of masters and students grew out of the cathedral school of Notre-Dame, and a struggle for autonomy against the bishop and chancellor led to a confirmation of the masters' privileges and rights through the first official statutes given to the University of Paris by the papal legate, Robert of Courson (d. 1219), in 1215.[7] In their struggle the masters had received support from the pope, Innocent III (1160–1216), but they had to pay for the protection by giving up some of their academic freedom. Henceforth, the masters could not pursue their theological studies in complete intellectual independence, but had to take part in the pope's and the universal church's struggle against heresies.

In this power struggle the masters and ecclesiastical authorities did not, however, represent completely separate parties. In fact, teaching as a master in theology in Paris often led to a high position within the church.[8] Out of the five theologians mentioned above, only Alan of Lille did not follow an ecclesiastical career. Peter the Chanter became bishop elect of Tournai, Peter of Poitiers and Praepositinus were both chancellors of Paris, and Stephen Langton ended his days as archbishop of Canterbury after having been a

---

[7] *CUP*, vol. I, 78–80, no. 20; G. Post, 'Parisian Masters as a Corporation 1200–1246', *Speculum*, 9 (1934), 421–5; S. C. Ferruolo, 'The Paris Statutes of 1215 Reconsidered', *History of Universities*, 5 (1985), 1–14.

[8] J. W. Baldwin, 'Masters at Paris from 1179 to 1215: a Social Perspective', in *Renaissance and Renewal*, 151.

cardinal. Innocent III and his legate Robert of Courson had studied together at Paris, and they had both been masters in theology. By giving Paris its first statutes they thus acted not merely as leaders of Christianity but also as ex-students of the university.

Robert of Courson renewed earlier prohibitions against the clergy studying law and medicine, and encouraged them to study theology. Honorius III (1216–27), the successor of Innocent III, weakened the study of law further by banning the teaching of Roman law in Paris (1219). The motives for this decision have been debated, but the obvious result was that Bologna remained the centre for legal studies, while Paris dominated theology.[9] Another way in which the pope exercised control over Parisian theology was in limiting the number of chairs. In 1207 Innocent set the maximum at eight, but in 1218 Honorius III made an exception to the rule, and already by 1230 the number was increased to twelve.[10]

The safeguarding of doctrinal purity was often entrusted to ex-masters: the condemnations of the teaching of Aristotle's natural philosophy at Paris in 1210 and 1215 were promulgated by Peter of Corbeil (d. 1222) and Robert of Courson, both former masters of theology, and Stephen Tempier (d. 1279), the man behind the condemnations of 1270 and 1277, had been not only a master in Paris but also chancellor.

Not until 1228, however, did a master of theology become bishop·of Paris. In that year William of Auvergne (d. 1249), then a deacon, was appointed bishop by Gregory IX (1227–41). The time of the appointment coincides with the prohibition against teaching natural philosophy in Paris, and it is possible that the pope felt it to be an advantage during a time of doctrinal instability to appoint as bishop a theologian who could appreciate and judge the compatibility of Aristotle's physics and Christian faith.

In Paris the theological faculty had had close ties with the bishop and chancellor from its very beginnings. Oxford on the other hand had no cathedral school, and the diocesan in Lincoln was not close enough to be able to exert the same power over the scholars as his colleague in Paris. The pope did not intervene in the affairs of the University of Oxford until 1254, when Innocent IV (1243–54) confirmed the privileges of the masters in his *Quaerentes in agro*.[11] The Parisian masters had been placed under papal protection much earlier through the confirmation of their privileges in 1215. Thereby the theological faculty at Paris had become responsible for the official doctrine of the church, and the teaching of the masters was closely supervised and, if necessary, corrected through condemnations from 1210 on. Oxford on the

---

[9] J. W. Baldwin, *Masters, Princes and Merchants. The Social Views of Peter the Chanter and his Circle*, vol. I (Princeton, 1970), 86ff.

[10] *CUP*, vol. I, 65, no. 5; 85, no. 27.

[11] For the relation between the papacy and Oxford University: C. H. Lawrence, 'The University in State and Church', in *History of Oxford*, 102–3.

other hand had more freedom in doctrinal matters, and there is no evidence of any intervention in the teachings of the masters from the church authorities before 1277. Nor did the popes ever make an attempt to limit the number of chairs in theology at Oxford.

Throughout the fourteenth century Paris and Oxford had the most important theological faculties. Paris retained its lead except for a few decades at the beginning of the century. There was a constant interaction between the two teaching centres until about 1350, mostly through English students going to Paris. Typically, the first known English theologian, Robert Pullen (d. 1146), taught in Paris for five years, and the next known lecturer in theology, Alexander Neckam (d. 1217), had studied there.[12] When war between the French and English kings in 1193–1204 prevented English students from going to Paris, theological studies prospered in Oxford. This tendency, however, was broken during the dispersion of the Oxonian masters in 1209–14. Many of the masters then went to Paris with its strong theological traditions, but the centre of education that mostly benefited from the migration of scholars was Cambridge, where a university was first opened in 1209 as a result of the secession.

THE MENDICANTS AND THE THEOLOGICAL FACULTIES: SYMBIOSIS AND CONFLICT

Until the fourteenth century, Paris, Oxford, and Cambridge were the only universities with the right to confer degrees in theology, but theology was by no means exclusively taught in these universities. The most important alternative to the universities was provided by the *studia* of the mendicant orders, which played the role of international faculties of theology in Germany, France, and, above all, Italy.

The Dominicans (or Preachers), the Franciscans (or Minors) and, from the middle of the thirteenth century, the Carmelites and the Austin friars were all mendicants. They were not bound to a monastery, but could settle in towns where they could devote themselves to studies. They all organized their studies in a similar way, the Preachers to some extent providing a model for this organization.[13]

The Dominican order had been founded in 1216 to combat heresies and preach orthodox doctrine, and study became the most important means to attain this goal. Already the earliest constitutions stated that every convent should have its own *lector* or teacher who had studied theology for four years, a rule that turned every convent into a school.[14] Besides the convent

---

[12] R. W. Southern, 'From Schools to University', in *History of Oxford*, 6–7.
[13] For the Dominican system of education: W. A. Hinnebusch, *The History of the Dominican Order*, vol. II (New York, 1973).
[14] M. W. Sheehan, 'The Religious Orders 1220–1370', in *History of Oxford*, 198.

schools there were provincial schools, and the most advanced teaching was given in the *studia generalia*, Dominican institutions open to students from all provinces.

The friars established schools in Paris, Oxford, and Cambridge, where they could not only benefit from the theological faculties at the universities, but also recruit students and teachers for the orders. Each mendicant order, except the English Carmelites, had a *studium generale* in these university towns. It would be wrong, however, to conceive of the religious schools as separate from the theological faculties of the universities. The first two masters who taught theology at Saint Jacques, the Dominican *studium* at Paris,[15] were in fact seculars: John of St Albans assumed his teaching around 1220 at the request of Honorius III, a supporter of the friars, and he was succeeded around 1225 by John of St Giles (*fl.* 1230–5).

The teachers of Saint Jacques obviously felt that their position differed from that of the university masters, for, when the latter left Paris to go on strike in March 1229, John of St Giles refused to join them. The Dominican Roland of Cremona (d. *c.* 1259) even 'incepted' as a master two months after the dispersion, thereby becoming the first Dominican master in theology in Saint Jacques. Possibly John of St Giles felt his position to be somewhat ambiguous, for in 1230 he joined the order in a spectacular way while delivering a sermon. On the other hand, all Dominican masters automatically belonged to the corporation of university masters. In 1230, two of the twelve chairs in theology were occupied by Preachers. The symbiosis extended to the students, for even non-Dominican students could attend lectures in Saint Jacques.

The Dominican and Franciscan schools in Paris benefited from the dispersion of the secular masters and gained influence in the university. The school of the Minors[16] acquired fame with the conversion of Alexander of Hales (d. 1245), a renowned university master, who was succeeded in the Franciscan chair by his students John of La Rochelle, Odo Rigaud (d. 1275), William of Meliton (d. 1257–60), and Saint Bonaventure (John of Fidanza, d. 1274), all distinguished scholars. At Oxford,[17] the Preachers acquired their first master in 1229–30, when Robert Bacon (d. 1248), a secular master, entered the order, thereby incorporating the Dominican school in the university. The Franciscans followed in kind with Robert Grosseteste (d. 1253), perhaps the most important of all secular masters who lectured (1230–5) to a

---

15 For the Dominican school in Paris: Hinnebusch, *History* (note 13), 37–9; J. A. Weisheipl, *Friar Thomas d'Aquino, His Life, Thought and Works* (Oxford, 1974), 54–67.
16 On the Franciscan *studium* in Paris: J. Moorman, *A History of the Franciscan Order* (Oxford, 1968), 131–3.
17 On the mendicant schools in Oxford: Sheehan, 'Religious orders' (note 14), 193–224; J. I. Catto, 'Theology and Theologians 1220–1320', in *History of Oxford*, 471–517; W. J. Courtenay, *Schools and Scholars in Fourteenth-Century England* (Princeton, 1987), 56–77.

mendicant order.[18] Furthermore, Grosseteste was succeeded by three other secular masters, and it was not until 1247 that the school acquired a Franciscan master. At Paris and Oxford the universities thus provided the Mendicant schools with their first teachers. But soon the friars recruited teachers from among themselves. Not only were they on a par with the secular masters, but they produced eminent theologians who attracted young students to the orders.

In the middle of the thirteenth century the secular masters both at Paris and Oxford reacted against the privileged position of the mendicants. In Paris the friars gained a temporary victory in 1255, thanks to the papal support in the bull *Quasi lignum vitae*. Between 1269 and 1271 the controversial questions were debated in the university classrooms in Paris by the Dominican Thomas Aquinas (d. 1274) and the secular Gerard of Abbeville (d. 1272). One of the issues was the acceptance of boys into religious orders: the seculars worried about the recruiting of novices from the young students in the arts faculty. Other matters of dispute, such as the role of evangelical poverty and spiritual perfection, had no direct bearing upon university life.[19]

At Oxford a conflict started about the same time as in Paris, but over a different matter.[20] The friars were not allowed by their order to study in the arts faculty, and in 1253 a decision was taken by the university that no one could become a master in theology unless he was first a master in arts. This would have been an effective way of stopping the friars from graduating in theology, had it not been for the dispensatory graces granted to candidates without the required degree in arts. Significantly enough, the decision was made when the Franciscans were no longer taught by secular masters, as they had been until 1247, but had built up a school of their own that could rival the teaching of the seculars. It is not surprising, therefore, that this decision was provoked by a Franciscan candidate for the degree in theology, Thomas of York (d. *c.* 1260). The Franciscans on their side widened the gap between themselves and the university by deciding during the general chapters of 1279 and 1292 that secular students were not allowed to attend lectures in philosophy in their schools.[21]

The conflict deepened between 1311 and 1314, when the Preachers

---

[18] For Robert Grosseteste and the Minors at Oxford: A. G. Little, 'The Franciscan School at Oxford in the Thirteenth Century', *Archivum Franciscanum Historicum*, 19 (1926), 803–74; D. Knowles, *The Religious Orders in England*, vol. I (Cambridge, 1948), 205–16; Sheehan, 'Religious Orders' (note 14), 197–8; R. W. Southern, *Robert Grosseteste: the Growth of an English Mind in Medieval Europe* (Oxford/New York, 1986).

[19] For the conflicts in Paris: Rashdall, *Universities*, vol. I, 370–97; Weisheipl, *Friar Thomas d'Aquino* (note 15), 80–92, 263–72; M. M. Dufeil, *Guillaume de Saint-Amour et la polémique universitaire Parisienne 1250–1259* (Paris, 1972).

[20] For the controversies at Oxford: Rashdall, *Universities*, vol. III, 70–4; Sheehan, 'Religious Orders' (note 14), 204–8.

[21] M. Biehl, 'Documenta-Statuta generalia ordinis edita in capitulis generalibus celebratis Narbonae . . .', *Archivum Franciscanum Historicum*, 34 (1941), 76.

appealed to the pope, complaining that the secular masters threatened their theological teaching in different ways. As in Paris, the university masters opposed the friars' fishing for novices among the young students, and in 1365 they tried in vain to forbid the friars from accepting any candidate under the age of eighteen.

At some universities, such as Montpellier and Bologna, the friars' *studia generalia* functioned as theological faculties for a long period of time before they were formally recognized as such. In Erfurt and Cologne there were important mendicant *studia generalia* more than a hundred years before universities were founded there. In Italy the friars practically monopolized the theological teaching in Naples, Florence, Pisa, Perugia, Bologna, Padua, and other towns. Through their great mobility the friars played an important role in keeping the channels of communication open between different *studia* and universities.

THE CURRICULUM

There is but scant material left to elucidate the organization of studies in the theological faculty at Paris.[22] The only extant thirteenth-century statutes (1215) dedicate a single paragraph to the theologians. The next surviving collections of statutes, issued between 1335 and 1387, reflect an already established practice, and shortly after 1389 a more comprehensive collection was formulated, repeating part of the old statutes in addition to new ones not to be found in any earlier extant document.[23] However, the meagre information concerning the theological faculty at Paris can be supplemented by reference to the statutes of Bologna (1364),[24] Toulouse (1366),[25] Heidelberg (1386),[26] Vienna (1389),[27] and Cologne (1393).[28] The theological faculties of these universities all followed the model of Paris, and their statutes – which are sometimes more systematically elaborated than those of their 'mother university' – contain detailed descriptions of certain practices that are only briefly mentioned or alluded to in the Parisian documents.

It was mentioned above (p. 416) that the decision taken at Oxford in 1253, to the effect that no one could become a master in theology unless he had

---

22 The most comprehensive survey is still P. Glorieux, 'L'enseignement au Moyen Age. Techniques et méthodes en usage à la Faculté de théologie de Paris au XIIIe siècle', *Archives d'histoire doctrinale et littéraire du Moyen Age*, 43 (1968), 65–186.

23 *CUP*, vol. I, 78–80, no. 20; vol. II, 691–3, no. 1188; vol. II, 697–703, no. 1189; vol. III, 143–4, no. 1319; vol. III, 441–2, no. 1534.

24 F. Ehrle, *I più antichi statuti della facoltà teologica dell'università di Bologna* (Bologna, 1932).

25 Fournier (ed.), *Statuts*, vol. I, 611–17, no. 670.

26 E. Winkelmann, *Urkundenbuch der Universität Heidelberg*, vol. I (Heidelberg, 1886), 20–3, no. 20.

27 R. Kink, *Geschichte der Universität Wien*, vol. II (Vienna, 1854), 93–127.

28 F. I. von Bianco, *Die alte Universität Köln und die späteren Gelehrten-Schulen dieser Stadt* (Cologne, 1855), 34–50.

served as master in the arts, gave rise to a conflict – or rather was the symptom of a conflict – between the seculars and mendicants. In the Paris statutes there is no mention of such a rule, possibly due to the papal support given to the religious orders in Paris.[29]

The textbooks of theology were merely the Bible and the *Sentences* of Peter Lombard. On the other hand, the 1228 constitution of the Dominican order stipulates that every student who was sent to a *studium generale* should bring with him at least three books in theology: the *Historia scholastica* of Peter Comestor, the *Sentences*, and a glossed Bible.[30] Students had to audit courses on the Bible and the *Sentences* for a certain number of years (varying between five and seven in Paris) before giving courses themselves. After the period of passive audition, the student could start lecturing as a *cursor* on two books of the Bible, one from the Old and another from the New Testament. The student then gave a series of more advanced lectures on the Bible as a *baccalarius biblicus* or *ordinarius* for two years. Before lecturing on the *Sentences*, the *baccalarii* had to act as respondents in a disputation.[31] The Paris statutes of 1387 and 1389 declare that the *baccalarius* may substitute acting as a respondent for his otherwise required two courses on the Bible. This shows that the study of the Bible was by this time overshadowed by the more speculative theology which came out of the aforesaid disputations.[32]

Those permitted to lecture on the *Sentences* were called *baccalarii Sententiarii*. They were required to introduce their lectures with a ceremony – described in the Bologna statutes – attended by the whole academic community. The incepting *baccalarius* began with a short sermon followed by an act of commitment to orthodoxy in which he stated that he would not assert anything against the teaching of the church. As a *Sententiarius* the student not only had doctrinal responsibility but was also entrusted with a certain degree of doctrinal independence. The Bologna statutes explain that those lecturing on the *Sentences* may sometimes attack the statements of the other bachelors, but in such a way that they do not in the heat of the dispute assert anything unorthodox that they would have to retract later. However, the bachelors were not allowed to question the teaching of the masters.

When the bachelor had finished his lectures on the *Sentences*, he was a *baccalarius formatus*, and remained so for four years, a period later (1389) reduced to three. During these years the bachelor was required to participate in the activities of the theological faculty and respond in an *aula*, a *vesperies*

---

[29] According to W.J. Courtenay, 'The Bible in the Fourteenth Century: Some Observations', *Church History*, 54 (1985), 181, the stronger position of the members of religious orders at Paris can be explained by the influence of the papacy – which favoured the religious orders – on the University of Paris.

[30] *CUP*, vol. I, 112, no. 57.   [31] Bazàn, 'Questions disputées' (note 4), 54.

[32] Cf. John Gerson's pleading in the 1390s for a return to the study of the Scripture: B. Smalley, 'The Bible in the Medieval Schools', in G. W. Lampe (ed.), *The Cambridge History of the Bible*, vol. II (Cambridge, 1969), 208.

(inaugural disputations of the masters), a *Sorbonica* (a disputation held in the college of Sorbonne), and a *quodlibetum* (a disputation on a question raised by anyone about any topic and held during Advent and Lent).[33] The teaching methods of the theological faculty included not only lectures and disputations but also sermons. The sermon crowned the formation of the student, and not until he was a *baccalarius formatus* was he allowed to preach to the academic community.

After the period of training (sixteen years for seculars, thirteen for regulars in Paris in 1335, fourteen and twelve years, respectively, in 1389) the bachelor was finally ready for the licence and the master's degree. The minimum age for graduating as a master was thirty-five, in Vienna and Cologne only thirty. Anyone holding the licence had to be in holy orders. The Bologna statutes include oaths that the new master had to take before starting to teach: first of all he swore fidelity and obedience to the pope, secondly he promised to safeguard orthodoxy in the faculty. Masters had to lecture, preside over disputations, and preach, but the Parisian statutes are silent about the content of their lectures and the frequence of their disputations and sermons. Again, the Bologna statutes are more helpful in making it clear that the number of disputations presided over by a master depended on the number of students who needed to participate in disputations in order to fulfil the requirements for a degree in theology.

In the case of the University of Oxford, the statutes, written in 1313, are rather summary.[34] When secular students, who were masters of arts, had completed seven years of audition in theology, they were ready to start lecturing on the *Sentences*. Those lacking the degree in arts (the mendicants) had to study philosophy in the arts faculty for eight years and complete nine years of audition in theology before lecturing on the *Sentences*.

On the whole, Oxford followed the same curriculum as Paris, an important divergence being that at Oxford the students lectured on the *Sentences* before lecturing on the Bible.[35] It is possible, however, that Oxford followed Paris to begin with by placing the lectures on the Bible before those on the *Sentences*, until a conflict between 1311 and 1314 between the chancellor and secular masters on the one hand and the Preachers on the other changed the order of study. There was by that time a strong anti-Dominican party at Oxford claiming that only those who had lectured on the *Sentences* were

33 For the different kinds of disputation: Bazàn, 'Questions disputées' (note 4).
34 H. S. Gibson (ed.), *Statuta antiqua universitatis Oxoniensis* (Oxford, 1931), 48–53. For the date of the statutes: G. Pollard, 'The Oxford Statute Book of the University', *Bodleian Library Record*, 8 (1967–72), 69–91.
35 A. G. Little and F. Pelster, *Oxford Theology and Theologians* c. AD 1282–1302, Publications of Oxford Historical Society, 96 (Oxford, 1934), 26, n. 3; Smalley, *Study* (note 2), 276 n. 2; Courtenay, *Schools and Scholars* (note 17), 43.

worthy of lecturing on the Bible.[36] The Dominicans answered that this was irrational, since the normal order of study would be to go from the interpretation of Scripture to the more advanced treatment of difficult questions in lectures on the *Sentences*. They also claimed that this change of order would stop those who were capable of lecturing on the Bible, but not on the *Sentences*, from pursuing their studies, and that Oxford ought to follow the Paris practice of giving two sets of lectures on the Bible before reading the *Sentences*.[37]

It seems that the Dominicans, who had to study the Bible in order to fulfil their goal of preaching, were less motivated to spend a year on purely speculative theology. The secular theologians on the other hand were not primarily moved by such pastoral considerations. In this conflict of interests (which was but one of many at this time), the chancellor and masters were victorious, thus proving once more that the friars at Oxford did not enjoy the same unchallenged position as their brothers at Paris.

Finally, one should note that the different teaching methods in the theological faculty – lectures, disputations, and sermons – gave rise to different genres of theological works: biblical commentaries, commentaries on the *Sentences*, disputed and quodlibetal questions, and sermons.[38]

THEOLOGY AND PHILOSOPHY IN PARIS AND OXFORD

In the thirteenth century, theologians in Paris could not ignore the works of Aristotle and his Arabic commentators, which, beginning in the second quarter of the twelfth century, were being translated into Latin. Aristotle's natural philosophy challenged the Christian theology of creation, and his definition of science could, at least to some extent, be applied to theology.

When in 1210 the ecclesiastical authorities banned Aristotle's *libri naturales* in Paris, it was the first official clash between the two world views, but the condemnation was primarily directed against the pantheistic heresies of Amalric of Bène (d.c. 1207) and his followers, and against the teaching of David of Dinant (*fl.* 1200), who was familiar with Aristotle's natural phil-

---

[36] H. Rashdall, 'The Friar Preachers versus the University', in M. Burrows (ed.), *Collectanea*, 2nd series, vol. XVI (Oxford, 1890), 223.

[37] Rashdall, 'Friar preachers' (note 36), 218.

[38] For a list of masters and biblical commentaries from the thirteenth century: C. Spicq, *Esquisse d'une histoire de l'exégèse latine au Moyen Age* (Paris, 1944). For a repertory of biblical commentaries: F. Stegmüller, *Repertorium biblicum medii aevi*, vols. I–VII (Madrid, 1949–61). For a repertory of *Sentences* commentaries: F. Stegmüller, *Repertorium Commentariorum in Sententias Petri Lombardi* (Würzburg, 1947); supplements to this fundamental work by V. Doucet in *Archivum Franciscanum Historicum* 47 (1954), 88–170, and J. Van Dyk in *Franciscan Studies*, 39 (1979), 255–315. For disputed and quodlibetal questions: Bazàn, 'Questions disputées' (note 4). For university sermons: J. B. Schneyer, *Repertorium der lateinischen Sermones des Mittelalters für die Zeit von 1150–1350*, Beiträge zur Geschichte der Philosophie und Theologie des Mittelalters, 43:6 (Münster, 1975).

osophy. Only after a command to burn the works of David of Dinant does there follow in the document a prohibition against lecturing, publicly or privately, on Aristotle's books on natural philosophy and their commentaries.[39] From the same period is a document condemning nine heretics, apparently followers of Amalric, to the flames, ending: 'We know that, because of these persons, some books were prohibited even to the learned.'[40] In the statutes of 1215, the prohibition of Aristotle's books on metaphysics and natural philosophy is still connected with the teaching of David of Dinant and Amalric of Bène.[41]

Only in 1228 do we come to a document whose sole purpose is to restrict the study of natural philosophy. This occurs in a letter from Pope Gregory IX, the eloquence of which reveals a carefully premeditated official statement written to provide guidelines for the future. The fact that it is directed to the regent masters of theology shows that the earlier prohibitions had not been very effective and that Aristotle's natural philosophy had penetrated even the faculty of theology. Gregory accuses theology of being dominated by philosophy, which should be its obedient servant, and of committing adultery with philosophical doctrines. The theologians, he says, have moved the limits set by the church fathers on the utilization of philosophy for the study of sacred Scripture. While trying to support faith with natural reason, they weaken faith, for nature believes what it has understood, whereas faith understands what it has believed. The pope finally commands the masters to teach pure theology without any leavening of worldly science.[42] This forceful admonition proves, if nothing else, that natural philosophy was used by theologians even after 1210 and 1215. The impression that the pope's letter made on the theologians is perhaps shown in a remark by the first Dominican master in Paris, Roland of Cremona (1229–30), that subtle disputations about the exterior senses belong to the philosophers and must be avoided by theologians, lest the latter be called physicians (*physici*).[43]

The pope's worries were shared by many theologians. Thus, William of Auxerre (d. 1231), the first theologian who made use of Aristotle's *libri naturales* in Paris, claimed in his *Summa aurea* of before 1220 that the articles of faith cannot be proved by appeal to human reason.[44] This shows that it was not the *libri naturales* in and of themselves that were controversial, but rather the use, or abuse, made of them in theology.

During the conflict of 1229, the masters who had gone on strike and left

---

[39] *CUP*, vol. I, 70, no. 11   [40] *CUP*, vol. I, 71–2, no. 12.   [41] *CUP*, vol. I, 78–80, no. 20.
[42] *CUP*, vol. I, 114–16, no. 59.
[43] D.A. Callus, 'The Function of the Philosopher in Thirteenth-century Oxford', in P. Wilpert (ed.), *Beiträge zur Berufsbewusstsein des mittelalterlichen Menschen*, Miscellanea Mediaevalia, 3 (Berlin, 1964), 157–8.
[44] J. Ribaillier (ed.), *Magistri Guillelmi Altissiodorensis Summa Aurea, Liber Primus*, Spicilegium Bonaventurianum, 16 (Paris/Grottaferrata, 1980), 15.

Paris were invited by Henry III to teach anywhere in England,[45] where there was no ban on the *libri naturales* of Aristotle, and in a letter of invitation from Toulouse it is openly stated that those who wish to look deep into nature's bosom may listen to lectures on the *libri naturales* that had been prohibited in Paris.[46] Whatever his expectations of William of Auvergne may have been, Gregory IX was obviously disappointed, and in a letter of 1229 he accused the bishop of having caused the dissent that made the masters leave Paris.[47] In his *Parens scientiarum* of 1231, in which he confirmed the privileges granted to the masters in 1215, he repeats his ban on the *libri naturales*, but with the mitigating remark: 'until they have been examined and purged from every suspicion of error'. He also repeats his exhortation of 1228 to the theologians not to show off as philosophers but only to dispute such questions as can be determined by appeal to theological books and the works of the church fathers.[48] A week later Gregory absolved those masters and scholars who had been condemned on account of their use of the *libri naturales*,[49] and about the same time he appointed a theological commission, of which William of Auxerre was a member, for the purpose of examining the books in question and excising their errors.[50] This examination never came to pass, possibly due to the death of William of Auxerre later that year.

The debate over the use of Aristotelian natural philosophy in theology is reflected in a collection of Parisian university sermons.[51] In a sermon preached in January 1231 the Dominican master John of St Giles criticizes those who prefer lengthy careers at the university to more fruitful work: 'When they come to theology they can hardly part from their science [*scientia sua*, i.e. philosophy], as is clear in certain persons, who cannot part from Aristotle in theology, bringing with them brass instead of gold, that is to say philosophical questions and opinions.'[52] Another Dominican, in a sermon belonging to the same collection, complains about those who use the language of philosophy in theology, 'for he who has studied metaphysics always talks about points and lines in theology'.[53]

During the 1230s, theologians like Philip the Chancellor (d.1236), William of Auvergne, and Roland of Cremona used Aristotle in their works, but within an Augustinian framework. Not until the 1240s did Aristotelian and, through the commentaries of Avicenna (Ibn Sina, d. 1037) and Averroës (Ibn Rushd, d. 1198), Arabic metaphysics pervade theology. In 1247, the papal legate Odo of Châteauroux (d. 1273) exiled the arts master John of Brescain, who had taught errors while mixing theology with logic. The legate expressed

45 *CUP*, vol. I, 119, no. 64.   46 *CUP*, vol. I, 129, no. 72.
47 See p. 413 and *CUP*, vol. I, 125–7, no. 69.
48 *CUP*, vol. I, 136–9, no. 79   49 *CUP*, vol. I, 143, no. 86
50 *CUP*, vol. I, 143–4, no. 87.
51 M.-M. Davy, *Les Sermons universitaires parisiens de 1230–1231. Contribution à l'histoire de la prédication médiévale* (Paris, 1931).
52 Davy, *Sermons* (note 51), 292.   53 Davy, *Sermons* (note 51), 341

his discontent at a situation in which logicians proceeded in a theological manner and theologians in a philosophical manner in their disputations. The masters, he concluded, should be content with the old limits set by the church fathers between sciences and faculties.[54]

One of the Dominican chairs was held that year by Albertus Magnus (d. 1280). While organizing the *studium generale* in the following year, 1248, in Cologne, he launched the project of writing expositions of all Aristotle's known works, in order to make them accessible to the Latin reader. In Albertus's view, while the fathers of the church were authorities in theology, Aristotle was the authority in natural philosophy, even if it would be wrong to regard him as infallible even in that area. By distinguishing the different areas of competence of theology and philosophy, Albertus contributed to the autonomy of the secular sciences, which were no longer seen merely as handmaidens of the queen, theology. On the other hand Albertus opposed the extreme reaction (such as the letter of Odo of Châteauroux) against the use of philosophy in theology, as coming from men who, like brute animals, blaspheme things of which they are ignorant.[55]

Another attempt to clarify the relations between philosophy and theology was made by Thomas Aquinas, who defined theology in a new way so that it should cohere with the Aristotelian notion of science. Ever since Alexander of Hales wrote his commentary on Peter Lombard's *Sentences*, the prologue of which was concerned with the epistemic status of theology, one was obliged to consider, at the opening of one's own commentary on the *Sentences*, whether theology is a science. By defining theology as a science, a *scientia* in the Aristotelian sense (even if it could not fulfil all requirements of a science), Aquinas broke with the tradition since Saint Augustine of defining *sacra pagina* or theology as wisdom, *sapientia*. As the other sciences have their principles known *per se*, theology, Aquinas claimed, has its articles of faith.[56] By regarding theology and the different branches of philosophy as different sciences, philosophy gained complete autonomy.[57] On the one hand, the definition of theology as a science strengthened its authority: if everything in a theological *summa* was deduced from the articles of faith, or at least consistent with them, its doctrines were not only orthodox but also scientifically correct. On the other hand, the liberation of philosophy from theology made

[54] *CUP*, vol. I, 206–8, no. 176.

[55] Albertus Magnus, *De somno et vigilia*, ed. S. C. A. Borgnet, Opera Omnia, 9 (Paris, 1890); E. A. Synan, 'Albertus Magnus and the Sciences', in J. A. Weisheipl (ed.), *Albertus Magnus and the Sciences. Commemorative Essays 1980* (Toronto, 1980), 10–11; M.-D. Chenu, *La Théologie comme science au XIII siècle* (Paris, 1957), 29 n. 4.

[56] Chenu, *Théologie comme science* (note 55), 64–71.

[57] J. Pinborg, 'Diskussionen um die Wissenschaftstheorie an der Artistenfakultät', in P. Wilpert (ed.), *Die Auseinandersetzungen an der Pariser Universität im XIII. Jahrhundert*, Miscellanea Mediaevalia, 10 (Berlin, 1976), 240.

it possible in the arts faculty to reason merely from scientific principles, even if the conclusions reached were unorthodox.

This is exactly what happened in the late 1260s, when masters such as Siger of Brabant (d. *c.* 1284) and Boethius of Dacia (d. *c.* 1284), influenced by an Averroistic reading of Aristotle, reached conclusions that were philosophically acceptable but contrary to Christian belief: namely, that the world is eternal, that terrestrial events are subject to the movement of the heavenly bodies, that there is only one human intellect, that there is no free will or choice, and that the soul is destroyed with the body and is unable to suffer punishment. These theses were condemned in thirteen articles by Stephen Tempier, bishop of Paris, in 1270.[58]

The members of the arts faculty thus realized that scientific autonomy was not tantamount to religious freedom, and in 1272 the masters of 'logical and natural science' issued a document stating that no member of their faculty could dispute questions on purely theological matters, such as the Trinity or incarnation. If a question touched both faith and philosophy it should be determined according to faith. If anyone lectured on a difficult passage or disputed a question with arguments that seemed to contradict faith, he should declare them totally erroneous or abstain from reading the text or adducing the arguments in question.[59] The masters incepting in the arts had to swear obedience to this statute until the fifteenth century, and in the fourteenth century the Parisian master of arts John Buridan (d. 1358), accused by some theologians of treating theological matters, complained that he could not possibly resolve the arguments contrary to faith in a question unless he was allowed to produce them.[60]

The atmosphere seems to have become increasingly suspicious at Paris, for in a statute of 1276 the masters decided that, because condemned doctrines had been taught at secret meetings, nobody could henceforth be allowed to give lectures privately, except in grammar and logic, where no subversive teaching could arise. All other lectures must be held in public places, where everybody could give a faithful report of the matters being taught.[61] In spite of this precaution, only four months later Pope John XXI (1276–7) (also known as Petrus Hispanus; he had studied arts at Paris and was the author of the *Summulae logicales*, a work that was later to become a standard text in its field) wrote to Bishop Stephen Tempier about certain errors that had been reported once again to be growing, asking him to make enquiries about them and to find out who taught them and where.[62] The bishop did more than that,

---

[58] *CUP*, vol. I, 486–7, no. 432.

[59] *CUP*, vol. I, 499–500, no. 441; P. Wilpert, 'Boethius von Dacien – die Autonomie der Philosophen', in Wilpert (ed.), *Beiträge* (note 43), 136–7.

[60] E. Grant, *A Source Book in Medieval Science*, (Cambridge, Mass., 1974), 50–1.

[61] *CUP*, vol. I, 538–9, no. 468.

[62] *CUP*, vol. I, 541–2, no. 471.

and on 7 March 1277 issued a list of 219 condemned articles.[63] These errors, he claimed, had been set forth by members of the arts faculty who had exceeded the limits of that faculty. He accused them of holding that the articles in question were true according to philosophy but not according to faith, as if there were two contrary truths. However, both Siger and Boethius, whom historians have come to regard as at least two of Tempier's targets, have been cleared by recent scholarship of the bishop's accusation of adhering to a double-truth theory.[64]

The list of 219 articles was drawn up by a commission of sixteen theologians (among them the Neo-Augustinian Henry of Ghent, d. 1293), who within the short compass of one month handed in the results of their enquiries on *schedulae*, or pieces of parchment. The articles were then lumped together, apparently without systematization, and condemned by the bishop. Even contemporary theologians, such as Godfrey of Fontaines (d. *c.* 1306) and Giles of Rome (d. 1316), thought that the condemnations were sometimes inconsistent, and that some of the condemned theses were indeed perfectly orthodox.[65]

The articles condemned repeat those of 1270, and many of them reflect an Aristotelian interpretation of nature that restricts God's power and human free will.[66] Some of the articles were directed against theology as such,[67] whereas some rejected theology as a science, on the grounds that certitude only follows from principles known *per se*, not from authority.[68] Those who held this view in the arts faculty clearly opposed the attempts made by Thomas Aquinas to give a scientific status to theology. On the other hand, some of Aquinas's doctrines were the target of the condemnations, which shows that the bishop's action was not exclusively aimed at members of the arts faculty, but was rather a reaction of conservative, Neo-Augustinian theologians against radical Aristotelians, whether in the arts faculty or among the theologians themselves.[69]

The line of demarcation thus did not run between the faculties of arts and theology, but between conservatives and radicals in both faculties. It has been suggested that the arts faculty's statute of 1272 was the work of a conserva-

---

[63] *CUP*, vol. I, 543–58, no. 473; R. Hissette, *Enquête sur les 219 articles condamnés à Paris le 7 mars 1277* (Louvain/Paris, 1977).

[64] F. Van Steenberghen, *Introduction à l'étude de la philosophie médiévale*, Philosophes médiévaux, 18 (Louvain, 1974), 557–63; Wilpert, 'Boethius von Dacien' (note 59), 149–52.

[65] J. F. Wippel, 'The Condemnations of 1270 and 1277 at Paris', *Journal of Medieval and Renaissance Studies*, 7 (1977), 195–6.

[66] P. Duhem, *Le Système du monde. Histoire des doctrines cosmologiques de Platon à Copernic*, vol. VI (Paris, 1954), 20–69; vol. VIII (Paris, 1958), 7–120; E. Grant, 'The Condemnation of 1277, God's Absolute Power, and Physical Thought in the Late Middle Ages', *Viator*, 10 (1979), 211–44.

[67] *CUP*, vol. I, 543–58, no. 473, arts. 152, 153, 175.

[68] *CUP*, vol. I, 543–58, no. 473, arts. 37, 150, 151.

[69] Wippel, 'Condemnations' (note 65), 184.

tive majority, opponents of the radical group to which Siger belonged. The controversy that led to the condemnations of 1277 was most fundamentally concerned with the area common to philosophy and theology, in which the objects of reason (*scibilia*) were also the objects of faith (*credibilia*). The radicals in both faculties claimed for philosophy the right to investigate all matters attainable by reason – *scibilia* – independently of the tenets of faith. The conservatives held that, when the truths revealed by faith – *credibilia* – could also be objects of philosophical investigation, the philosophers should determine their questions in accordance with faith or abstain from raising them.[70]

During the decades between the entry of Aristotle into theology and the condemnations (1240–70), much theological activity focused on the relations between faith and reason. This fostered an interest in metaphysics as a bridge between Aristotle's philosophy and Christian revelation.[71] One result was the theological syntheses of Albertus Magnus, Bonaventure, and Thomas Aquinas.

The first English theologian to use natural philosophy in theology was Alexander Neckam, who taught theology at Oxford shortly before 1200.[72] This was the beginning of a long tradition in Oxford of combining biblical and scientific studies. In the late 1220s, Robert Grosseteste made a synthesis of Genesis, Aristotle's *De caelo*, and Arabic Neoplatonism in his metaphysical treatise *De luce* (On light), in which the foundations of reality were described as mathematical, with God as a creative mathematician.[73] Other examples of a harmonious relationship between theology and philosophy can be found in the works of the Dominican Simon of Hinton (*fl.* 1250–60) and the Franciscan Thomas Docking (*fl.* 1260–5), who made use of optics and other natural sciences in order to elucidate the literal sense of the Bible.[74]

At Oxford, the use of logic and philosophy in theology never provoked negative reactions from the authorities, and there are no prohibitions against philosophy in the Oxford statutes. On the other hand, there were tensions between the biblical and speculative aspects of theology. In Paris, lectures on Scripture focused on moral instruction, whereas theological questions were kept for lectures on the *Sentences*; in Oxford, theologians like Grosseteste, Simon of Hinton, and Thomas Docking made theological questions part of their lectures on the Bible, and Grosseteste equated theology with biblical study. The Dominicans Richard Fishacre (d. 1248) and Robert Kilwardby

---

[70] Wilpert, 'Boethius von Dacien' (note 59), 139.
[71] E. A. Moody, 'Empiricism and Metaphysics in Medieval Philosophy', in E. A. Moody, *Studies in Medieval Philosophy, Science, and Logic (Collected Papers 1933–1969)* (Berkeley, 1975), 287–304.
[72] R. W. Hunt, *The Schools and the Cloister. The Life and Writings of Alexander Nequam (1157–1216)*, ed. M. Gibson (Oxford, 1984).
[73] J. McEvoy, *The Philosophy of Robert Grosseteste* (Oxford, 1982), 149–80.
[74] Catto, 'Theology and Theologians' (note 17), 493–4.

(d. 1279), as well as the Franciscan Richard Rufus (*fl.* 1250–5), all of whom belong to the generation of theologians who wrote the earliest commentaries on the *Sentences* in Oxford, adhered to the Parisian practice, and advocated separation of speculative theology from Bible study. But it has been pointed out that the two areas of theology were not kept strictly apart, and that establishing the *Sentences* as a textbook for speculative theology did not prevent theologians from continuing to insert *quaestiones* into their biblical commentaries.[75]

The introduction of the *Sentences* as a textbook in the theological programme of study at Oxford was deplored in the 1260s by the Franciscan Roger Bacon (d. *c.* 1292). The theologians of this day, he complains, put all their pride in lectures on the *Sentences*, and in many places, such as Bologna, *quaestiones* are only allowed in that context. If Bacon is right, and *quaestiones* were in fact not allowed in biblical courses, lectures on the *Sentences* must have been more prestigious, since they provided the teachers with an opportunity to show their acuity in theological discussions and disputations.[76] A later Oxford statute shows that Bacon may have been exaggerating, but that there was some truth to his statement: it asserts that those who lecture on the Bible, either *biblice* or *cursorie*, must not introduce *quaestiones* other than *literales*, that is to say questions arising from the text itself, the *litera*, and consequently directly relevant to the biblical passage lectured on.[77]

For the decades after Tempier's condemnations in 1277, it is impossible to treat the theological faculties of Paris and Oxford separately.

The leading theologians at Paris, Giles of Rome, Henry of Ghent, and Godfrey of Fontaines, were concerned with philosophical questions such as the unity or plurality of forms, the relationship between essence and existence, and that between matter and form.[78] The shadow of the condemnations of 1277 is apparent in the biblical lectures of Henry of Ghent, the reading of which has been compared to 'walking through an exhibition of errors'.[79]

For the period between 1265 and 1280, in sharp contrast to Paris, there is little evidence of theological activities at Oxford, but after 1277 the controversies concerning metaphysical issues were brought from Paris to Oxford by scholars such as Robert Kilwardby, John Pecham (d. 1292), and Roger Marston (d. *c.* 1303). Since the discussion at Oxford was carried out by men with a past at Paris, it was more often aimed at Paris theologians than at Oxford colleagues.[80]

On 18 March 1277, only eleven days after the condemnation in Paris,

[75] Smalley, *Study* (note 2), 275–80; Catto 'Theology and theologians' (note 17), 492–4.
[76] Little, 'Franciscan School' (note 18), 809.
[77] See note 34.
[78] J. F. Wippel, *The Metaphysical Thought of Godfrey of Fontaines. A Study in Late Thirteenth-Century Philosophy* (Washington, DC, 1981).
[79] Smalley, 'Bible in Medieval Schools' (note 32), 212.
[80] Catto, 'Theology and Theologians' (note 17), 496–8.

Robert Kilwardby, archbishop of Canterbury, condemned thirty errors, four of which concerned grammar, ten logic, and sixteen natural philosophy.[81] Some of the 219 articles condemned at Paris had been directed against different doctrines of Thomas Aquinas, but out of the Oxford articles as many as one-third were related to a doctrine held by Aquinas, that concerning the unity of form. Kilwardby affirms that the errors in question were condemned with the approval of all regent and non-regent masters at Oxford, which shows that the condemnations were not directed against a certain party at Oxford, but were addressed to a debate whose centre was in Paris. It is noteworthy that at Paris the doctrine of the unity of form was never officially condemned, in spite of some steps taken in that direction by Stephen Tempier.[82] At Oxford, the problem had been discussed since the 1240s, but it was not until after 1277 that the views in question followed confessional lines, so that Dominicans advocated unity and Franciscans plurality.[83]

The condemnations of Kilwardby put an end to the doctrinal peace at Oxford. In 1278 the English Franciscan William of la Mare (*fl.* 1275) produced a list of errors found in the writings of Aquinas, and in 1280 it was published under the title of *Correctorium*. In 1282 the Franciscan general chapter declared that Aquinas's *Summa theologica* should not be copied by any member of the order without the corrections made by William of la Mare.

The attacks on Aquinas's doctrines in the condemnations of Paris and Oxford and in the *Correctorium* of la Mare naturally provoked a reaction from the Dominicans, first in a series of *Correctoria Correctorii*, or, as they were called, *Correctoria Corruptorii*, by English and French Dominicans between 1282 and 1285.[84] The second reaction came in 1286, when the Dominican general chapter decided that Aquinas's doctrine should be promoted and defended, by threat of suspension.[85] In December of that year, the dissent was aggravated when in their quodlibetal questions the secular masters opposed the privileges of the mendicants.[86] The following year, the Augustinian general chapter reacted by declaring that all present and future works by one of their own, Giles (Aegidius) of Rome, who had been expelled from the theological faculty of Paris between 1278 and 1285, but had reconciled himself to the pope, should be defended by the teachers and students of the order.[87]

The development of schools of thought within theology – Thomism and Aegidianism – was an act of defence produced by the climate of censure and

---

[81] *CUP*, vol. I, 558–60, no. 474.   [82] *CUP*, vol. I, 624–6, no. 517.

[83] Catto, 'Theology and theologians' (note 17), 497–8.

[84] P. Glorieux, ' "Pro et contra Thomam". Un survol de cinquante années', *Studia Anselmiana*, 63 (1974), 255–87; M. D. Jordan, 'The Controversy of the "correctoria" and the Limits of Metaphysics', *Seculum*, 57 (1982), 292–314.

[85] *CUP*, vol. II, 6, no. 536.   [86] Wippel, *Metaphysical Thought* (note 78), xic.

[87] *CUP*, vol. I, 633–4, no. 522; vol. II, 12, no. 542.

opposition that reigned in both Paris and Oxford. As a result of this intellectual climate, theological discussion was no longer presented in broad syntheses, but more fragmentarily in lists of corrections, in which literary works
were criticized point by point, in *quaestiones* and quodlibets. It is hardly a
coincidence that quodlibetal questions, which had appeared in the theological
faculty of Paris around 1230, became popular at Paris in the 1260s, a period of
doctrinal conflicts, and that they were presumably introduced in Oxford in
the seventies by the Franciscan John Pecham, one of the theologians who
brought the controversies of Paris to England.[88]

The atmosphere of the 1280s is well captured in a series of letters written
by John Pecham, archbishop of Canterbury, who in 1284 had ratified the
condemnations of his predecessor.[89] In the first of these, sent to the chancellor and regent masters of Oxford, he defends himself against an accusation
from the Dominicans of having acted against their order. According to
Pecham, the Dominicans called the opinions of Aquinas 'the opinions of their
order', and some of them had said officially that their teaching was more
truthful than that of any other contemporary order. In another letter of
1285[90] Pecham writes that the teachings of the two orders (i.e. the Dominicans and the Franciscans) are radically opposed on every point of discussion.
One of them (obviously the Dominican order) has rejected the teaching of the
church fathers and relies almost totally on the philosophers. The Augustinian
outlook of Pecham is also apparent in his letter to the Bishop of Lincoln of
the same year, in which he insists that he does not dislike the study of philosophy as long as it is a servant of the theological mysteries, but that he is
against the worldly novelties that go against philosophical truth (i.e. the truth
of a philosophy that is the servant of theology) and were introduced into
theology twenty years earlier (i.e around 1265).[91]

But it would be a mistake to think that these – or later – Thomists were
Aristotelians in the same way as their revered doctor had been. Most Thomists, such as Robert of Orford (d. *c.* 1300) and Hervé Nedellec (d. 1323),
were first and foremost zealous defenders of Aquinas's works against such
critics as Henry of Ghent.[92] In a study of Oxford University sermons of
1290–3, it has been shown that none of them mentions either the controversial doctrine of Aquinas or the ban on it.[93] A possible explanation of this is
that crises and controversies at the university were by this time ventilated in
quodlibets rather than in sermons.

In the 1280s Oxford equalled Paris for the first time as a centre for theo-

---

[88] Catto, 'Theology and Theologians' (note 17), 478.
[89] *CUP*, vol. I, 624–6, 626–7, 634–5, nos. 517, 518, 523.
[90] *CUP*, vol. I, 626–7, no. 518.   [91] *CUP*, vol. I, 634–5, no. 523.
[92] Glorieux, ' "Pro et contra Thomam" ' (note 84).
[93] B. Smalley, 'Oxford University Sermons 1290–1293', in J. J. G. Alexander and M. T. Gibson
(eds.), *Medieval Learning and Literature. Essays presented to Richard W. Hunt* (Oxford,
1976), 316–25.

logical discussions and its star continued to rise until its superiority was established in the first half of the fourteenth century. The main actors on the Oxford scene at that time were Franciscans, more vital than the Dominicans, who were tied to the official Thomist doctrine. The first in a row of prominent Oxford Franciscans was Duns Scotus (d. 1308), who used the works of a Parisian master, Henry of Ghent, as his point of departure. Scotus was the first Oxford master who strongly influenced Paris, where theology was soon to be dominated by his pupils.[94]

From the 1330s onwards the Hundred Years War brought to an end the interchange of scholars between the Universities of Paris and Oxford. A lack of creativity among Parisian scholars during this period has been blamed on the conservatism of John XXII (1316–34).[95] On the other hand, the pope in Avignon does not seem to have been able to bridle the Paris masters; in 1317 he reproached them in a letter for being deceived by philosophy and for devoting themselves to philosophical questions and subtleties,[96] and, during the dispute that arose in 1331–2 over the pope's controversial views on the beatific vision, the unanimous opposition of the Paris masters led to his final retraction.[97]

At Oxford, intellectual life after 1320 was characterized by the absence of schools of thought of any kind.[98] During the previous decades the Franciscans had opposed the teaching of the Dominicans, especially that of Aquinas, without tying themselves to any doctrinal leader of their own. This fostered a critical and open attitude that made it possible for somebody like William of Ockham (d. 1349) to make an eclectic use of the writings both of Franciscan predecessors – above all Duns Scotus – and secular masters. In his works on logic Ockham often brought up physical problems, and this became a standard procedure in the following generation of Oxford scholars, especially in the group called the 'Oxford calculators' or, sometimes, the Mertonians.[99] Whether they belonged to the Merton school or not, when the scholars became students in the faculty of theology they used the methods they had previously applied in logic and physics. The theological questions, as formulated once and for all by Peter Lombard, provided these students – who by this stage of their formation were advanced philosophers – with a new and

---

[94] Catto, 'Theology and Theologians' (note 17), 505; C. Bérubé, 'La première école scotiste', in Z. Kaluza and P. Vignaux (eds.), *Preuve et raisons à l'université de Paris. Logique, ontologie et théologie au XIV siècle* (Paris, 1984), 9–24.

[95] W. J. Courtenay, 'The Role of English Thought in the Transformation of University Education in the Late Middle Ages', in J. M. Kittelson and P. J. Transue (eds.), *Rebirth, Reform and Resilience. Universities in Transition 1300–1700* (Columbus, Ohio, 1984), 119.

[96] *CUP*, vol. II, 200–1, no. 741.   [97] *CUP*, vol. II, 414–42, nos. 970–87.

[98] Courtenay, *Schools and Scholars* (note 17), 190–2.

[99] E. D. Sylla, 'The Oxford Calculators', in N. Kretzmann, A. Kenny, and J. Pinborg (eds), *The Cambridge History of Later Medieval Philosophy* (Cambridge, 1982), 540–63.

challenging set of problems. They investigated them by using analytical languages developed in the arts faculty.[100]

It has been pointed out[101] that the major areas in which these analytical languages – often connected with measurement – were applied were the central theological issues of the period: will, justification, grace, merit, reward, sin; that is to say the changeable and measurable components of the relation between God and man. The degree to which philosophy was pursued within a theological context is well illustrated by the fact that parts of some fourteenth-century commentaries on the *Sentences* circulated separately as treatises in natural philosophy.[102]

The development of this characteristic Oxford theology (it later received the epithet 'English' on the continent) follows chronologically upon the defeat of the Dominicans at Oxford and the composition of new statutes, under the anti-Dominican chancellor Henry of Harclay (d. 1317) in 1313, which stipulated that lectures on the *Sentences* should precede those on the Bible.[103] It is possible that the Oxonian masters' interest in the methods and content of the arts faculty teaching caused a change in the curriculum (if there *was* a change in 1313 and not merely codification of already existing practice), but it is equally possible that the rule itself, by making possible a continuation of philosophical investigations within the theological faculty, favoured the growth of Oxford theology. Whether or not any such connection exists, it is a fact that the Dominicans, who were gravely affected by the rule, do not seem to have played any significant part in the development of the new 'logical' and 'physical' theology.

In 1340–5 Paris regained its prominence in theology and entered a creative period characterized by the absence of schools of thought, as in Oxford twenty years earlier. The scholarly interchange between Paris and Oxford, interrupted by the Hundred Years War, was restored indirectly by German, east European, and Italian mendicant students, who kept Paris and Oxford informed of each other. English theologians, for example, went to the mendicant *studia* in Bologna and many Franciscan students were sent from Assisi, Bologna, and other Italian convents to Oxford. German centres of education that had close contact with England in the first half of the fourteenth century were Cologne and Erfurt.[104]

One example of this indirect contact between Paris and Oxford is the Austin friar Gregory of Rimini (d. 1358), who had studied in Italy and England and taught at Bologna and in other Italian cities before reading the *Sentences* at Paris in 1343. With him begins a new era in Paris theology, no

---

100 J. E. Murdoch, 'From Social to Intellectual Factors: an Aspect of the Unitary Character of Later Medieval Learning', in J. E. Murdoch and E. D. Sylla (eds.), *The Cultural Context of Medieval Learning* (Dordrecht/Boston, 1975), 271–348.

101 Murdoch, 'Social to intellectual factors' (note 100), 291.

102 Murdoch, 'Social to intellectual factors' (note 100), 276.

103 See note 34. See also p. 419–20.   104 Courtenay, *Schools and Scholars* (note 17), 163.

longer dominated by Dominicans and Franciscans but by Austin friars and Cistercians. In 1335 the pope granted them *studia generalia* in Paris, Oxford, Toulouse, and Montpellier, with the proviso that Paris should be the most prominent centre of study.[105] The Cistercians and Austin friars were closely associated intellectually in the fourteenth century.[106] Gregory of Rimini introduced to Paris the kind of theology that had been developed at Oxford in the second quarter of the fourteenth century.

The invasion of theology by mathematics and logic was accepted at Oxford, where mathematics and natural philosophy had never been officially banned from theology, but met with resistance at Paris, where there was a long tradition of prohibiting philosophizing in theology. Already in 1344 and 1345 there were signs of what was coming, when the Dominican and Augustinian general chapters both condemned the *doctrinae peregrinae*, 'strange doctrines',[107] a quotation from Hebrews 13:9 probably aimed at the English theology that had found its way to Paris through Gregory of Rimini. The gravity of the danger felt by the authorities is shown in a letter written by Clement VI (1342–52) in 1346 to the masters and students in Paris.[108] He complains that the philosophers devote themselves to *extraneae doctrinae sophisticae*, foreign sophistical doctrines that are said to be taught in some other universities,[109] and that they adhere to strange opinions. What is even more deplorable, the pope continues, is that many theologians do not care for the study of the Bible,[110] but entangle themselves in philosophical questions, trivial disputations, suspect opinions, and divers strange teachings. The forcefulness of the papal document had not been equalled since 1228, when Gregory IX warned the theologians against letting natural philosophy penetrate theology.[111]

The letter of 1346 did not have the desired effect and in the following year fifty articles collected from the works of John of Mirecourt (*fl.* 1344–7) and others were condemned by the Austin friar Hugolino of Orvieto (d. 1373).[112] Eight of these were concerned with assertions to the effect that Christ as man was capable of erring and even of lying, the rest with what makes human acts

[105] *CUP*, vol. II, 448–50, no. 992.
[106] D. Trapp, 'Augustinian Theology of the 14th Century. Notes on Editions, Marginalia, Opinions and Book-lore', *Augustiniana*, 6 (1956), 251.
[107] *CUP*, vol. II, 550, no. 1091; A. Zumkeller, 'Die Augustinerschule des Mittelalters: Vertreter und Philosophisch-Theologische Lehre', *Analecta Augustiniana*, 27 (1964), 170.
[108] *CUP*, vol. II, 587–9, no. 1125.
[109] Sylla has shown in 'Oxford Calculators' (note 99), 545, that the most typical works of the Oxford calculators were connected with the disputations *de sophismatibus* in the arts faculty.
[110] This is confirmed by the decline of the Biblical commentaries in Paris after 1340: J. Verger, 'L'exégèse de l'université', in P. Riché and G. Lobrichon (eds.), *Le Moyen Age et la Bible* (Paris, 1984), 224.
[111] *CUP*, vol. I, 114–16, no. 59. The biblical quotation *doctrinis variis et peregrinis*, 'diverse and strange doctrines', is used in Gregory IX's letter as well, but there it refers to natural philosophy.
[112] *CUP*, vol. II, 610–13, no. 1147.

meritorious or non-meritorious and with claims that God is the cause of sin as well as of just actions. Nothing is said explicitly about philosophizing in theology, but it may have been the feeling of Hugolino of Orvieto and others that the use of the *subtilitates Anglicanae* led to heresies such as the propositions condemned.

The resistance and condemnations of the pope and conservative theologians seem to have been less effective than the censure in 1277. That is at least the impression given by the Cistercian Peter Ceffons, who had read the *Sentences* in 1348–9 together with Hugolino of Orvieto. He defends the use of *subtilitas* in theology,[113] and claims that criticism of the use of logic in theology is simply due to ignorance, an ignorance that leads to errors.[114] The criticism of Tempier's condemnations in 1277 delivered by Giles of Rome had led to his expulsion from the theological faculty of Paris, but at this time the church authorities no longer had the last word in doctrinal matters.

After 1350, there was a decline in Oxford theology, partly due to the black death. With the exception of John Wyclif (d. 1384), whose unorthodox views on the Eucharist were condemned at the university in 1382, there were hardly any well-known theologians at Oxford between 1350 and 1500.[115]

THE END OF THE PARISIAN–OXONIAN MONOPOLY

The year 1347 was a milestone in the history of theological faculties, not only because of the doctrinal controversies in Paris but because the highest theological education, until then practically monopolized by Paris and Oxford, was then decentralized by the foundation in Prague of a university with a theological faculty. This was the first German university, although the mendicants previously had important schools in Prague.

Many similar cases can be found in Italy, where theology had more or less been abandoned to the mendicants. A great number of the theological faculties founded towards the middle of the fourteenth century were Italian, and many of these, for example in Pisa, Perugia, Bologna, and Padua, merely conferred a new status on already existing schools of theology. The change in status from *studium generale* to university seems to have changed little in reality, since in Bologna only 24 of the 447 masters of theology from the period between 1364 and 1500 were secular; the rest were mainly mendicants.[116]

---

113 For references: Trapp, 'Augustinian Theology' (note 106), 187.
114 For references: J. E. Murdoch, ' "Subtilitates Anglicanae" in Fourteenth-century Paris: John of Mirecourt and Peter Ceffons', in M. P. Cosman and B. Chandler (eds.), *Machaut's World. Science and Art in the Fourteenth Century*, Annals of the New York Academy of Sciences, 314 (New York, 1978), 64, 80 n. 78.
115 Courtenay, *Schools and Scholars* (note 17), 359–65; J. A. Robson, *Wyclif and the Oxford Schools* (Cambridge, 1961).
116 Rashdall, *Universities*, vol. I, 252.

The theological faculty of Bologna is especially interesting because its foundation reflects the controversies that had shaken Paris in the late 1340s. When the Austin friar Hugolino of Orvieto, who had played an active role in the condemnations of 1347, drew up the statutes of a theological faculty in Bologna in 1364 he used the Parisian organization as a model and appended a list of the articles condemned in Paris.[117]

The main target of the censure of 1347 had been the excessive use of *subtilitates* and methods originating in the sophistic disputations in the arts faculty; Hugolino of Orvieto warned against this kind of abuse not only by appending the list of propositions condemned, but also in the text of the statutes. He there prohibits the use of 'divers strange doctrines' proffered in obscure and non-traditional language by means of sophisms and fruitless (*vanae*) questions that lead to aberrations.[118] Hugolino also asserts that not only those who manifestly oppose truth are fighting against orthodoxy, but also those who chant in chorus words that serve to cover and mask (*concinant verborum involucra*) strange (*peregrinae* can also mean 'foreign') novelties, so that less learned men hold them to be brilliant, whereas their subtlety (*subtilitas*) is nothing but ignorance.[119] Those guilty of such errors must humbly promise before the masters to correct their teaching.[120]

When the University of Paris received new statutes in 1366,[121] two years after the statutes of Bologna, there was for the first time in any Parisian collection of statutes a prohibition against treating logical or philosophical questions or matters while reading the *Sentences*. Exceptions could be made if the text itself required the use of logic or philosophy or if it was necessary in order to solve a problem. The temptation to treat purely logical problems in a theological context was obviously greater in lectures on the *Sentences* than in those on the Bible. It is noteworthy that philosophical methods were not banned in and of themselves; what was condemned was philosophizing for its own sake. The prohibition is repeated in the Toulouse statutes of the same year and in the Parisian collection of statutes of 1389,[122] but both these collections repeat everything concerning the theological faculty contained in the Paris statutes of 1366 and therefore do not indicate any new crisis. In the statutes of Vienna, where reference is constantly made to the customs of Paris, it is stipulated that those lecturing on the Bible or the *Sentences* must not treat philosophical or logical matters, but may use philosophy, logic, and the other arts when the difficulty of the theological matter to be explained so requires.[123] The same rule is laid down in the statutes of Cologne.[124]

Although the Parisian–Oxonian monopoly was broken after 1347, the Bologna statutes testify to the prestige that the older theological faculties still

---

[117] For an edition of the statutes, see note 24.   [118] Ehrle, *I più antichi statuti* (note 24), 20.
[119] Ehrle, *I più antichi statuti* (note 24), 48.   [120] Ehrle, *I più antichi statuti* (note 24), 50–1.
[121] *CUP*, vol. III, 143–4. no. 1319.   [122] See note 25 and *CUP*, vol. II, 697–703, no. 1189.
[123] See note 27.   [124] See note 28.

enjoyed in 1364, by stipulating that no bachelor who had read the *Sentences* in another university would be automatically accepted for further studies in Bologna, unless he had read them in Paris, Oxford, or Cambridge.[125]

For the period 1350–65 there are few sources for Paris theology. An important source of information is three theological student notebooks attributed earlier to John of Falisca but recently ascribed to Stephen Gaudet.[126] The questions and arguments reported are mainly concerned with problems about future contingents, predestination, and determinism, and they reflect the growing habit among theologians of the second half of the fourteenth century to read the *Sentences secundum alium*, 'according to somebody else'.

From 1365 to the Great Schism the theological faculty at Paris was dominated by German scholars.[127] An exception is the Frenchman Peter of Ailly (d. 1420), a nominalist of reputation, the teacher of John Gerson (d. 1429), and chancellor of the university. One of the main fields for theological activity during these years was the application of logic in Trinitarian speculation.[128]

THE GREAT SCHISM AND THE THEOLOGICAL FACULTIES

With the Great Schism that divided the church between 1378 and 1418, the Parisian–Oxonian hegemony was definitively broken. In 1379 the majority of the theological faculty in Paris voted for Clement VII,[129] the Avignon pope, who had the support of the French kings, but two German theologians, Henry of Langenstein (also of Hesse) (d. 1397) and Conrad of Gelnhausen (d. 1390), composed treatises in which they recommended that a general council should be formed as a way of putting an end to the schism.[130] The 'conciliar way', *via concilii*, was officially adopted by the university in 1381,[131] but in the same year Paris turned pro-Clementine, and a close friend of Clement VII, John Blanchard, was appointed chancellor of the university. The appointment caused scholars from countries that supported Urban VI, the Roman pope and rival of Clement VII, to leave Paris.[132]

The exodus of scholars – mostly of German origin – from Paris had more

---

125 Ehrle, *I più antichi statuti* (note 24), 32–3.
126 P. Glorieux, 'Jean de Falisca: la formation d'un maître en théologie au XIVe siècle', *Archives d'Histoire Doctrinale et Littéraire du Moyen Age*, 33 (1966), 23–104; Z. Kaluza, *Thomas de Cracovie. Contribution à l'histoire du collège de Sorbonne* (Wrocław, 1978), 60–108.
127 W. J. Courtenay, *Adam Wodeham: an Introduction to his Life and Writings* (Leiden, 1978), 140.
128 A. Maierù, 'Logique et théologie trinitaire dans le moyen-âge tardif: deux solutions en présence', in M. Asztalos (ed.), *The Editing of Theological and Philosophical Texts from the Middle Ages* (Stockholm, 1986), 185–212.
129 *CUP*, vol. III, 565–72, no. 1624.
130 A. E. Bernstein, *Pierre d'Ailly and the Blanchard Affair. University and Chancellor of Paris at the Beginning of the Great Schism* (Leiden, 1978), 36.
131 *CUP*, vol. III, 582, no. 1637.   132 Bernstein, *Pierre d'Ailly* (note 130), 45–6.

important consequences for university life than any of the previous academic dispersions, since the scholars not only went to already existing universities but also contributed to the foundation and organization of new ones. The chancellor of Prague University even tried to transfer the Paris University to Prague,[133] just as the Universities of Toulouse and Oxford had invited Parisian masters in 1229, but the universities that really benefited from the exodus were those of Vienna, where Henry of Langenstein and Henry Totting of Oyta (d. 1396) drew up the statutes in 1389, Heidelberg, which hosted Conrad of Gelnhausen and Marsilius of Inghen (d. 1396), an ex-rector of Paris, and Cologne.[134] These three universities were all founded by Urban VI, who was only too pleased to weaken the position of Clementist Paris by issuing bulls confirming new universities, whereas Clement VII avoided establishing new theological faculties. An important exception is Erfurt, founded in 1379 by the Avignon pope.

All these new universities were modelled on the University of Paris. Vienna and Cologne also made use of the Bologna statutes of 1364. In their statutes they both include a paragraph, not to be found in any extant Paris or Bologna statutes, which has a certain interest, since it obviously refers to a Parisian practice that the authors did not wish to see in these new universities. The paragraph says that the theme chosen for the *collatio* belonging to the *principia*[135] must consist of a whole sentence taken from the Bible, not merely one word or syllable.[136] The Vienna statutes then proceed to a lengthy condemnation of neologisms and other stylistic abuses.

A similar criticism of new and inappropriate terminology in theology is delivered by the Paris chancellor John Gerson in his *Contra curiositatem studentium*, a reform programme for the theological faculty written in 1402.[137] Gerson criticizes the new words invented by the '*formalizantes*', the successors of Duns Scotus, who, like the Franciscan John of Ripa (*fl.* 1350), introduced a formal distinction and other unnecessary notions into Trinitarian speculations, thereby complicating matters more than explaining them. In this context Gerson praises Henry Totting of Oyta, who, as one of the authors of the Vienna statutes, had reacted against terminological innovations in a similar way.

Gerson defines the relations that should obtain between the different sciences and ascribes to theology the traditional role of *domina*, mistress,

---

133 *CUP*, vol. III, 548–9, no. 1642.   134 See note 132.

135 The sermon introducing the lectures on the *Sentences*. See p. 418.

136 For editions of the Vienna and Cologne statutes, see notes 27 and 28. Peter Ceffons, the *enfant terrible* of Paris in the mid-fourteenth century, had actually chosen the single letter (O) as a theme (from 'Omega' in Revelation 1) for his *collationes* of the *principia* to his lectures on the *Sentences*: D. Trapp, 'Peter Ceffons of Clairvaux', *Recherches de Théologie Ancienne et Médiévale*, 24 (1957), 106.

137 J. Gerson, *Oeuvres complètes*, ed. P. Glorieux, vol. III (Tournai, 1962), 224–49; also C. Burger, *Aedificatio, Fructus, Utilitas. Johannes Gerson als Professor der Theologie und Kanzler der Universität Paris* (Tübingen, 1986), 45–55.

over the other sciences that are but *ancillae*, handmaidens. He recommends a return to the old rule that members of arts faculties should not treat purely theological matters[138] and repeats the warning given in the statutes of 1366 against introducing purely logical or philosophical matters into theology. He also criticizes theologians who fill their books and classes with sophisms and introduce strange doctrines. This sounds like an echo of the Paris condemnations of 1347.[139] An echo of Bishop Tempier's preface to the condemnations of 1277 can be heard in Gerson's claim that the articles of faith can never be contrary to natural philosophy. In the spirit of Gregory IX's letter of 1228, Gerson asserts that natural philosophy cannot approach the level of knowledge of the articles of faith and that the philosophers have to accept the limitations of their science. Transcending these limits would impose limits on God's freedom in a way that leads to determinism. The theologians on the other hand must realize that their science is limited to what is revealed in the holy Scriptures. The two great faults in contemporary theologians, he says, are *curiositas*, the wish to know things that are unattainable or harmful to know, and *singularitas*, the wish to prove oneself superior by turning to strange and unusual teachings. Instead of searching for innovations and questioning well-known doctrines, theologians should be content with traditional knowledge.

In a letter of 1400 to Peter of Ailly[140] Gerson had recommended some ways of returning to a more traditional theology: more emphasis on the study of the Bible, rejection of sophisms in theology, and a concentration on books 2–4 of the *Sentences* instead of paying almost exclusive attention to book 1 (the place where Trinitarian speculations belong).[141]

It seems as if, as a chancellor of the University of Paris, Gerson had studied the bulls, condemnations, statutes, and other documents from earlier times and found support in them for a return to a more traditional theology. He deplored the contemporary habit of defending and attacking doctrines according to schools or religious orders.[142] This was a burning problem in his days, when the Dominicans were expelled from the university as a result of a controversy that started in 1387 when the Dominican John of Monzon (d. *c.* 1412) asserted that the doctrine of the Immaculate Conception was contrary to faith.[143] There was a strong reaction against his opinion at the university, where the Immaculate Conception had been celebrated officially since 1380.[144] To restore order, Gerson allowed the Dominicans to come back in 1403.

According to Gerson, to avoid doctrinal confusion theology should be

---

[138] Cf. the statute of 1272, mentioned on p. 424, and note 59.   [139] See p. 432.
[140] Gerson, *Oeuvres complètes* (note 137), vol. II, 23–8.
[141] Cf. a similar statement in the statutes of 1389, *CUP*, vol. II, 697–703, no. 1189.
[142] Gerson, *Oeuvres complètes* (note 137), vol. III, 239.
[143] *CUP*, vol. III, 486–533, nos. 1557–83.   [144] *CUP*, vol. III, 297–8, no. 1456.

taught at only one university, or at least there should not be more than one theological faculty in France. This sole university – obviously Paris – should be an uncorrupt source from which the other theological faculties could flow like rivers.[145] That very metaphor was in fact used for Paris in the statutes of the Universities of Vienna and Cologne.[146] Already in 1387, in the controversy concerning the Immaculate Conception, the dean of the theological faculty at Paris had proclaimed that this faculty was the seat (*sedes*) of Catholic truth and enjoyed the highest authority in questions of orthodoxy.[147] This was no less than a challenge to the authority of the Holy See, weakened through the Schism. During the Council of Pisa in 1409, Gerson presented a theory according to which the church as Christ's mystical body can convoke a council with authority to appoint or depose popes and condemn heretical propositions.[148] In a council like the one Gerson had in mind, the theologians would be invested with a special authority, a kind of 'academic infallibility'.[149]

It has been noted that university institutions influenced the structure of the Councils of Constance (1414–18) and Basle (1431–49), and during the latter council a theory was elaborated that gave even more power to the council than in Gerson's programme: the council itself was now seen as the representative of Christ's mystical body.[150]

Gerson brought to an end an epoch in the history of the theological faculty at Paris. For two hundred years the ecclesiastical and academic authorities had collaborated to preserve the faculty as a universally recognized guardian of orthodoxy. When the papacy faltered during the Schism the theological faculty was ready to assume papal authority. It had secured its position by maintaining tradition and rejecting strange foreign doctrines, whether in the form of Greek natural philosophy, Arabic metaphysics, or English subtleties.

VIA ANTIQUA AND VIA MODERNA

The fifteenth century witnessed the return of school traditions, with a dividing line between the realists (*reales, antiqui*) and the nominalists (*nominales, moderni*).[151] These two main groups represented two different methods or

---

[145] Gerson, *Oeuvres complètes* (note 137), vol. III, 248.

[146] For editions of the Vienna and Cologne statutes, see notes 27 and 28. In the 1389 statutes of Paris (*CUP*, vol. II, 697–703, no. 1189), it is stated that, if a student in theology has received his training elsewhere than at Paris, two years at that other school will count as one year at Paris.

[147] *CUP*, vol. III, 486, no. 1557.

[148] S. E. Ozment, 'The University and the Church. Patterns of Reform in Jean Gerson', *Medievalia et Humanistica*, new series, 1 (1970), 117.

[149] J. B. Morrall, *Gerson and the Great Schism* (Manchester, 1960), 80.

[150] A. Black, 'The Universities and the Council of Basle: Ecclesiology and Tactics', *Annuarium historiae conciliorum*, 6 (1974), 341, 345–6.

[151] For a discussion of the use of the term nominalism: W. J. Courtenay, 'Nominalism and Late Medieval Religion', in C. Trinkaus (ed.) with H. A. Oberman, *The Pursuit of Holiness in the Late Medieval and Renaissance Religion* (Leiden, 1974), 26–59.

ways of teaching in the faculties of arts and theology, the *via antiqua* and the *via moderna*.[152] There were, however, important differences within each system, depending on whether one followed the realism of Albertus Magnus, Thomas Aquinas, or Duns Scotus, or the nominalism of William of Ockham (regarded as the initiator of the nominalist school), John Buridan, or Marsilius of Inghen. By the middle of the fifteenth century the University of Padua had two chairs in theology, one according to the *via sancti Thomae*, occupied by a Dominican, and another following the *via Scoti*, occupied by a Franciscan.[153]

In Paris and in many German universities founded in the fifteenth century, the different teaching methods gave rise to conflicts between adherents to the different *viae*. In Prague, realism became connected with the national Czech party and an ecclesiastical reform movement, the leader of which was John Huss (d. 1415), who was influenced by the extreme realism of Wyclif. In 1409 the nominalists had to leave Prague, and many of them went to Leipzig, where a new university was founded. This accidental connection between realism and Hussite heresies, fortified at the Council of Constance, where the nominalist Peter of Ailly played an important part in condemning Huss, seems to have promoted nominalism in some European universities in the first half of the fifteenth century.[154]

When the Universities of Vienna, Heidelberg, and Cologne were founded, the scholars who had left Paris due to the Schism brought nominalism with them. In Cologne there was a reaction in 1415, when it was decided that the arts faculty should return to the teaching methods that had prevailed before the arrival of the Parisian masters.[155] In 1425, Count Louis III cautioned against realism on the ground that it could lead to heresies, as in Prague.[156] In Heidelberg Wyclifite errors were also invoked to stop realist teaching in 1412, but in 1452 the rector prohibited insult to either of the two *viae*, and proclaimed that the students were free to follow either way. From a document issued three years later, it is clear that the two *viae* had almost the status of two separate faculties, for it is stated that no student could transfer from one *via* to another without fulfilling the requirements of that other *via*.[157]

---

152 See A. Zimmermann (ed.), *Antiqui und Moderni*, Miscellanea Mediaevalia, 9 (Berlin/New York, 1974), especially N. W. Gilbert, 'Ockham, Wyclif, and the "via moderna" ', 85–125, and A. Gabriel, ' "Via antiqua" and "via moderna" and the Migration of Paris Students and Masters to the German Universities in the Fifteenth Century', 439–83. Also 'Ancients and Moderns: a Symposium', with papers by W. J. Courtenay, C. Trinkaus, and H. A. Oberman, and a comment by N. W. Gilbert, *Journal of the History of Ideas*, 48 (1987), 3–50.
153 P. O. Kristeller, *Le Thomisme et la Pensée italienne de la renaissance* (Montreal/Paris, 1967), 46.
154 Rashdall, *Universities*, vol. III, 214–33; P. De Vooght, *L'hérésie de Jean Huss* (Louvain, 1960).
155 G. Ritter, *Via antiqua und via moderna auf den deutschen Universitäten des XV. Jahrhunderts*, Studien zur Spätscholastik, 2 (Heidelberg, 1922), 42.
156 F. Ehrle, 'Der Sentenzkommentar Peters von Candia', *Franziskanische Studien*, 9 (1925), 282.
157 Winkelmann, *Urkundenbuch* (note 26), 165, 173f., 193.

In 1474 King Louis XI forbade the teaching of nominalism at Paris, and recommended the teaching of Aristotle and Averroës, Albertus Magnus, Thomas Aquinas, Giles of Rome, Alexander of Hales, Duns Scotus, Saint Bonaventure, and other realists, instead of the new doctors: William of Ockham, John of Mirecourt, Gregory of Rimini, John Buridan, Peter of Ailly, Marsilius of Inghen, Adam Wodeham (d. 1358), John Dorp, Albert of Saxony (d. 1390), and other nominalists. The nominalists wrote a document defending themselves, which is historically interesting, since it gives the main characteristics of realist and nominalist teachings and a survey of the persecutions of nominalism from the days of Ockham onwards. The ban was lifted in 1481.[158]

In the second half of the fifteenth century realism, especially its Thomistic species, became the prevailing way, starting in the Dominican convents in Germany, where the *Summa theologica* of Thomas Aquinas replaced Lombard's *Sentences* as a textbook. This innovation found its way into German universities and was also introduced somewhat later into Italian universities. Among the foremost representatives of this Thomist revival were John Capreolus (d. 1444), called *princeps Thomistarum*, who taught in France in the first half of the fifteenth century, and Thomas de Vio (Cardinal Cajetanus, d. 1534), who taught at Padua and Pavia at the turn of the century and wrote a commentary on the *Summa theologica*.[159] About the same time or a few decades later the system of two *viae* was abolished in many universities.

In the middle of the fourteenth century humanism and scholasticism coexisted peacefully in some universities. English Dominicans and Franciscans had an interest in classical literature, the French Cistercian Peter Ceffons quoted the classics in his commentary on the *Sentences* while defending logical subtleties, and Prague was a centre of humanism and nominalism.[160] At Tübingen, one of the latest continental universities to be founded in the fifteenth century, the humanist Henry Bebel (d. 1518), who taught poetics and rhetoric, dedicated poems to the ex-rector Gabriel Biel (d. 1495), who had himself been influenced by the nominalists Ockham, Peter of Ailly, and Gerson;[161] but scholastic theology was defeated when humanism became united with a movement calling for a return to the study of the Bible. When humanists like Lorenzo Valla (d. 1457) applied to the Bible textual criticism that had been developed for the study of the classics,[162] they came close to the conception of theology as an interpretation of the holy Scriptures with the help of the secular sciences, the view put forth by Saint Augustine in his *De doctrina christiana*.

---

[158] Ehrle, 'Sentenzkommentar' (note 156), 310–16; L. Thorndike, *University Records and Life in the Middle Ages* (New York, 1944), 355–60.

[159] Kristeller, *Thomisme* (note 153), 34, 36f., 53.

[160] B. Smalley, *English Friars and Antiquity in the Early Fourteenth Century* (Oxford, 1960); Trapp, 'Peter Ceffons' (note 136); Kaluza, *Thomas de Cracovie* (note 126), 55–7.

[161] H. A. Oberman, *The Harvest of Medieval Theology. Gabriel Biel and Late Medieval Nominalism* (Cambridge, Mass., 1963), 17.

[162] S. I. Camporeale, *Lorenzo Valla. Umanesimo e teologia* (Florence, 1972).

The faculty of theology

SELECT BIBLIOGRAPHY

Bazàn, B. C., Wippel, J. F., Fransen, G., and Jacquart, D. *Les Questions disputées et les questions quodlibétiques dans les facultés de théologie, de droit et de médecine*, Typologie des sources du Moyen Age occidental, ed. L. Genicot, fasc. 44–5, Turnhout, 1985.

Catto, J. I. 'Theology and theologians 1220–1320', in J. I. Catto (ed.), *The History of the University of Oxford*, Vol. I, *The Early Oxford Schools*, Oxford, 1984, 471–517.

Chenu, M.-D. *La Théologie comme science au XIIIé siècle*, Paris, 1957.

Courtenay, W. J. *Schools and Scholars in Fourteenth-century England*, Princeton, 1987.

Ehrle, F. *I più antichi statuti della facoltà teologica dell'università di Bologna*, Bologna, 1932.

de Ghellinck, J. *Le Mouvement théologique du XIIe siècle*, Bruges/Brussels, 1948; reprint, 1969.

Glorieux, P. 'L'enseignement au Moyen Age. Techniques et méthodes en usage à la Faculté de théologie de Paris au XIIIe siècle', *Archives d'histoire doctrinale et littéraire du Moyen Age*, 43 (1968), 65–186.

Landgraf, A. M. *Introduction à l'histoire de la littérature théologique de la scholastique naissante*, Montreal/Paris, 1973.

Leff, G. *Paris and Oxford Universities in the Thirteenth and Fourteenth Centuries*, New York, 1968.

Little, A. G. and Pelster, F. *Oxford Theology and Theologians* c. AD 1282–1302, Publications of Oxford Historical Society, 96, Oxford, 1934.

Paré, G., Brunet, A., and Tremblay, P. *La Renaissance du XIIe siècle. Les écoles et l'enseignement*, Paris/Ottawa, 1933.

Ritter, G. *Via antiqua und via moderna auf den deutschen Universitäten des XV. Jahrhunderts*, Studien zur Spätscholastik, 2, Heidelberg, 1922.

Schneyer, J. B. *Repertorium der lateinischen Sermones des Mittelalters für die Zeit von 1150–1350*, Beiträge zur Geschichte der Philosophie und Theologie des Mittelalters, 43:6, Münster, 1975.

Sheehan, M. W. 'The religious orders 1220–1370', in J. I. Catto (ed.), *The History of the University of Oxford*, vol. I, *The Early Oxford Schools*, Oxford, 1984, 193–224.

Smalley, B. 'The Bible in the Medieval Schools', in G. W. Lampe (ed.), *The Cambridge History of the Bible*, vol. II, Cambridge, 1969, 197–220.

Smalley, B. *The Study of the Bible in the Middle Ages*, Oxford, 1983.

Spicq, C. *Esquisse d'une histoire de l'exégèse latine au Moyen Age*, Paris, 1944.

Stegmüller, F. *Repertorium biblicum medii aevi*, vols. I–VII, Madrid, 1949–61.

Stegmüller, F. *Repertorium commentariorum in Sententias Petri Lombardi*, Würzburg, 1947.

Verger, J. 'L'exégèse de l'université', in P. Riché and G. Lobrichon (eds.), *Le Moyen Age et la Bible*, Paris, 1984, 199–232.

Zimmermann, A. (ed.) *Antiqui und Moderni*, Miscellanea Mediaevalia, 9, Berlin/New York, 1974.

Zumkeller, A. 'Die Augustinerschule des Mittelalters: Vertreter und Philosophisch-Theologische Lehre', *Analecta Augustiniana*, 27 (1964), 167–262.

EPILOGUE: THE RISE OF HUMANISM

WALTER RÜEGG

WALTER RÜEGG

THE EPOCHAL CONSCIOUSNESS OF HUMANISM

In his ground-breaking book, *Die Entstehung der Universitäten des Mittelalters bis 1400*, published in 1885, Denifle justified his closing date by saying that 'the fifteenth century everywhere witnessed the emergence of a new situation'.[1] Kaufmann in his 'prehistory' of the *Geschichte der deutschen Universitäten*,[2] which he dedicated to the University of Bologna for its jubilee of 1888, differed from Denifle and included the fifteenth century in the second volume, which dealt with the 'origin and development of the German universities up to the end of the Middle Ages'. Most historians agree that there is a dividing line somewhere around 1500. Some of them, particularly social historians and historians of science, see that dividing line as coming much later; they say that, until the 'scientific revolution' of the seventeenth century or the 'industrial revolution' of the eighteenth century, little change had occurred in social structure from what it had been in the Middle Ages.[3]

The introduction to volume II will treat this problem. Here, however, we are interested in the sense in which the fifteenth century 'witnessed the emergence of a new situation'. As the text, list, and maps of chapter 2 show, the universities continued, despite the deep economic, religious, and political crises which shook Europe between 1350 and 1450, to expand during the fifteenth century. Around 1500, universities also existed at the periphery in Uppsala, Aberdeen, Palma, and Cracow. Within the central areas from

---

[1] Denifle, *Entstehung*, xxvi.   [2] Kaufmann, *Deutsche Universitäten*, vol. I, xiff.
[3] E. R. Curtius, *Europäische Literatur und lateinisches Mittelalter* (Berne, 1954), 29–33; N. Hammerstein, 'Bildungsgeschichtliche Traditionszusammenhänge zwischen Mittelalter und früher Neuzeit', in *Der Übergang zur Neuzeit und die Wirkung von Traditionen. Vorträge, gehalten auf der Tagung der Joachim Jungius Gesellschaft der Wissenschaften, Hamburg 13. u. 14. Oktober 1977* (Göttingen, 1978), 32–6. On periodization: P. E. Hübinger, 'Spätantike und frühes Mittelalter, ein Problem historischer Periodenbildung (1952)', in P. E. Hübinger (ed.), *Zur Frage der Periodengrenze zwischen Altertum und Mittelalter* (Darmstadt, 1969), 145–64.

Louvain and Vienna to Ferrara and Alcalá, the map of the universities became dense. Yet the character of the universities did not change fundamentally during this time. The faculties continued to become diversified, theology was taken up in most universities. The salaries of the professors were increasingly paid by secular authorities and the universities were ever more subjected to the supervision of the municipal or princely authorities. None of those were new phenomena; they were rather accentuations of tendencies already at work in the thirteenth and fourteenth centuries. The same was true of the substance and methods of scholastic doctrine. These continued to develop and led to sharp controversies but they remained within the framework of scholastic philosophy and raised no questions of an epistemological nature or concerning ways of teaching scholastic philosophy.

Nevertheless, there was increasing competition from certain intellectual and educational tendencies which, since the nineteenth century, have been referred to as humanism. Like all such designations of 'isms', humanism is a party label. It was first used in 1808 by Niethammer, a philosopher and educationalist in the Bavarian government, in a polemic against an educational reform which aspired to establish practical training of the kind already being offered at the Philanthropinum in Dessau, for which he coined the term 'Philanthropinism',[4] claiming that it encouraged the animality of the child while humanism called forth its humanity. By humanism, Niethammer meant a curriculum based on liberal education and the teaching of language, which had dominated secondary education all over Europe since the fifteenth century and which, in expressions like *humaniora* (1617) or humanity (1484), humanities (1703), and *humanités* (1673),[5] could be traced back to the Ciceronian idea of the *studia humanitatis*.[6]

The latter term had been taken up in 1369 by Coluccio Salutati (1331–1406), the Florentine secretary of state and humanist;[7] it referred, like terms such as *studia humaniora*, to the goals of the new intellectual movement set in motion by Petrarch (1304–74) and to the content of the new academic disciplines. It is quite understandable, therefore, that historians designated this movement as humanism and that, after 1869, they referred to the entire epoch from 1350 to about 1550 by the new concept of 'humanism'.[8] In distinction from the term 'Renaissance', which began to be used at about the same time

---

[4] F. J. Niethammer, *Der Streit des Philantropinismus und des Humanismus in der Theorie des Erziehungs – Unterrichts unserer Zeit* (Jena, 1808); W. Rüegg, *Cicero und der Humanismus, formale Untersuchungen über Petrarca und Erasmus* (Zurich, 1946), 1ff.; E. Kessler, *Das Problem des frühen Humanismus* (Munich, 1968), 9.

[5] H. Schulz, *Deutsches Fremdwörterbuch* (Strasburg, 1913); *Oxford English Dictionary* (Oxford, 1971); E. Littré, *Dictionnaire de la langue française* (Paris, 1874), s.v.

[6] W. Rüegg, 'Prolegomena zu einer Theorie der humanistischen Bildung', *Gymnasium*, 92 (1985), 307–17.

[7] References in A. von Martin, *Coluccio Salutati und das humanistische Lebensideal, ein Kapitel aus der Genesis der Renaissance* (Leipzig, 1916), 106.

[8] See select bibliography.

to designate the epoch of the renewal of all aspects of life, 'humanism' was confined to educational and literary cultures.

What was new in humanism? According to ideas which are still widely current, humanism rediscovered the ancient authors, who, as representatives of pagan antiquity, had fallen into oblivion. According to this view, humanism helped the secular notions of the ancients to make their way against Christian religious sentiment and against the scholastic philosophy. Today, however, this view has been shown to be inadequate. Medieval studies have quite rightly reminded us of the point of shining light in the 'dark' ages and have shown that Charlemagne had already taken in hand the revival of classical forms of culture and thought. (This was the basis of the myth, mentioned in the first chapter, of the Carolingian foundation of the University of Paris.) The importance of the renewal of interest in classical works in the twelfth century has been established, and the concept of the Renaissance as well as that of humanism has been applied to works and activities of the early and high Middle Ages. Secular, and even pagan tendencies, can be seen as early as the thirteenth century, for example in the study of Aristotle in the universities. It has also been shown that typical humanists, from Petrarch to Erasmus, espoused religious views and that many of them were much influenced by scholasticism. We may therefore ask once more, what was new in humanism?

First of all, it was the common awareness of persons then living that a new epoch was opening in the course of which literature and art, which had slumbered in darkness for centuries, had awakened into a new life. Those who experienced this awareness called the 'dark' interval between the great migration and the fourteenth century the *medium aevum* or *media tempestas*, or the 'middle epoch'.[9] This was new. There were already writers in the twelfth century who thought of themselves as moderns – some superior to, others inferior to, the ancients. Nevertheless, they did not link the distinction between past and present with a consciousness of a historically demarcated epoch, any more than did Joachim of Floris (*c.* 1132–1202) with his three eschatologically defined ages of the world.[10]

THE QUEST FOR NEW SYMBOLS OF SECURITY

Petrarch and his successors did not designate the Middle Ages as dark ages because they were ignorant of their science and literature but because they could detect no 'light' there, no insights which would illuminate life, no

[9] J. Voss, *Das Mittelalter im historischen Denken Frankreichs. Untersuchungen zur Geschichte des Mittelalterbegriffes und der Mittelalterdeutung von der zweiten Hälfte des 16. bis zur Mitte des 19. Jahrhunderts* (Munich, 1972), 22ff.

[10] A. J. Gurevich, *Categories of Medieval Culture* (London, 1986), chs. 2 and 4.

words which could warm the human heart.[11] The rise of humanism occurred during a period of severe political and economic crises, the Great Schism, the Hundred Years War in the west, the decline of the imperial house and the conflict for supremacy among the various territorial powers in the Empire itself, in Burgundy, and in Italy, and the Turkish menace in the east. All these took place against the background of a cessation of economic growth, financial crises, famine, and, not least, the Black Death. The result was a deepened sense of existential menace. These disasters caused the age of humanism to be called 'the most psychically disturbed era in European history', an epoch marked by 'psychological shock', by the fear of death, and by the dance of death.[12]

The psychological insecurity was evidence of the fact that it was not only external conditions which were disturbed but that the crisis had penetrated into the understanding which individuals had of themselves and the world. The cliché of the dark Middle Ages is an expression of the preoccupation with crisis on the part of an urban service society, which, with the increasing importance of rationalized means of communication and exchange, had come into conflict with its traditional values. The day-to-day experiences of these urban classes, which became ever more powerful, were deprived of transcendental legitimization and were often contrary to the conceptions and norms professed by the church, as illustrated by the conflict between the growing importance of a money economy and the condemnation of usury by the church.[13] The main religious problem for the new urban ruling classes was to reconcile their mundane activities with the norms of the traditional transcendental order, while finding a form of religion that was no longer bound to the hierarchical structure of that order but which gave the social dimension an ethical meaning of its own. The humanists did not aim to emancipate men from the bonds of medieval religiosity and solidarity. Rather, it was their intention to overcome the religious and social crises by participating in the search for 'new symbols of security'.[14]

---

[11] Concerning the concept of the 'dark ages': T. E. Mommsen, 'Petrarch's Conception of the "Dark Ages" (1942)' in T. E. Mommsen, *Medieval and Renaissance Studies*, ed. E. F. Rice (Ithaca, N.Y., 1959), 106–29; E. Garin, 'Medio Evo e tempi bui: concetto e polemiche nella storia del pensiero dal XV al XVIII secolo', in V. Branca (ed.), *Concetto, Storia, Miti e Immagini del medio Evo* (Florence, 1973), 199–224. Concerning the symbolism of light: W. Rüegg, 'Die scholastische und die humanistische Bildung im Trecento (1960)', in W. Rüegg, *Anstösse, Aufsätze und Vorträge zur dialogischen Lebensform* (Frankfurt, 1973), 126.

[12] Lynn White Jr, 'Death and the Devil', in R. S. Kinsman (ed.), *The Darker Vision of the Renaissance*, UCLA Center for Medieval and Renaissance Studies Contributions, 6 (Berkeley/Los Angeles/London, 1974), 26; M. Hébert, 'La mort: impact réel et choc psychologique', in C. Sutto (ed.), *Le Sentiment de la mort au Moyen-Age, Etudes présentées au Cinquième colloque de l'Institut d'études médiévales de l'Université de Montréal* (Quebec, 1979), 10.

[13] B. Nelson, *The Ideal of Usury: From Tribal Brotherhood to Universal Otherhood* (Chicago, 1949; 2nd edn enlarged, 1969), 5, 28.

[14] Concerning search for new symbols of security: H. A. Oberman, 'The Shape of Late Medieval Thought: the Birthpangs of the Modern Era', in C. Trinkaus and H. Oberman (eds.), *The Pursuit of Holiness in Late Medieval and Renaissance Religion* (Leiden, 1974), 11.

The specifically humanistic search for such new symbolic configurations made *humanitas* itself the symbol of the human security which it sought. It is true that the questioning of the human condition and especially the discrepancy between the dignity of man made in the image of God and his miserable vulnerability to his earthly fate has a long tradition. This tradition was carried forward by the humanists with particular intensity.[15] Nevertheless, the humanity of the human being is a logical triviality and only makes sense if humanity is so much endangered that not only dignity or some other human value but humanity itself as a boundary value becomes the object of special endeavours in moral education.

Human beings are educated in interaction with other human beings in a given environment and in the intellectual reflection on familiar experiences transmitted orally. The psychological insecurity which characterized the epoch of humanism is evidence that traditional institutions could no longer form the person – whether because those professions which used rational and particularly written means of communication and exchange could find no appropriate models for human self-understanding in their own family traditions and their own milieu, or because the procedures of rational criticism, promoted by the universities, alienated traditional groups like the nobility from their own orally transmitted models.

The *studia humanitatis* replaced the missing or alienated family traditions of political and social experiences with the study of literary testimonies of alien humanity. They made the analysis of language into the most important part of the educational formation of a human being. Expressions such as *studia humanitatis*, *studia humaniora*, and *litterae humanitatis* conceive of these efforts as a cybernetic process: through his interaction with textual testimonies of alien *humanitas*, the individual human being gives form in language and forms his own *humanitas*. He educates himself thereby into a morally responsible human being who achieves autonomy through a mastery of language. The *studia humanitatis* were from the very beginning identical with the *eruditio moralis*. The humanists discovered in the classical Christian and pagan writers, such as Augustine and Cicero, Aristotle and Jerome, human models for their own moral education. They found in the dialogue with ancient authors a new security in the performance of their social roles. Unlike their medieval predecessors, they did not evaluate their books in relation to the Christian road to salvation, but treated them rather as human partners in a dialogue over time and space. Humanists of various standing, including the professor and later diplomat Vergerio (1370–1444), Saint Bernardino of Siena (1380–1444), the teacher Guarino da Verona (1374–1460), the statesman and political philosopher Machiavelli (1469–1527), and the cosmopolitan scholar Erasmus of Rotterdam (about 1466–1536), called books

---

[15] W. Kölmel, *Aspekte des Humanismus* (Münster, 1981), 187–8.

friends, to whom one could address questions and who could answer them, and in whose company one felt at ease, whose soul met one's own soul in reading, and who gave one strength.[16]

Philosophically, the humanists took the sophistic definition of man, which had been developed further by Isocrates and Cicero, as an entity distinguished from animals by the use of language. By the use of language man establishes social institutions, formulates values, and forms images of reality. Through language he also experiences the ineffable mystery of transcendence in the Word of God and he attempts to delineate it in poetry. Scholars in recent decades have established the affinity between various Italian humanists and scholastic nominalism, which placed language as a system of signs in this world and which gave prominence to the human will in comparison with the intellect.[17] For the humanists, language was both a result and a cause of relations and interactions in the process of the forming of the individual, and in his conduct in public life, between present and past, between man and nature, between man and God.

The humanists experienced this dialogic meaning of language in the ancient authors, Christian as well as pagan, to a greater extent than in scholastic writings. For this reason, they spoke of 'reanimation', of 'new flowering', not of antiquity but of poetry as the most inclusive term for the formation of human knowledge by language. In about 1360, Salutati ascribed to Petrarch the merit of having helped the grey and long-forgotten muses to regain a new youthfulness and of having caused the dry stream of poetry to flow once more. At about the same time, Boccaccio praised Dante because it was by him that the dead art of poetry was revived. It was the state of poetry which the Florentine historian Filipo Villani in about 1381 used as the criterion to define, for the first time, the temporal dimension of the interval between antiquity and the present. Villani said that, around 400 AD, poetry, as a consequence of the niggardliness and feebleness of the emperor and in part because of the negative attitude of the church, became senile and sank into a neglected and unrespected condition until Dante 'recalled it into the light of day from the abyss of darkness, reached out his hand to it and helped the recumbent figure to stand erect on its own feet'.[18] Around 1400, Florence was praised as the 'florescence' (*florentia*) because eloquence and culture were awakened simultaneously and called back from Hell.

---

[16] Evidence in W. Rüegg, 'Das antike Vorbild in Mittelalter und Renaissance (1953)', in Rüegg, *Anstösse* (note 11), 91–111, especially 106–8; W. Rüegg, 'Christliche Brüderlichkeit und humanistische Freundschaft (1976)', in W. Rüegg, *Bedrohte Lebensordnung, Studien zur humanistischen Soziologie* (Zurich/Munich, 1978), 107–24.

[17] K. O. Apel, 'Die Idee der Sprache in der Tradition des Humanismus von Dante bis Vico', *Archiv für Begriffsgeschichte*, 8 (1963), 12ff.; W. Kölmel, 'Scolasticus literator, Die Humanisten und ihr Verhältnis zur Scholastik', *Historisches Jahrbuch*, 93 (1973), 327–35; Oberman, 'Shape of the Late Medieval Thought' (note 14), 14.

[18] B. L. Ullman, 'Renaissance, the Word and the Underlying Concept (1952)', in B. L. Ullman, *Studies in the Italian Renaissance*, (Rome, 1955), 11–25.

It is true that, as a result of this attitude, the language of classical prose authors and, in particular, the Ciceronian style were often slavishly imitated, but it must also be recognized that many of the great humanists – from Salutati to Valla (1407–57) up to Erasmus – were strongly critical of the aping of the classical style. What was important was not the classical model of language but the concrete attitude and disposition which were embodied in it. Since, in it, Cicero said, every word has its meaning in the community in which it is placed, the moderns must express themselves differently from the ancients and can even be superior to them.[19] Thus, living persons in dialogue with the authors of antiquity could discover 'new symbols of security', and develop their own understanding of themselves and the world.

By comparing their own situation with the different historical situation depicted in the works they read, personalities, epochs, and symbolic forms of the past could be perceived in their own perspective. Antiques were no longer used merely as spoils for present use, but rather as elements for the symbolic reconstruction of past societies and epochs. In this sense, classical antiquity was 'rediscovered' as a distant historical epoch. At the same time the humanists tried to replace the mythical foundations of their own city or country by historical research into their sources. It has often been a cause of wonderment how the same humanists who promoted the cultivation of classical Latin could also be the most active champions of national literature and history. This source of bewilderment is the false identification of humanism with the pure imitation of antiquity. It was the dialogical perspective of the past that enabled both worlds to be recognized as entities in their own right.

THE HUMANISTIC MOVEMENT IN EDUCATION

Etienne Gilson, the great student of scholastic philosophy, spoke of the fifteenth and sixteenth centuries as the *aetas Ciceroniana*, which replaced the *aetas Aristotelica* of the thirteenth and fourteenth centuries. According to his argument, the philosophy which was represented by the name of Aristotle and which dominated scholasticism had to yield place to humanistic writings and, hence, to Cicero, *orator noster*. The centre of gravity of the image of the world and of human beings shifted from the nature of things to the nature of human beings, who as social beings, were defined by the use of language. One typically Ciceronian element in humanism was the definition of man as *homo loquens*. Accordingly, the *orator* was granted the highest position in the hierarchy of human beings and in the classification of types of knowledge. Instead of ranking them in accordance with the greater or lesser capacity to comprehend the real world, individuals and the various branches

---

[19] Rüegg, 'Scholastische und humanistische Bildung' (note 11), 112ff., 135.

of knowledge were classified by their value as instruments for the employment of words as the 'bonds and norms of societies'.[20]

Humanism first appeared outside the universities, and after a few generations it was assimilated by the main centres of society. For them, words, as the 'bonds and norms of societies', were parts of their daily experience. Among the most important humanists were to be found municipal, royal, and papal officials, notaries and teachers, aristocrats and kings, members of religious orders and princes of the church, bankers and wealthy merchants, and publishers and free-lance authors. They were, for the most part, university graduates, who carried on their humanistic studies alongside the practice of their professional and official duties.[21] Their studies found direct application in the more effective mastery of the spoken and written word in business, in politics, in the courts, in the chancelleries, and in diplomacy. It was said of the humanistic pen of the Florentine secretary of state, Salutati, that it did more damage to the enemy than a thousand cavalrymen.[22] More important, however, was the conviction that the acquisition of a moral education by the *studia humanitatis* enabled one to act responsibly as a member of one's family and one's society.[23]

No less important was the spiritually liberating effect of the *studia humanitatis*. They were regarded not as the opposite of Christian piety but as its complement. This was expressed in symbolic form by the humanistic Duke Federigo da Montefeltro (1422–82) in the three artistically arranged rooms in which he spent his leisure hours when he was at his *palazzo ducale* in Urbino: two small chapels next to each other and identical in size and shape were the foci of spiritual and emotional contemplation. One was for divine worship, the other for approaching the Muses. Directly over these two 'small sanctuaries' – *sacella* – was the study, the *studiolo*, of the duke. Still today, the duke is represented on panelled walls as the embodiment of human virtues in the midst of the symbols of the service of God and the Muses. On the walls above, the famous painting by Berruguete shows him with his son, in the midst of twenty-eight paintings depicting philosophers, poets, and scholars of antiquity, the Middle Ages, and his own times. They symbolize the intellectual society in which he could acquire the moral and political foundations of his *vita activa*.[24]

[20] E. Gilson, 'Le message de l'humanisme', in F. Simone (ed.), *Culture et politique en France à l'époque de l'Humanisme et de la Renaissance* (Turin, 1974), 4.

[21] C. Bec, *Les Marchands écrivains. Affaires et humanisme à Florence* (Paris/The Hague, 1967); P. Burke, *The Italian Renaissance. Culture and Society in Italy, 1420–1540* (Cambridge, 1986); L. Martines, *Power and Imagination, City-states in Renaissance Italy* (New York, 1979), 191–217 (ch. II, 'Humanism: a Program for Ruling Classes').

[22] F. Novati (ed.), *Epistolario di Coluccio Salutati*, vol. IV (Rome, 1905), 247ff., 514.

[23] M. B. Becker, 'Aspects of Lay Piety in Early Renaissance Florence', in Trinkaus and Oberman (eds.), *Pursuit of Holiness* (note 14), 177–99.

[24] W. Rüegg, 'Die befreiende Kraft der Studia humanitatis (1961)', and 'Der Humanist als Diener Gottes und der Musen (1967)', in Rüegg, *Anstösse* (note 11), 138–67, especially 149, 162ff.; P.

Even the militarily successful *condottiere* sought and found, in the dialogue of individuals with individuals of the past and present and of individual human beings with nature and the Word of God, 'new symbols of security'. Between the Scylla of traditional systems of concepts and values which were in contradiction with daily experiences and the Charybdis of the modern relativity of all values, the humanistic educational experience, of words as 'bonds and norms', led along a path of society culminating in the overcoming of the identity crises of the age. It did this through the provision of a scheme for interpreting the self and the world; it was a scheme with a bounded perspective, but the boundaries could be subjected to conscious reflection and thereby the scheme could be opened up to other perspectives.

Concepts and values as the forms in which definitions of the interpersonal situation are expressed became the objects of discursive dialogue. This was also manifested in the structure of argument. It was not intended primarily to analyse and evaluate, in a dialectical-logical way, various propositions and doctrines with a view to establishing their abstract truth. Rather the propositions and doctrines were regarded as assertions of individuals in historical situations, which were to be understood in the light of those situations and in confrontation with one's own situation. The effort to discover by textual comparison and criticism the most authentic form of these statements and to locate them historically was not a result of the work of academic scholars in universities. Salutati was the first of the humanists who practised textual criticism and historical research. His successor as the secretary of state of Florence, Leonardo Bruni (1370–1444), has been regarded as 'the first modern historian'.[25]

The continuous dialogue, whether explicit or implicit, with contemporary or historical figures influenced not only the type of argumentation. Works dealing with moral philosophy, pedagogy, politics, theology, and natural science also took the form of dialogues, letters, and speeches. From the fourteenth to the sixteenth centuries, they appeared alongside and indeed supplanted the genres of sentences, *summae*, and tractates. There were dialogues in which various conflicting standpoints or doctrines as well as personal experiences and reflections were presented by various proponents: letters recounting personal experiences and evaluative reflections arising from them were exchanged between individuals and often developed into collections of correspondence, which the humanists edited themselves. They also favoured the literary genre of speeches which were addressed to a more diffuse audience of listeners or a group of readers widely dispersed. These genres were not limited to the cognitive clarification of particular subject-matters or

Rotondi, *Il Palazzo Ducale di Urbino*, vol. I (Urbino, 1950) 357–82; W. Liebenwein, *Studiolo. Die Entstehung eines Raumtypes und seine Entwicklung bis um 1600* (Berlin, 1977), 83–99.
[25] B. L. Ullman, 'Leonardo Bruni and Humanistic Historiography (1946)', in Ullman, *Studies* (note 18), 322, 344.

topics. They introduced the affective, and even the dramatic, elements of social action as well.[26]

The humanistic idea of language also influenced the art of the Renaissance; it did so indirectly through the teaching of the *studia humanitatis*, which engendered a humanistic disposition (*habitus*) in the artist. (Panofsky has demonstrated something very much akin to this for the relationship between scholastic philosophy and Gothic architecture.)[27] A more direct connection between humanistic ideas and the art of the Renaissance may be seen in the application of rhetorical concepts in the theory and practice of art.[28]

The dialogic structure of the *studia humanitatis* found its realization in new, non-university institutions. In Florence, around the turn of the fifteenth century, citizens, clerics, and university teachers met regularly in private circles with Salutati in order to carry on learned discussions. In 1454, the first academy was established in the house of the humanist Rinuccini (1419–99); there, within a framework of fixed statutes and rules, citizens met for common readings and the interpretation of classical authors as well as for lectures and discussions about general scientific or scholarly topics. This form of regular learned dialogues between educated laymen soon spread. It was first reproduced in Ficino's 'Platonic academy', in Florence (1462), and subsequently reproduced in Rome, Naples, Venice, Ofen, Cracow, Heidelberg, Ingolstadt, Augsburg, and Vienna. It provided the stimulus for the learned societies and academies which, alongside the universities, spread all over Europe in the second half of the sixteenth century, and became some of the most important agents of the progress of science and scholarship in modern times.[29]

This early form of 'continuing education' in scientific and scholarly subjects had its complement in the efforts of the humanists to work out a pattern of secondary education as a preparation for study at the university as well as for political leadership and economic enterprise. They were also interested in physical training, education in mathematics and languages, humanistic general education, and education for the formation of moral character. From Salutati and Vergerio to Erasmus, Budé (1468–1540), and Vives (1492–1540), almost all outstanding humanists made recommendations for the reform of education, partly along the lines of Cicero, Quintilian, Plutarch, and Basilius, in letters or in full educational treatises, which they addressed to the political or ecclesiastical authorities. Vittorino da Feltre (1378–1446) and Guarino da Verona (1374–1460) created in country-houses successful models of humanistic

[26] C. Vasoli, 'The Renaissance Concept of Philosophy', in C. B. Schmitt and G. Steiner (eds.), *The Cambridge History of Renaissance Philosophy* (Cambridge, 1988), 57–74.

[27] See chapter 1, p. 28.

[28] G. Kaufmann, 'Sprache und Kunst in der Renaissance', *Wolfenbütteler Abhandlungen zur Renaissanceforschung*, 1 (1981), 237–65.

[29] T. Klaniczay, 'Celtis und die sodalitas litteraria per Germaniam', *Chloe, Beihefte zur Daphnis*, 6 (1987), 79–108.

educational communities. Through hostels, colleges, and *gymnasia* these models were as influential, if not more so, in the promotion of the spread of humanism north of the Alps as the humanists who were university teachers.[30]

Eloquentia together with *sapientia* constituted the elements of the morally responsible capacity to persuade by skill in the use of language. The importance of persuasion in the *vita activa* was expressed in the term *orator*, the title which those who cultivated the *studia humanitatis* in the fifteenth century gave themselves.[31] They often supplemented it with the title of *poeta*. Poetry for them was the broadest category of human knowledge and for that reason – despite Gilson's view – they regarded the *poeta*, and not the *orator*, as the highest representative of the *studia humanitatis*.[32] The laurel wreath of the poet, the *laurea*, was regarded as the highest honour by Italian or German humanists and it was mostly bound up with the right to teach in a university.[33]

THE ENTRY OF HUMANISM INTO THE UNIVERSITIES

The rise of the word 'humanist' was an indication that the *studia humanitatis* had found their own distinctive and recognized place in the universities. The word *humanista* appeared in an Italian letter of the rector of the University of Pisa in 1490, and as the Latin title for the incumbent of the new chair of *litterae humanitatis* at the University of Bologna in 1512. It was used analogously to the more common university designations such as *artista*, *legista*, *canonista*. From 1515 it was also used for persons who, outside the universities, represented the *studia humaniora*, like the famous printer and scholar Aldus Manutius (1450–1515) and Erasmus; it thus entered into common usage.[34]

This does not by any means show that it was only in the sixteenth century that humanism became established in the universities. The date when this occurred depends on what one means by humanism. If one understands it to mean only that classical authors, particularly poets, were taught in universities, then one must go back to the beginnings of the universities. At the University of Valencia in Spain, the term *auctorista* was used in 1220 alongside *teologus*, *decretista*, and *logicus*; the same usage appeared a century

---

[30] E. Garin, *L'educazione umanistica in Italia, testi scelti e illustrati* (Bari, 1949); E. Garin, *L'educazione in Europa: Problemi e programmi* (Bari, 1957); A. Grafton and L. Jardine, *From Humanism to the Humanities: Education and the Liberal Arts in Fifteenth and Sixteenth Century Europe* (London, 1986).

[31] G. Billanovich, 'Auctorista, humanista, orator', *Rivista di cultura classica e medioevale*, 7 (1965), 160ff.

[32] F. d'Episcopo, *Civiltà della parola*, vol. I, *Il Rinascimento, La rivolta della poesia* (Naples, 1984).

[33] E. H. Wilkins, 'The Coronation of Petrarch', *Speculum*, 18 (1943), 156–97.

[34] A. Campana, 'The Origins of the Word "Humanist"', *Journal of the Warburg and Courtauld Institutes*, 9 (1946), 60–73.

earlier in the monastery at Hirsau to designate the teacher of classical authors.[35]

If one understands by humanism the return to antiquity, then its beginnings are to be found at the University of Padua, which, in 1315, awarded to the poet Mussato the first poet's crown since ancient times; this was the laurel wreath. Therewith he acquired the right to teach. It was at the University of Padua that the lawyer Lovato Lovati (1241–1309) wrote poetry and also analysed the classical metrical forms and 'discovered' the tomb of the legendary founder of the city of Padua, the Trojan hero Antenor.[36] But one may also say that humanism began in the University of Bologna, where in 1321, Giovanni del Virgilio was appointed by the municipality as *auctorista*, with the task of lecturing on the 'great authors' of antiquity and on versification as well. His commentary on Ovid's *Metamorphoses* shows, however, that there can be no question of his having dealt with the text in the humanistic way, i.e. 'dialogically' in the sense understood on p. 447 ff.[37] In general – and this remains to be made more precise in its academic application – these and other *auctoristae* have been called 'proto-humanists'.

When and how such 'proto-humanists' became humanistic teachers belongs to the 'dark ages' of the history of universities. Giuseppe Billanovich, who is probably the greatest authority on this subject, has said that, 'in order to understand how Gothic Europe changed into humanistic Europe, it is necessary to reconstruct the physiognomies and voices of those old teachers, tracing their influence and their testimony by pursuing the meandering, toilsome but necessary road of research in archives and manuscripts'.[38]

Various reasons have been adduced to explain why humanism was assimilated or, as some scholars think, was initiated in the Italian universities a century sooner than it appeared in universities elsewhere. The lack of theological faculties in the Italian universities was considered helpful for the introduction of teaching about classical pagan authors. The emphases placed on legal studies and their practical significance for lay professions like the notarial one, the high prestige of Roman law, and not least the especially intensive training of students for written transactions in law and business through the *artes dictandi* together could have led to the situation in which the classical authors were introduced as models for the use of language in written intercourse. Italians could have become better acquainted with the classical authors who had been rediscovered in the French renaissance of the twelfth century when, during the exile of the popes in Avignon, they became more familiar with the achievements of French culture.

---

[35] Billanovich, 'Auctorista' (note 31), 148.

[36] R. Weiss, *The Renaissance Discovery of Classical Antiquity* (Oxford, 1969), 18ff.

[37] Text in F. Ghisalberti, 'Giovanni del Virgilio', *Giornale Dantesco*, 34 (1933), 3–110.

[38] G. Billanovich, 'Giovanni del Virgilio, Pietro da Moglio, Francesco da Fiano', *Italia medievale e umanistica*, 6 (1963), 203.

Yet these explanations do not elucidate the following facts: as we have seen, for the humanists, the church fathers and contemporary poetry were at least equally important with the classical authors. The *Divina Commedia* was no epistolary guide, any more than the *Confessions* of Saint Augustine. If humanism was caused by the emphasis placed on legal studies at Italian universities, it would have had to invade first the law faculty, which, in Italy, did not require a diploma from the arts faculty for admission. But humanism was able to break out of the faculty of arts only much later and only against very strong resistance from the faculty of law. It is also interesting to note that humanistic jurisprudence – as demonstrated in chapter 12 – was called *mos gallicus*, as a French phenomenon, which was contrasted with the *mos italicus*.[39]

Positivistic explanations always fall short of giving satisfaction. External circumstances at best provide conditions which are more favourable to new developments, as was the case with the weaknesses of the professional *collegia* in Italian universities, which enabled individual teachers, and outsiders too, to have greater influence on the formation of the curriculum. Conclusive knowledge can, however, be achieved only by carefully developing the material to be found in the sources. But, in so far as we can say anything on the basis of existing research, it was not the university teachers but former students of the university and the notarial schools at Bologna – Petrarch and Salutati, respectively – who first brought together classical texts in a systematic form and who interpreted them by the methods of philological and historical criticism.[40] Even though they themselves did not wish to be university teachers – Petrarch on personal grounds, Salutati because of his obligations as secretary of state – through their personal and epistolary connections, they none the less had an important influence in turning the professors of grammar and rhetoric at the universities of northern Italy to humanistic studies. Humanistic studies in these universities made such progress that, by 1415, according to Billanovich, 'Gothic Italy very soon became humanistic Italy'.[41]

Two examples can indicate, even if they do not explain, this gradual penetration of 'dialogic' humanism into the faculties of arts. Towards the end of the fourteenth century, a protégé of Salutati, Antonio Loschi, who became an official in Milan, wrote the first humanistic exposition of rhetoric. It had a direct influence on a former fellow student of Loschi, Gasparino Barzizza. Barzizza became well known as professor of grammar and rhetoric at Pavia (1403–7), and of rhetoric and moral philosophy at Padua (1407–21), and above all through his studies of Cicero. As a teacher, who later opened his

[39] Cf. p. 392.
[40] On Petrarch: G. Billanovich, *Petrarca letterato, I, Lo scrittoio del Petrarca* (Rome, 1947). On Salutati: B. L. Ullman. *The Humanism of Coluccio Salutati* (Padua, 1963), 95–114.
[41] Billanovich, 'Giovanni del Virgilio' (note 38), 322.

own private school, as a philologist, and as the author of various textbooks, as well as through his extensive correspondence, he – like many similar members of the ever denser network of participants in the humanistic dialogue – contributed to the establishment of humanism at the universities in his own generation and in the next one.[42]

The second example of the inclusion of humanism in the universities is the introduction of the study of Greek. This is often still attributed to the conquest of Constantinople by the Turks in 1453 and to the emigration of Greek scholars to Italy which immediately followed. Already in 1320, the Council of Vienna had decided to promote the study of Hebrew, Greek, Arabic, and Aramaic at the Universities of Paris, Oxford, Bologna, and Salamanca, in order to make missionary work more effective; but it had only sporadic effects and did not establish a regular study of Greek. Between 1360 and 1362, a Calabrian, Leoncino Pilato, taught Greek at the University of Florence, on Boccaccio's recommendation. But his teaching was so inadequate that no trace remains of it. It was a merit of Salutati that, after careful preparation – flattering letters, the sending of students, generous support by the authorities – he brought Chrysoloras, a highly educated Byzantine diplomat, to Florence for three years in 1397. He induced a number of talented students to study Greek so intensively that they later, like the already mentioned 'first modern historian', Leonardo Bruni, who translated Greek authors into Italian in the new humanistic way,[43] taught Greek in various universities and purchased, in the course of their travels, hundreds of Greek manuscripts. In this manner, Greek authors were already at home in the west before 1453.[44]

By the middle of the fifteenth century, the *studia humanitatis* were already firmly established in the faculties of arts in the Italian universities.[45] This was essentially a result of indirect and of direct external initiative, as the two examples cited indicate; they represent a general tendency. In many places, the leading strata were interested in forms of education which would permit them to perform their professional and official tasks more adequately and with enhanced legitimacy. They were also interested in having these new forms of education introduced into the universities,[46] and they were often willing to meet some of the costs of these innovations. For example, at the University of Florence in 1432, the humanist Filelfo was paid 224 Florentine guilders, *ad legendam rhetoricam et poesiam*, while his philosophical col-

---

[42] W. Rüegg, 'Cicero – Orator noster', in W. Ludwig (ed.), *Eloquence et rhétorique chez Cicéron*, Entretiens sur l'Antiquité classique, 28 (Vandoeuvres/Geneva, 1982), 283ff.

[43] H. Harth, 'Leonardo Brunis Selbstverständnis als Übersetzer', *Archiv für Kulturgeschichte*, 50 (1968), 41–63.

[44] R. Weiss, *Medieval and Humanist Greek* (Padua, 1977); Grafton and Jardine, *Humanism to Humanities* (note 30), 99–121.

[45] Grafton and Jardine, *Humanism to Humanities* (note 30), 62.

[46] Martines, *Power and Imagination* (note 21), 202ff.; however, the author does not see the significance of the psychological stabilization for the upper classes.

league received only 160 guilders, the teacher of civil law 130 guilders, and the teacher of medicine 150 guilders. The remuneration of the professors of Greek, Chrysoloras and, sixty years later, Argyropoulos, were even more princely: the former received 250 guilders and the latter 400 guilders.[47] Even if not all cities and rulers were at the same level as Florence, which was both rich and devoted to humanism, the humanists were not the poor devils which they were made out to be by many literary caricatures, showing them as unstable characters who had to flatter the rich in order to keep themselves alive. They often moved from one university to another or combined their professorship with a governmental post – arrangements for which we have more understanding nowadays than did our predecessors in the nineteenth century.

In the middle of the quattrocento, the *studia humanitatis* led to far-reaching reforms in certain disciplines within the faculties of arts at the universities, notably in grammar and rhetoric. These reforms required turning to the sources, although the famous battle-cry *Ad fontes* was not a creation of the humanists but of the historians of the nineteenth century. In certain universities they even penetrated into the third discipline of the *trivium*, dialectics, in which they pressed for a humanistic logic.[48] Poetics, history, and moral philosophy were added to the traditional disciplines, as may be inferred from the sketch drawn in 1444 for a classificatory scheme made for the library of Cosimo de Medici, by the later Pope Nicholas V.[49]

THE IMPACT OF HUMANISM ON THE BEGINNINGS OF THE MODERN UNIVERSITY

As the humanistic outlook acquired social recognition and, with it, establishment in university teaching, so the original humanistic polemic against scholastic philosophy was turned into a polemic between the faculties and between the humanists themselves. The issues at stake were primarily methodological ones, regarding the irrefutability of the ancient authorities as against the historical criticism of the sources, and ultimately about the epistemological status of linguistic configurations.

Lorenzo Valla was a teacher of rhetoric at Pavia from 1431 to 1436, then secretary of the humanistic King Alfonso of Aragon in Naples, and, finally, from 1447 until his death in 1457, in the service of the humanistic Pope Nicholas V and concurrently professor of rhetoric at the University of Rome. Through his programme to develop the logic of spoken discourse, *gram-*

---

[47] E. Garin, 'La concezione de l'Università in Italia nell'età del Rinascimento', in *Les Universités européennes du XIVe au XVIIIe siècle. Aspects et problèmes* (Geneva, 1967), 92.

[48] L. Jardine, 'Humanistic Logic', in Schmitt and Steiner (eds.), *Cambridge History* (note 26), 173–98.

[49] Text in P. O. Kristeller, *Renaissance Thought, the Classic, Scholastic and Humanist Strains* (New York, 1961), 162.

matice, by interpreting an author in terms of his understanding of language and his situation, he had a very far-flung influence. His method of historical criticism of texts permitted him to show in 1440 that the 'donation of Constantine', which had been used to legitimate the earthly power of the papacy, was a forgery. His annotations of the New Testament in 1444 were the first effort at historical exegesis of the Bible, which was then developed further by Erasmus. His *Elegantiae* – also produced in 1444 – in which he analysed the Latin language as a living expression of the changing self-understanding of human beings, with the purpose of laying the foundations for correct Latin usage, remained for centuries the most important textbook of Latin style. His *Dialecticae disputationes* – much like present work on this subject – attempted to erect logic on a foundation of the grammar of normal speech. This was then carried further by the major works of two followers, the Dutch humanist Rudolf Agricola, *De inventione dialectica*, and the French philosopher, Petrus Ramus (1515–72), whose influence spread to Germany, England, and then America.[50] It was already clear in the writings of Valla that the humanists, through their teaching in the *trivium*, could reach out beyond the disciplinary boundaries of the faculty of arts and could thereby come into conflict with the other faculties. As a result of such expansion, Valla had to flee from his professorship in Pavia because of the physical dangers arising from his violent persecution at the hands of the members of the faculty of law; in Rome he was protected from the attacks of the theologians only because he enjoyed the favour of the pope. But even less critical humanists could not avoid dealing with works in the natural sciences, law, and theology when they collected Latin and Greek works and attempted to establish their right textual form and therewith to interpret them. In their study of mathematics, they drew in part upon important, newly discovered, ancient sources.[51] The same was true of their work on astronomical and natural science texts, some of which were translated from the Greek for the first time; they made available for the first time in the west the complete text of Lucretius' atomic theory. These works became important in the development of the natural sciences. George of Peurbach (1423–61) who, as a *magister artium* of the University of Vienna, had studied from 1440 to 1450 in Ferrara, Bologna, and Padua, lectured on astronomy and on Latin authors in Vienna from 1454 onward. This joining of the 'two cultures' was self-evident for later humanists.[52]

In the Italian universities, the physicians, and *artistae* belonged to the same

[50] Grafton and Jardine, *Humanism to Humanities* (note 30), 71–8; P. O. Kristeller, *Acht Philosophen der italienischen Renaissance* (Weinheim, 1986), 17–31 (translation of P. O. Kristeller, *Eight Italian Philosophers of the Italian Renaissance*, Stanford, 1964). Cf. C. Vasoli, *La dialettica e la retorica dell'Umanesimo, 'Invenzione' e 'Metodo' nella cultura del XV et XVI secolo* (Milan, 1968).
[51] P. I. Rose, *The Italian Renaissance of Mathematics* (Geneva, 1975).
[52] M. Boas, *The Scientific Renaissance 1450–1630* (London, 1962), ch. 1.

faculty. Nevertheless, until 1500, as is shown in chapter 11, humanism had only an indirect influence on medical studies. In the sixteenth century this changed. One may speak of their influence as indirect because many physicians had received a humanistic education; many also carried on humanistic studies and, by means of translations and commentaries on the newly available medical writings, made ancient medicine known at a historical distance.[53] Niccolò Leoniceno (1428–1524) is a striking example. Until his death, he taught medicine, mathematics, and Greek philosophy at Ferrara for sixty years, and translated Galen and Hippocrates into Latin and Roman historians into Italian. By his application of the humanistic methods of textual criticism to medical works, he stirred up vehement academic controversies but his influence was felt far beyond Italy. Erasmus praised him as a humanistic renewer of medicine.[54]

More direct was the relationship between humanism and theology. The church fathers, and particularly Saint Augustine, were from the very beginning among the favourite authors of the humanists. The humanists edited their writings, wrote commentaries on them, and, if necessary, translated them. In their lectures and writings on moral philosophy, the humanists had repeatedly to deal with theological arguments; for example, Salutati dealt with existential questions during plagues with respect to divine providence and free-will. The critical treatments of the text of the New Testament by Valla and later by Erasmus were occasions for deeply penetrating theological discussions, which had long-lasting and profound repercussions on the attempts at ecclesiastical reform and on the Reformation.[55]

The relationship both to the law as such and to the practice of law was not an easy one. Many humanists had studied and practised law. Petrarch retained a deep repugnance for legal hair-splitting as a result of his own years as a law student. He preferred the simple moral laws of Cicero. In the first of many disputations about the ranking of the faculties, Salutati decided against medicine and for law on the ground that man is ennobled by law.[56] But his protégés Bruni and Poggio (1380–1459) condemned the lawyers, ridiculed the law, and praised medicine as a true science.[57] Many lawyers remained inter-

---

[53] G. Baader, 'Medizinische Theorie und Praxis zwischen Arabismus und Renaissance Humanismus', and A. Buck, 'Die Rezeption des Humanismus an der juristischen und medizinischen Fakultäten der italienischen Universitäten', in G. Keil, B. Moeller, and W. Trusen (eds.), *Der Humanismus und die oberen Fakultäten*, Mitteilung XIV der Kommission für Humanismusforschung (Weinheim, 1987), 185–213, 276ff. Cf. E. Schmitz and G. Keil (eds.), *Humanismus und Medizin*, Mitteilung XI der Kommission für Humanismusforschung (Weinheim, 1984).

[54] M. J. C. Lowry, 'Niccolò Leoniceno', in P. G. Bietenholz (ed.), *Contemporaries of Erasmus. A Biographical Register of the Renaissance and Reformation*, vol. II (Toronto, 1986), 323.

[55] H. Lutz, 'Humanismus und Reformation (1972)', in H. Lutz, *Politik, Kultur und Religion im Werdeprozess der frühen Neuzeit, Aufsätze und Vorträge* (Graz, 1984), 3–14; C. Trinkaus, 'The Religious Thought of the Italian Humanists and the Reformers: Anticipation or Autonomy?', in Trinkaus and Oberman (eds.), *Pursuit of Holiness* (note 14), 339–66.

[56] Cf. p. 28.   [57] A. Buck, 'Rezeption des Humanismus' (note 53), 270–9.

ested in humanistic topics and were on friendly terms with humanists. Nevertheless, as mentioned earlier, humanistic methods encountered bitter resistance in the Italian faculties of law. The humanistic principles of historical textual criticism were introduced into legal studies only in the sixteenth century, and then as *mos gallicus*, by an Italian professor of law, Alciatus (1492–1550). 'Legal humanism produced in the florescence of Italian humanism only forerunners and dispositions but scarcely results and performances.'[58]

THE EMERGENCE OF HUMANISM OUTSIDE ITALY

This last observation does not apply only to the reception of humanistic methods and the substance of humanistic thought in the university faculties. Aside from France, where humanism had an early flowering before the crisis of 1418, humanism, beyond the borders of Italy, expanded into the universities only after the middle of the fifteenth century, and it became enduringly established only after 1500. Nevertheless, it is worthwhile examining the details of some of its less successful precursors. To do so will permit us to perceive the social conditions under which the expansion of humanism spread. For the most part, its patrons and adherents were to be found among the secular and spiritual princes; then *iter italicum* brought the graduates and the texts of the *studia humanitatis* into courts, cities, and universities beyond the Alps. Finally, mostly on the initiative of the political authorities rather than that of the universities, humanists, at first mostly of Italian origin, began to be charged with the teaching of humanistic subjects in some faculties of arts or in colleges.

Petrarch engaged in an intimate correspondence with Charles IV (1316–87). In 1356, as the ambassador of the Visconti, he had sought out the emperor in Prague, whereupon Archbishop Arnost of Prague, Bishop Johann Ocko of Olmütz, and above all the imperial chancellor, Bishop Johann von Neumark, became his admirers and followers. This did not, however, last and it had no serious impact on the University of Prague, which had been founded by Charles in 1348. It was only in the sixteenth century that the University of Prague made a place for humanism.

The humanistic interest of the Hungarian king, Louis of Anjou (1322–82), had an indirect influence on the short-lived University of Pécs (1376 to *c.* 1440); the king corresponded with Petrarch and Salutati and he opened his chancery to the humanistic stylistic forms. Sermons at the University of Pécs

[58] H. E. Troje, 'Die Literatur des gemeinen Rechts unter dem Einfluss des Humanismus', in H. Coing (ed.), *Handbuch der Quellen und Literatur der neueren europäischen Privatrechtsgeschichte, Bd 2: Neuere Zeit (1500–1800)*, vol. I (Munich, 1977), 614; see also Buck, 'Rezeption des Humanismus' (note 53), 269–79; K. H. Burmeister, *Das Studium der Rechte im Zeitalter des Humanismus im deutschen Rechtsbereich* (Wiesbaden, 1974), 26f. 151–60; E. Meuthen, *Kölner Universitätsgeschichte*, vol. I, *Die alte Universität* (Cologne/Vienna, 1988), 215ff.

contain humanistic ideas and passages. It is still uncertain how much the graduates of this university, who increasingly came from the lower nobility, from the bourgeoisie, and even from the less prosperous peasants, and who sought to follow secular careers, contributed to the diffusion of humanistic ideas. In any case, King Louis laid the foundation on which humanists of ensuing generations could build.[59] Sigismund (1368–1437), king of Hungary, Bohemia, and Germany, and later emperor, brought Piero Paolo Vergerio (1370–1444), who was the author of the first humanistic educational tract, from the Council at Constance to Ofen. Vergerio was active at the court up to the very end of his life, as an inspirer and educator of the first Hungarian humanists, including the later archbishop of Gran, Johannes Vitez (c. 1400–72). Hungarian humanism was an affair of the court. Vitez was a teacher of and chancellor to the humanistic king, Matthias Corvinus (1440–90); his nephew, Janus Pannonius (1434–72), whom he sent to Guarino and who may be regarded as the greatest Hungarian humanist, was Matthias's vice-chancellor. The *studia humanitatis* were cultivated above all in learned circles, the first of which began in 1440 in Vitez's house, followed in 1470 by Matthias in his court, and in 1497 by the *contubernium* in Buda of the *sodalitas literaria Danubiana*. There, Italian humanists and intellectuals from all over central Europe met; these 'academies' formed real centres for the diffusion of humanism in Hungary, Bohemia, and Poland. They had their counterpart in the humanistic libraries. Vitez created the first significant library of central Europe at his episcopal court in Grosswardein, while Matthias built up the largest and most splendid library outside Rome, namely the *Biblioteca Corvina*. Of the various short-lived Hungarian universities of the fifteenth century, only the University of Pozsony, founded by Matthias and existing between 1465 and 1492, showed any trace of humanistic influence.[60]

The humanistic interests of the higher prelates had a much more far-reaching influence in every respect on the University of Cracow, which was re-established in 1400. The forerunner was Cardinal Olesnicky, who was archbishop of Cracow from 1423 until his death in 1455; he participated in a very lively correspondence with Italian humanists. Humanism entered the University of Cracow in 1439 when Gregory of Sanok, following his studies at Cracow and in Italy, began to deliver humanistic lectures. They met with

---

[59] E. Kovacs, 'Die Gründung der Universität Pecs und ihre Bedeutung für die ungarische Kultur', in *Universités Européennes* (note 47), 42–7.

[60] T. Klaniczay, E. Kushner, and A. Stegmann (eds.), *L'Epoque de la Renaissance 1400–1600*, vol. I, *L'Avènement de l'esprit nouveau (1400–1480)* (Budapest, 1988), 135; T. Klaniczay, *Mattia Corvino e l'umanesimo italiano*, Accademia Nazionale dei Lincei, anno CCCLXXI – 1974, Quad. N.202 (Rome, 1974); T. Klaniczay, 'Le mouvement académique à la Renaissance et le cas de la Hongrie', *Hungarian Studies* 2:1 (1986), 13–34; T. Klaniczay, 'Das Contubernium des Johannes Vitéz, Die ersten ungarische "Akademie"', in K. Benda, T. von Beggay, H. Glass, and K. Lengyel (eds.), *Forschungen über Siebenbürgen und seine Nachbarn, Festschrift für A. T. Szabo und Z. Jako* (Munich, 1988), 227–43.

such great interest that, in 1449, a professorship of poetry and rhetoric was created. In 1440, Gregory followed Vitez to Hungary; and until 1450 he participated as tutor of the sons of Hunyadi at Vitez's humanistic *contubernium*. Afterwards he returned to Poland in 1451, was elevated to the archbishopric of Lemberg by Olesnicky, and made his residence into a centre of humanistic culture in Poland. The Italian humanist, Callimachus Experiens, took refuge there before he became, in Cracow, a tutor of the royal princes in 1472 and then secretary of the king; he stood in a close relationship with the university. The university soon became recognized as a centre for astronomy; after 1450, many leading Cracow astronomers went to Italy to acquire a doctorate in medicine and to train themselves further in the *studia humanitatis*. Copernicus, who studied *artes* in Cracow from 1491 to 1495, was the most important of the beneficiaries of the humanistic combination of mathematical and astronomical sciences with philological criticism. The humanistic courses of study at Cracow, which included Greek from 1499 onwards, attracted many students from central Europe and as far west as Switzerland.[61]

The true 'apostle of humanism' in the empire was Aeneas Sylvius, later Pope Pius II,[62] who, in connection with his role at the Council of Basle, was appointed to the imperial chancellery in Vienna in 1442 and remained in the service of Frederick III until 1455. At first he criticized the University of Vienna for its neglect of letters, poetics, music, and arithmetic in favour of dialectics;[63] he regarded it as more important to attract young princes to humanistic studies. Later, he exercised his right as *poeta laureatus* to deliver humanistic lectures. Following his example, such lectures were held regularly – although with interruptions – from 1450 onwards. In 1454 the astronomer, George of Peurbach, taught Latin classics, and his pupil and friend, Regiomontanus, did the same in 1461. After the decline of the university in the 1480s, Emperor Maximilian I, supported by Perger, the humanistic superintendent of the university, exerted himself to bring about a humanistic reform of the latter against the resistance of the scholastically dominated arts faculty. Humanism acquired a firm position in the University of Vienna only in 1497, when the emperor appointed the German 'arch-humanist', Conrad Celtis, to a newly established professorship for poetics and rhetoric. When the faculty would not swallow its pride, he created a separate educational centre alongside the faculty, namely, the *Collegium poetarum et mathematicorum*; the *Collegium* enjoyed the privilege of the coronation of poets which conferred the teaching qualification, i.e. the *venia legendi*.[64]

[61] L. Hajdukiewicz and M. Karas, *Die Jagellonen-Universität, Tradition – Gegenwart – Perspektiven* (Cracow, 1977), 26–34; M. Markowski, 'Astronomie an der Krakauer Universität im XV. Jahrhundert', in *Universities in the Late Middle Ages*, 267.

[62] G. Voigt and M. Lehnerdt, *Die Wiederbelebung des classischen Alterthums oder das erste Jahrhundert des Humanismus*, vol. II, 3rd edn (Berlin, 1893), 277.

[63] Enea Silvio Piccolomini, *Epistolae*, vol. I, ed. R. Wolkan, (Vienna, 1909), 81ff.

[64] A. Lhotsky, *Die Wiener Artistenfakultät 1365–1497* (Vienna, 1965).

In other parts of the Empire, too, where the reception of humanism has been well investigated,[65] it was primarily ecclesiastical and secular princes, like the bishop of Worms and chancellor of the University of Heidelberg, Johann von Dahlberg (1455–1503), who encouraged and supported humanistic learning in their palaces and universities – in part, personally as patrons of centres of humanistic *sodalitates* and, in part, through their counsellors and officials, who had been humanistically trained in Italy. But humanism was also well received in the cities, which were gaining in collective self-consciousness. This reception was partly the achievement of influential individuals like Albrecht von Eyb (1420–75), head of the cathedral at Bamberg and Eichstätt, Sigismund Gossenbrot, mayor of Augsburg in 1458, or Hans Pirckheimer, the Nuremberg patrician who, with Eyb in Bologna in 1448, had been introduced to the *studia humanitatis*; his collection of humanistic manuscripts is now in the British Museum. His son Johannes and his nephew Willibald, who was a member of the municipal council of Nuremberg (1498), were also very active as humanists. The *studia humanitatis* were given an institutional position in municipal schools; some of these, like the schools at Rottweil, Münster, and Schlettstadt, became genuine forcing-houses of humanism. Basle, through the joint activities of schools, the university, and publishing houses, developed into a centre of humanistic culture, prominent and influential throughout Europe.

'Itinerant humanists', both Italian and German, who had studied in Italy were the first representatives of humanism in the German universities. They taught mainly outside the programme of the faculties, on the basis of invitations by the territorial sovereign. Luder was a good example of the situation. Although he had no university degree, he was the first person to deliver humanistic lectures in German universities. Between 1456 and 1470, Luder offered a new programme of humanistic teaching in Heidelberg, Erfurt, Leipzig, Basle and Vienna. He did this in two senses: as an outsider he had to make propaganda for his lectures by means of special publicity.[66]

Not only were the humanists imposed on the faculties of arts, they were often paid on a princely scale; their remuneration exceeded by far the ordinary salary of a *magister*.[67] The municipal universities made efforts to

---

[65] H. O. Burger, *Renaissance, Humanismus, Reformation, Deutsche Literatur im europäischen Kontext* (Bad Homburg/Berlin/Zurich, 1969); L. W. Spitz, 'The Course of German Humanism', in H. A. Oberman (ed.), with T. A. Brady, *Iter Italicum, the Profile of the Italian Renaissance in the Mirror of the European Transformation* (Leiden, 1975), 371–436; E. Meuthen, 'Charakter und Tendenzen des deutschen Humanismus', in H. Angermeier (ed.), *Säkulare Aspekte der Reformationszeit*, Schriften des Historischen Kollegs, Kolloquien 3 (Munich/Vienna, 1983), 217–66.

[66] L. Bertalot, 'Humanistische Vorlesungsankündigungen in Deutschland im 15. Jahrhundert (1915)', in L. Bertalot *Studien zum italienischen und deutschen Humanismus*, vol. I, ed. P. O. Kristeller, (Rome, 1975), 219–27.

[67] L. Boehm, 'Humanistische Bildungsbewegung und mittelalterliche Universitätsverfassung, Aspekte zur frühneuzeitlichen Reformgeschichte der deutschen Universitäten', in *Universities*

provide humanistic teaching. Basle established its first salaried post in *arte humanitatis sive oratoria* in 1464. Similar efforts were made in Cologne, it was only in 1515 that it came to be regarded as a fortress of scholasticism and hence the object of humanistic polemics. Taken as a whole, tendencies towards humanistic teaching existed in most German universities before 1500. Nevertheless, it was only after 1516 that the structures of the universities, first of all in Wittenberg, were reformed in a humanistic direction.[68]

In England, too, humanism was at first a private affair of princes who, through their diplomatic missions, were impressed by Italian humanists. Thus, the bishop of Winchester and later cardinal of England, Henry Beaufort, engaged the services of the famous humanist Poggio Bracciolini at the Council of Constance. But he did not do much for the *humaniora* during Poggio's sojourn in London from 1418 to 1423. The situation was rather different in the case of his rival, the regent of the English crown, Duke Humphrey of Gloucester (1391–1447). He was not only an interested and generous patron of Italian humanists, some of whom he took into his service and others of whom dedicated their translations and essays to him. He also assembled a valuable humanistic library, parts of which now form the basis of the Bodleian Library in Oxford. His example was emulated by other English aristocrats, who collected humanistic books and gathered learned humanists around themselves. A generation later, it was the *iter italicum* which introduced members of the aristocracy, as well as those who later became tutors and officials, to the *studia humanitatis*. These were given institutional status as prerequisites for other studies at the end of the fifteenth century by certain colleges, for example, Magdalen College, Oxford, in 1480. Humanistic studies, however, really penetrated into the universities only in the sixteenth century.[69]

Humanism was even more an affair of the court in the Iberian peninsula. King John II of Castile and León (1405–54) had very close relationships with Italian humanists. Alfonso, V, king of Aragon, Catalonia, and Naples (1396–1458), surrounded himself with a genuinely humanistic court. Later Italian humanists at the Portuguese court led the efforts to make the new discoveries known in Latin. After 1464, other Italian humanists were appointed to the professorships of astrology and poetics at the University of Salamanca. The *studia humanitatis* set down deep roots in Salamanca at the end of the century through the activities of two scholars who had studied in Italy; these were the Latinist, Antonio de Nebrija (1444–1522), and Aires Barbosa, who

of the Late Middle Ages, 329–41; O. Herding, 'Pädagogik, Politik, Geschichte', in *L'Humanisme allemand (1480–1540): XVIIIe Colloque international de Tours* (Munich/Paris, 1979), 114–16.
68 Meuthen, *Kölner Universitätsgeschichte* (note 58), 204–9.
69 W. E. Pantin, 'The Conception of the Universities in England in the Period of the Renaissance', in *Universités européennes* (note 47), 101–13; D. Hay, 'England and the Humanities in the Fifteenth Century', in Oberman (ed.), with Brady, *Iter Italicum* (note 65), 305–67.

was appointed to the first professorship of Greek in 1495. The University of Alcalá, which was founded in 1499 through the efforts of the humanistic Cardinal Ximenes, opened its doors only in 1508. In Portugal, too, humanism became established only during the sixteenth century.[70]

Ever since Petrarch, who called a Dutch friend 'his Socrates', there had been in the Netherlands scattered individual intellectuals interested in humanism. Nevertheless, one may speak of a reception of humanism in the Netherlands only after 1465. Its reception occurred primarily in schools like the one in Deventer under Alexander Hegius (1483–98) and in learned circles like the 'academy' of Adwerth, which was a monastery near Groningen, to which the important humanists, Wessel Gansfort (1419–85) and Rudolf Agricola (1443–85), belonged in the years around 1470. It is significant that Gansfort and Agricola first taught at universities outside the Netherlands, the former at Paris, where Agricola and Reuchlin were among his students, the latter at Ferrara and Heidelberg. It is true that, in Louvain, there was a professorship for poetics in the law faculty in 1477–8 and that, in the faculty of arts, a professorship for rhetoric had existed since 1444. Nevertheless, the incumbents of these chairs were primarily interested in mathematics and law. It was only with the establishment of the *Collegium trilingue* in 1517 that the efflorescence of humanism in Louvain began.[71]

In France, humanism developed at first mostly in close association with Italian humanism. The papal court at Avignon, which fostered contacts between Italian and French intellectuals, contributed to this. The high officials of the papal and royal chancelleries, like Jean de Montreuil (1354–1418) and Nicolas de Clamanges (1365–1437), gave currency to the humanistic ideas of their Italian colleagues. Both had become acquainted with the Latin classics at the Collège de Navarre in Paris. Nicolas, before he took up his new duties as apostolic secretary, gave lectures on those subjects at the collège de Navarre; in 1393 he was elected rector of the university. In addition to these two, there was a third former pupil of the Collège de Navarre, the eminent theologian, preacher, and ecclesiastical politician, Gerson (1363–1429), who was chancellor of the University of Paris from 1396 and its most influential representative at the Council of Constance. Together with Clamanges and Montreuil, Gerson may be regarded as the founder of the first generation of French humanism.

With the dissolution of many of the colleges in 1418, humanism suffered a

[70] F. Rico, 'Nebrija, Aires Barbosa et l'humanisme de leur temps'; A. da Costa Ramalho, 'Quelques aspects de l'introduction de l'humanisme au Portugal'; L. de Matos, 'L'expansion portugaise dans la littérature latine de la Renaissance'; and L. de Albuquerque, 'Science et l'humanisme dans la Renaissance portugaise', in *L'Humanisme portugais et l'Europe. Actes du XXIe Colloque international d'études humanistes, Tours 3–13 juillet 1978* (Paris, 1984), 245–6, 33–49, 402–6, 419–35.
[71] J. IJsewijn, 'The Coming of Humanism in the Low Countries', in Oberman (ed.), with Brady, *Iter Italicum* (note 65), 193–301, especially 203, 230, 235, 276.

severe reverse. It is true that later on the English regent, Humphrey of Gloucester, gave a stimulus to humanistic studies not only in Paris but also at the University of Caen, which had been founded by the English king. In Aix, Angers, and Avignon, the *studia humanitatis* were cultivated in the context of relations with Italy. After 1440, former pupils of the Collegè de Navarre also lectured on humanistic subjects. But it was only after the reform of the faculty of arts at the University of Paris from 1452 onwards that there was a genuine upsurge of humanism. It was not only the arrival of Italian humanists of high standing in Paris which opened the new phase of humanism in France. In 1453, Guillaume Fichet (1433–c. 1480) began an influential career as a humanistic teacher at the Collège de la Sorbonne. In 1470, together with his colleague Heynlin, he established a printing-press at the Sorbonne which was the first in France to print humanistic texts. However, they both left Paris in 1473. It was only a decade later that a Christian and nationally oriented humanism became established, thanks to a pupil of Fichet, the general of the Trinitarian order, Robert Gaguin (c. 1433–1502); he counted among his pupils Erasmus of Rotterdam. Lefèvre d'Etaples (1455–1536) continued this tradition with the zeal of the Reformation. Taken as a whole, humanism in the fifteenth century played a relatively modest part in the French universities. The *studia humanitatis* offered only optional lectures, and teaching was confined to individual colleges. Humanistic reforms occurred only in the sixteenth century, and even then as a result of much strenuous exertion.[72]

BOOK-PUBLISHING AS THE ALLY OF HUMANISM

Fichet's foundation of a printing-press at the Sorbonne shows what importance humanism attached to the printing of books. But, in the fifteenth century, we find only precursors of this development, which in the sixteenth century became a significant feature of universities. It is true that Gutenberg's invention of printing by the use of separately cast and combinable characters was not driven by humanistic motives. The famous 42-line Bible was the first product of Gutenberg's press and it appeared in 1455. Almost half of the nearly 30,000 incunabula titles printed before 1501 were editions of the Bible, liturgical works, breviaries, and other religious writings; nearly 30 per cent were literary works of antiquity, the earlier Middle Ages, and contemporary times; 10 per cent were legal and natural scientific works.[73]

The printing of books served the objectives of humanism in two ways. First, the humanists, as we have seen, met other persons through books and for that reason they were driven by the desire to possess as many books as possible. This demand was met by copying offices like that of the Florentine Vespasiano de Bisticci (1421–98), which produced expensive de luxe editions.

[72] *Universités en France*, 131–3; D. Cecchetti, *Il primo umanesimo francese* (Turin, 1987).
[73] L. Febvre and H. -J. Martin, *L'Apparition du livre* (Paris, 1971), 351.

The printing of books permitted the less propertied humanists to build up their own libraries. The qualitative aspect was as important as the quantitative one. Salutati noted with regret in 1400 that the critical improvement of the flawed traditional texts, which he had inaugurated through systematic comparison of manuscripts, was a wasted labour of love because every copyist made new mistakes. With the coming of the printed book, the critically edited text could be reproduced in as many copies as desired. This presupposed, of course, special care in the setting of type.

The printing business expanded very rapidly, since it led to a speedy growth of fortunes. It developed outside the guilds and their norms of quality. It was easier to become a printer than to become a baker, Erasmus said contemptuously. Alongside the innumerable producers of mass products, there appeared, as a result of the humanists' efforts to obtain authentic texts, printers who themselves had been trained as scholars and who collaborated closely with learned men. A typical example of this type of printer was Aldus Manutius, who had gone through and taught the *studia humanitatis*, including Greek – particularly in Rome and Ferrara – and who, when he was forty years of age, founded a printing office in Venice in 1490. In order to publish Greek classics correctly, he surrounded himself with a circle of learned friends who were Greeks and teachers of Greek. This circle acquired the name and statute of a 'new academy', *Neakademias nomos.*[74]

Manutius and, above all, his collaborator Erasmus of Rotterdam were examples of the significance which the printing of books had for the development of humanism outside the universities. Erasmus was the first free-lance writer of the Occident who lived only for and from his publications; he rejected various invitations to become a university teacher or a high ecclesiastical official. His influence as the most significant representative and propagator of Christian humanism, and as a forerunner of the Protestant Reformation and the Catholic reforms of the sixteenth century, was a result not only of his extended correspondence but of his role in the printing of books and in the book trade. He worked directly at the proof-reading table, first with Aldus Manutius and then later with Johannes and Hieronymus Froben in Basle, where he read the proofs of his latest work while at the same time he was busy writing another one. He sold his own humanistic output, which included more than 160 works and which were distinguished by the fact that he was one of the first to receive royalties, and by his combination of personal attention to the design of his books by artists like Urs Graf and Hans Holbein with advertising and distributing them. He praised the art of book-printing as the highest of all

---

[74] M. Lowry, *The World of Aldus Manutius. Business and Scholarship in Renaissance Venice* (Oxford, 1979), 8, 196.

arts because it permitted a continuous dialogue with the most educated and most pious men of all time.[75]

Book-printing had far-reaching consequences for university teaching. Teaching in the Middle Ages was dominated by the spoken word in lectures and in disputations, as well as by the ideas which were presented and elaborated in those oral forms. When the ordinary student began to buy books, the written word became dominant in university teaching. Not only were the sources made more immediately and more comprehensively accessible, but commentaries, textbooks, and polemics ceased to be monopolized by teachers and could be purchased in the market. Thus, diverse views and new insights could speedily become objects of intensive discussions and of individual debates within the larger scientific community. It was not only the physical universe which expanded so vastly by the end of the fifteenth century. Thanks to humanism and its connection with book-printing, the world of knowledge and ideas in the universities expanded in all its historical depths and its diverse manifestations to an extent which could only be fully developed in subsequent centuries.

Humanism is a phenomenon of the transition from the Middle Ages to modern times. Humanism, especially in the universities, was built on medieval foundations. The emphasis which the humanists laid on the differences between themselves and medieval intellectual methods and beliefs shows how deep the medieval imprint was on them; they felt themselves nearly overwhelmed by it and found it very difficult to go their own way, especially in the universities. In so far as they placed at the centre of their intellectual interests the understanding which human beings have of themselves and the world, and the social activities of human beings as potential sources of conflict, they opened up a new epoch in the history of universities. In this new epoch, human experience and its translation in verbal and mathematical form became the task of the 'scientific revolution' – or, more precisely expressed, the substantive extension, empirical deepening, methodological reformation, and conceptual systematization of the results of scientific and scholarly research and their communication through teaching.

[75] W. Rüegg, 'Erasmus von Rotterdam', in S. Corsten, G. Pflug, and F. A. Schmidt-Kunsemüller (eds.), *Lexikon de gesamten Buchwesens*, vol. II (Stuttgart, 1989), 476–7.

SELECT BIBLIOGRAPHY

Baron, H. *The Crisis of Early Italian Renaissance, Civic Humanism and Republican Liberty in an Age of Classicism and Tyranny*, 2 vols., Princeton, 1955; revised one-volume edition with an epilogue, Princeton, 1966.

Baron, H. *In Search of Florentine Civic Humanism, Essays on the Transition from Medieval to Renaissance Thought*, 2 vols., Princeton, 1988.

Baxandall, M. *Giotto and the Orators, Humanist Observers of Painting in Italy and the Discovery of Pictorial Composition*, Oxford, 1971.

Bibliographie internationale de l'Humanisme et de la Renaissance (Geneva), 1 (1969), and subsequent annual volumes.

Buck, A. *Humanismus, seine europäische Entwicklung in Dokumenten und Darstellungen*, Freiburg/Munich, 1987.

Cochrane, R. *Historians and Historiography in the Italian Renaissance*, Chicago, 1982.

Garin, E. *La cultura filosofica del Rinascimento italiano*, Florence, 1961; 2nd edn, 1979.

Garin, E. *La disputa delle arti nel Quattrocento*, Florence, 1947.

Garin, E. *Der italienische Humanismus*, Berne, 1947.

Grafton, A. and Jardine, L. *From Humanism to the Humanities, Education and the Liberal Arts in Fifteenth and Sixteenth Century Europe*, London, 1986.

Kohl, B. J. *Renaissance Humanism, 1300–1550. A Bibliography of Materials in English*, New York/London, 1985.

Kristeller, P. O. 'The Curriculum of the Italian Universities from the Middle Ages to the Renaissance', *Proceedings of the Patristic, Mediaeval and Renaissance Conference*, 7 (1984), 1–15.

Kristeller, P. O. 'Humanism and Scholasticism in the Italian Renaissance (1944–45)', in P. O. Kristeller, *Studies in Renaissance Thought and Letters*, Rome, 1956.

Kristeller, P. O. 'Humanism', in C. B. Schmitt and G. Steiner, (eds.), *The Cambridge History of Renaissance Philosophy*, Cambridge, 1988, 113–37.

Martines, L. *Power and Imagination, City-states in Renaissance Italy*, New York, 1979.

Mitteilungen der Senatskommission für Humanismusforschung der DFG Deutsche Forschungsgemeinschaft, vol. XI, *Humanismus und Medizin*, ed. E. Schmitz and G. Keil, Weinheim, 1984; vol. XII, *Humanismus im Bildungswesen des 15. und 16. Jahrhunderts*, ed. W. Reinhard, Weinheim, 1984, vol. XIV, *Der Humanismus und die oberen Fakultäten*, ed. G. Keil, B. Moeller, and W. Trusen, Weinheim, 1987.

Müller, G. *Mensch und Bildung im italienischen Renaissance – Humanismus, Vittorino da Feltre und das humanistische Erziehungsdenken*, Baden-Baden, 1984.

Schmitt, C. B. and Steiner, G. (eds.) *The Cambridge History of Renaissance Philosophy*, Cambridge, 1988.

Trinkaus, C. 'Humanism', in *Encyclopedia of World Art*, vol. VI, New York, 1962, 702–43.

Trinkaus, C. and Oberman, H. A. (eds.) *The Pursuit of Holiness in Late Medieval and Renaissance Religion. Papers from the University of Michigan Conference*, Leiden, 1974.

Les Universités européennes du XIVe au XVIIIe siècle: aspects et problèmes. Actes du colloque international à l'occasion du VIe centenaire de l'université Jagellonne de Cracovie, 6–8 Mai 1964, Geneva, 1967.

Verger, J. (ed.) *Histoire des universités en France*, Toulouse, 1986, 77–137.

Wuttke, D. 'Dürer et Celtis, l'an 1500 considéré comme l'époque de l'humanisme allemand', in *XVIIIe Colloque international de Tours, L'Humanisme allemand (1480–1540)*, Munich/Paris, 1979.

EDITORS' NOTE ON THE
INDEXES

For practical reasons, the index has been divided into two parts: a list of names of persons, and an index of geographical places and subjects.

The first index contains the names of all the persons mentioned in the volume. In the case of medieval scholars and personalities, the alphabetical order used is that of the Christian or given name rather than the family surname. For the humanists, usually better known under their patronymic, this is the name that features in the alphabetical list. Authors' works have not been included in the indexes.

The geographical and subject index has been carefully edited. In other words, the various subjects which appear in the text are not necessarily reproduced as such or under a place name in the index. Instead, we have preferred to group entries under a more general heading, and we have included only subjects which are directly relevant for the history of universities. For all references to individual persons, the reader should consult the name index (with the obvious exception of Aristotle and Aristotelianism). Place names are given in the English form, when this exists, followed by the (modern) country and county, *Land, département* or province. For the sake of historical accuracy, the name commonly used at the time is listed. The present place name or other variants are shown in brackets after the entry concerned. Wherever possible, people have been identified and places located.

The two indexes have been compiled with the help of Johan Hanselaer in Ghent. We are most grateful to him for his diligent work and attention to detail.

NAME INDEX

470

GEOGRAPHICAL AND SUBJECT
INDEX